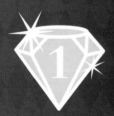

JoJo's BIZARRE ADVENTURE

HIROHIKO ARAKI

PART 4 ★ DIAMOND IS UNBREAKABLE

1

JoJo's
BIZARRE ADVENTURE

PART 4 ★ DIAMOND IS UNBREAKABLE

CONTENTS

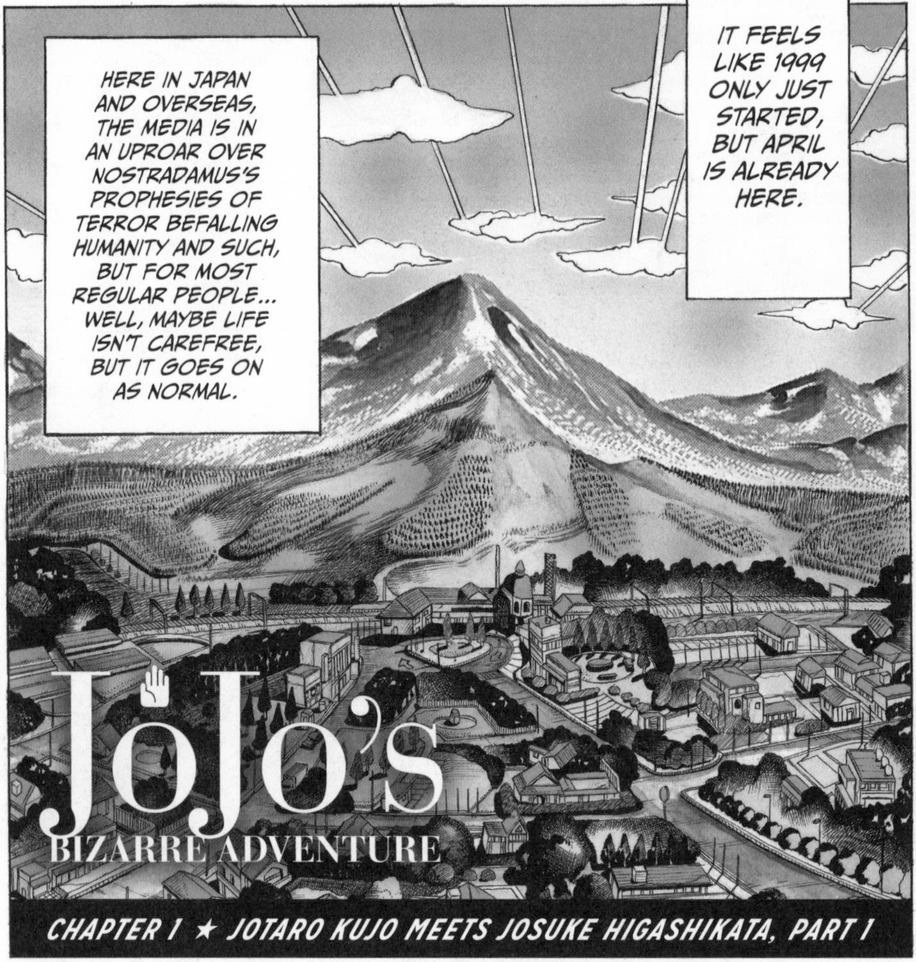
IT FEELS LIKE 1999 ONLY JUST STARTED, BUT APRIL IS ALREADY HERE.
HERE IN JAPAN AND OVERSEAS, THE MEDIA IS IN AN UPROAR OVER NOSTRADAMUS'S PROPHESIES OF TERROR BEFALLING HUMANITY AND SUCH, BUT FOR MOST REGULAR PEOPLE... WELL, MAYBE LIFE ISN'T CAREFREE, BUT IT GOES ON AS NORMAL.
JoJo's
BIZARRE ADVENTURE
CHAPTER 1 ★ JOTARO KUJO MEETS JOSUKE HIGASHIKATA, PART 1

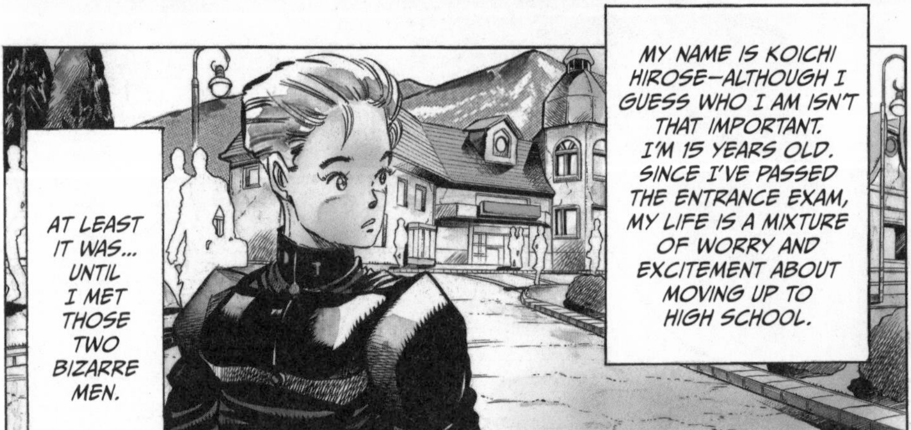
MY NAME IS KOICHI HIROSE—ALTHOUGH I GUESS WHO I AM ISN'T THAT IMPORTANT. I'M 15 YEARS OLD. SINCE I'VE PASSED THE ENTRANCE EXAM, MY LIFE IS A MIXTURE OF WORRY AND EXCITEMENT ABOUT MOVING UP TO HIGH SCHOOL.
AT LEAST IT WAS... UNTIL I MET THOSE TWO BIZARRE MEN.

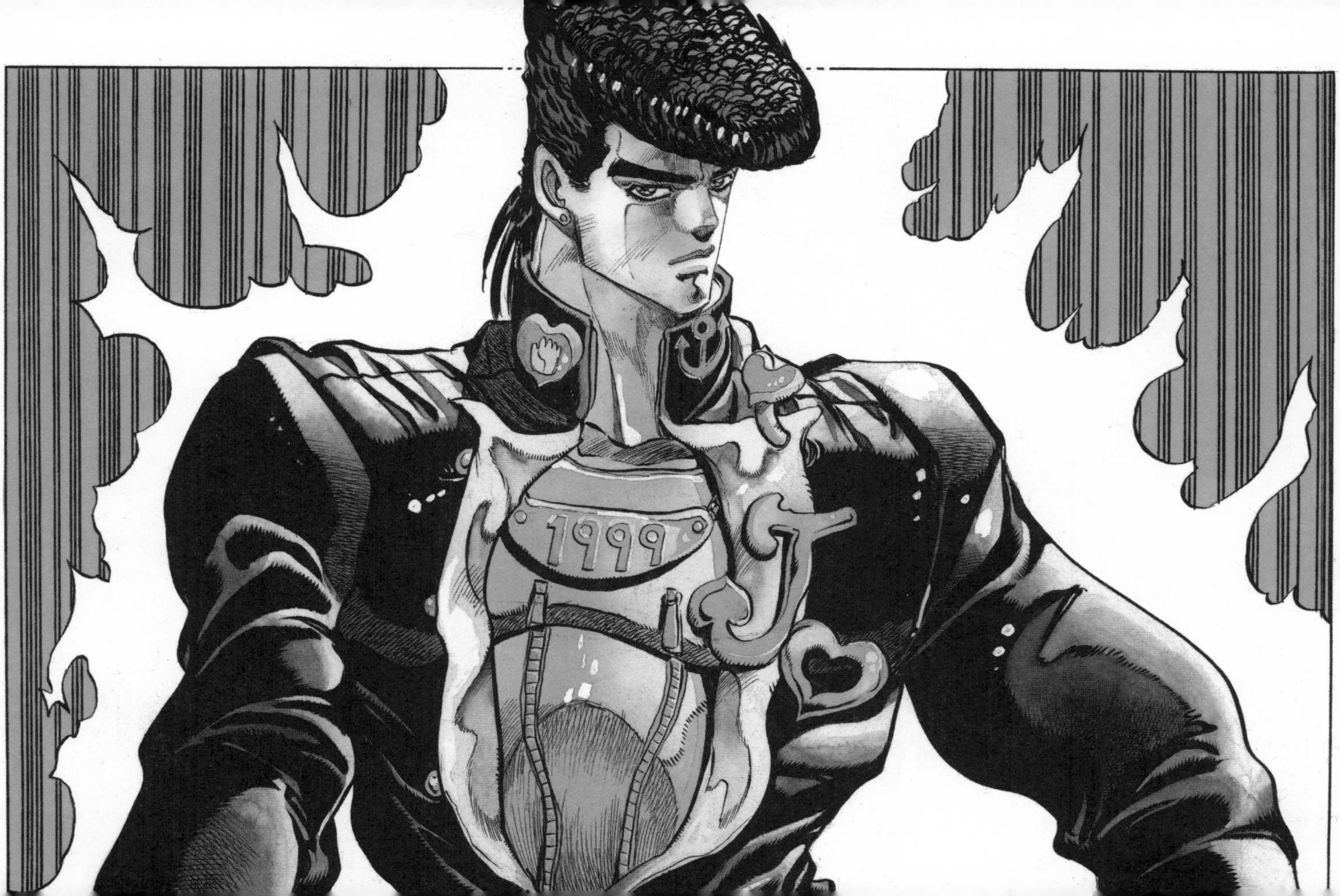
1999

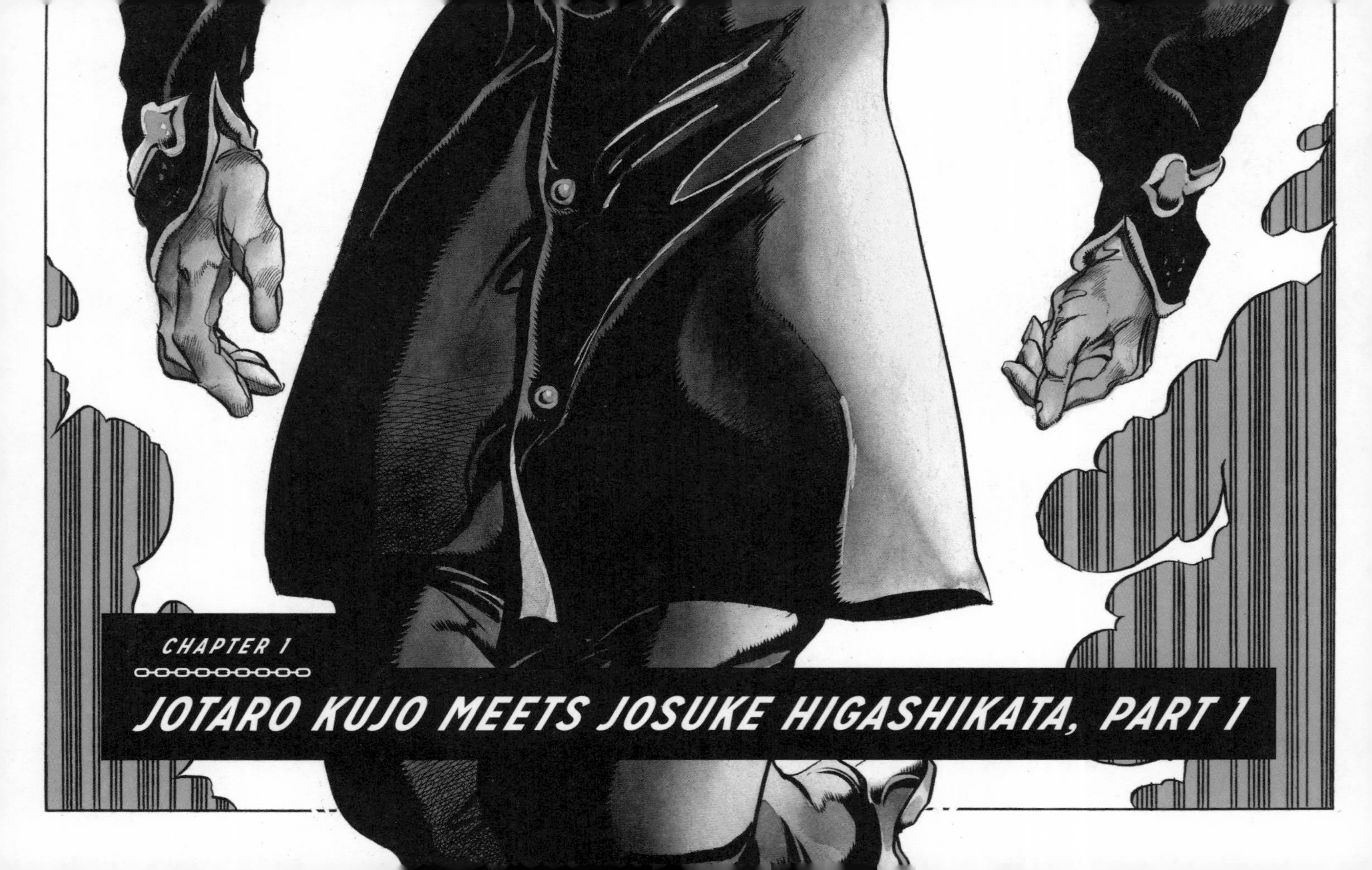
CHAPTER 1
JOTARO KUJO MEETS JOSUKE HIGASHIKATA, PART 1

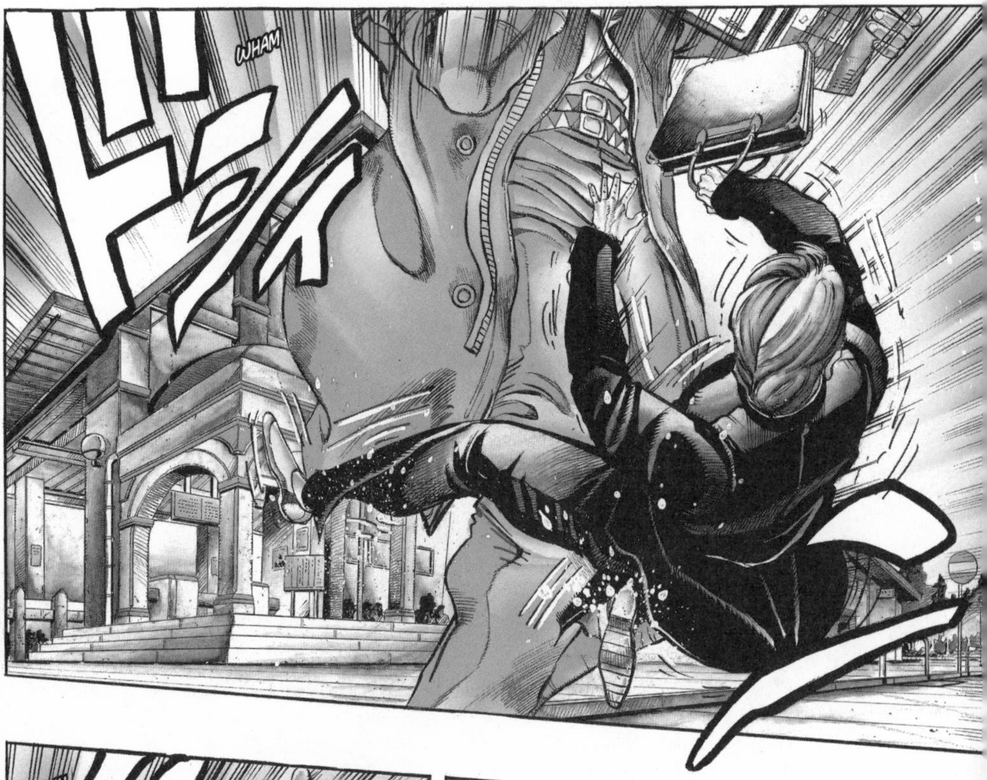
WHAM
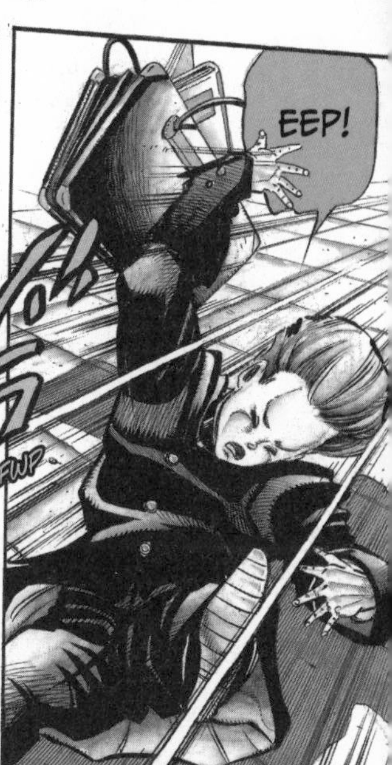
EEP!
FWP
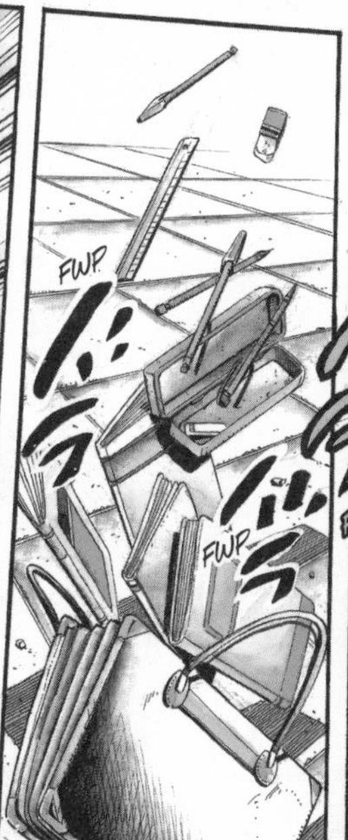
FWP
FWP
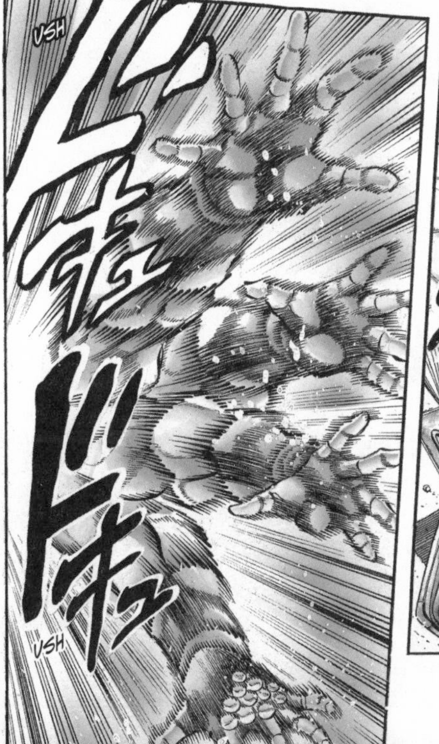
VSH
VSH

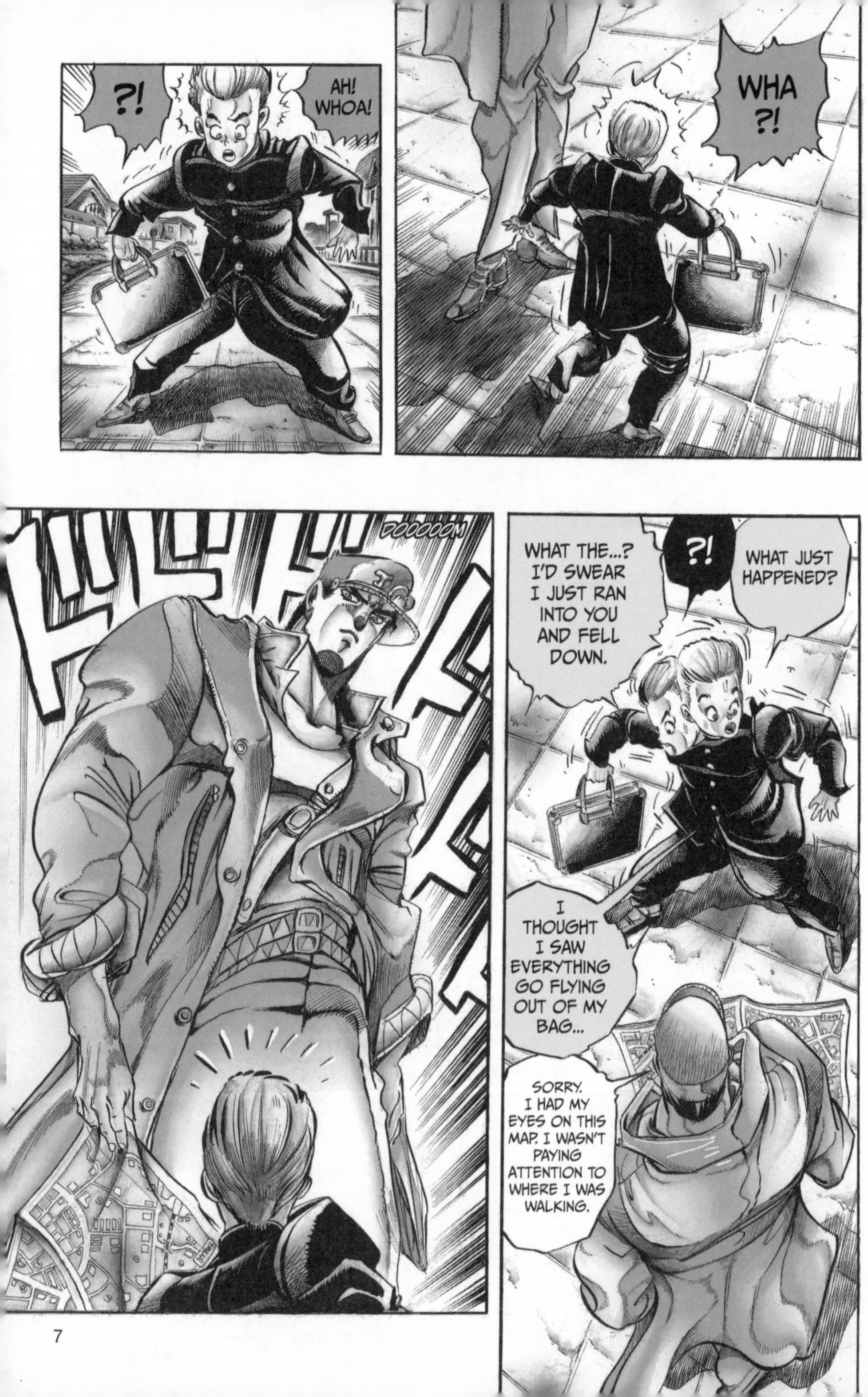
WHA ?!
AH! WHOA!
?!
WHAT JUST HAPPENED?
?!
WHAT THE...? I'D SWEAR I JUST RAN INTO YOU AND FELL DOWN.
I THOUGHT I SAW EVERYTHING GO FLYING OUT OF MY BAG...
SORRY. I HAD MY EYES ON THIS MAP. I WASN'T PAYING ATTENTION TO WHERE I WAS WALKING.
DOOOOOOM

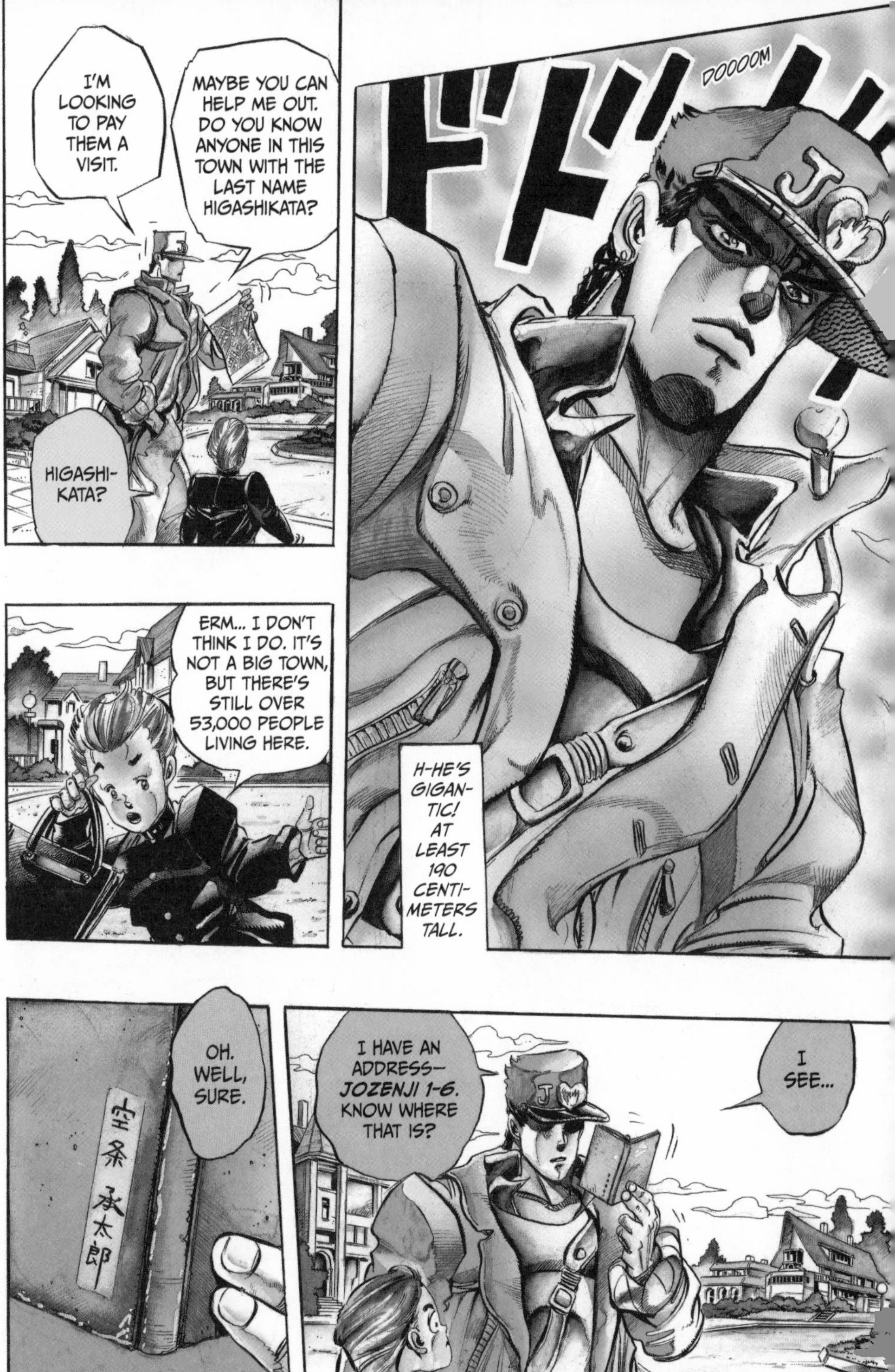
DOOOOM
H-HE'S GIGANTIC! AT LEAST 190 CENTIMETERS TALL.
MAYBE YOU CAN HELP ME OUT. DO YOU KNOW ANYONE IN THIS TOWN WITH THE LAST NAME HIGASHIKATA?
I'M LOOKING TO PAY THEM A VISIT.
HIGASHI-KATA?
ERM... I DON'T THINK I DO. IT'S NOT A BIG TOWN, BUT THERE'S STILL OVER 53,000 PEOPLE LIVING HERE.
I SEE...
I HAVE AN ADDRESS—JOZENJI 1-6. KNOW WHERE THAT IS?
OH. WELL, SURE.
空条承太郎

NAME ON BOOK: JOTARO KUJO

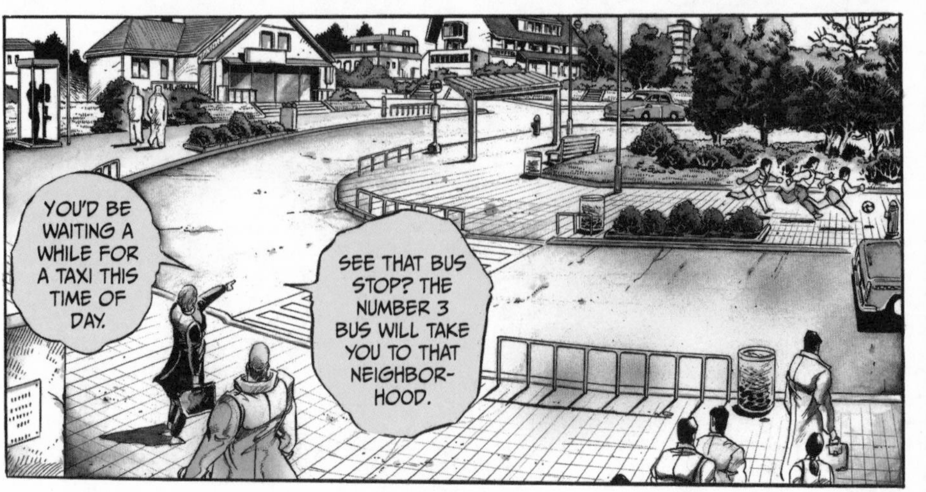
YOU'D BE WAITING A WHILE FOR A TAXI THIS TIME OF DAY.
SEE THAT BUS STOP? THE NUMBER 3 BUS WILL TAKE YOU TO THAT NEIGHBOR-HOOD.

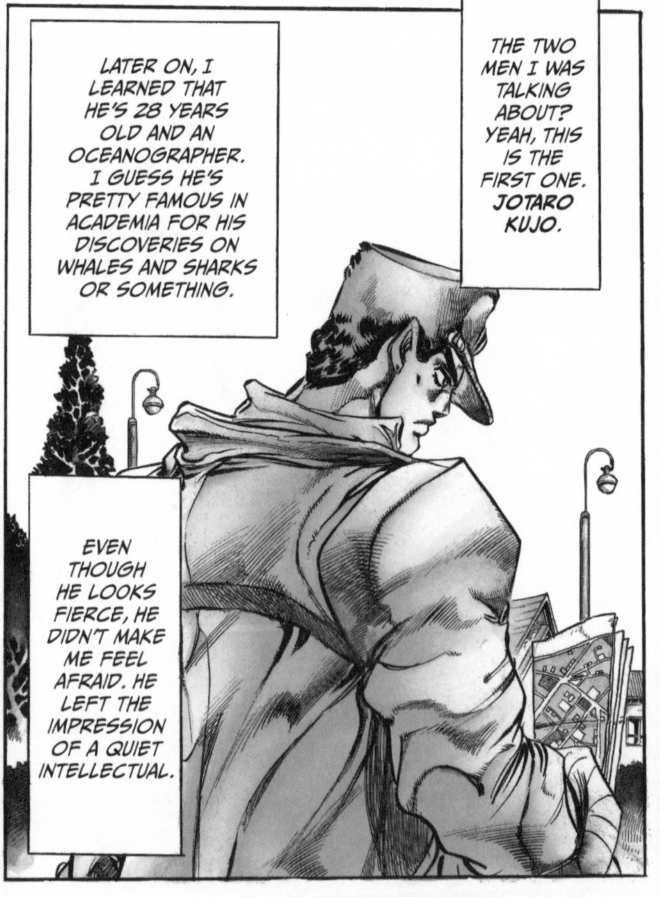
THE TWO MEN I WAS TALKING ABOUT? YEAH, THIS IS THE FIRST ONE. **JOTARO KUJO.**
LATER ON, I LEARNED THAT HE'S 28 YEARS OLD AND AN OCEANOGRAPHER. I GUESS HE'S PRETTY FAMOUS IN ACADEMIA FOR HIS DISCOVERIES ON WHALES AND SHARKS OR SOMETHING.
EVEN THOUGH HE LOOKS FIERCE, HE DIDN'T MAKE ME FEEL AFRAID. HE LEFT THE IMPRESSION OF A QUIET INTELLECTUAL.

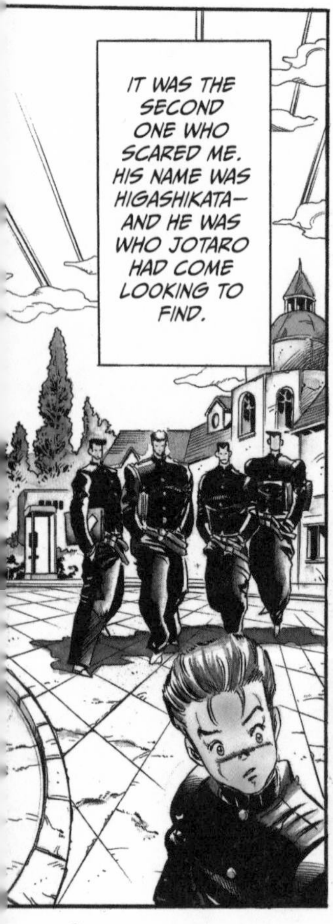
IT WAS THE SECOND ONE WHO SCARED ME. HIS NAME WAS HIGASHIKATA— AND HE WAS WHO JOTARO HAD COME LOOKING TO FIND.

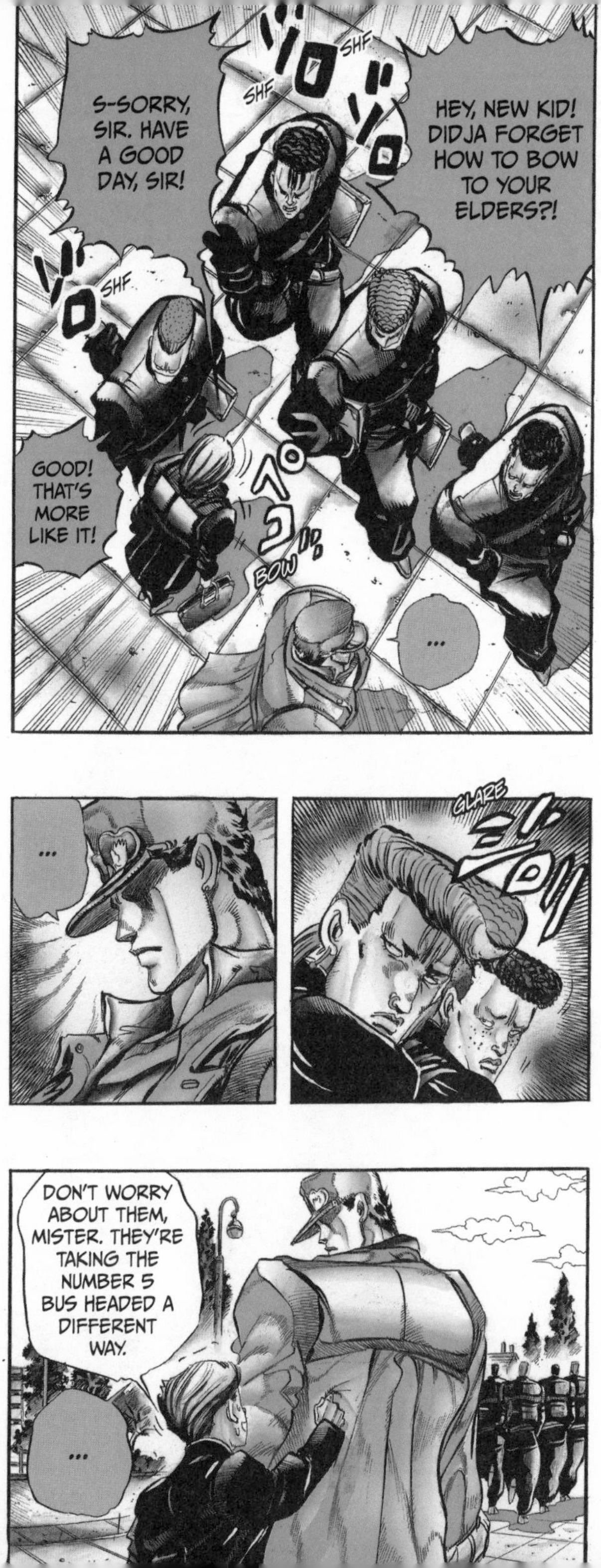
SHF
HEY, NEW KID! DIDJA FORGET HOW TO BOW TO YOUR ELDERS?!
SHF
S-SORRY, SIR. HAVE A GOOD DAY, SIR!
SHF
GOOD! THAT'S MORE LIKE IT!
BOW
...
GLARE
...
DON'T WORRY ABOUT THEM, MISTER. THEY'RE TAKING THE NUMBER 5 BUS HEADED A DIFFERENT WAY.
...

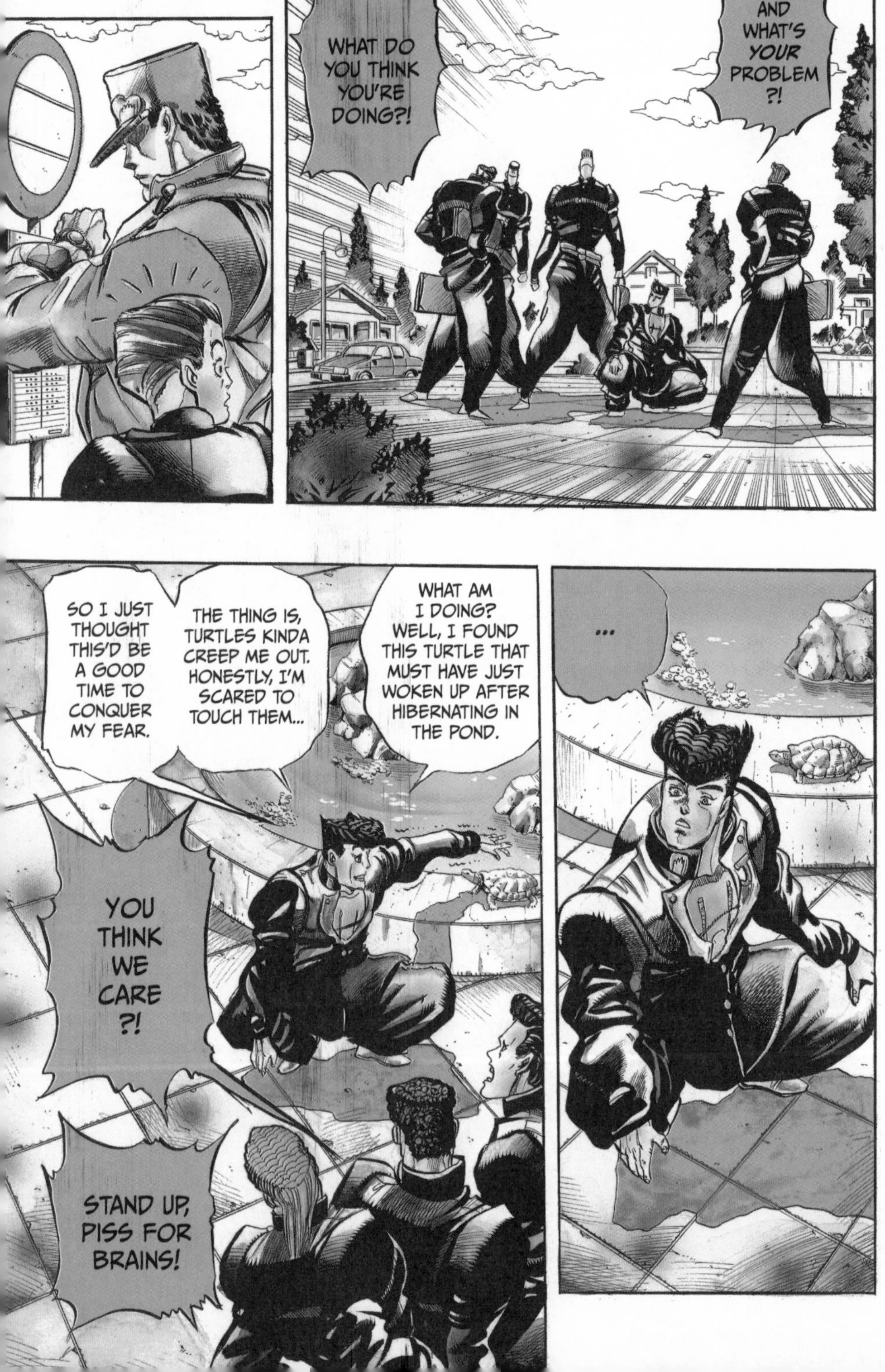
AND WHAT'S *YOUR* PROBLEM ?!
WHAT DO YOU THINK YOU'RE DOING?!
...
WHAT AM I DOING? WELL, I FOUND THIS TURTLE THAT MUST HAVE JUST WOKEN UP AFTER HIBERNATING IN THE POND.
THE THING IS, TURTLES KINDA CREEP ME OUT. HONESTLY, I'M SCARED TO TOUCH THEM...
SO I JUST THOUGHT THIS'D BE A GOOD TIME TO CONQUER MY FEAR.
YOU THINK WE CARE ?!
STAND UP, PISS FOR BRAINS!

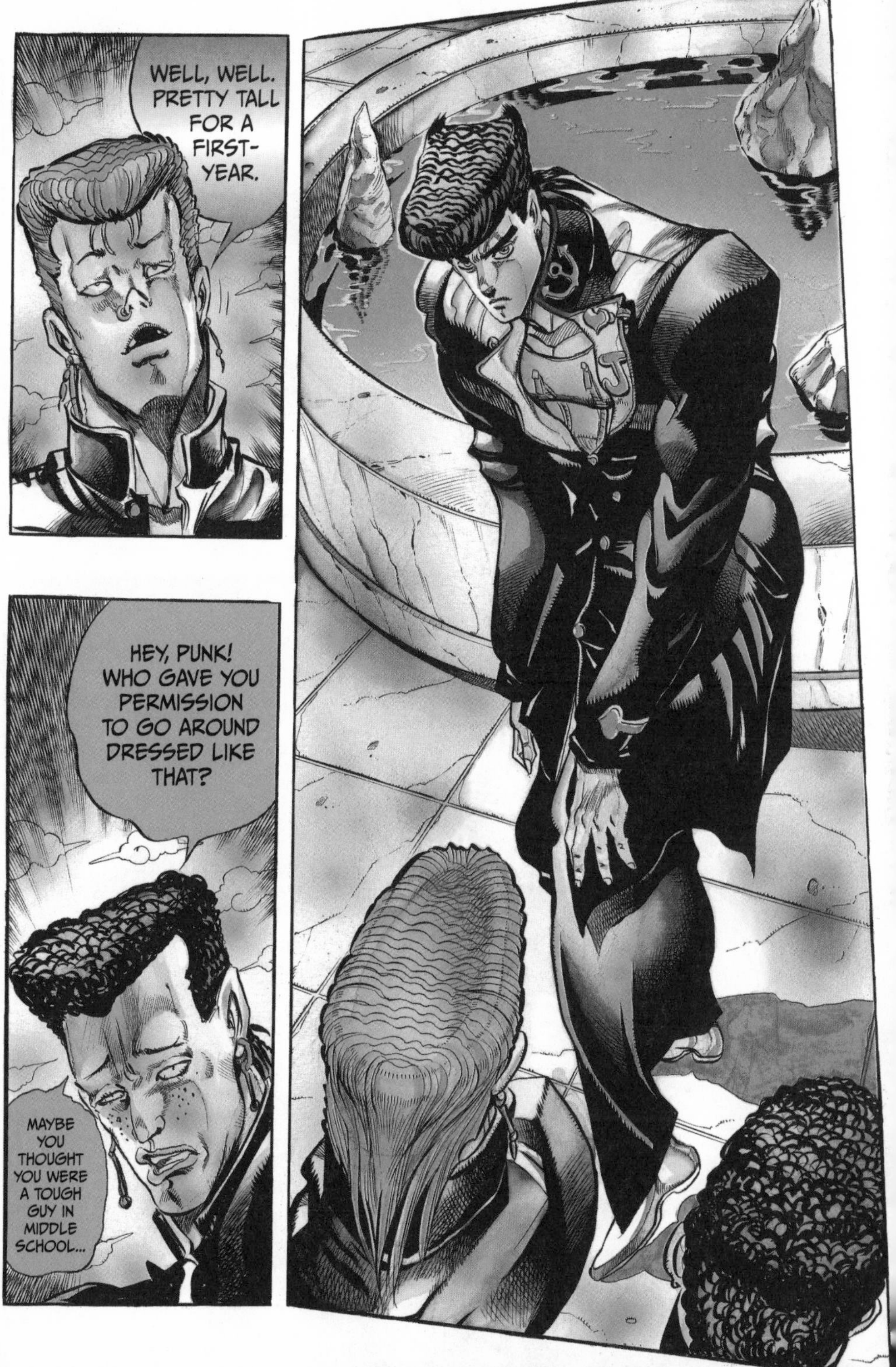
WELL, WELL. PRETTY TALL FOR A FIRST-YEAR.
HEY, PUNK! WHO GAVE YOU PERMISSION TO GO AROUND DRESSED LIKE THAT?
MAYBE YOU THOUGHT YOU WERE A TOUGH GUY IN MIDDLE SCHOOL...

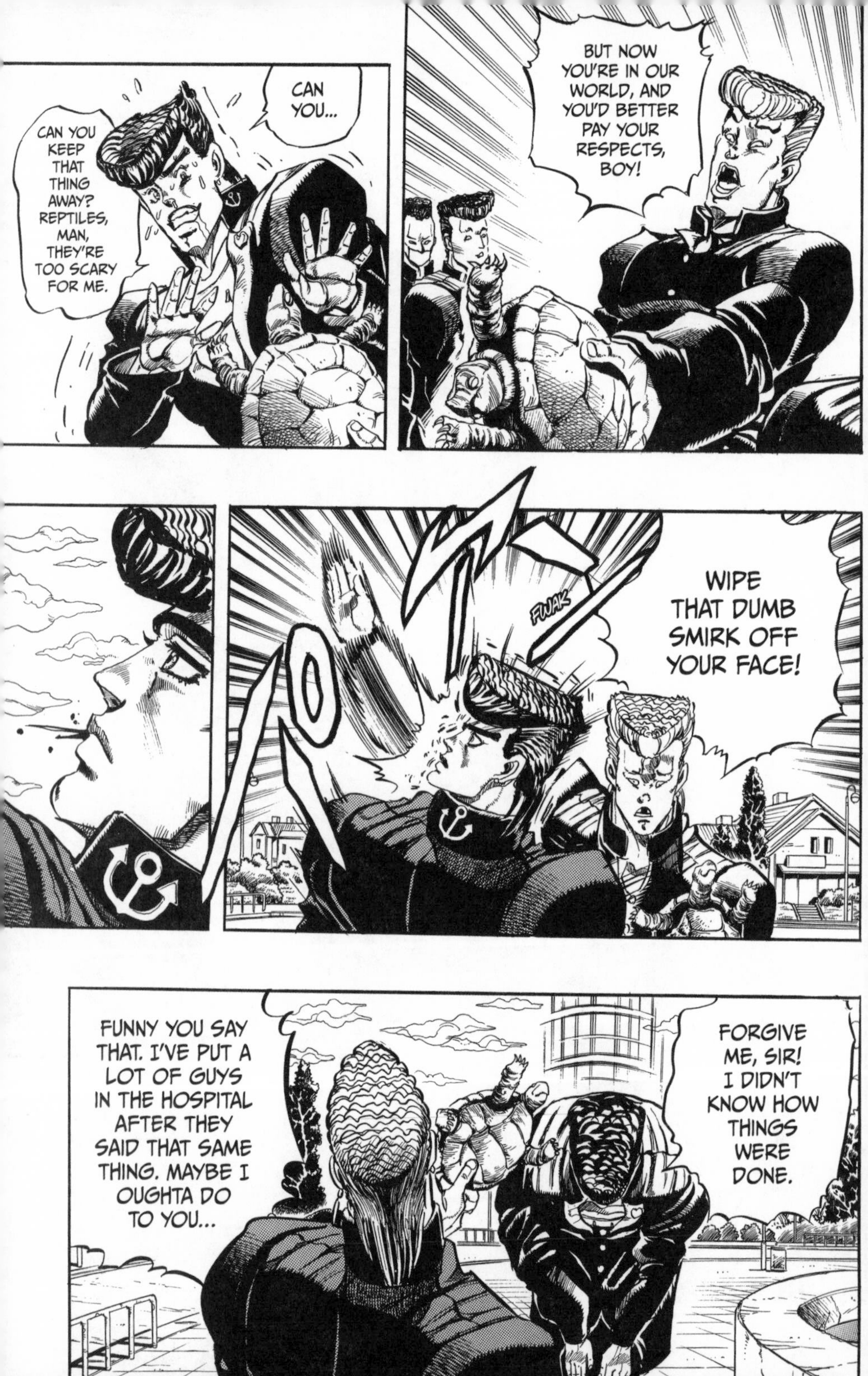
BUT NOW YOU'RE IN OUR WORLD, AND YOU'D BETTER PAY YOUR RESPECTS, BOY!
CAN YOU...
CAN YOU KEEP THAT THING AWAY? REPTILES, MAN, THEY'RE TOO SCARY FOR ME.
WIPE THAT DUMB SMIRK OFF YOUR FACE!
FWAK
FORGIVE ME, SIR! I DIDN'T KNOW HOW THINGS WERE DONE.
FUNNY YOU SAY THAT. I'VE PUT A LOT OF GUYS IN THE HOSPITAL AFTER THEY SAID THAT SAME THING. MAYBE I OUGHTA DO TO YOU...

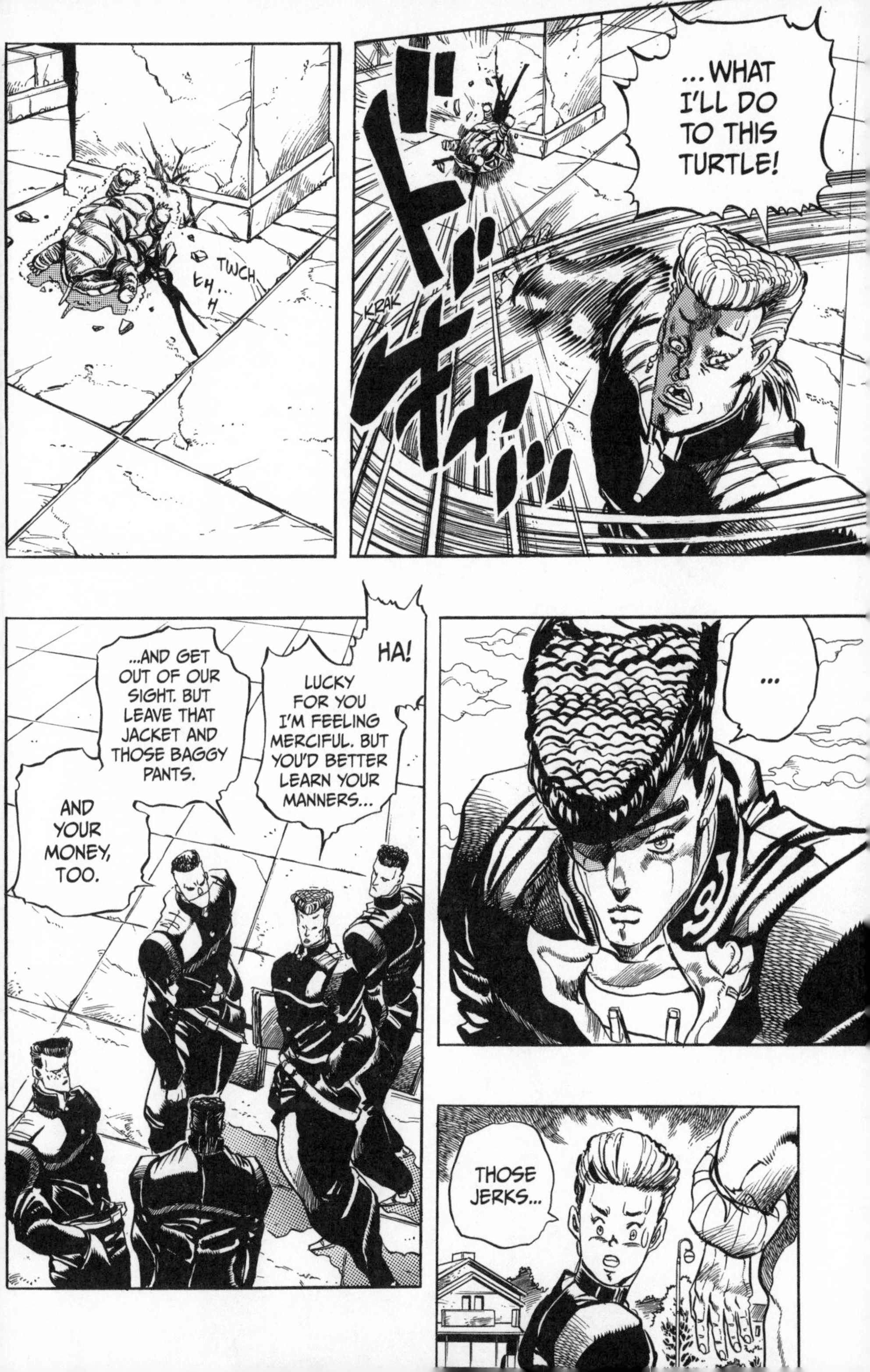
...WHAT I'LL DO TO THIS TURTLE!
ドギャ
KRAK
TWCH
...
HA!
LUCKY FOR YOU I'M FEELING MERCIFUL. BUT YOU'D BETTER LEARN YOUR MANNERS...
...AND GET OUT OF OUR SIGHT. BUT LEAVE THAT JACKET AND THOSE BAGGY PANTS.
AND YOUR MONEY, TOO.
THOSE JERKS...

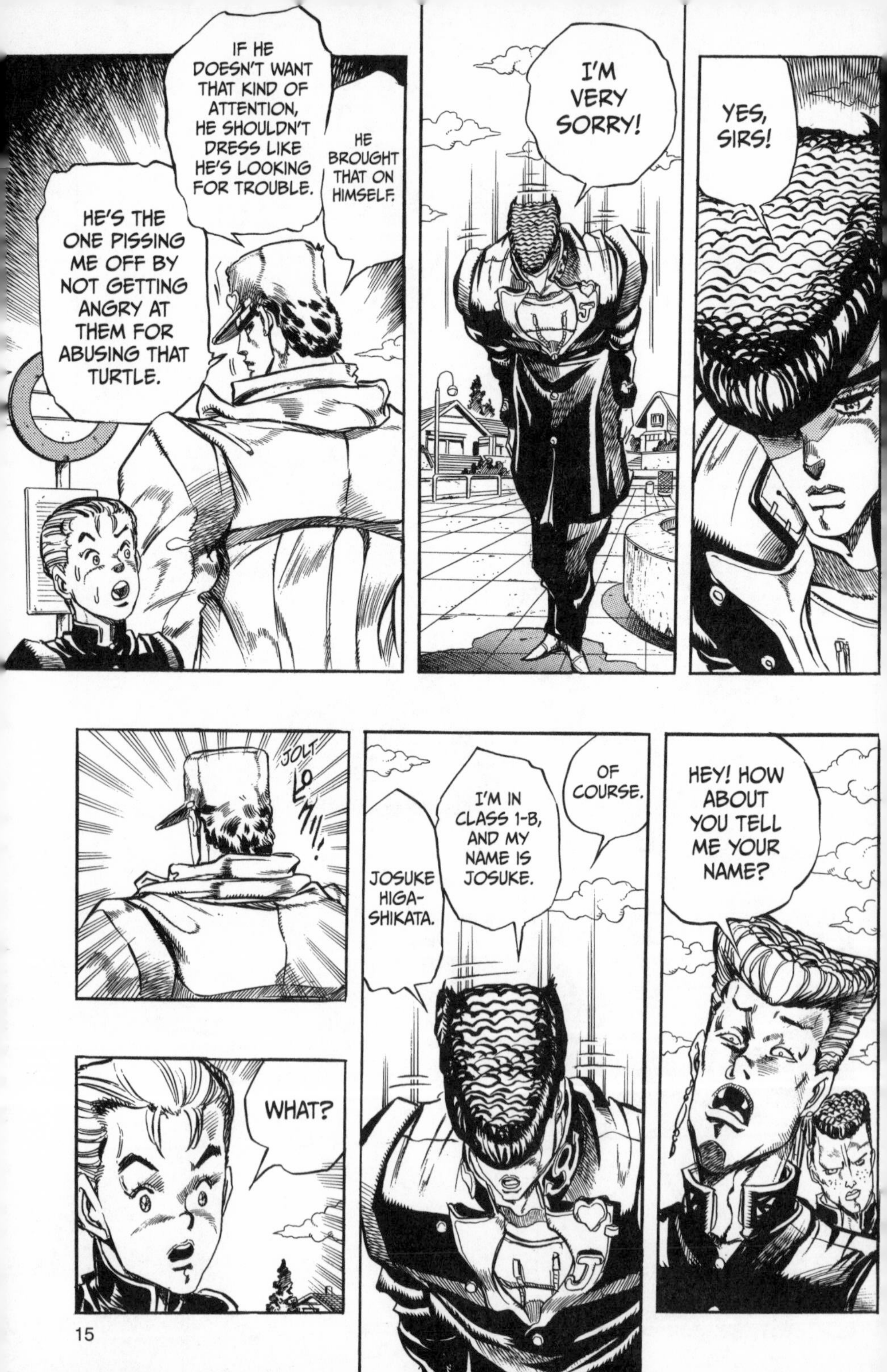
YES, SIRS!
I'M VERY SORRY!
IF HE DOESN'T WANT THAT KIND OF ATTENTION, HE SHOULDN'T DRESS LIKE HE'S LOOKING FOR TROUBLE.
HE BROUGHT THAT ON HIMSELF.
HE'S THE ONE PISSING ME OFF BY NOT GETTING ANGRY AT THEM FOR ABUSING THAT TURTLE.
HEY! HOW ABOUT YOU TELL ME YOUR NAME?
OF COURSE.
I'M IN CLASS 1-B, AND MY NAME IS JOSUKE.
JOSUKE HIGA-SHIKATA.
JOLT
WHAT?

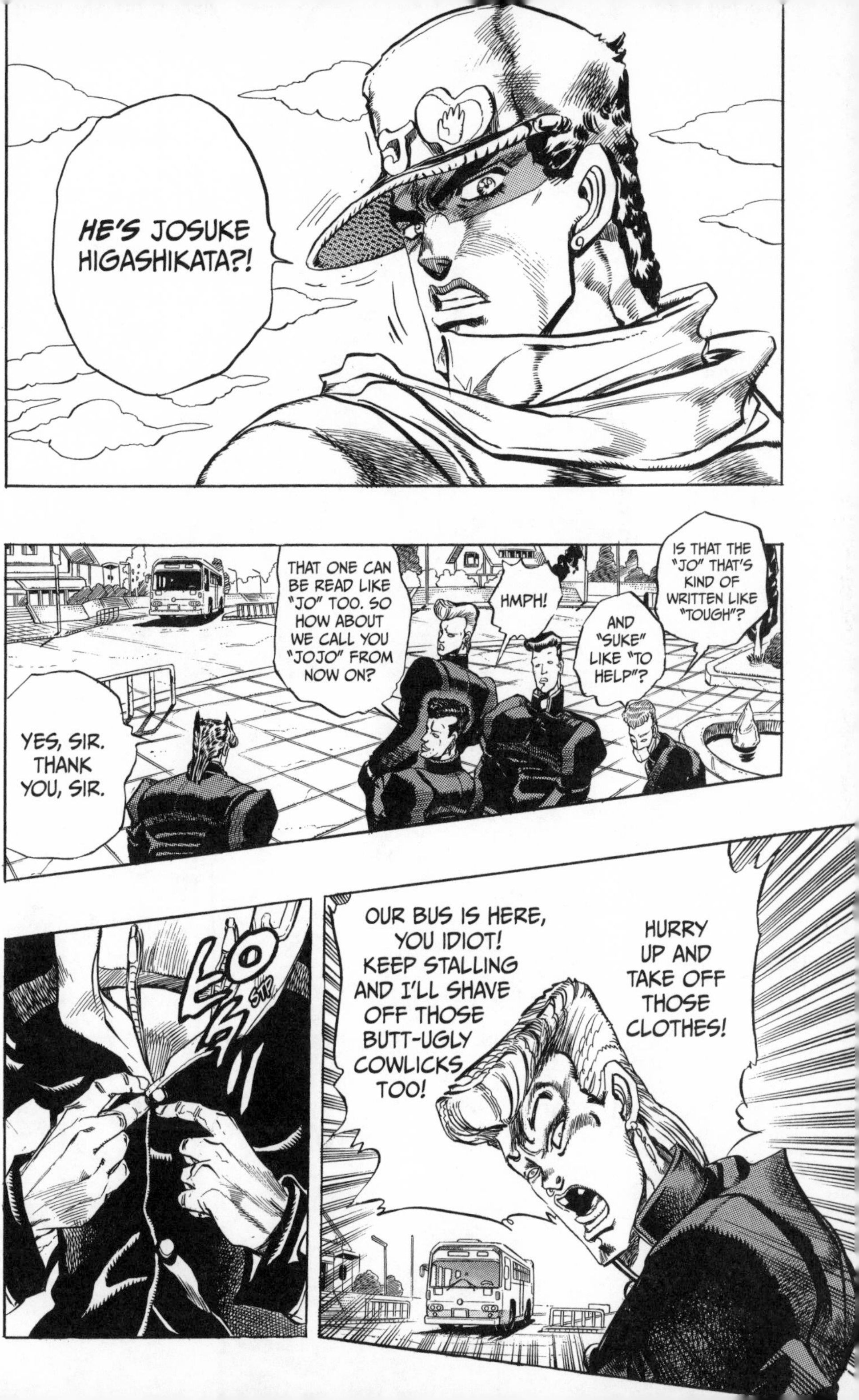
HE'S JOSUKE HIGASHIKATA?!
IS THAT THE "JO" THAT'S KIND OF WRITTEN LIKE "TOUGH"?
AND "SUKE" LIKE "TO HELP"?
HMPH!
THAT ONE CAN BE READ LIKE "JO" TOO. SO HOW ABOUT WE CALL YOU "JOJO" FROM NOW ON?
YES, SIR. THANK YOU, SIR.
HURRY UP AND TAKE OFF THOSE CLOTHES!
OUR BUS IS HERE, YOU IDIOT! KEEP STALLING AND I'LL SHAVE OFF THOSE BUTT-UGLY COWLICKS TOO!
STP

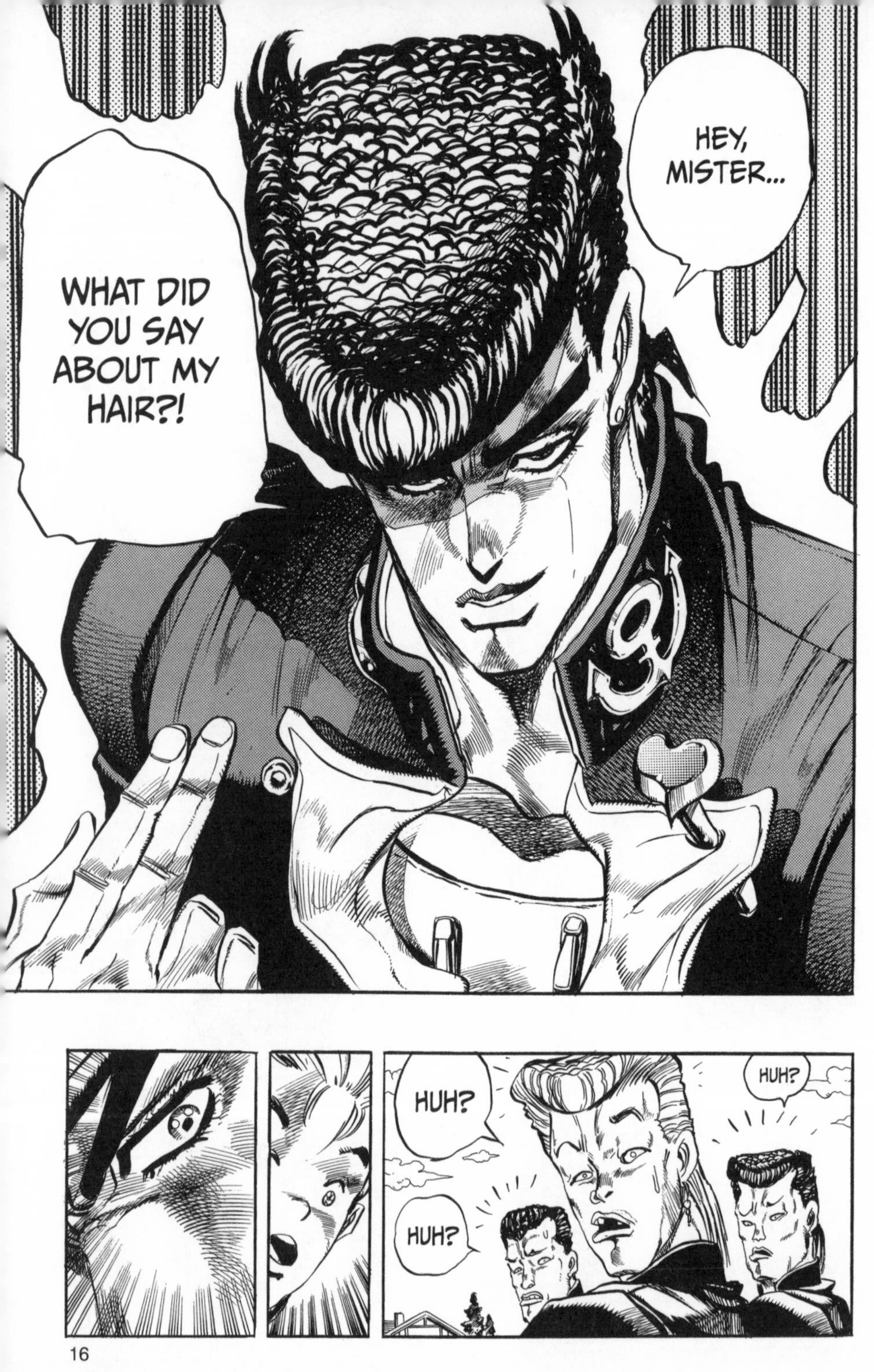
HEY, MISTER...
WHAT DID YOU SAY ABOUT MY HAIR?!
HUH?
HUH?
HUH?

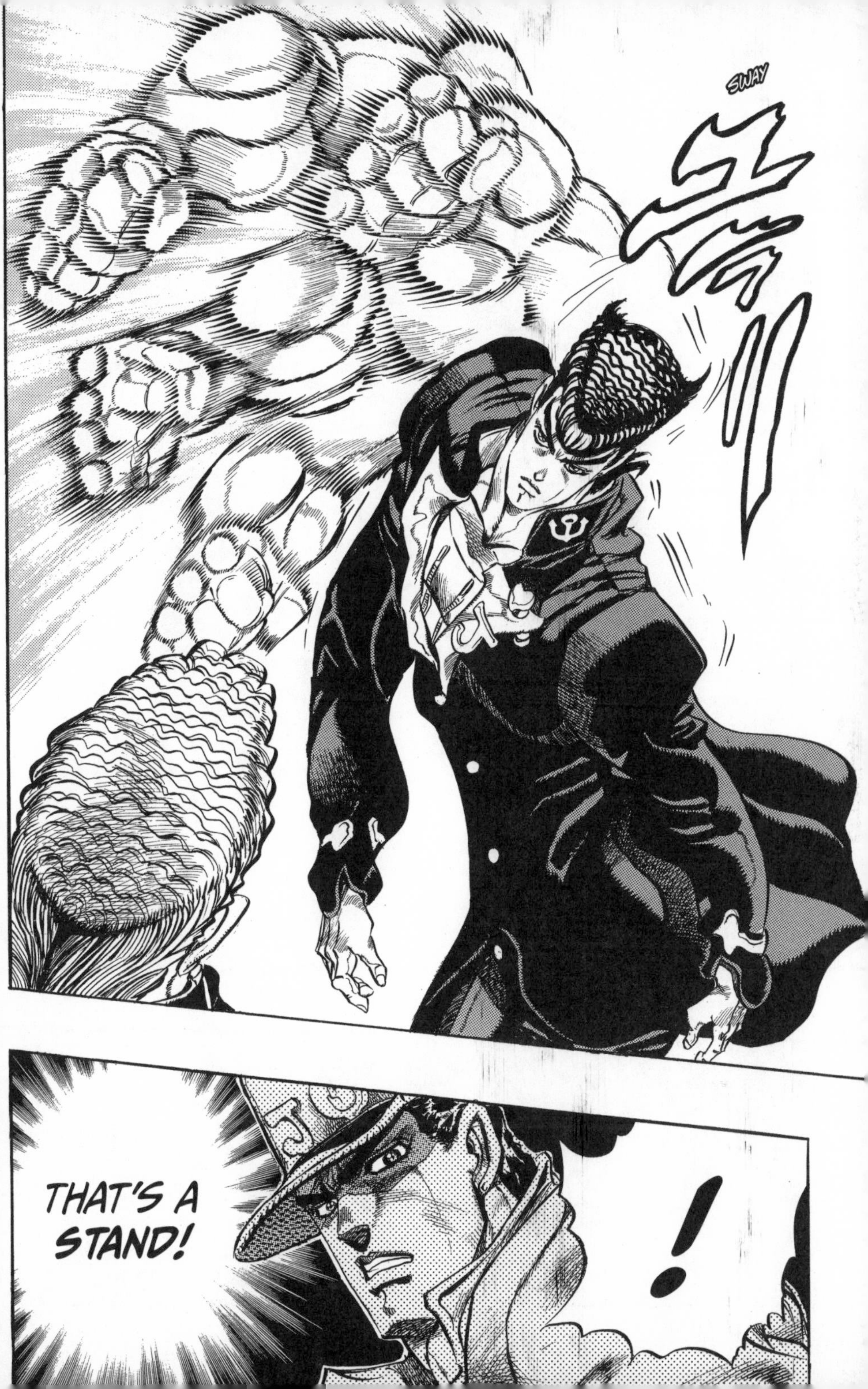
SWAY
THAT'S A STAND!
!

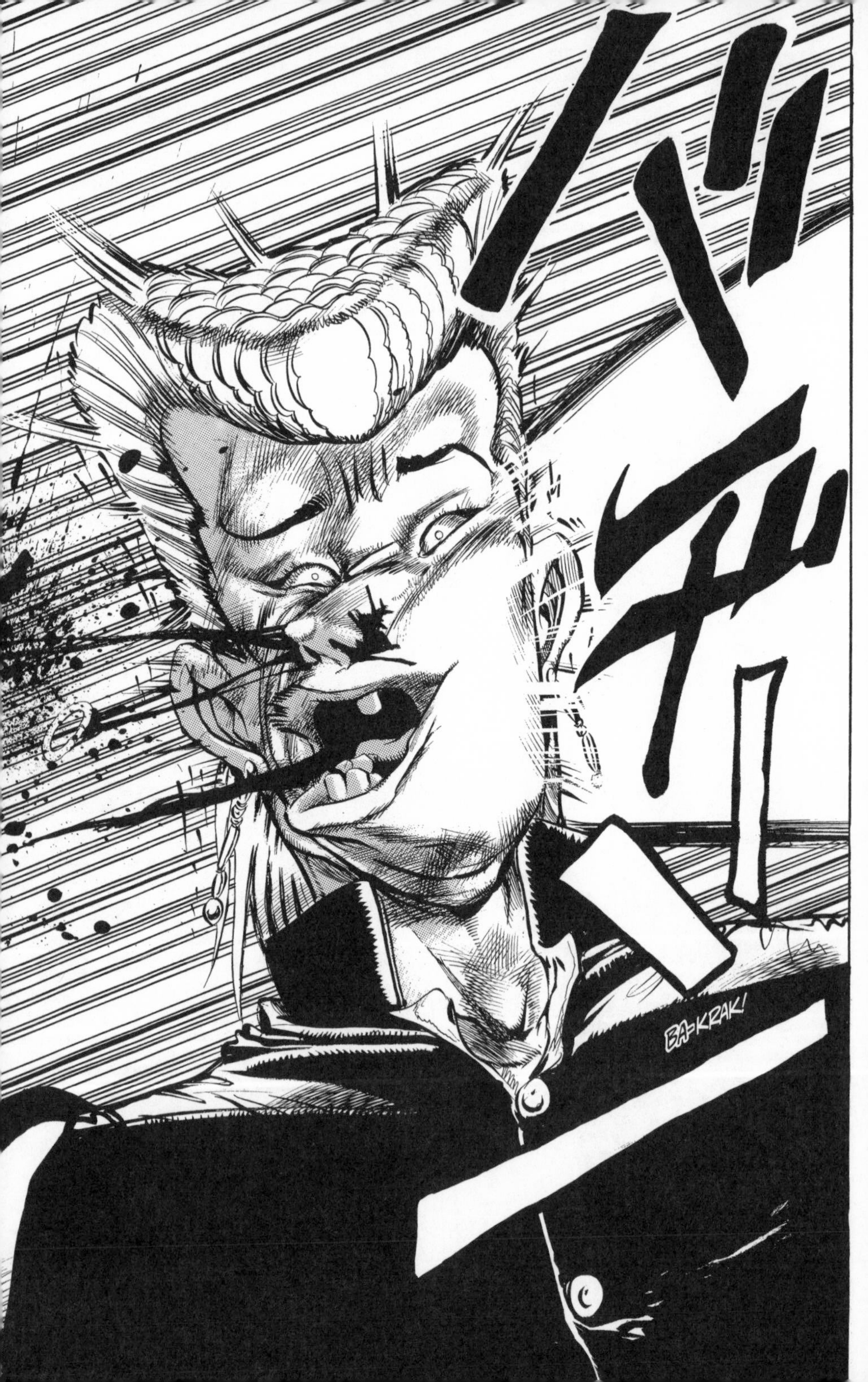
BA-KRAK!

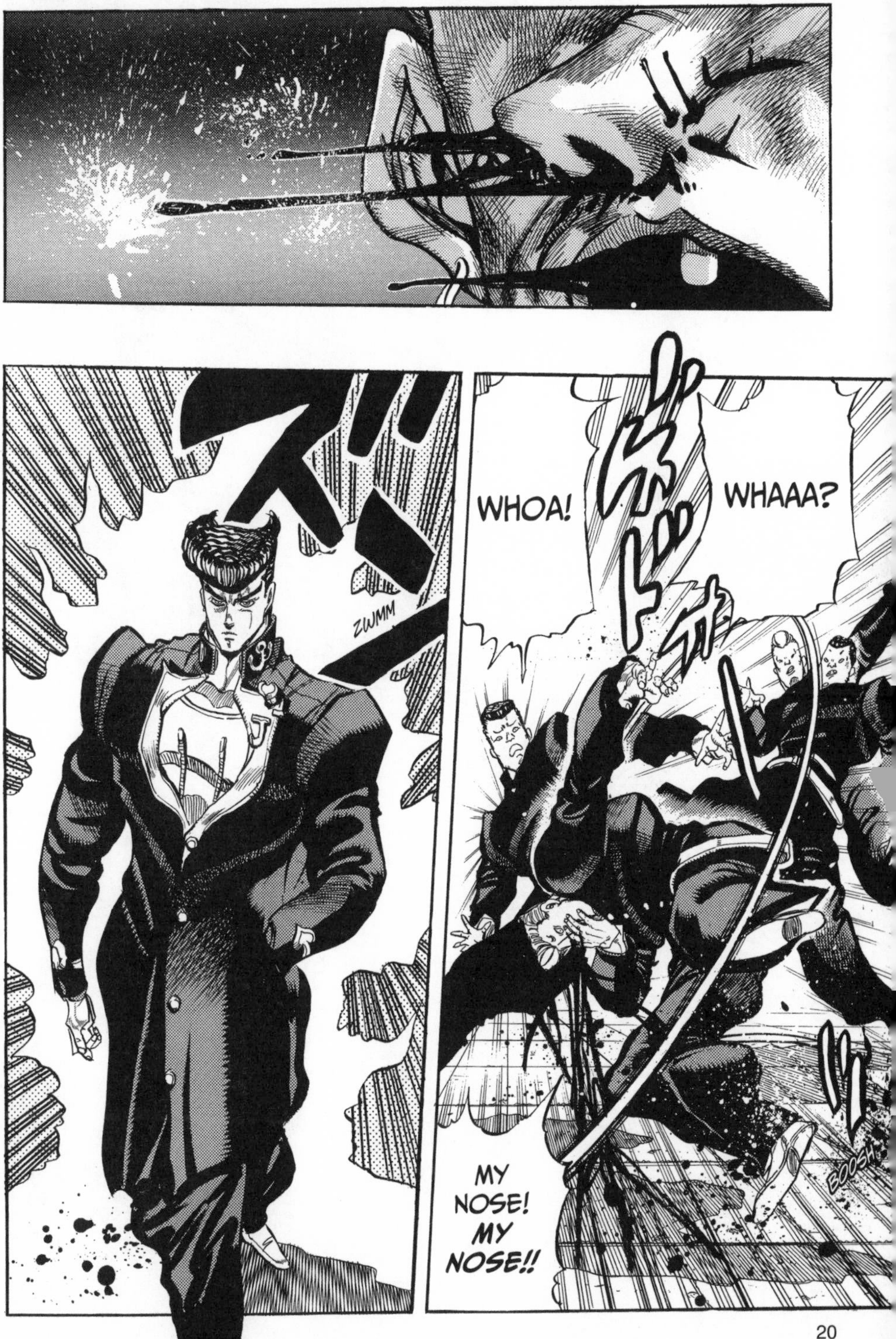
WHAAA?
WHOA!
BOOSH
MY NOSE! MY NOSE!!
ZWUMM

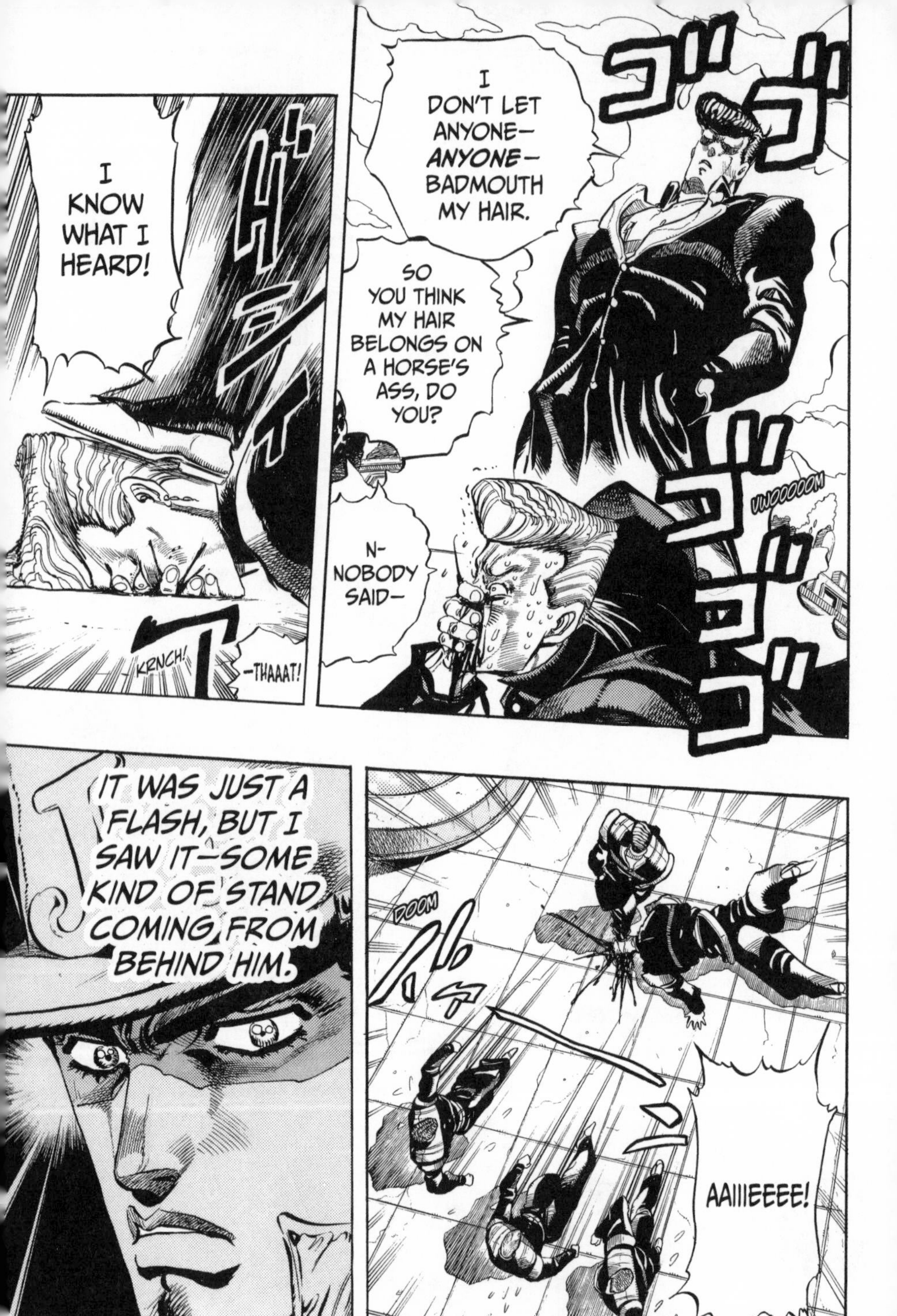
I DON'T LET ANYONE— ANYONE— BADMOUTH MY HAIR.
SO YOU THINK MY HAIR BELONGS ON A HORSE'S ASS, DO YOU?
...
N-NOBODY SAID—
VWOOOOOM
I KNOW WHAT I HEARD!
KRNCH!
—THAAAT!
DOOM
AAIIIEEEE!
IT WAS JUST A FLASH, BUT I SAW IT—SOME KIND OF STAND COMING FROM BEHIND HIM.

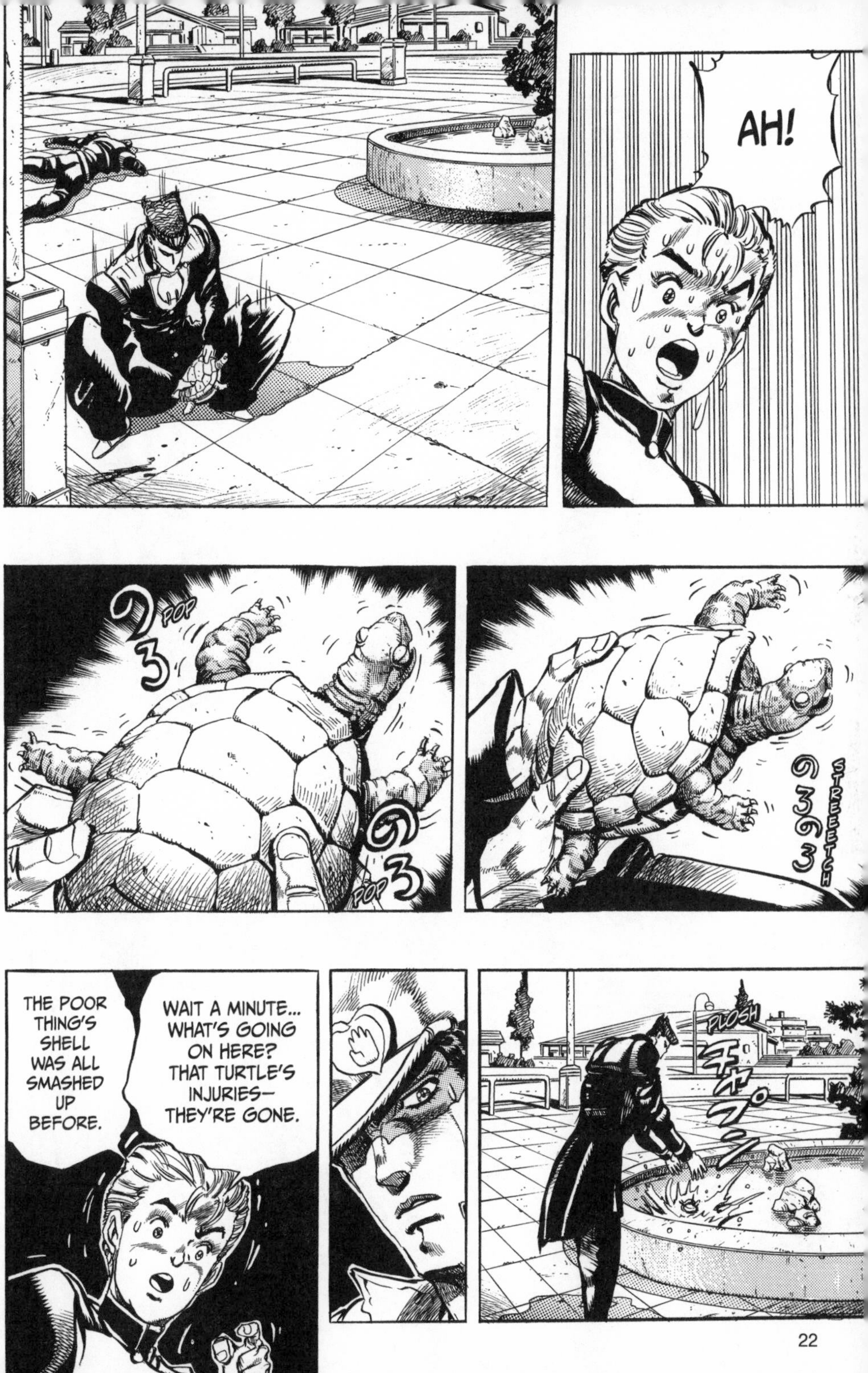
AH!
STREEETCH
POP
POP
PLOSH
WAIT A MINUTE... WHAT'S GOING ON HERE? THAT TURTLE'S INJURIES— THEY'RE GONE.
THE POOR THING'S SHELL WAS ALL SMASHED UP BEFORE.

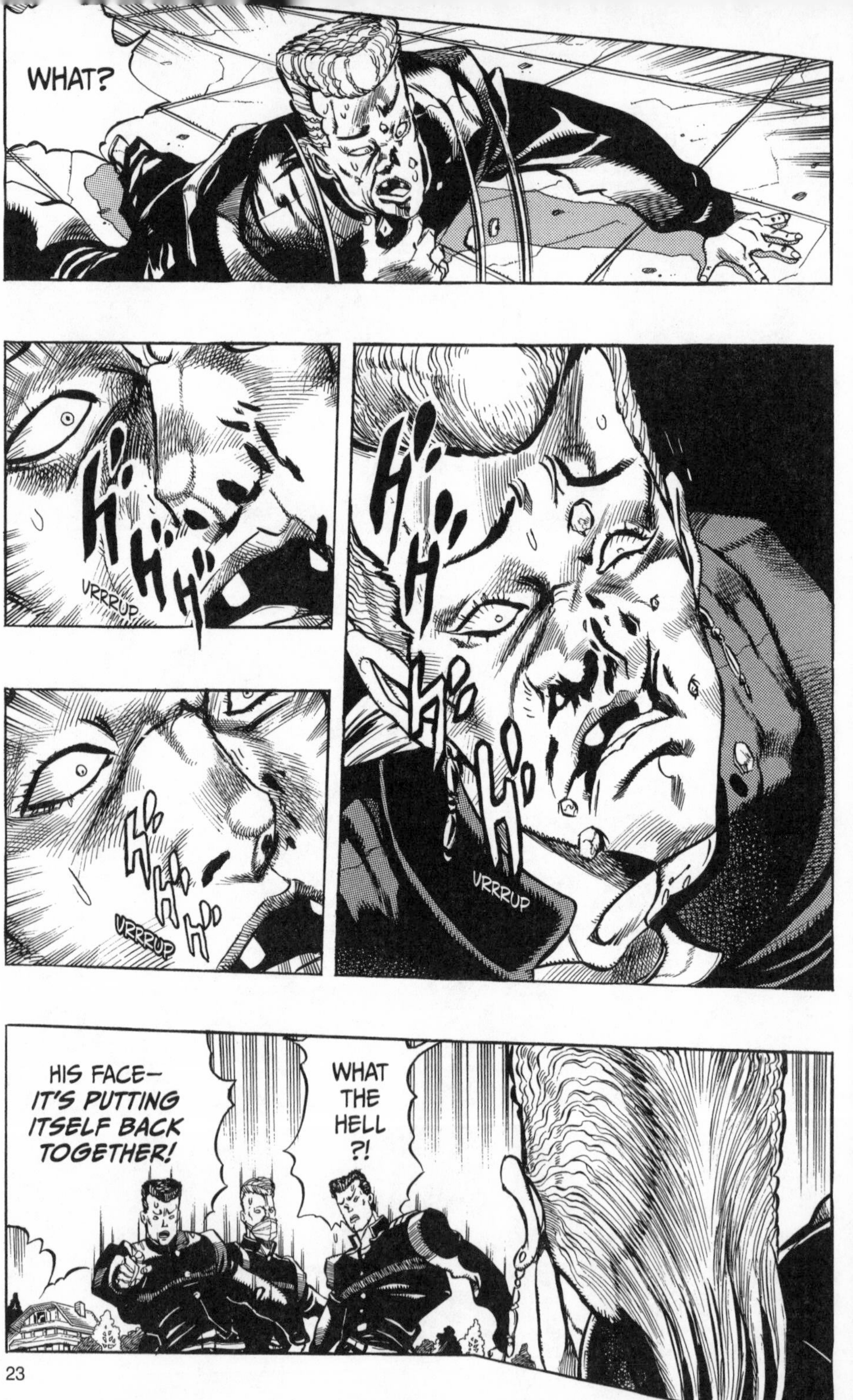
WHAT?
URRRUP
URRRUP
URRRUP
WHAT THE HELL ?!
HIS FACE— IT'S PUTTING ITSELF BACK TOGETHER!

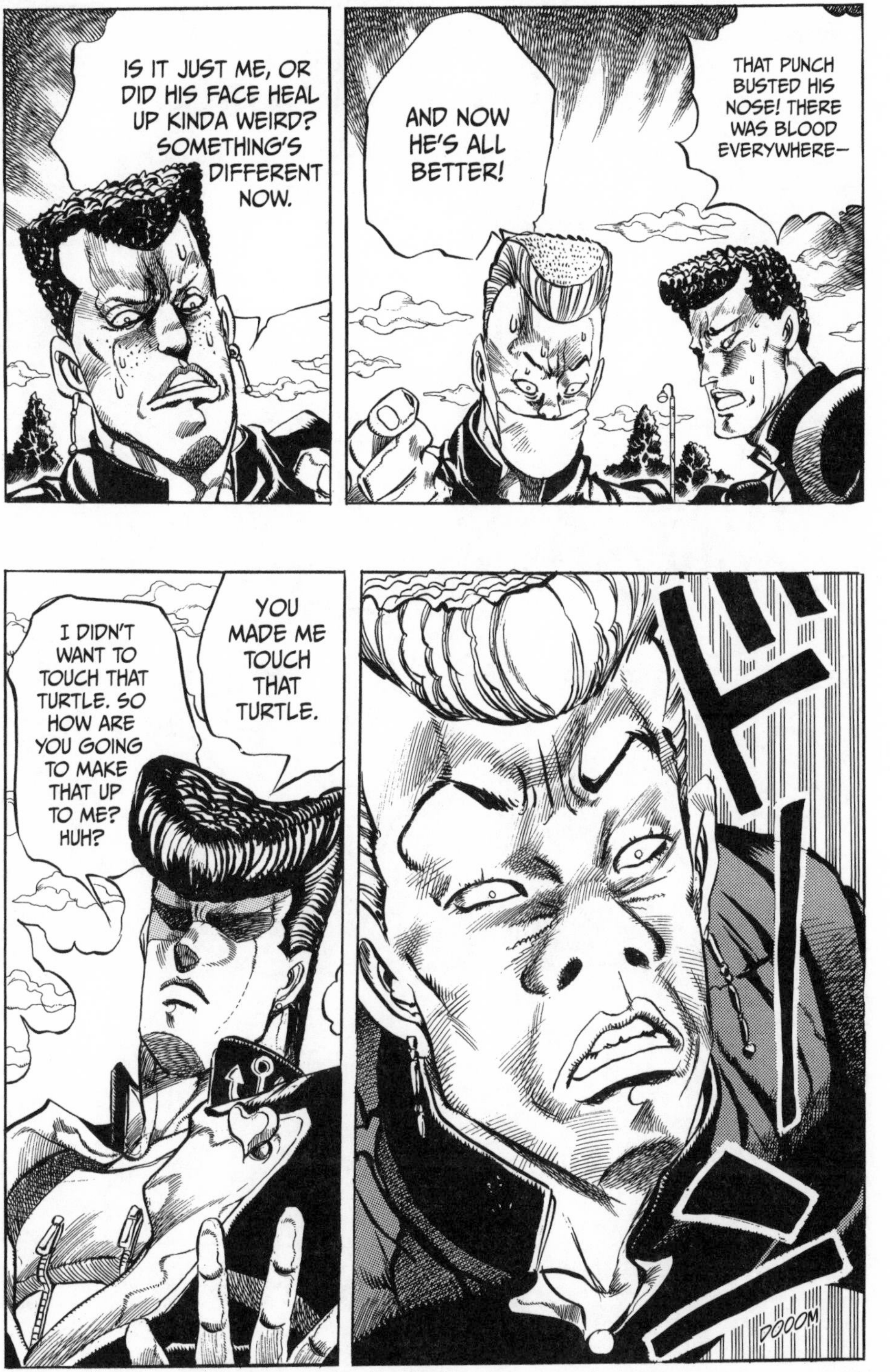
THAT PUNCH BUSTED HIS NOSE! THERE WAS BLOOD EVERYWHERE—
AND NOW HE'S ALL BETTER!
IS IT JUST ME, OR DID HIS FACE HEAL UP KINDA WEIRD? SOMETHING'S DIFFERENT NOW.
DOOOM
YOU MADE ME TOUCH THAT TURTLE.
I DIDN'T WANT TO TOUCH THAT TURTLE. SO HOW ARE YOU GOING TO MAKE THAT UP TO ME? HUH?

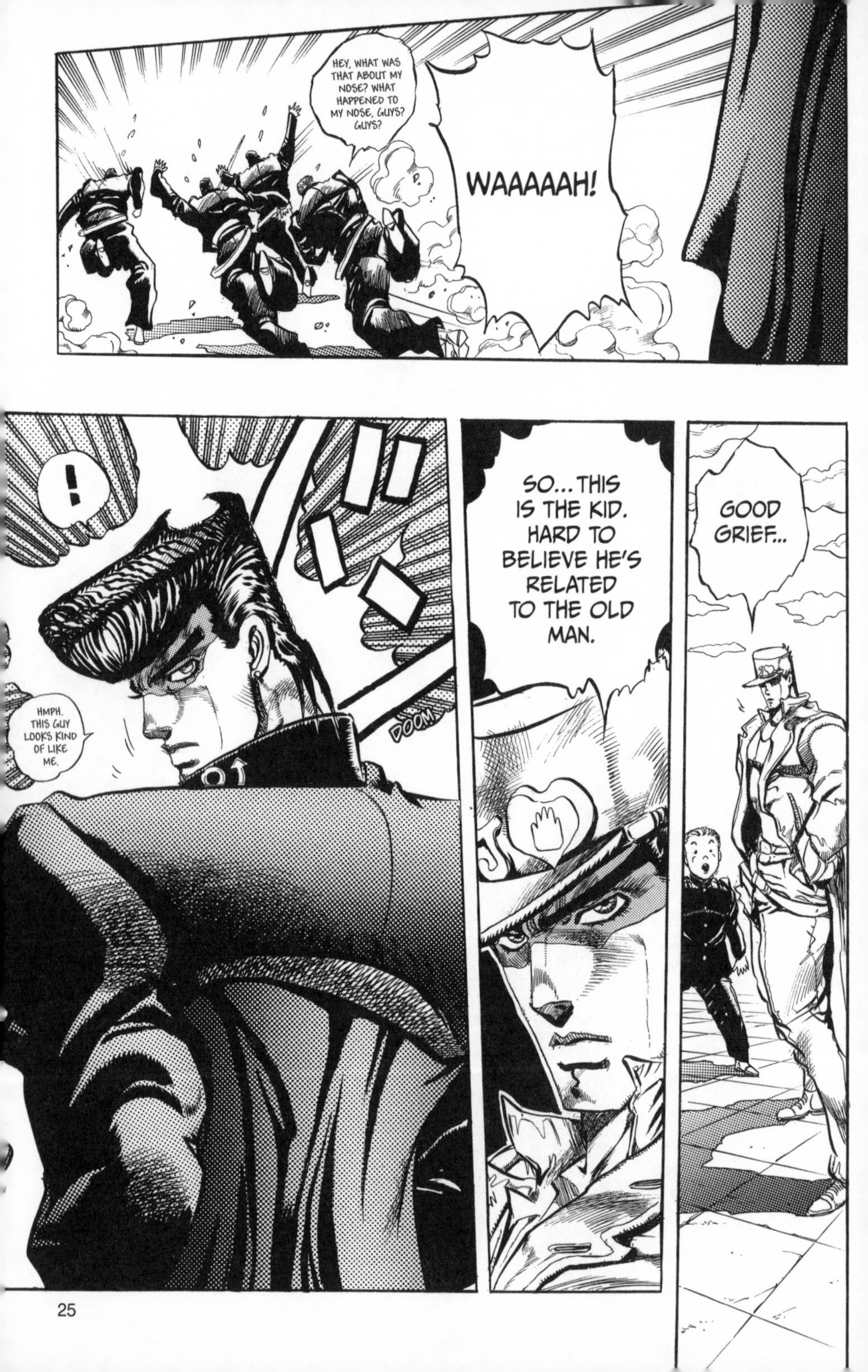
WAAAAAH!
HEY, WHAT WAS THAT ABOUT MY NOSE? WHAT HAPPENED TO MY NOSE, GUYS? GUYS?
GOOD GRIEF...
SO... THIS IS THE KID. HARD TO BELIEVE HE'S RELATED TO THE OLD MAN.
!
HMPH. THIS GUY LOOKS KIND OF LIKE ME.
DOOM

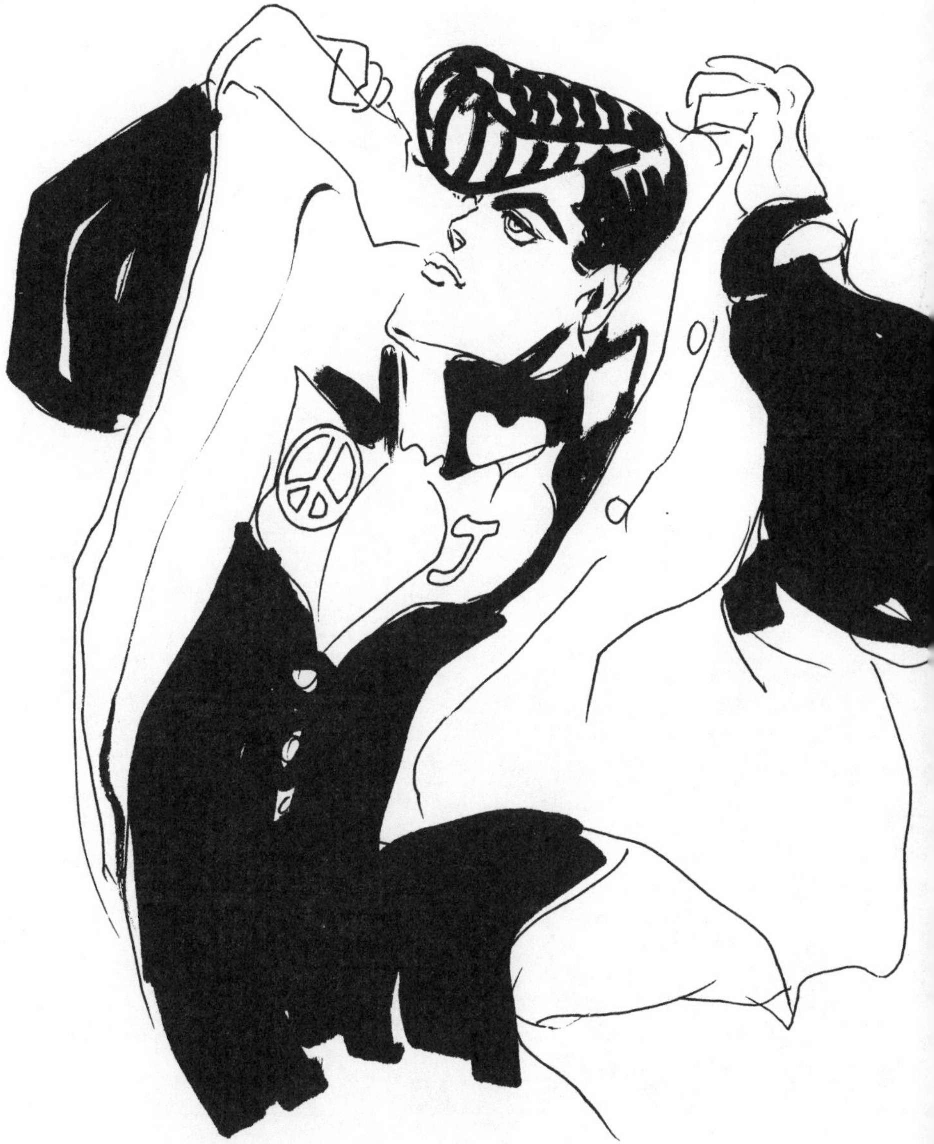

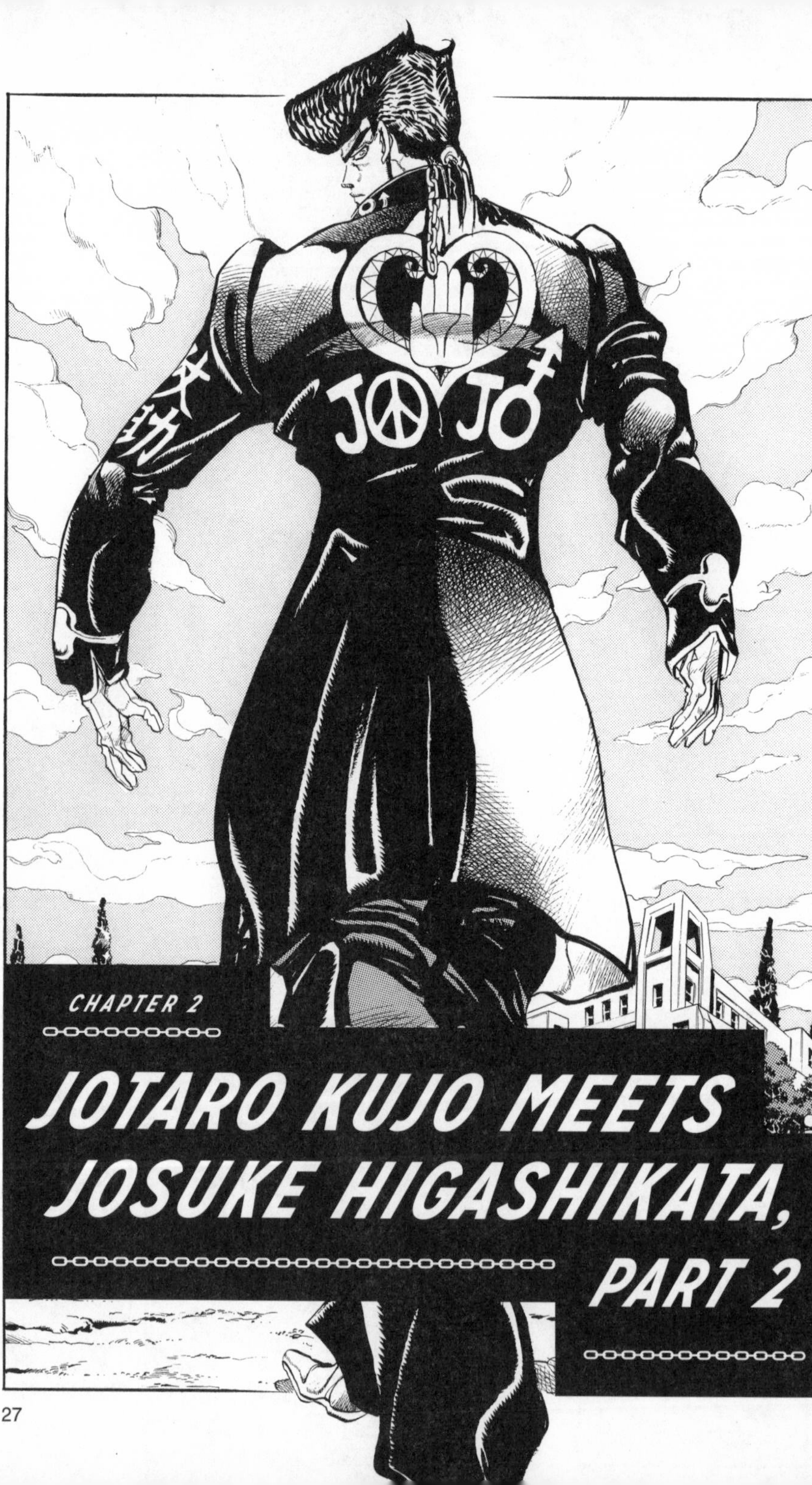
JOJO
CHAPTER 2
JOTARO KUJO MEETS JOSUKE HIGASHIKATA, PART 2

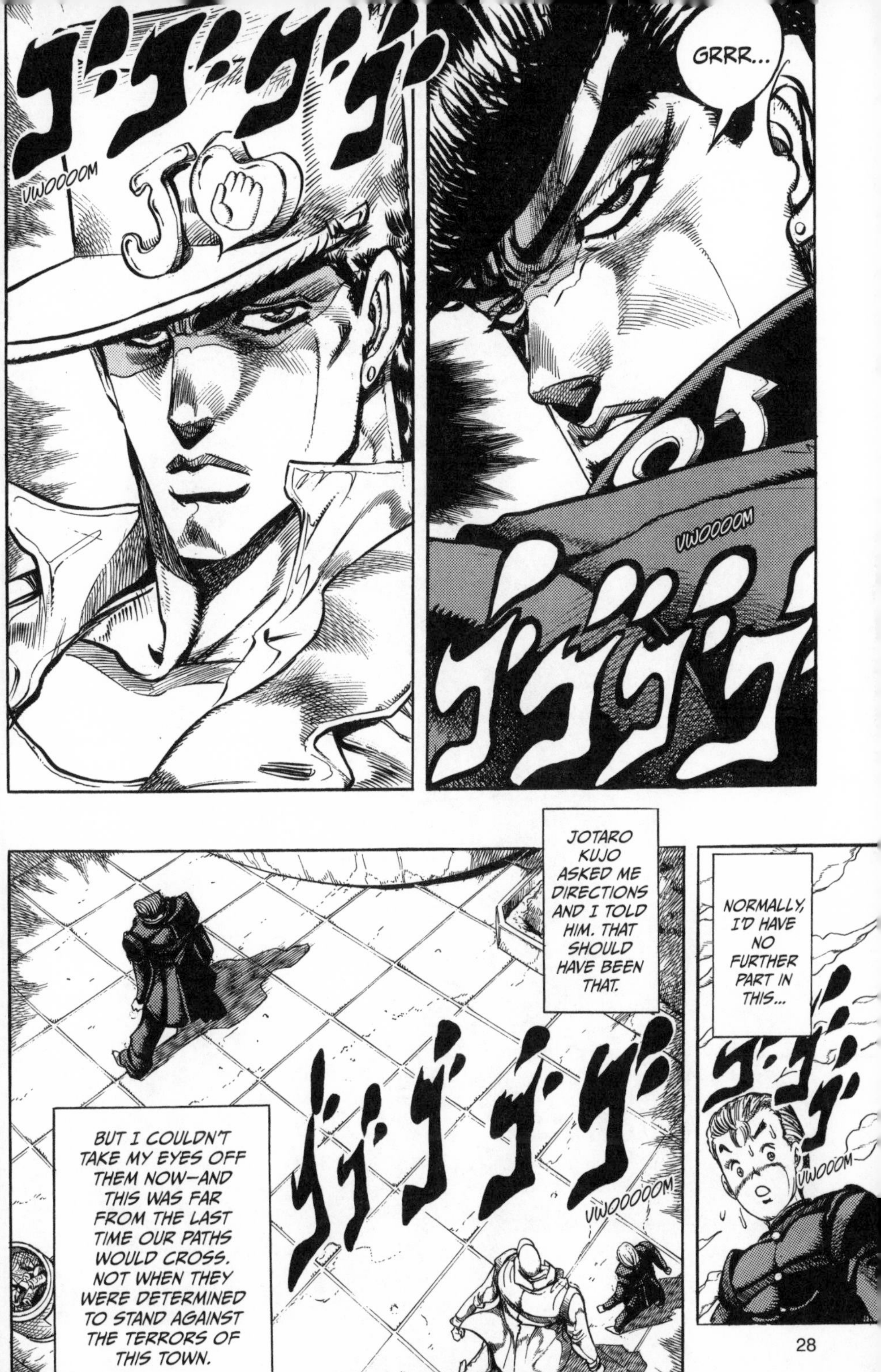
GRRR...
VWOOOOM
VWOOOOM
NORMALLY, I'D HAVE NO FURTHER PART IN THIS...
VWOOOM
JOTARO KUJO ASKED ME DIRECTIONS AND I TOLD HIM. THAT SHOULD HAVE BEEN THAT.
VWOOOOOM
BUT I COULDN'T TAKE MY EYES OFF THEM NOW—AND THIS WAS FAR FROM THE LAST TIME OUR PATHS WOULD CROSS. NOT WHEN THEY WERE DETERMINED TO STAND AGAINST THE TERRORS OF THIS TOWN.

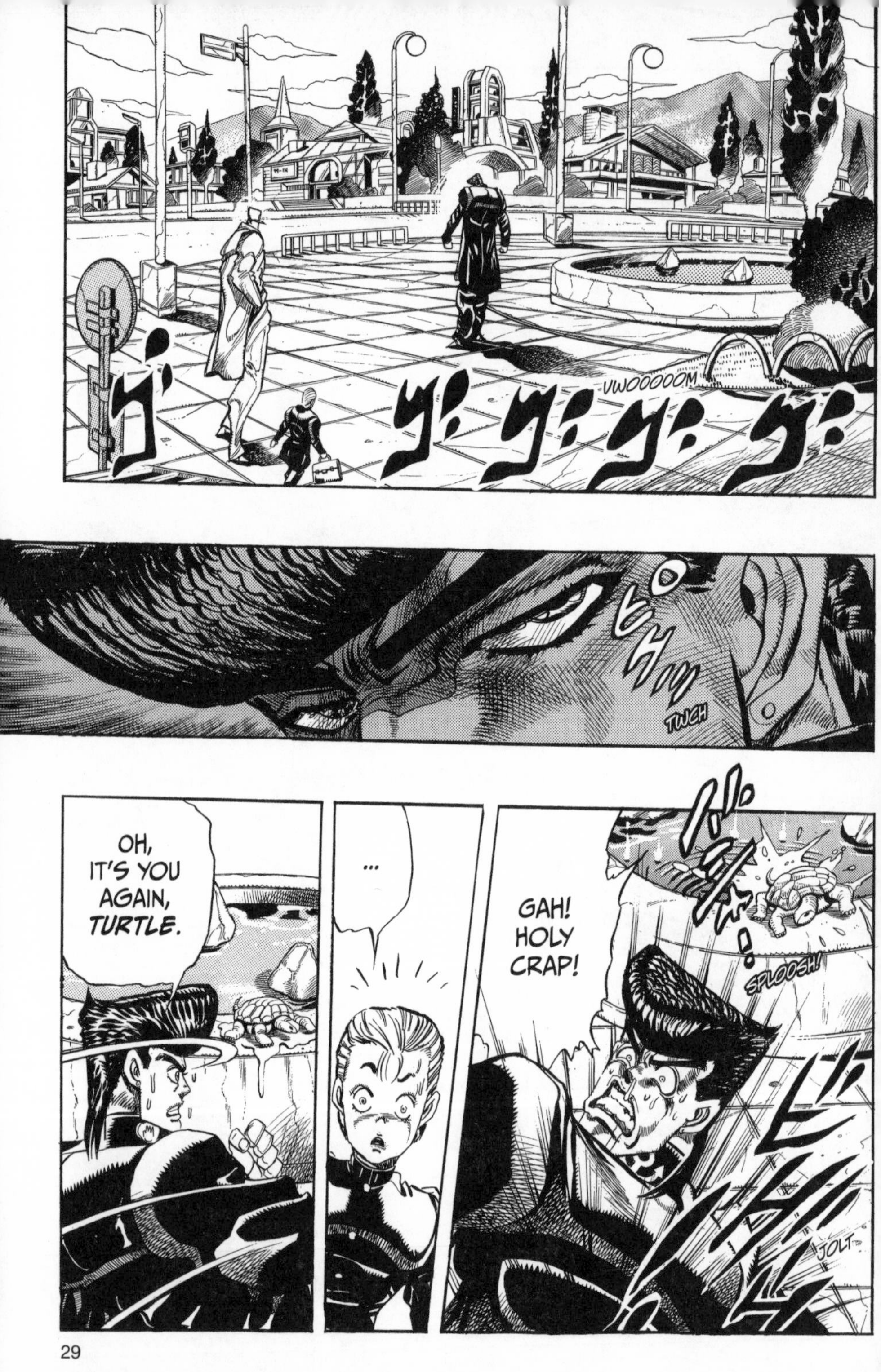
VWOOOOOM
TWCH
GAH! HOLY CRAP!
SPLOOSH!
JOLT
...
OH, IT'S YOU AGAIN, *TURTLE*.

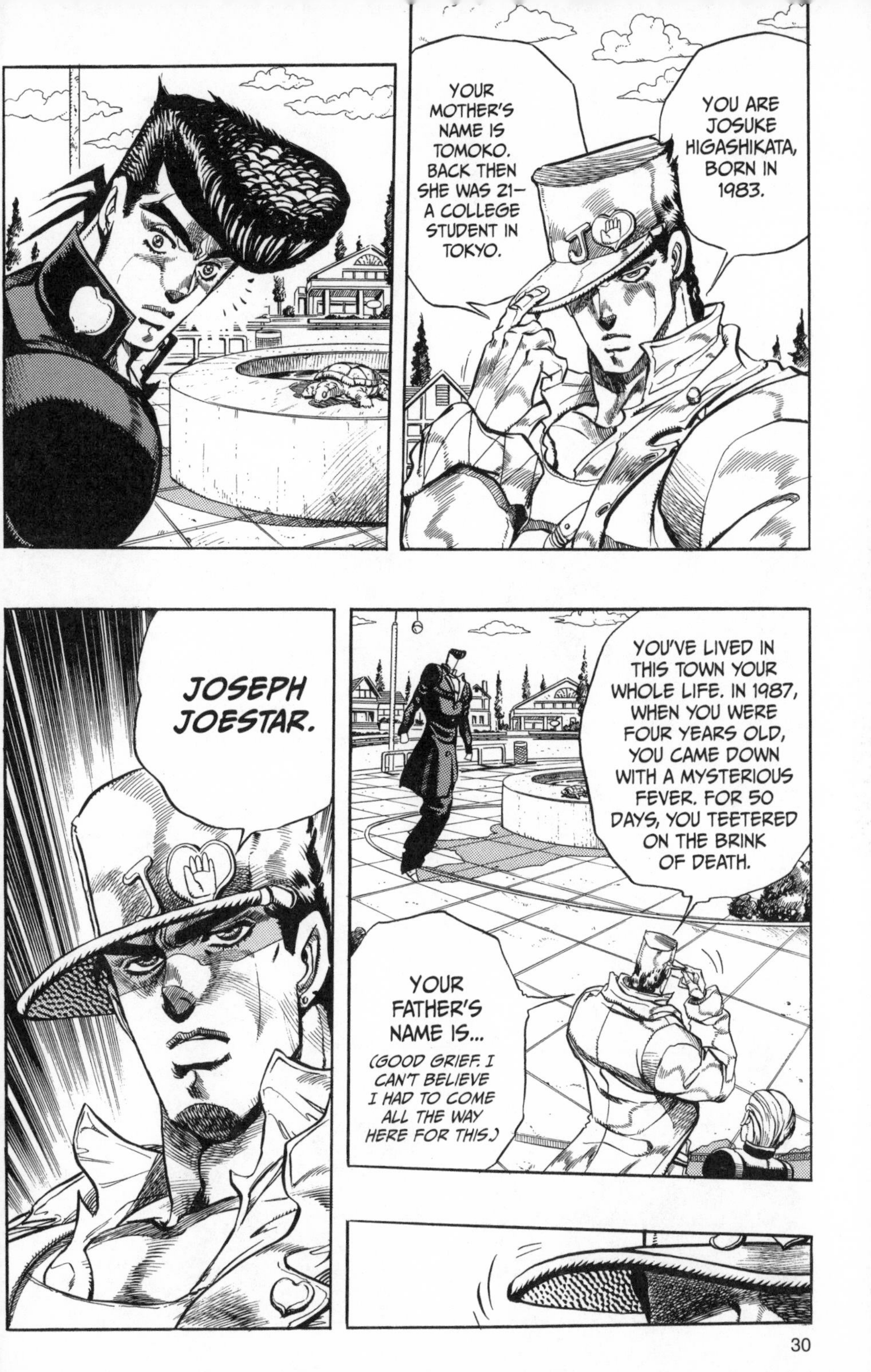
YOU ARE JOSUKE HIGASHIKATA, BORN IN 1983.
YOUR MOTHER'S NAME IS TOMOKO. BACK THEN SHE WAS 21— A COLLEGE STUDENT IN TOKYO.
YOU'VE LIVED IN THIS TOWN YOUR WHOLE LIFE. IN 1987, WHEN YOU WERE FOUR YEARS OLD, YOU CAME DOWN WITH A MYSTERIOUS FEVER. FOR 50 DAYS, YOU TEETERED ON THE BRINK OF DEATH.
YOUR FATHER'S NAME IS...
(GOOD GRIEF. I CAN'T BELIEVE I HAD TO COME ALL THE WAY HERE FOR THIS.)
JOSEPH JOESTAR.

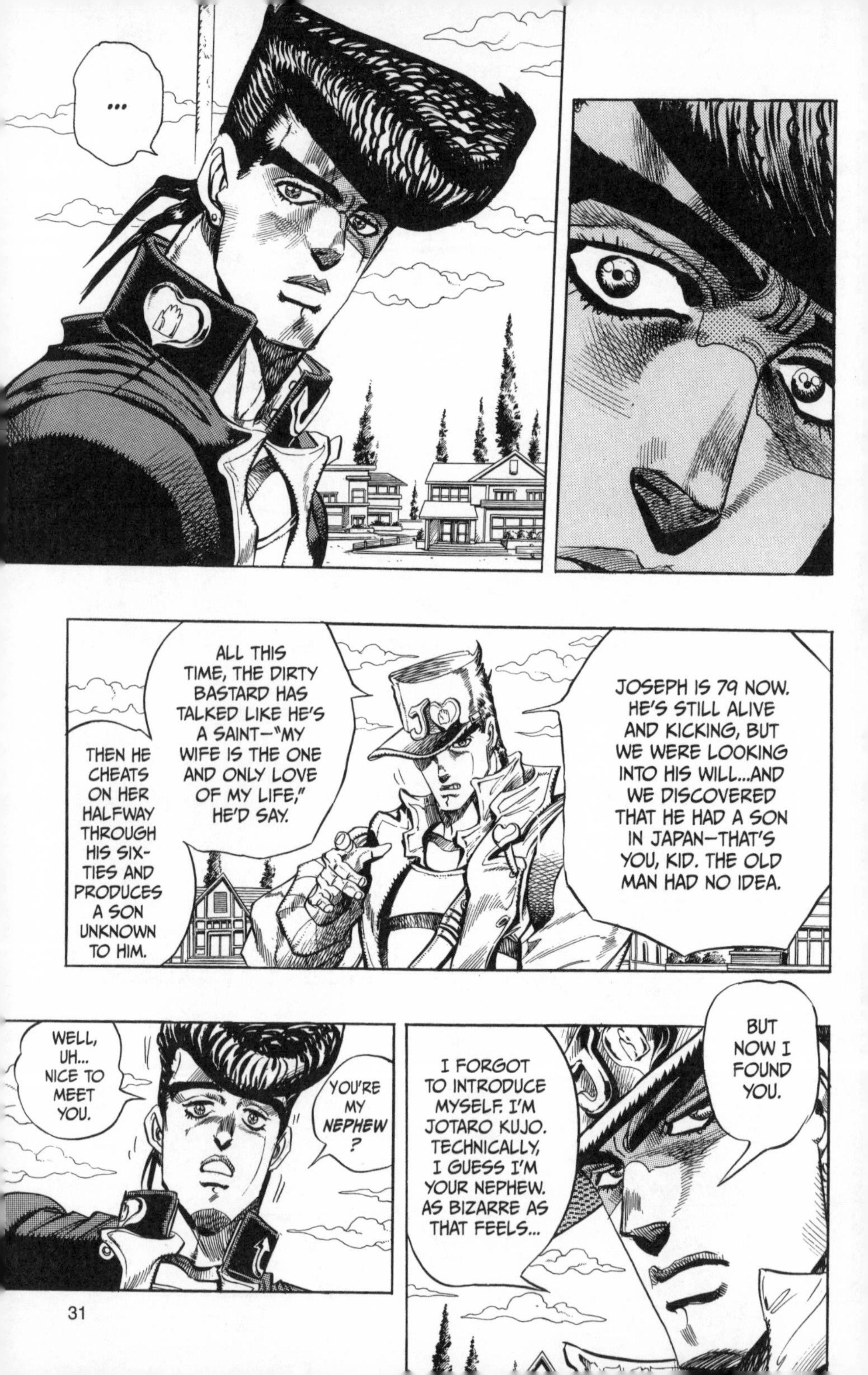
...
JOSEPH IS 79 NOW. HE'S STILL ALIVE AND KICKING, BUT WE WERE LOOKING INTO HIS WILL...AND WE DISCOVERED THAT HE HAD A SON IN JAPAN—THAT'S YOU, KID. THE OLD MAN HAD NO IDEA.
ALL THIS TIME, THE DIRTY BASTARD HAS TALKED LIKE HE'S A SAINT—"MY WIFE IS THE ONE AND ONLY LOVE OF MY LIFE," HE'D SAY.
THEN HE CHEATS ON HER HALFWAY THROUGH HIS SIX-TIES AND PRODUCES A SON UNKNOWN TO HIM.
BUT NOW I FOUND YOU.
I FORGOT TO INTRODUCE MYSELF. I'M JOTARO KUJO. TECHNICALLY, I GUESS I'M YOUR NEPHEW. AS BIZARRE AS THAT FEELS...
YOU'RE MY *NEPHEW*?
WELL, UH... NICE TO MEET YOU.

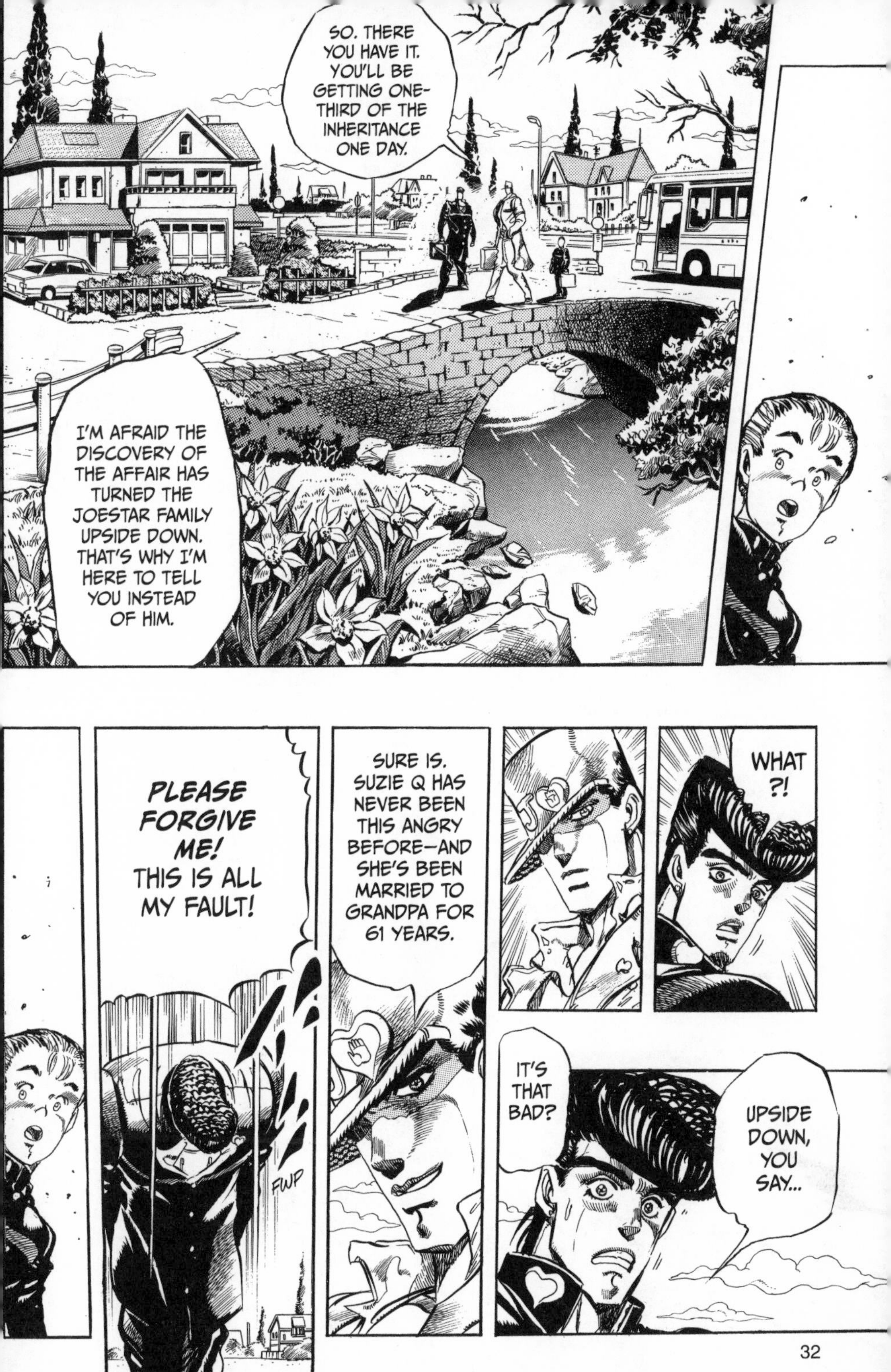
SO. THERE YOU HAVE IT. YOU'LL BE GETTING ONE-THIRD OF THE INHERITANCE ONE DAY.
I'M AFRAID THE DISCOVERY OF THE AFFAIR HAS TURNED THE JOESTAR FAMILY UPSIDE DOWN. THAT'S WHY I'M HERE TO TELL YOU INSTEAD OF HIM.
WHAT ?!
UPSIDE DOWN, YOU SAY...
IT'S THAT BAD?
SURE IS. SUZIE Q HAS NEVER BEEN THIS ANGRY BEFORE—AND SHE'S BEEN MARRIED TO GRANDPA FOR 61 YEARS.
PLEASE FORGIVE ME! THIS IS ALL MY FAULT!
FWUP

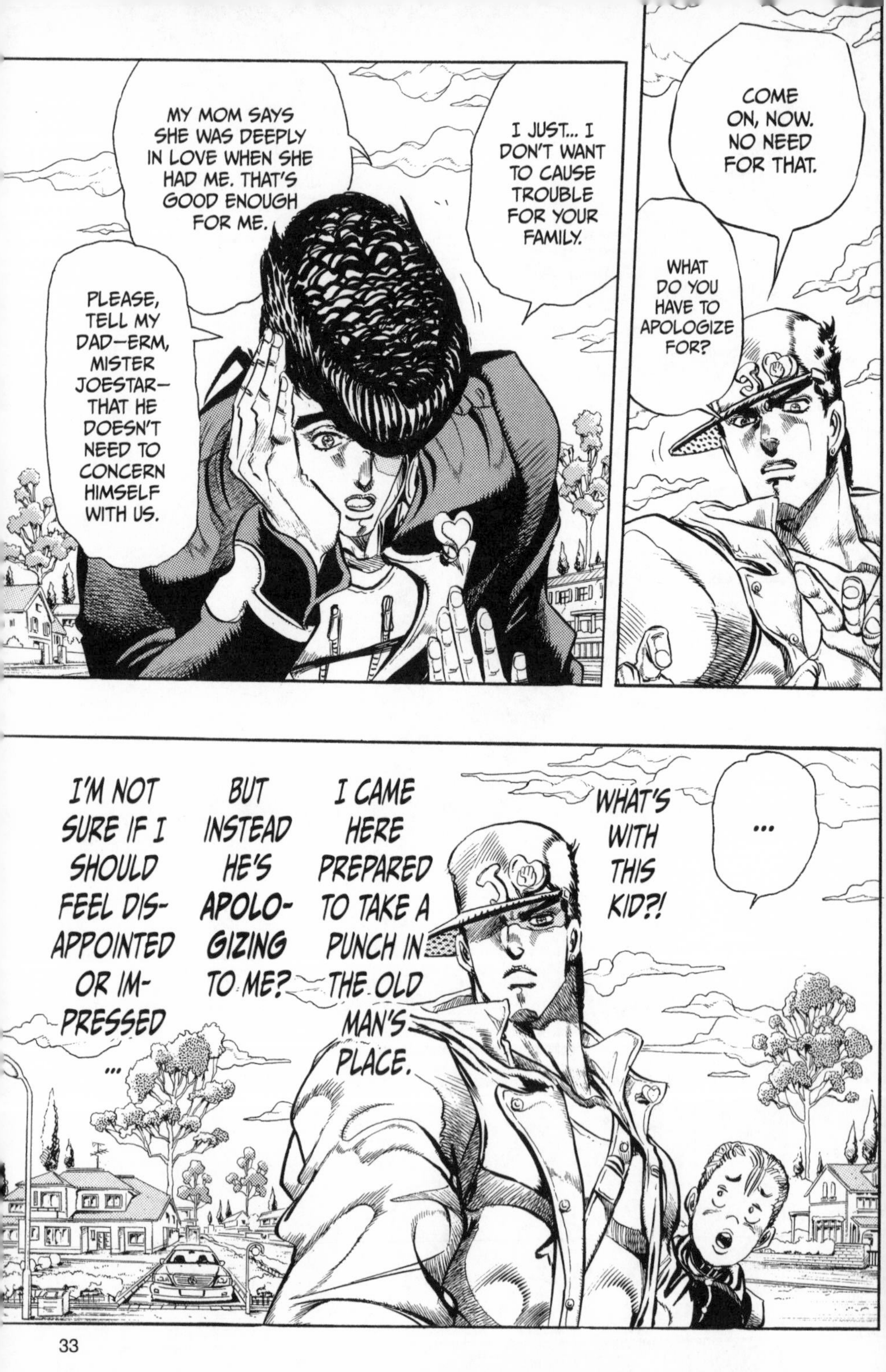
COME ON, NOW. NO NEED FOR THAT.
WHAT DO YOU HAVE TO APOLOGIZE FOR?
I JUST... I DON'T WANT TO CAUSE TROUBLE FOR YOUR FAMILY.
MY MOM SAYS SHE WAS DEEPLY IN LOVE WHEN SHE HAD ME. THAT'S GOOD ENOUGH FOR ME.
PLEASE, TELL MY DAD—ERM, MISTER JOESTAR—THAT HE DOESN'T NEED TO CONCERN HIMSELF WITH US.
...
WHAT'S WITH THIS KID?!
I CAME HERE PREPARED TO TAKE A PUNCH IN THE OLD MAN'S PLACE.
BUT INSTEAD HE'S APOLO-GIZING TO ME?
I'M NOT SURE IF I SHOULD FEEL DIS-APPOINTED OR IM-PRESSED...

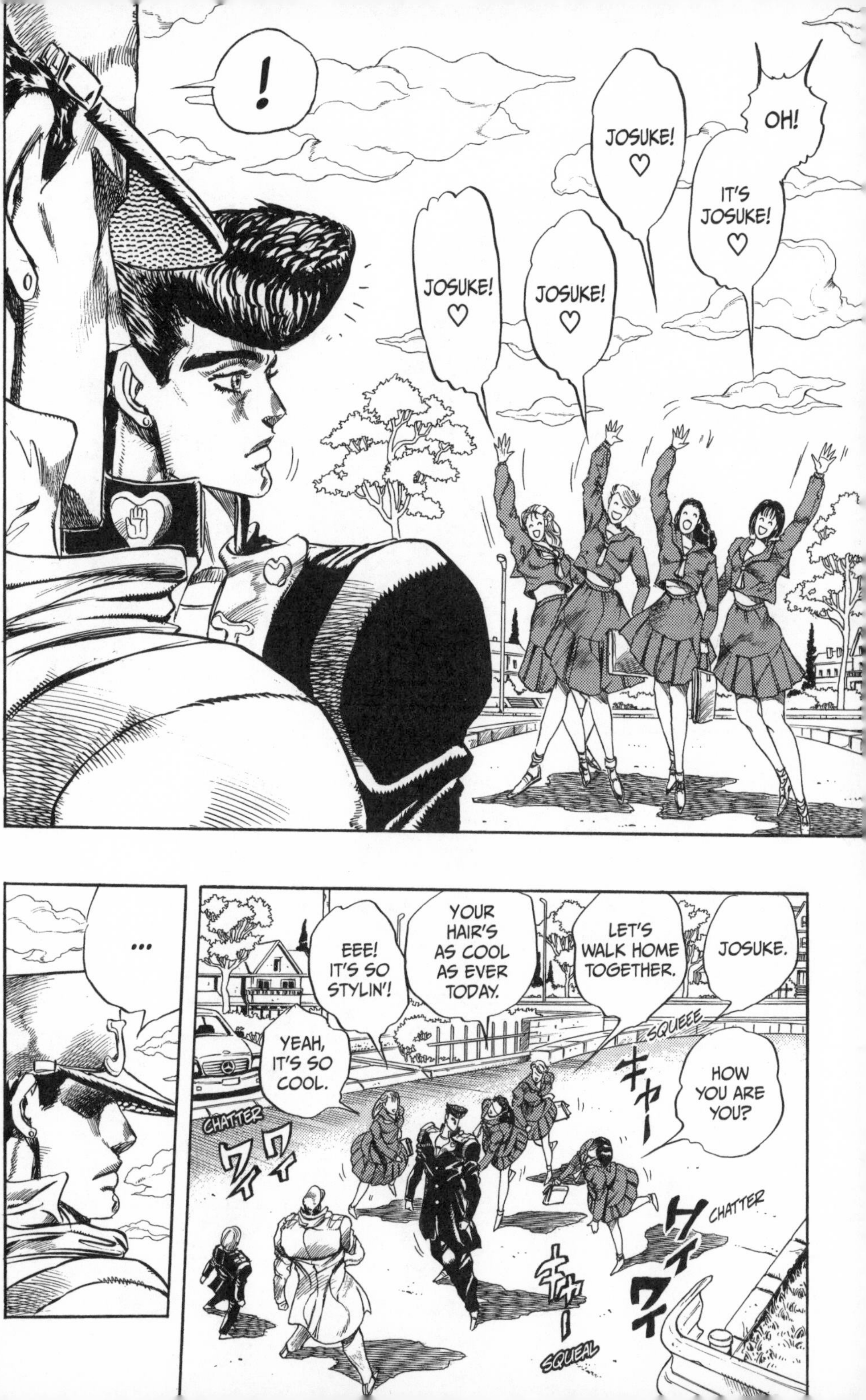
OH!
IT'S JOSUKE! ♡
JOSUKE! ♡
JOSUKE! ♡
JOSUKE! ♡
!
JOSUKE.
LET'S WALK HOME TOGETHER.
YOUR HAIR'S AS COOL AS EVER TODAY.
EEE! IT'S SO STYLIN'!
SQUEEE
キャー
HOW YOU ARE YOU?
YEAH, IT'S SO COOL.
CHATTER
ワイワイ
CHATTER
ワイワイ
キャー
SQUEAL
...

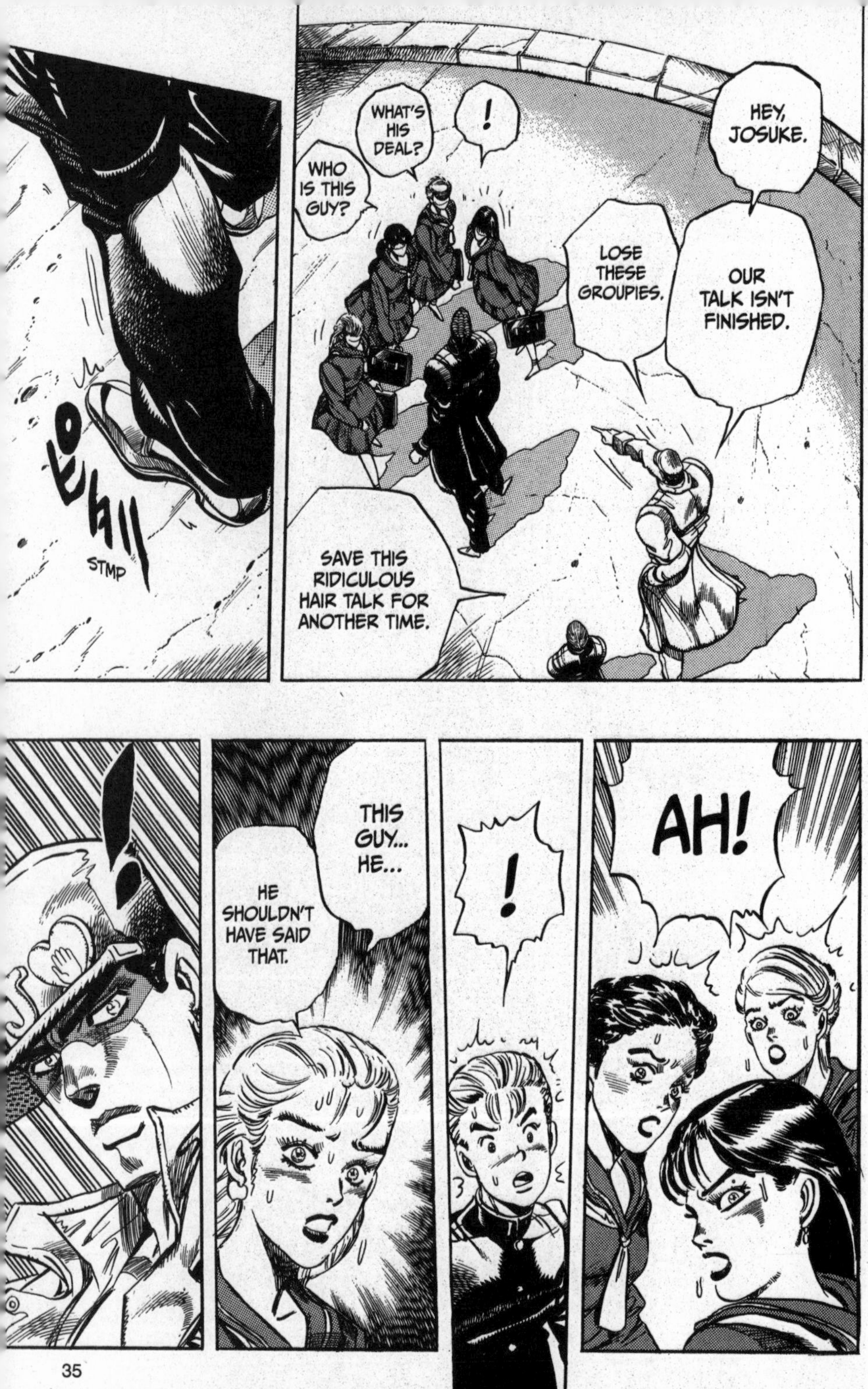
HEY, JOSUKE.
OUR TALK ISN'T FINISHED.
LOSE THESE GROUPIES.
!
WHAT'S HIS DEAL?
WHO IS THIS GUY?
SAVE THIS RIDICULOUS HAIR TALK FOR ANOTHER TIME.
STMP
AH!
!
THIS GUY... HE...
HE SHOULDN'T HAVE SAID THAT.

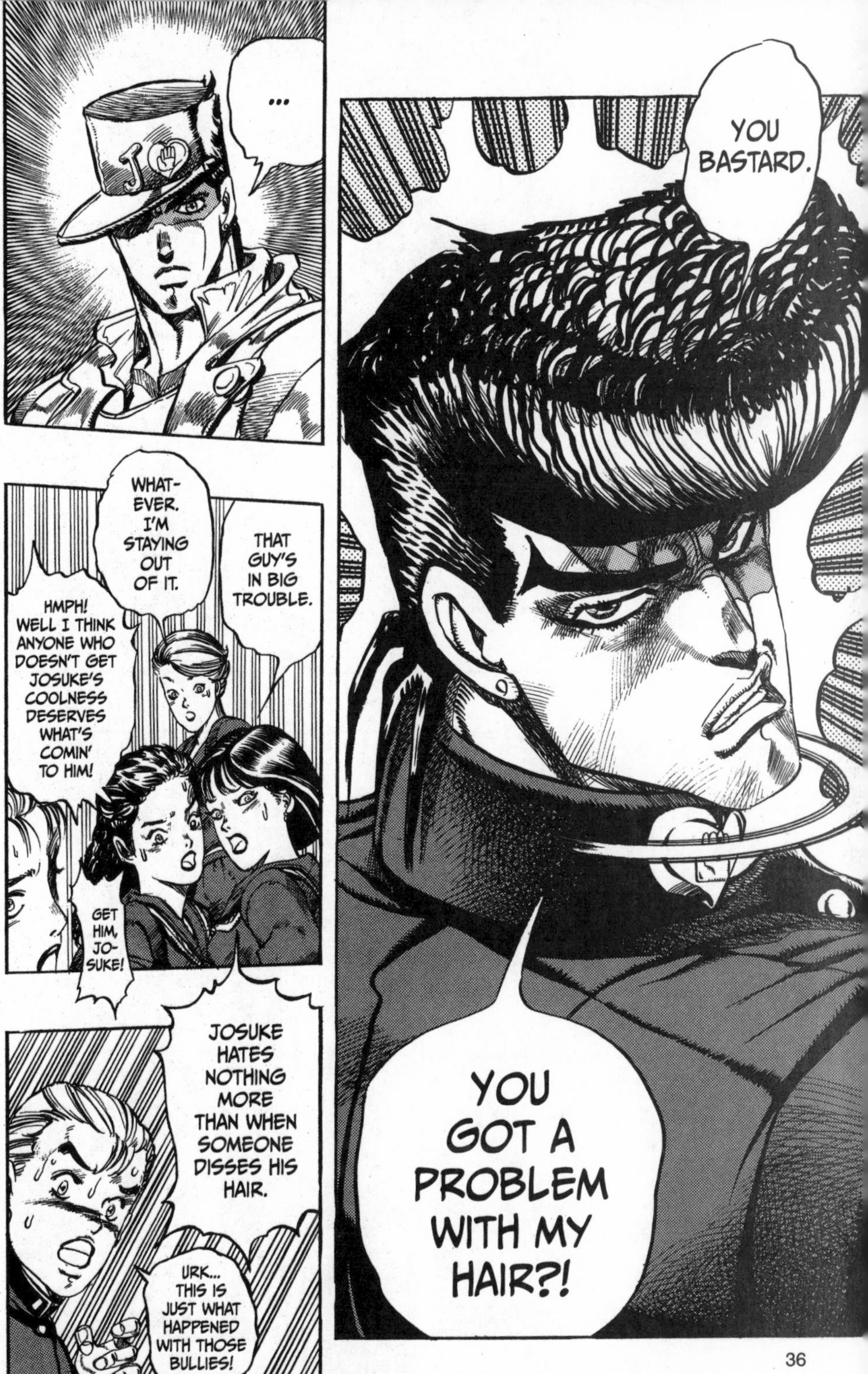
YOU BASTARD.
YOU GOT A PROBLEM WITH MY HAIR?!
...
THAT GUY'S IN BIG TROUBLE.
WHAT-EVER. I'M STAYING OUT OF IT.
HMPH! WELL I THINK ANYONE WHO DOESN'T GET JOSUKE'S COOLNESS DESERVES WHAT'S COMIN' TO HIM!
GET HIM, JO-SUKE!
JOSUKE HATES NOTHING MORE THAN WHEN SOMEONE DISSES HIS HAIR.
URK... THIS IS JUST WHAT HAPPENED WITH THOSE BULLIES!

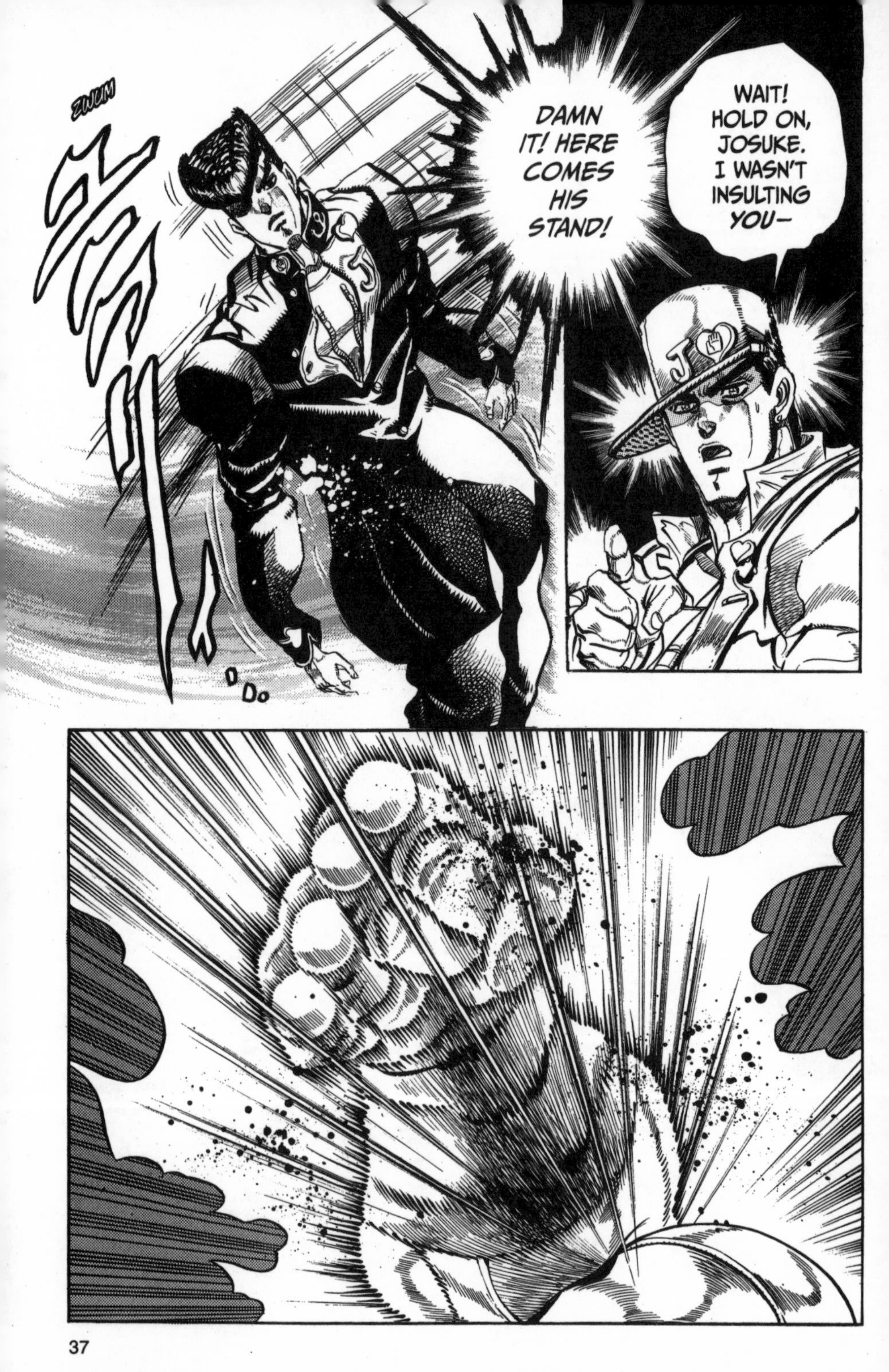
WAIT! HOLD ON, JOSUKE. I WASN'T INSULTING YOU—
DAMN IT! HERE COMES HIS STAND!
ZWUM
D Do

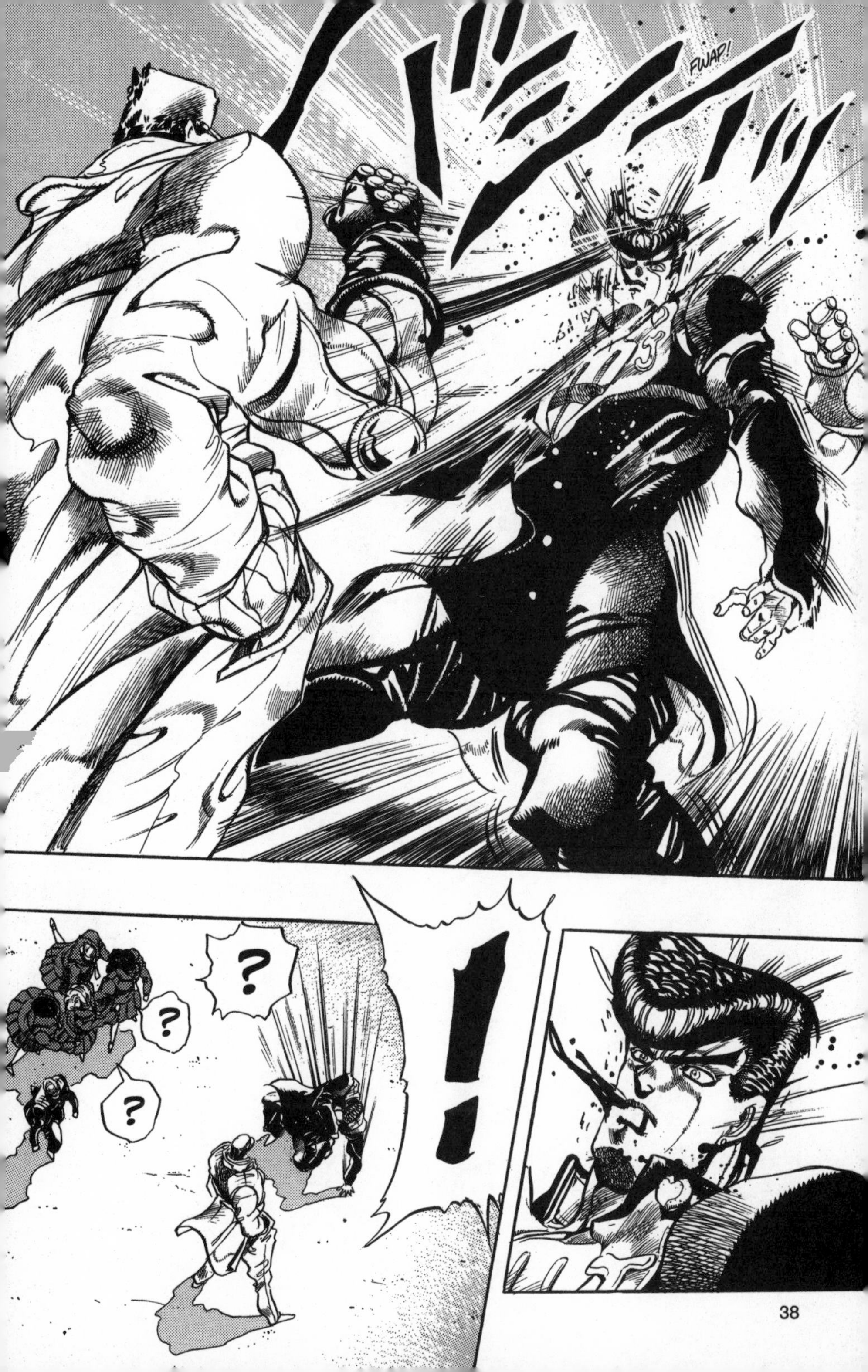
FWAP!
!
?
?
?

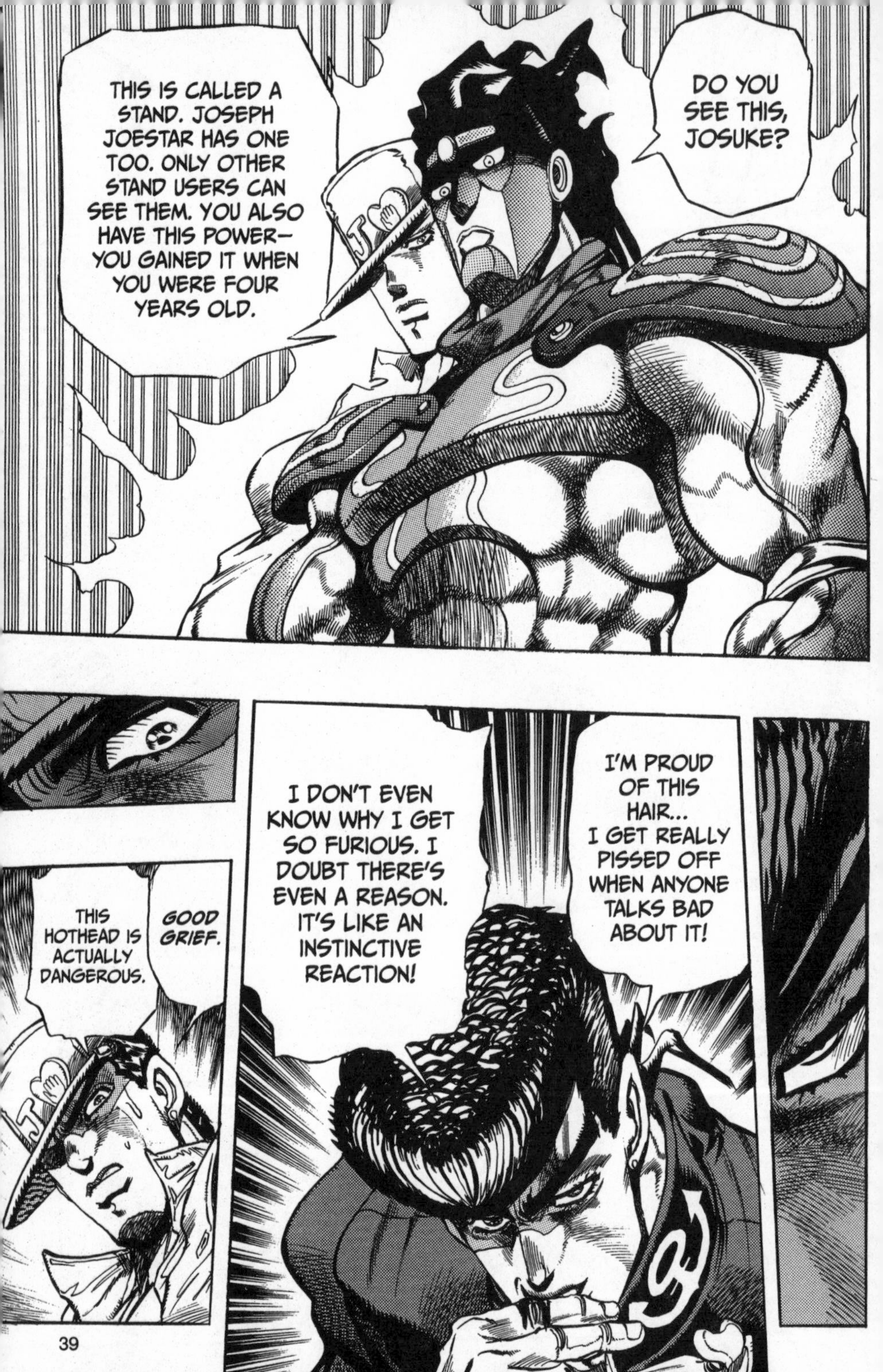
DO YOU SEE THIS, JOSUKE?
THIS IS CALLED A STAND. JOSEPH JOESTAR HAS ONE TOO. ONLY OTHER STAND USERS CAN SEE THEM. YOU ALSO HAVE THIS POWER— YOU GAINED IT WHEN YOU WERE FOUR YEARS OLD.
I'M PROUD OF THIS HAIR... I GET REALLY PISSED OFF WHEN ANYONE TALKS BAD ABOUT IT!
I DON'T EVEN KNOW WHY I GET SO FURIOUS. I DOUBT THERE'S EVEN A REASON. IT'S LIKE AN INSTINCTIVE REACTION!
GOOD GRIEF.
THIS HOTHEAD IS ACTUALLY DANGEROUS.

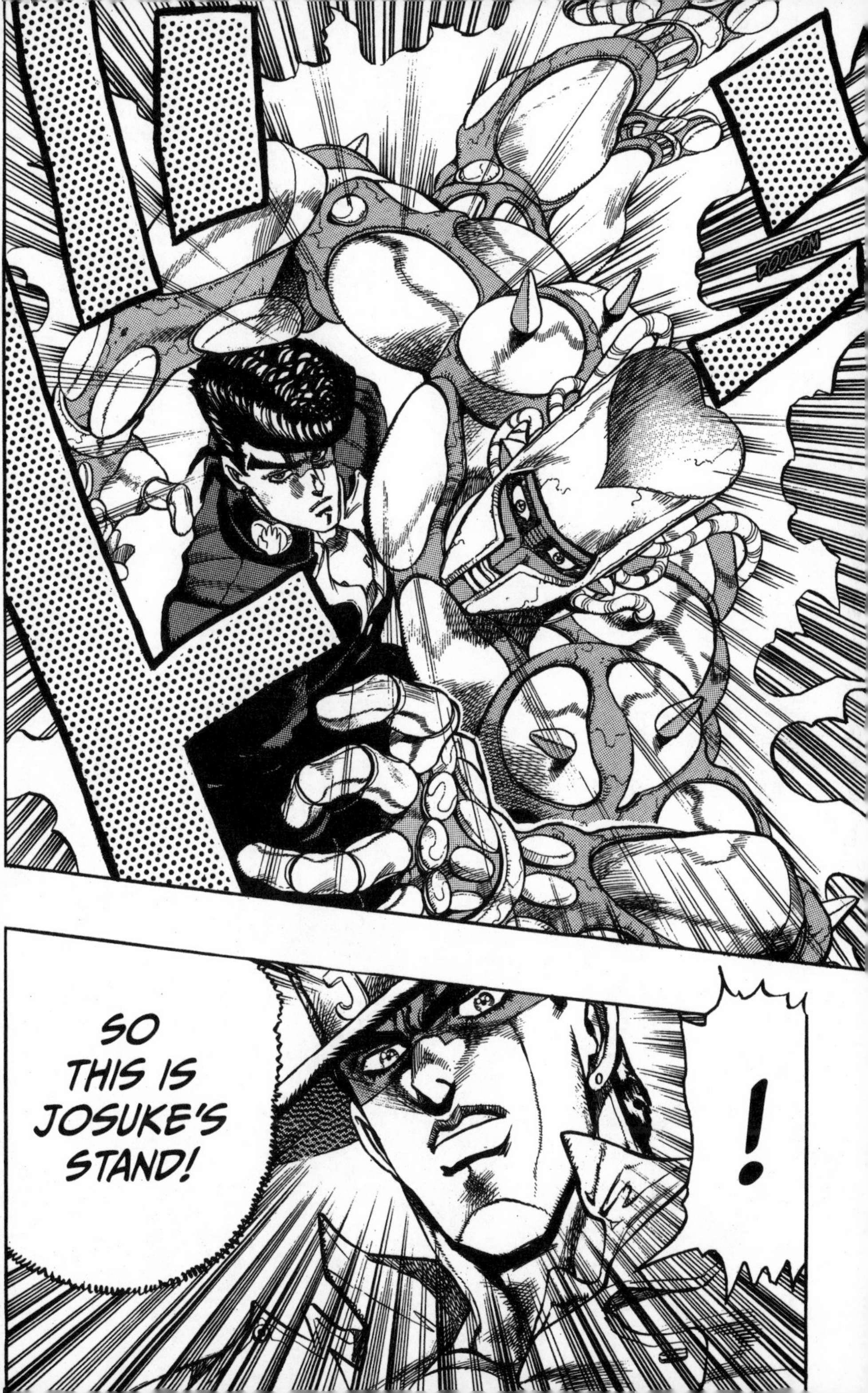
DOOOOM
SO THIS IS JOSUKE'S STAND!
!

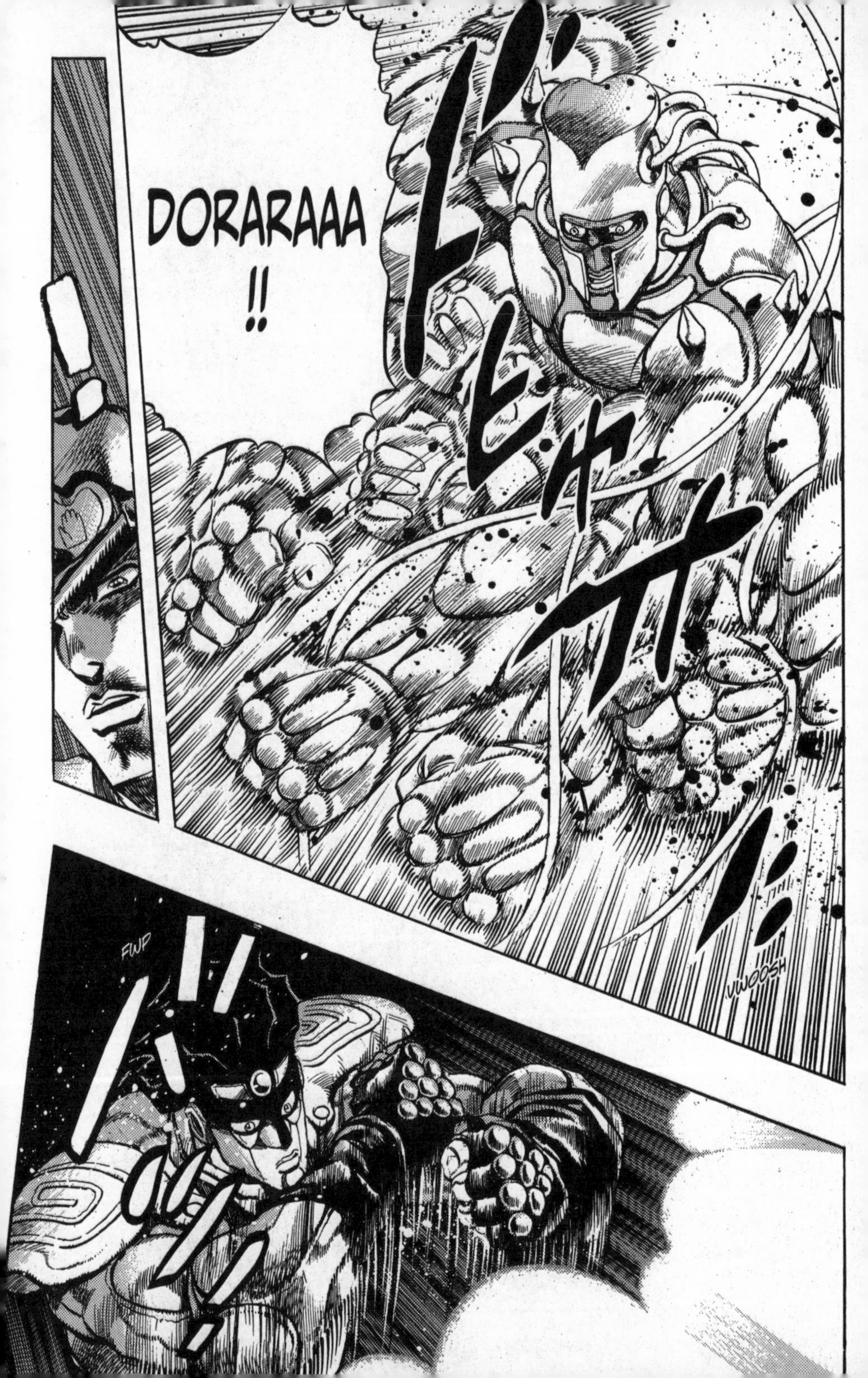

DORARAAA
!!
VWOOSH
!
FWP

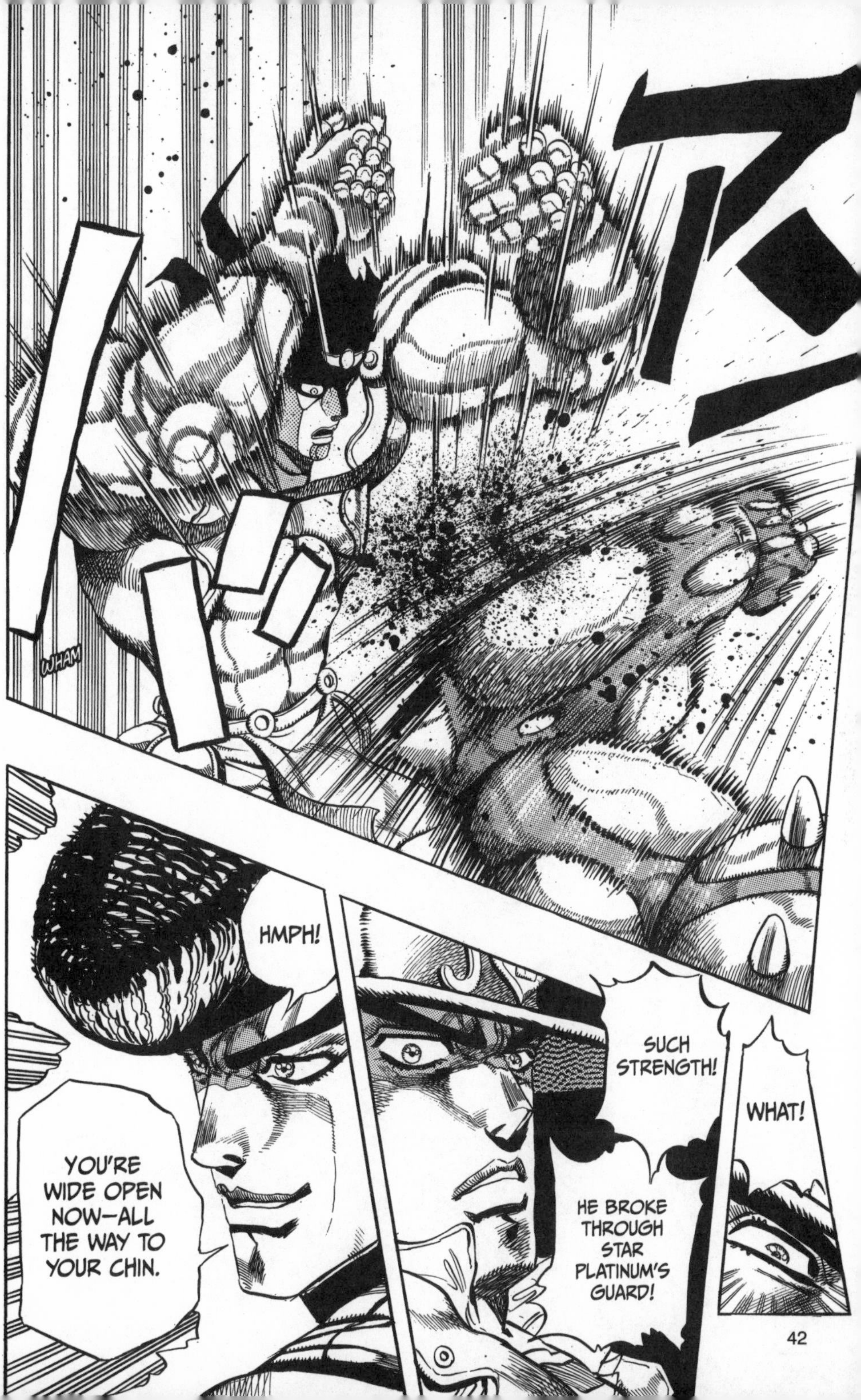
WHAM
WHAT!
SUCH STRENGTH!
HE BROKE THROUGH STAR PLATINUM'S GUARD!
HMPH!
YOU'RE WIDE OPEN NOW—ALL THE WAY TO YOUR CHIN.

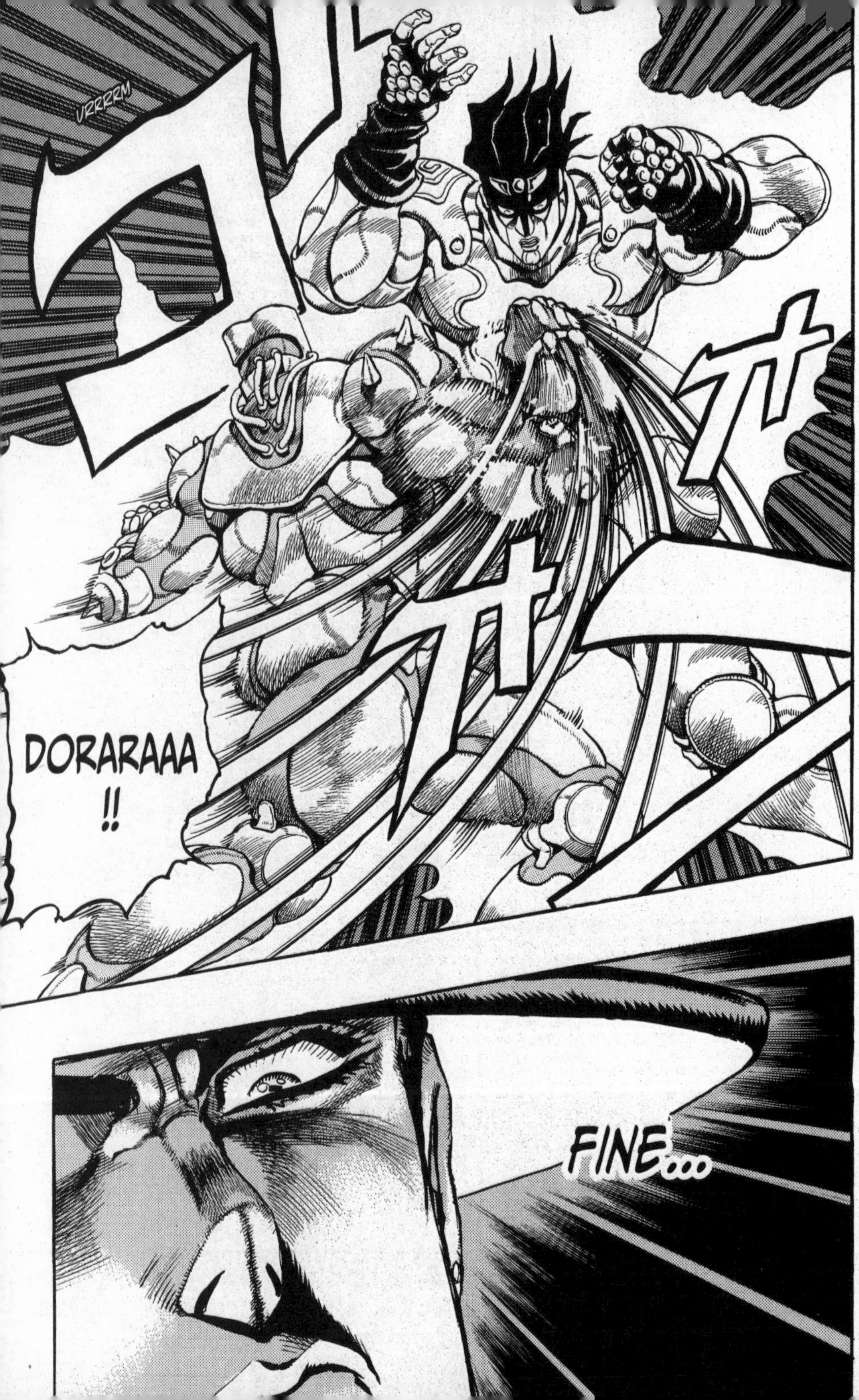
URRRRM
DORARAAA !!
FINE...

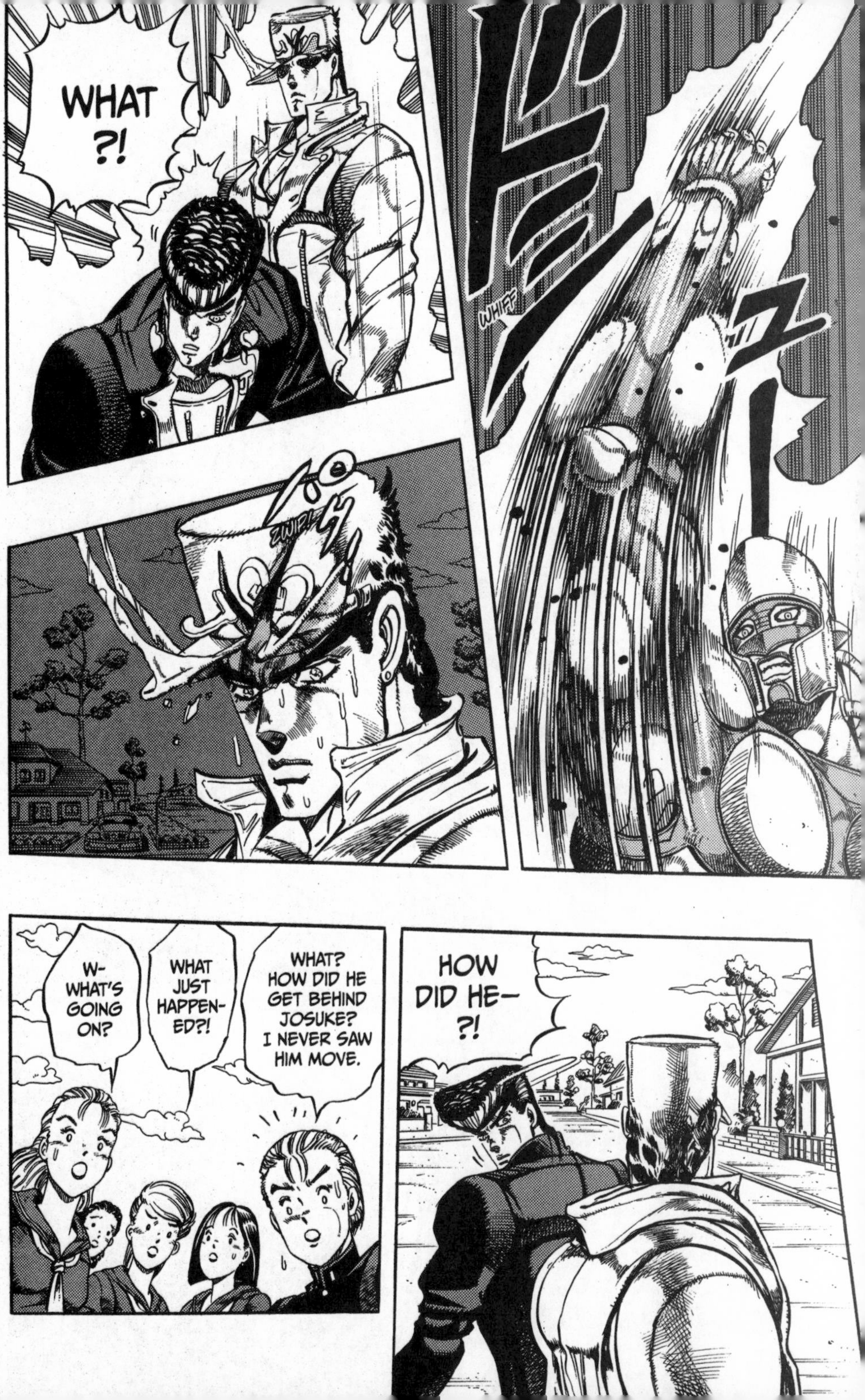
WHIFF
WHAT ?!
ZWIP!
HOW DID HE— ?!
WHAT? HOW DID HE GET BEHIND JOSUKE? I NEVER SAW HIM MOVE.
WHAT JUST HAPPEN-ED?!
W- WHAT'S GOING ON?

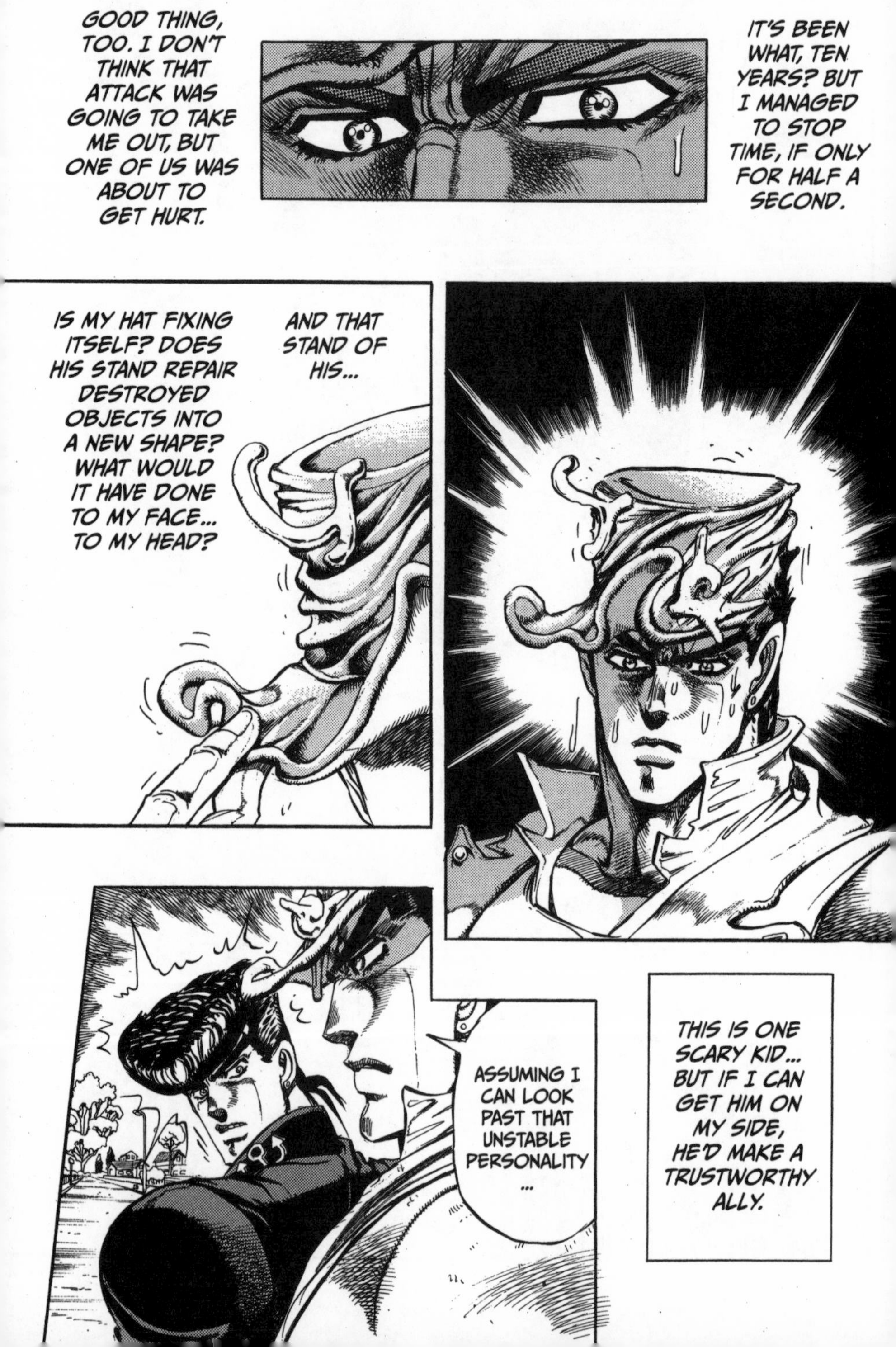
IT'S BEEN WHAT, TEN YEARS? BUT I MANAGED TO STOP TIME, IF ONLY FOR HALF A SECOND.
GOOD THING, TOO. I DON'T THINK THAT ATTACK WAS GOING TO TAKE ME OUT, BUT ONE OF US WAS ABOUT TO GET HURT.
AND THAT STAND OF HIS...
IS MY HAT FIXING ITSELF? DOES HIS STAND REPAIR DESTROYED OBJECTS INTO A NEW SHAPE? WHAT WOULD IT HAVE DONE TO MY FACE... TO MY HEAD?
THIS IS ONE SCARY KID... BUT IF I CAN GET HIM ON MY SIDE, HE'D MAKE A TRUSTWORTHY ALLY.
ASSUMING I CAN LOOK PAST THAT UNSTABLE PERSONALITY...

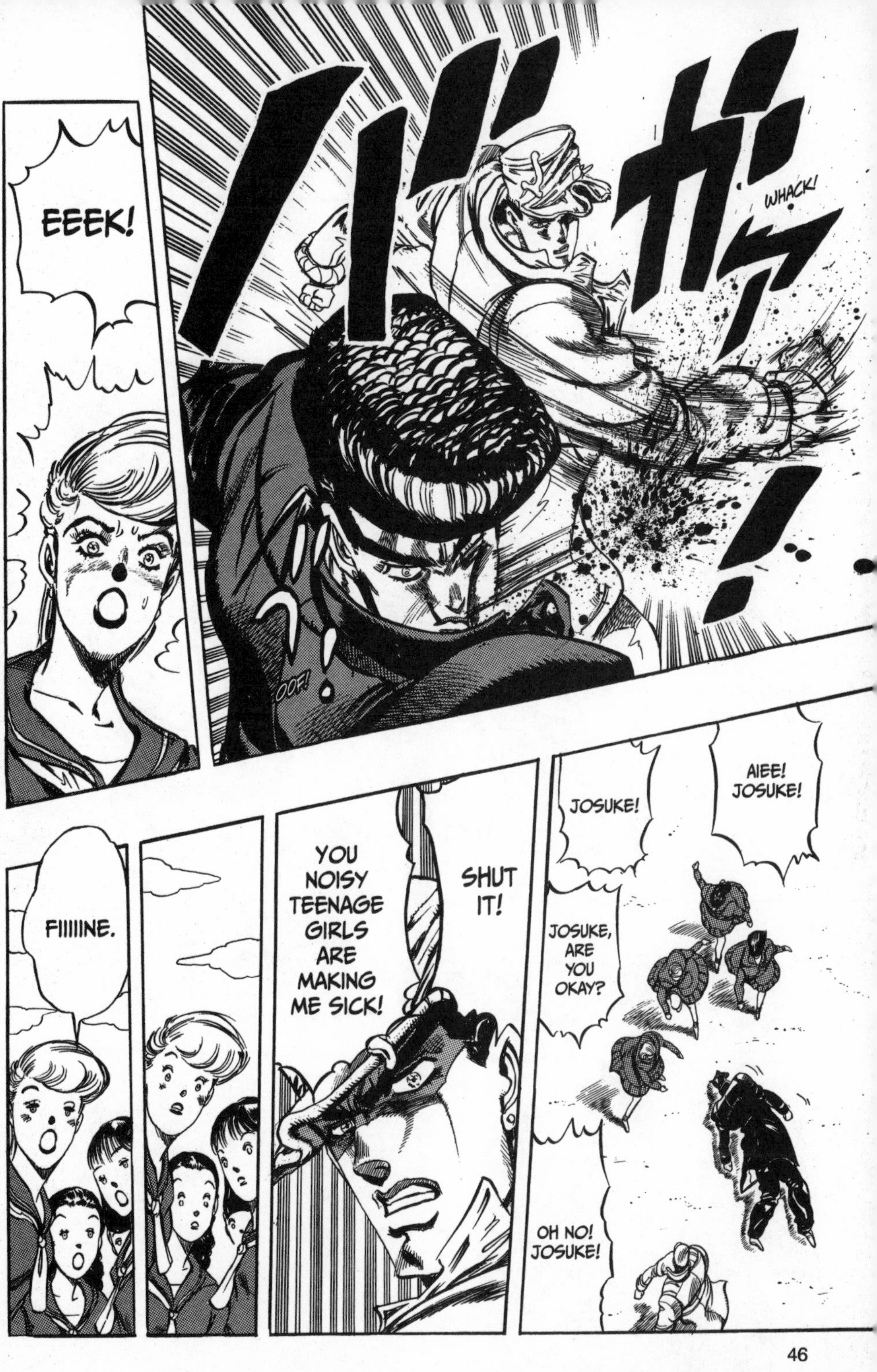
WHACK!
OOF!
EEEK!
AIEE! JOSUKE!
JOSUKE!
JOSUKE, ARE YOU OKAY?
OH NO! JOSUKE!
SHUT IT!
YOU NOISY TEENAGE GIRLS ARE MAKING ME SICK!
FIIIIINE.

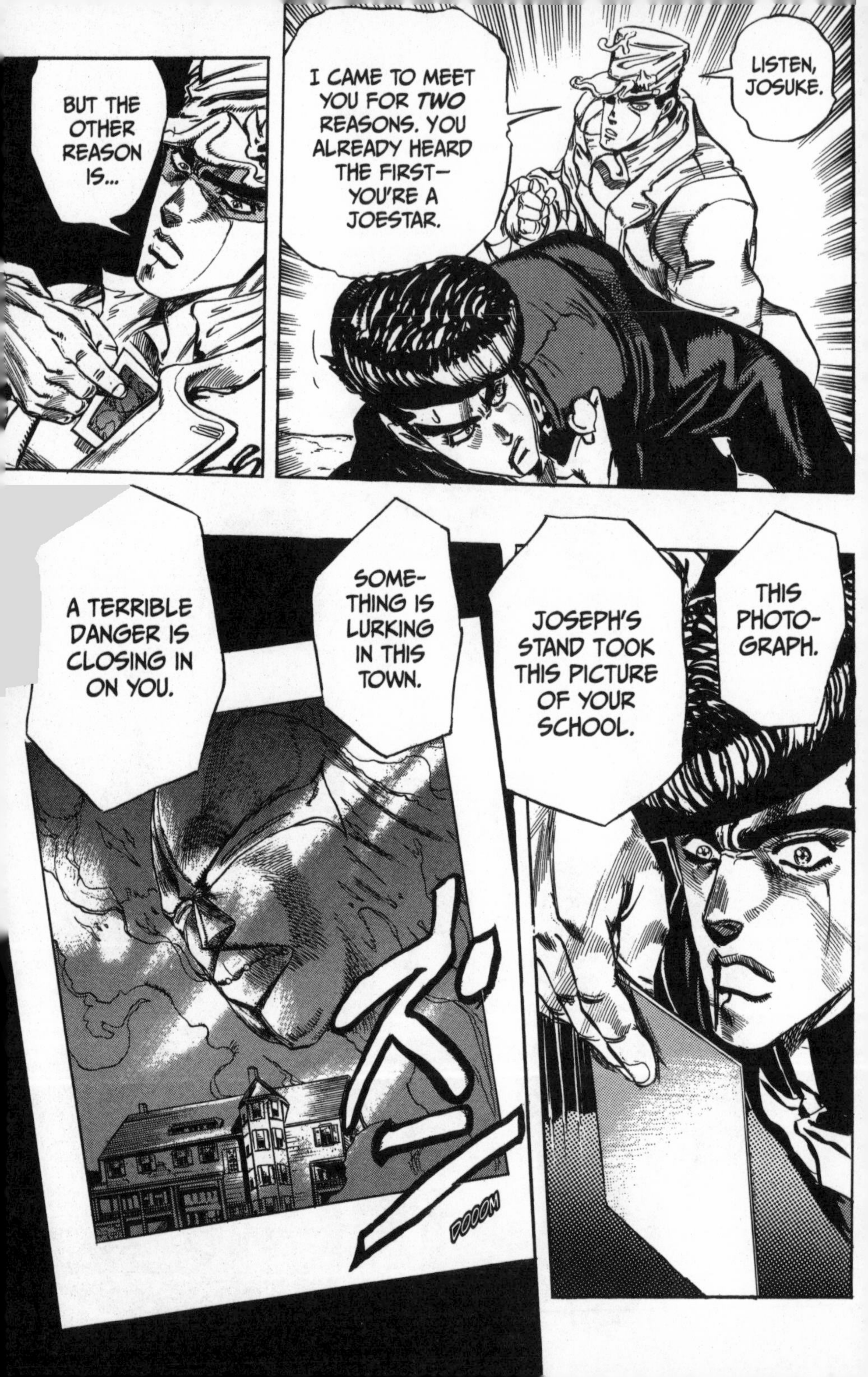
LISTEN, JOSUKE.
I CAME TO MEET YOU FOR *TWO* REASONS. YOU ALREADY HEARD THE FIRST— YOU'RE A JOESTAR.
BUT THE OTHER REASON IS...
THIS PHOTOGRAPH.
JOSEPH'S STAND TOOK THIS PICTURE OF YOUR SCHOOL.
SOMETHING IS LURKING IN THIS TOWN.
A TERRIBLE DANGER IS CLOSING IN ON YOU.
DOOOM

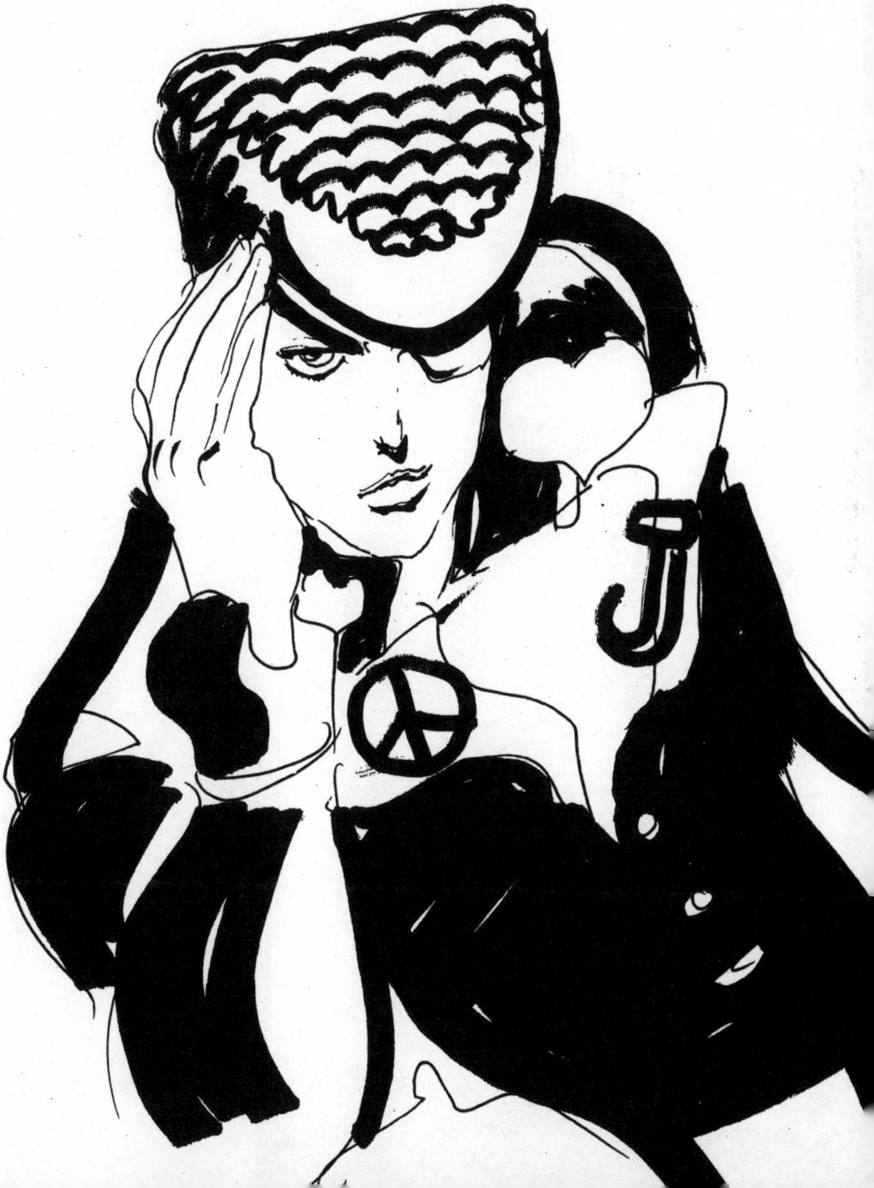

CHAPTER 3

JOTARO KUJO MEETS JOSUKE HIGASHIKATA, PART 3

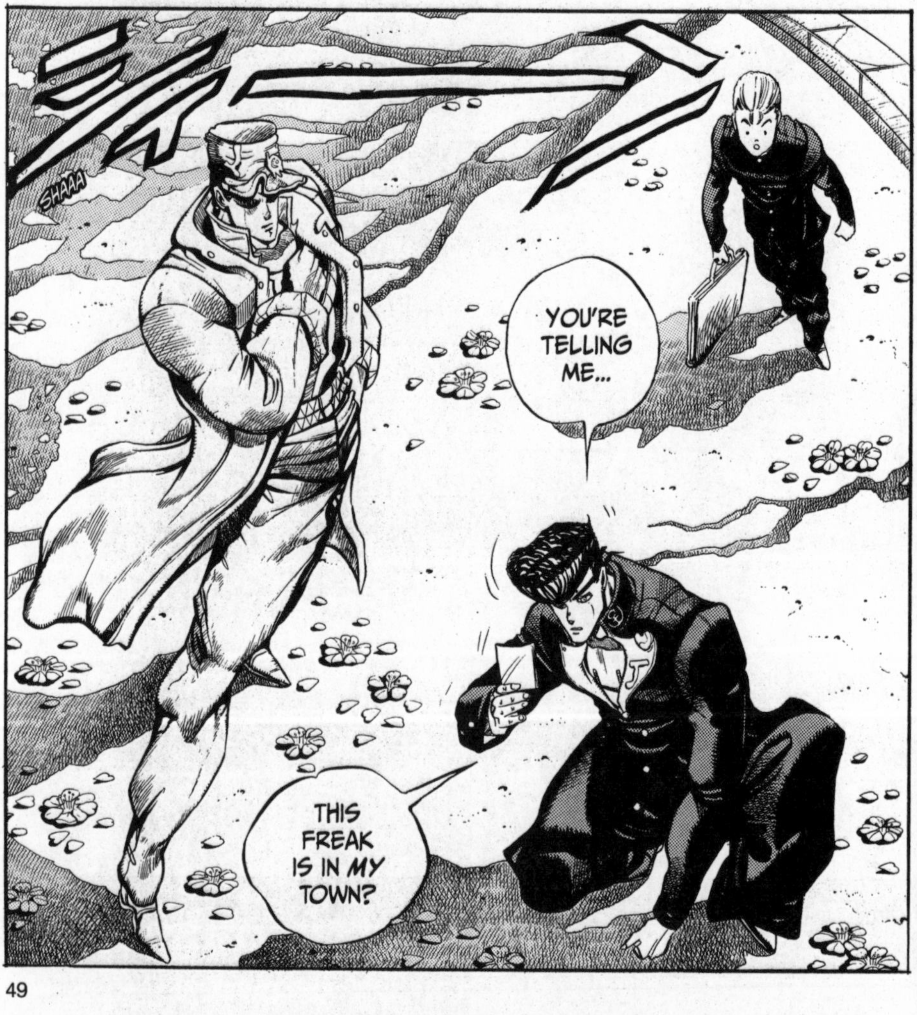
YOU'RE TELLING ME...
SHAAA
THIS FREAK IS IN *MY* TOWN?

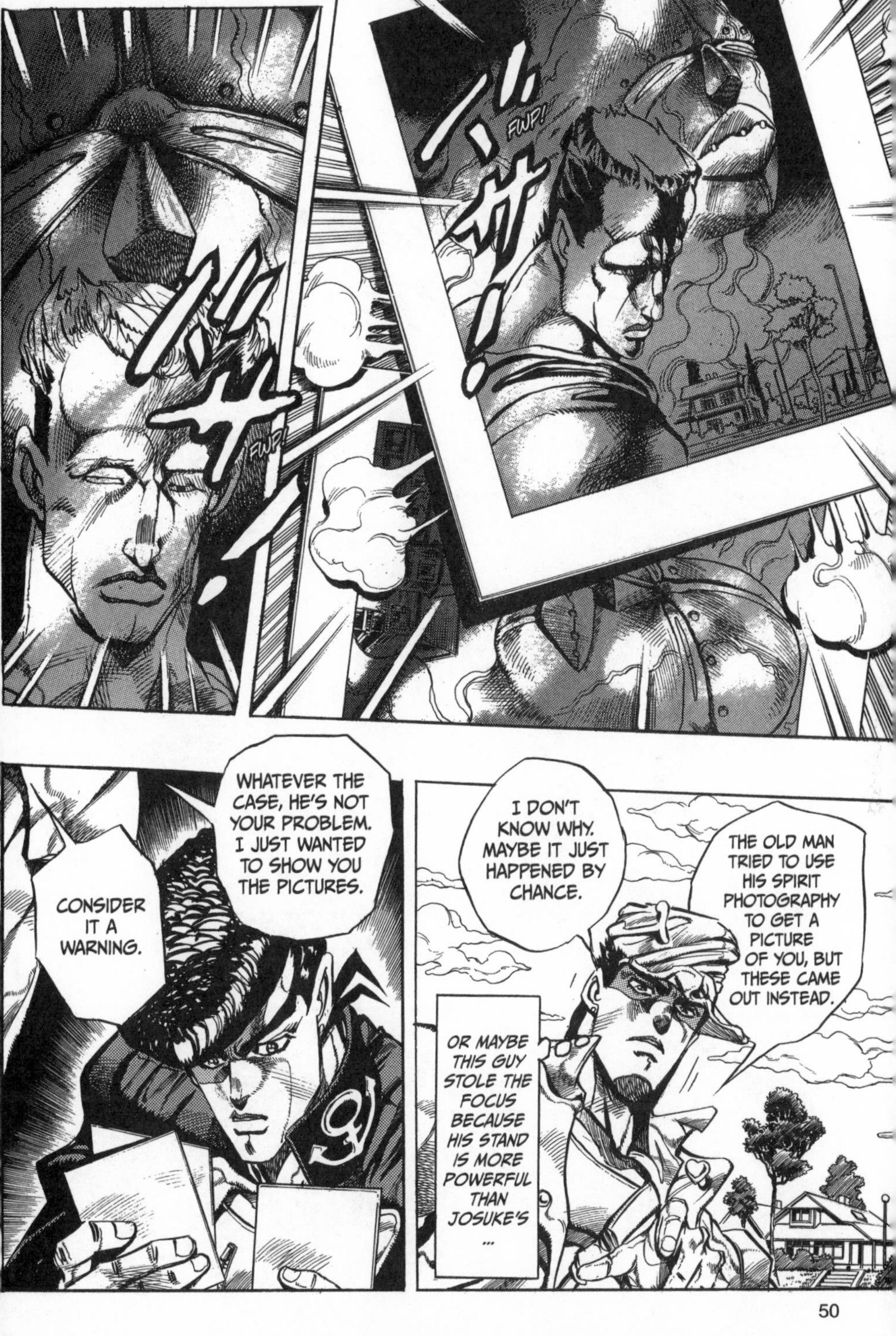
FWP!
FWP!
THE OLD MAN TRIED TO USE HIS SPIRIT PHOTOGRAPHY TO GET A PICTURE OF YOU, BUT THESE CAME OUT INSTEAD.
I DON'T KNOW WHY. MAYBE IT JUST HAPPENED BY CHANCE.
OR MAYBE THIS GUY STOLE THE FOCUS BECAUSE HIS STAND IS MORE POWERFUL THAN JOSUKE'S ...
WHATEVER THE CASE, HE'S NOT YOUR PROBLEM. I JUST WANTED TO SHOW YOU THE PICTURES.
CONSIDER IT A WARNING.

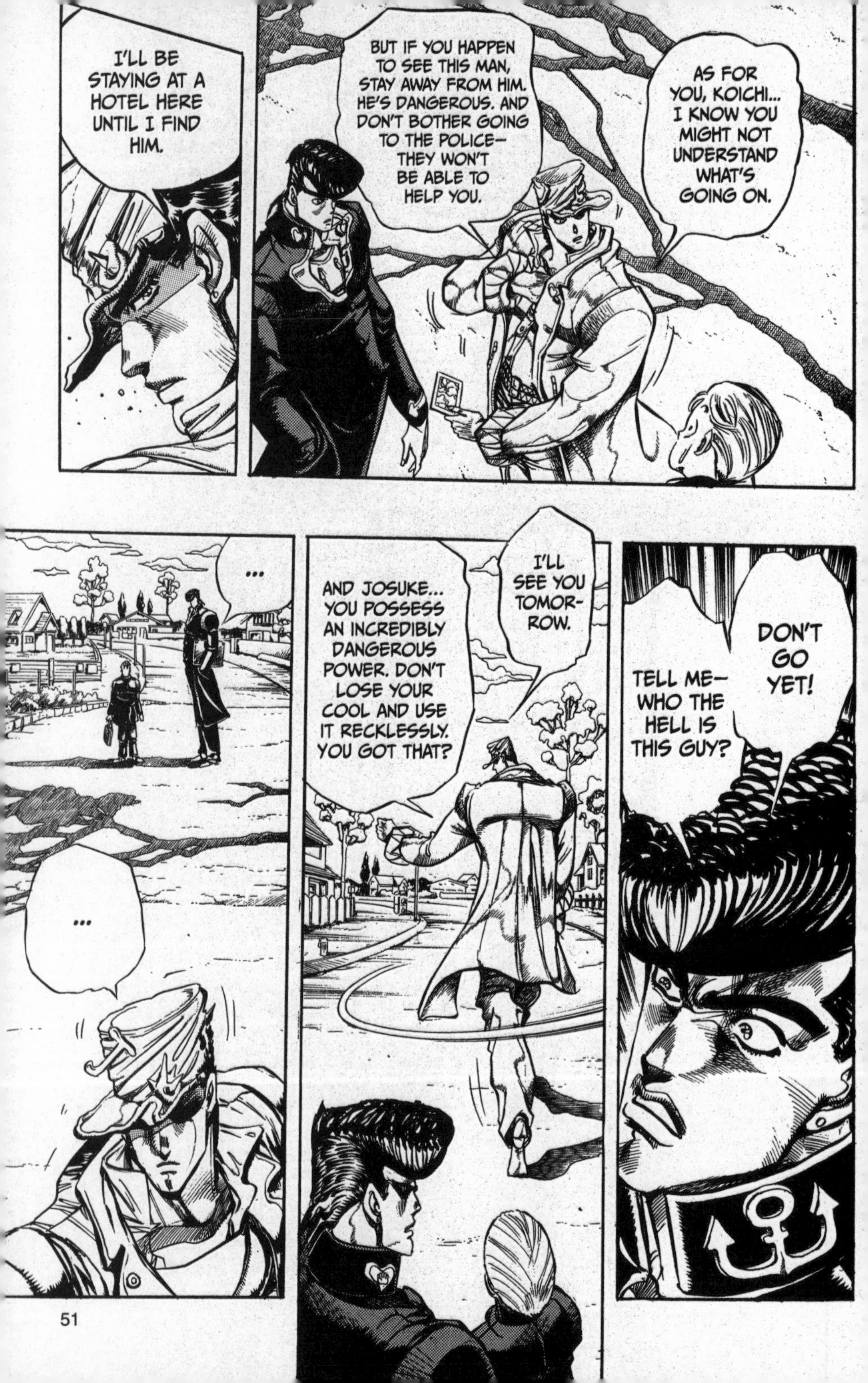
AS FOR YOU, KOICHI... I KNOW YOU MIGHT NOT UNDERSTAND WHAT'S GOING ON.
BUT IF YOU HAPPEN TO SEE THIS MAN, STAY AWAY FROM HIM. HE'S DANGEROUS. AND DON'T BOTHER GOING TO THE POLICE— THEY WON'T BE ABLE TO HELP YOU.
I'LL BE STAYING AT A HOTEL HERE UNTIL I FIND HIM.
DON'T GO YET!
TELL ME— WHO THE HELL IS THIS GUY?
I'LL SEE YOU TOMORROW.
AND JOSUKE... YOU POSSESS AN INCREDIBLY DANGEROUS POWER. DON'T LOSE YOUR COOL AND USE IT RECKLESSLY. YOU GOT THAT?
...
...

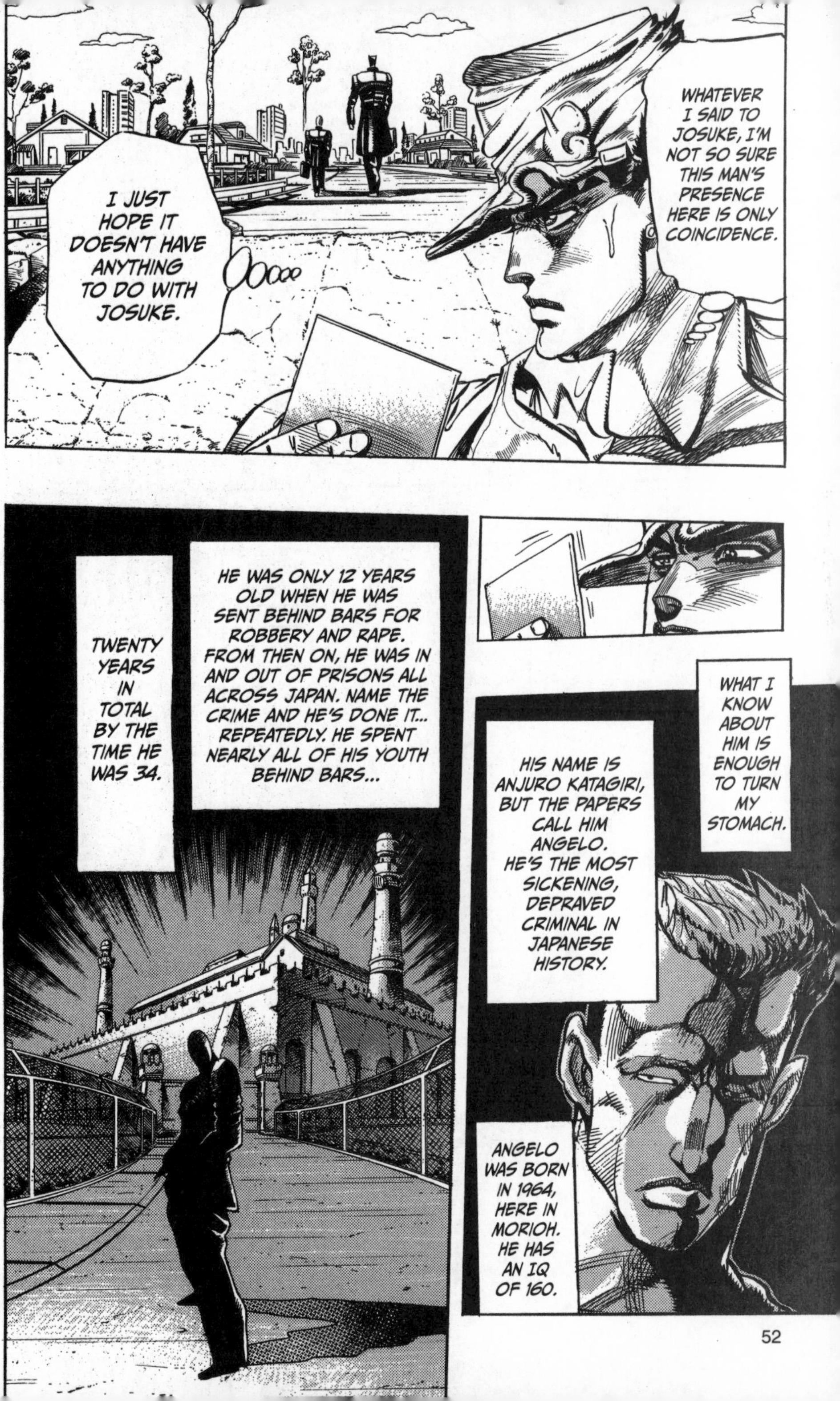
WHATEVER I SAID TO JOSUKE, I'M NOT SO SURE THIS MAN'S PRESENCE HERE IS ONLY COINCIDENCE.
I JUST HOPE IT DOESN'T HAVE ANYTHING TO DO WITH JOSUKE.
WHAT I KNOW ABOUT HIM IS ENOUGH TO TURN MY STOMACH.
HIS NAME IS ANJURO KATAGIRI, BUT THE PAPERS CALL HIM ANGELO. HE'S THE MOST SICKENING, DEPRAVED CRIMINAL IN JAPANESE HISTORY.
ANGELO WAS BORN IN 1964, HERE IN MORIOH. HE HAS AN IQ OF 160.
HE WAS ONLY 12 YEARS OLD WHEN HE WAS SENT BEHIND BARS FOR ROBBERY AND RAPE. FROM THEN ON, HE WAS IN AND OUT OF PRISONS ALL ACROSS JAPAN. NAME THE CRIME AND HE'S DONE IT... REPEATEDLY. HE SPENT NEARLY ALL OF HIS YOUTH BEHIND BARS...
TWENTY YEARS IN TOTAL BY THE TIME HE WAS 34.

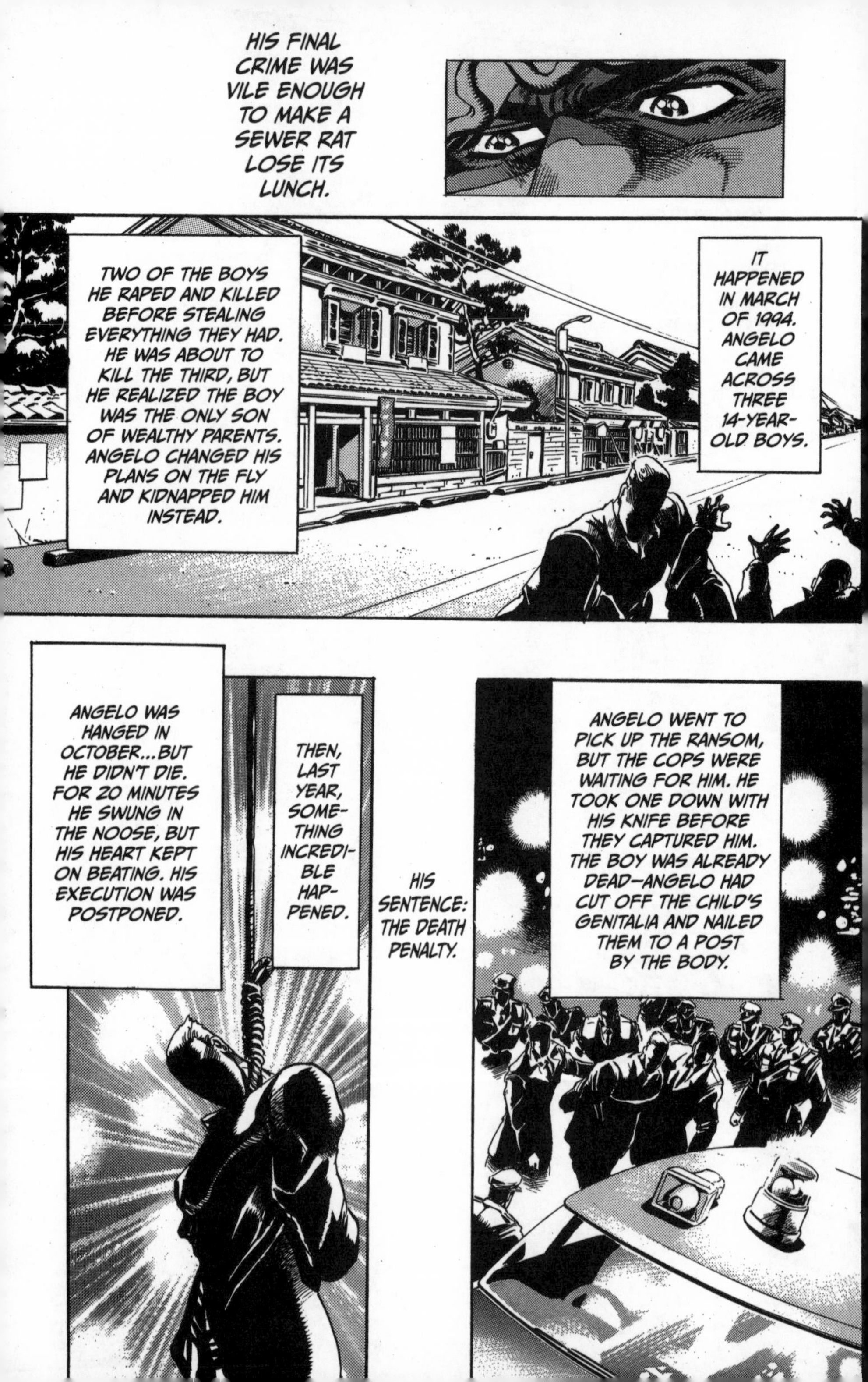
HIS FINAL CRIME WAS VILE ENOUGH TO MAKE A SEWER RAT LOSE ITS LUNCH.
IT HAPPENED IN MARCH OF 1994. ANGELO CAME ACROSS THREE 14-YEAR-OLD BOYS.
TWO OF THE BOYS HE RAPED AND KILLED BEFORE STEALING EVERYTHING THEY HAD. HE WAS ABOUT TO KILL THE THIRD, BUT HE REALIZED THE BOY WAS THE ONLY SON OF WEALTHY PARENTS. ANGELO CHANGED HIS PLANS ON THE FLY AND KIDNAPPED HIM INSTEAD.
ANGELO WENT TO PICK UP THE RANSOM, BUT THE COPS WERE WAITING FOR HIM. HE TOOK ONE DOWN WITH HIS KNIFE BEFORE THEY CAPTURED HIM. THE BOY WAS ALREADY DEAD—ANGELO HAD CUT OFF THE CHILD'S GENITALIA AND NAILED THEM TO A POST BY THE BODY.
HIS SENTENCE: THE DEATH PENALTY.
ANGELO WAS HANGED IN OCTOBER...BUT HE DIDN'T DIE. FOR 20 MINUTES HE SWUNG IN THE NOOSE, BUT HIS HEART KEPT ON BEATING. HIS EXECUTION WAS POSTPONED.
THEN, LAST YEAR, SOMETHING INCREDIBLE HAPPENED.

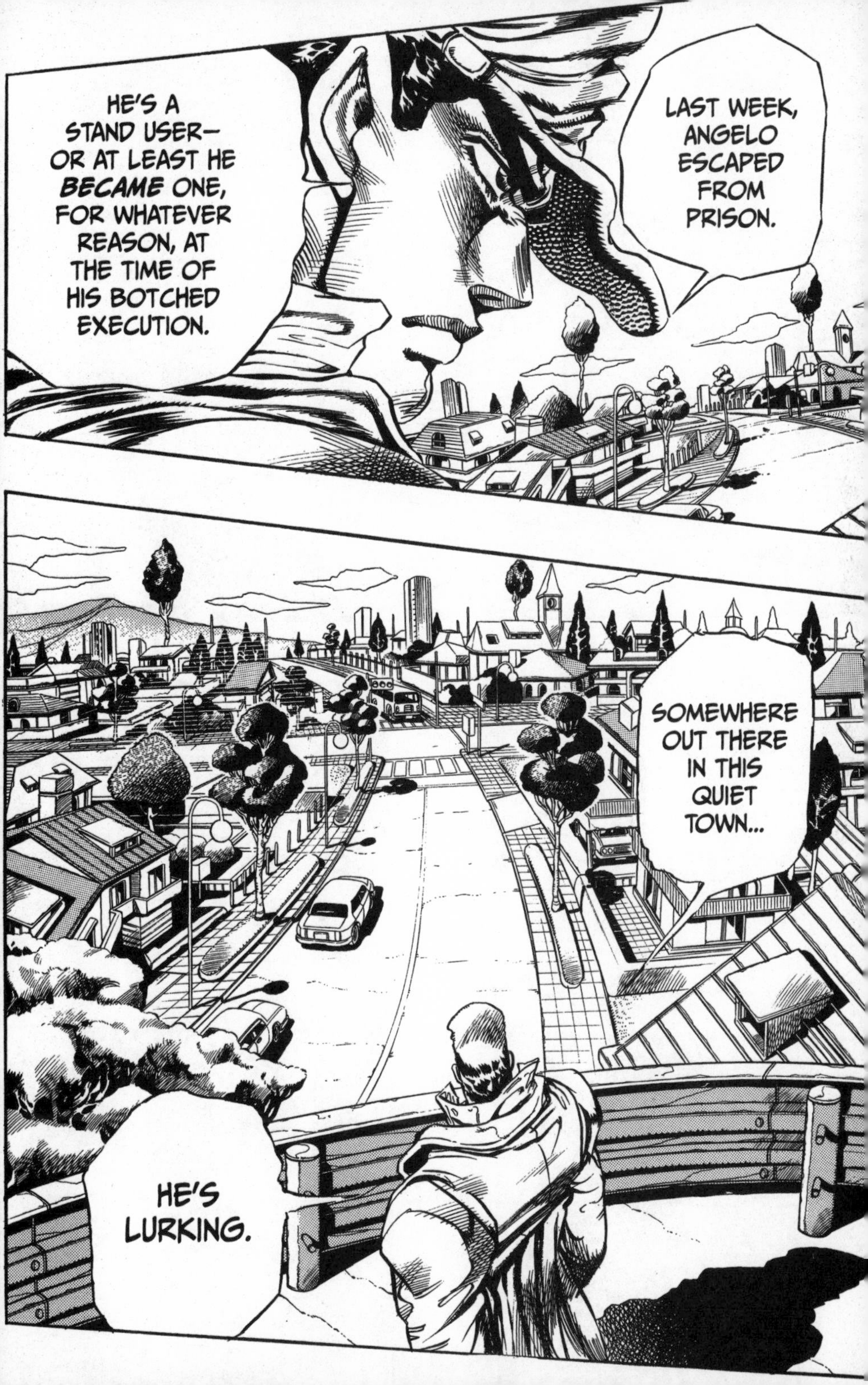
LAST WEEK, ANGELO ESCAPED FROM PRISON.
HE'S A STAND USER— OR AT LEAST HE *BECAME* ONE, FOR WHATEVER REASON, AT THE TIME OF HIS BOTCHED EXECUTION.
SOMEWHERE OUT THERE IN THIS QUIET TOWN...
HE'S LURKING.

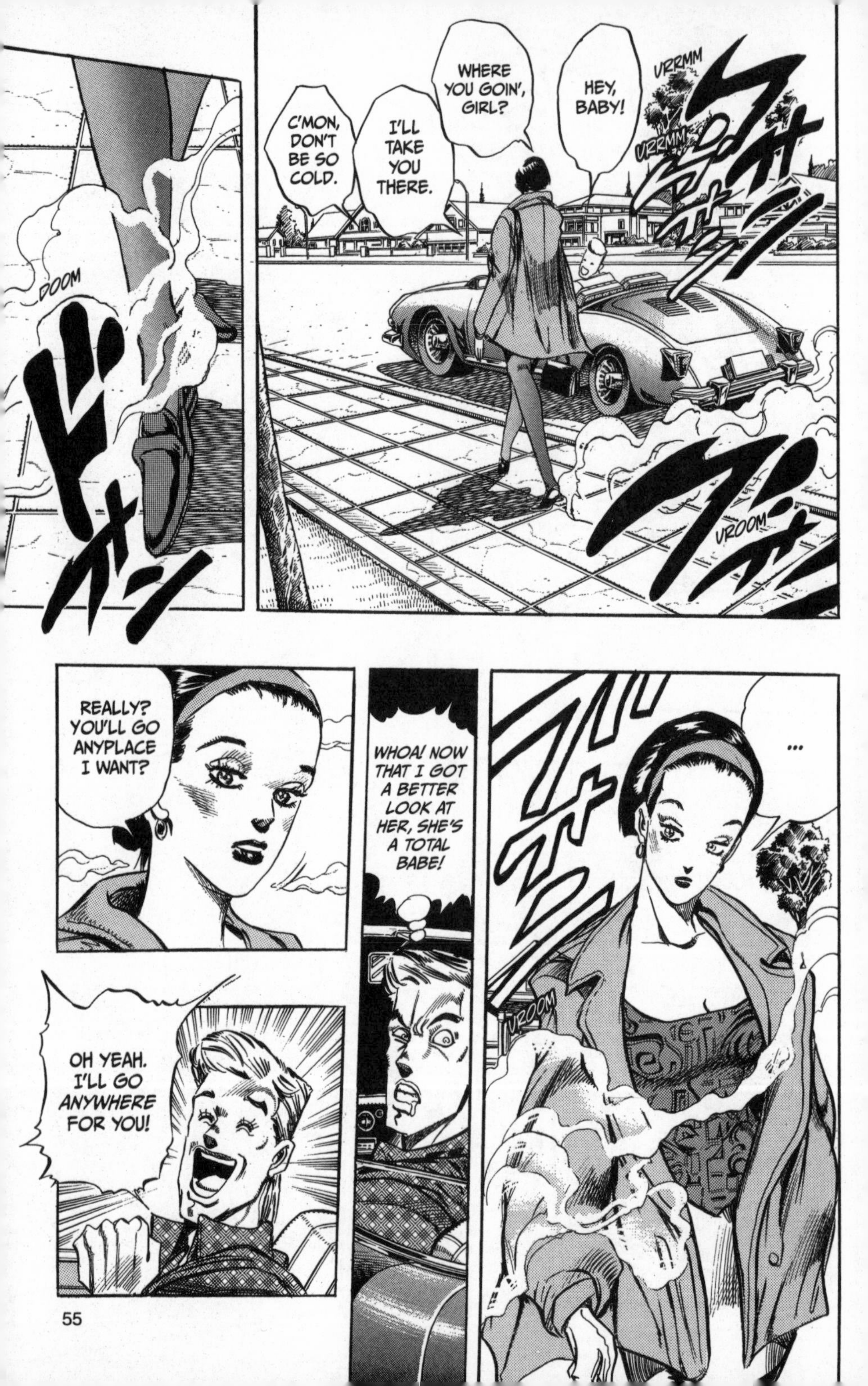
URRMM
URRMM
HEY, BABY!
WHERE YOU GOIN', GIRL?
I'LL TAKE YOU THERE.
C'MON, DON'T BE SO COLD.
VROOM
DOOM
...
VROOM
WHOA! NOW THAT I GOT A BETTER LOOK AT HER, SHE'S A TOTAL BABE!
REALLY? YOU'LL GO ANYPLACE I WANT?
OH YEAH. I'LL GO ANYWHERE FOR YOU!

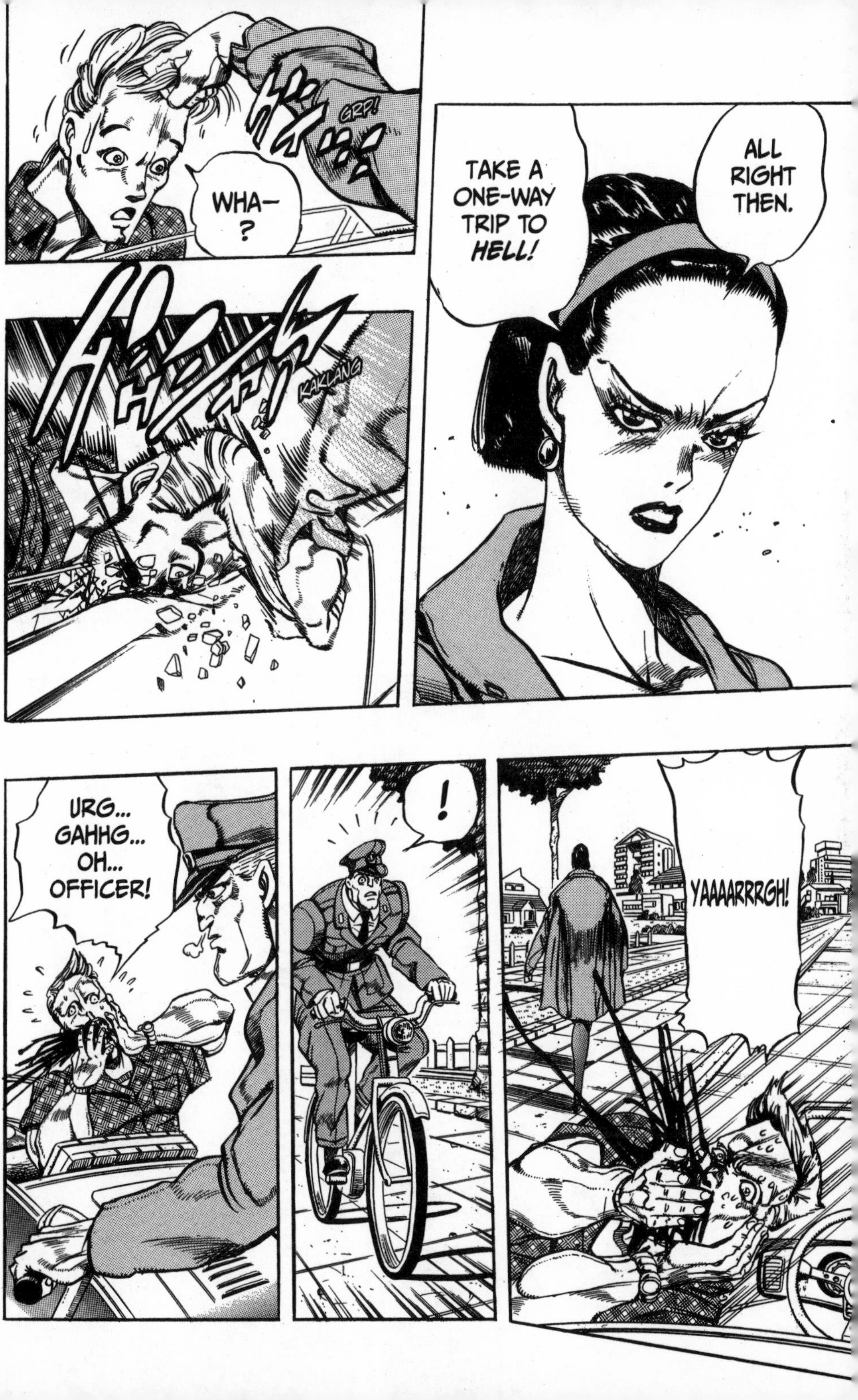
ALL RIGHT THEN.
TAKE A ONE-WAY TRIP TO HELL!
GRP!
WHA—?
KAKLANG
YAAAARRRGH!
!
URG... GAHHG... OH... OFFICER!

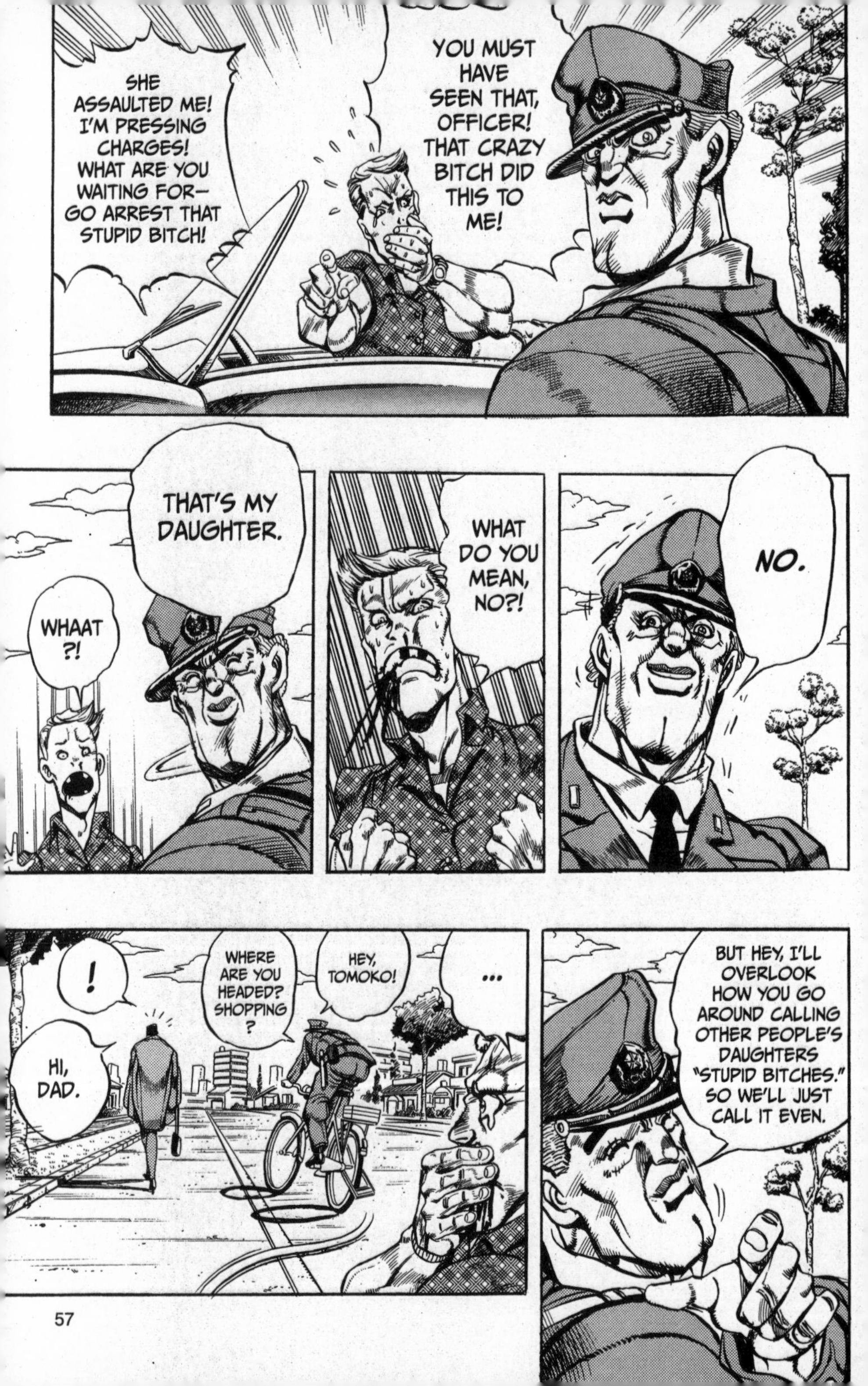
YOU MUST HAVE SEEN THAT, OFFICER! THAT CRAZY BITCH DID THIS TO ME!
SHE ASSAULTED ME! I'M PRESSING CHARGES! WHAT ARE YOU WAITING FOR— GO ARREST THAT STUPID BITCH!
NO.
WHAT DO YOU MEAN, NO?!
THAT'S MY DAUGHTER.
WHAAT ?!
BUT HEY, I'LL OVERLOOK HOW YOU GO AROUND CALLING OTHER PEOPLE'S DAUGHTERS "STUPID BITCHES." SO WE'LL JUST CALL IT EVEN.
...
HEY, TOMOKO!
WHERE ARE YOU HEADED? SHOPPING ?
!
HI, DAD.

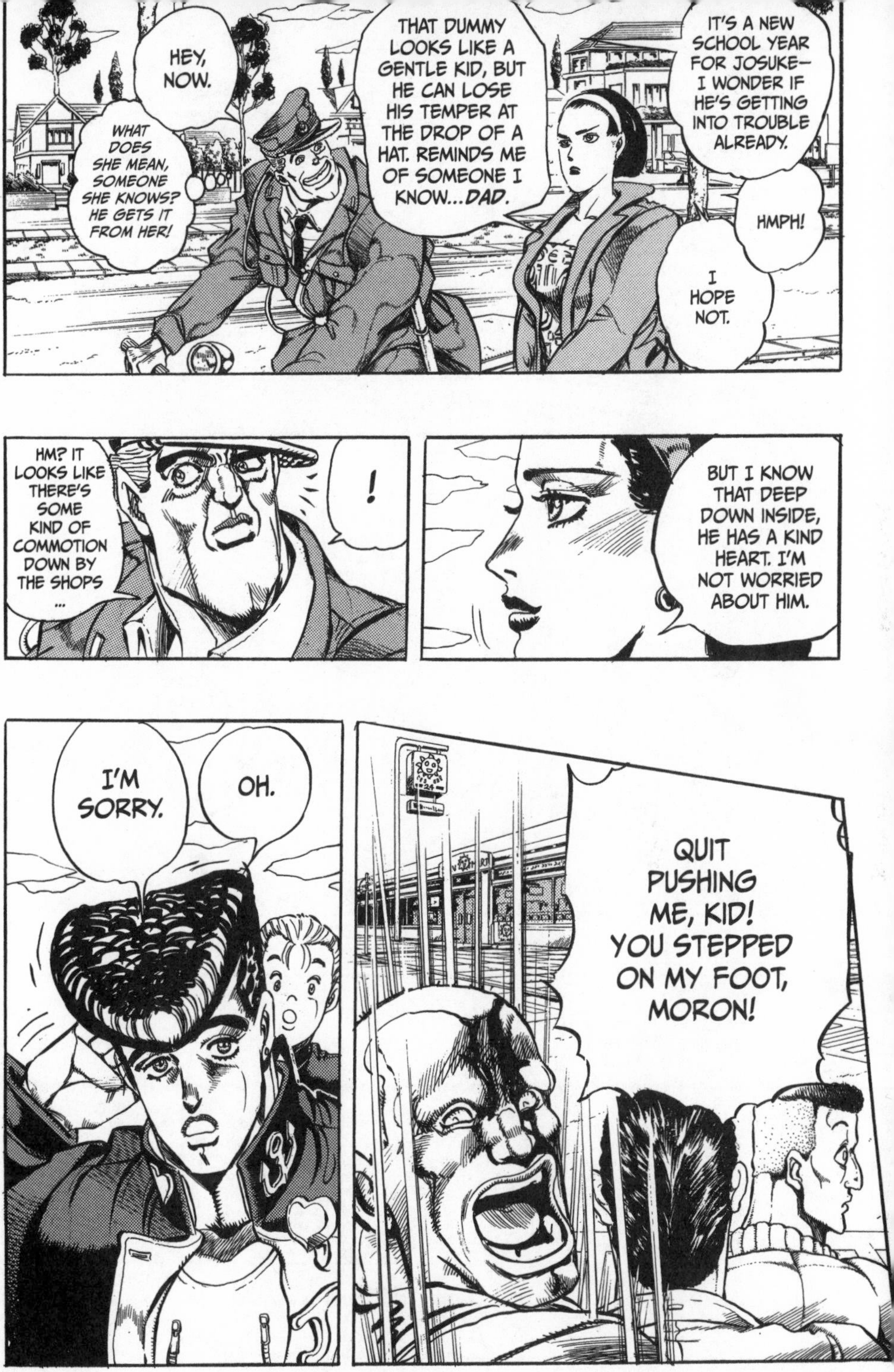

IT'S A NEW SCHOOL YEAR FOR JOSUKE— I WONDER IF HE'S GETTING INTO TROUBLE ALREADY.
HMPH!
I HOPE NOT.
THAT DUMMY LOOKS LIKE A GENTLE KID, BUT HE CAN LOSE HIS TEMPER AT THE DROP OF A HAT. REMINDS ME OF SOMEONE I KNOW...*DAD*.
HEY, NOW.
WHAT DOES SHE MEAN, SOMEONE SHE KNOWS? HE GETS IT FROM HER!
BUT I KNOW THAT DEEP DOWN INSIDE, HE HAS A KIND HEART. I'M NOT WORRIED ABOUT HIM.
!
HM? IT LOOKS LIKE THERE'S SOME KIND OF COMMOTION DOWN BY THE SHOPS ...
QUIT PUSHING ME, KID! YOU STEPPED ON MY FOOT, MORON!
OH.
I'M SORRY.

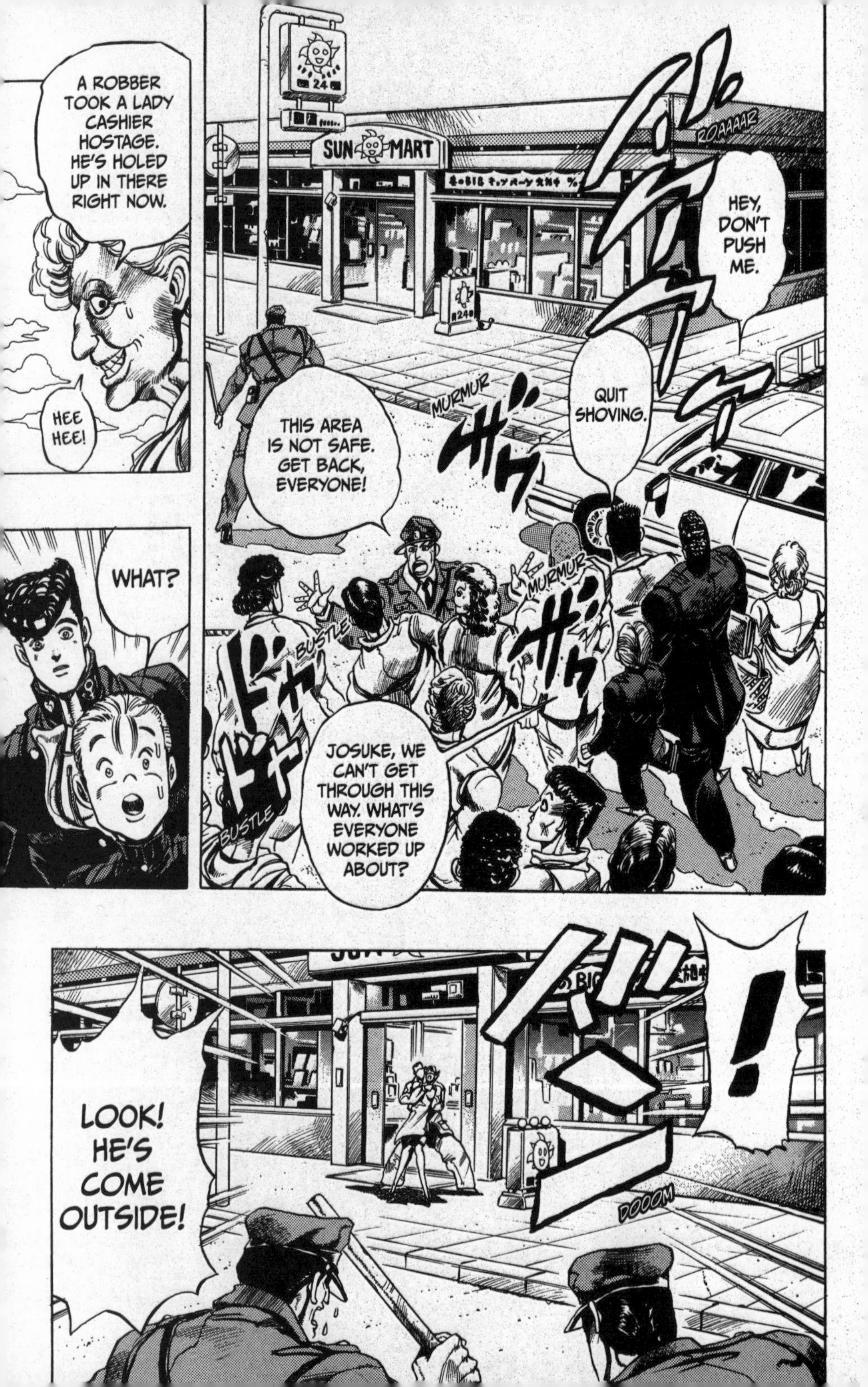
SUN MART
24
ROAAAAR
HEY, DON'T PUSH ME.
QUIT SHOVING.
MURMUR
THIS AREA IS NOT SAFE. GET BACK, EVERYONE!
MURMUR
BUSTLE
BUSTLE
JOSUKE, WE CAN'T GET THROUGH THIS WAY. WHAT'S EVERYONE WORKED UP ABOUT?
A ROBBER TOOK A LADY CASHIER HOSTAGE. HE'S HOLED UP IN THERE RIGHT NOW.
HEE HEE!
WHAT?
DOOOM
LOOK! HE'S COME OUTSIDE!

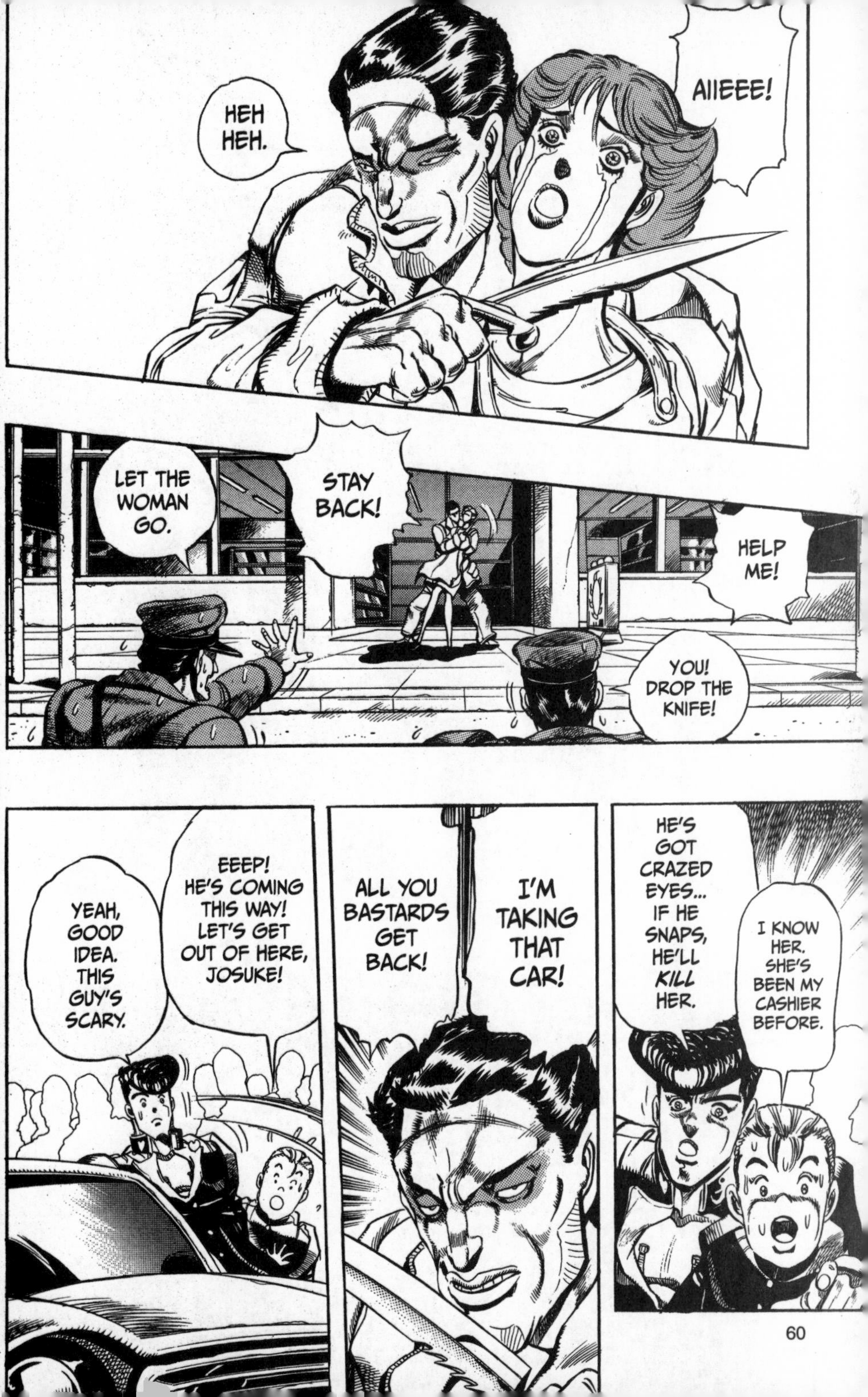
AIIEEE!
HEH HEH.
HELP ME!
STAY BACK!
LET THE WOMAN GO.
YOU! DROP THE KNIFE!
I KNOW HER. SHE'S BEEN MY CASHIER BEFORE.
HE'S GOT CRAZED EYES... IF HE SNAPS, HE'LL *KILL* HER.
I'M TAKING THAT CAR!
ALL YOU BASTARDS GET BACK!
EEEP! HE'S COMING THIS WAY! LET'S GET OUT OF HERE, JOSUKE!
YEAH, GOOD IDEA. THIS GUY'S SCARY.

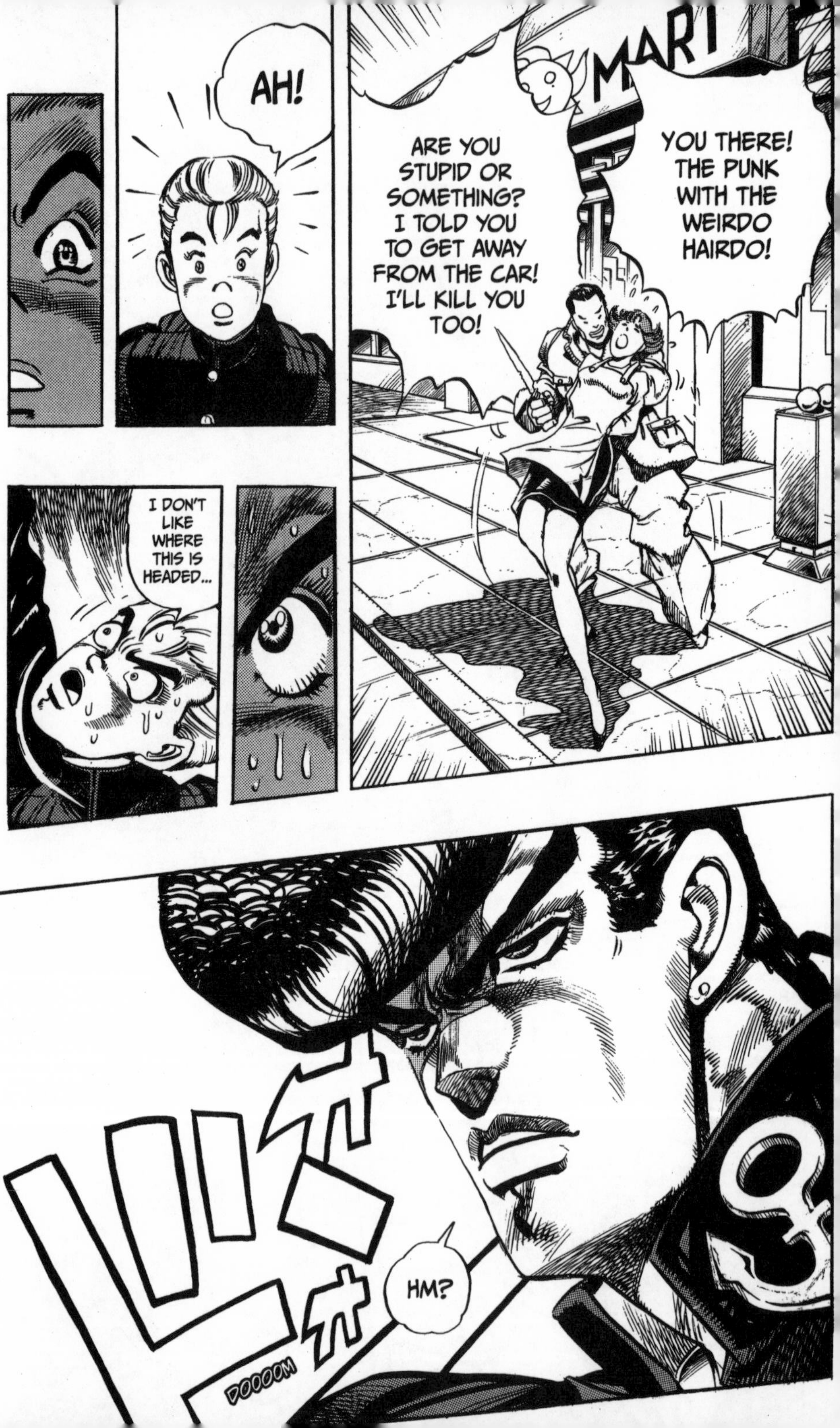
MARI
YOU THERE! THE PUNK WITH THE WEIRDO HAIRDO!
ARE YOU STUPID OR SOMETHING? I TOLD YOU TO GET AWAY FROM THE CAR! I'LL KILL YOU TOO!
AH!
I DON'T LIKE WHERE THIS IS HEADED...
HM?
DOOOOM

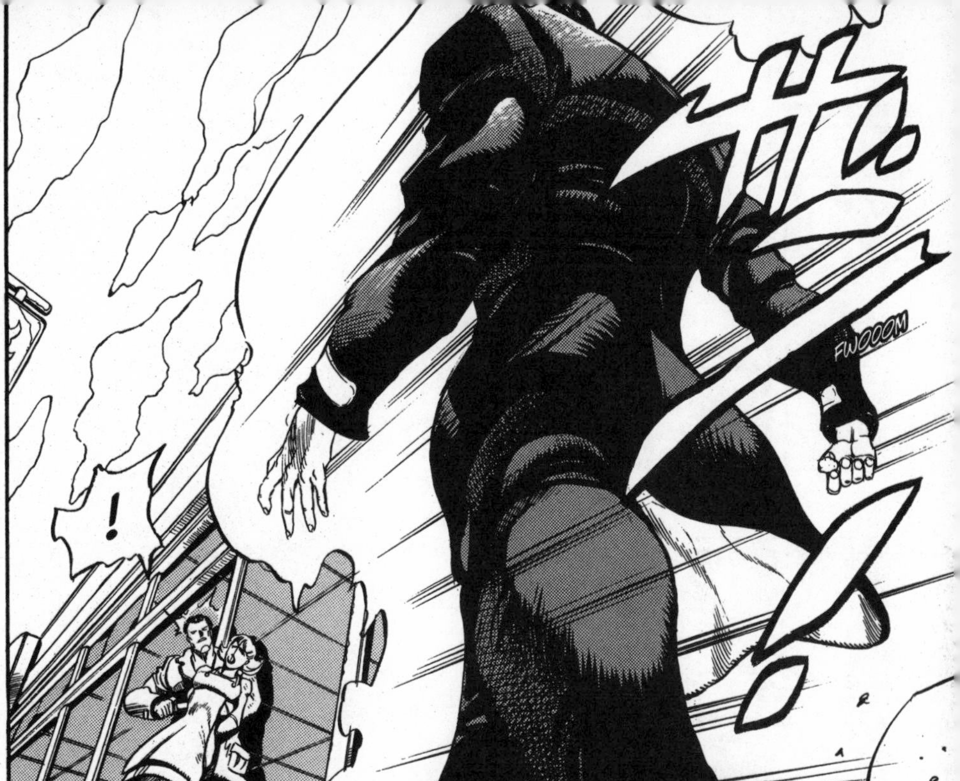
!
FWOOOM
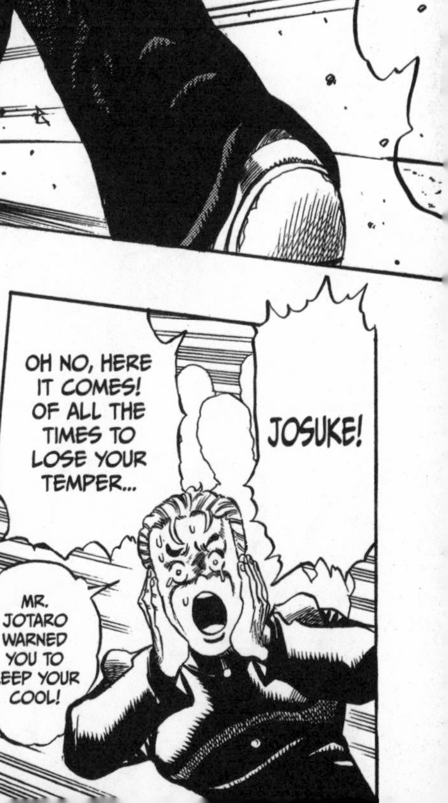
JOSUKE!
OH NO, HERE IT COMES! OF ALL THE TIMES TO LOSE YOUR TEMPER...
MR. JOTARO WARNED YOU TO KEEP YOUR COOL!
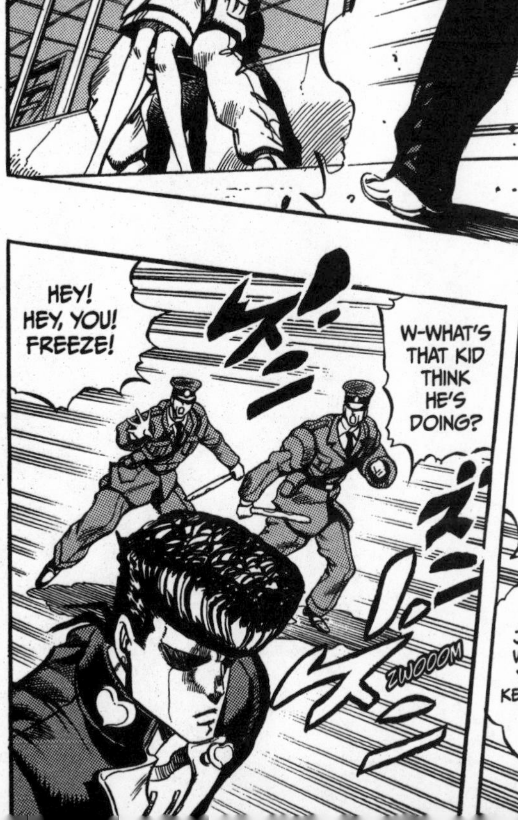
W-WHAT'S THAT KID THINK HE'S DOING?
HEY! HEY, YOU! FREEZE!
ZWOOOM

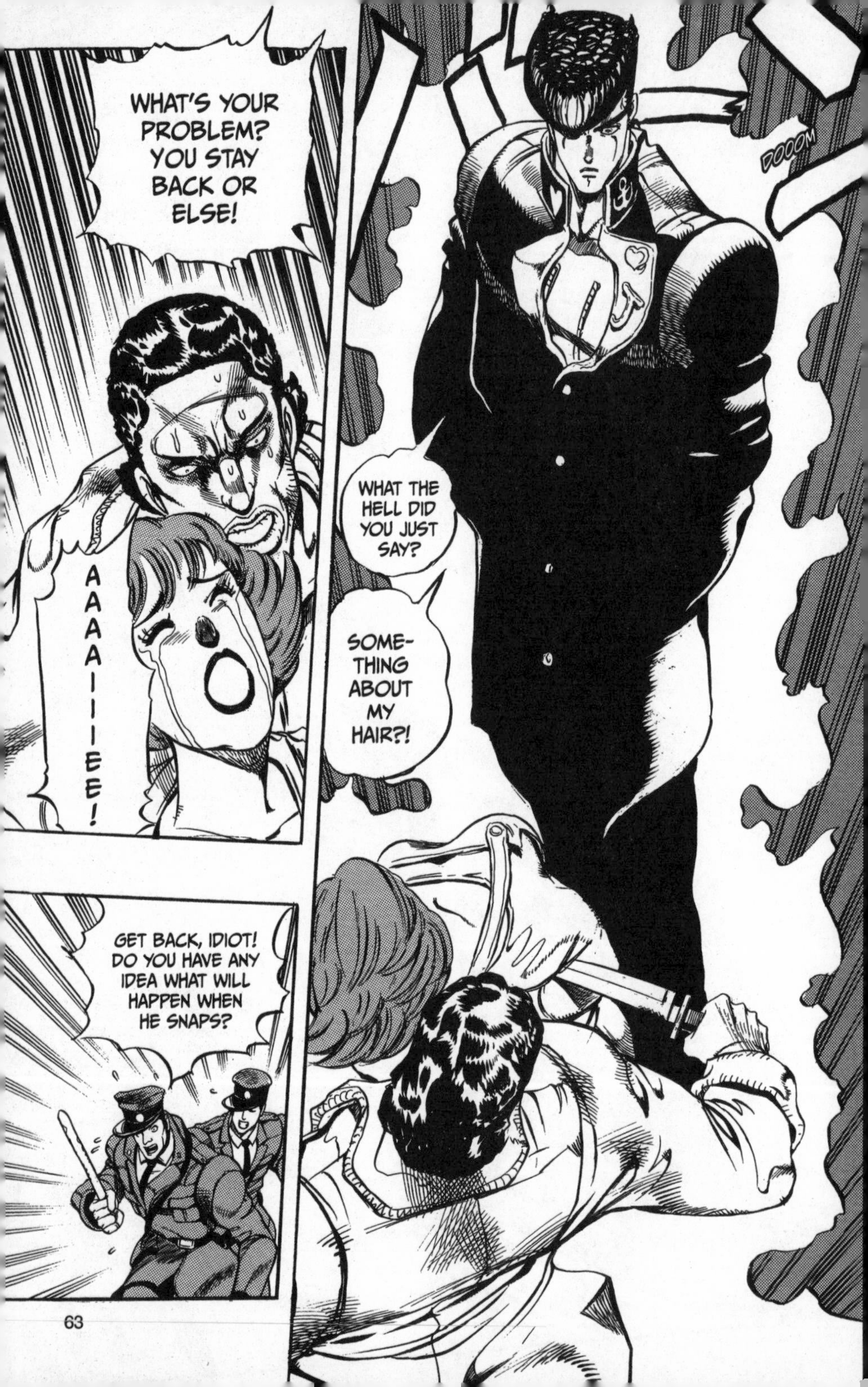
DOOOM
WHAT THE HELL DID YOU JUST SAY?
SOME-THING ABOUT MY HAIR?!
WHAT'S YOUR PROBLEM? YOU STAY BACK OR ELSE!
AAAAIIIIEE!
GET BACK, IDIOT! DO YOU HAVE ANY IDEA WHAT WILL HAPPEN WHEN HE SNAPS?

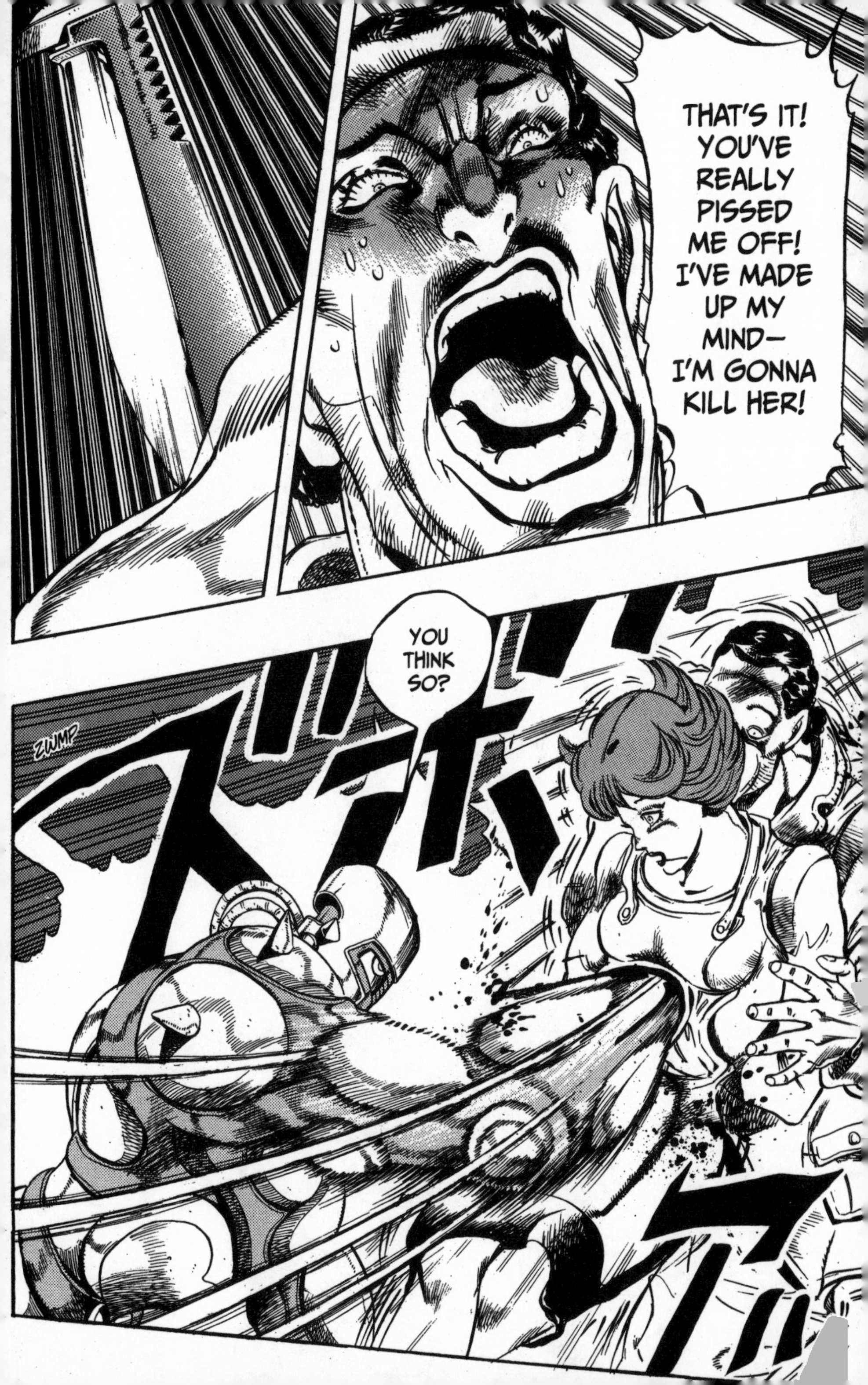
THAT'S IT! YOU'VE REALLY PISSED ME OFF! I'VE MADE UP MY MIND— I'M GONNA KILL HER!
YOU THINK SO?
ZWMP

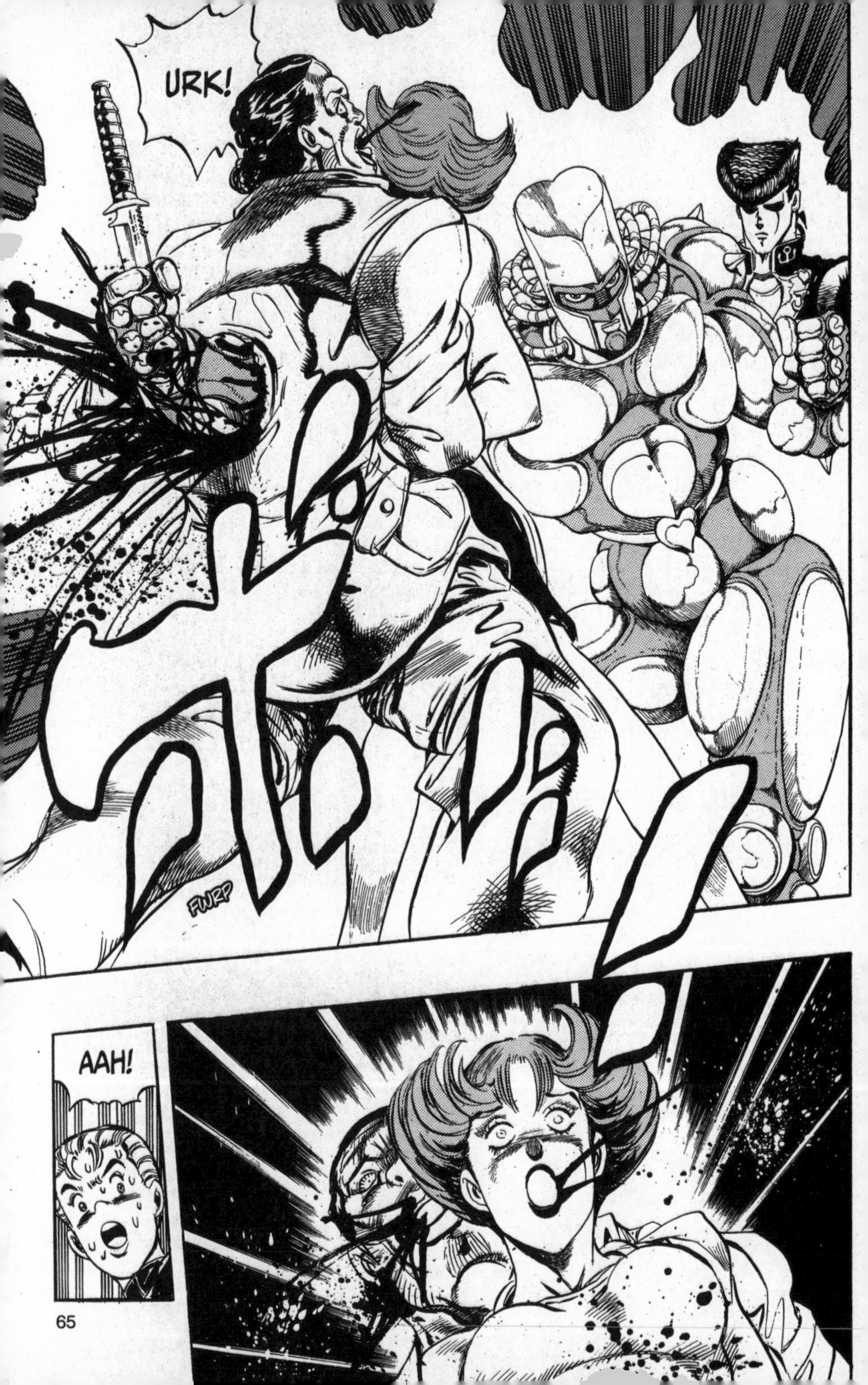
URK!
FWRP
AAH!

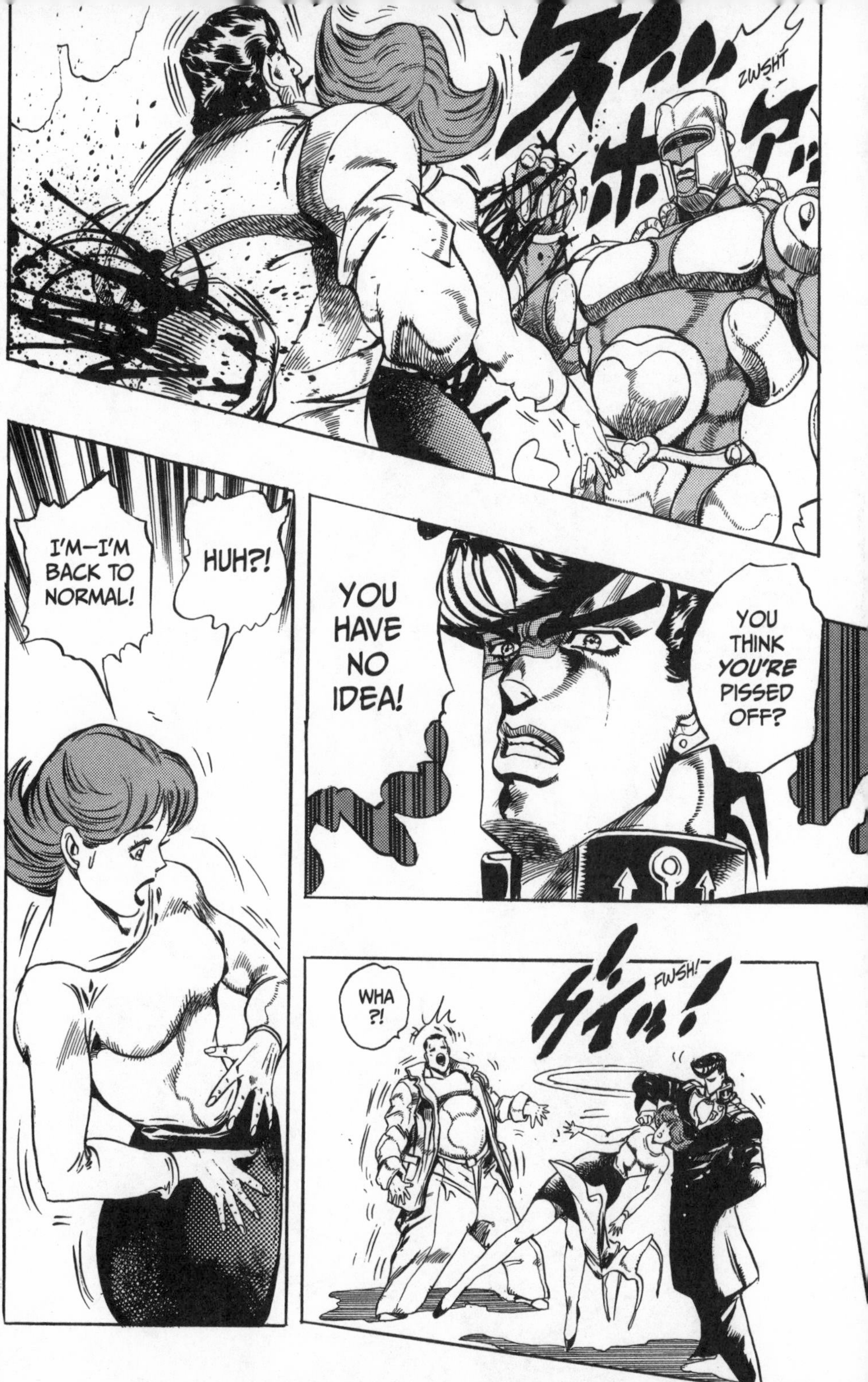
ZWSHT
YOU THINK *YOU'RE* PISSED OFF?
YOU HAVE NO IDEA!
FWSH!
WHA ?!
HUH?!
I'M—I'M BACK TO NORMAL!

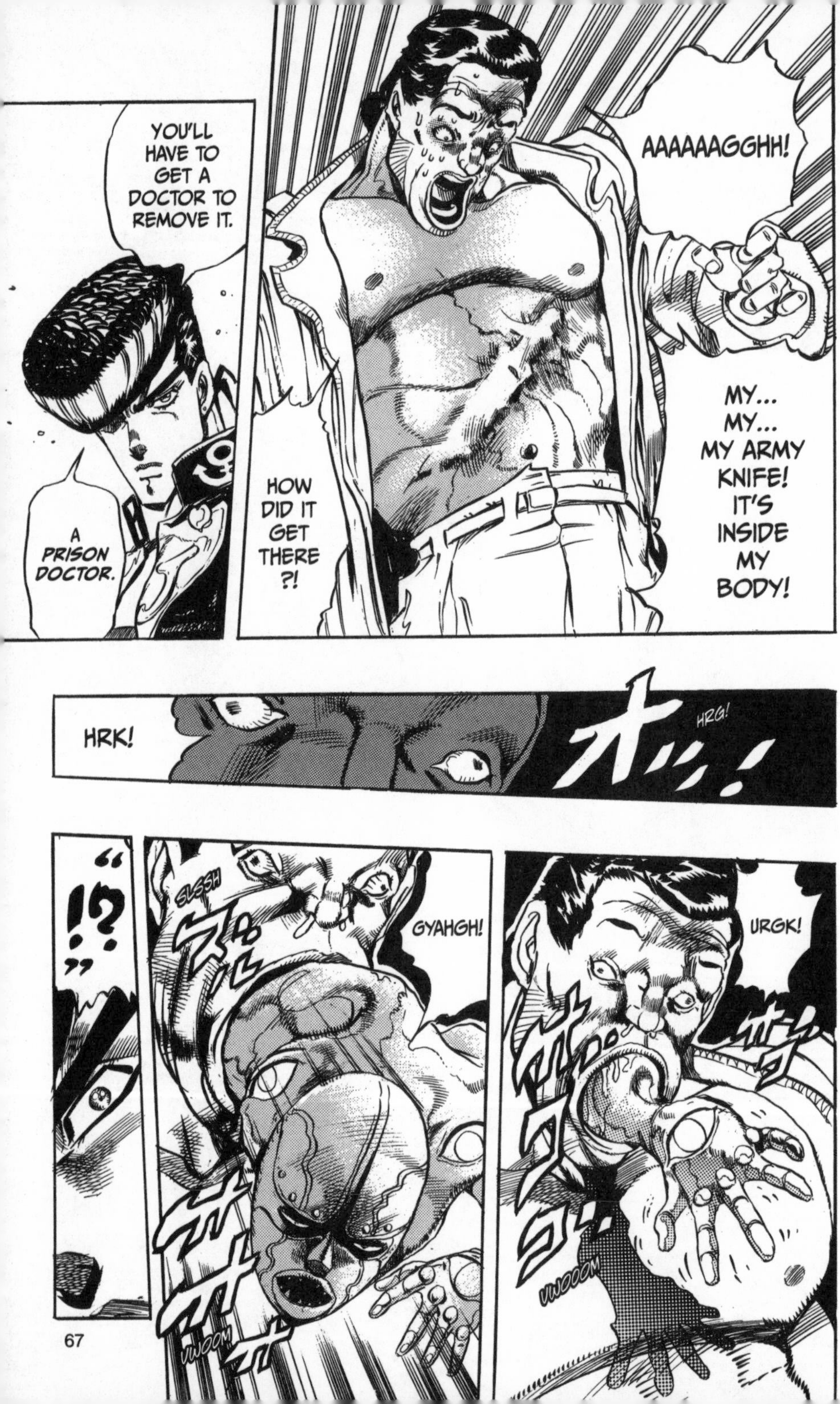
AAAAAAGGHH!
MY... MY... MY ARMY KNIFE! IT'S INSIDE MY BODY!
HOW DID IT GET THERE ?!
YOU'LL HAVE TO GET A DOCTOR TO REMOVE IT.
A PRISON DOCTOR.
HRG!
HRK!
URGK!
UWOOOM
GYAHGH!
SLSSH
UWOOM
"!?"

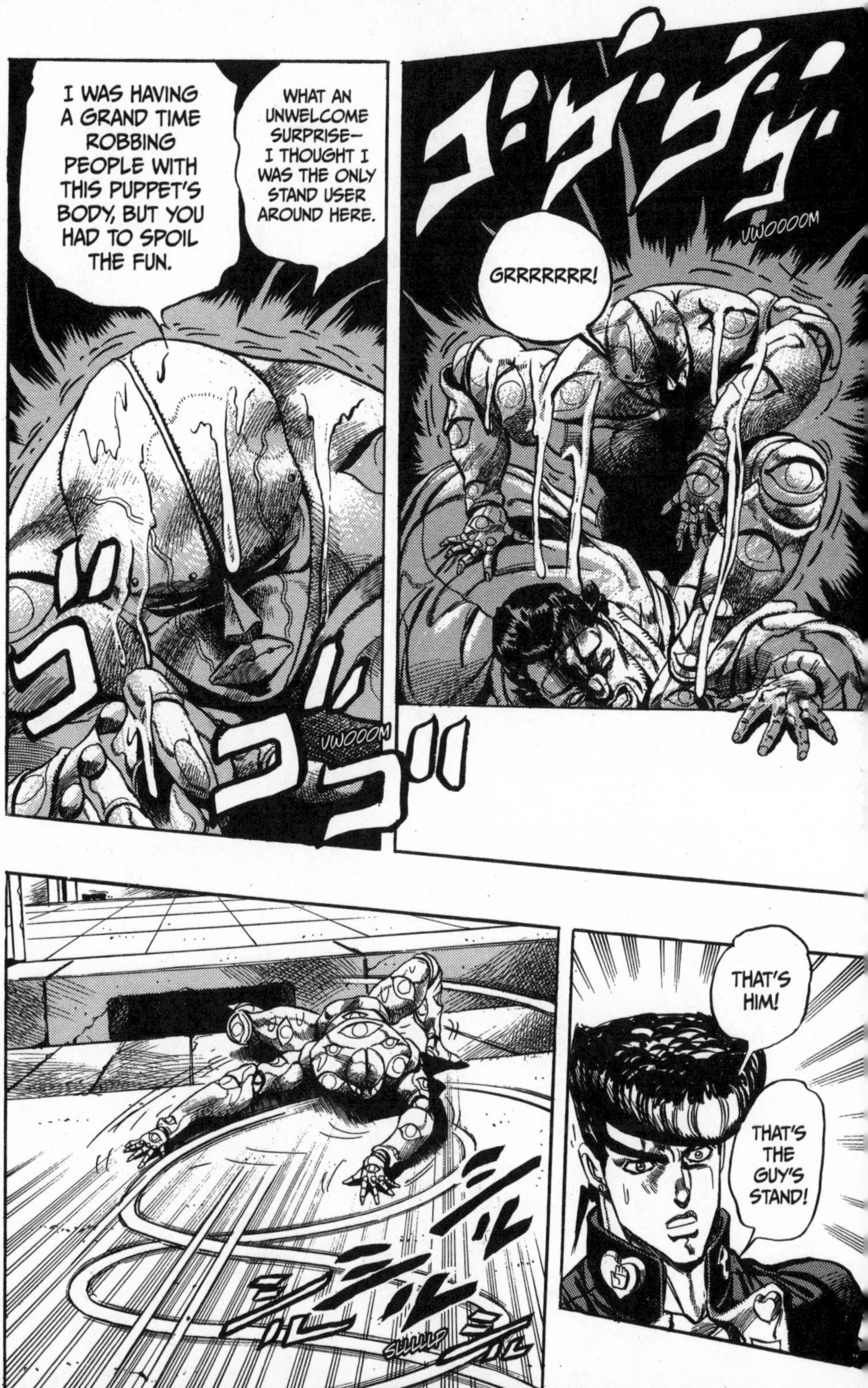
GRRRRRR!
VWOOOOM
WHAT AN UNWELCOME SURPRISE— I THOUGHT I WAS THE ONLY STAND USER AROUND HERE.
I WAS HAVING A GRAND TIME ROBBING PEOPLE WITH THIS PUPPET'S BODY, BUT YOU HAD TO SPOIL THE FUN.
VWOOOM
THAT'S HIM!
THAT'S THE GUY'S STAND!

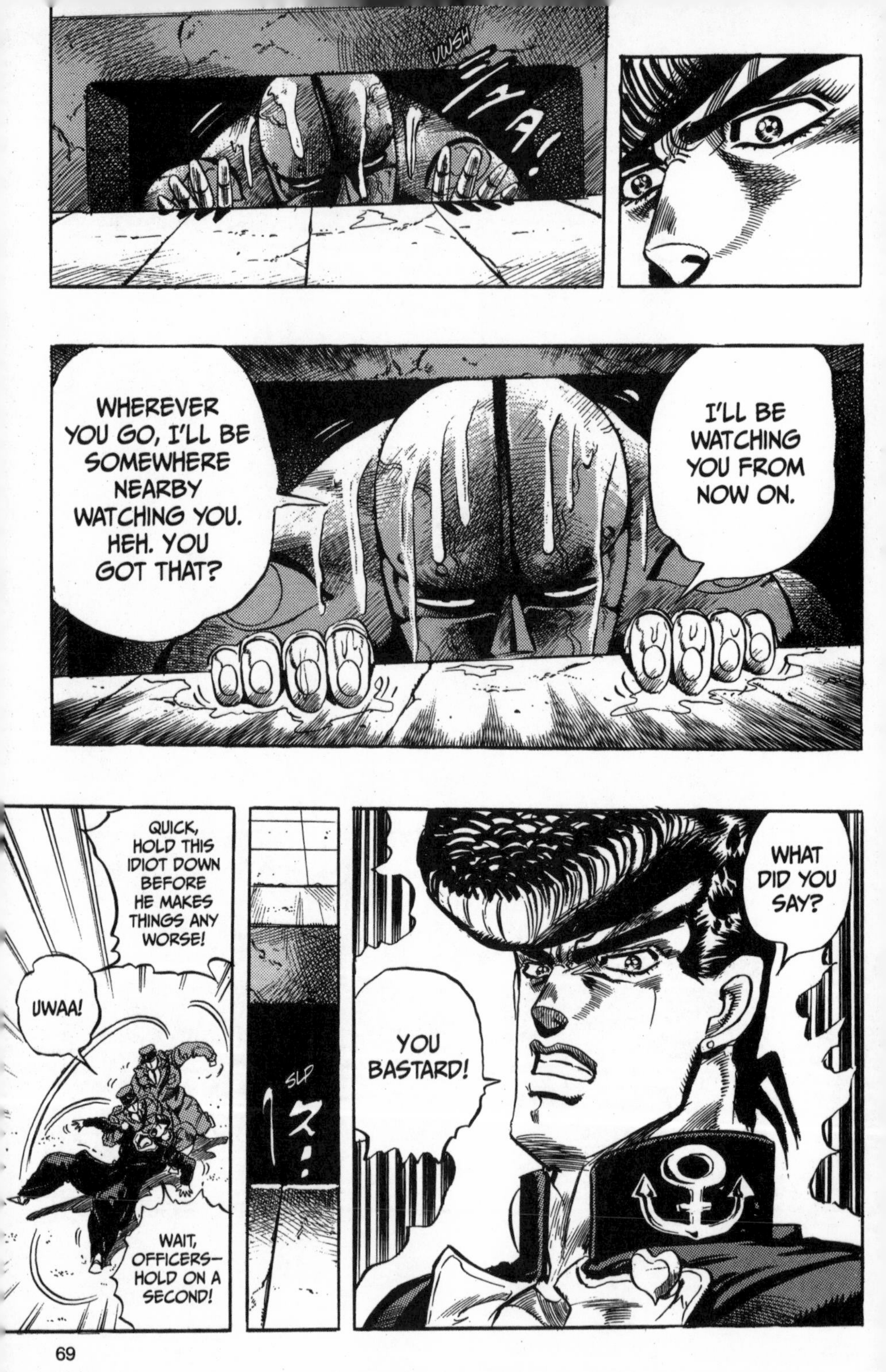
VWSH
I'LL BE WATCHING YOU FROM NOW ON.
WHEREVER YOU GO, I'LL BE SOMEWHERE NEARBY WATCHING YOU. HEH. YOU GOT THAT?
WHAT DID YOU SAY?
YOU BASTARD!
SLP
QUICK, HOLD THIS IDIOT DOWN BEFORE HE MAKES THINGS ANY WORSE!
UWAA!
WAIT, OFFICERS— HOLD ON A SECOND!

CHAPTER 4

JOSUKE HIGASHIKATA MEETS ANGELO, PART 1

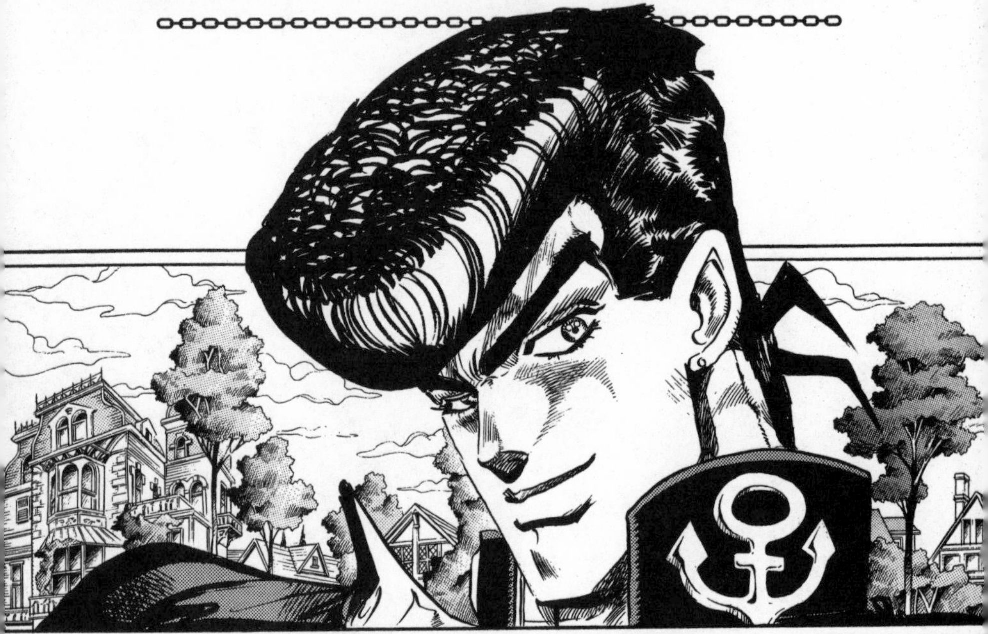

JOSUKE HIGASHIKATA

Birth Sign: Gemini **Blood Type:** B **Current Age (in 1999):** 16 (first year in high school)
Father: Joseph Joestar (79) **Grandfather:** Ryohei Higashikata (55), policeman
Grandmother: Deceased **Mother:** Tomoko Higashikata (36), teacher
Height: 185 cm (and still growing) **Medical History:** A mysterious fever nearly killed him in 1987 (age 4)
Hobbies: Video games, listening to Prince CDs **Favorite phrases:** "dorara," "great"

Personality: Gentle, but loses his temper if anyone insults his hair.

Josuke: I don't know why that pisses me off, but I can't help what makes me mad.
Tomoko: I know that deep down inside, he has a kind heart. Even if he gets a little rambunctious sometimes, I'm not worried that he'll go too far.
Ryohei: She's wrong—he's dangerous.
Jotaro: ...
Some punk: I'll kill him!
Some kid: He's dumb.
Pachinko parlor manager: I would never say anything bad about a loyal patron.

Stand: As yet unnamed.

Ability: Can repair things that have been broken, but if Josuke is angry, his Stand might not repair things back exactly how they were.

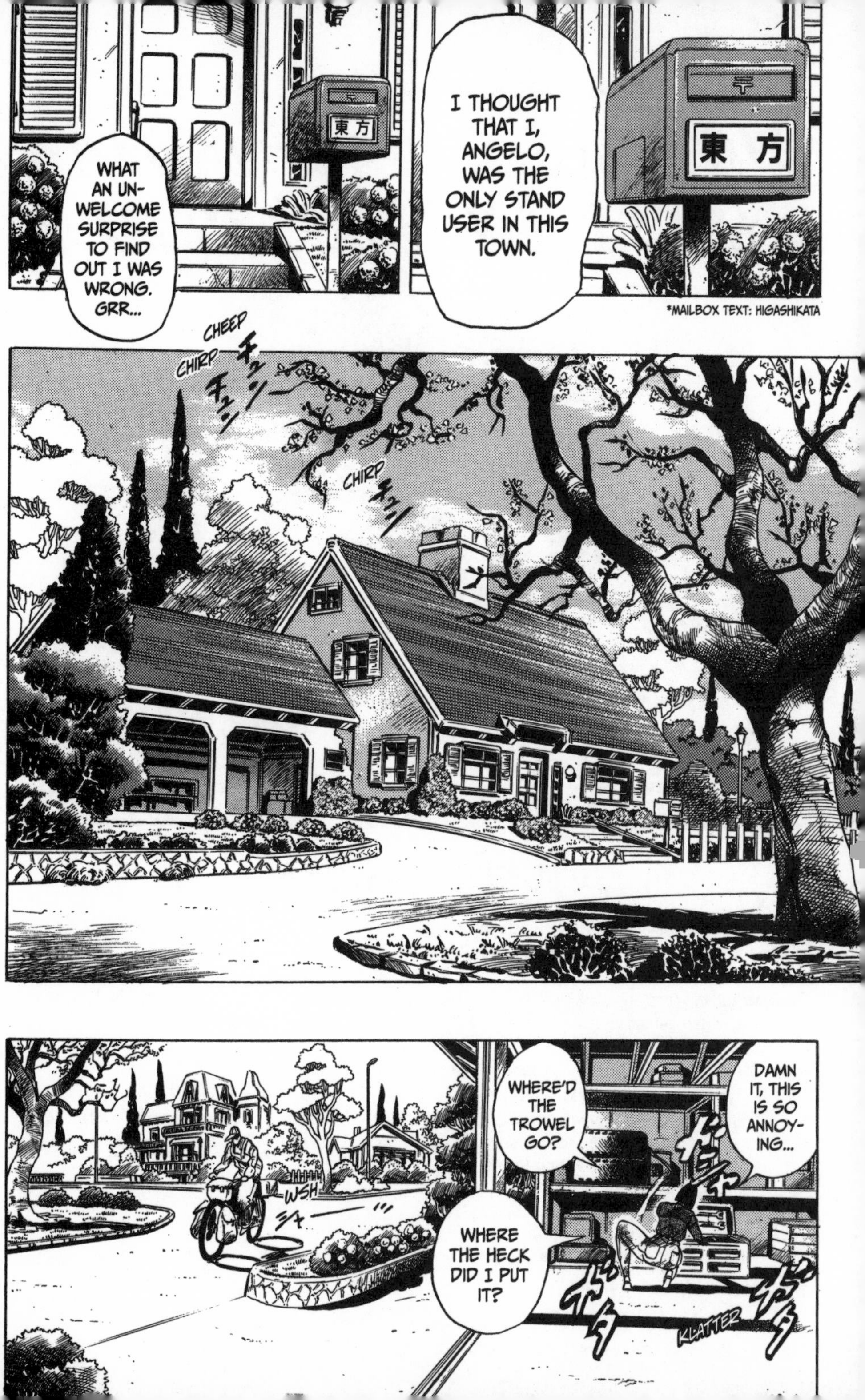
東方
I THOUGHT THAT I, ANGELO, WAS THE ONLY STAND USER IN THIS TOWN.
東方
WHAT AN UN-WELCOME SURPRISE TO FIND OUT I WAS WRONG. GRR...
*MAILBOX TEXT: HIGASHIKATA
CHEEP
CHIRP
CHIRP
DAMN IT, THIS IS SO ANNOY-ING...
WHERE'D THE TROWEL GO?
WHERE THE HECK DID I PUT IT?
KLATTER
WSH

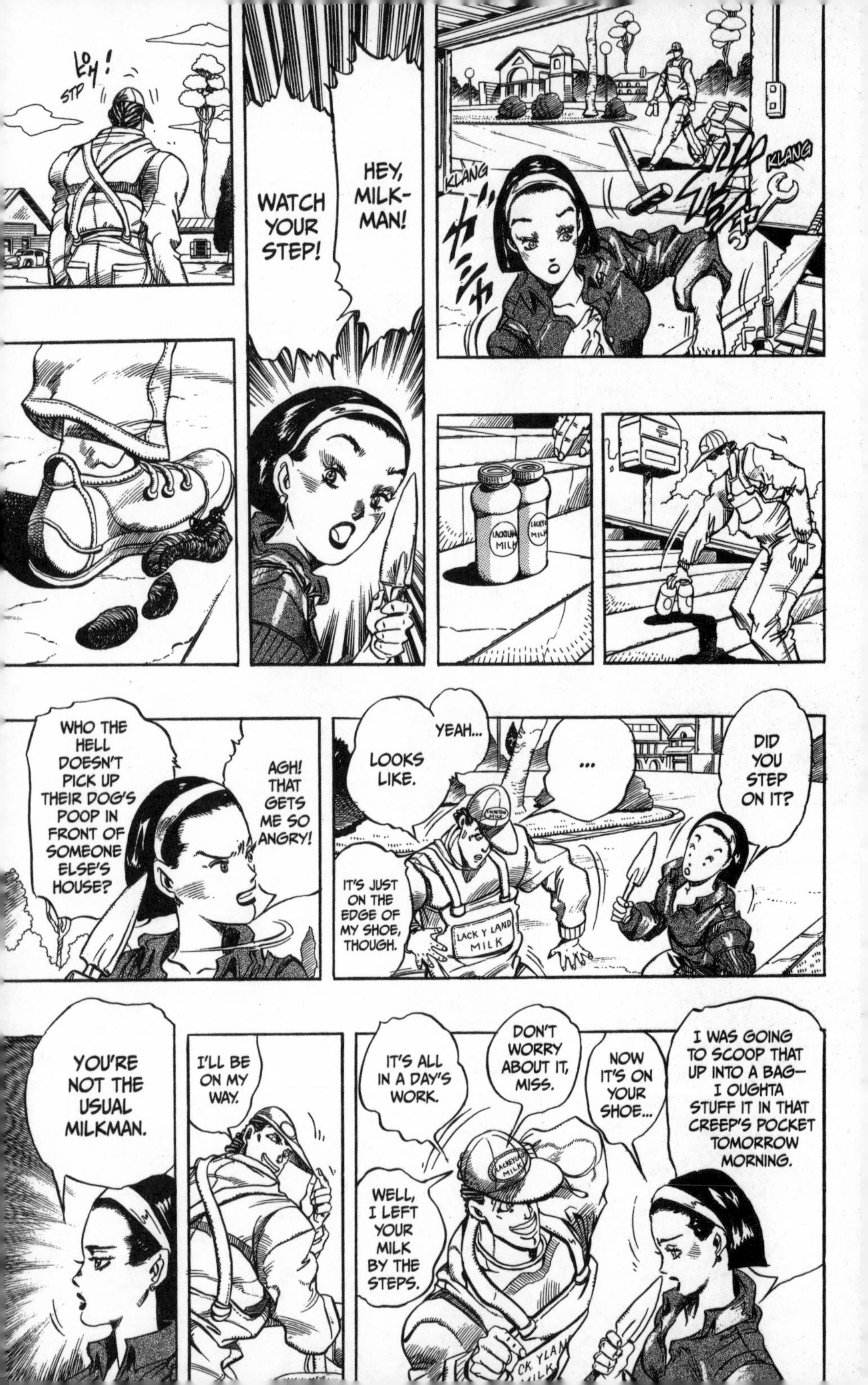
KLANG
KLANG
HEY, MILK-MAN!
WATCH YOUR STEP!
STP
DID YOU STEP ON IT?
...
YEAH... LOOKS LIKE.
IT'S JUST ON THE EDGE OF MY SHOE, THOUGH.
AGH! THAT GETS ME SO ANGRY!
WHO THE HELL DOESN'T PICK UP THEIR DOG'S POOP IN FRONT OF SOMEONE ELSE'S HOUSE?
I WAS GOING TO SCOOP THAT UP INTO A BAG— I OUGHTA STUFF IT IN THAT CREEP'S POCKET TOMORROW MORNING.
NOW IT'S ON YOUR SHOE...
DON'T WORRY ABOUT IT, MISS.
IT'S ALL IN A DAY'S WORK.
WELL, I LEFT YOUR MILK BY THE STEPS.
I'LL BE ON MY WAY.
YOU'RE NOT THE USUAL MILKMAN.

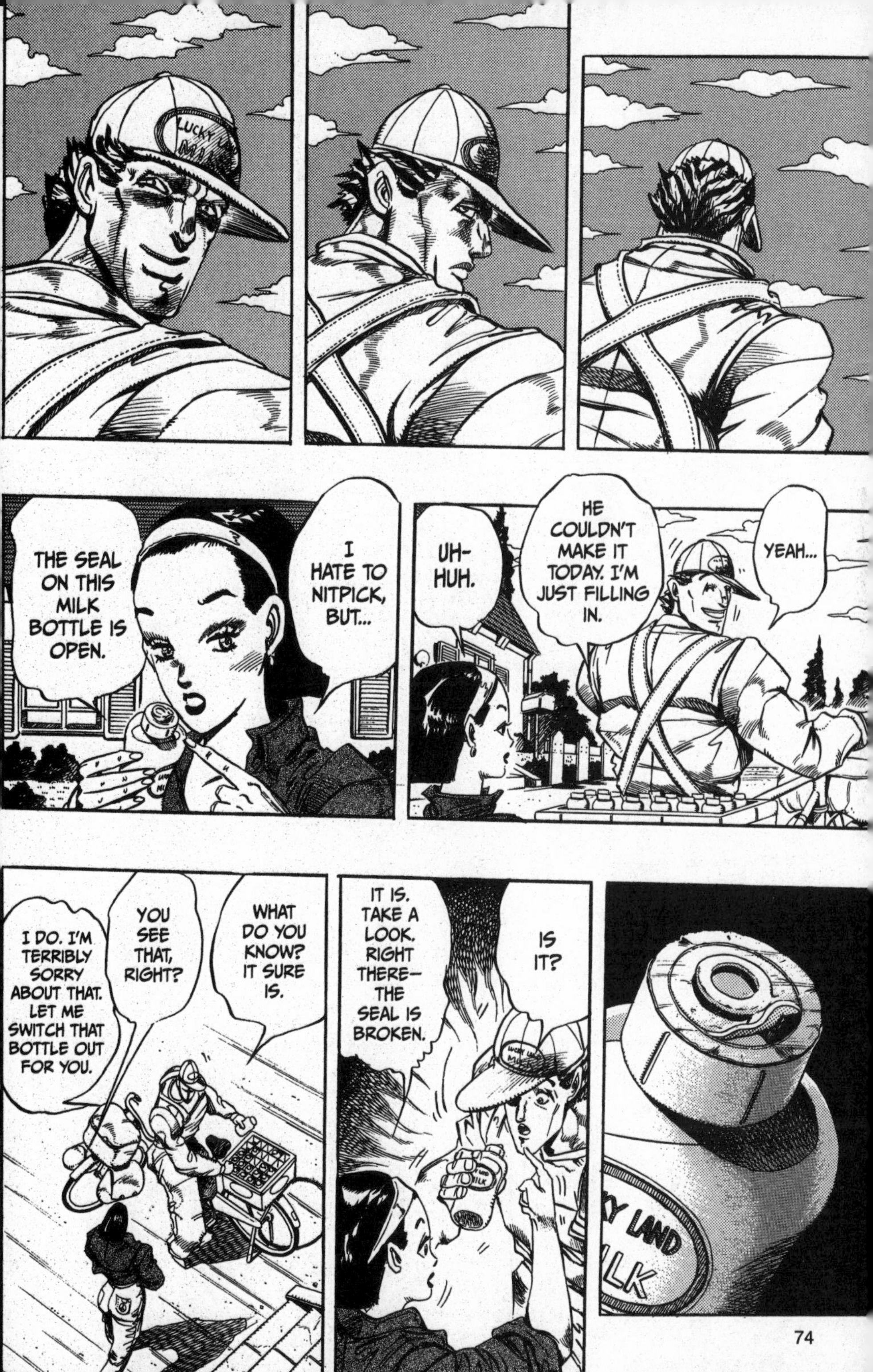
YEAH...
HE COULDN'T MAKE IT TODAY. I'M JUST FILLING IN.
UH-HUH.
I HATE TO NITPICK, BUT...
THE SEAL ON THIS MILK BOTTLE IS OPEN.
IS IT?
IT IS. TAKE A LOOK. RIGHT THERE— THE SEAL IS BROKEN.
WHAT DO YOU KNOW? IT SURE IS.
YOU SEE THAT, RIGHT?
I DO. I'M TERRIBLY SORRY ABOUT THAT. LET ME SWITCH THAT BOTTLE OUT FOR YOU.

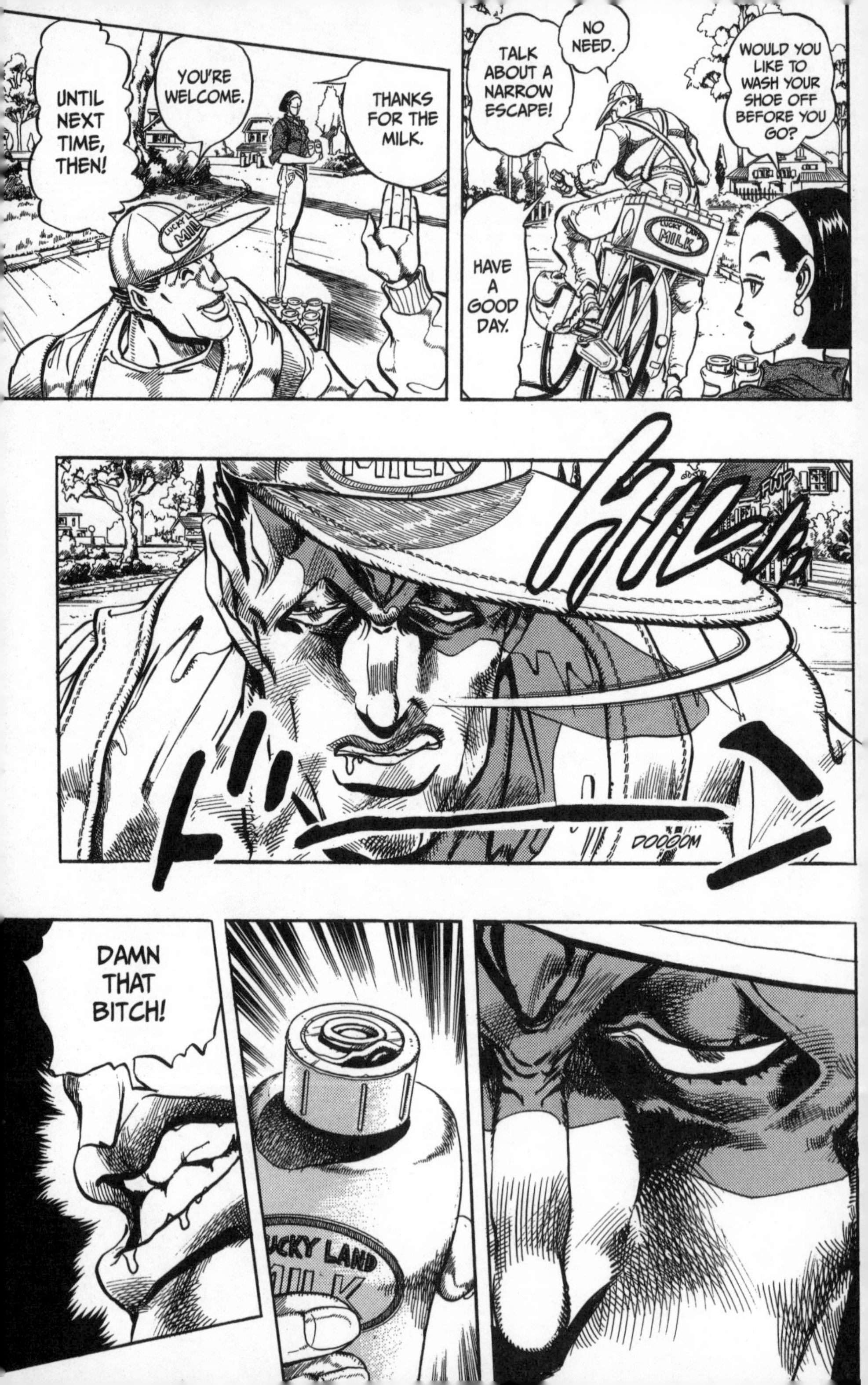

WOULD YOU LIKE TO WASH YOUR SHOE OFF BEFORE YOU GO?
NO NEED.
TALK ABOUT A NARROW ESCAPE!
HAVE A GOOD DAY.
THANKS FOR THE MILK.
YOU'RE WELCOME.
UNTIL NEXT TIME, THEN!
FWP
DOOOOM
DAMN THAT BITCH!

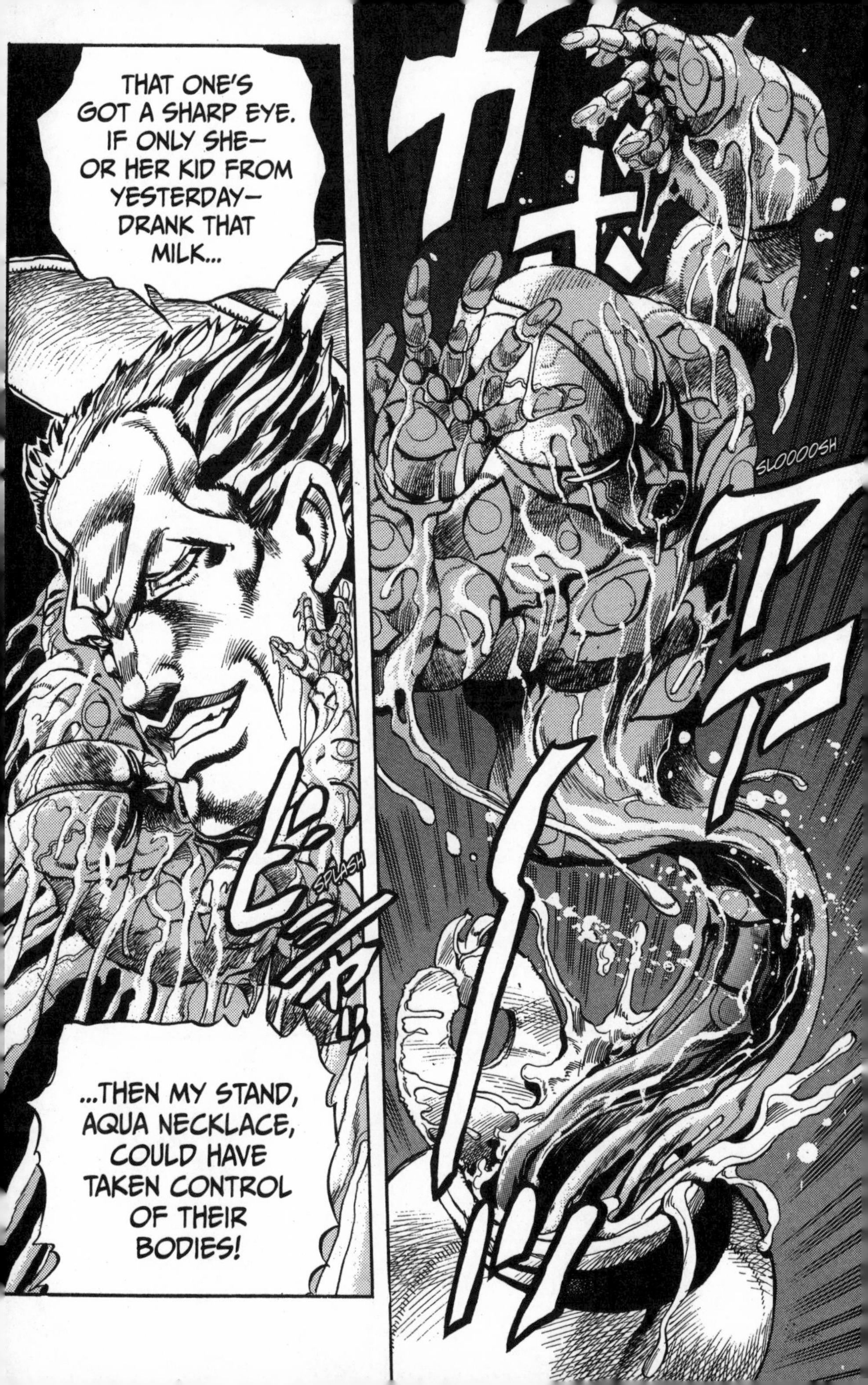
SLOOOOSH
THAT ONE'S GOT A SHARP EYE. IF ONLY SHE—OR HER KID FROM YESTERDAY—DRANK THAT MILK...
SPLASH
...THEN MY STAND, AQUA NECKLACE, COULD HAVE TAKEN CONTROL OF THEIR BODIES!

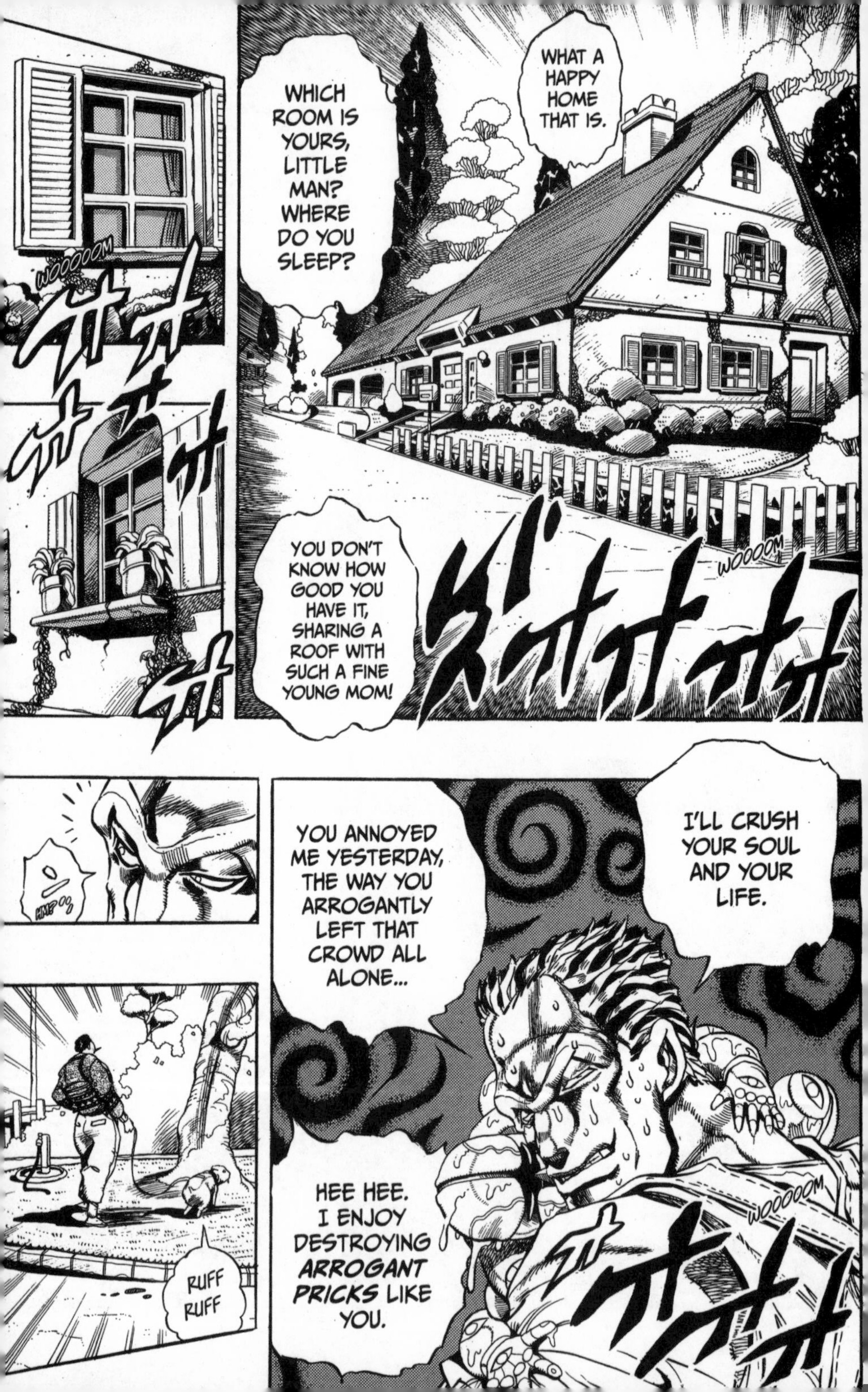
WHAT A HAPPY HOME THAT IS.
WHICH ROOM IS YOURS, LITTLE MAN? WHERE DO YOU SLEEP?
YOU DON'T KNOW HOW GOOD YOU HAVE IT, SHARING A ROOF WITH SUCH A FINE YOUNG MOM!
WOOOOM
WOOOOOM
I'LL CRUSH YOUR SOUL AND YOUR LIFE.
YOU ANNOYED ME YESTERDAY, THE WAY YOU ARROGANTLY LEFT THAT CROWD ALL ALONE...
HEE HEE. I ENJOY DESTROYING *ARROGANT PRICKS* LIKE YOU.
WOOOOOM
HM?
RUFF RUFF

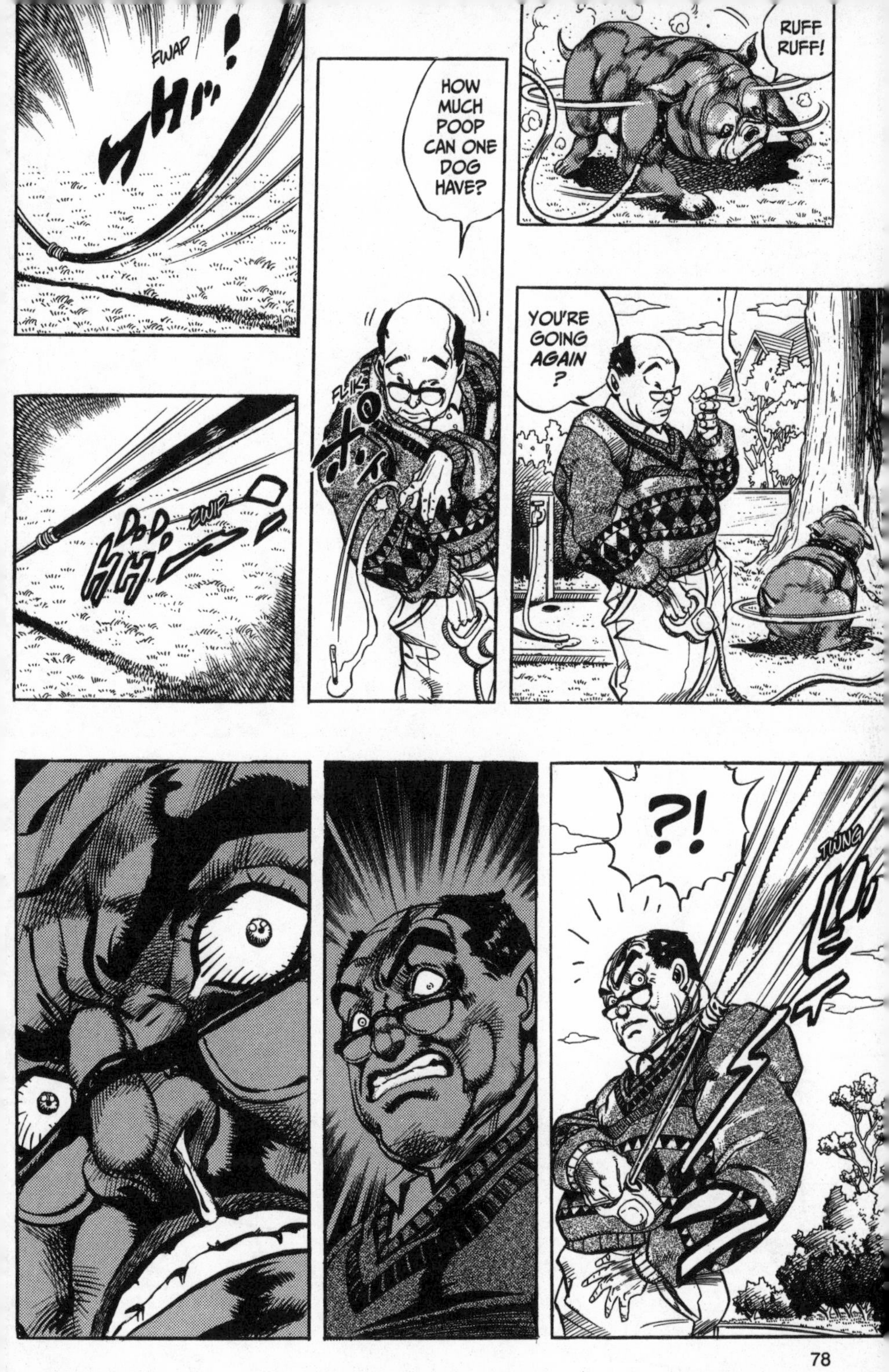
RUFF RUFF!
YOU'RE GOING AGAIN?
HOW MUCH POOP CAN ONE DOG HAVE?
FLIKS
FWAP
ZWIP
?!
TWNG

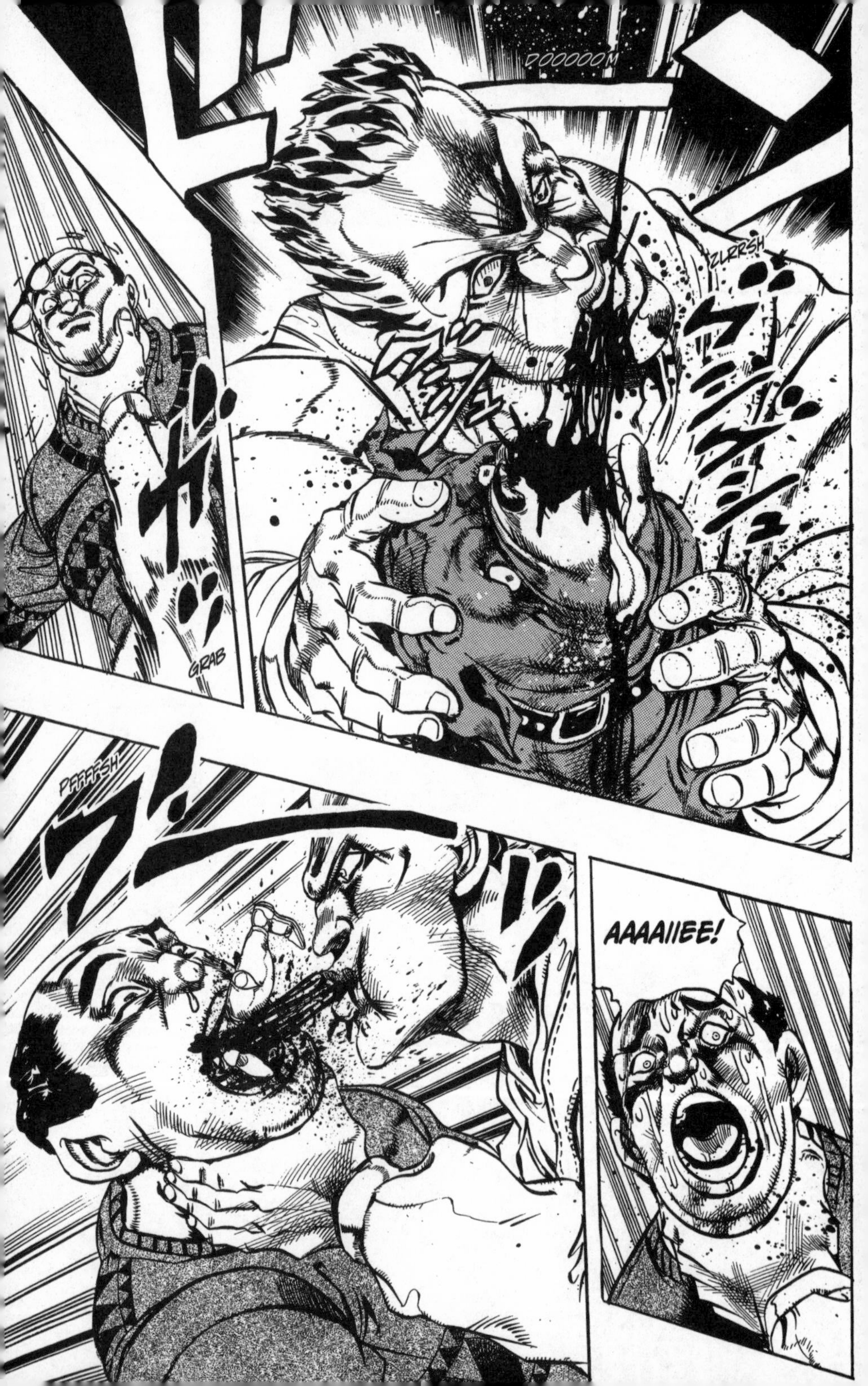
DOOOOOM
ZLRRSH
GRAB
AAAAIIEE!
PARRRSH

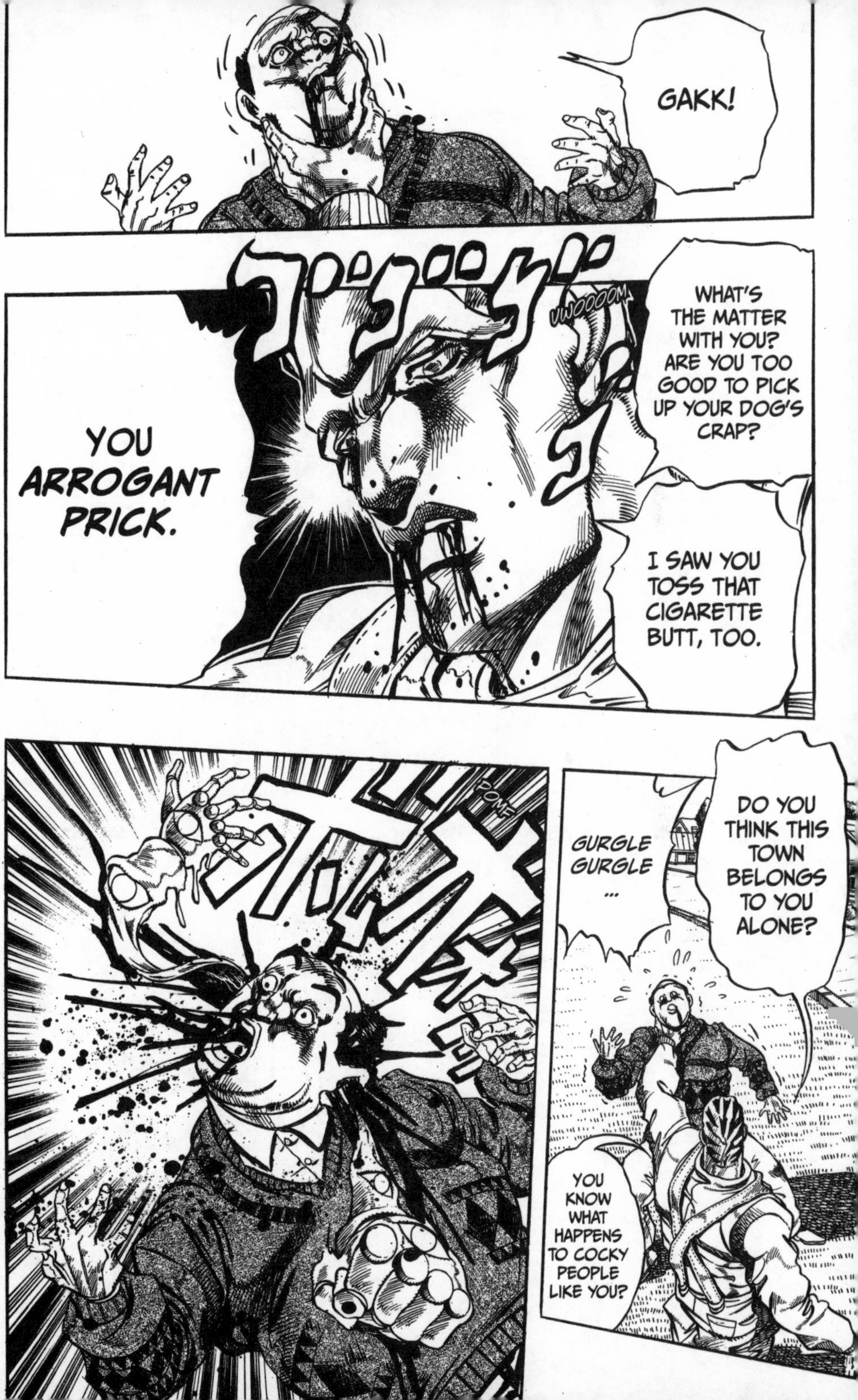
GAKK!
WHAT'S THE MATTER WITH YOU? ARE YOU TOO GOOD TO PICK UP YOUR DOG'S CRAP?
UWOOOOM
I SAW YOU TOSS THAT CIGARETTE BUTT, TOO.
YOU ARROGANT PRICK.
DO YOU THINK THIS TOWN BELONGS TO YOU ALONE?
GURGLE GURGLE ...
YOU KNOW WHAT HAPPENS TO COCKY PEOPLE LIKE YOU?
POMF

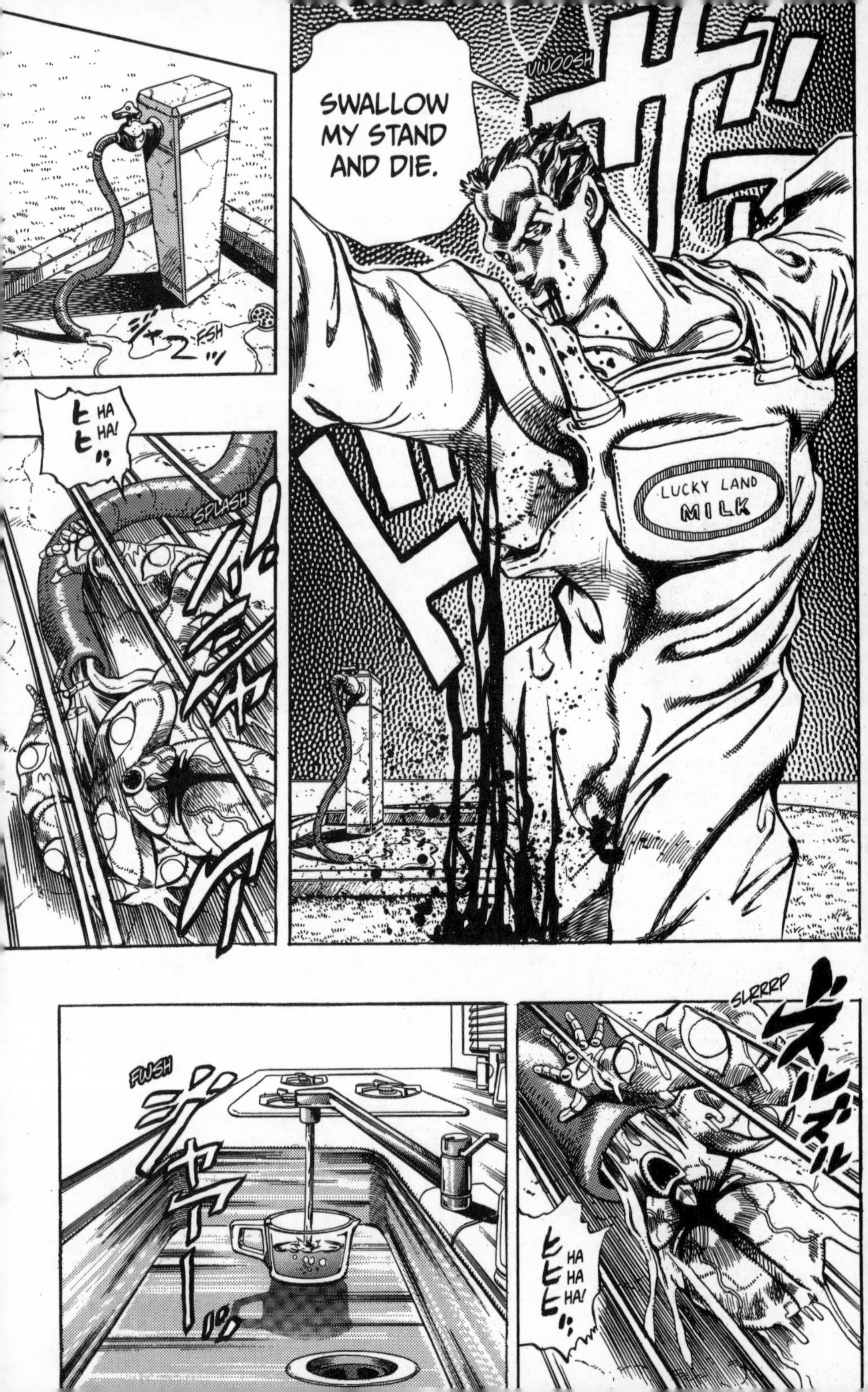
VWOOSH
SWALLOW MY STAND AND DIE.
LUCKY LAND MILK
FSH
HA HA!
SPLASH
SLURRP
HA HA HA!
FWSH

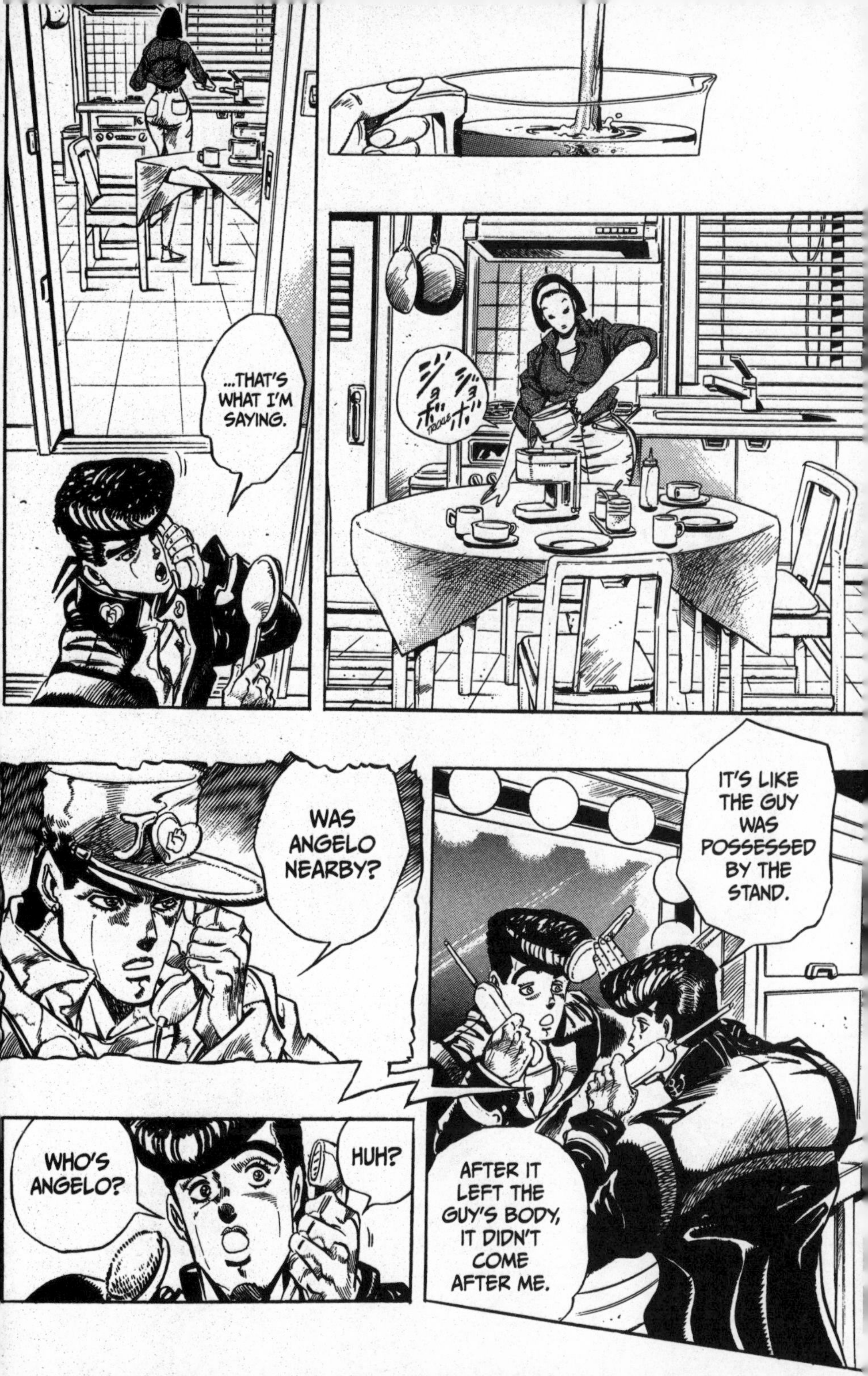
ジョボジョボ
TRICKLE
...THAT'S WHAT I'M SAYING.
IT'S LIKE THE GUY WAS POSSESSED BY THE STAND.
AFTER IT LEFT THE GUY'S BODY, IT DIDN'T COME AFTER ME.
WAS ANGELO NEARBY?
HUH?
WHO'S ANGELO?

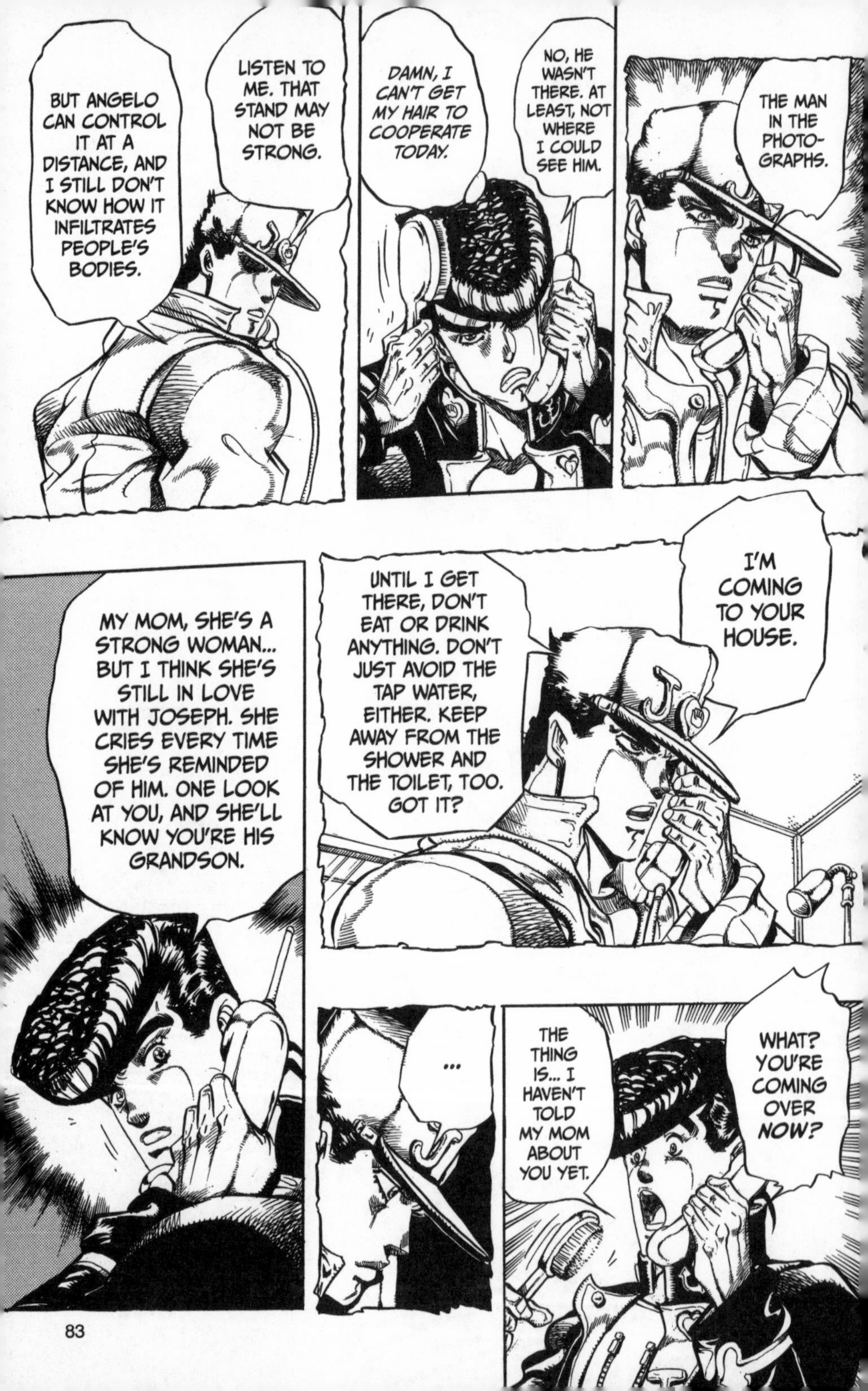
THE MAN IN THE PHOTO-GRAPHS.
NO, HE WASN'T THERE. AT LEAST, NOT WHERE I COULD SEE HIM.
DAMN, I CAN'T GET MY HAIR TO COOPERATE TODAY.
LISTEN TO ME. THAT STAND MAY NOT BE STRONG.
BUT ANGELO CAN CONTROL IT AT A DISTANCE, AND I STILL DON'T KNOW HOW IT INFILTRATES PEOPLE'S BODIES.
I'M COMING TO YOUR HOUSE.
UNTIL I GET THERE, DON'T EAT OR DRINK ANYTHING. DON'T JUST AVOID THE TAP WATER, EITHER. KEEP AWAY FROM THE SHOWER AND THE TOILET, TOO. GOT IT?
WHAT? YOU'RE COMING OVER *NOW?*
THE THING IS... I HAVEN'T TOLD MY MOM ABOUT YOU YET.
...
MY MOM, SHE'S A STRONG WOMAN... BUT I THINK SHE'S STILL IN LOVE WITH JOSEPH. SHE CRIES EVERY TIME SHE'S REMINDED OF HIM. ONE LOOK AT YOU, AND SHE'LL KNOW YOU'RE HIS GRANDSON.

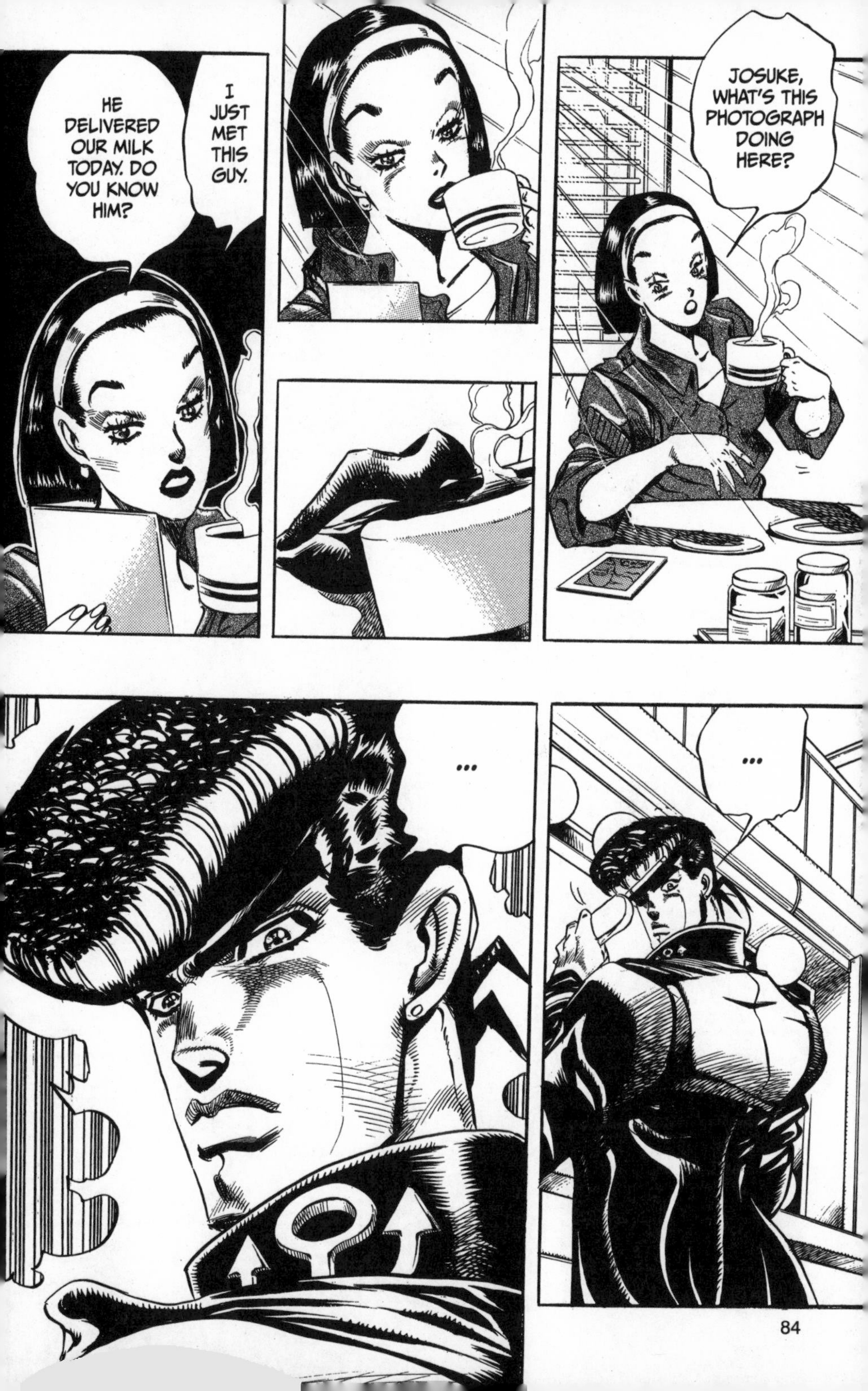
JOSUKE, WHAT'S THIS PHOTOGRAPH DOING HERE?
I JUST MET THIS GUY.
HE DELIVERED OUR MILK TODAY. DO YOU KNOW HIM?
...
...

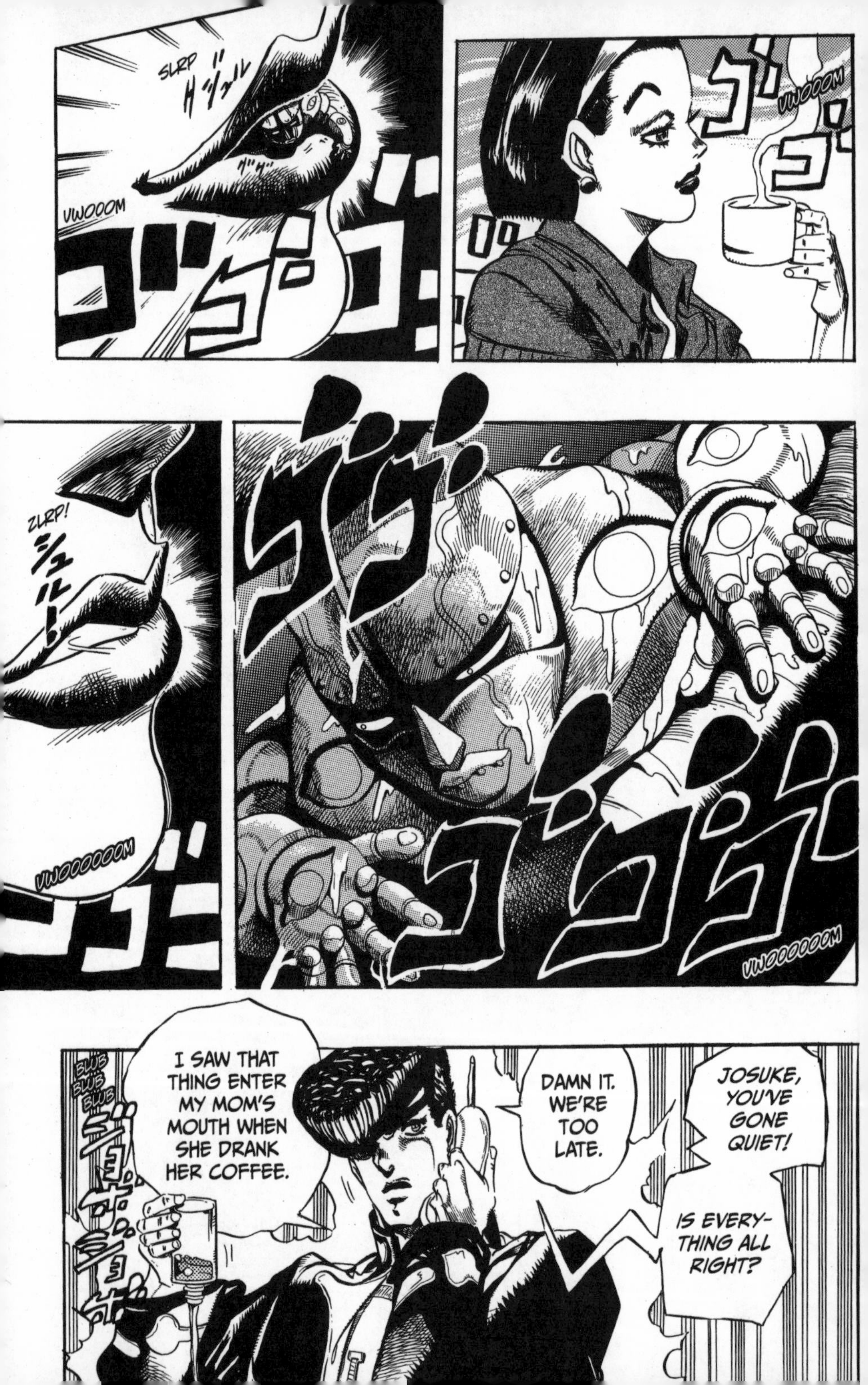
VWOOOM
SLRP
VWOOOM
VWOOOOOOM
ZLRP!
VWOOOOOOM
JOSUKE, YOU'VE GONE QUIET!
IS EVERY-THING ALL RIGHT?
DAMN IT. WE'RE TOO LATE.
I SAW THAT THING ENTER MY MOM'S MOUTH WHEN SHE DRANK HER COFFEE.
BLUB BLUB BLUB

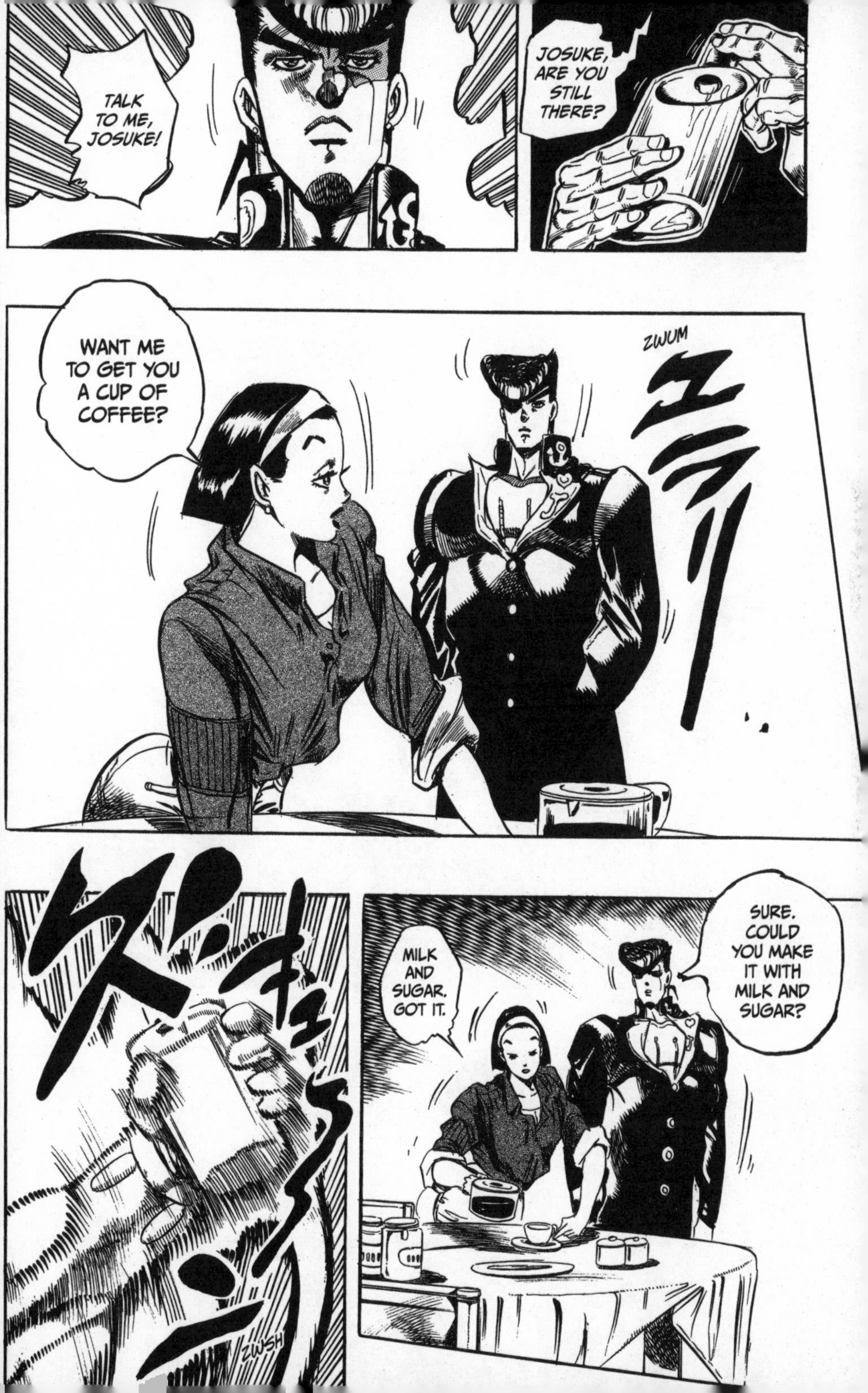
JOSUKE, ARE YOU STILL THERE?
TALK TO ME, JOSUKE!
WANT ME TO GET YOU A CUP OF COFFEE?
ZWUM
SURE. COULD YOU MAKE IT WITH MILK AND SUGAR?
MILK AND SUGAR. GOT IT.
ZWSH

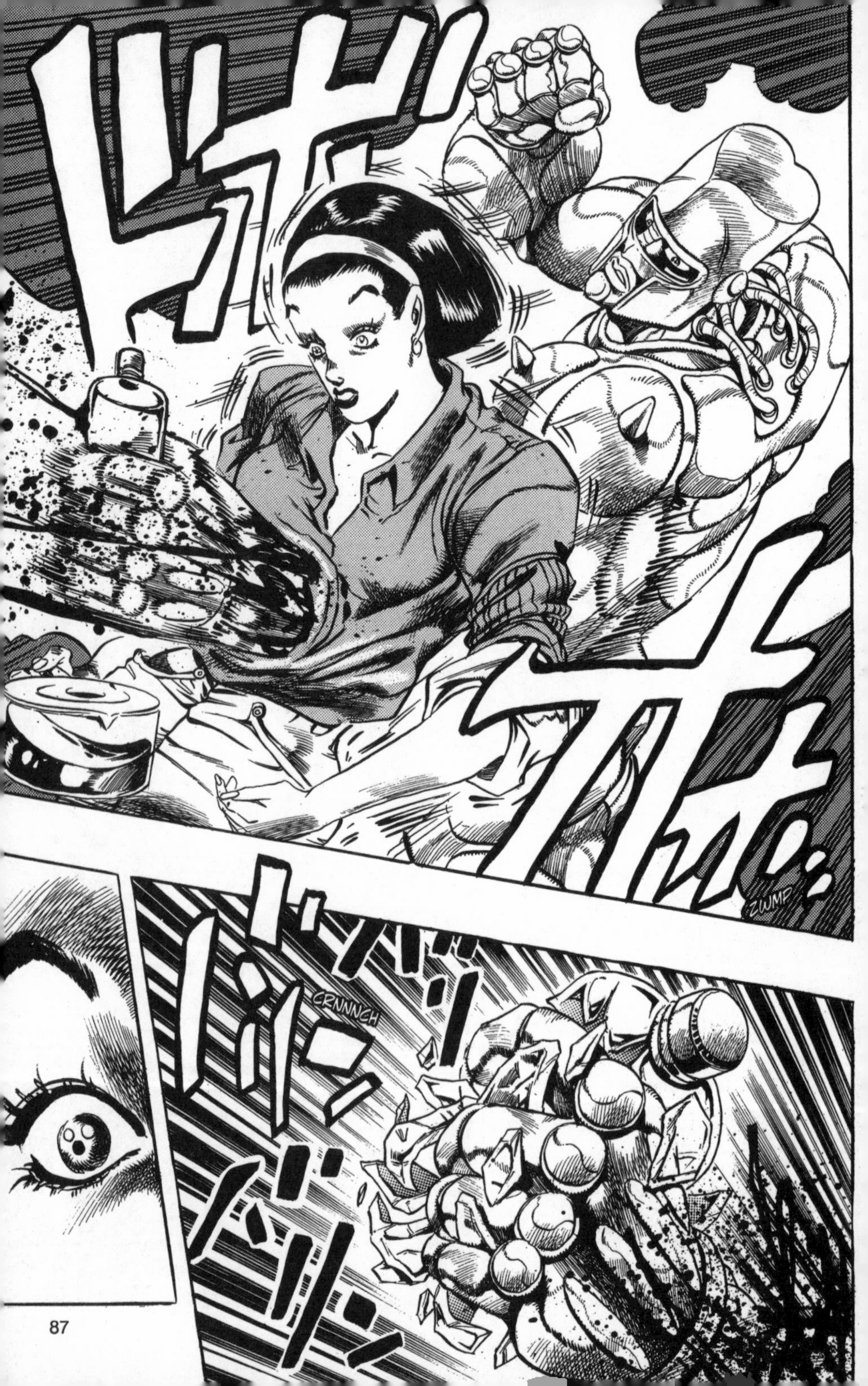
ZWUMP
CRNNNCH

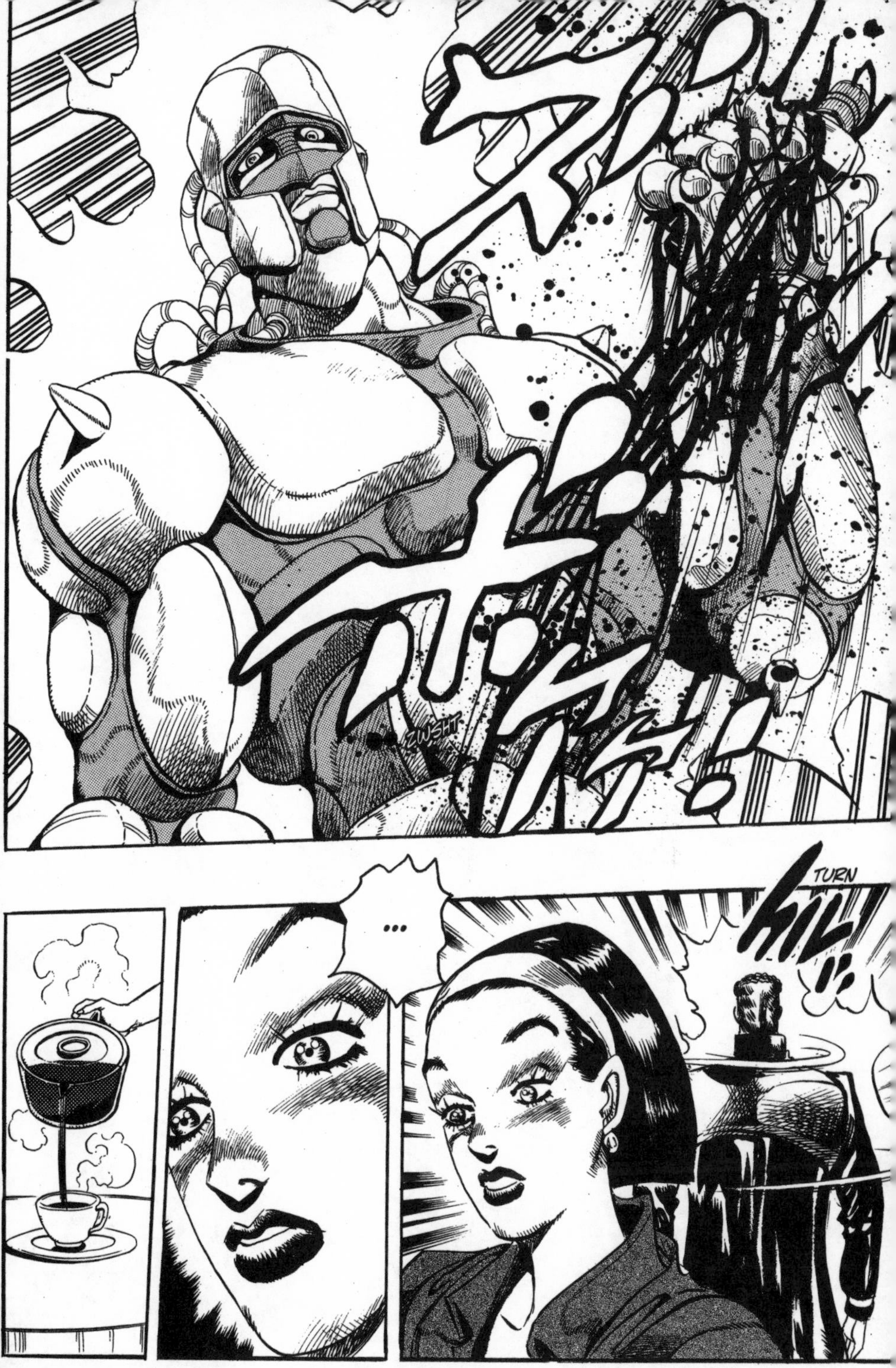
ZWSHT
TURN
...

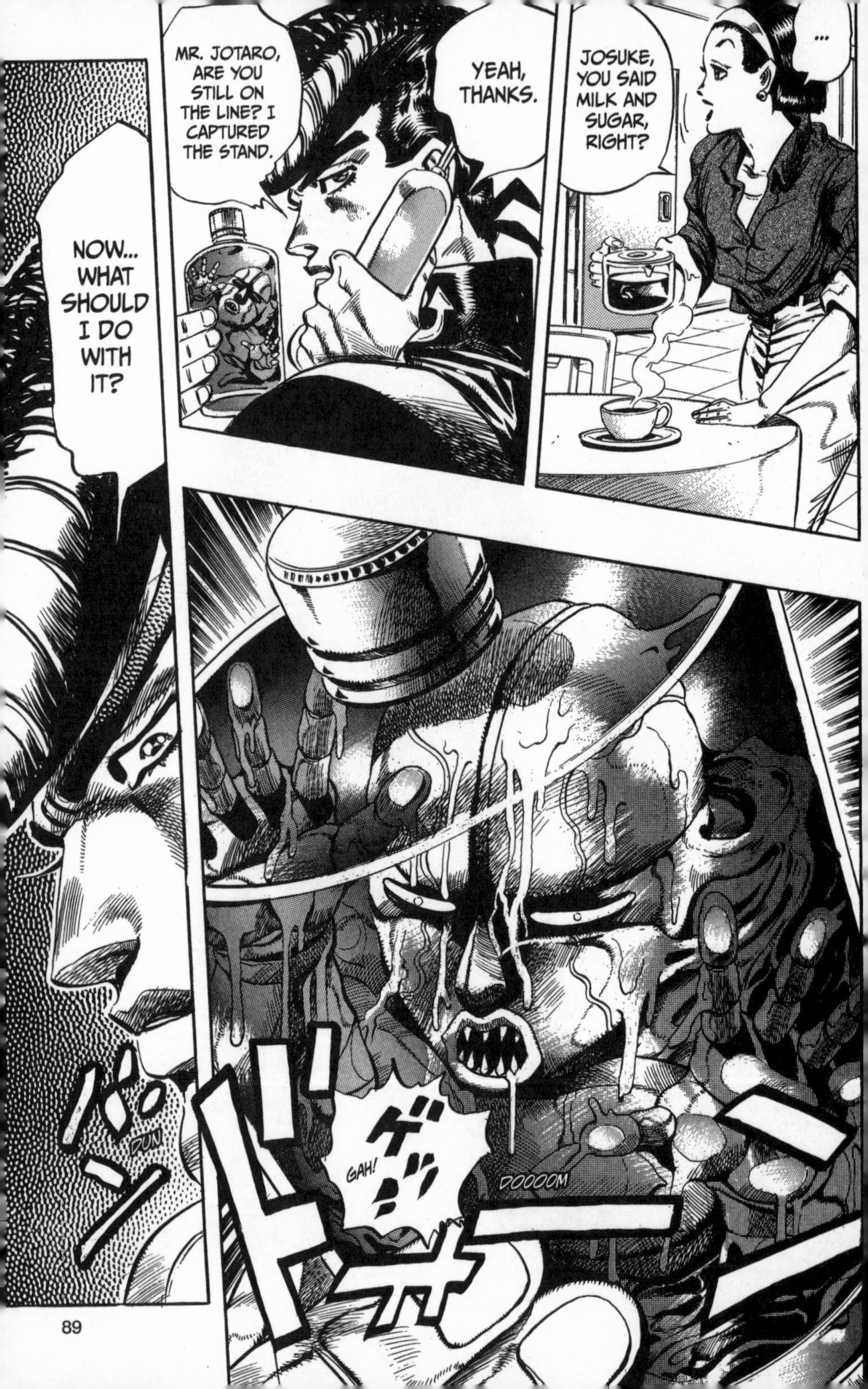
...
JOSUKE, YOU SAID MILK AND SUGAR, RIGHT?
YEAH, THANKS.
MR. JOTARO, ARE YOU STILL ON THE LINE? I CAPTURED THE STAND.
GAH!
DOOOOM
NOW... WHAT SHOULD I DO WITH IT?
DUN

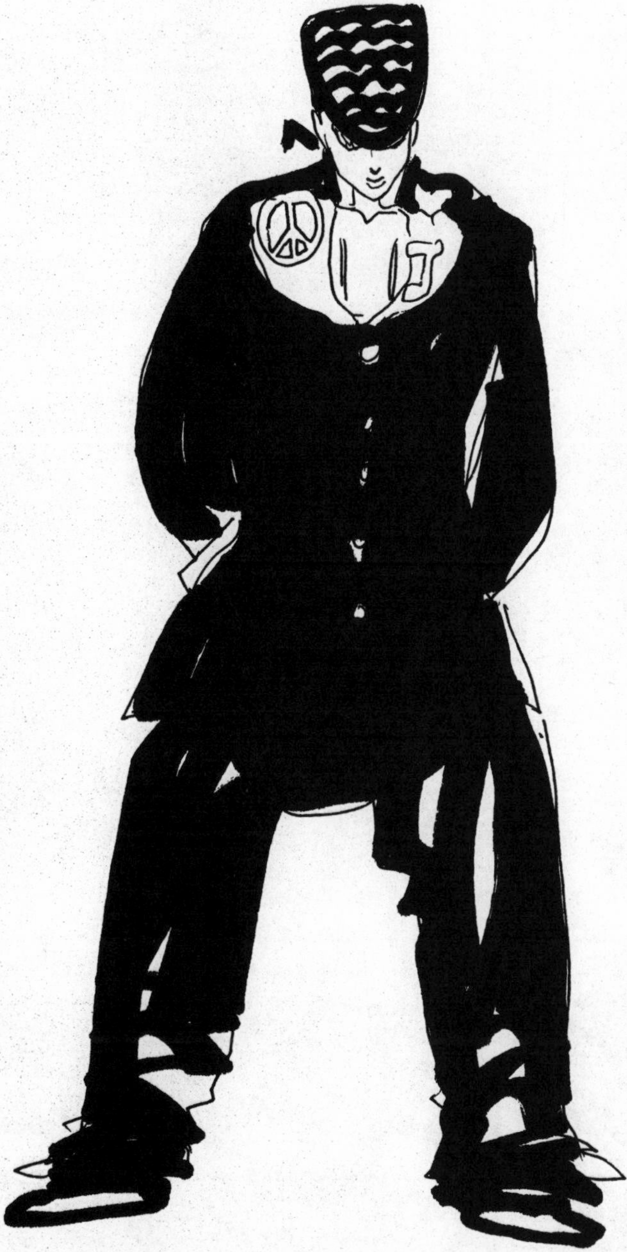

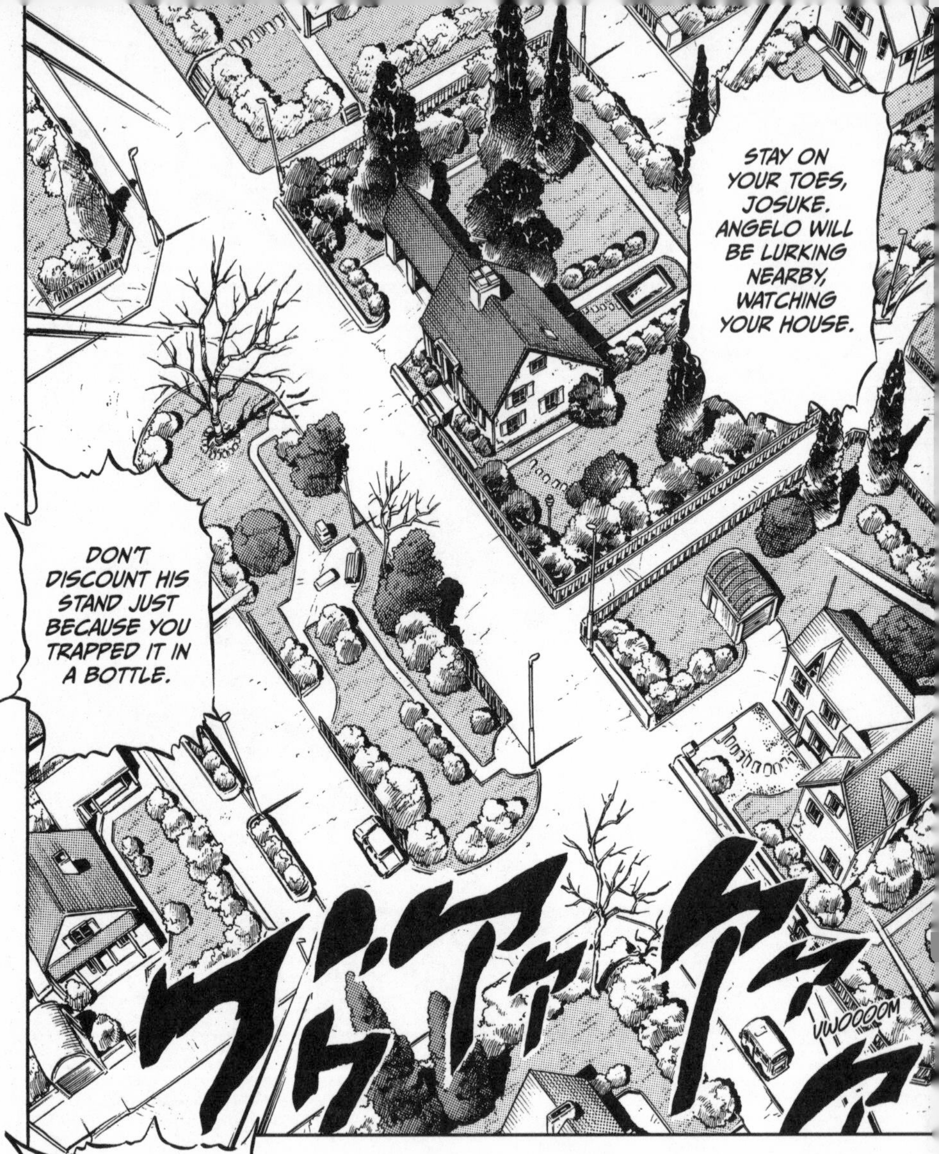
STAY ON YOUR TOES, JOSUKE. ANGELO WILL BE LURKING NEARBY, WATCHING YOUR HOUSE.
DON'T DISCOUNT HIS STAND JUST BECAUSE YOU TRAPPED IT IN A BOTTLE.
VWOOOOM
HIS STAND IS LIKE LIQUID. IT CAN EVEN DISGUISE ITSELF AS COFFEE OR MILK. I THINK WE'RE GOING TO NEED MORE THAN JUST OUR FISTS TO STOP IT... DON'T LET THAT BOTTLE OUT OF YOUR SIGHT UNTIL I GET THERE. GOT IT?

CHAPTER 5

JOSUKE HIGASHIKATA MEETS ANGELO, PART 2

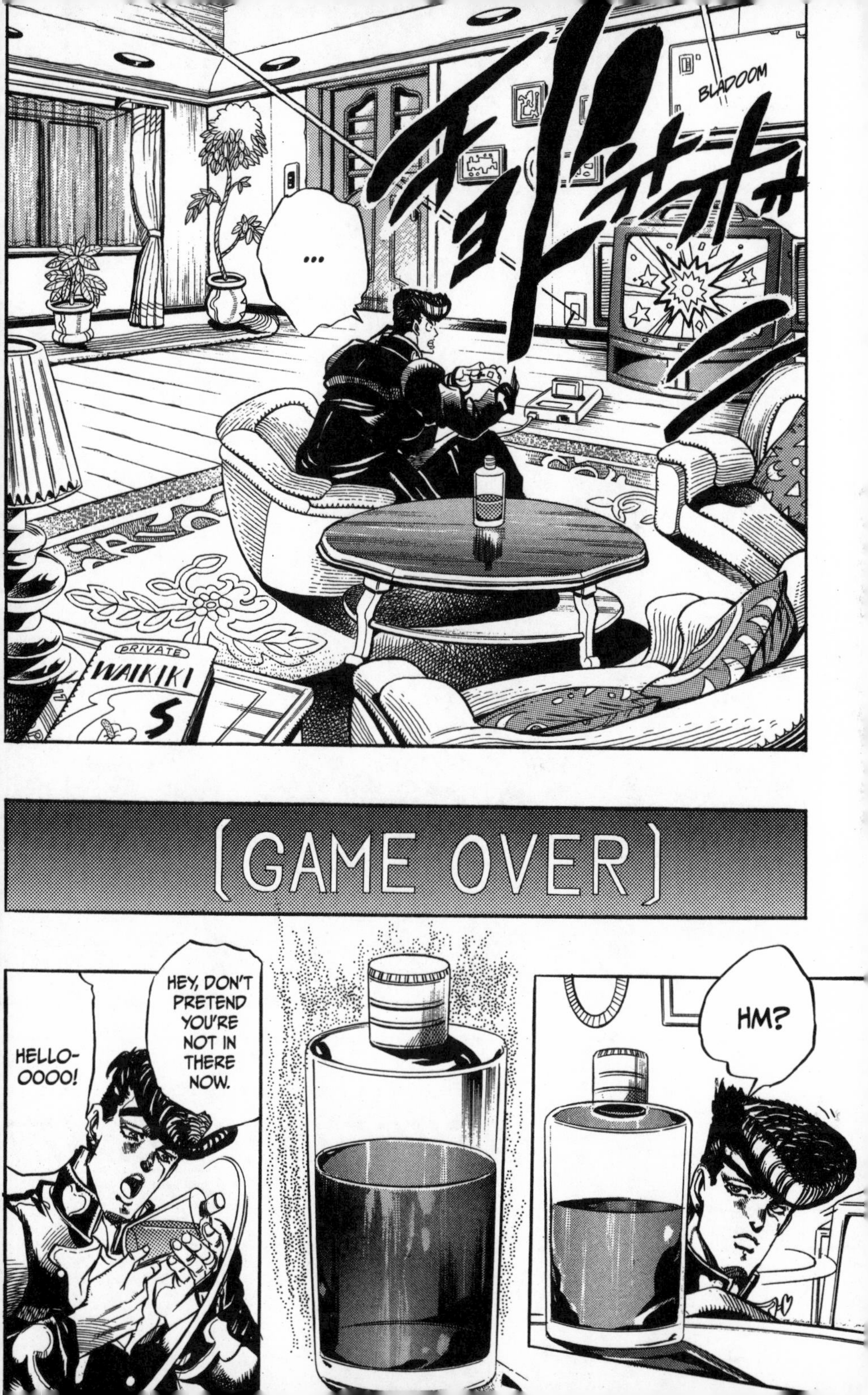
BLADOOM
...
(GAME OVER)
HM?
HEY, DON'T PRETEND YOU'RE NOT IN THERE NOW.
HELLO-OOOO!

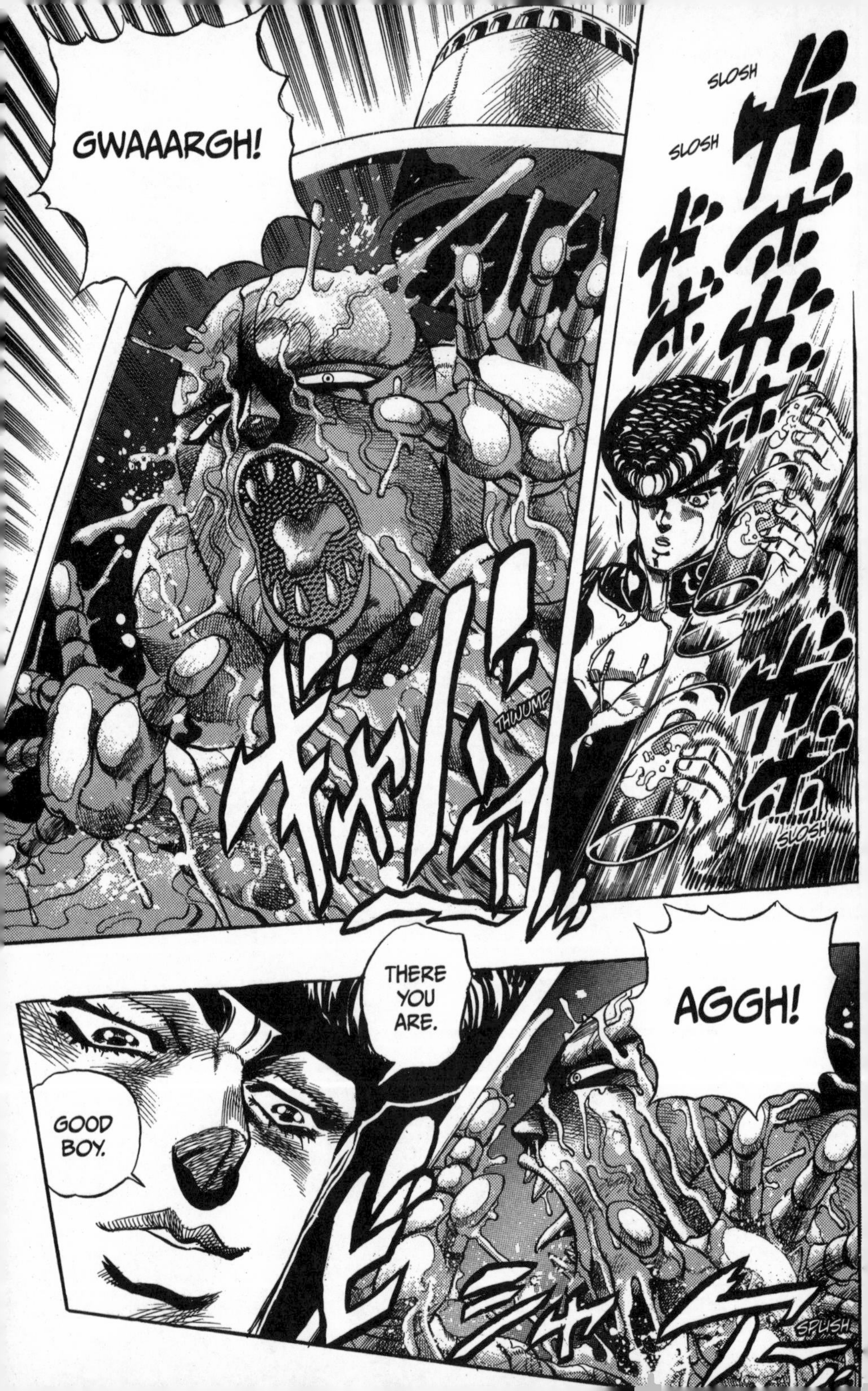
SLOSH
SLOSH
SLOSH
GWAAARGH!
THWUMP
AGGH!
SPLUSH
THERE YOU ARE.
GOOD BOY.

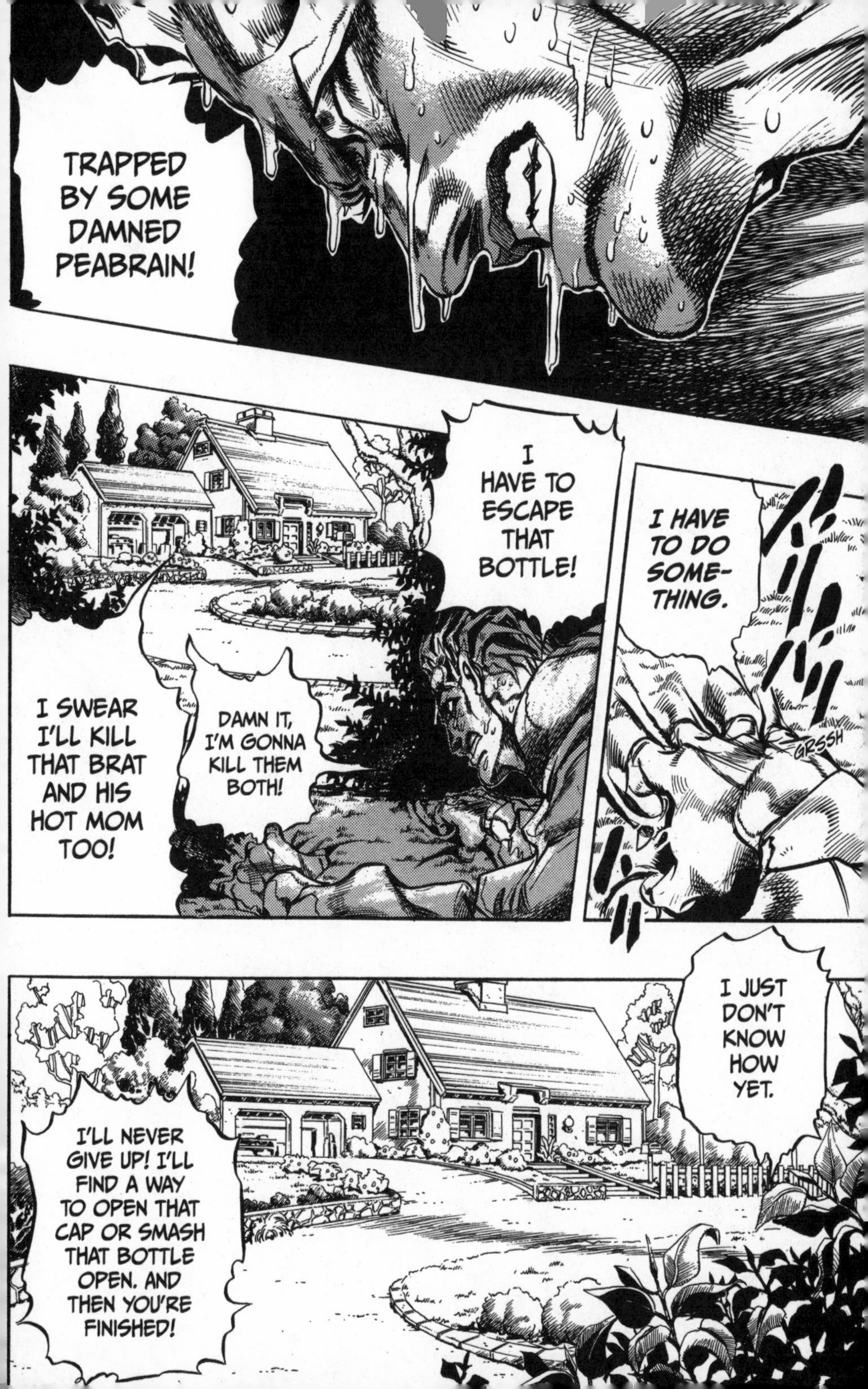
TRAPPED BY SOME DAMNED PEABRAIN!
I HAVE TO DO SOME-THING.
GRSSH
I HAVE TO ESCAPE THAT BOTTLE!
DAMN IT, I'M GONNA KILL THEM BOTH!
I SWEAR I'LL KILL THAT BRAT AND HIS HOT MOM TOO!
I JUST DON'T KNOW HOW YET.
I'LL NEVER GIVE UP! I'LL FIND A WAY TO OPEN THAT CAP OR SMASH THAT BOTTLE OPEN. AND THEN YOU'RE FINISHED!

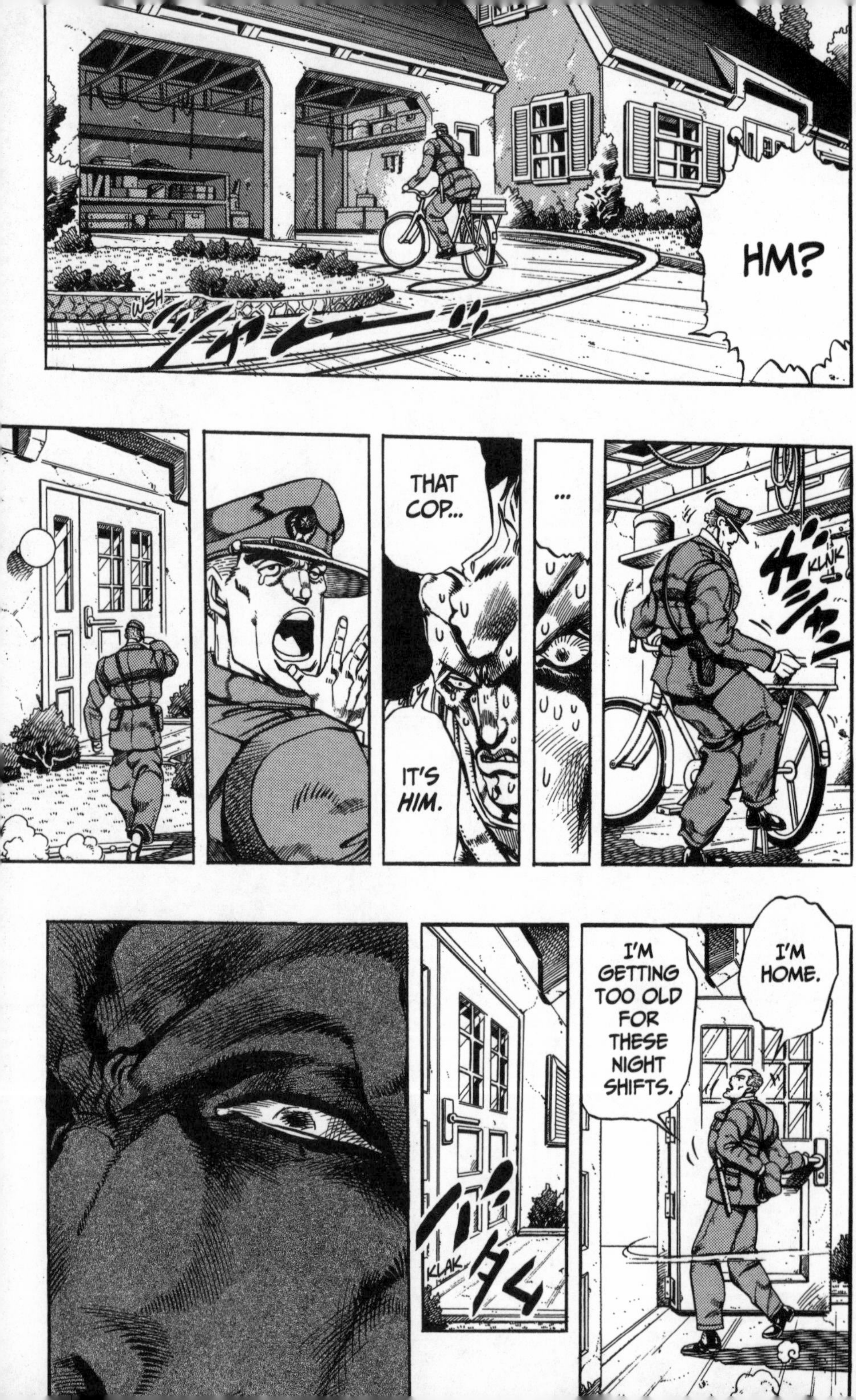
HM?
WSH
KLNK
...
THAT COP...
IT'S HIM.
I'M HOME.
I'M GETTING TOO OLD FOR THESE NIGHT SHIFTS.
KLAK

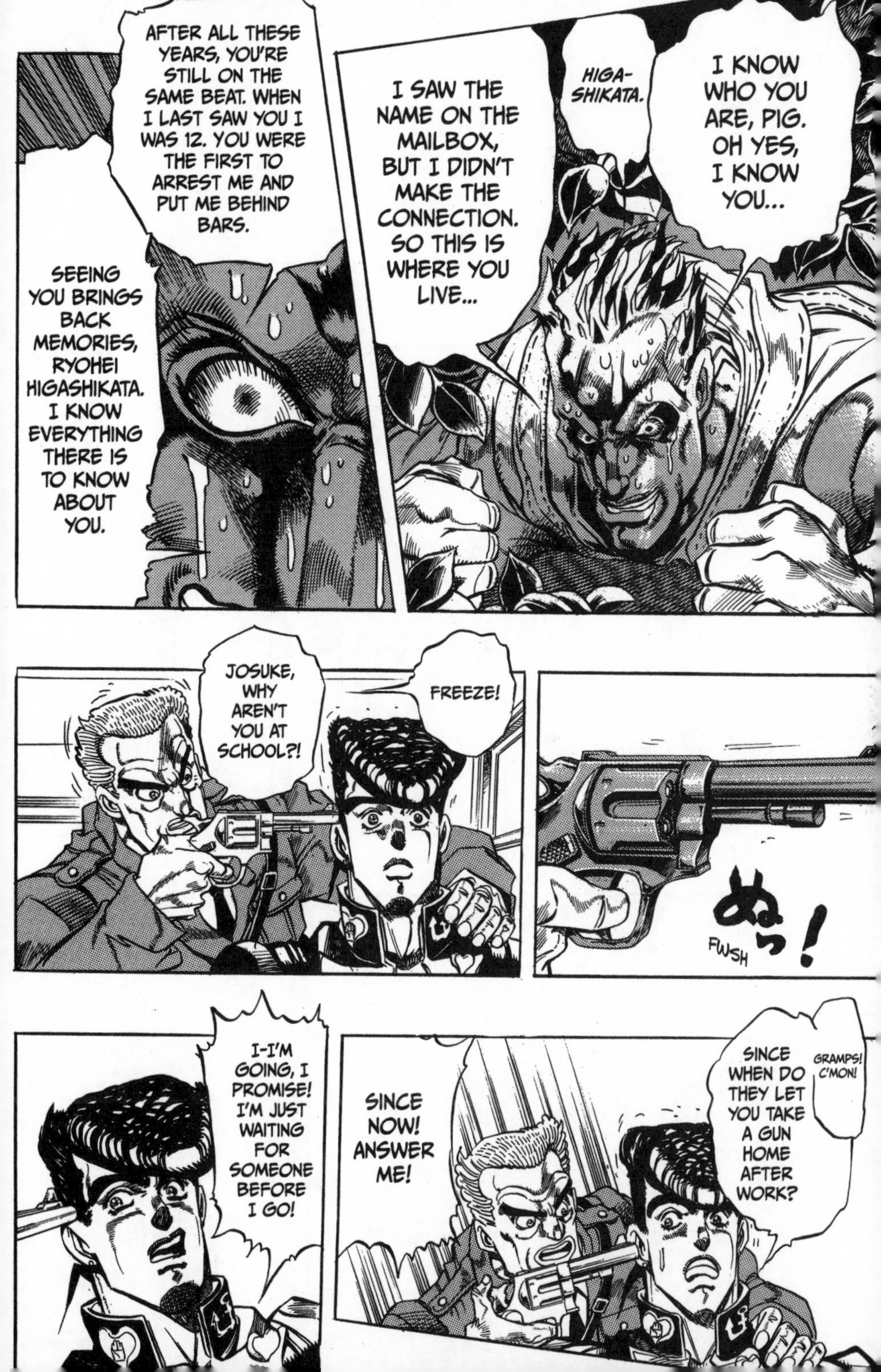
I KNOW WHO YOU ARE, PIG. OH YES, I KNOW YOU...
HIGA-SHIKATA.
I SAW THE NAME ON THE MAILBOX, BUT I DIDN'T MAKE THE CONNECTION. SO THIS IS WHERE YOU LIVE...
AFTER ALL THESE YEARS, YOU'RE STILL ON THE SAME BEAT. WHEN I LAST SAW YOU I WAS 12. YOU WERE THE FIRST TO ARREST ME AND PUT ME BEHIND BARS.
SEEING YOU BRINGS BACK MEMORIES, RYOHEI HIGASHIKATA. I KNOW EVERYTHING THERE IS TO KNOW ABOUT YOU.
ぬっ!
FWSH
FREEZE!
JOSUKE, WHY AREN'T YOU AT SCHOOL?!
GRAMPS! C'MON!
SINCE WHEN DO THEY LET YOU TAKE A GUN HOME AFTER WORK?
SINCE NOW! ANSWER ME!
I-I'M GOING, I PROMISE! I'M JUST WAITING FOR SOMEONE BEFORE I GO!

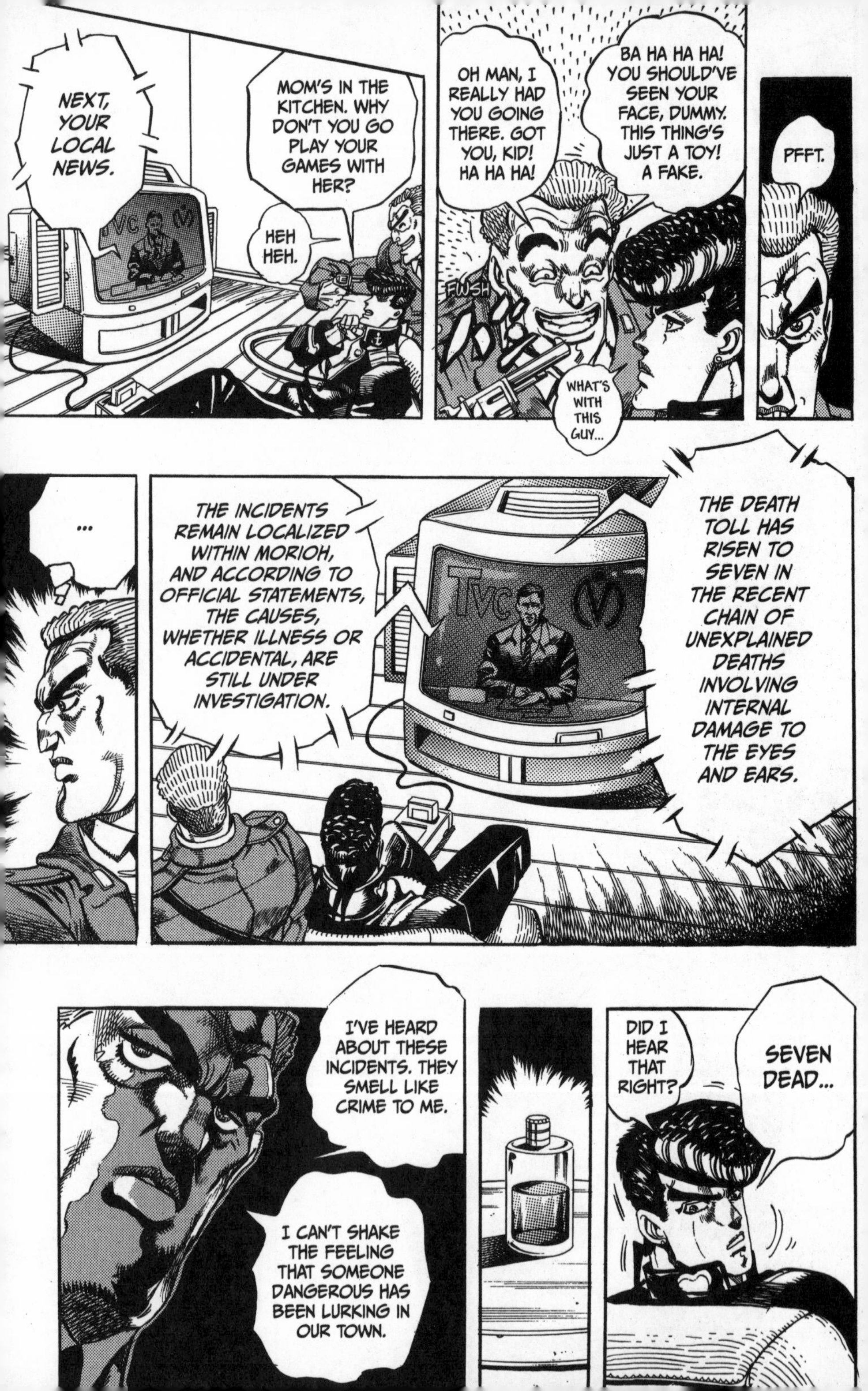
PFFT.
BA HA HA HA! YOU SHOULD'VE SEEN YOUR FACE, DUMMY. THIS THING'S JUST A TOY! A FAKE.
OH MAN, I REALLY HAD YOU GOING THERE. GOT YOU, KID! HA HA HA!
FWSH
WHAT'S WITH THIS GUY...
MOM'S IN THE KITCHEN. WHY DON'T YOU GO PLAY YOUR GAMES WITH HER?
NEXT, YOUR LOCAL NEWS.
HEH HEH.
THE DEATH TOLL HAS RISEN TO SEVEN IN THE RECENT CHAIN OF UNEXPLAINED DEATHS INVOLVING INTERNAL DAMAGE TO THE EYES AND EARS.
THE INCIDENTS REMAIN LOCALIZED WITHIN MORIOH, AND ACCORDING TO OFFICIAL STATEMENTS, THE CAUSES, WHETHER ILLNESS OR ACCIDENTAL, ARE STILL UNDER INVESTIGATION.
...
SEVEN DEAD...
DID I HEAR THAT RIGHT?
I'VE HEARD ABOUT THESE INCIDENTS. THEY SMELL LIKE CRIME TO ME.
I CAN'T SHAKE THE FEELING THAT SOMEONE DANGEROUS HAS BEEN LURKING IN OUR TOWN.

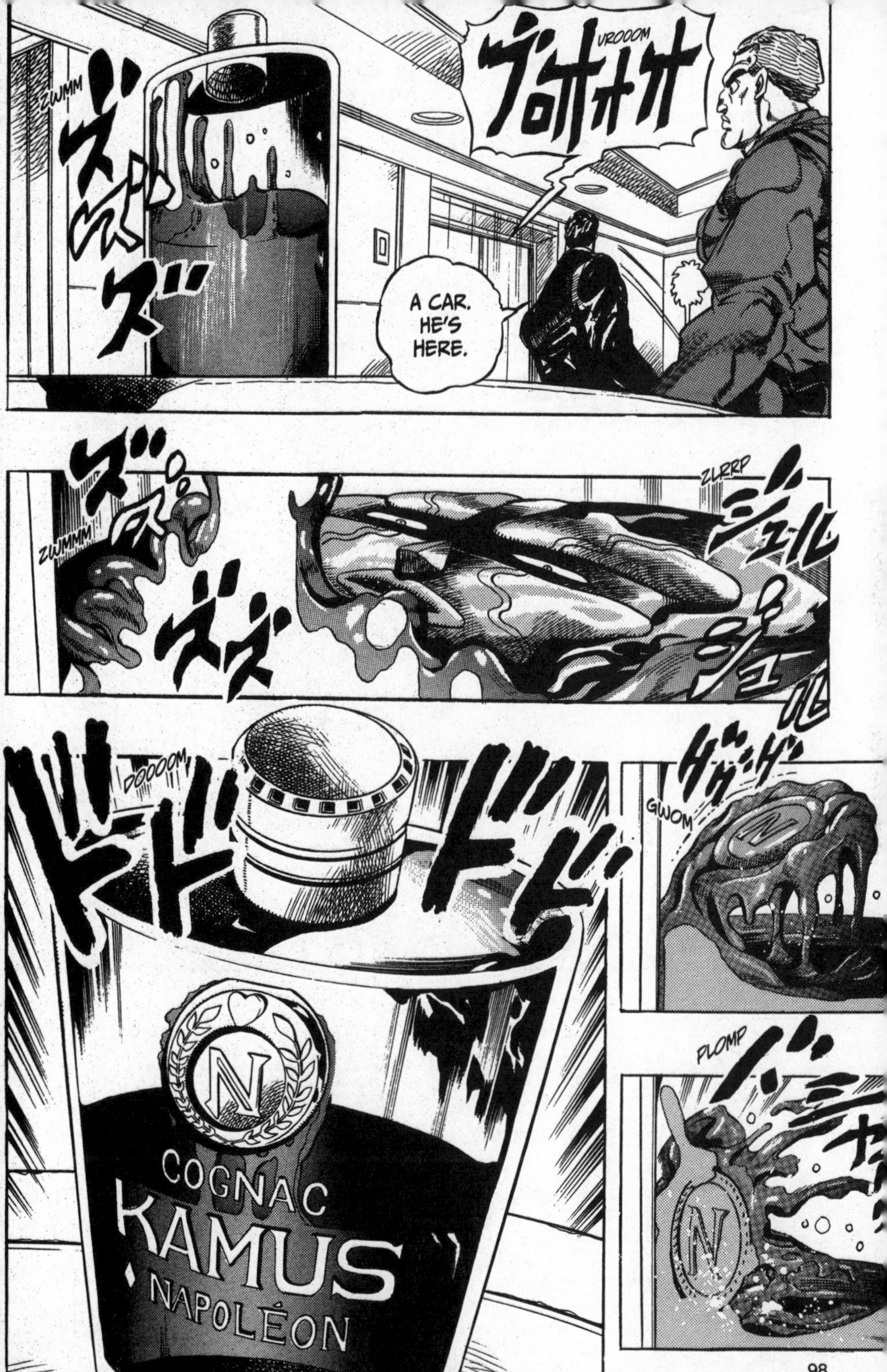
VROOOM
A CAR. HE'S HERE.
ZWMM
ZLRRP
ZWMMM
GWOM
PLOMP
DOOOOM
COGNAC
KAMUS
NAPOLÉON

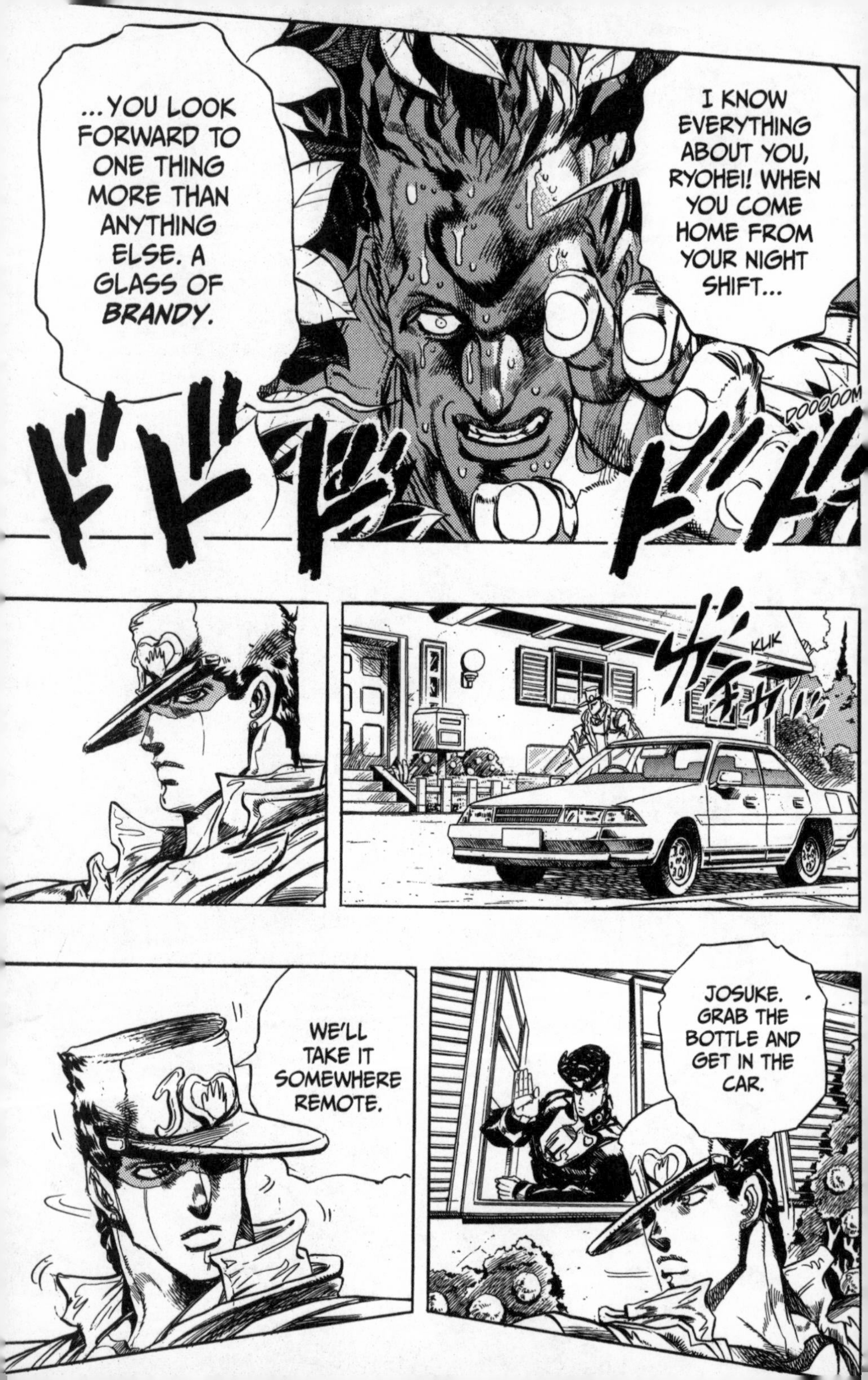
I KNOW EVERYTHING ABOUT YOU, RYOHEI! WHEN YOU COME HOME FROM YOUR NIGHT SHIFT...
...YOU LOOK FORWARD TO ONE THING MORE THAN ANYTHING ELSE. A GLASS OF *BRANDY*.
DOOOOOM
KUK
JOSUKE. GRAB THE BOTTLE AND GET IN THE CAR.
WE'LL TAKE IT SOMEWHERE REMOTE.

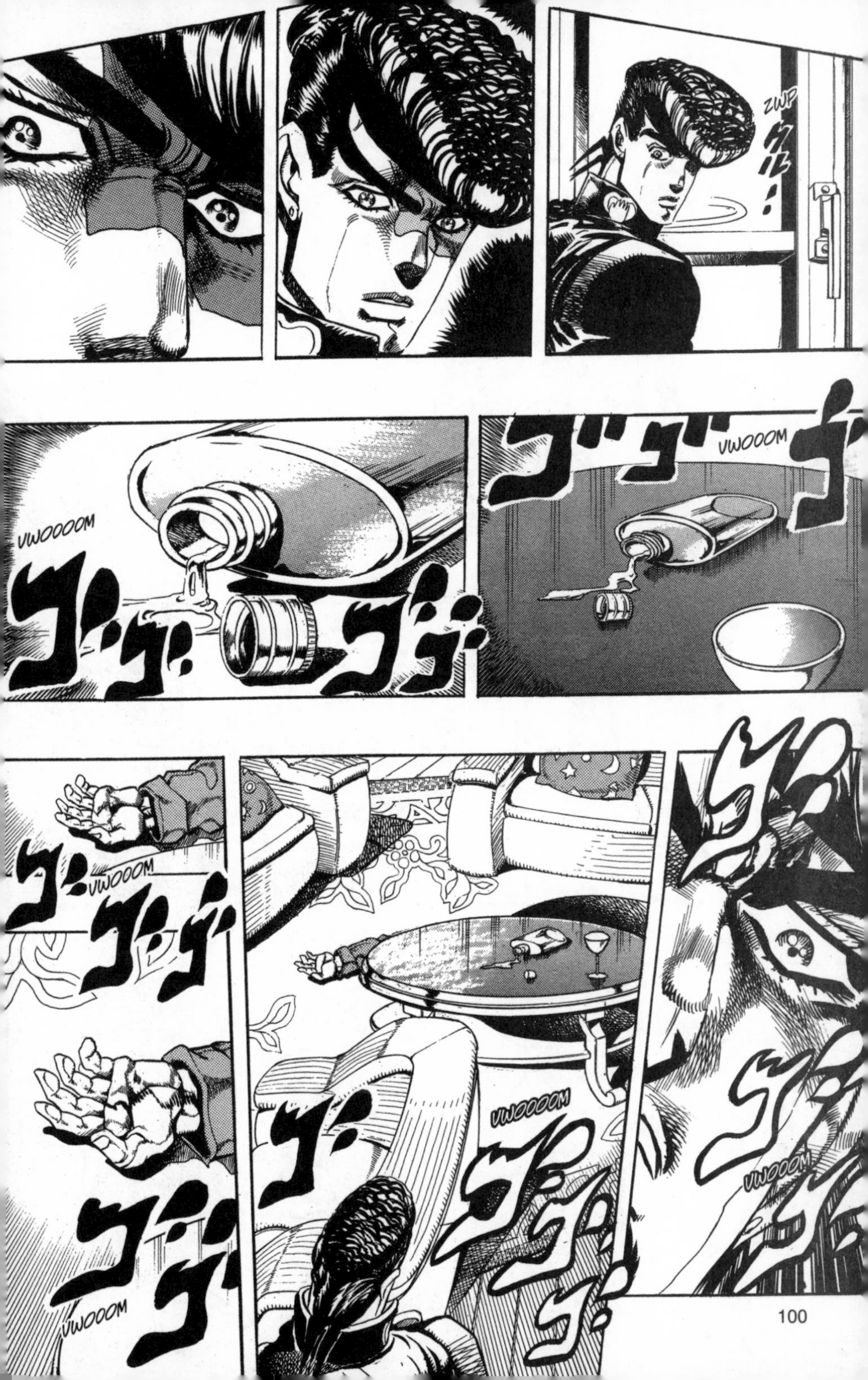
ZWP
VWOOOM
VWOOOOM
VWOOOM
VWOOOM
VWOOOM
VWOOOM

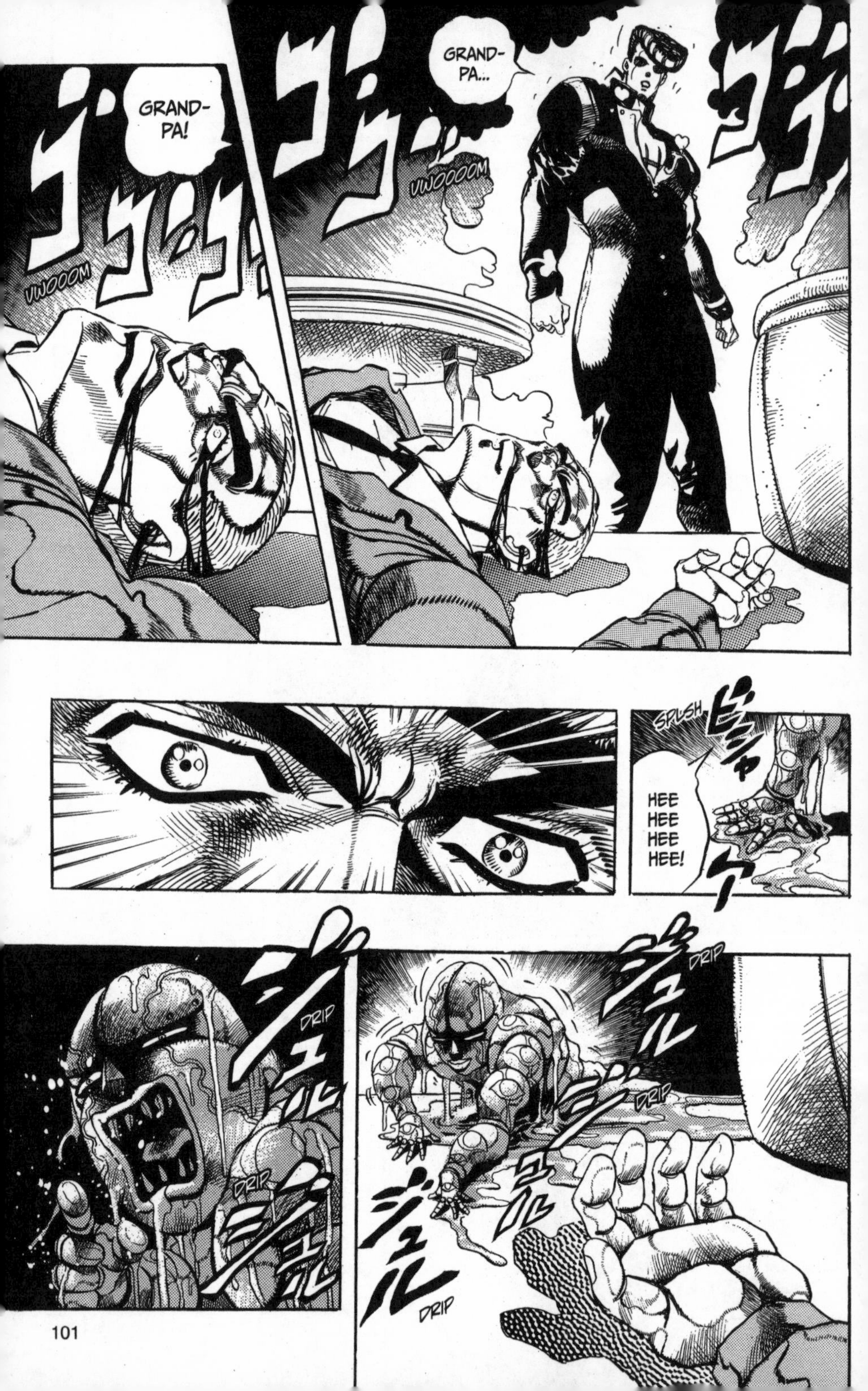
GRAND-PA...
VWOOOOM
GRAND-PA!
VWOOOM
SPLSH
HEE HEE HEE HEE!
DRIP
DRIP
DRIP
DRIP
DRIP

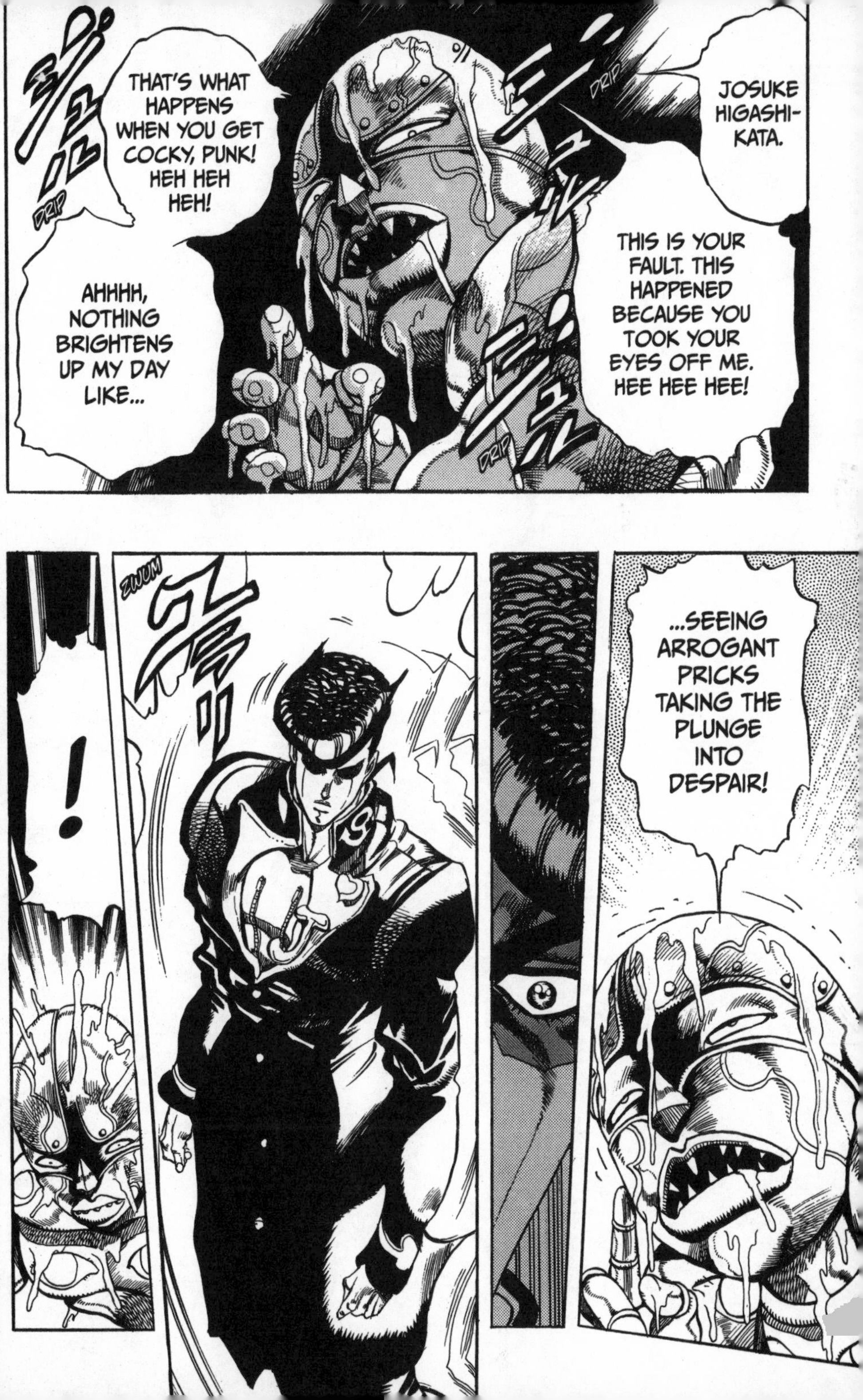

DRIP
JOSUKE HIGASHI-KATA.
THIS IS YOUR FAULT. THIS HAPPENED BECAUSE YOU TOOK YOUR EYES OFF ME. HEE HEE HEE!
DRIP
DRIP
THAT'S WHAT HAPPENS WHEN YOU GET COCKY, PUNK! HEH HEH HEH!
AHHHH, NOTHING BRIGHTENS UP MY DAY LIKE...
...SEEING ARROGANT PRICKS TAKING THE PLUNGE INTO DESPAIR!
ZWUM
!

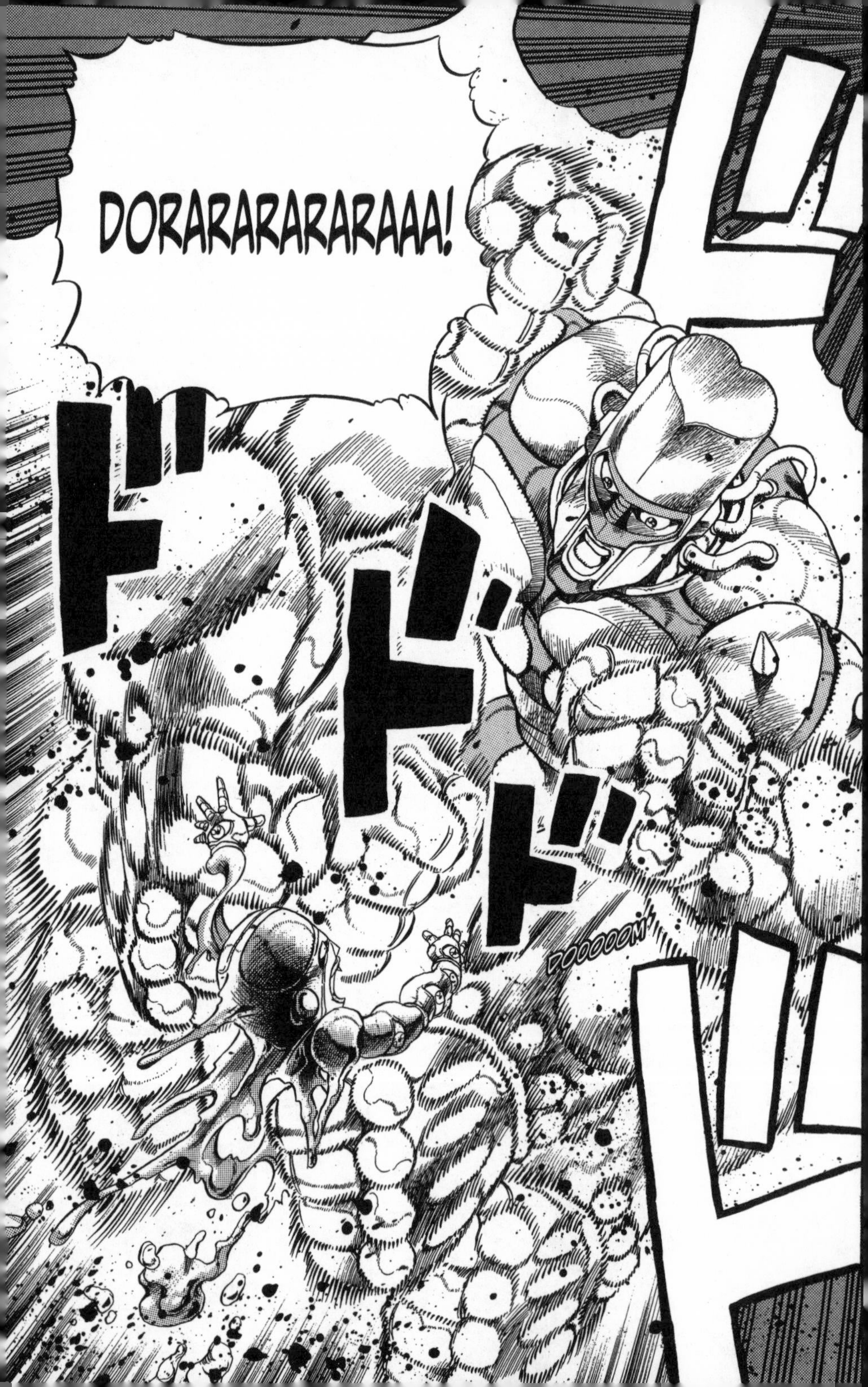
DORARARARARAAA!
ドドドド
DOOOOOOM

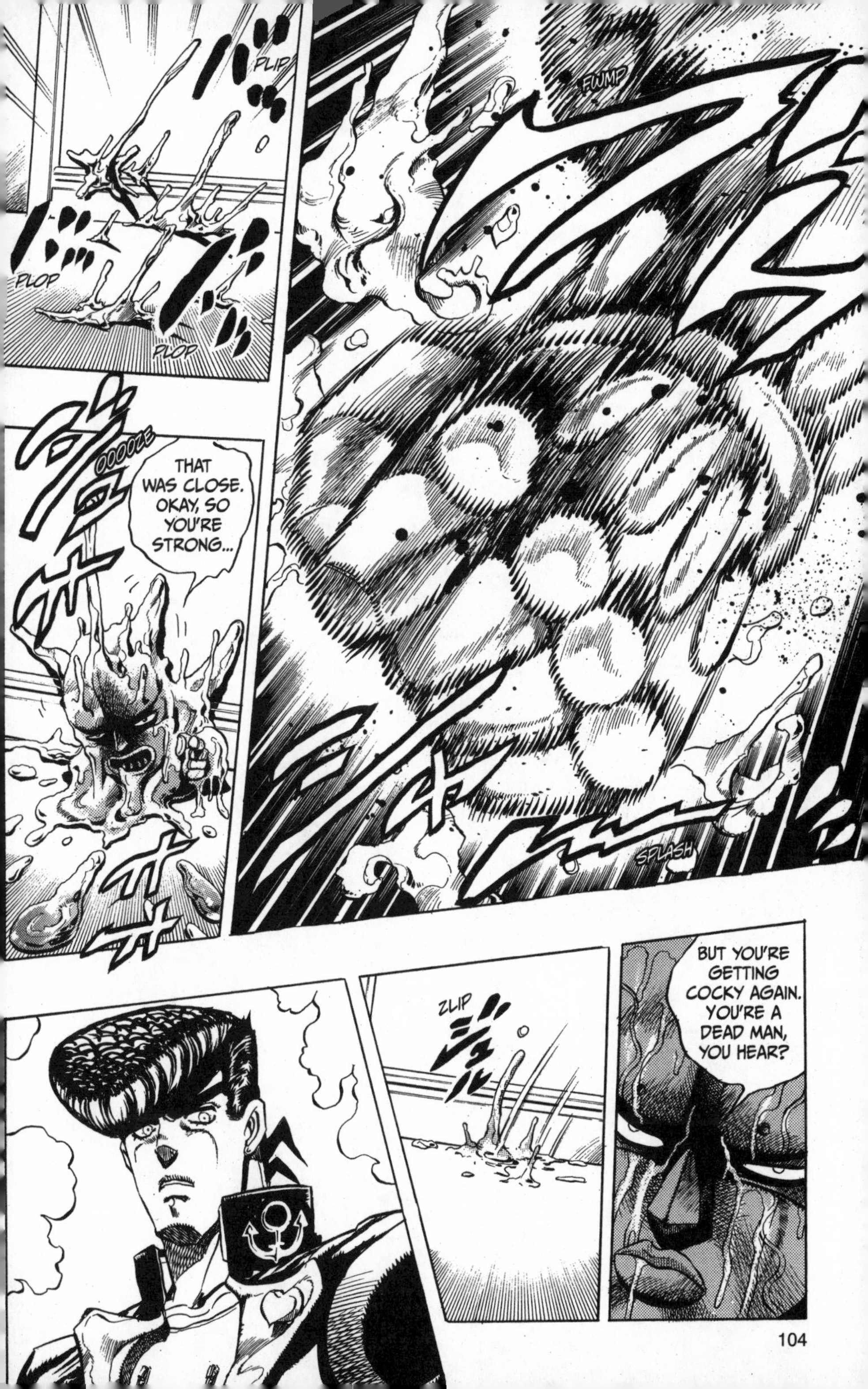
FWUMP
SPLASH
PLIP
PLOP
PLOP
OOOOZE
THAT WAS CLOSE. OKAY, SO YOU'RE STRONG...
BUT YOU'RE GETTING COCKY AGAIN. YOU'RE A DEAD MAN, YOU HEAR?
ZLIP

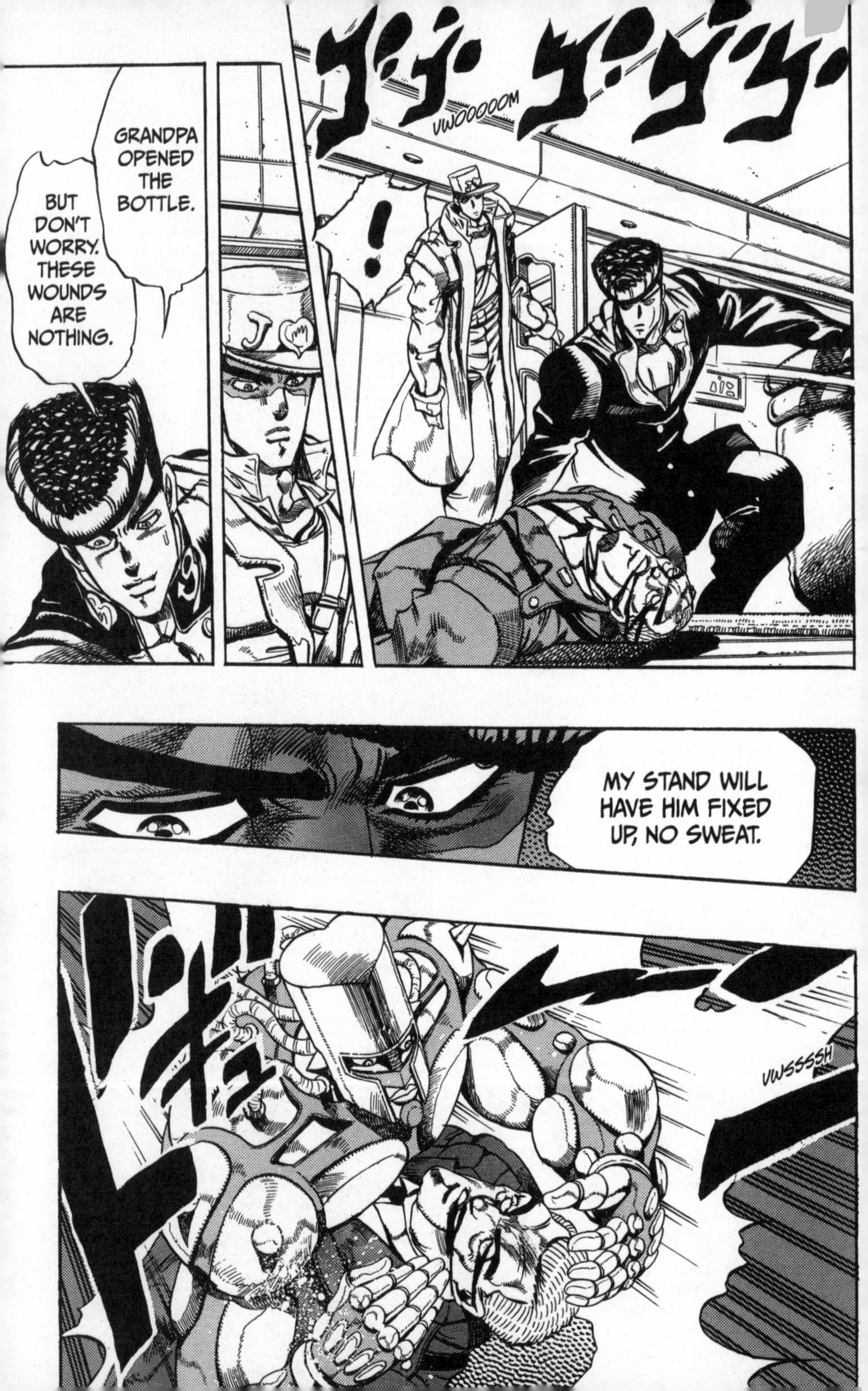
VWOOOOOM
!
GRANDPA OPENED THE BOTTLE.
BUT DON'T WORRY. THESE WOUNDS ARE NOTHING.
MY STAND WILL HAVE HIM FIXED UP, NO SWEAT.
VWSSSSH

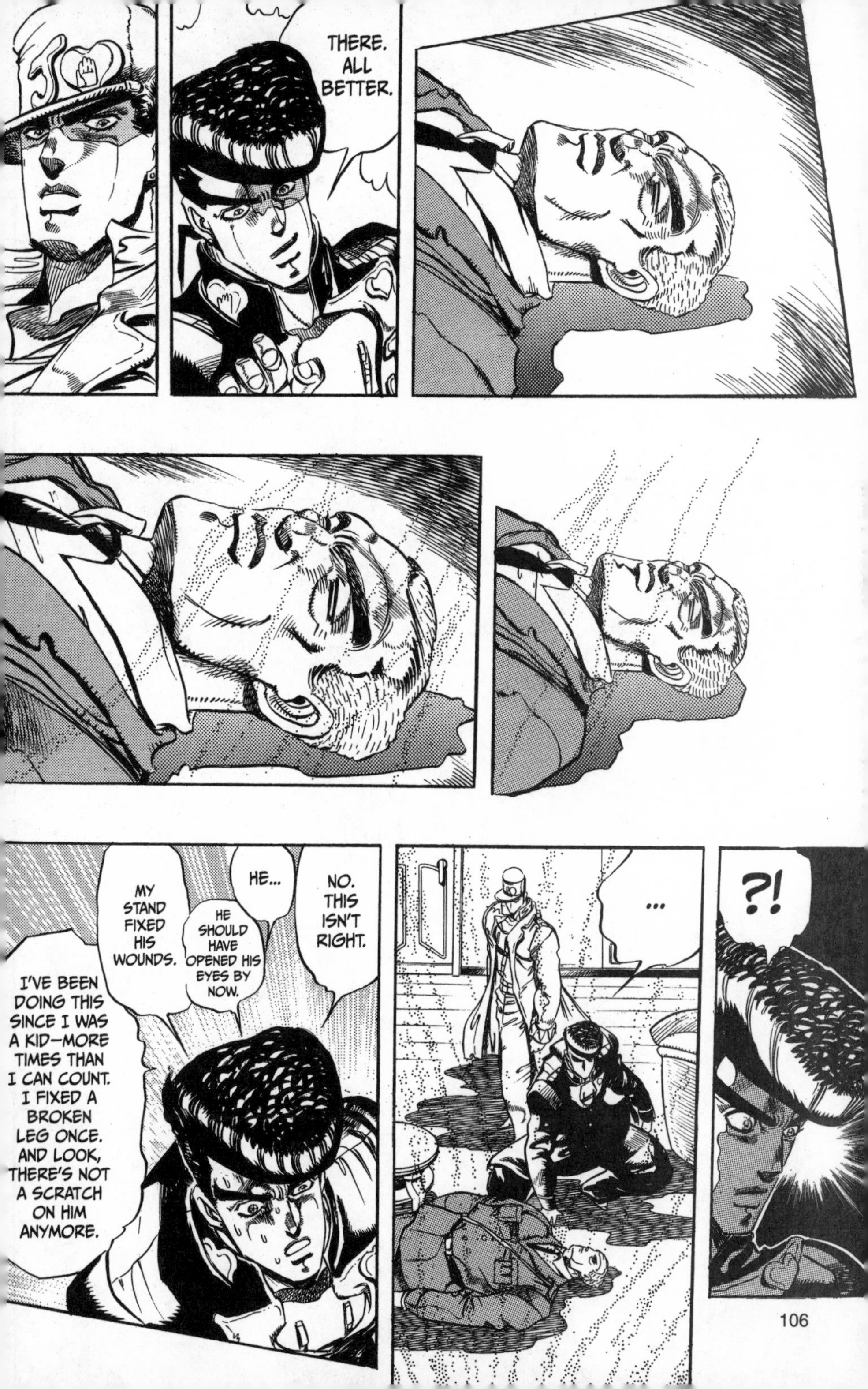
THERE. ALL BETTER.
?!
...
NO. THIS ISN'T RIGHT.
HE...
HE SHOULD HAVE OPENED HIS EYES BY NOW.
MY STAND FIXED HIS WOUNDS.
I'VE BEEN DOING THIS SINCE I WAS A KID—MORE TIMES THAN I CAN COUNT. I FIXED A BROKEN LEG ONCE. AND LOOK, THERE'S NOT A SCRATCH ON HIM ANYMORE.

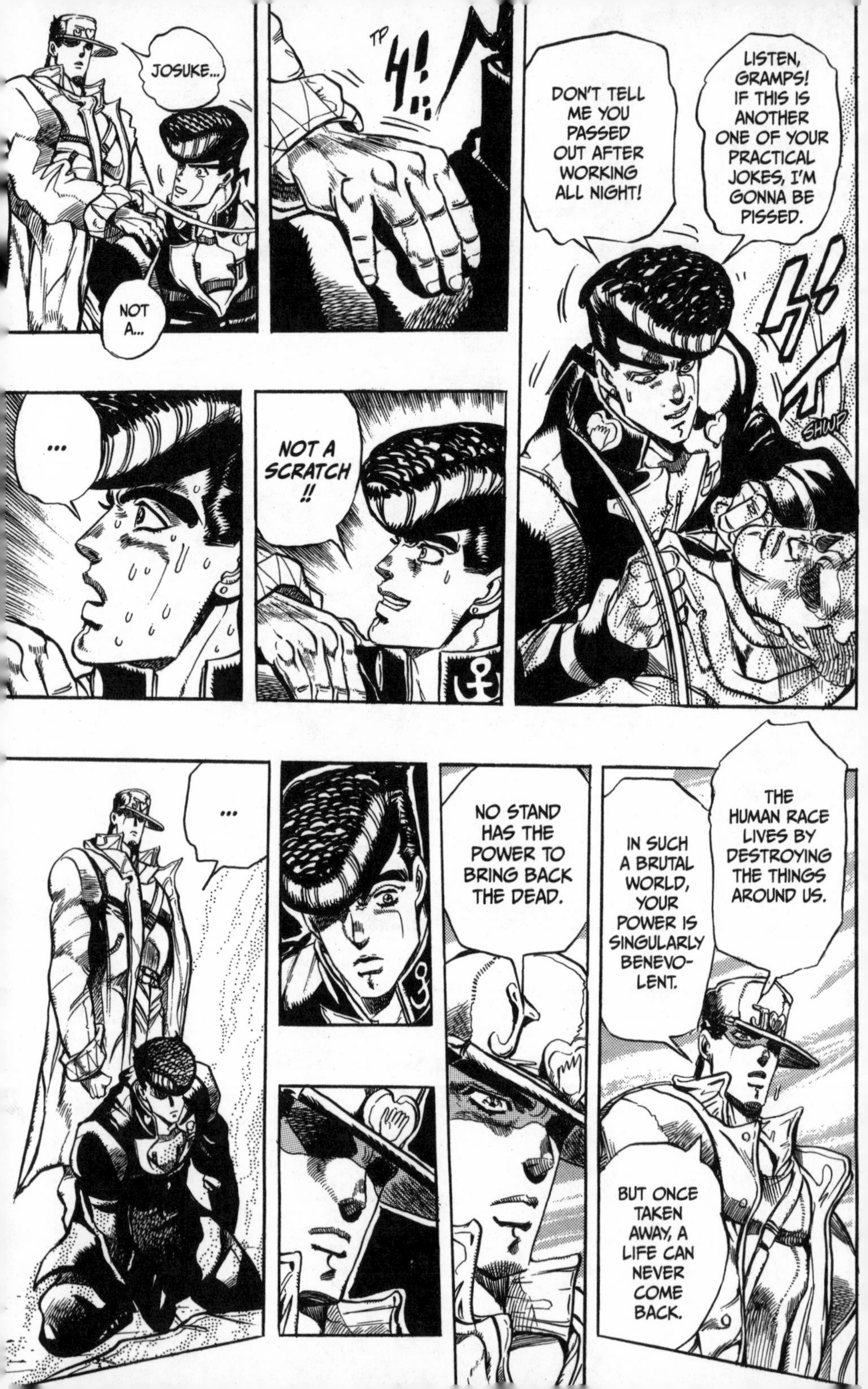
LISTEN, GRAMPS! IF THIS IS ANOTHER ONE OF YOUR PRACTICAL JOKES, I'M GONNA BE PISSED.
DON'T TELL ME YOU PASSED OUT AFTER WORKING ALL NIGHT!
SHWP
TP
JOSUKE...
NOT A...
NOT A SCRATCH !!
...
THE HUMAN RACE LIVES BY DESTROYING THE THINGS AROUND US.
IN SUCH A BRUTAL WORLD, YOUR POWER IS SINGULARLY BENEVOLENT.
BUT ONCE TAKEN AWAY, A LIFE CAN NEVER COME BACK.
NO STAND HAS THE POWER TO BRING BACK THE DEAD.
...

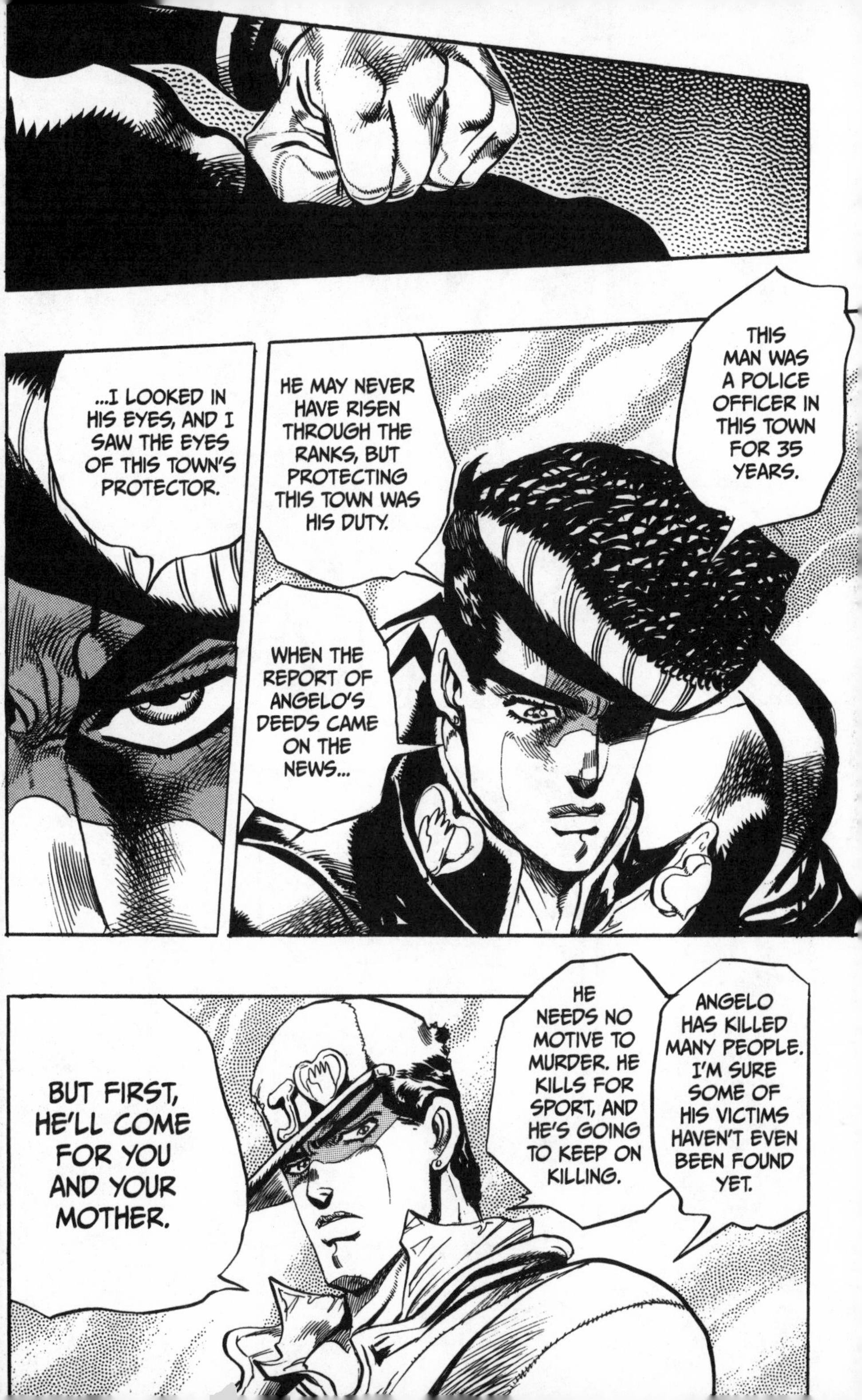
THIS MAN WAS A POLICE OFFICER IN THIS TOWN FOR 35 YEARS.
HE MAY NEVER HAVE RISEN THROUGH THE RANKS, BUT PROTECTING THIS TOWN WAS HIS DUTY.
WHEN THE REPORT OF ANGELO'S DEEDS CAME ON THE NEWS...
...I LOOKED IN HIS EYES, AND I SAW THE EYES OF THIS TOWN'S PROTECTOR.
ANGELO HAS KILLED MANY PEOPLE. I'M SURE SOME OF HIS VICTIMS HAVEN'T EVEN BEEN FOUND YET.
HE NEEDS NO MOTIVE TO MURDER. HE KILLS FOR SPORT, AND HE'S GOING TO KEEP ON KILLING.
BUT FIRST, HE'LL COME FOR YOU AND YOUR MOTHER.

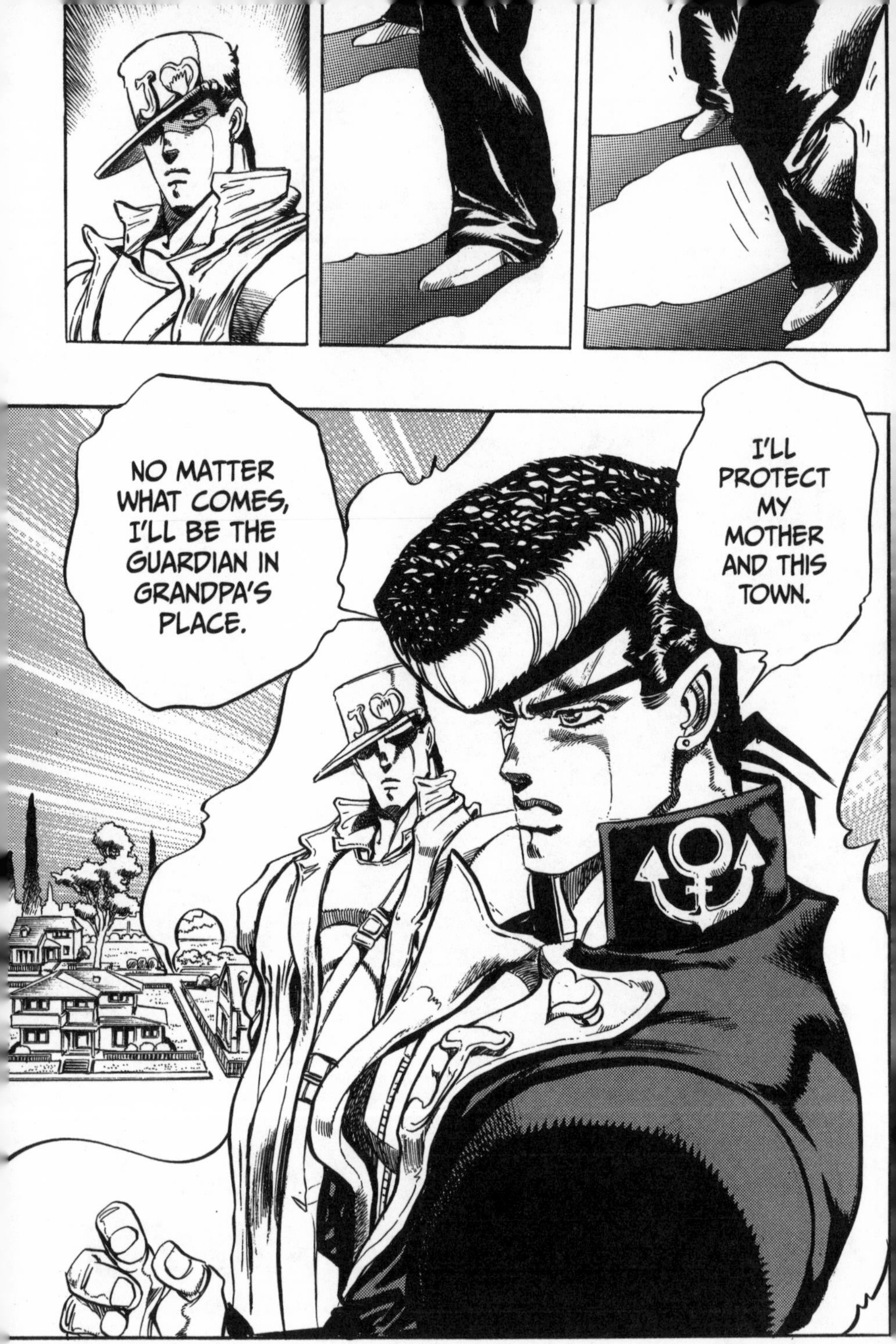
I'LL PROTECT MY MOTHER AND THIS TOWN.
NO MATTER WHAT COMES, I'LL BE THE GUARDIAN IN GRANDPA'S PLACE.

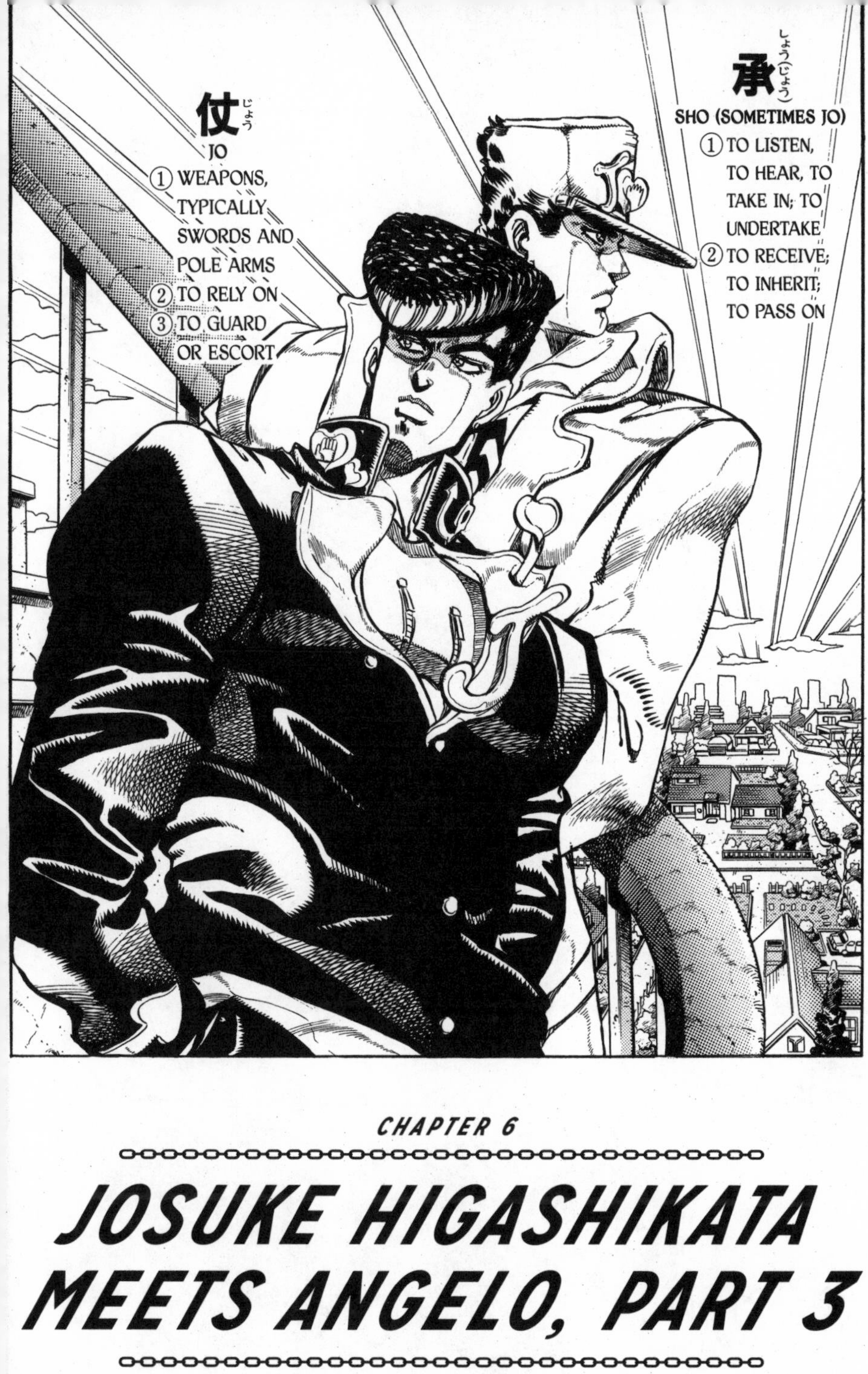
承 しょう(じょう)
SHO (SOMETIMES JO)
① TO LISTEN, TO HEAR, TO TAKE IN; TO UNDERTAKE
② TO RECEIVE; TO INHERIT; TO PASS ON
仗 じょう
JO
① WEAPONS, TYPICALLY SWORDS AND POLE ARMS
② TO RELY ON
③ TO GUARD OR ESCORT

CHAPTER 6

JOSUKE HIGASHIKATA MEETS ANGELO, PART 3

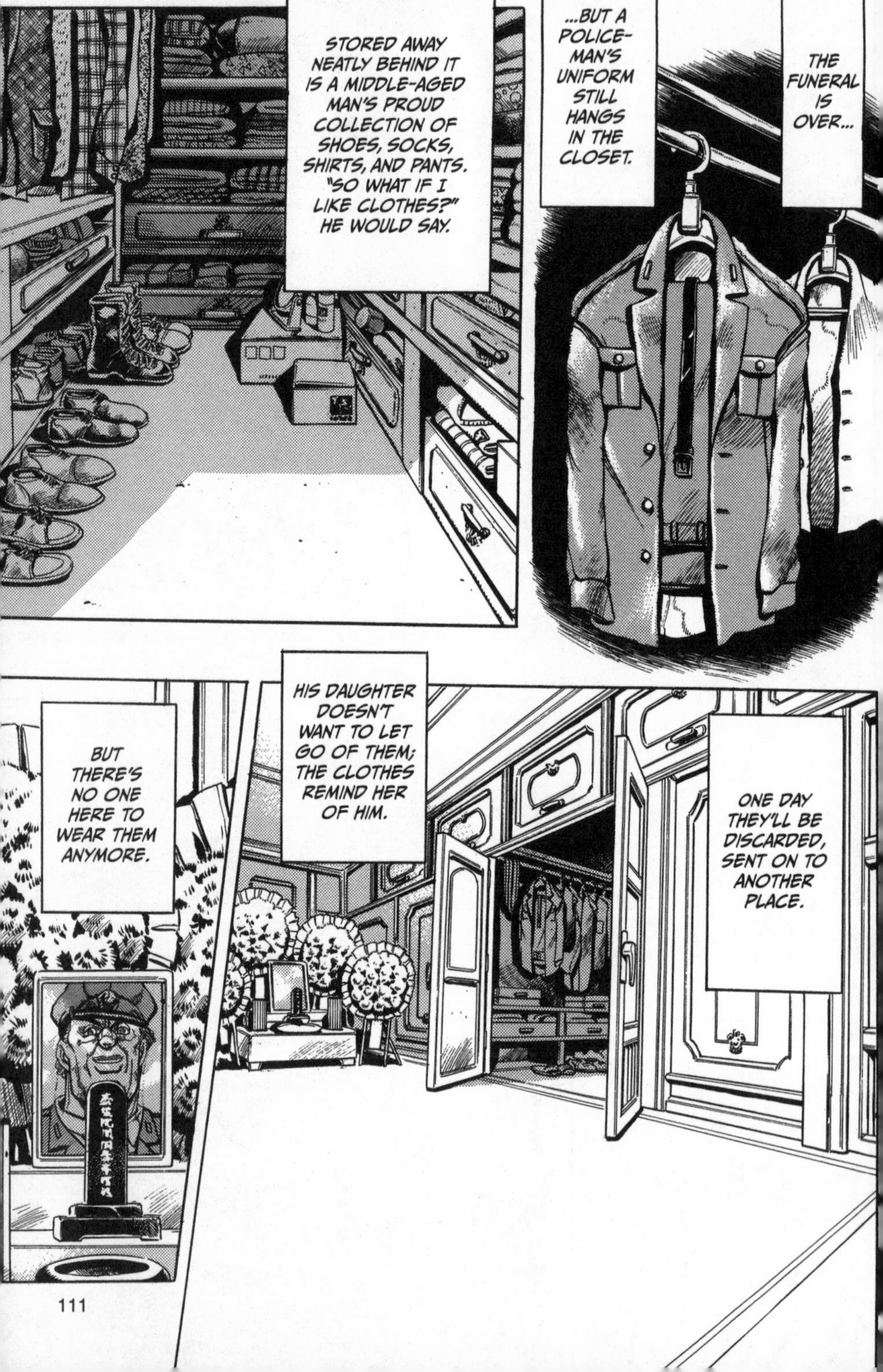
THE FUNERAL IS OVER...
...BUT A POLICE-MAN'S UNIFORM STILL HANGS IN THE CLOSET.
STORED AWAY NEATLY BEHIND IT IS A MIDDLE-AGED MAN'S PROUD COLLECTION OF SHOES, SOCKS, SHIRTS, AND PANTS. "SO WHAT IF I LIKE CLOTHES?" HE WOULD SAY.
ONE DAY THEY'LL BE DISCARDED, SENT ON TO ANOTHER PLACE.
HIS DAUGHTER DOESN'T WANT TO LET GO OF THEM; THE CLOTHES REMIND HER OF HIM.
BUT THERE'S NO ONE HERE TO WEAR THEM ANYMORE.

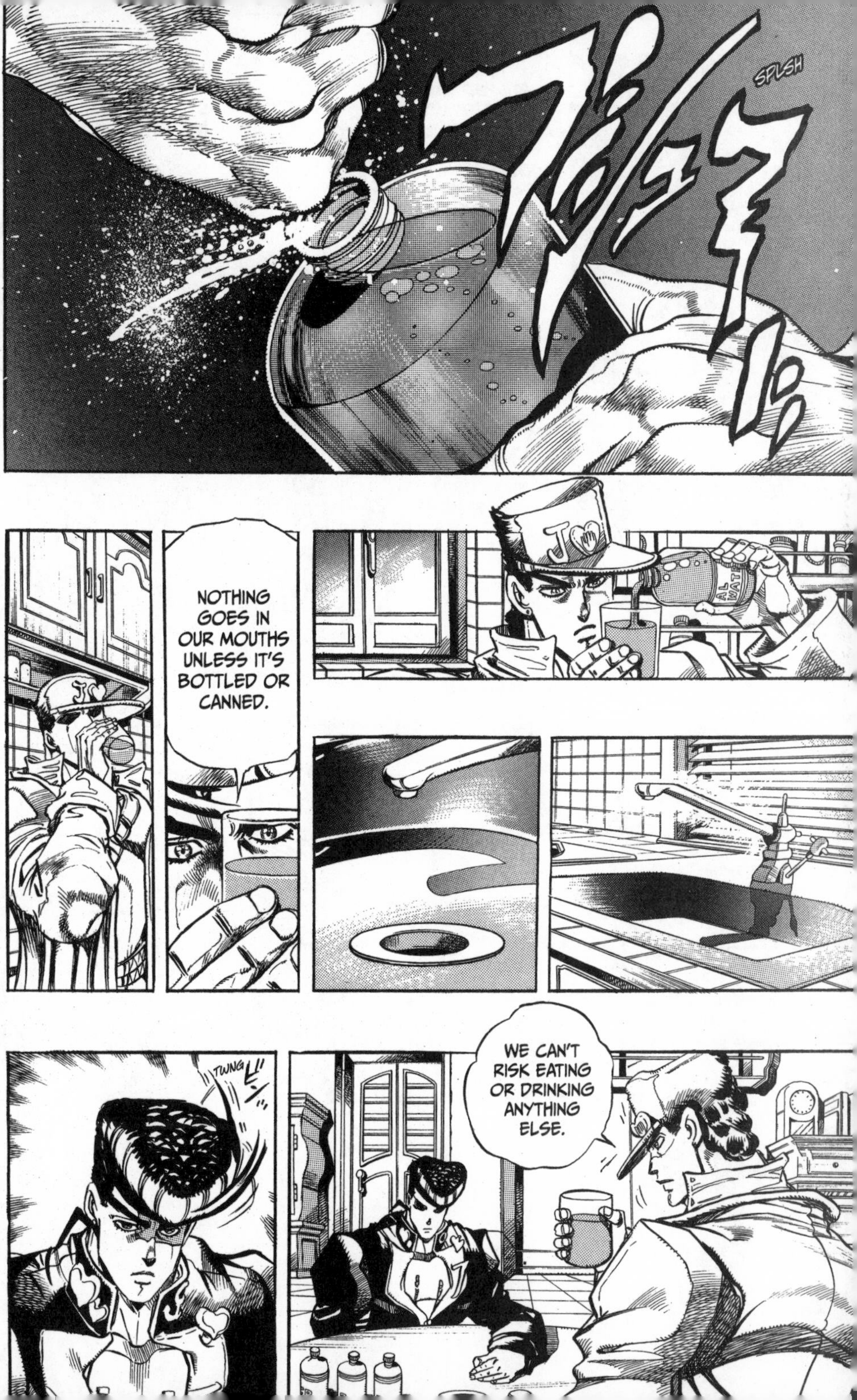
SPLSH
NOTHING GOES IN OUR MOUTHS UNLESS IT'S BOTTLED OR CANNED.
WE CAN'T RISK EATING OR DRINKING ANYTHING ELSE.
TWNG

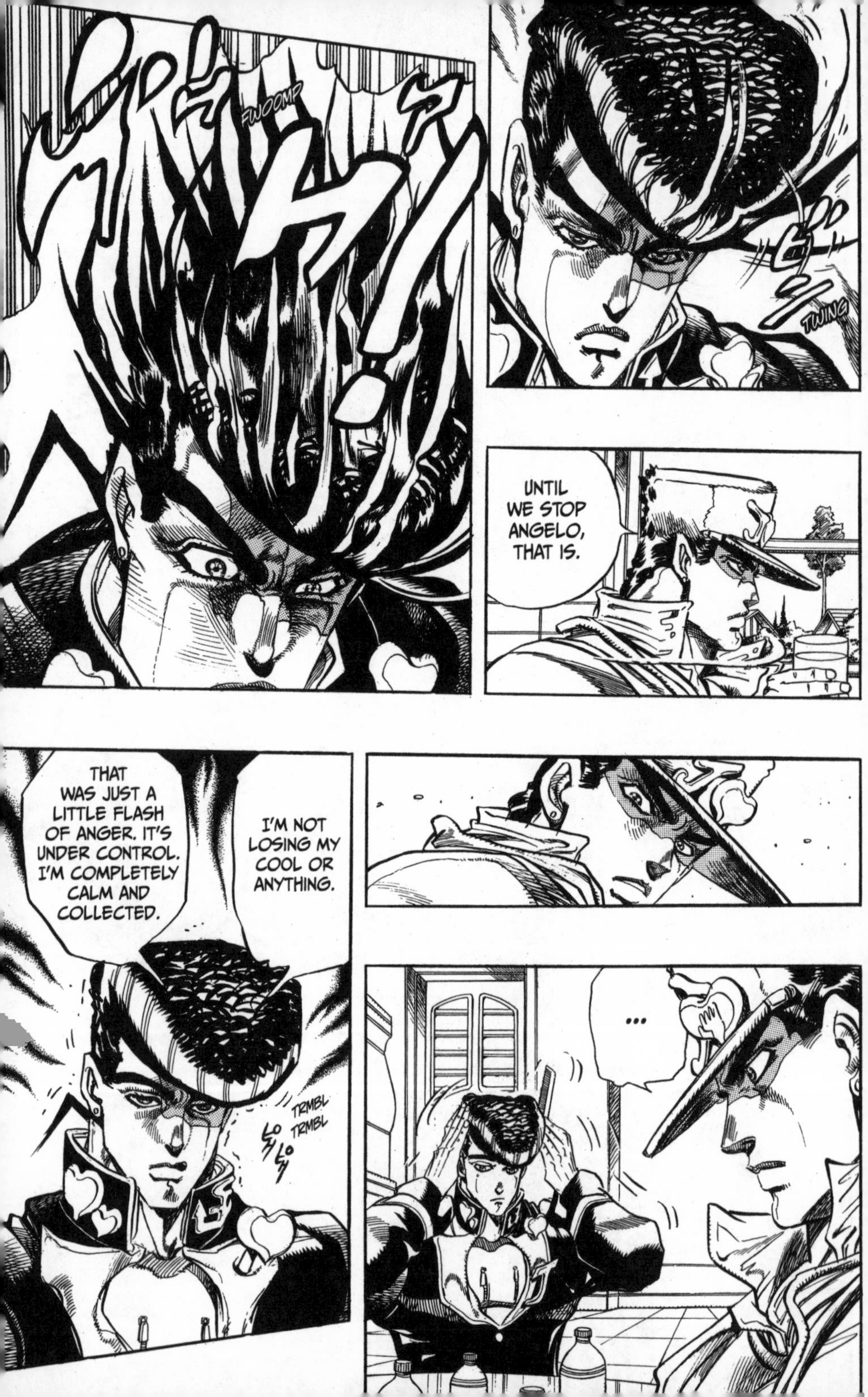
TWING
UNTIL WE STOP ANGELO, THAT IS.
FWOOMP
...
THAT WAS JUST A LITTLE FLASH OF ANGER. IT'S UNDER CONTROL. I'M COMPLETELY CALM AND COLLECTED.
I'M NOT LOSING MY COOL OR ANYTHING.
TRMBL TRMBL

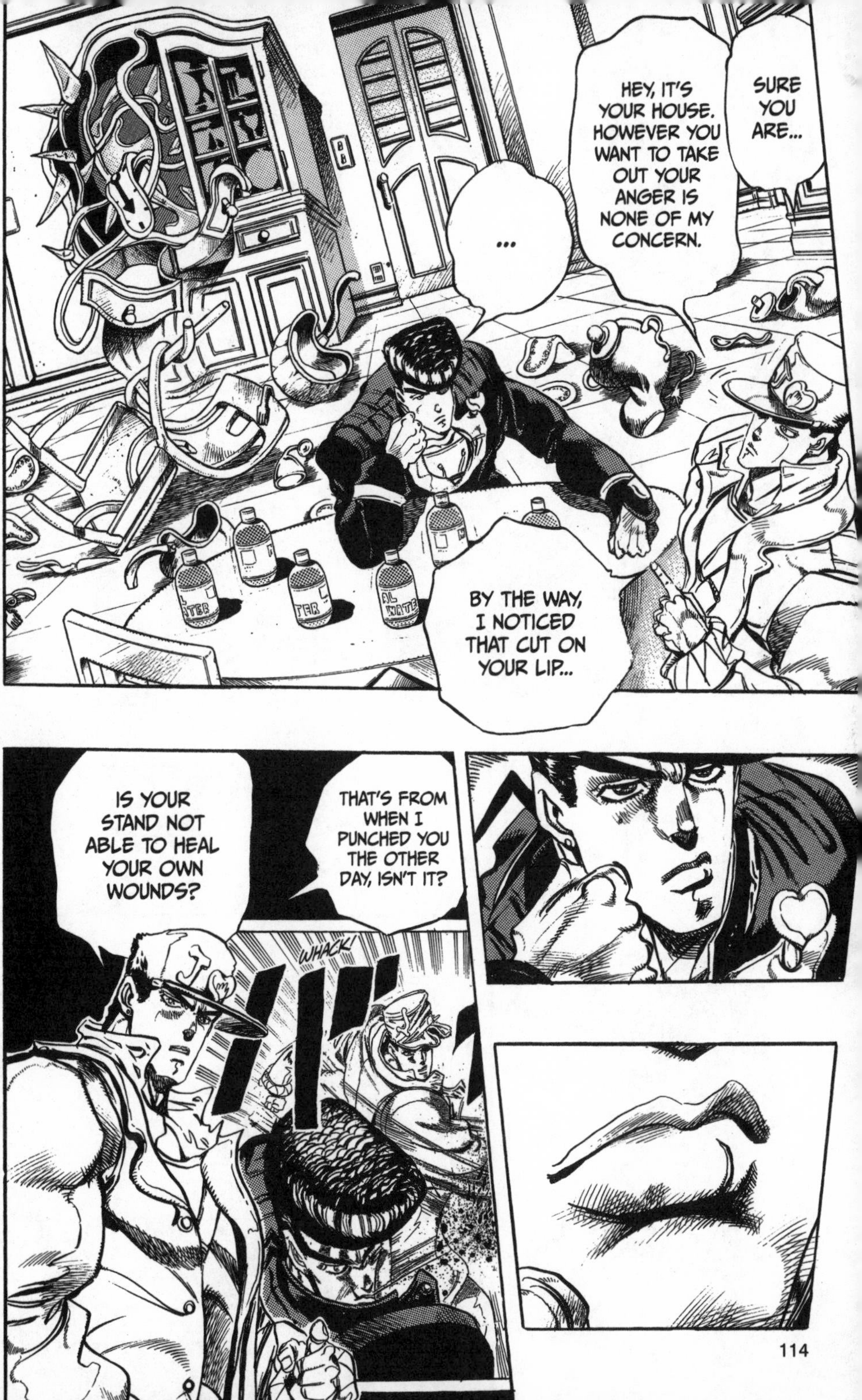
SURE YOU ARE...
HEY, IT'S YOUR HOUSE. HOWEVER YOU WANT TO TAKE OUT YOUR ANGER IS NONE OF MY CONCERN.
...
BY THE WAY, I NOTICED THAT CUT ON YOUR LIP...
THAT'S FROM WHEN I PUNCHED YOU THE OTHER DAY, ISN'T IT?
IS YOUR STAND NOT ABLE TO HEAL YOUR OWN WOUNDS?
WHACK!

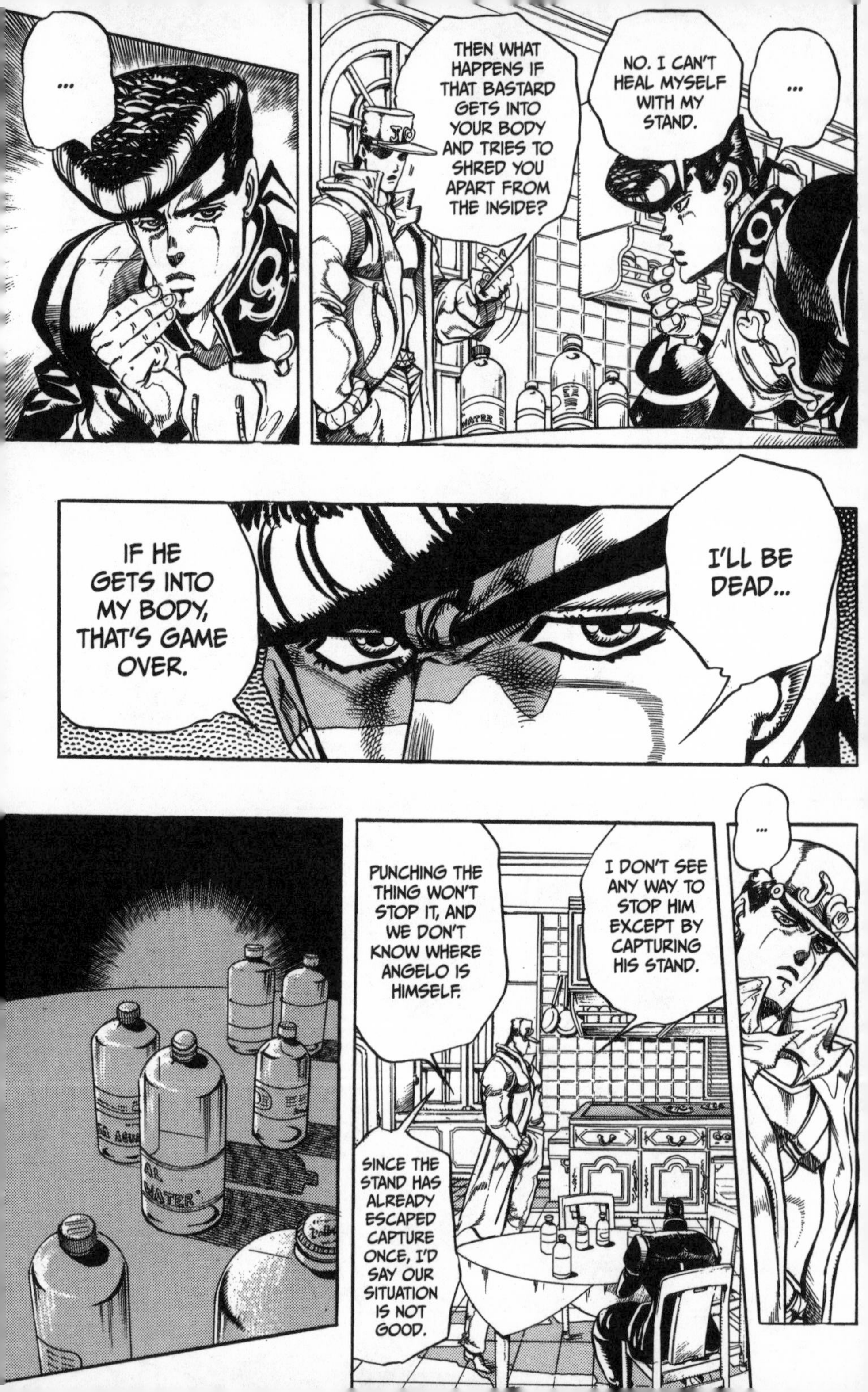
...
NO. I CAN'T HEAL MYSELF WITH MY STAND.
THEN WHAT HAPPENS IF THAT BASTARD GETS INTO YOUR BODY AND TRIES TO SHRED YOU APART FROM THE INSIDE?
...
I'LL BE DEAD...
IF HE GETS INTO MY BODY, THAT'S GAME OVER.
...
I DON'T SEE ANY WAY TO STOP HIM EXCEPT BY CAPTURING HIS STAND.
PUNCHING THE THING WON'T STOP IT, AND WE DON'T KNOW WHERE ANGELO IS HIMSELF.
SINCE THE STAND HAS ALREADY ESCAPED CAPTURE ONCE, I'D SAY OUR SITUATION IS NOT GOOD.

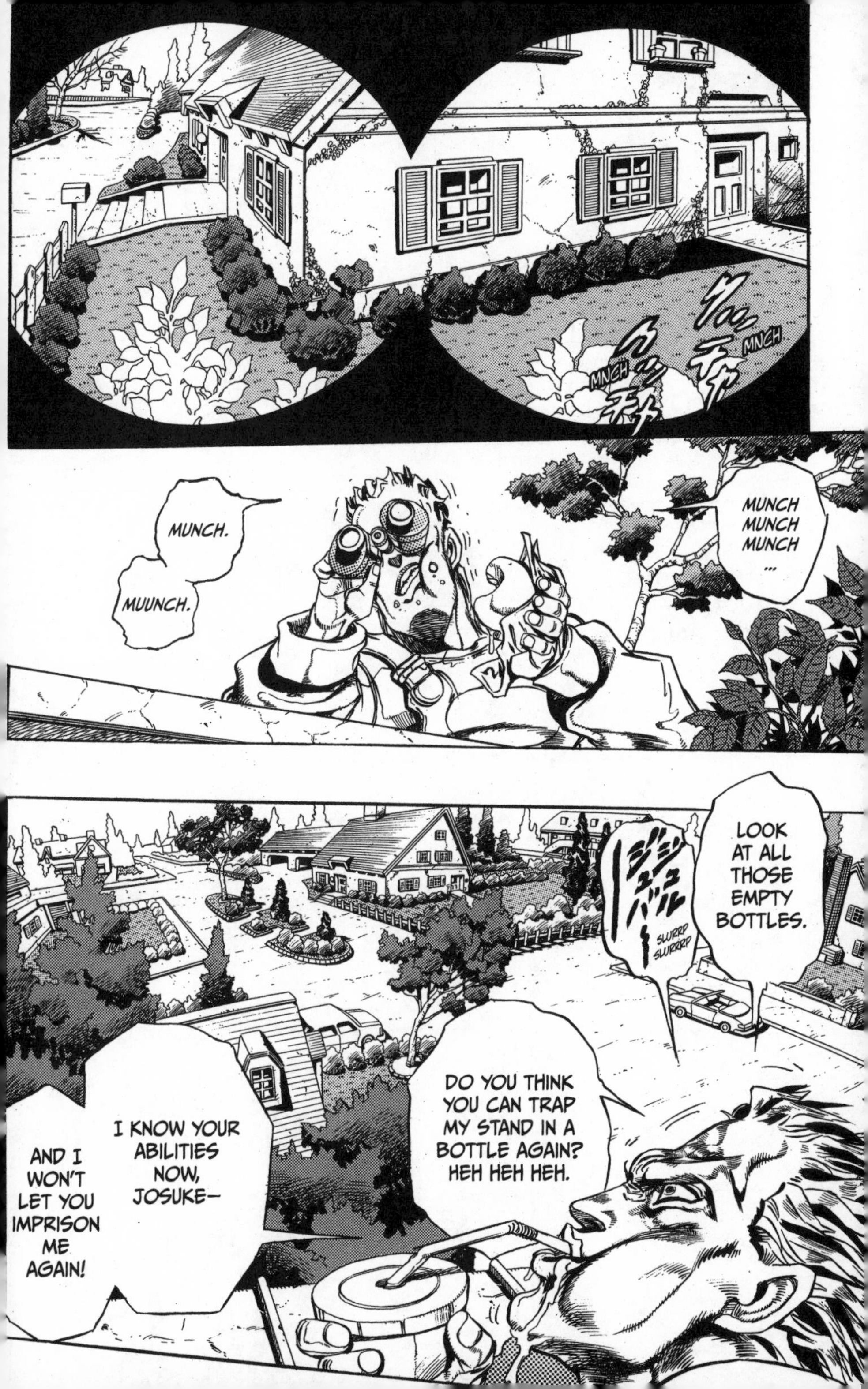
MNCH
MNCH
MUNCH MUNCH MUNCH ...
MUNCH.
MUUNCH.
LOOK AT ALL THOSE EMPTY BOTTLES.
SLURRP SLURRRP
DO YOU THINK YOU CAN TRAP MY STAND IN A BOTTLE AGAIN? HEH HEH HEH.
I KNOW YOUR ABILITIES NOW, JOSUKE—
AND I WON'T LET YOU IMPRISON ME AGAIN!

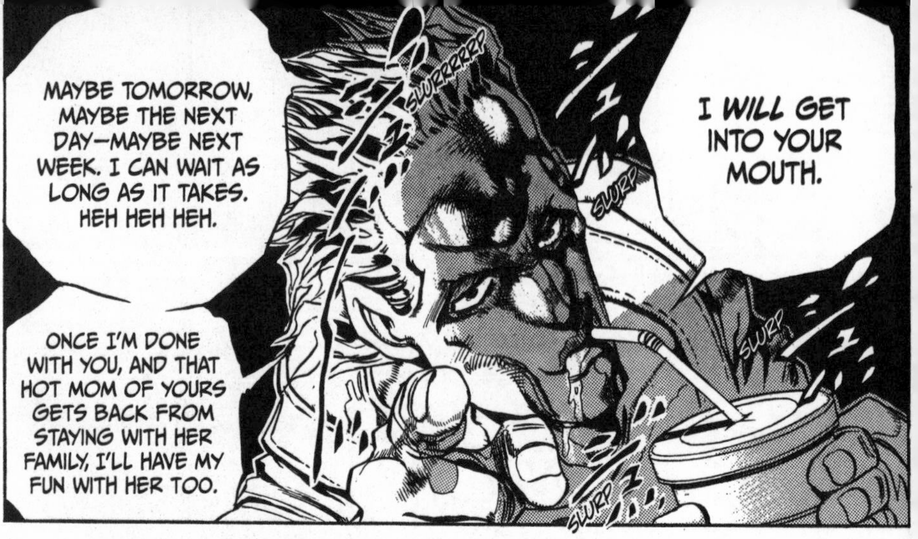
I *WILL* GET INTO YOUR MOUTH.
MAYBE TOMORROW, MAYBE THE NEXT DAY—MAYBE NEXT WEEK. I CAN WAIT AS LONG AS IT TAKES. HEH HEH HEH.
SLURRRRRP
SLURP
SLURP
ONCE I'M DONE WITH YOU, AND THAT HOT MOM OF YOURS GETS BACK FROM STAYING WITH HER FAMILY, I'LL HAVE MY FUN WITH HER TOO.
SLURP

THREE DAYS LATER

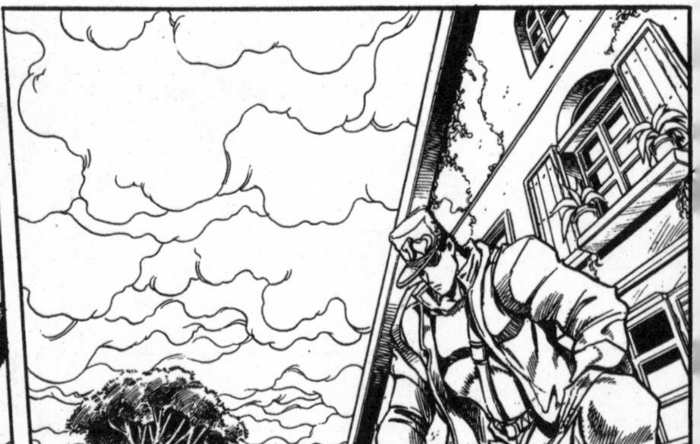

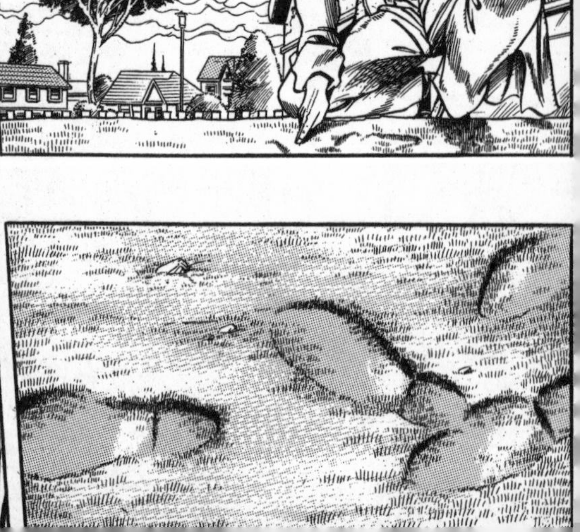

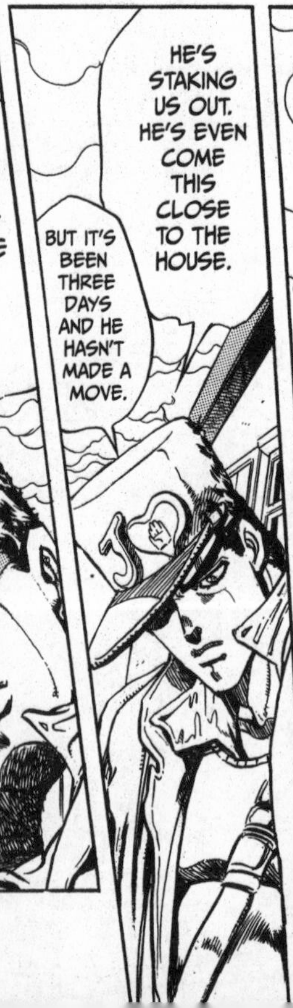
HE'S STAKING US OUT. HE'S EVEN COME THIS CLOSE TO THE HOUSE.
BUT IT'S BEEN THREE DAYS AND HE HASN'T MADE A MOVE.

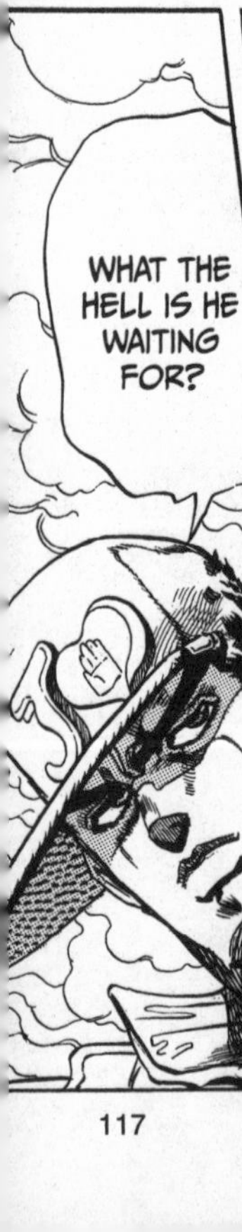
WHAT THE HELL IS HE WAITING FOR?

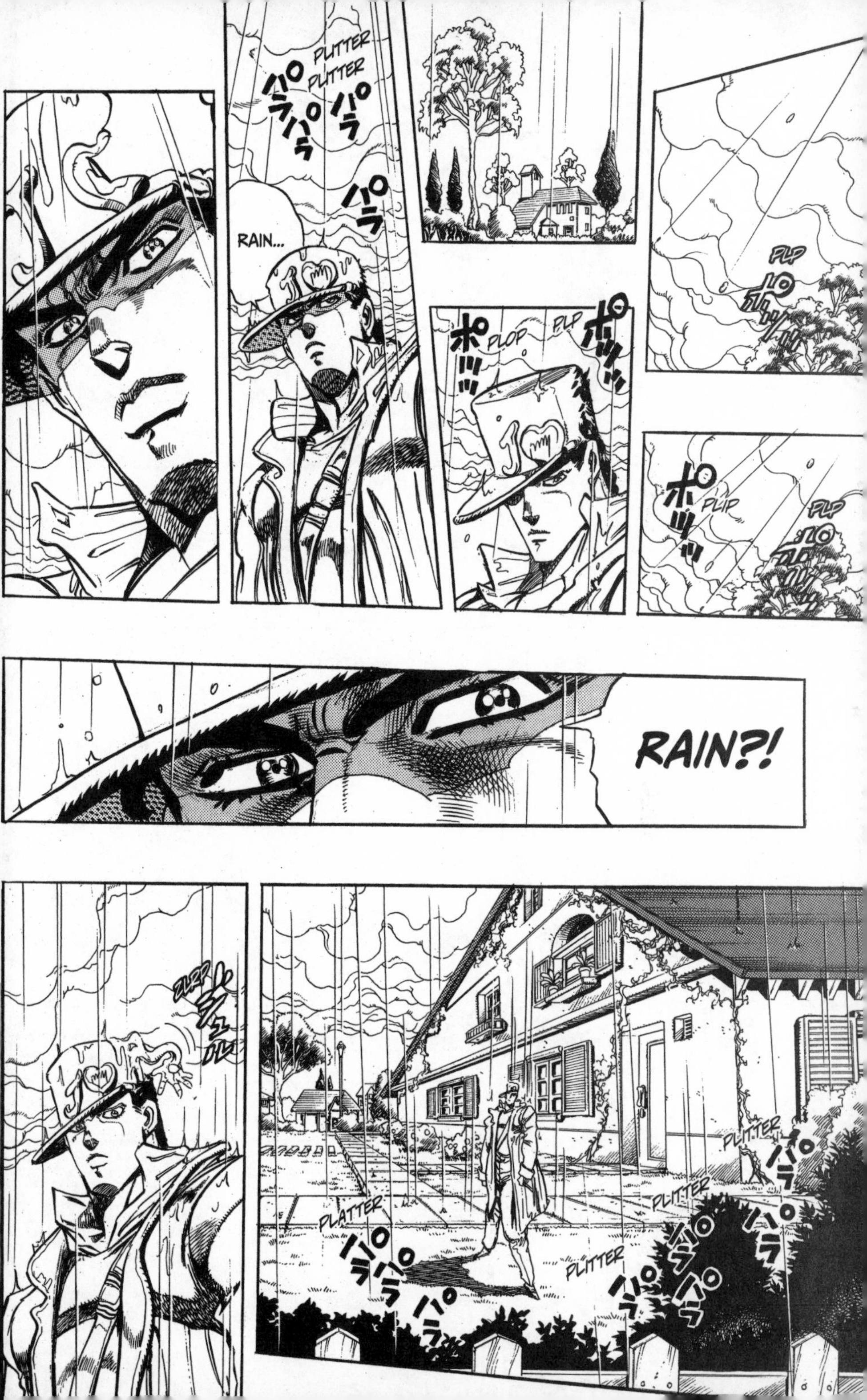
PLP
PLIP
PLP
PLP
PLOP
PLITTER
PLITTER
RAIN...
RAIN?!
PLITTER
PLITTER
PLITTER
PLATTER
ZLRP

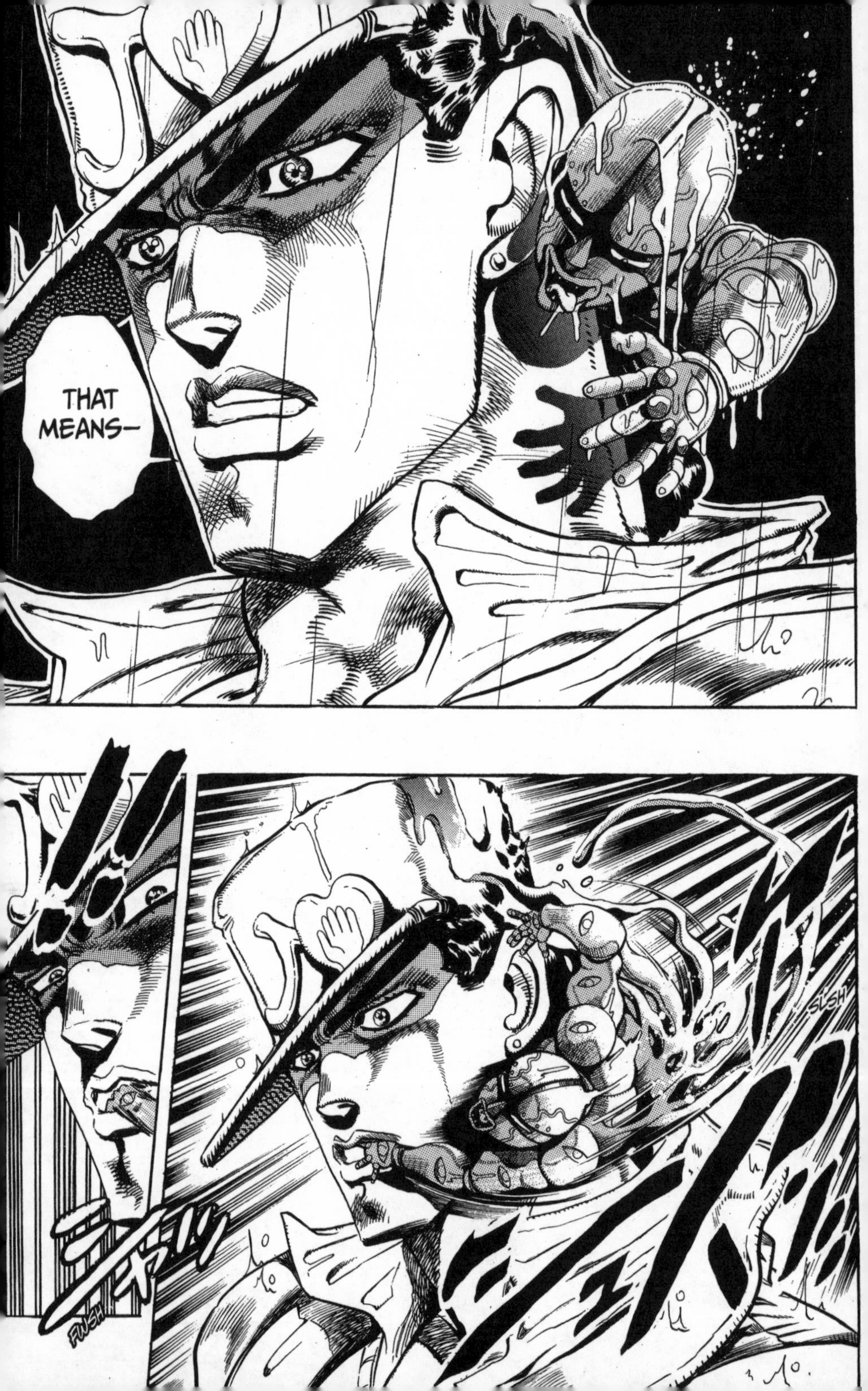
THAT MEANS—
SLSH
FWSH

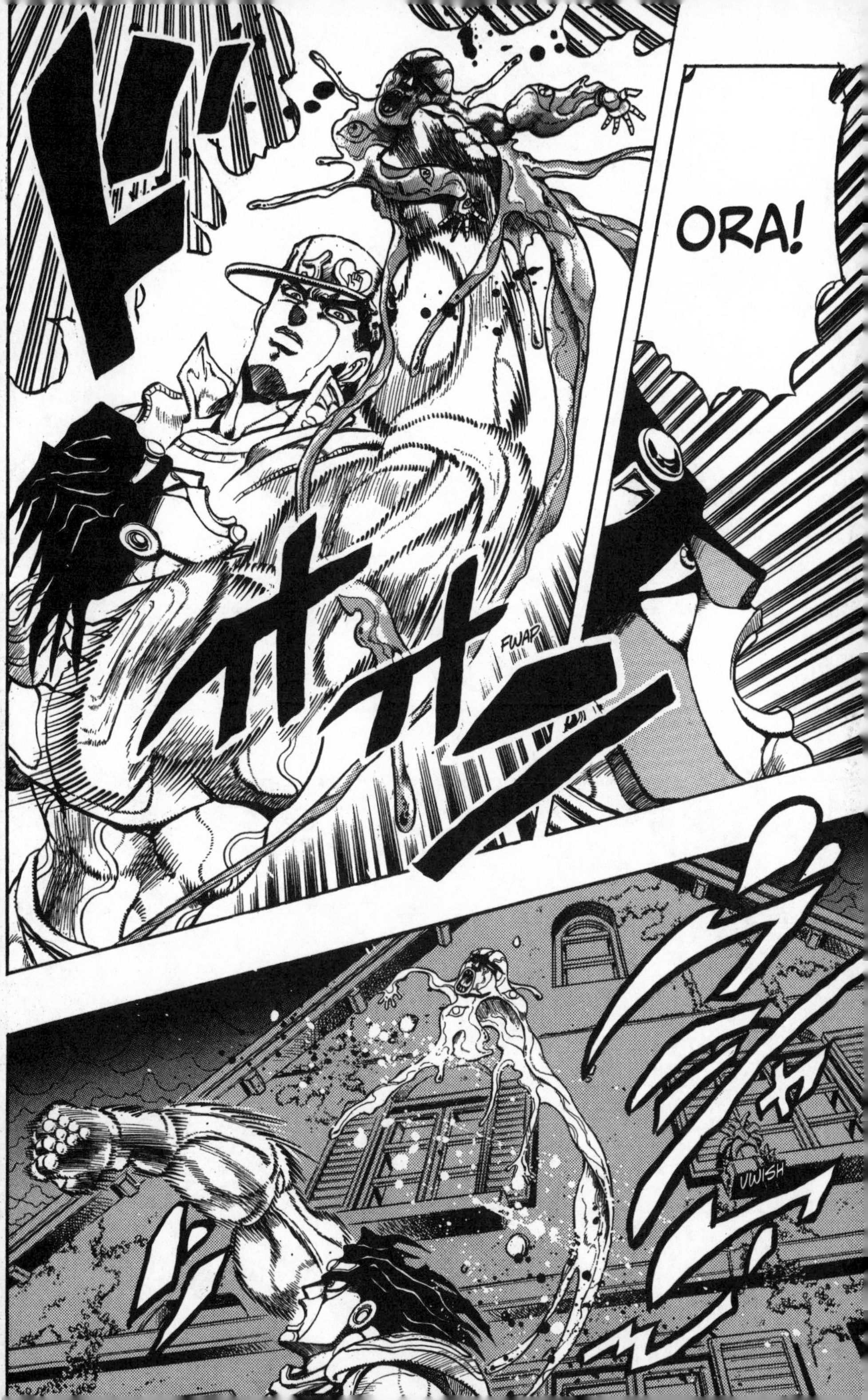
ORA!
FWAP
VWISH

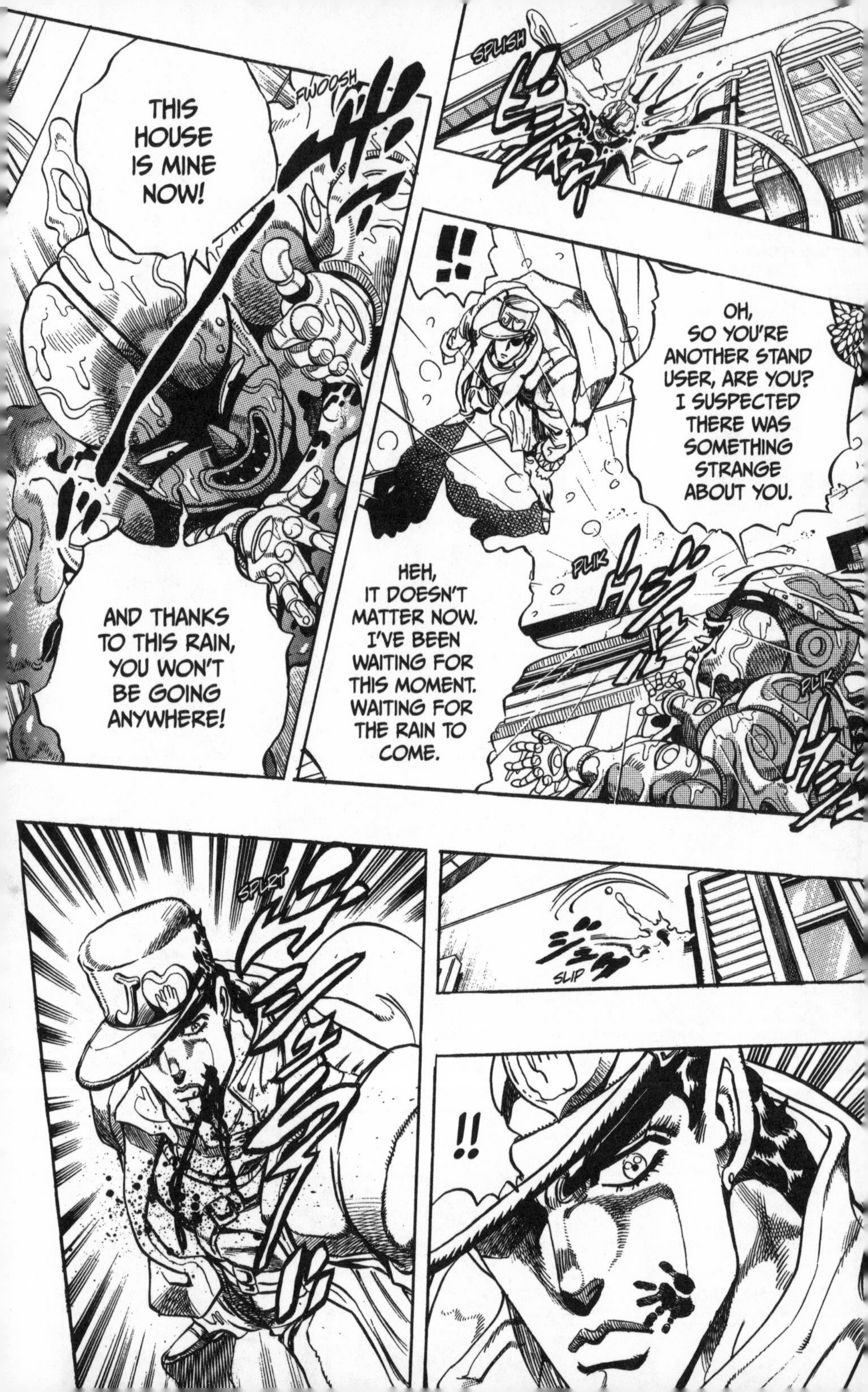
SPLISH
!!
OH, SO YOU'RE ANOTHER STAND USER, ARE YOU? I SUSPECTED THERE WAS SOMETHING STRANGE ABOUT YOU.
PLIK
PLIK
HEH, IT DOESN'T MATTER NOW. I'VE BEEN WAITING FOR THIS MOMENT. WAITING FOR THE RAIN TO COME.
FWOOSH
THIS HOUSE IS MINE NOW!
AND THANKS TO THIS RAIN, YOU WON'T BE GOING ANYWHERE!
SLIP
!!
SPLRT

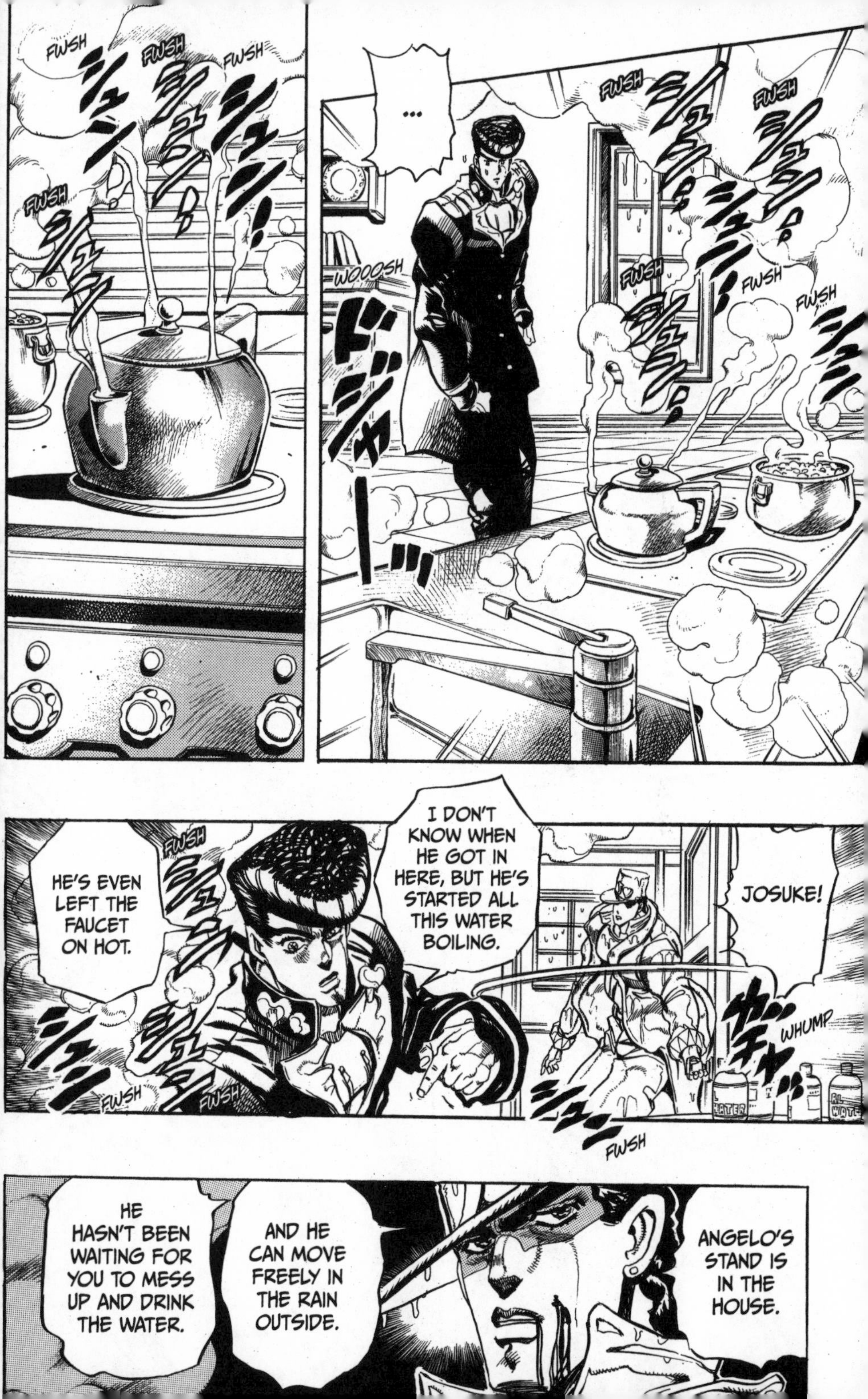

...
FWSH
FWSH
FWSH
FWSH
WOOOSH
FWSH
FWSH
FWSH
FWSH
FWSH
JOSUKE!
WHUMP
I DON'T KNOW WHEN HE GOT IN HERE, BUT HE'S STARTED ALL THIS WATER BOILING.
FWSH
HE'S EVEN LEFT THE FAUCET ON HOT.
FWSH
FWSH
FWSH
ANGELO'S STAND IS IN THE HOUSE.
AND HE CAN MOVE FREELY IN THE RAIN OUTSIDE.
HE HASN'T BEEN WAITING FOR YOU TO MESS UP AND DRINK THE WATER.

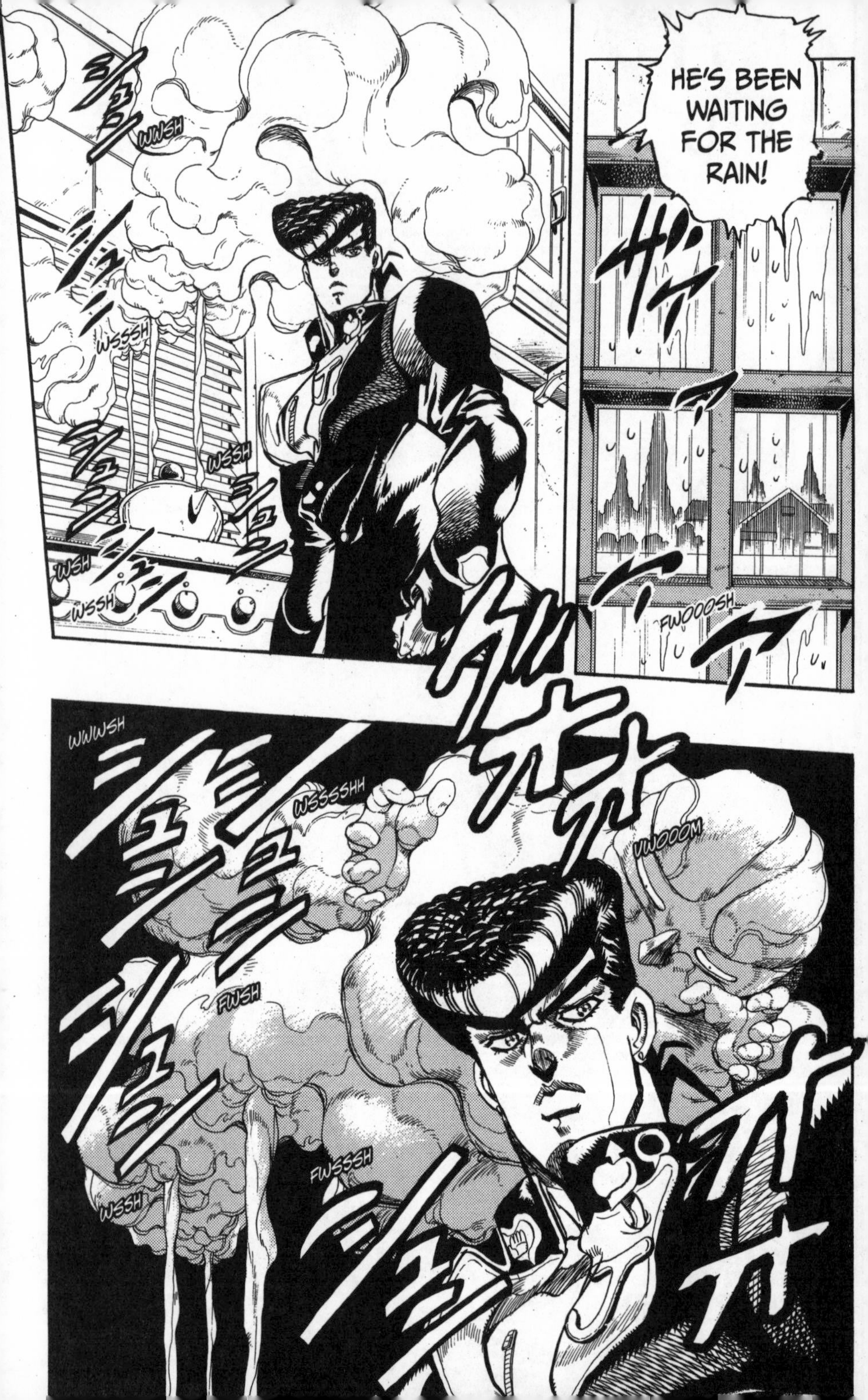
HE'S BEEN WAITING FOR THE RAIN!
FWOOOSH
WWSH
WSSSH
WSSH
WSH
WSSH
VWOOOM
WSSSSHH
WWWSH
FWSH
FWSSSH
WSSH

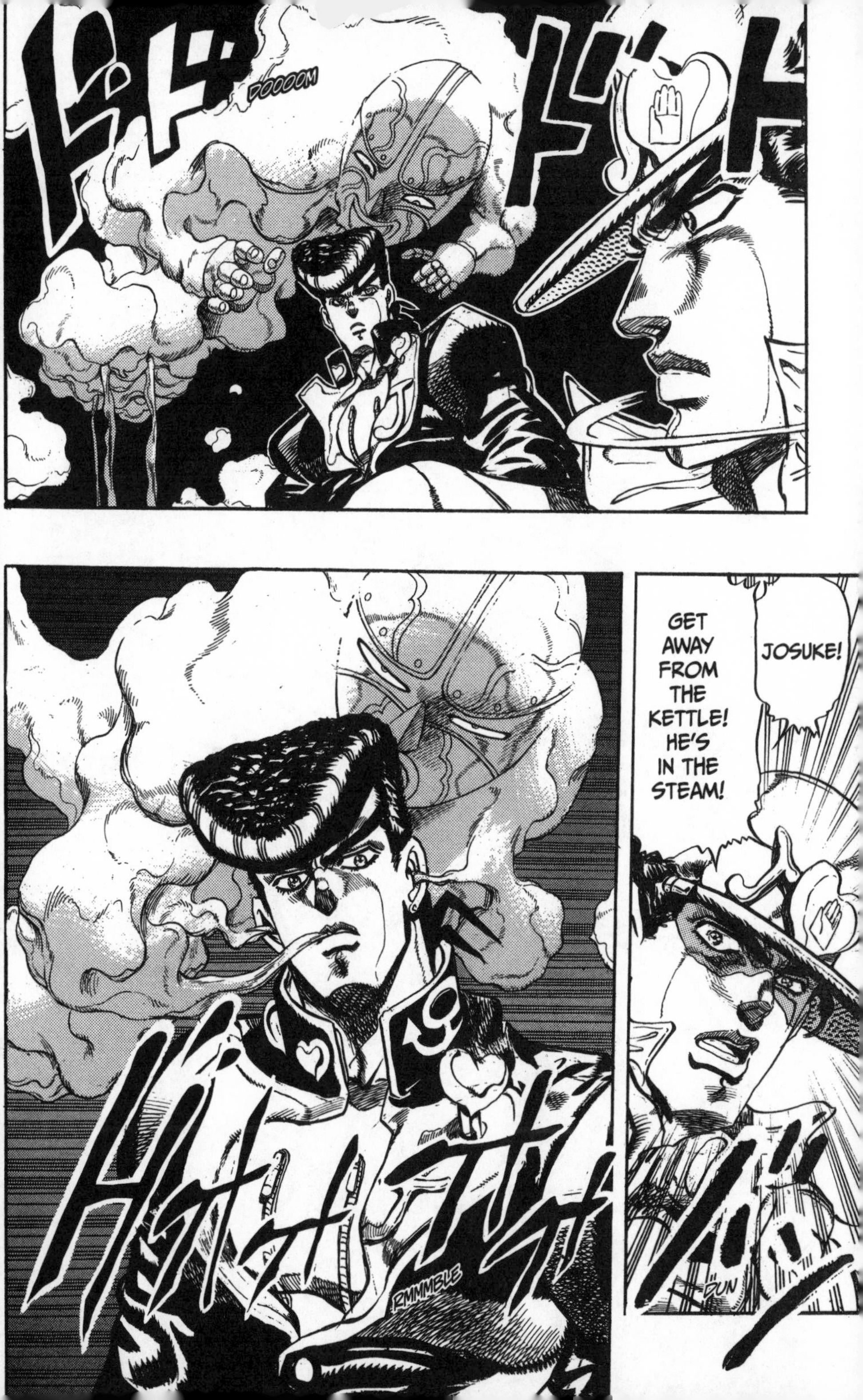
DOOOOM
JOSUKE!
GET AWAY FROM THE KETTLE! HE'S IN THE STEAM!
DUN
RMMMBLE

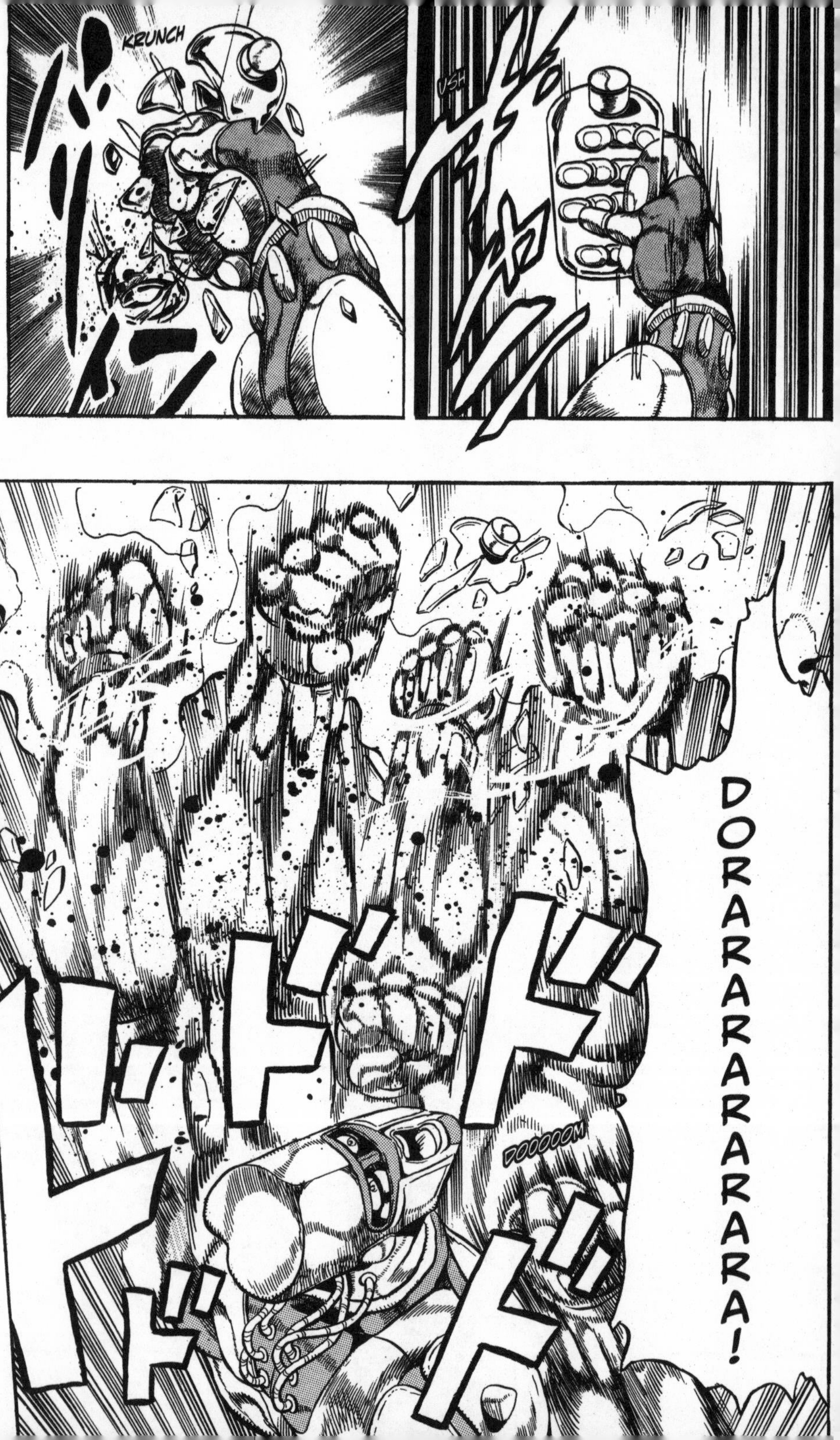
USH
KRUNCH
DORARARARARARARA!
DOOOOOM

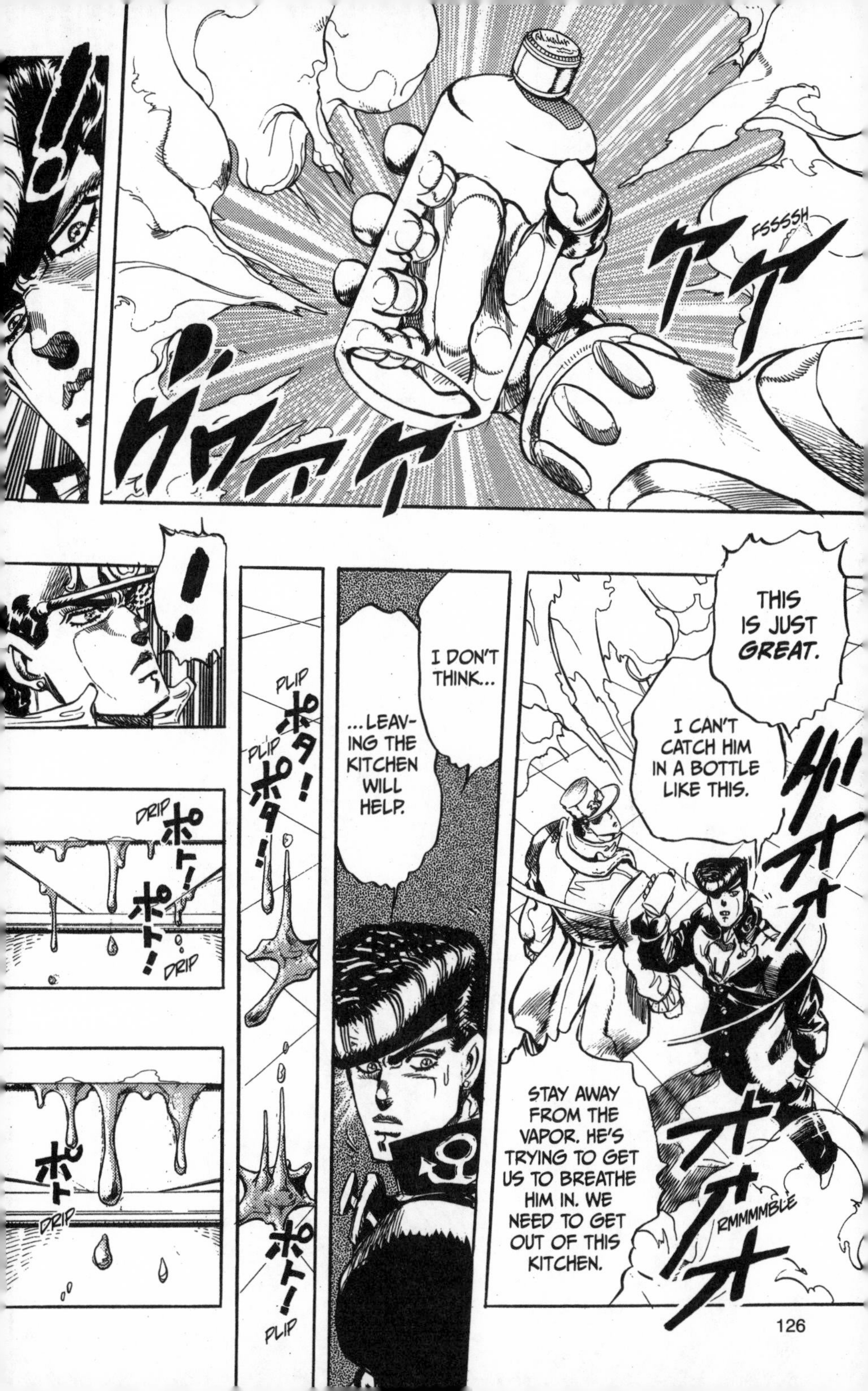
FSSSSH
THIS IS JUST GREAT.
I CAN'T CATCH HIM IN A BOTTLE LIKE THIS.
STAY AWAY FROM THE VAPOR. HE'S TRYING TO GET US TO BREATHE HIM IN. WE NEED TO GET OUT OF THIS KITCHEN.
RMMMMBLE
I DON'T THINK...
...LEAVING THE KITCHEN WILL HELP.
PLIP
PLIP
PLIP
!
DRIP
DRIP
DRIP

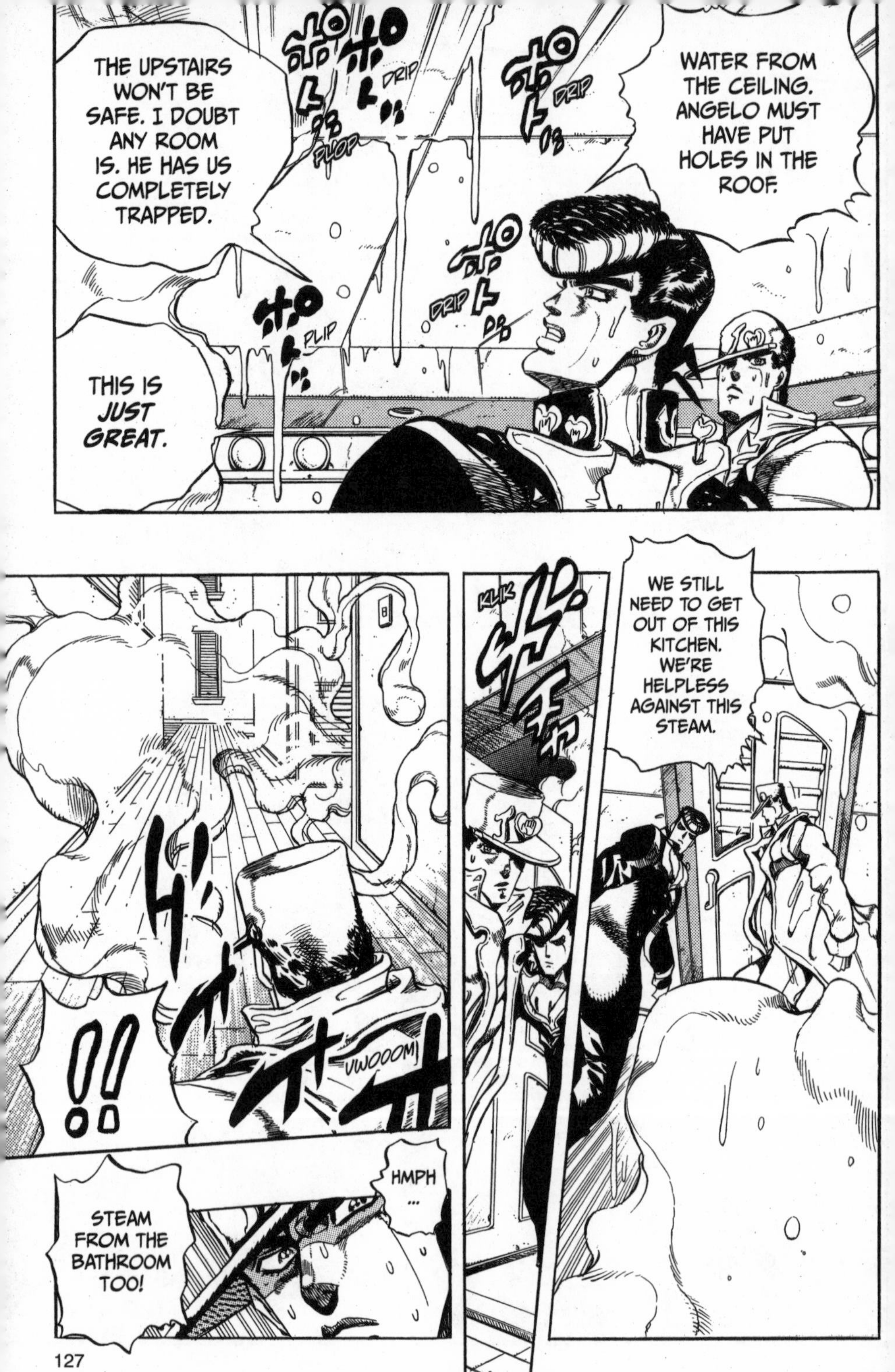
WATER FROM THE CEILING. ANGELO MUST HAVE PUT HOLES IN THE ROOF.
DRIP
DRIP
PLOP
DRIP
PLIP
THE UPSTAIRS WON'T BE SAFE. I DOUBT ANY ROOM IS. HE HAS US COMPLETELY TRAPPED.
THIS IS JUST GREAT.
KLIK
WE STILL NEED TO GET OUT OF THIS KITCHEN. WE'RE HELPLESS AGAINST THIS STEAM.
VWOOOM
!!
HMPH ...
STEAM FROM THE BATHROOM TOO!

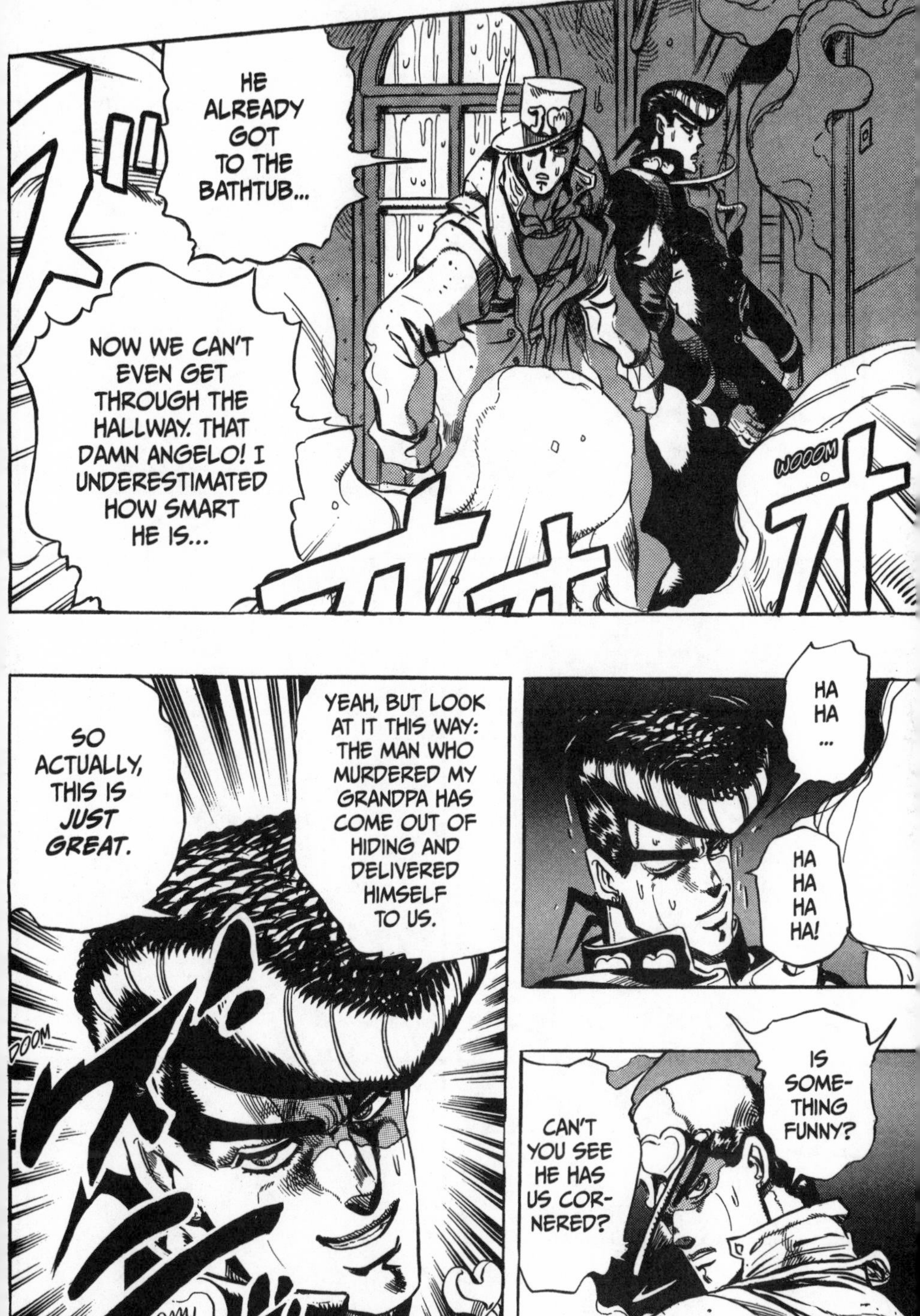
HE ALREADY GOT TO THE BATHTUB...
NOW WE CAN'T EVEN GET THROUGH THE HALLWAY. THAT DAMN ANGELO! I UNDERESTIMATED HOW SMART HE IS...
WOOOM
HA HA ...
HA HA HA HA!
IS SOME-THING FUNNY?
CAN'T YOU SEE HE HAS US COR-NERED?
YEAH, BUT LOOK AT IT THIS WAY: THE MAN WHO MURDERED MY GRANDPA HAS COME OUT OF HIDING AND DELIVERED HIMSELF TO US.
SO ACTUALLY, THIS IS *JUST GREAT.*
DOOM

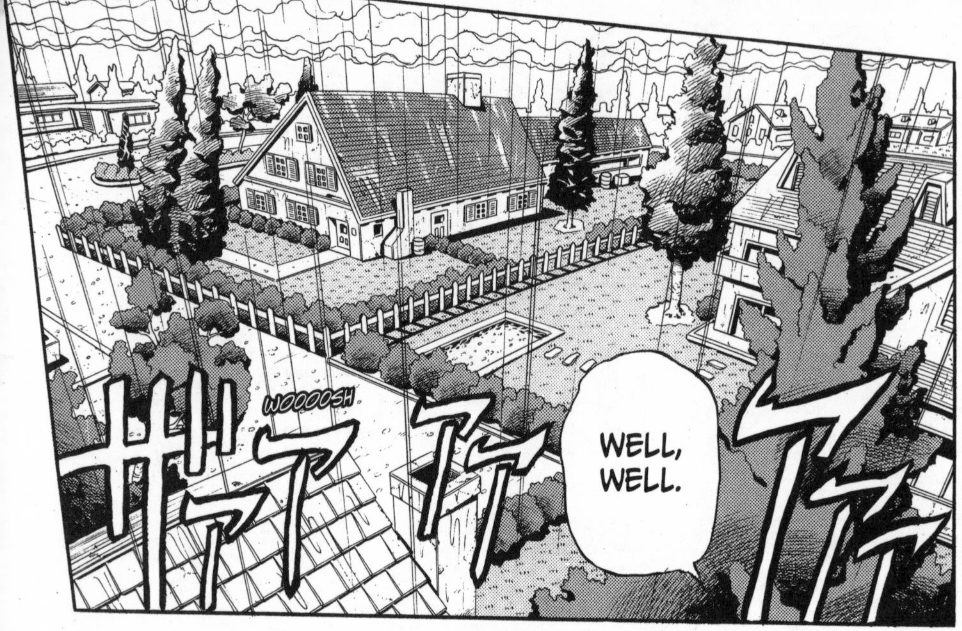
WOOOOSH
WELL, WELL.

CHAPTER 7

JOSUKE HIGASHIKATA MEETS ANGELO

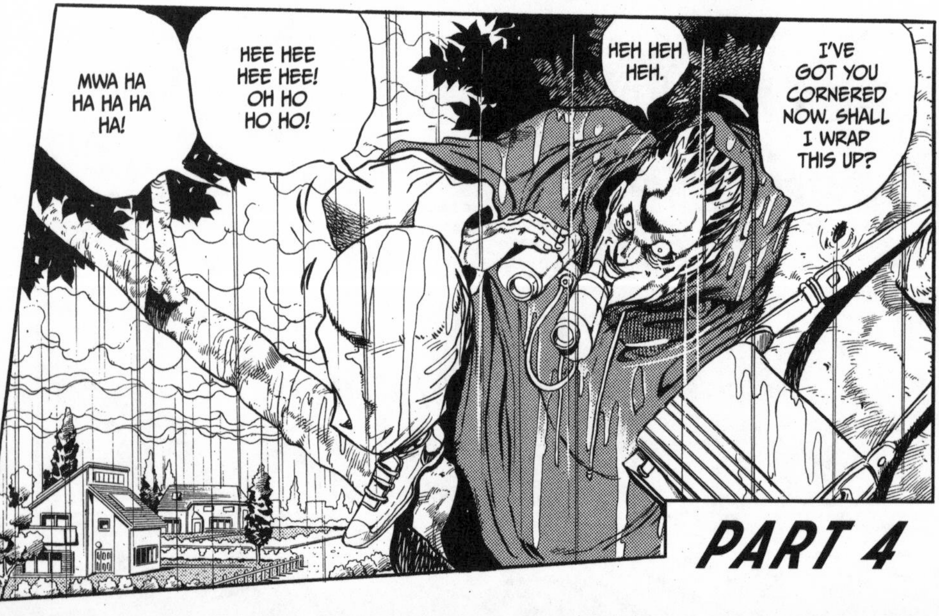
I'VE GOT YOU CORNERED NOW. SHALL I WRAP THIS UP?
HEH HEH HEH.
HEE HEE HEE HEE! OH HO HO HO!
MWA HA HA HA HA HA!

PART 4

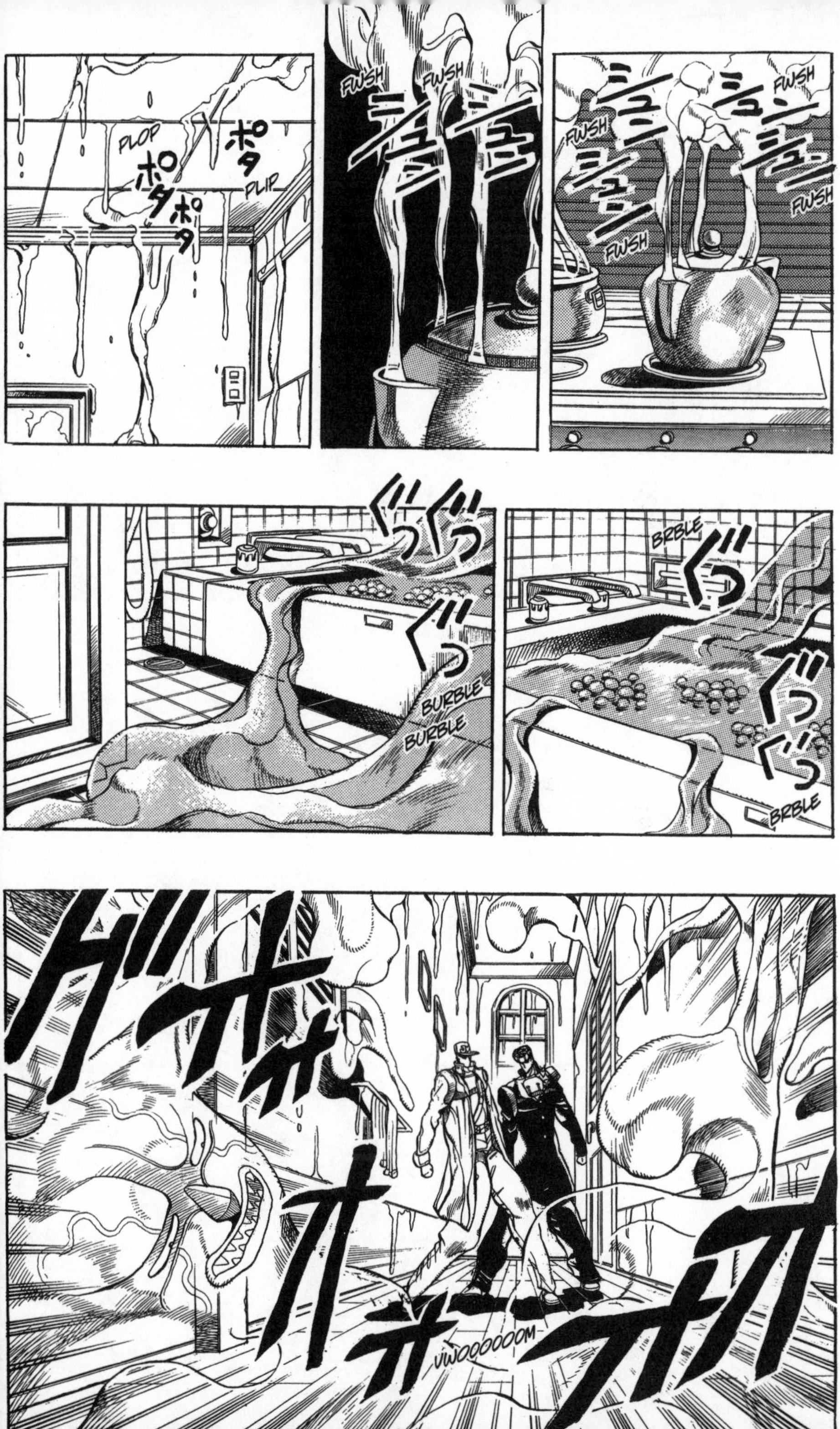

FWSH
FWSH
FWSH
FWSH
FWSH
FWSH
PLOP
PLIP
BRBLE
BRBLE
BURBLE
BURBLE
VWOOOOOOM

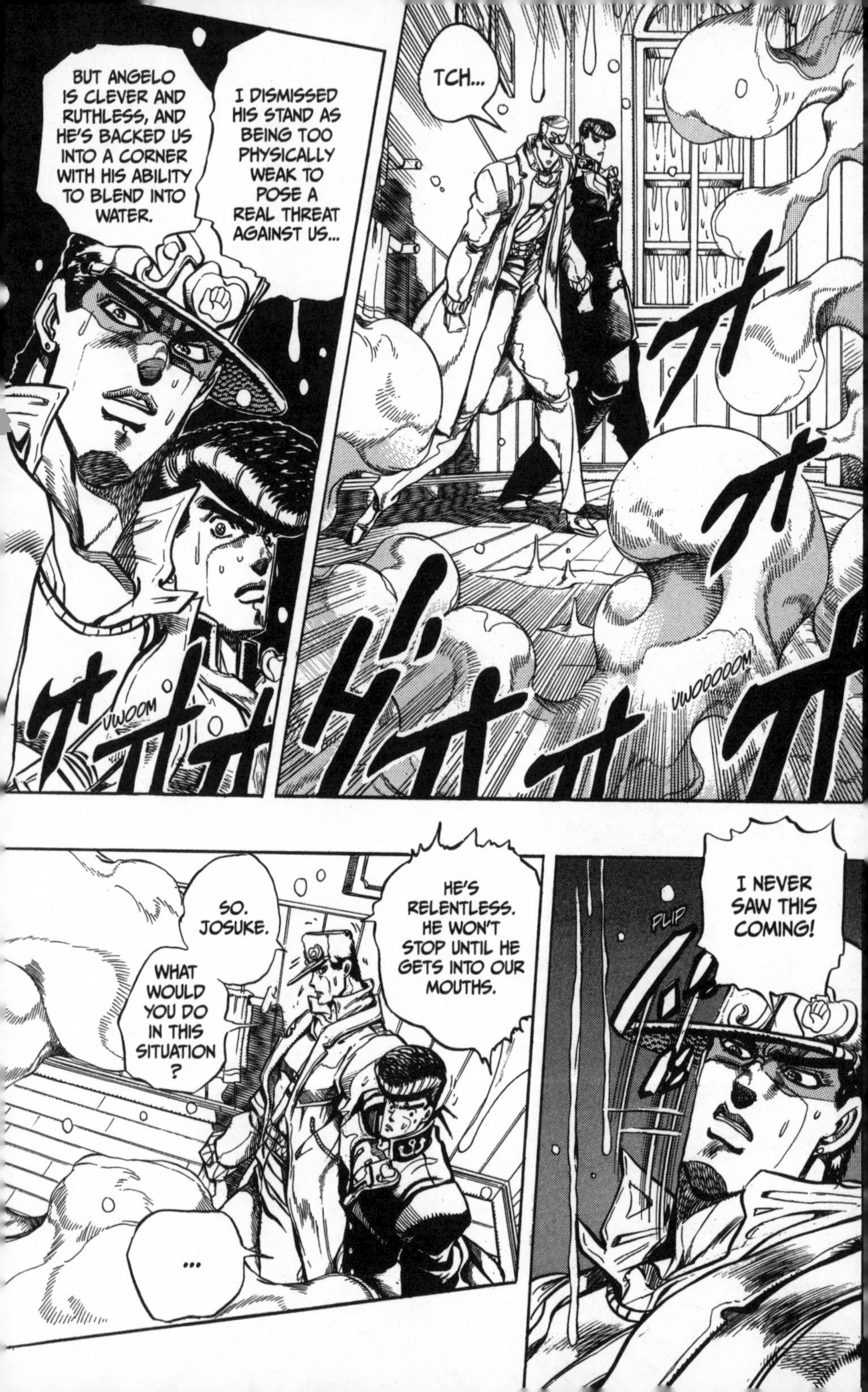
TCH...
VWOOOOOM
I DISMISSED HIS STAND AS BEING TOO PHYSICALLY WEAK TO POSE A REAL THREAT AGAINST US...
BUT ANGELO IS CLEVER AND RUTHLESS, AND HE'S BACKED US INTO A CORNER WITH HIS ABILITY TO BLEND INTO WATER.
VWOOM
I NEVER SAW THIS COMING!
PLIP
HE'S RELENTLESS. HE WON'T STOP UNTIL HE GETS INTO OUR MOUTHS.
SO. JOSUKE.
WHAT WOULD YOU DO IN THIS SITUATION?
...

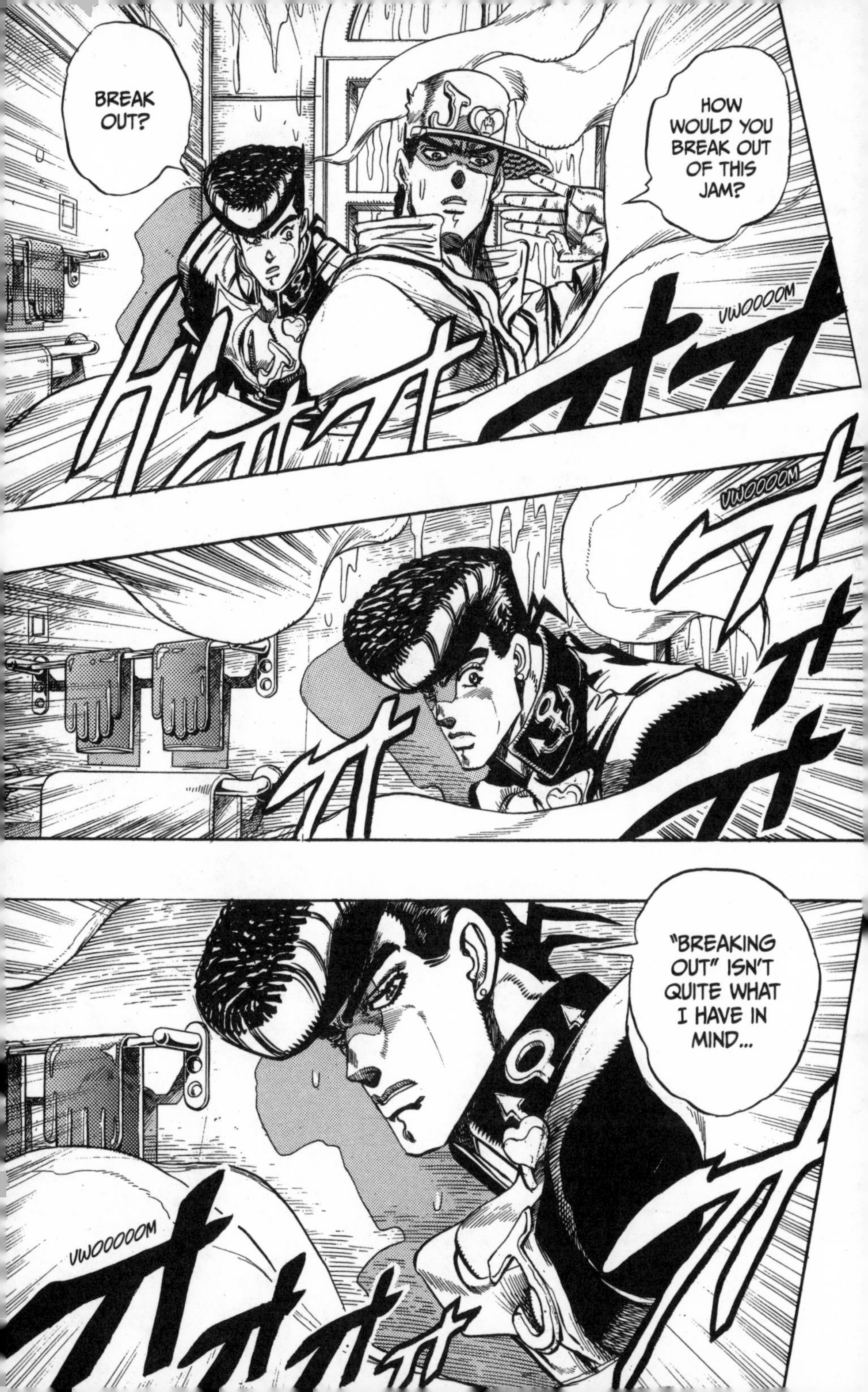
HOW WOULD YOU BREAK OUT OF THIS JAM?
BREAK OUT?
VWOOOOM
VWOOOOM
"BREAKING OUT" ISN'T QUITE WHAT I HAVE IN MIND...
VWOOOOOM

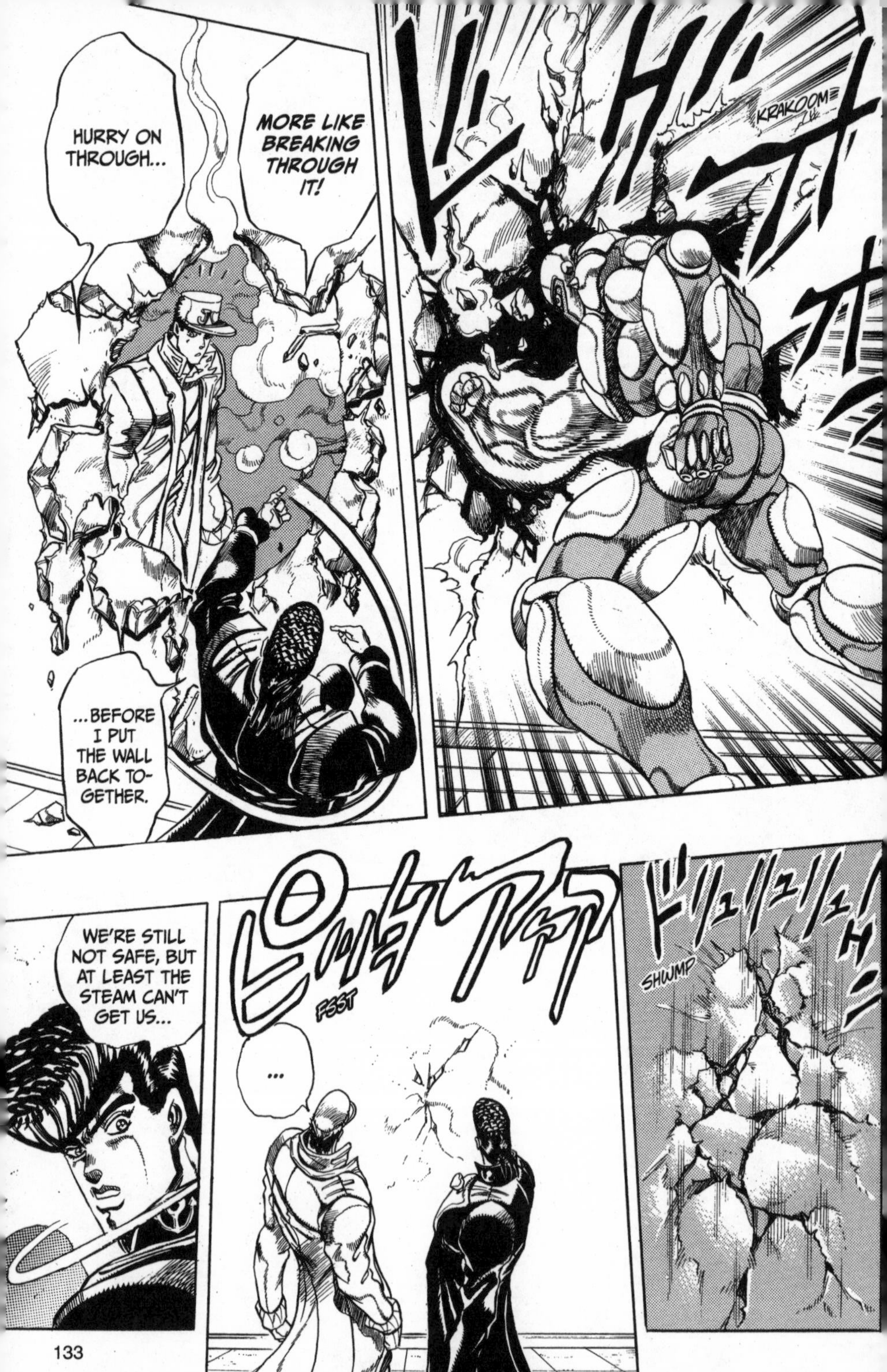
KRAKOOM
MORE LIKE BREAKING THROUGH IT!
HURRY ON THROUGH...
...BEFORE I PUT THE WALL BACK TO-GETHER.
SHWUMP
FSST
...
WE'RE STILL NOT SAFE, BUT AT LEAST THE STEAM CAN'T GET US...

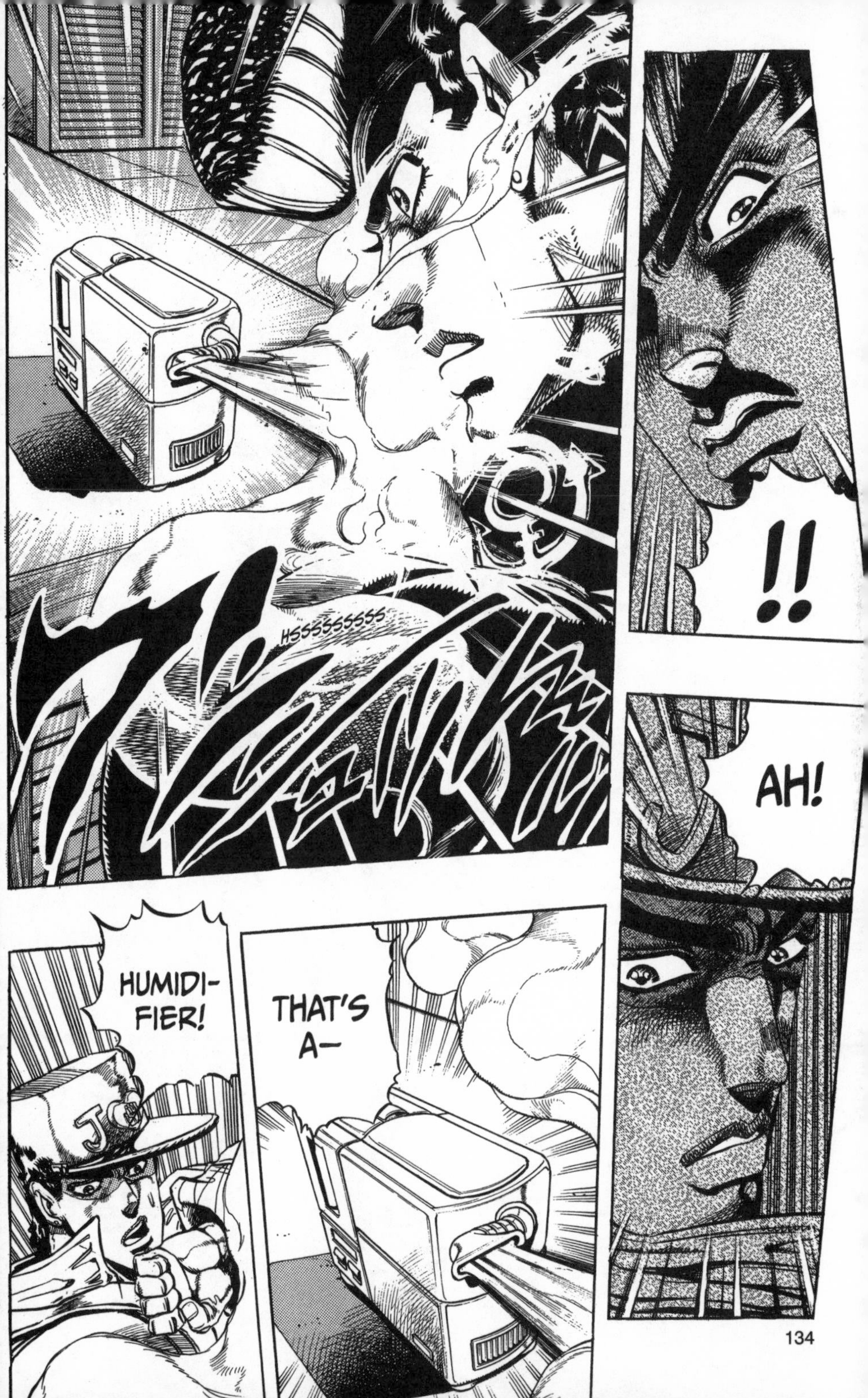
!!
HSSSSSSSSS
AH!
THAT'S A—
HUMIDI-
FIER!

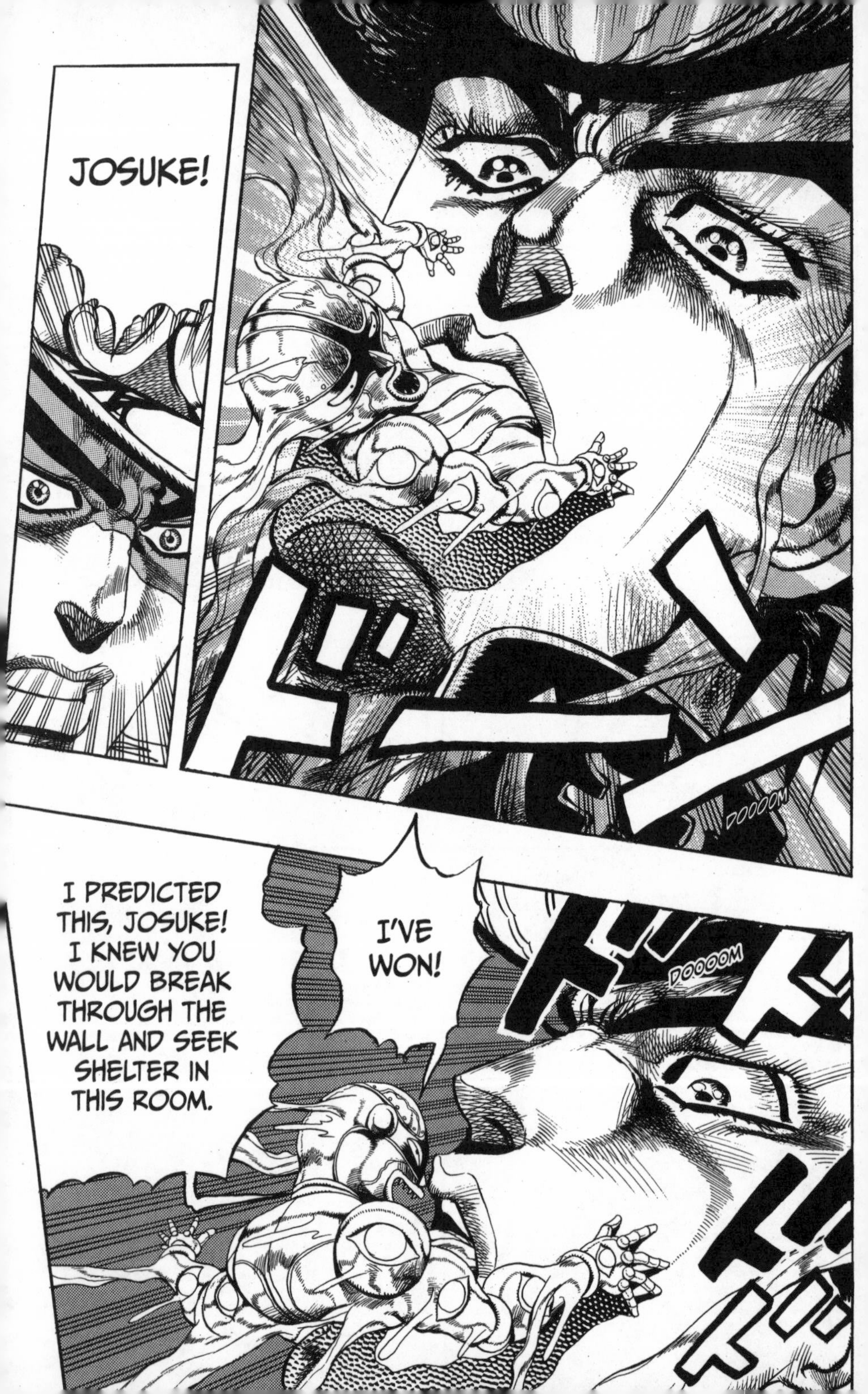
DOOOOM
JOSUKE!
DOOOOM
I'VE WON!
I PREDICTED THIS, JOSUKE! I KNEW YOU WOULD BREAK THROUGH THE WALL AND SEEK SHELTER IN THIS ROOM.

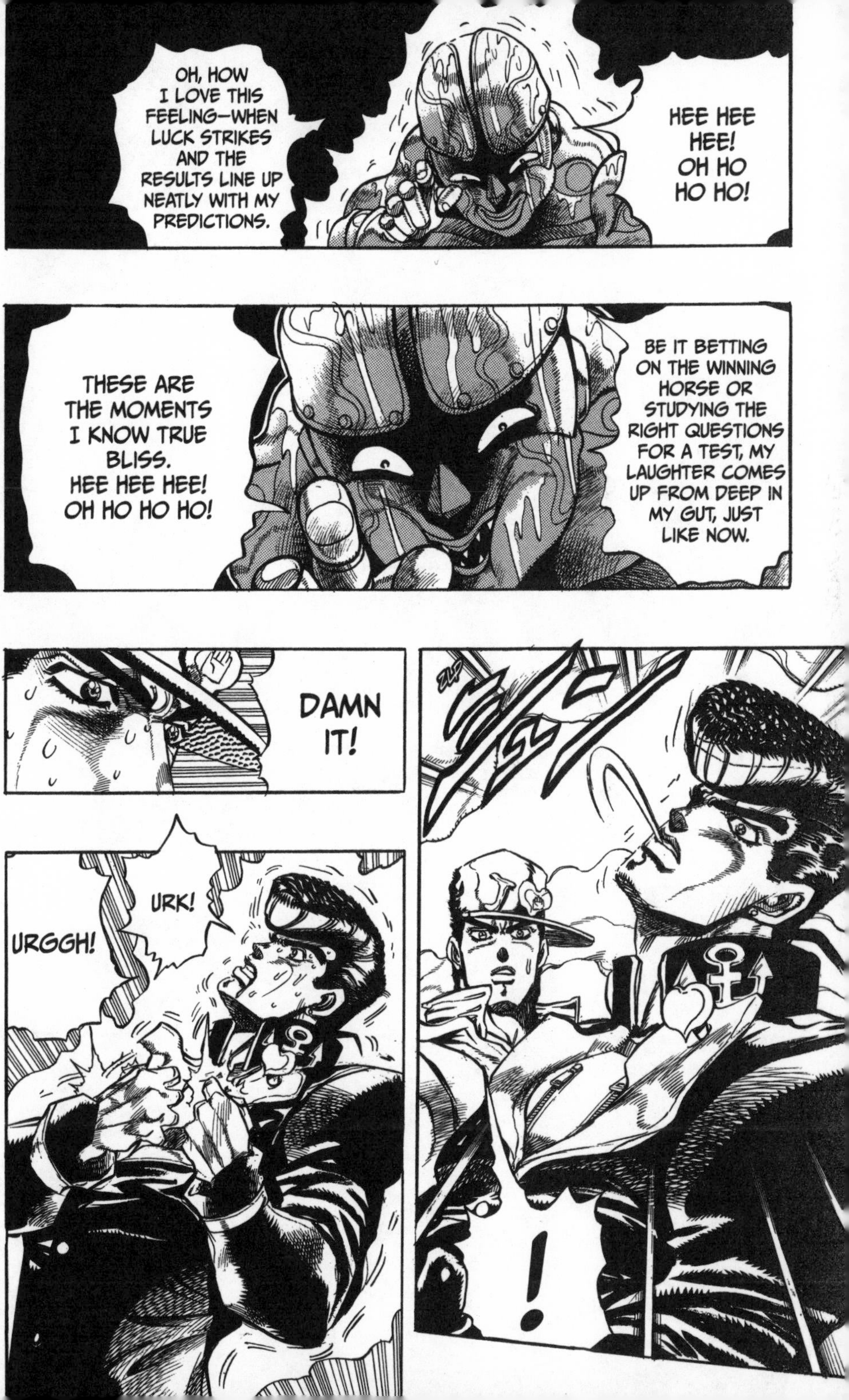
HEE HEE HEE! OH HO HO HO!
OH, HOW I LOVE THIS FEELING—WHEN LUCK STRIKES AND THE RESULTS LINE UP NEATLY WITH MY PREDICTIONS.
BE IT BETTING ON THE WINNING HORSE OR STUDYING THE RIGHT QUESTIONS FOR A TEST, MY LAUGHTER COMES UP FROM DEEP IN MY GUT, JUST LIKE NOW.
THESE ARE THE MOMENTS I KNOW TRUE BLISS. HEE HEE HEE! OH HO HO HO!
!
DAMN IT!
URK!
URGH!

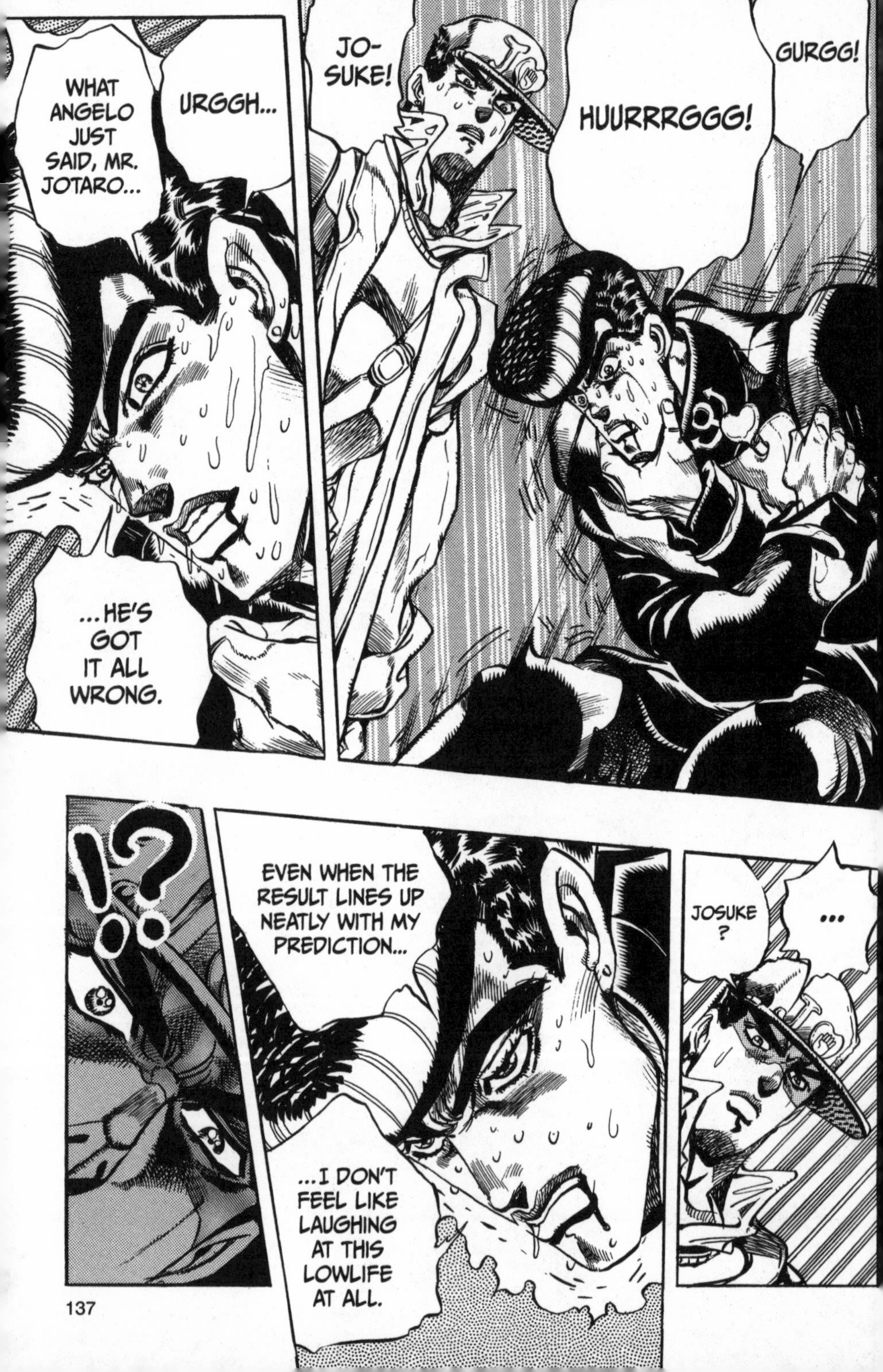
GURGG!
HUURRRGGG!
JO-SUKE!
URGGH...
WHAT ANGELO JUST SAID, MR. JOTARO...
...HE'S GOT IT ALL WRONG.
...
JOSUKE?
EVEN WHEN THE RESULT LINES UP NEATLY WITH MY PREDICTION...
...I DON'T FEEL LIKE LAUGHING AT THIS LOWLIFE AT ALL.
!?

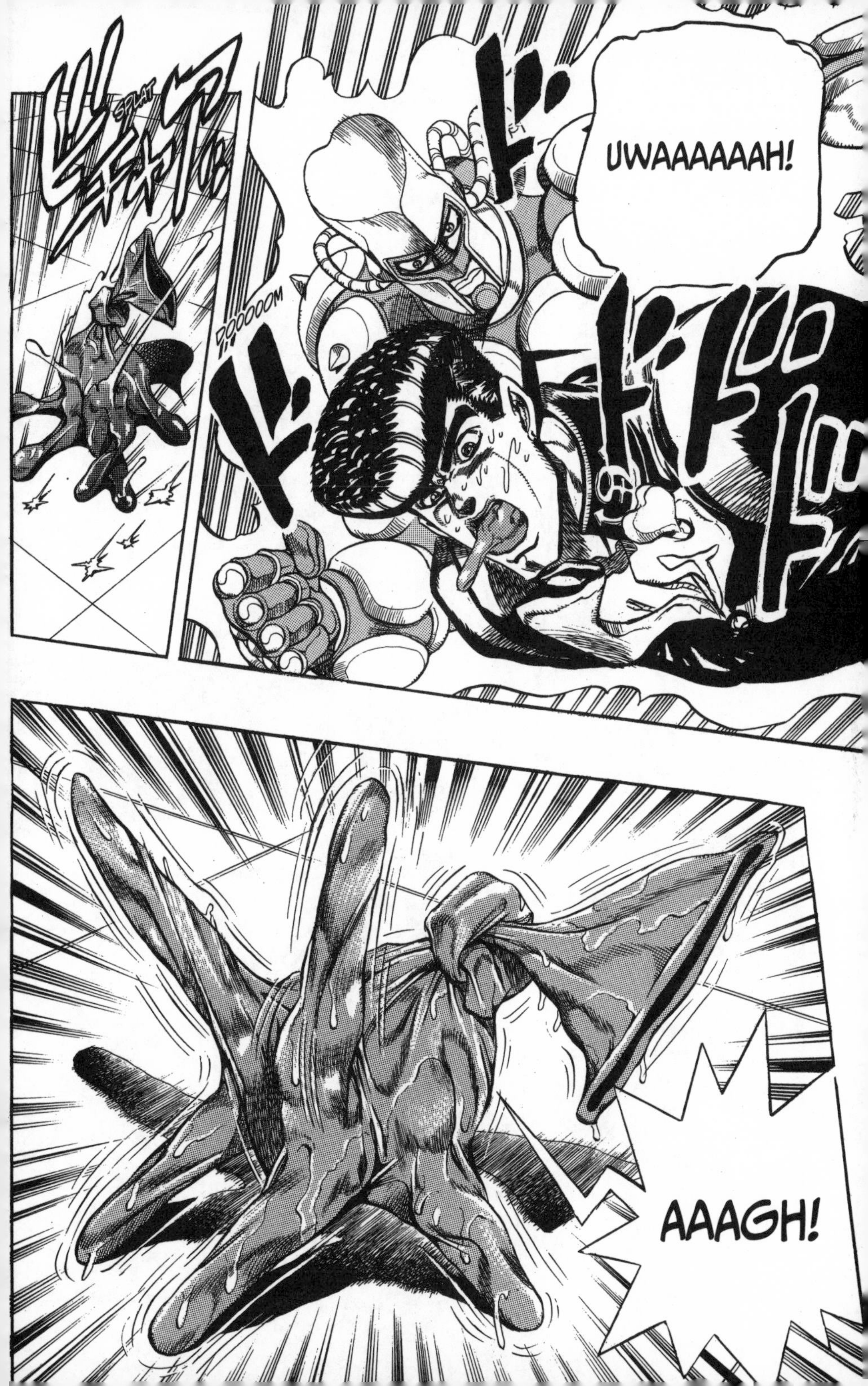
UWAAAAAAH!
DOOOOOM
SPLAT
AAAGH!

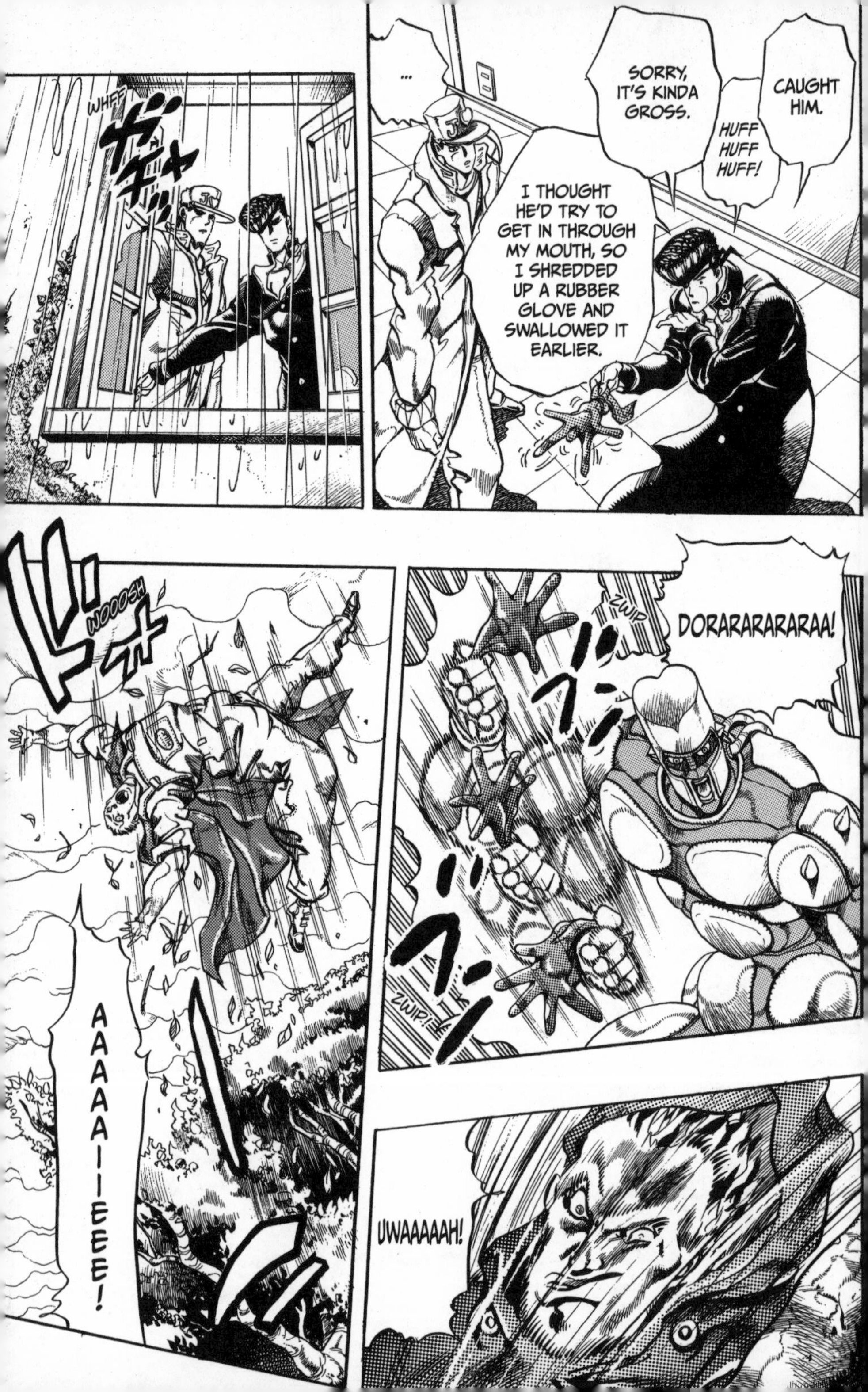
CAUGHT HIM.
HUFF HUFF HUFF!
SORRY, IT'S KINDA GROSS.
I THOUGHT HE'D TRY TO GET IN THROUGH MY MOUTH, SO I SHREDDED UP A RUBBER GLOVE AND SWALLOWED IT EARLIER.
...
WHFF
DORARARARARAA!
ZWIP
ZWIP!
UWAAAAAH!
WOOOSH
AAAAAIIEEEE!

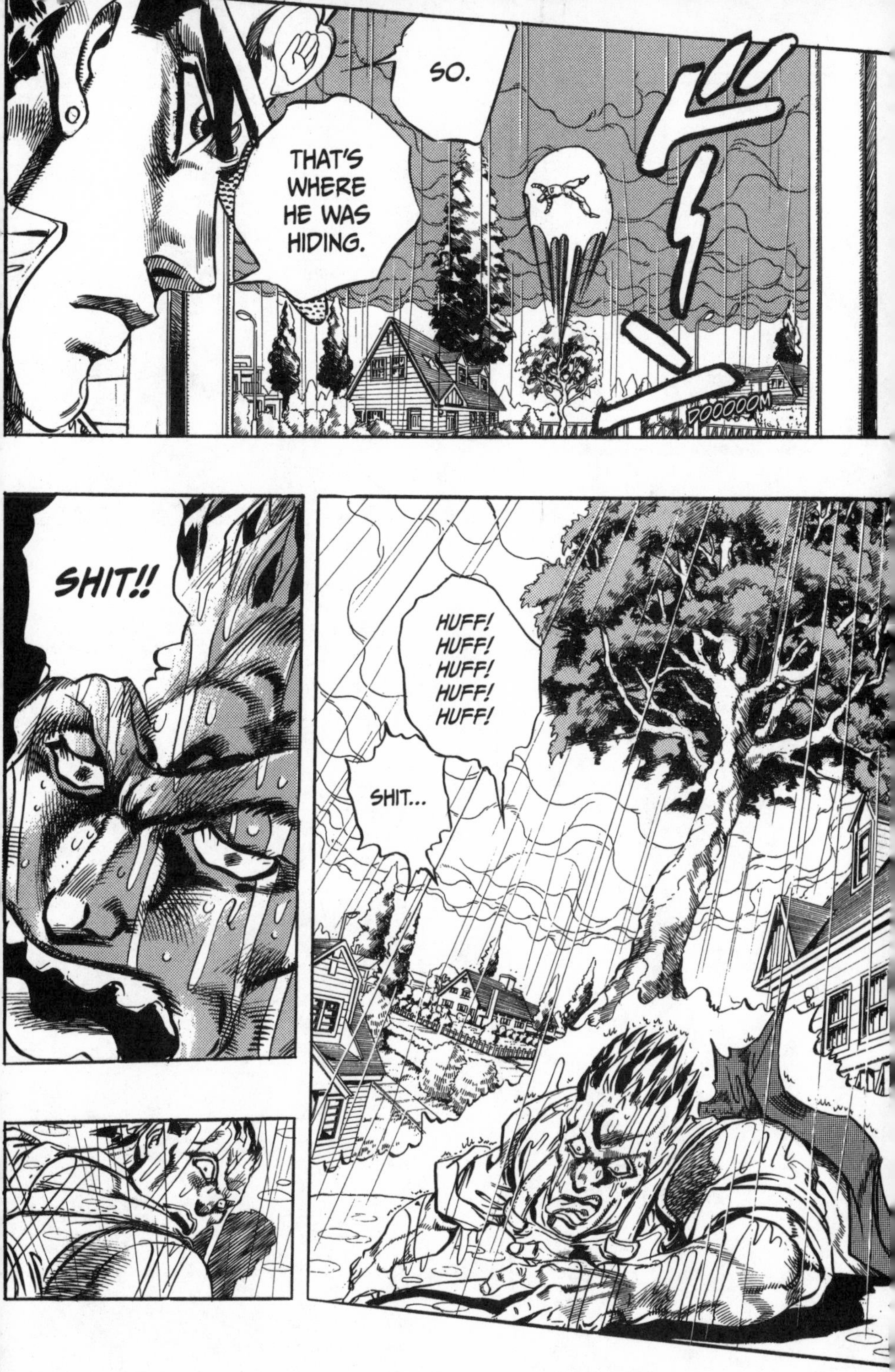
SO.
THAT'S WHERE HE WAS HIDING.
DOOOOOM
HUFF! HUFF! HUFF! HUFF! HUFF!
SHIT...
SHIT!!

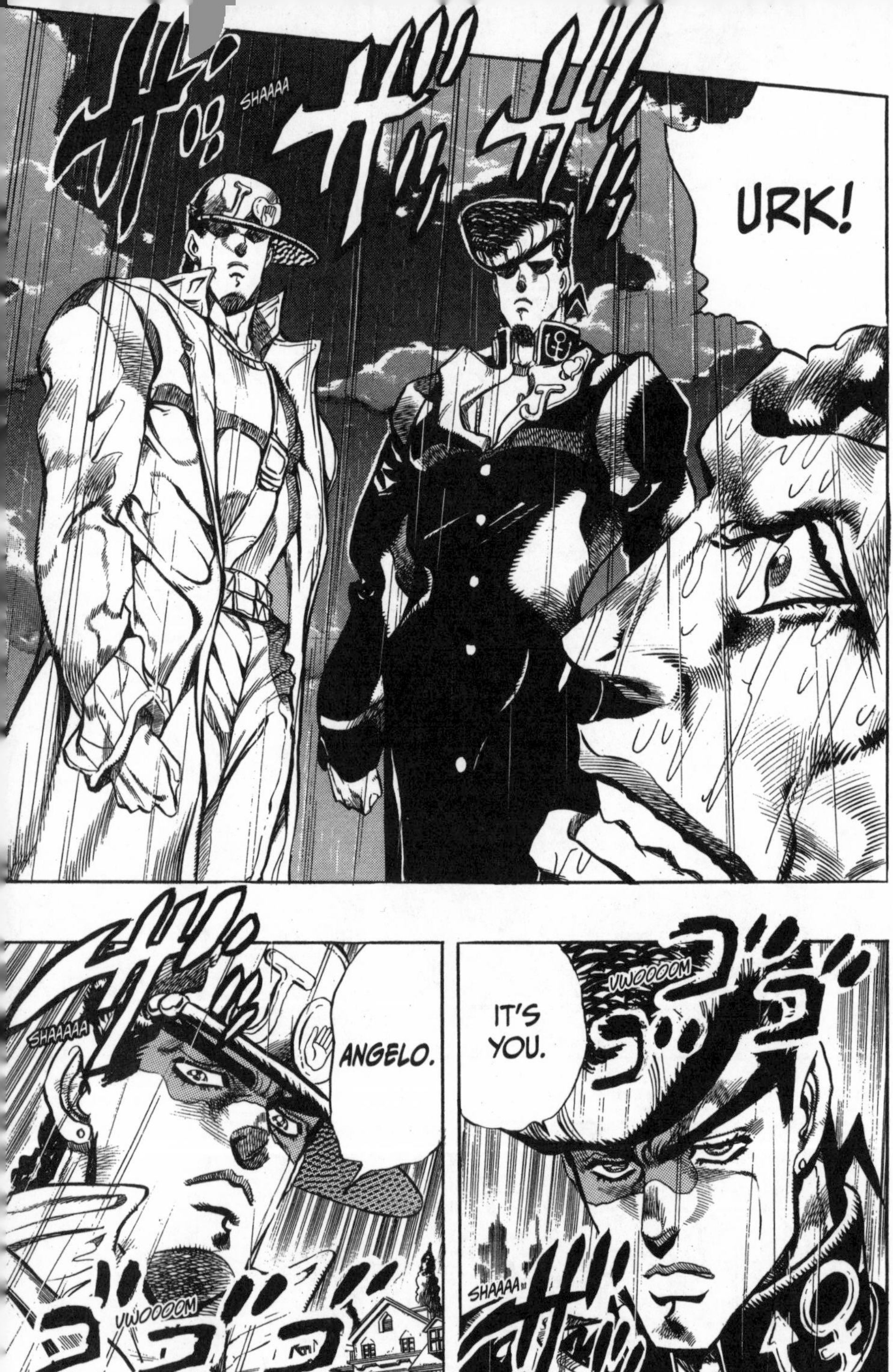
SHAAAA
URK!
VWOOOOM
IT'S YOU.
SHAAAA
SHAAAAA
ANGELO.
VWOOOOM

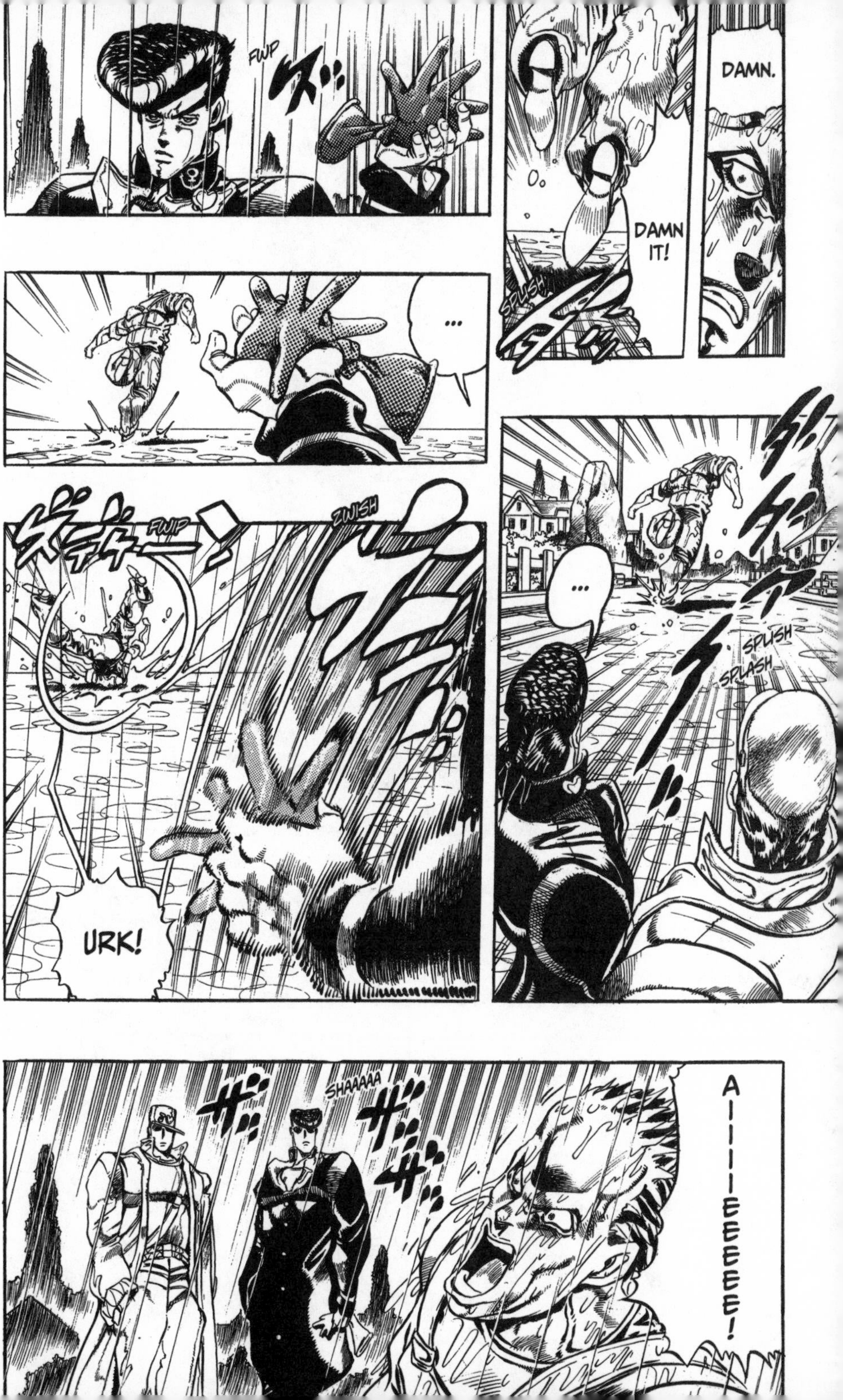
DAMN.
DAMN IT!
SPLISH
FWIP
...
...
SPLUSH
SPLASH
FWIP
ZWISH
URK!
SHAAAAA
AIIIIEEEEEE!

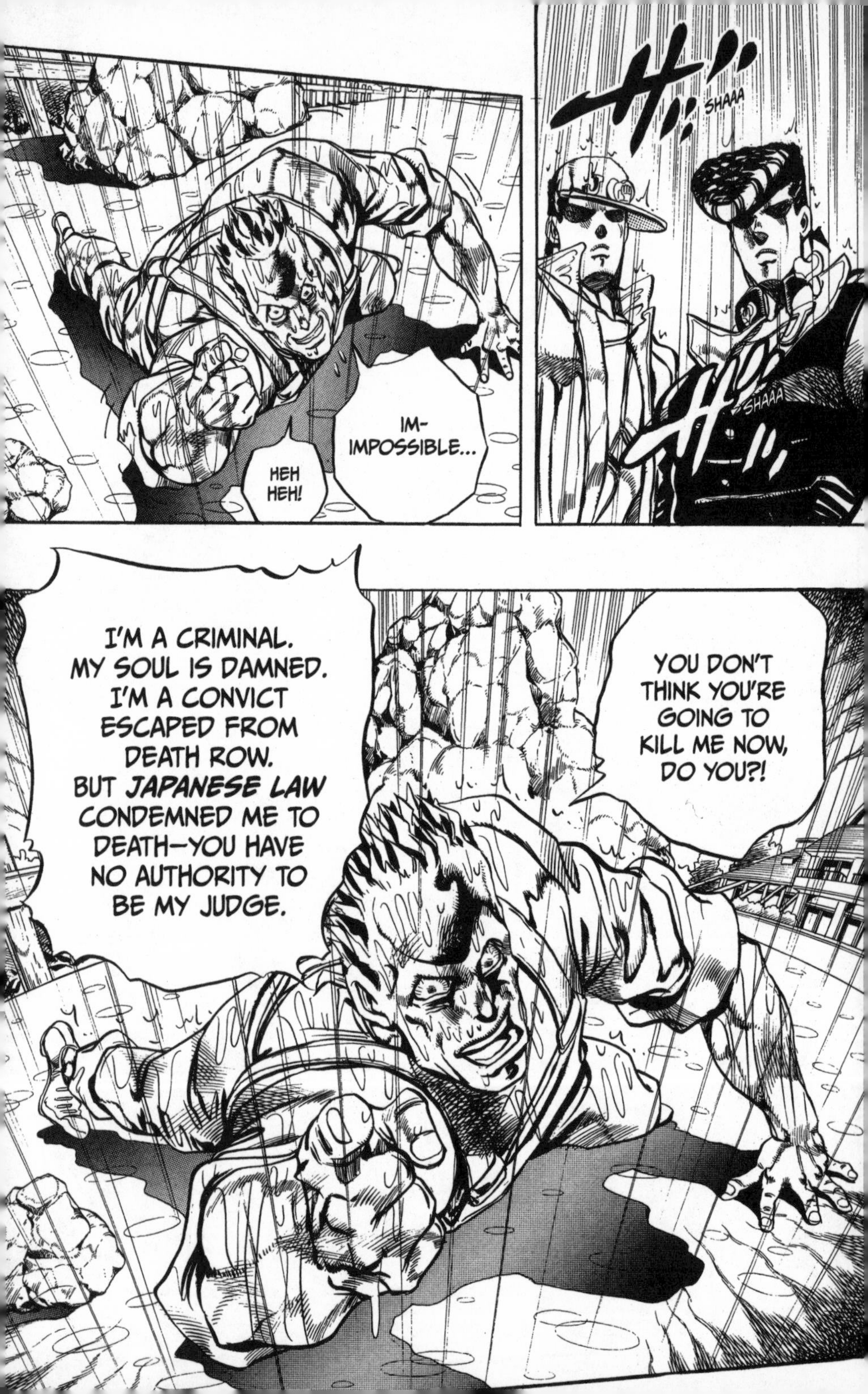
SHAAA
SHAAA
IM-IMPOSSIBLE...
HEH HEH!
YOU DON'T THINK YOU'RE GOING TO KILL ME NOW, DO YOU?!
I'M A CRIMINAL. MY SOUL IS DAMNED. I'M A CONVICT ESCAPED FROM DEATH ROW. BUT *JAPANESE LAW* CONDEMNED ME TO DEATH—YOU HAVE NO AUTHORITY TO BE MY JUDGE.

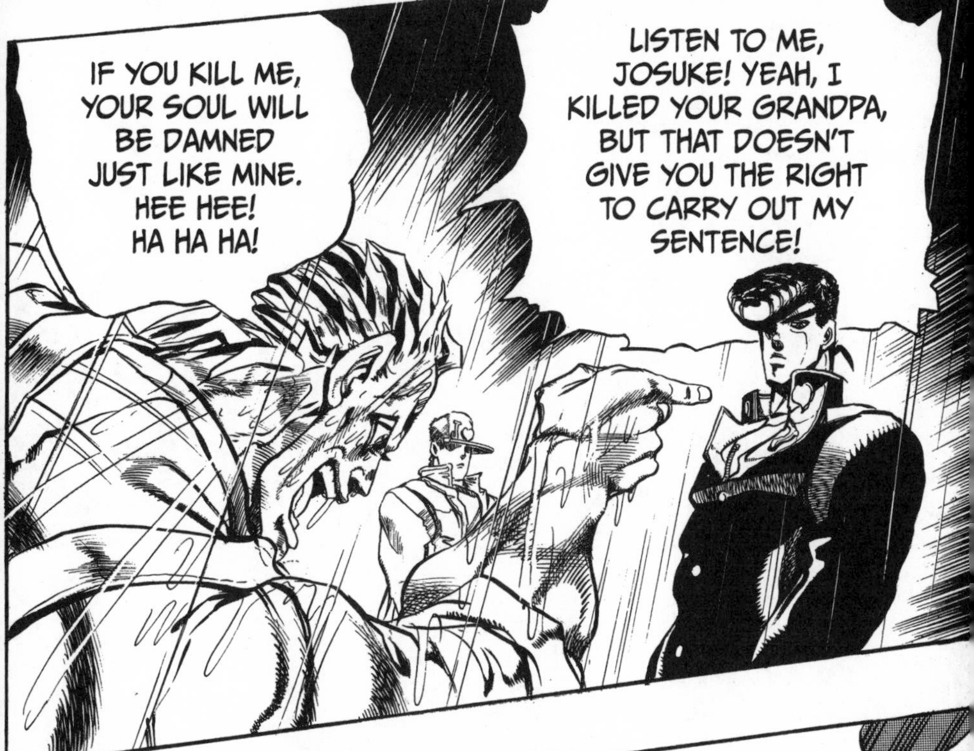
LISTEN TO ME, JOSUKE! YEAH, I KILLED YOUR GRANDPA, BUT THAT DOESN'T GIVE YOU THE RIGHT TO CARRY OUT MY SENTENCE!
IF YOU KILL ME, YOUR SOUL WILL BE DAMNED JUST LIKE MINE. HEE HEE! HA HA HA!
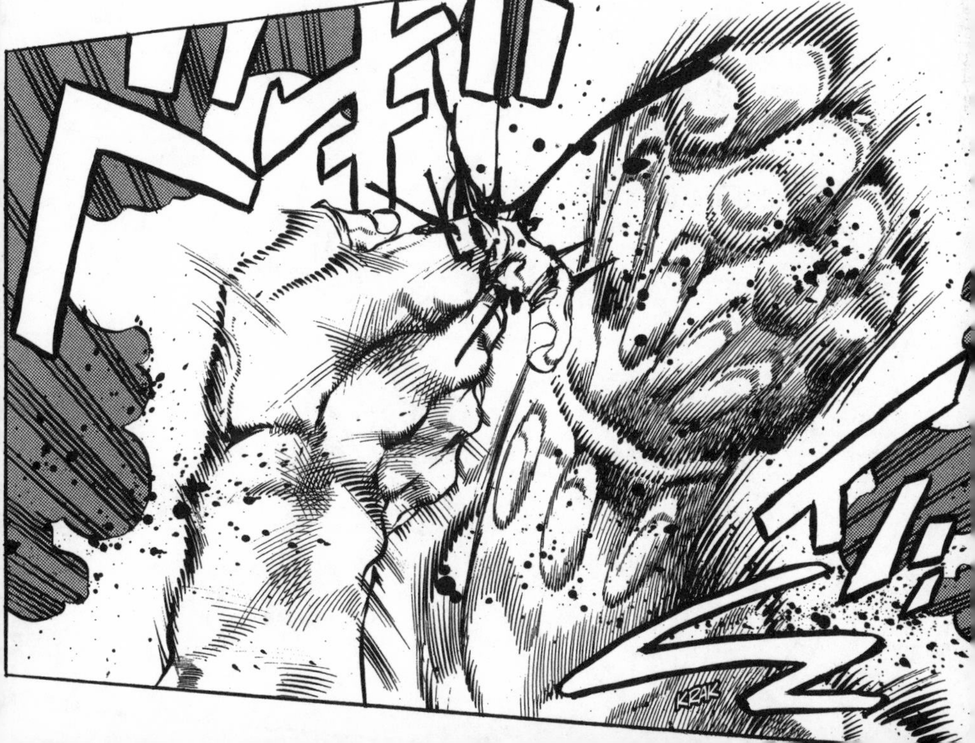
KRAK

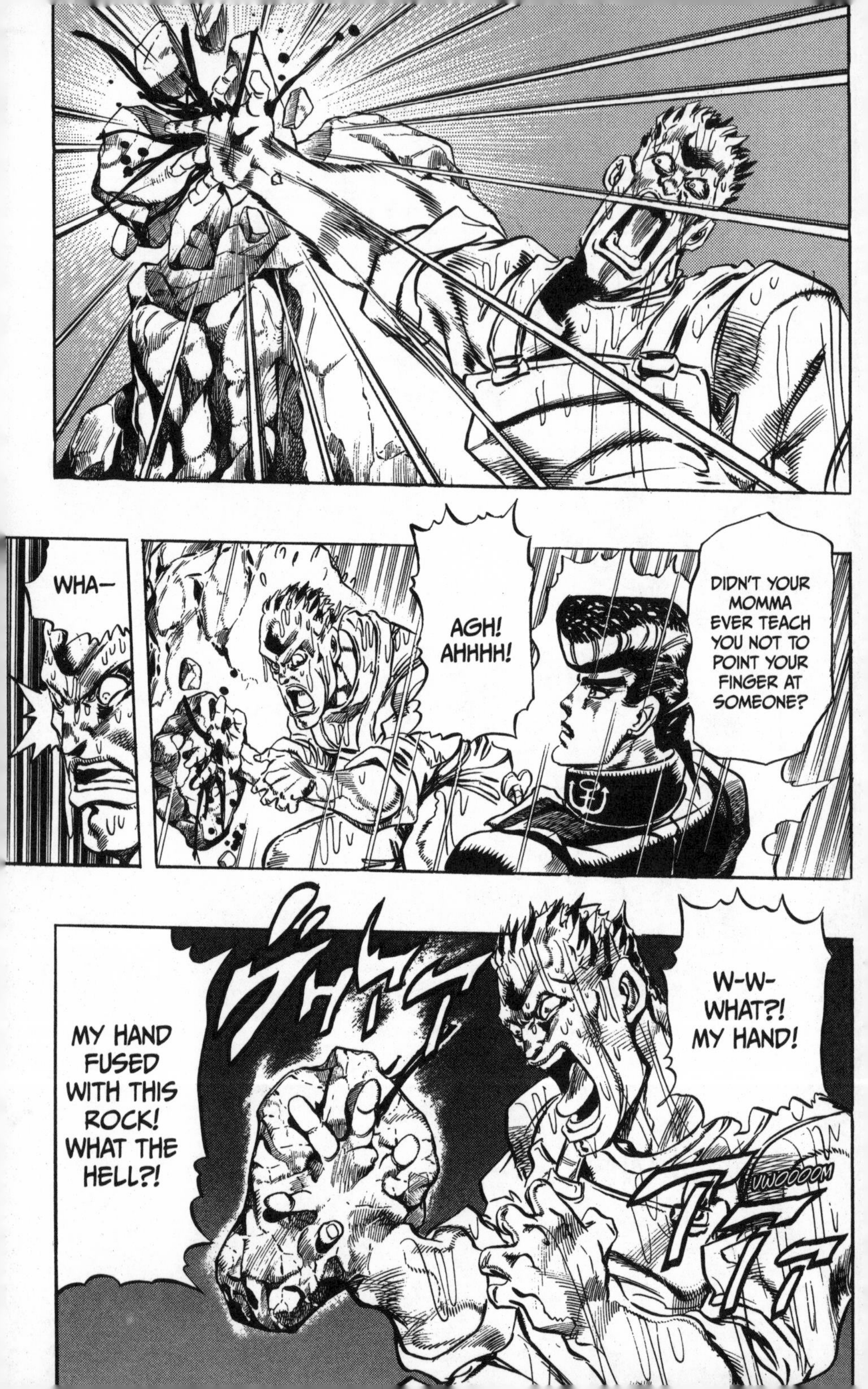

DIDN'T YOUR MOMMA EVER TEACH YOU NOT TO POINT YOUR FINGER AT SOMEONE?
AGH! AHHHH!
WHA–
W-W- WHAT?! MY HAND!
MY HAND FUSED WITH THIS ROCK! WHAT THE HELL?!
VWOOOOM

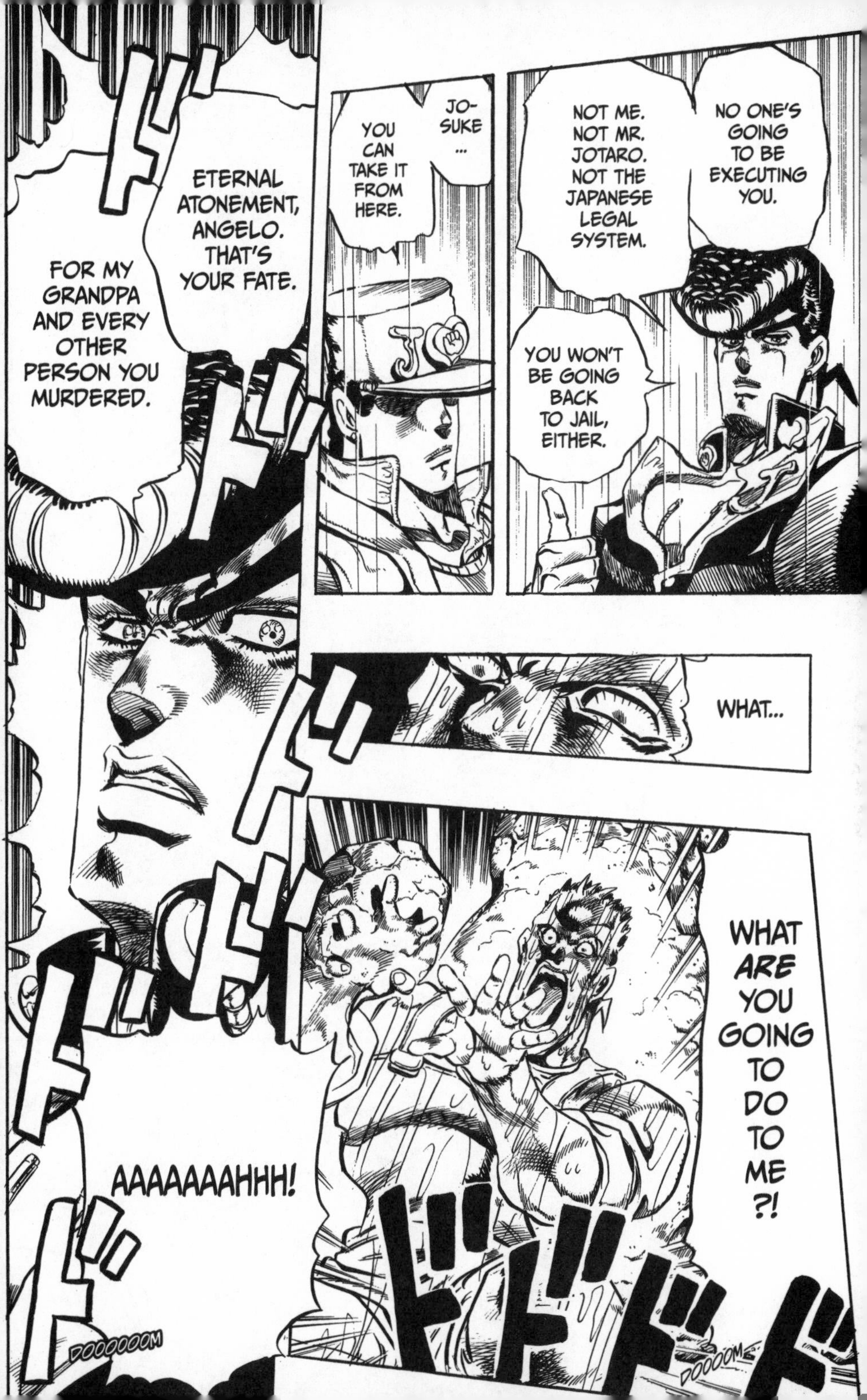
NO ONE'S GOING TO BE EXECUTING YOU.
NOT ME. NOT MR. JOTARO. NOT THE JAPANESE LEGAL SYSTEM.
YOU WON'T BE GOING BACK TO JAIL, EITHER.
JO-SUKE ...
YOU CAN TAKE IT FROM HERE.
WHAT...
WHAT ARE YOU GOING TO DO TO ME ?!
DOOOOM
ETERNAL ATONEMENT, ANGELO. THAT'S YOUR FATE.
FOR MY GRANDPA AND EVERY OTHER PERSON YOU MURDERED.
AAAAAAAHHH!
DOOOOOOM

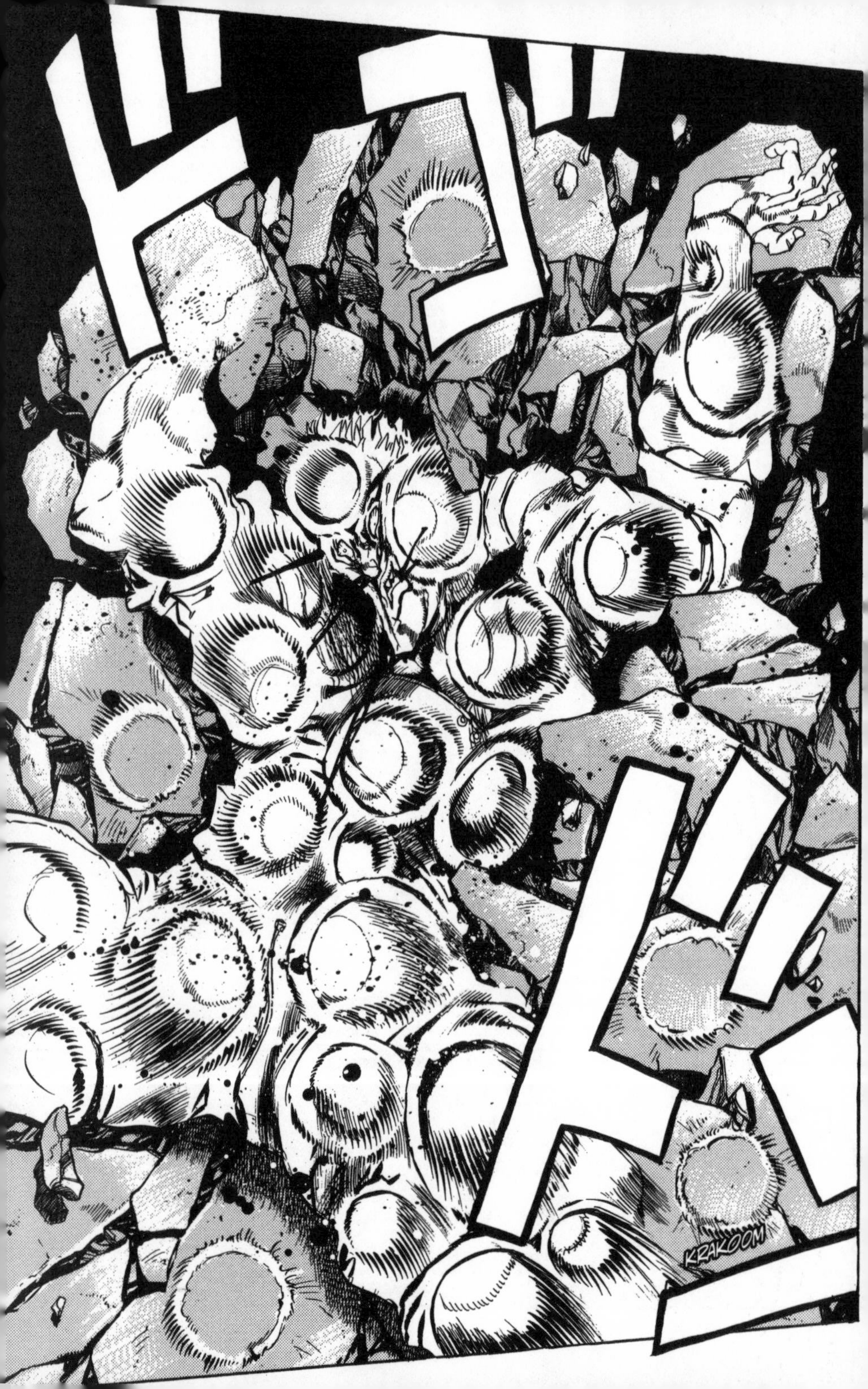
ドゴ
ドド
KRAKOOM

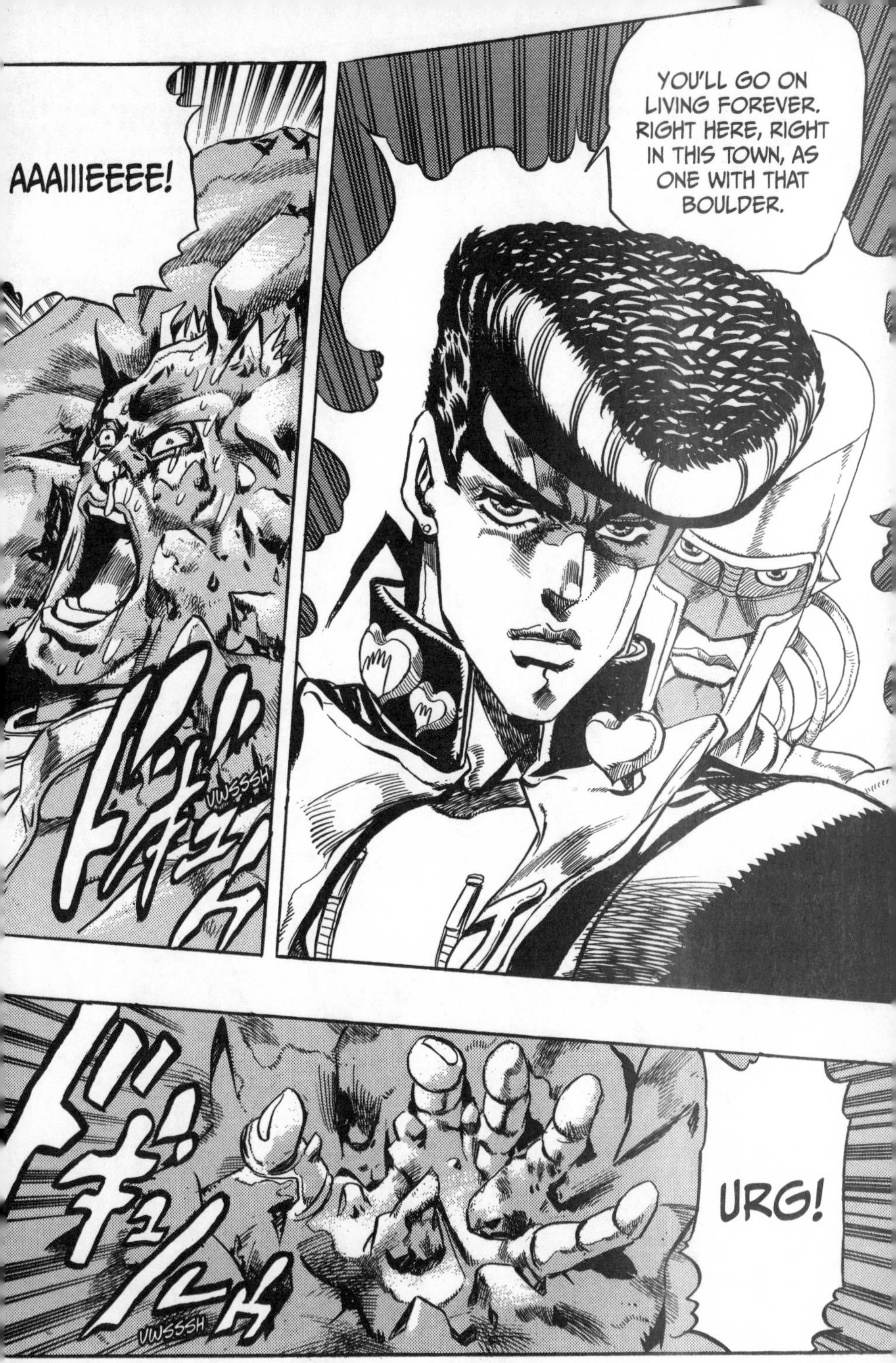
YOU'LL GO ON LIVING FOREVER. RIGHT HERE, RIGHT IN THIS TOWN, AS ONE WITH THAT BOULDER.
AAAIIIEEEE!
VWSSSH
URG!
VWSSSH

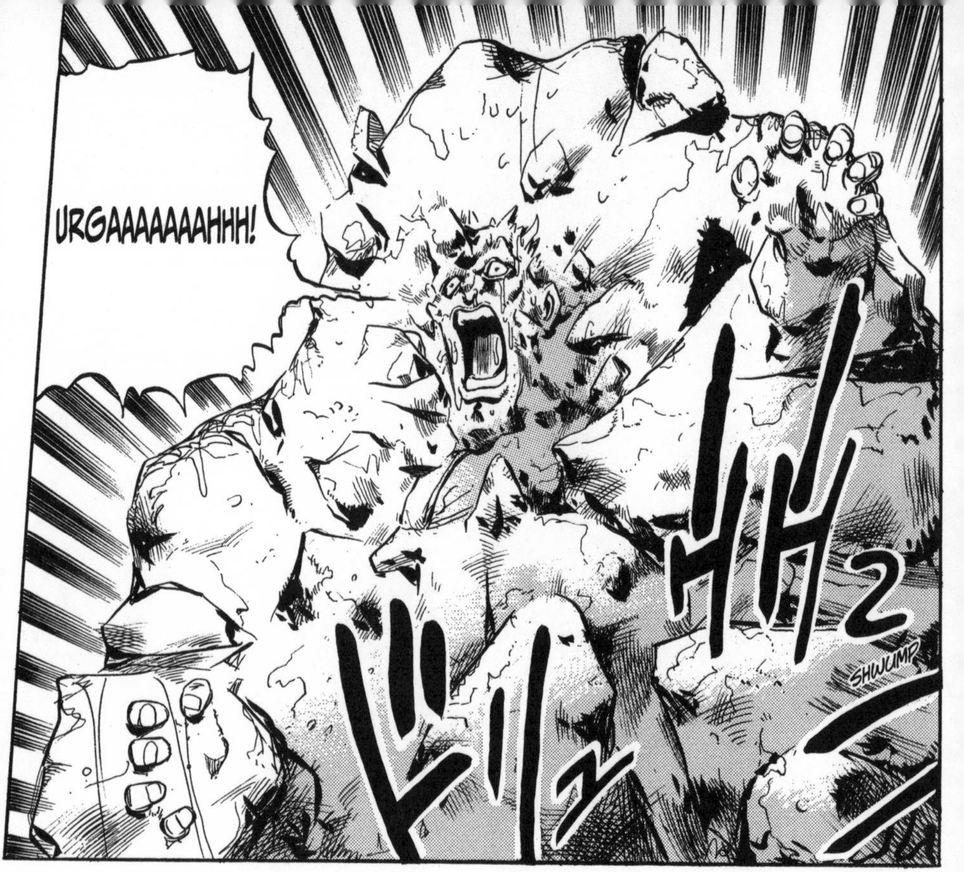
URGAAAAAAAHHH!
SHWUMP

MAKING A MORE PLEASANT TOWN
MORIOH PLACES OF INTEREST #1: "ANGELO'S ROCK"
DIRECTIONS: 1 MINUTE WALK FROM THE JOZENJI BUS ROUTE'S #3 STOP

DESPITE ITS CREEPY APPEARANCE, ANGELO'S ROCK HAS ENDEARED ITSELF TO LOCAL RESIDENTS AS A CONVENIENT LANDMARK AND AS A MEETING PLACE FOR COUPLES HEADING OUT ON A DATE.

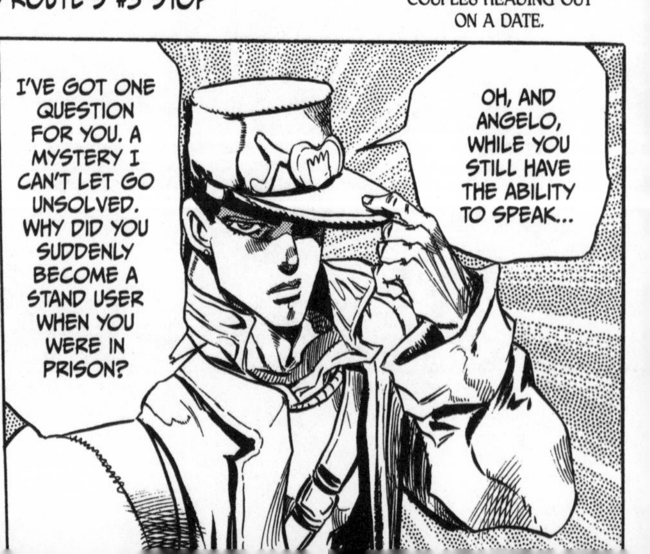
OH, AND ANGELO, WHILE YOU STILL HAVE THE ABILITY TO SPEAK...
I'VE GOT ONE QUESTION FOR YOU. A MYSTERY I CAN'T LET GO UNSOLVED. WHY DID YOU SUDDENLY BECOME A STAND USER WHEN YOU WERE IN PRISON?

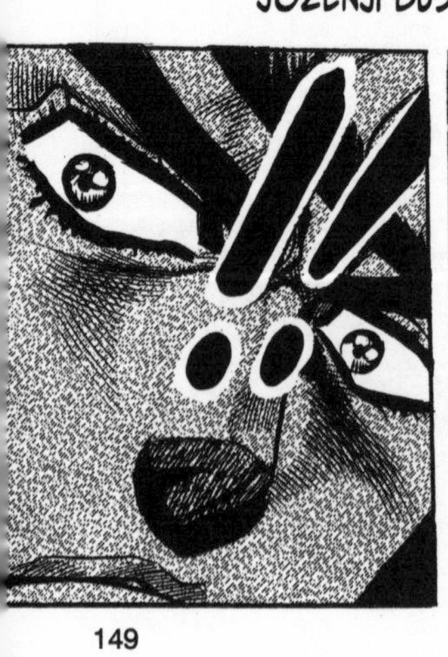

CHAPTER 8

JOSUKE HIGASHIKATA MEETS ANGELO, PART 5

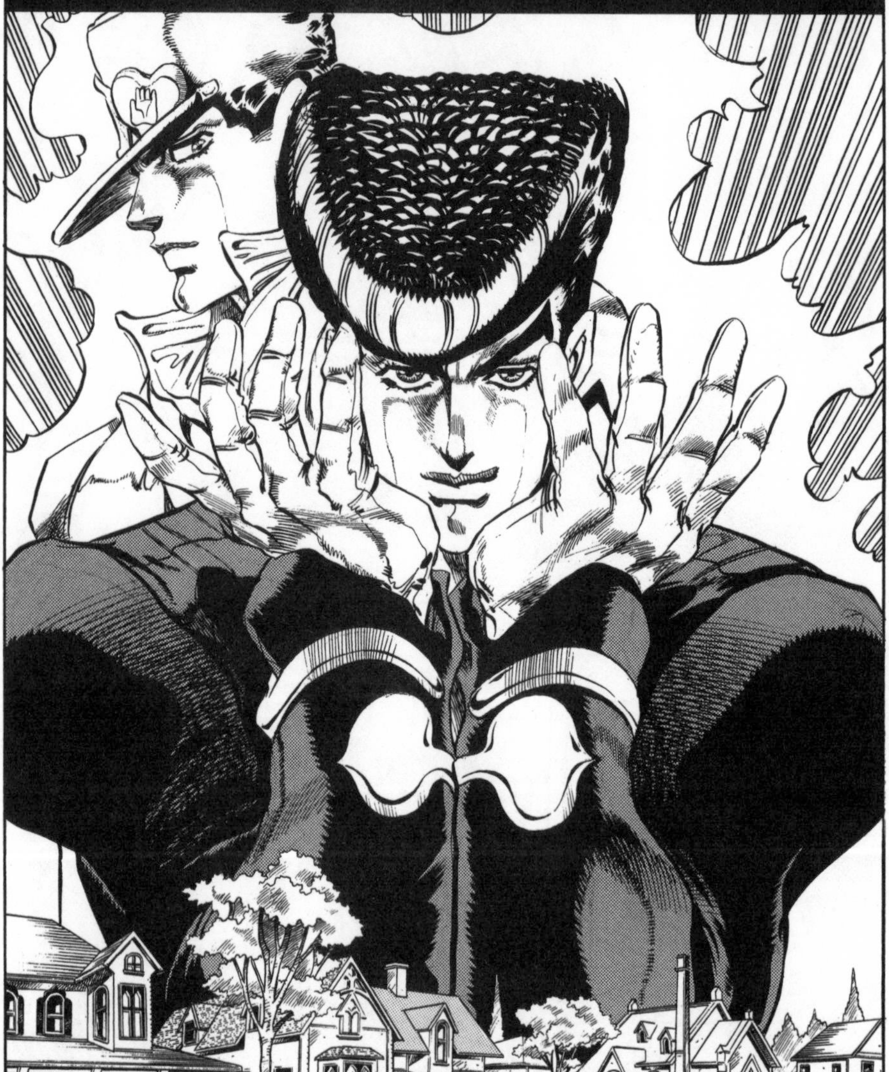

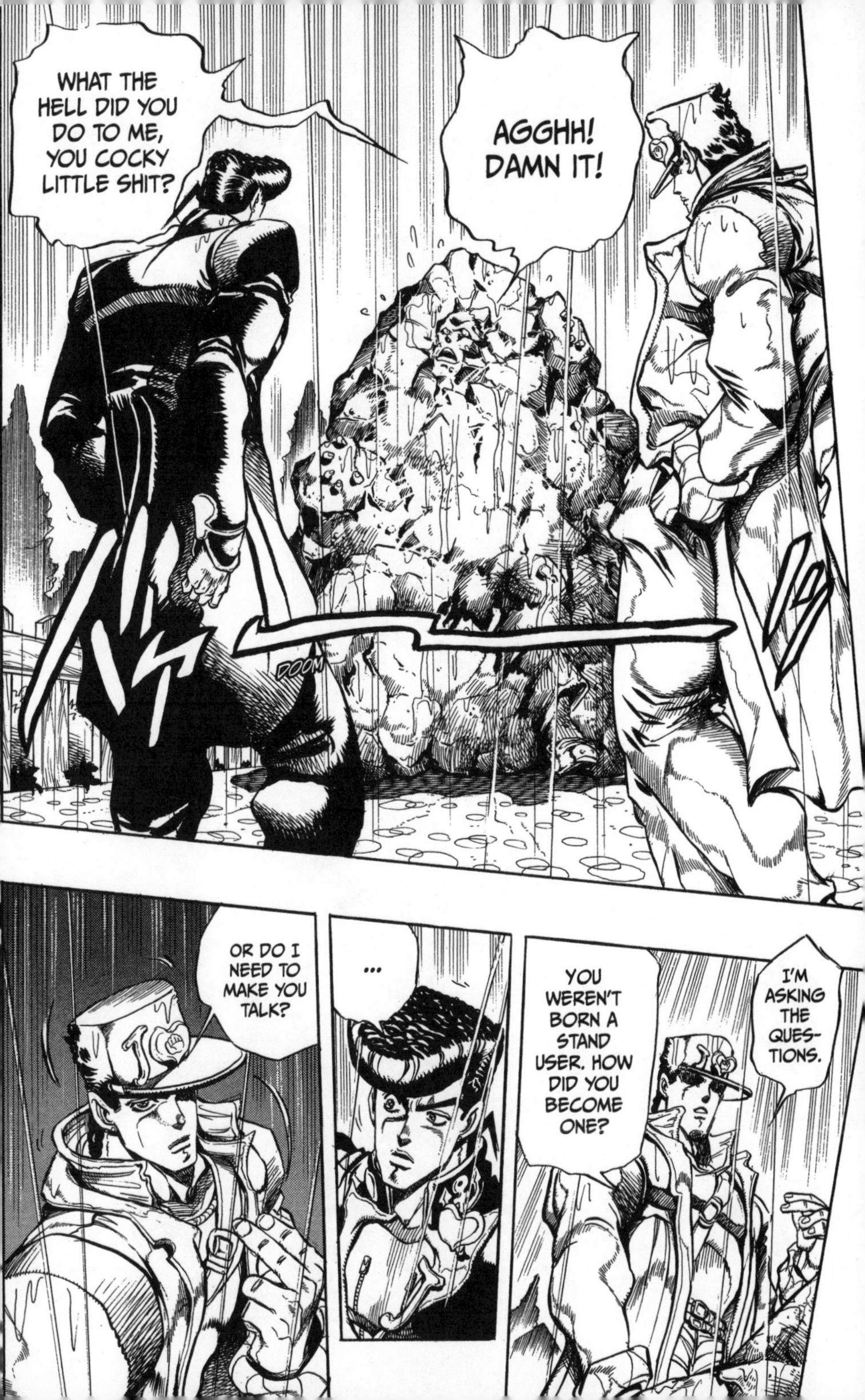
AGGHH! DAMN IT!
WHAT THE HELL DID YOU DO TO ME, YOU COCKY LITTLE SHIT?
DOOM
I'M ASKING THE QUES-TIONS.
YOU WEREN'T BORN A STAND USER. HOW DID YOU BECOME ONE?
...
OR DO I NEED TO MAKE YOU TALK?

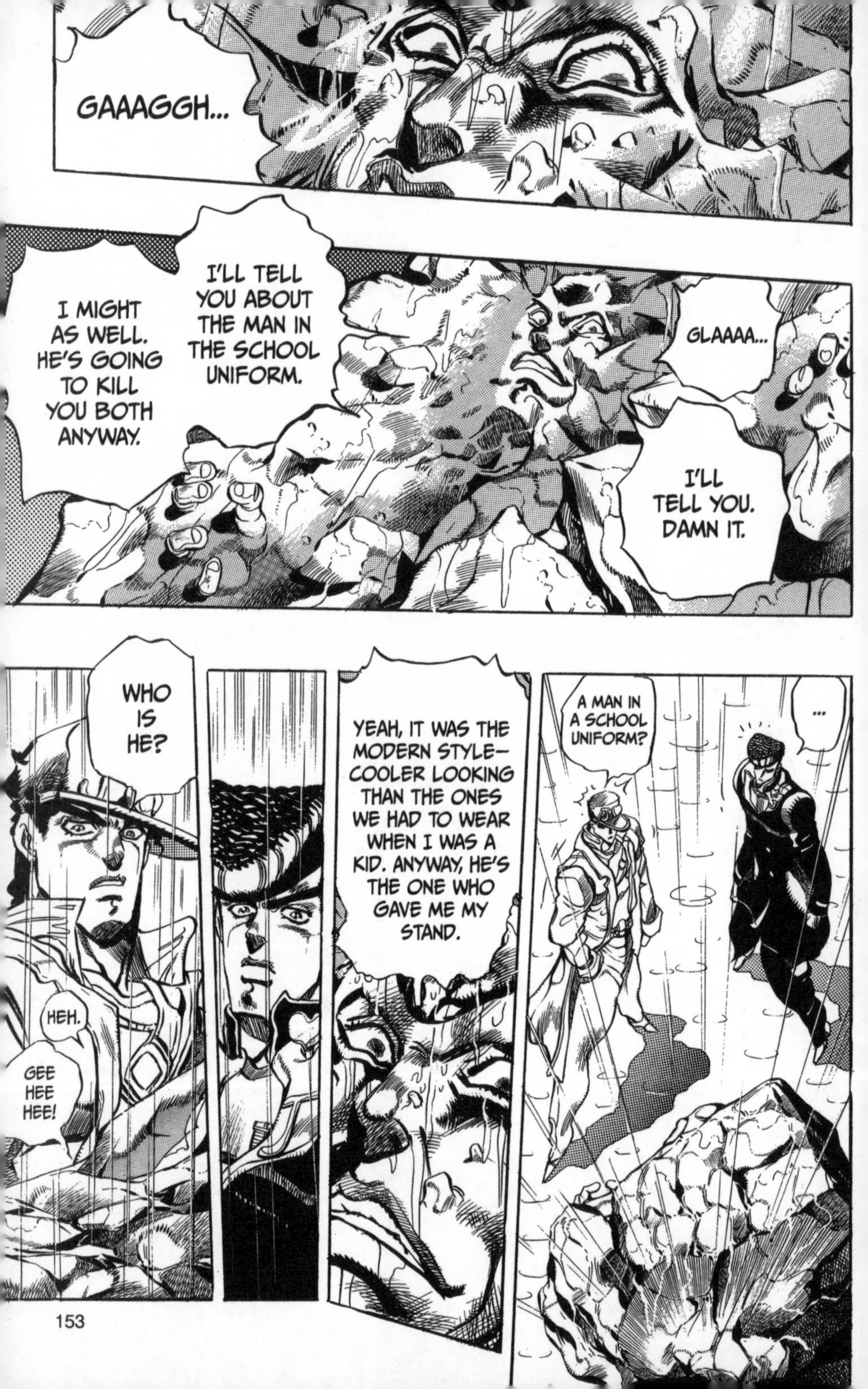
GAAAGGH...
GLAAAA...
I'LL TELL YOU. DAMN IT.
I'LL TELL YOU ABOUT THE MAN IN THE SCHOOL UNIFORM.
I MIGHT AS WELL. HE'S GOING TO KILL YOU BOTH ANYWAY.
...
A MAN IN A SCHOOL UNIFORM?
YEAH, IT WAS THE MODERN STYLE—COOLER LOOKING THAN THE ONES WE HAD TO WEAR WHEN I WAS A KID. ANYWAY, HE'S THE ONE WHO GAVE ME MY STAND.
WHO IS HE?
HEH.
GEE HEE HEE!

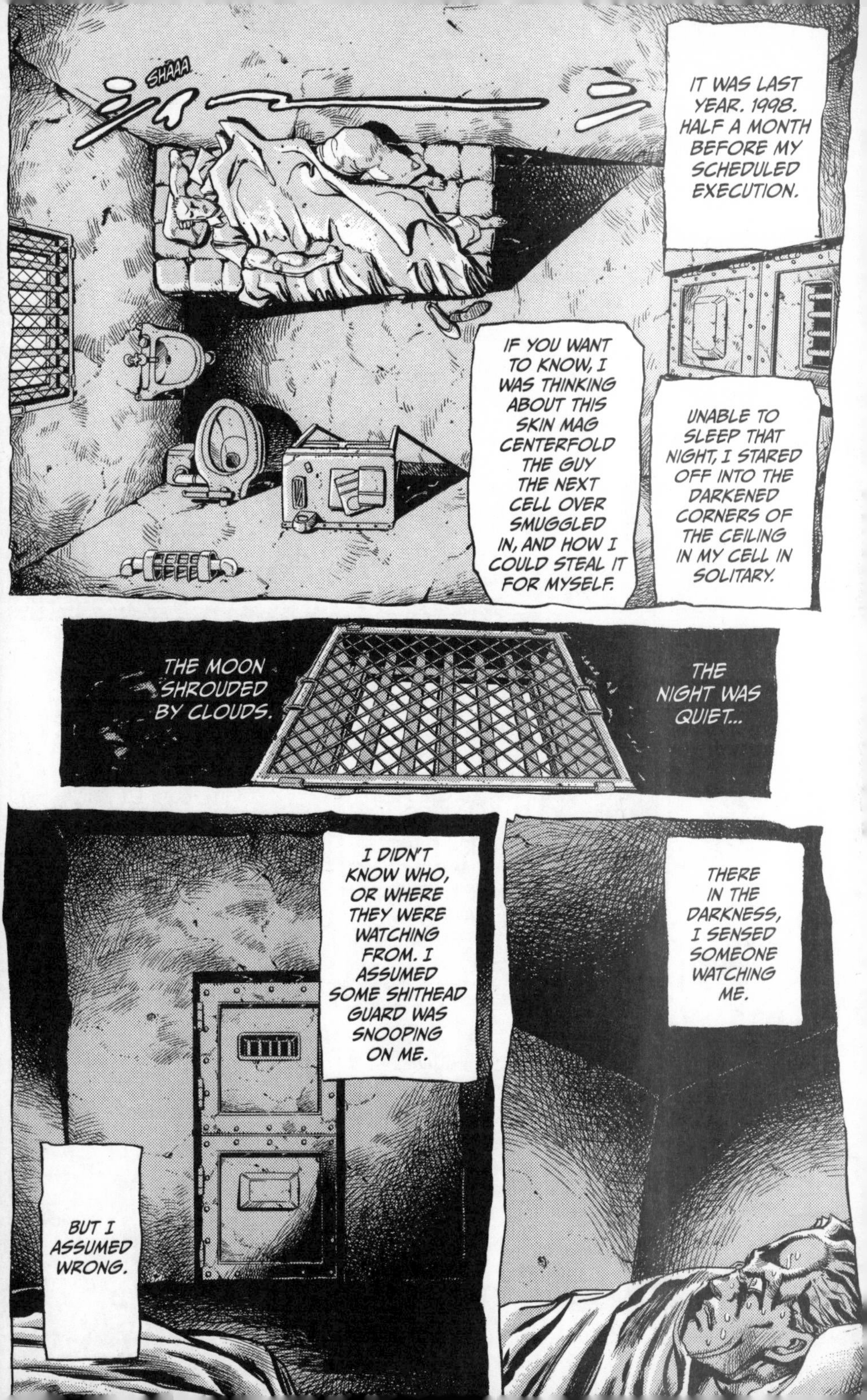

IT WAS LAST YEAR. 1998. HALF A MONTH BEFORE MY SCHEDULED EXECUTION.
UNABLE TO SLEEP THAT NIGHT, I STARED OFF INTO THE DARKENED CORNERS OF THE CEILING IN MY CELL IN SOLITARY.
IF YOU WANT TO KNOW, I WAS THINKING ABOUT THIS SKIN MAG CENTERFOLD THE GUY THE NEXT CELL OVER SMUGGLED IN, AND HOW I COULD STEAL IT FOR MYSELF.
SHAAA
THE NIGHT WAS QUIET...
THE MOON SHROUDED BY CLOUDS.
THERE IN THE DARKNESS, I SENSED SOMEONE WATCHING ME.
I DIDN'T KNOW WHO, OR WHERE THEY WERE WATCHING FROM. I ASSUMED SOME SHITHEAD GUARD WAS SNOOPING ON ME.
BUT I ASSUMED WRONG.

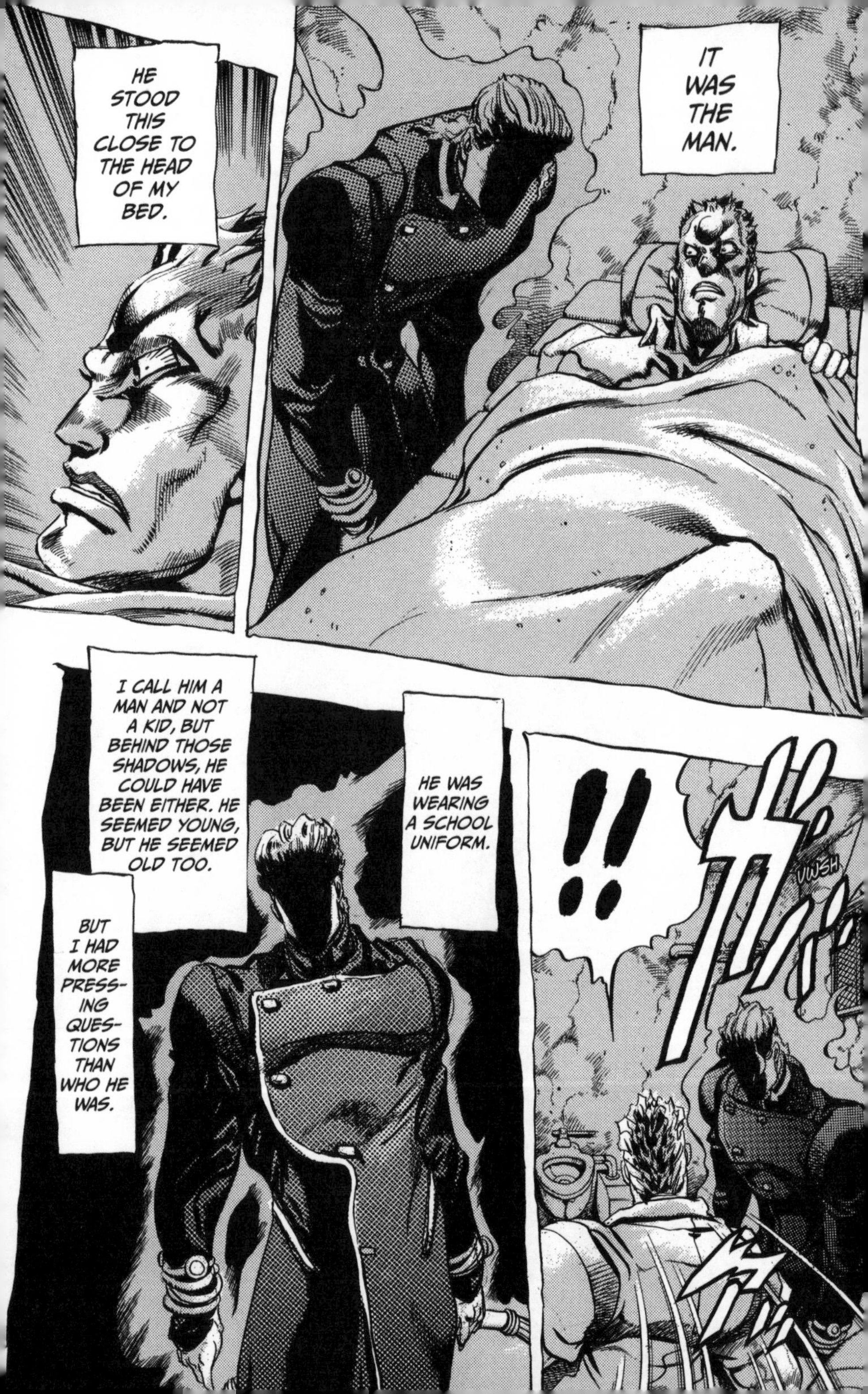
IT WAS THE MAN.
HE STOOD THIS CLOSE TO THE HEAD OF MY BED.
!!
VWSH
HE WAS WEARING A SCHOOL UNIFORM.
I CALL HIM A MAN AND NOT A KID, BUT BEHIND THOSE SHADOWS, HE COULD HAVE BEEN EITHER. HE SEEMED YOUNG, BUT HE SEEMED OLD TOO.
BUT I HAD MORE PRESSING QUESTIONS THAN WHO HE WAS.

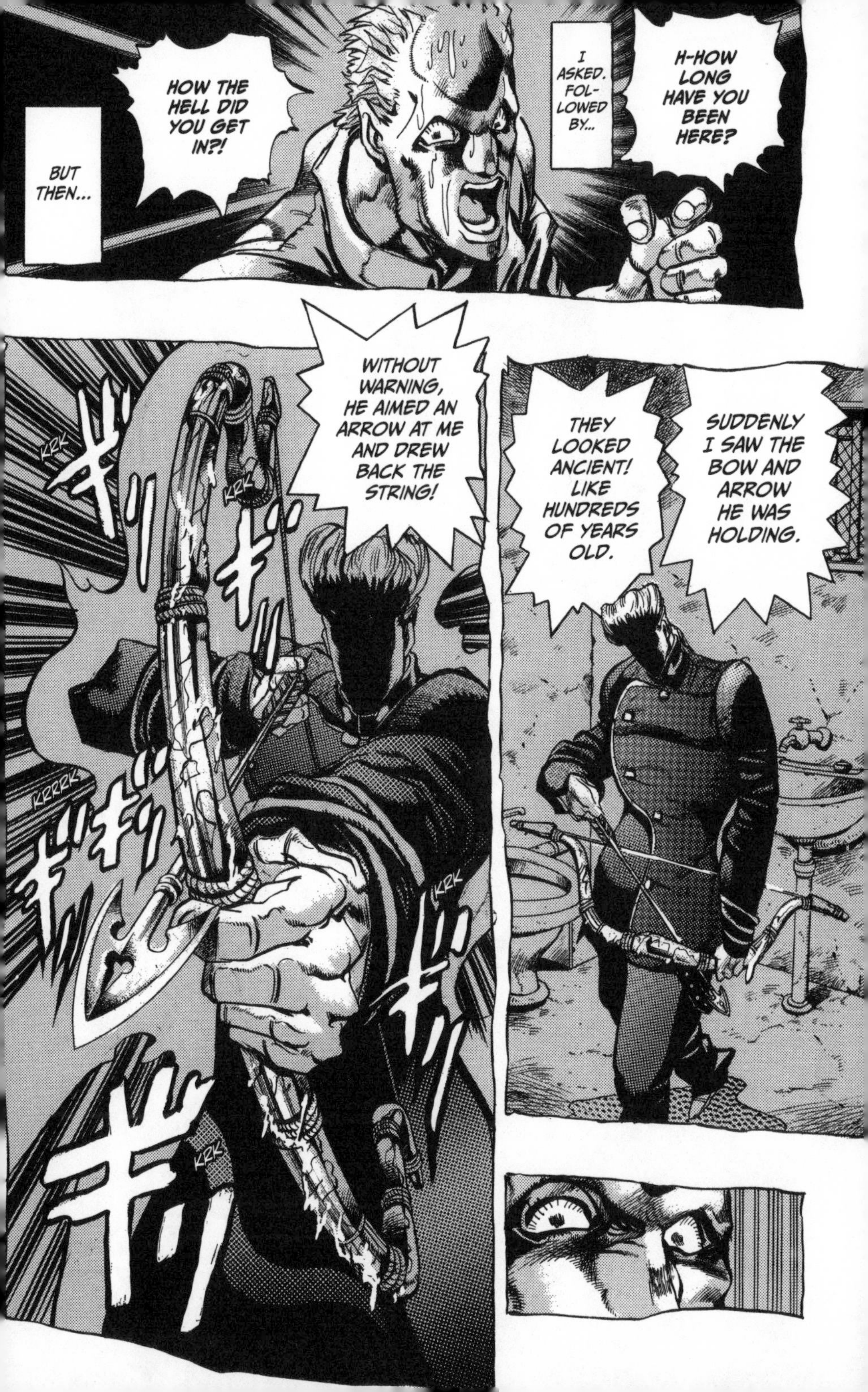
H-HOW LONG HAVE YOU BEEN HERE?
I ASKED. FOL-LOWED BY...
HOW THE HELL DID YOU GET IN?!
BUT THEN...
SUDDENLY I SAW THE BOW AND ARROW HE WAS HOLDING.
THEY LOOKED ANCIENT! LIKE HUNDREDS OF YEARS OLD.
WITHOUT WARNING, HE AIMED AN ARROW AT ME AND DREW BACK THE STRING!
KRK
KRK
KRRRK
KRK
KRK

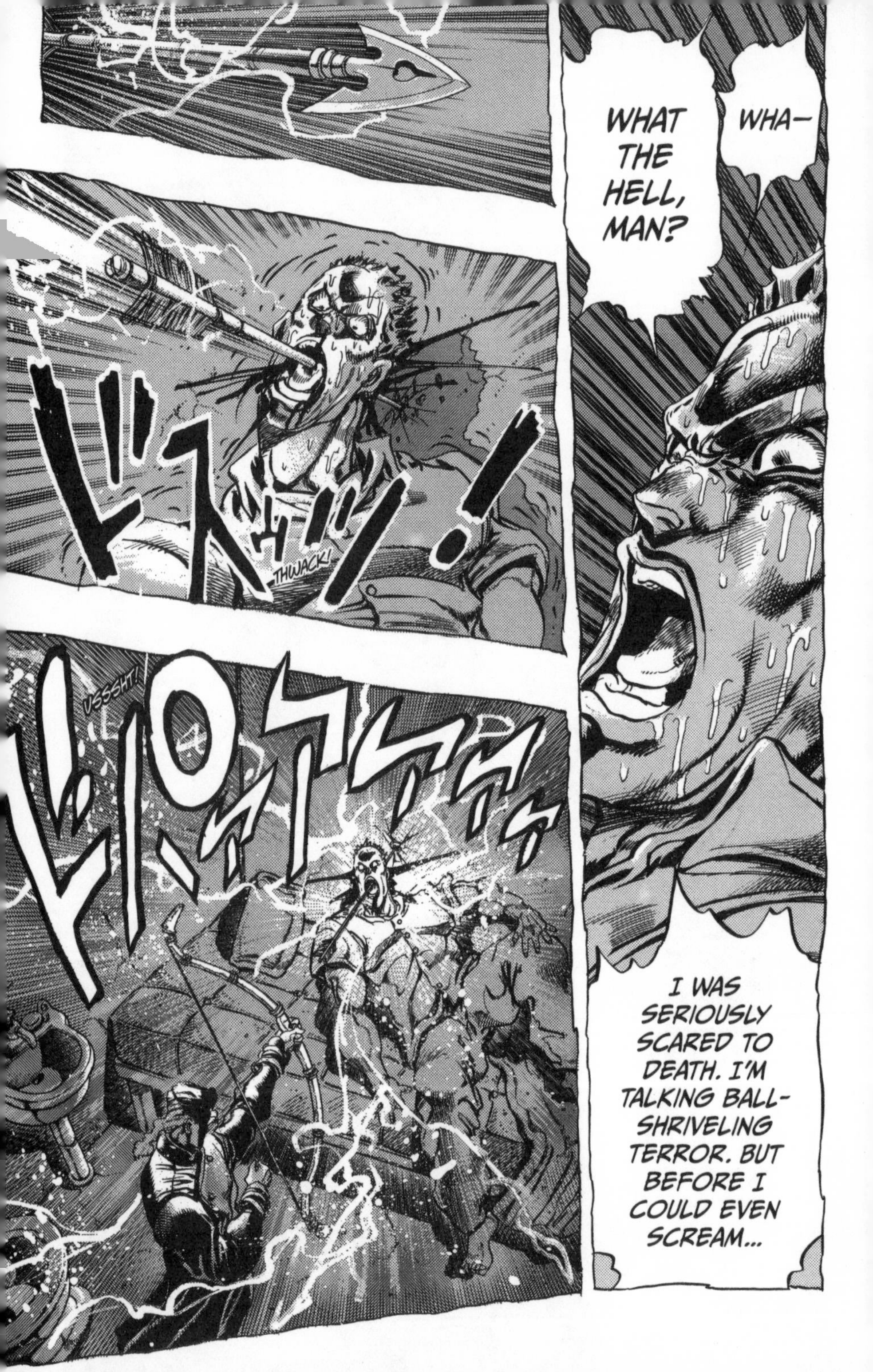
WHA—
WHAT THE HELL, MAN?
I WAS SERIOUSLY SCARED TO DEATH. I'M TALKING BALL-SHRIVELING TERROR. BUT BEFORE I COULD EVEN SCREAM...
THWACK!
USSSHT!

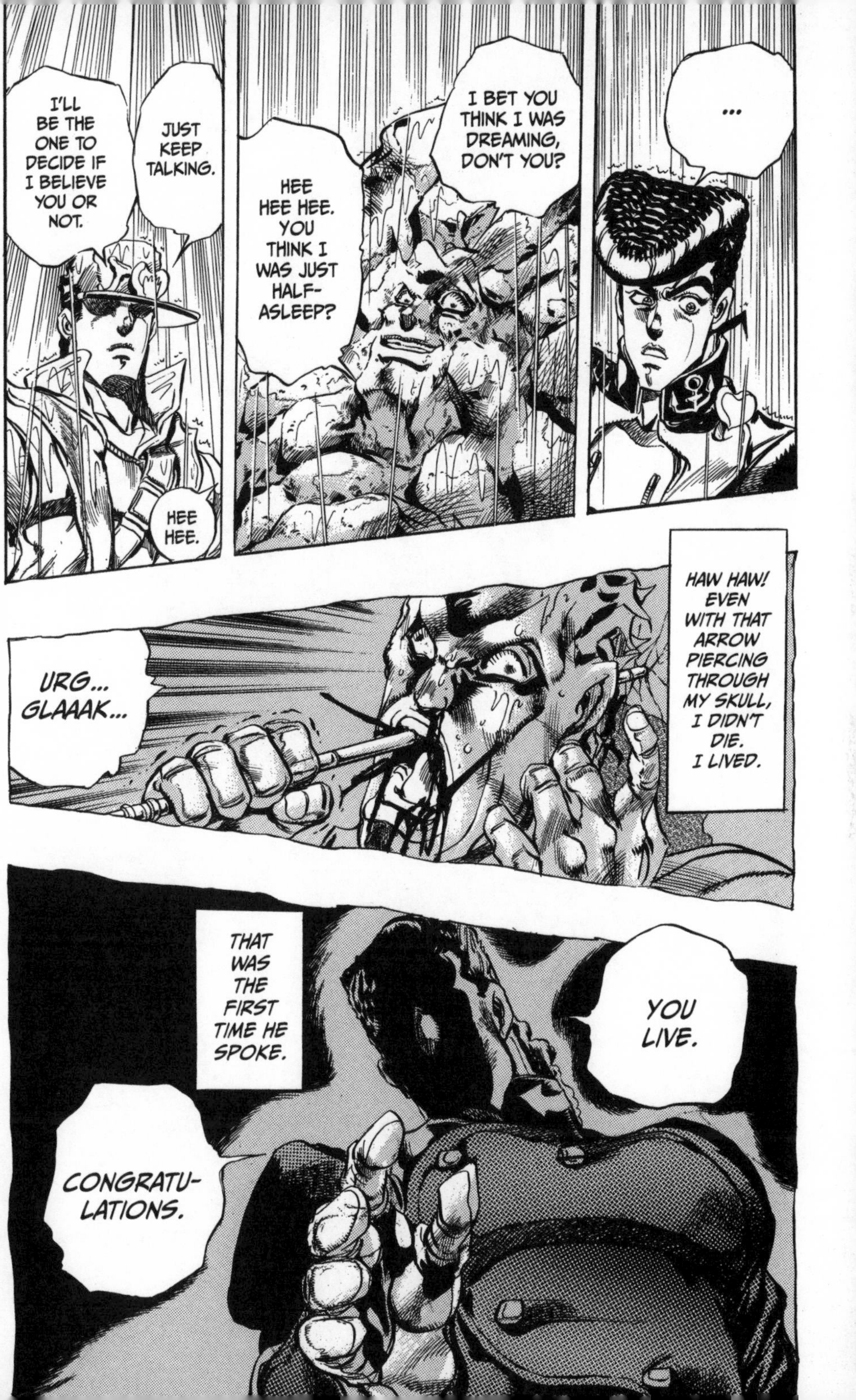
...
I BET YOU THINK I WAS DREAMING, DON'T YOU?
HEE HEE HEE. YOU THINK I WAS JUST HALF-ASLEEP?
JUST KEEP TALKING.
I'LL BE THE ONE TO DECIDE IF I BELIEVE YOU OR NOT.
HEE HEE.
HAW HAW! EVEN WITH THAT ARROW PIERCING THROUGH MY SKULL, I DIDN'T DIE. I LIVED.
URG... GLAAAK...
THAT WAS THE FIRST TIME HE SPOKE.
YOU LIVE.
CONGRATU-LATIONS.

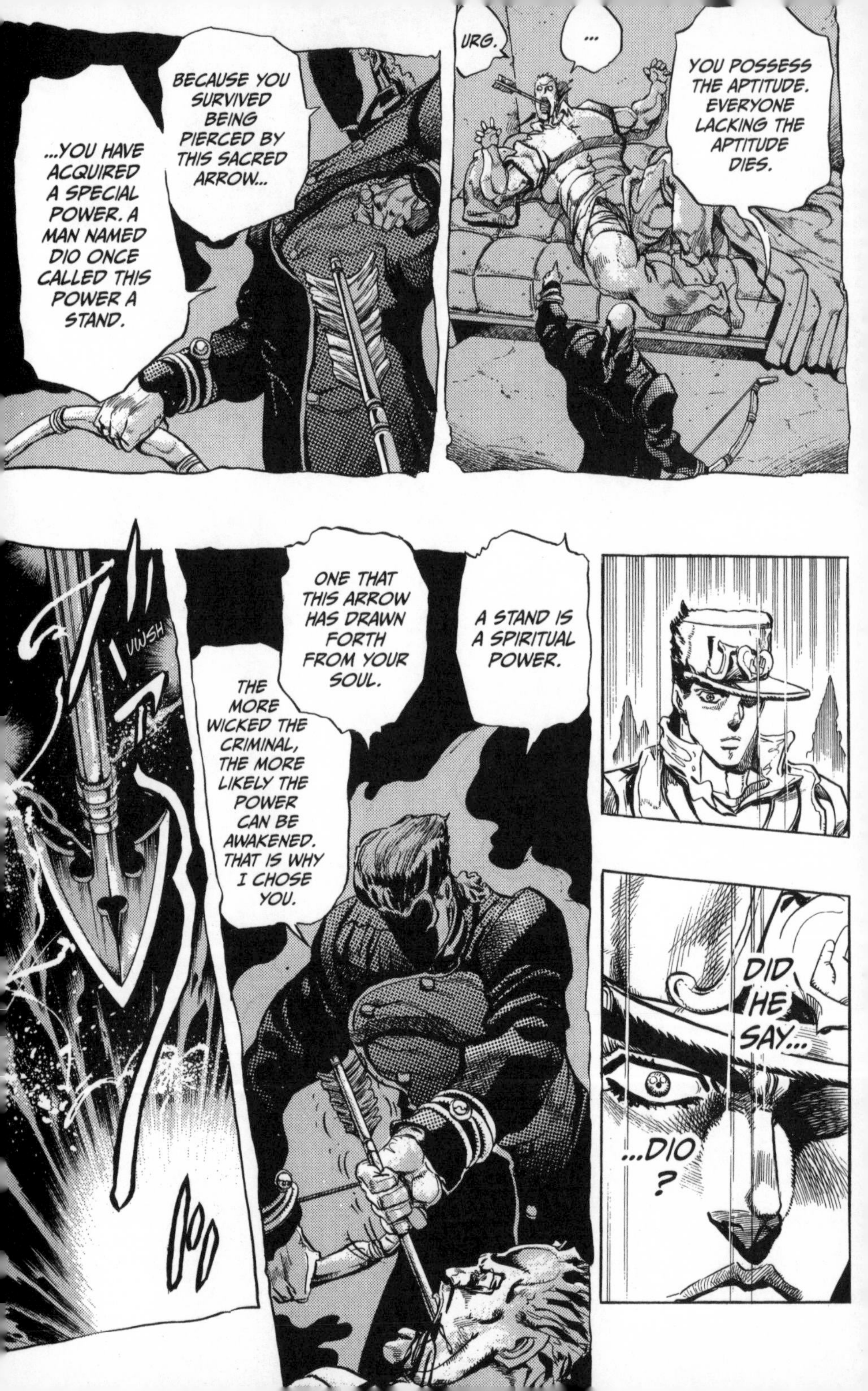

YOU POSSESS THE APTITUDE. EVERYONE LACKING THE APTITUDE DIES.
...
URG.
BECAUSE YOU SURVIVED BEING PIERCED BY THIS SACRED ARROW...
...YOU HAVE ACQUIRED A SPECIAL POWER. A MAN NAMED DIO ONCE CALLED THIS POWER A STAND.
DID HE SAY...
...DIO?
A STAND IS A SPIRITUAL POWER.
ONE THAT THIS ARROW HAS DRAWN FORTH FROM YOUR SOUL.
THE MORE WICKED THE CRIMINAL, THE MORE LIKELY THE POWER CAN BE AWAKENED. THAT IS WHY I CHOSE YOU.
VWSH

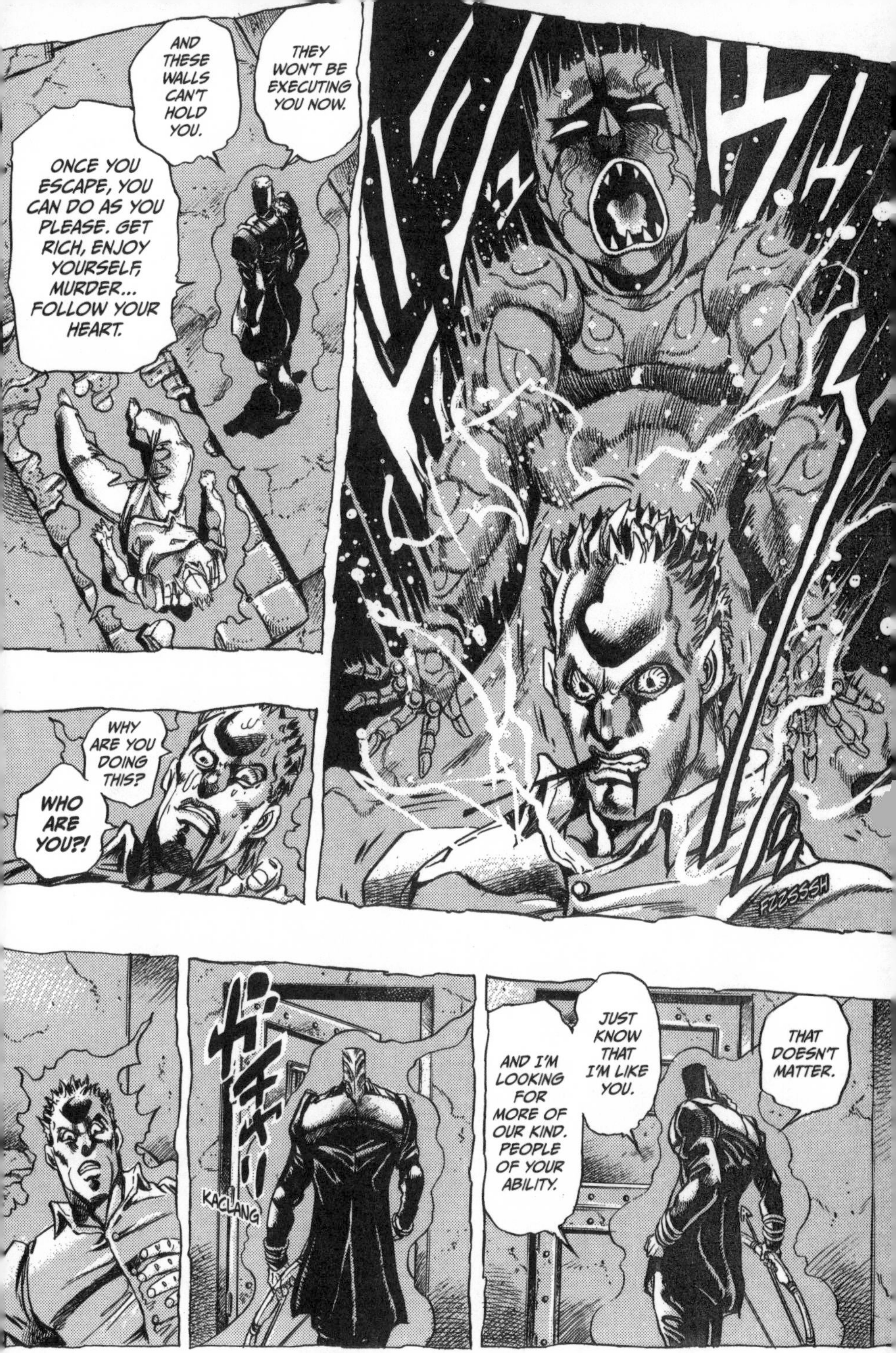
FZZSSSH
THEY WON'T BE EXECUTING YOU NOW.
AND THESE WALLS CAN'T HOLD YOU.
ONCE YOU ESCAPE, YOU CAN DO AS YOU PLEASE. GET RICH, ENJOY YOURSELF, MURDER... FOLLOW YOUR HEART.
WHY ARE YOU DOING THIS?
WHO ARE YOU?!
THAT DOESN'T MATTER.
JUST KNOW THAT I'M LIKE YOU.
AND I'M LOOKING FOR MORE OF OUR KIND. PEOPLE OF YOUR ABILITY.
KACLANG

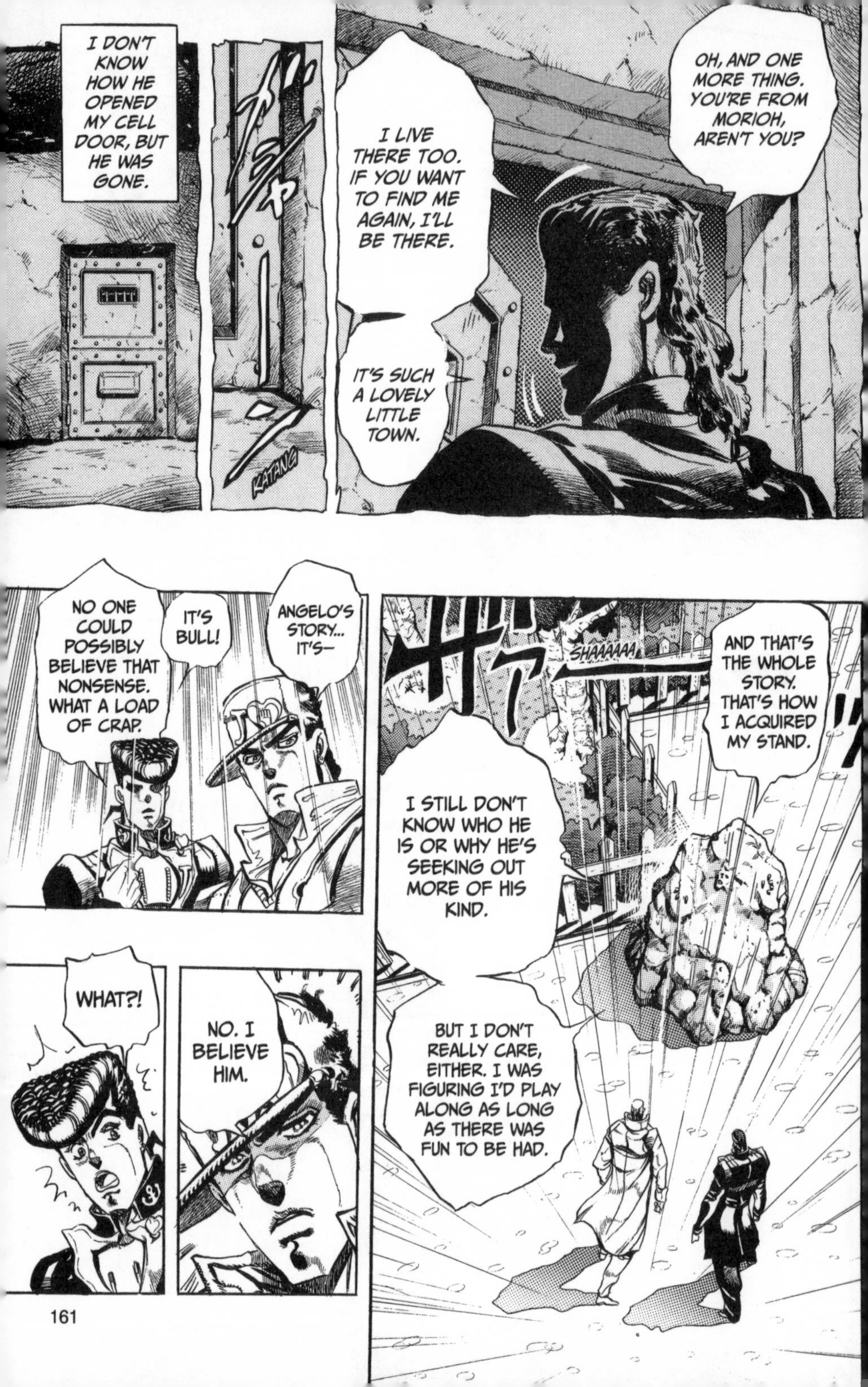
OH, AND ONE MORE THING. YOU'RE FROM MORIOH, AREN'T YOU?
I LIVE THERE TOO. IF YOU WANT TO FIND ME AGAIN, I'LL BE THERE.
IT'S SUCH A LOVELY LITTLE TOWN.
KATANG
I DON'T KNOW HOW HE OPENED MY CELL DOOR, BUT HE WAS GONE.
SHAAAAAA
AND THAT'S THE WHOLE STORY. THAT'S HOW I ACQUIRED MY STAND.
I STILL DON'T KNOW WHO HE IS OR WHY HE'S SEEKING OUT MORE OF HIS KIND.
BUT I DON'T REALLY CARE, EITHER. I WAS FIGURING I'D PLAY ALONG AS LONG AS THERE WAS FUN TO BE HAD.
ANGELO'S STORY... IT'S—
IT'S BULL!
NO ONE COULD POSSIBLY BELIEVE THAT NONSENSE. WHAT A LOAD OF CRAP.
NO. I BELIEVE HIM.
WHAT?!

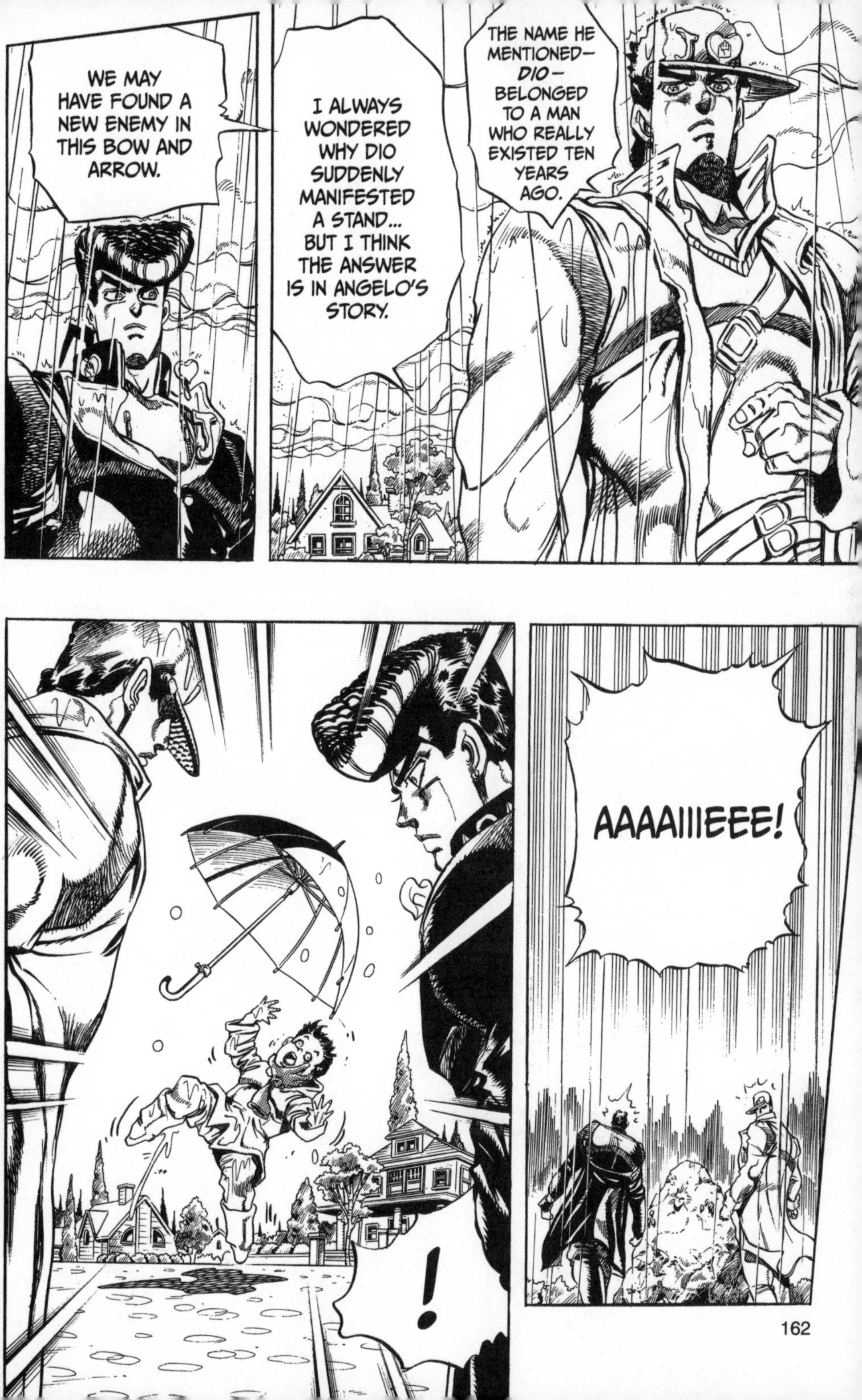
THE NAME HE MENTIONED— DIO— BELONGED TO A MAN WHO REALLY EXISTED TEN YEARS AGO.
I ALWAYS WONDERED WHY DIO SUDDENLY MANIFESTED A STAND... BUT I THINK THE ANSWER IS IN ANGELO'S STORY.
WE MAY HAVE FOUND A NEW ENEMY IN THIS BOW AND ARROW.
AAAAIIIEEE!
!

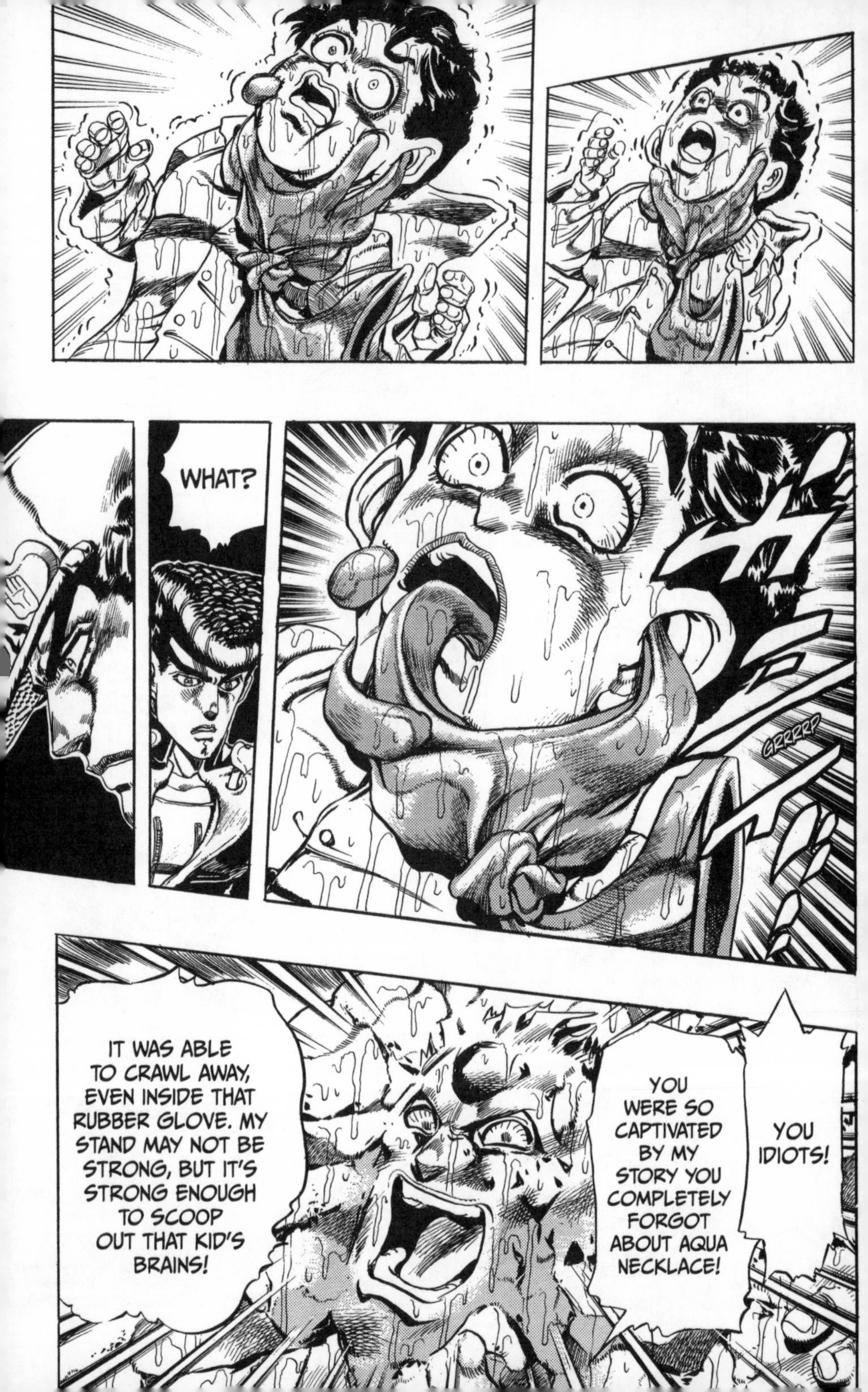
GRRRRP
WHAT?
YOU IDIOTS!
YOU WERE SO CAPTIVATED BY MY STORY YOU COMPLETELY FORGOT ABOUT AQUA NECKLACE!
IT WAS ABLE TO CRAWL AWAY, EVEN INSIDE THAT RUBBER GLOVE. MY STAND MAY NOT BE STRONG, BUT IT'S STRONG ENOUGH TO SCOOP OUT THAT KID'S BRAINS!

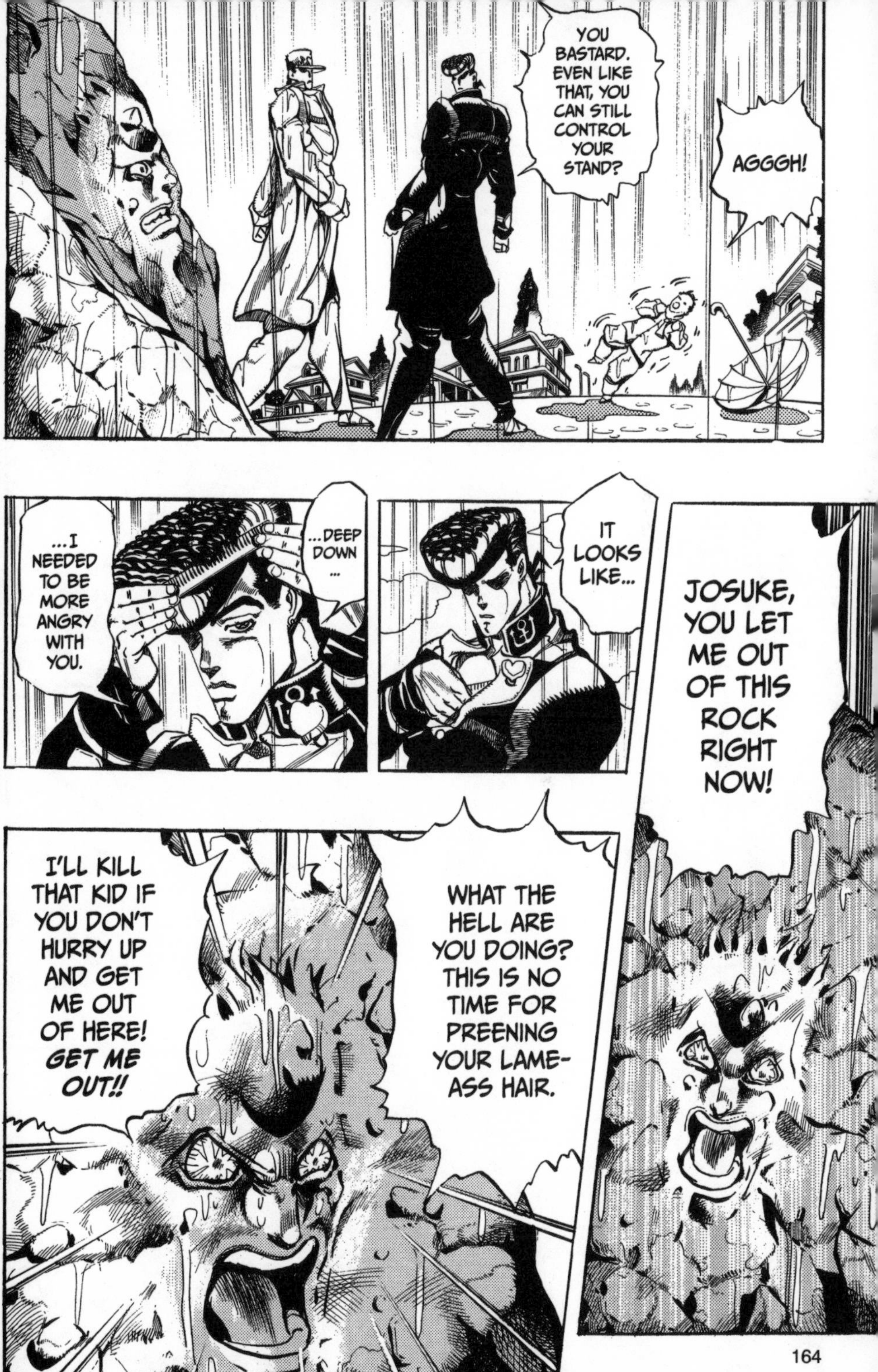
YOU BASTARD. EVEN LIKE THAT, YOU CAN STILL CONTROL YOUR STAND?
AGGGH!
JOSUKE, YOU LET ME OUT OF THIS ROCK RIGHT NOW!
IT LOOKS LIKE...
...DEEP DOWN ...
...I NEEDED TO BE MORE ANGRY WITH YOU.
WHAT THE HELL ARE YOU DOING? THIS IS NO TIME FOR PREENING YOUR LAME-ASS HAIR.
I'LL KILL THAT KID IF YOU DON'T HURRY UP AND GET ME OUT OF HERE! *GET ME OUT!!*

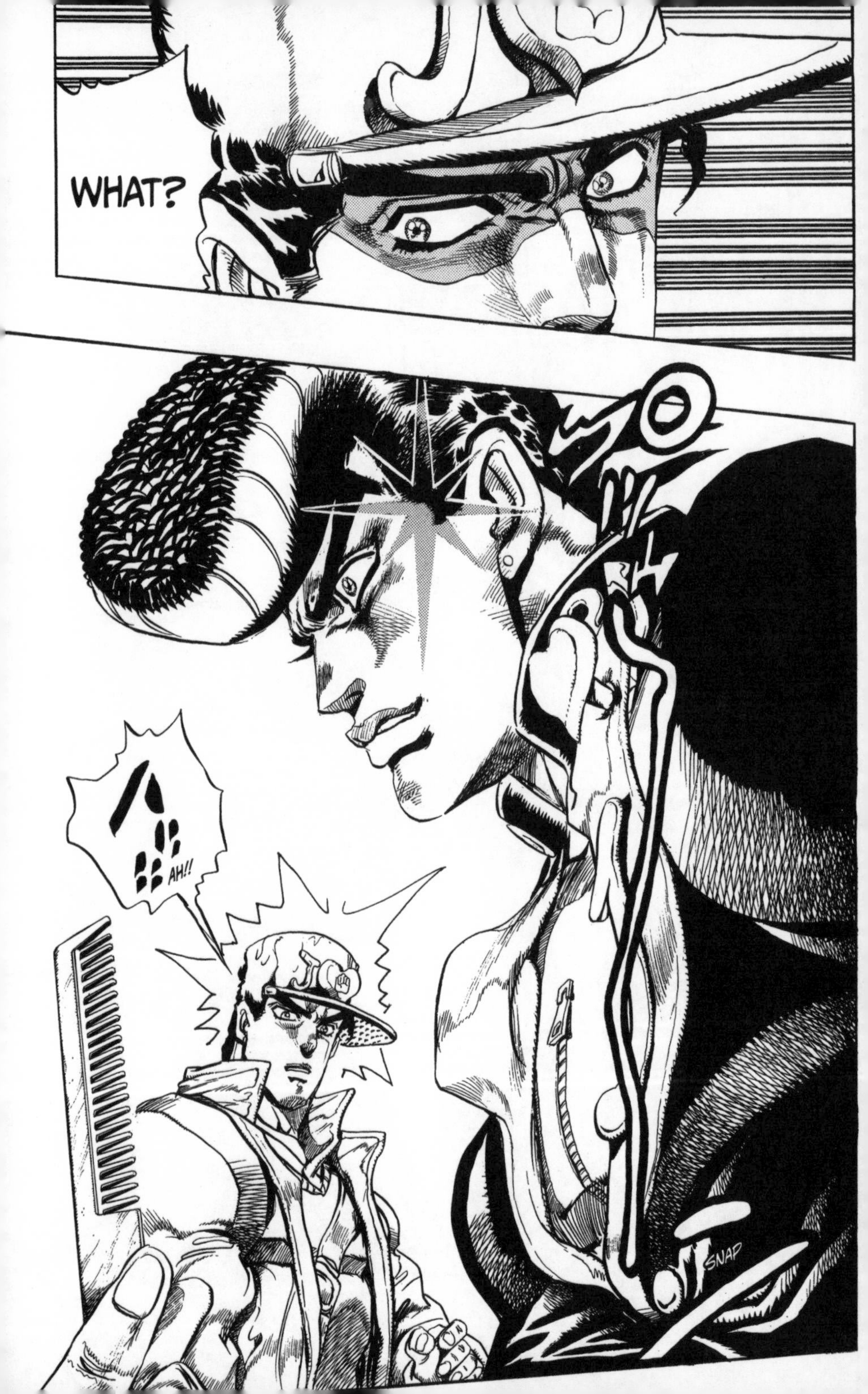
WHAT?
ハ!!
AH!!
SNAP

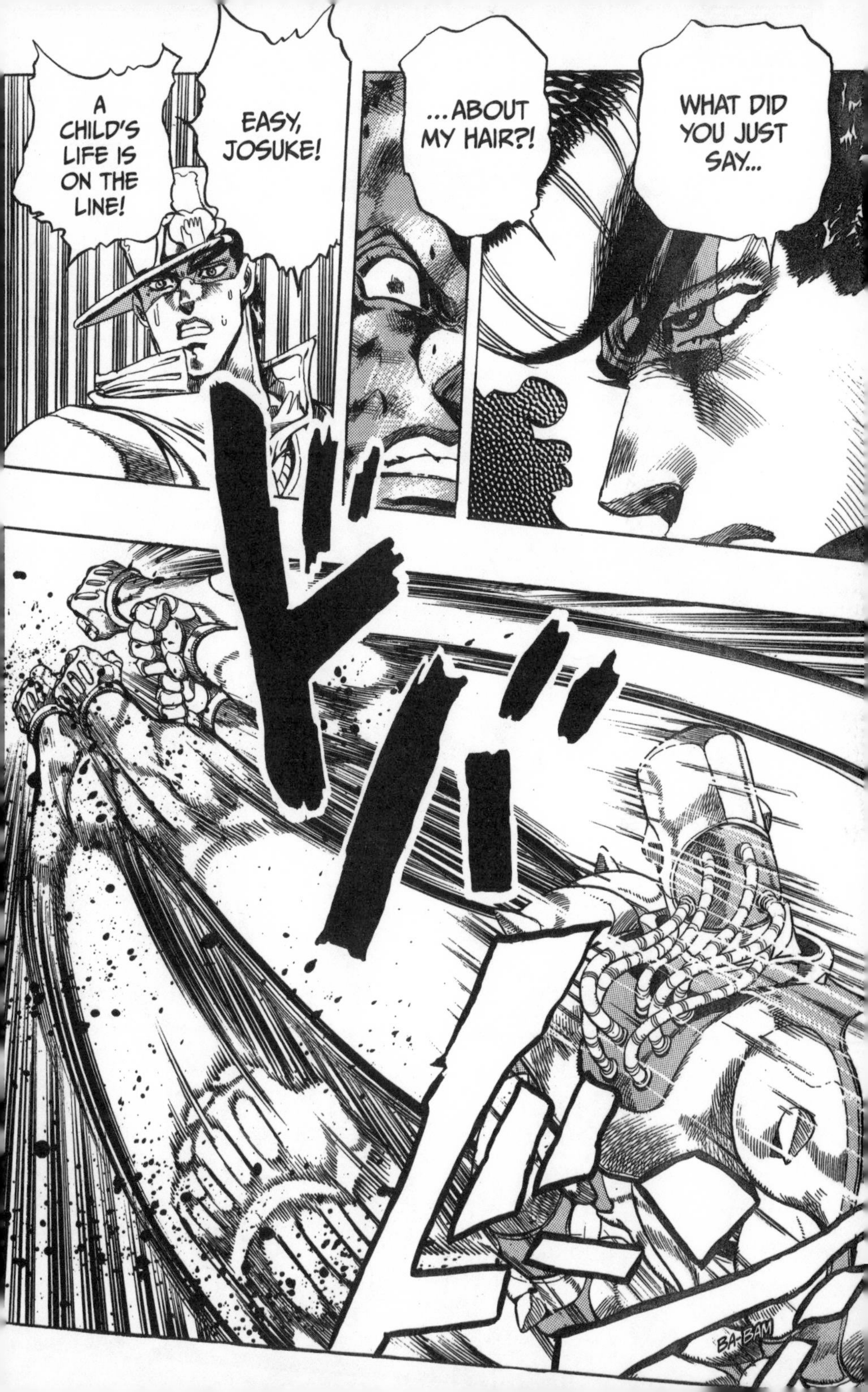
WHAT DID YOU JUST SAY...
...ABOUT MY HAIR?!
EASY, JOSUKE!
A CHILD'S LIFE IS ON THE LINE!
BA-BAM

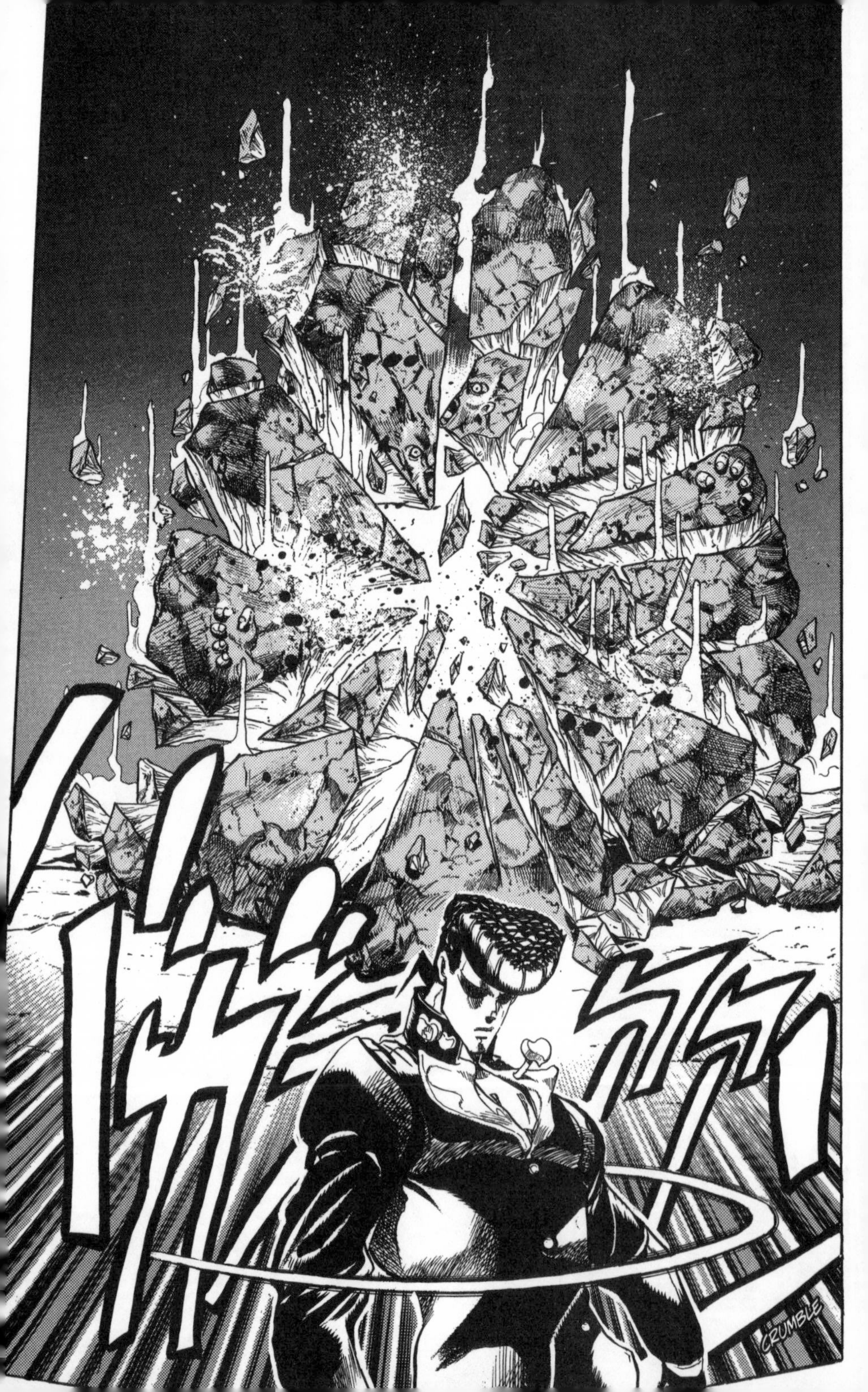
CRUMBLE

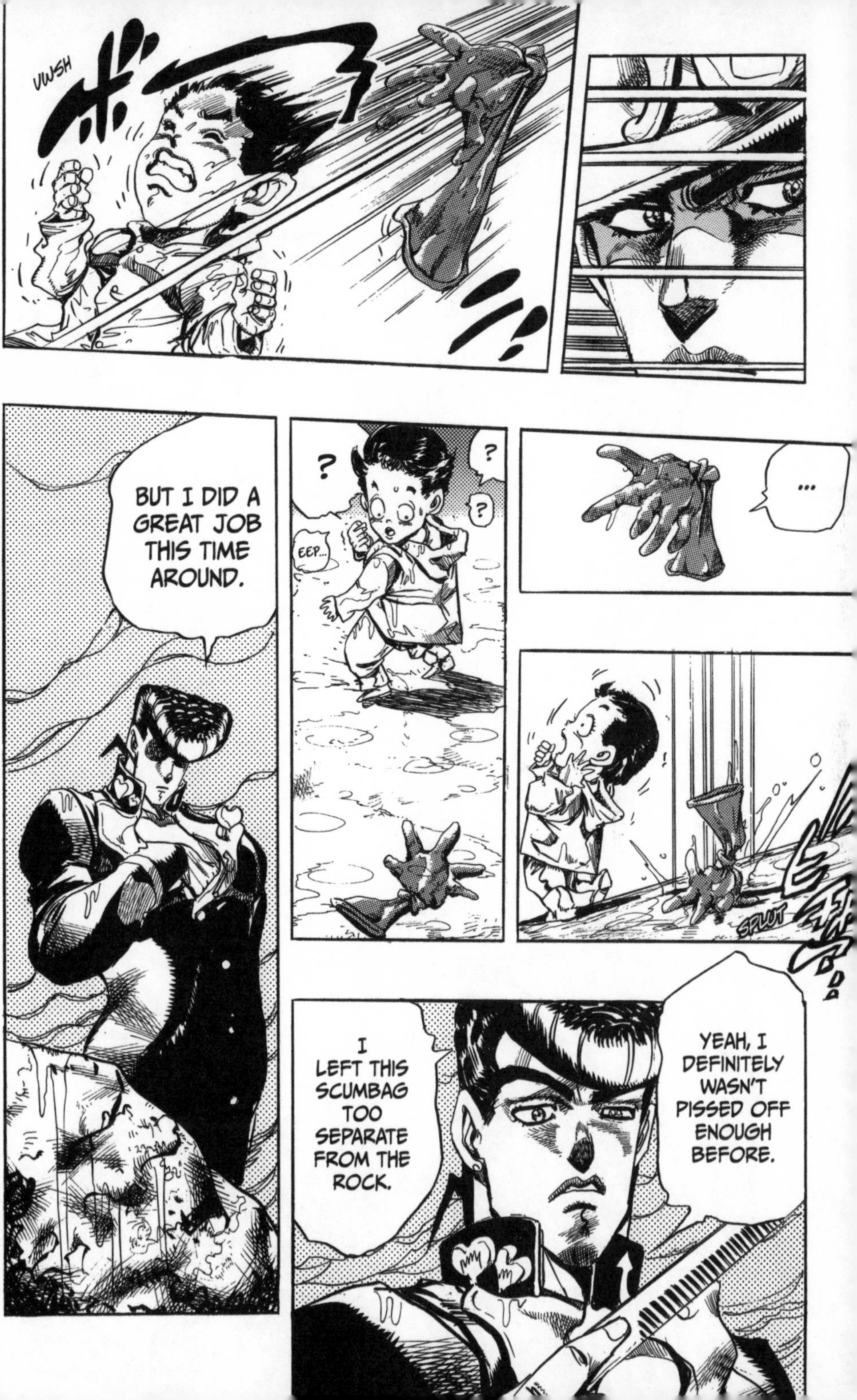
VWSH
...
SPLUT
?
?
EEP...
?
BUT I DID A GREAT JOB THIS TIME AROUND.
YEAH, I DEFINITELY WASN'T PISSED OFF ENOUGH BEFORE.
I LEFT THIS SCUMBAG TOO SEPARATE FROM THE ROCK.

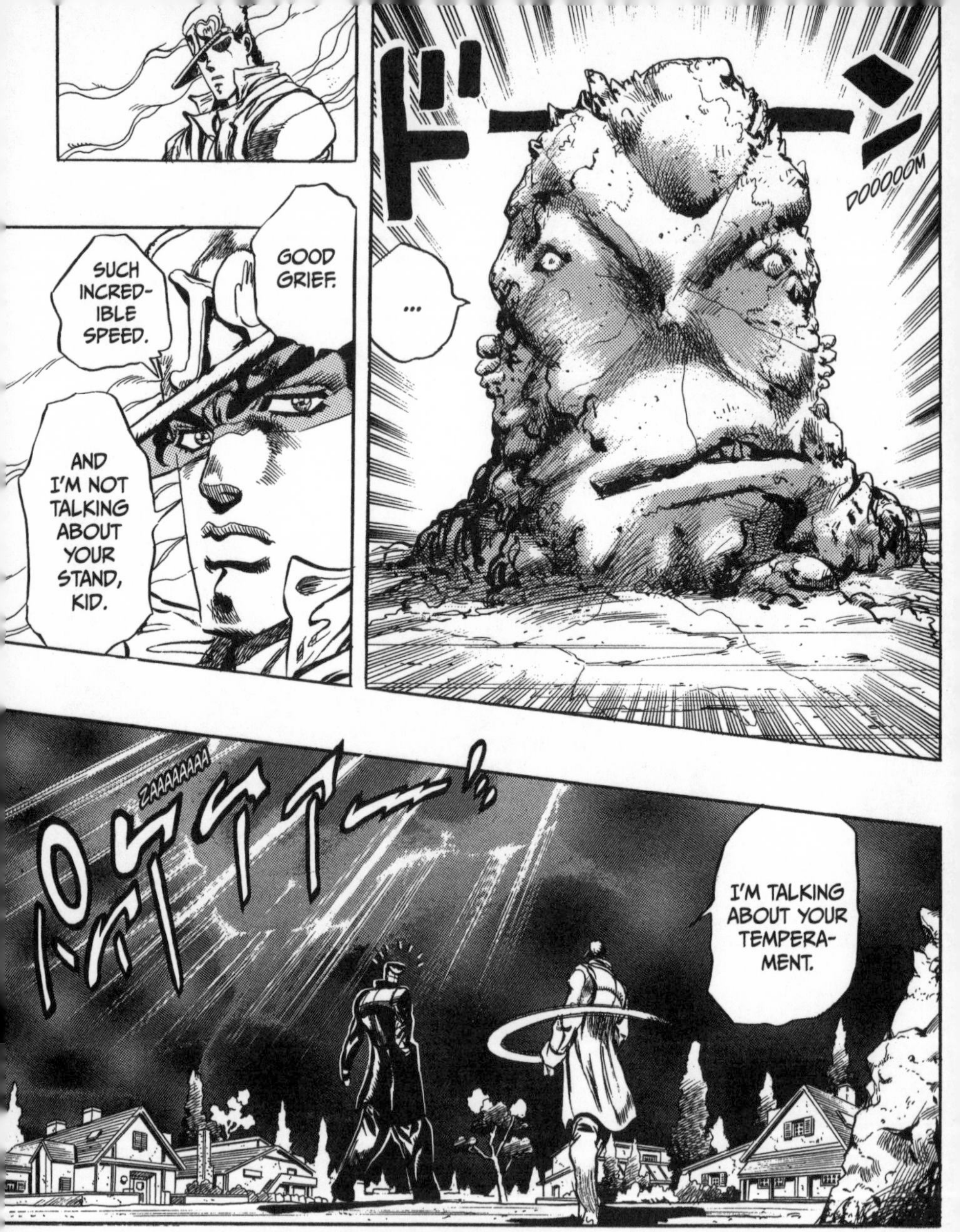
DOOOOOM
...
GOOD GRIEF.
SUCH INCRED-IBLE SPEED.
AND I'M NOT TALKING ABOUT YOUR STAND, KID.
I'M TALKING ABOUT YOUR TEMPERA-MENT.
ZAAAAAAAA

JOSUKE HIGASHIKATA

STAND NAME:

(NAMED BY JOTARO KUJO)

SHINING DIAMOND

ABILITY: CAN REPAIR THINGS THAT HAVE BEEN BROKEN, BUT IF JOSUKE IS ANGRY, HIS STAND MIGHT NOT PUT THINGS BACK EXACTLY HOW THEY WERE.

(1) KOTODAI
(2)
WHERE JOSUKE AND JOTARO MET
TRAIN STATION
(3)
(1)
CEMETERY
DOWNTOWN
MORIOH GRAND HOTEL
COMMERCIAL AREA
(2)
JOZENJI
WHERE ANGELO'S STAND WAS FIRST ENCOUNTERED
JOSUKE'S HOUSE
ANGELO'S ROCK
(3)
(4)

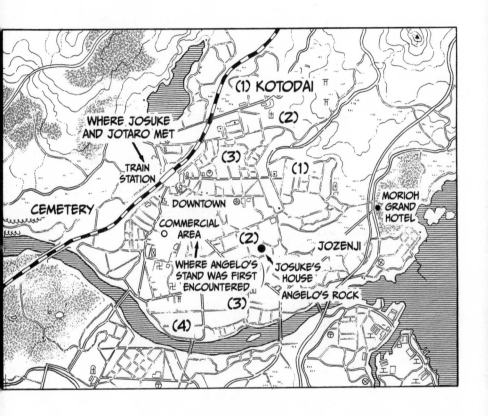

CHAPTER 9 ★ THE NIJIMURA BROTHERS, PART 1

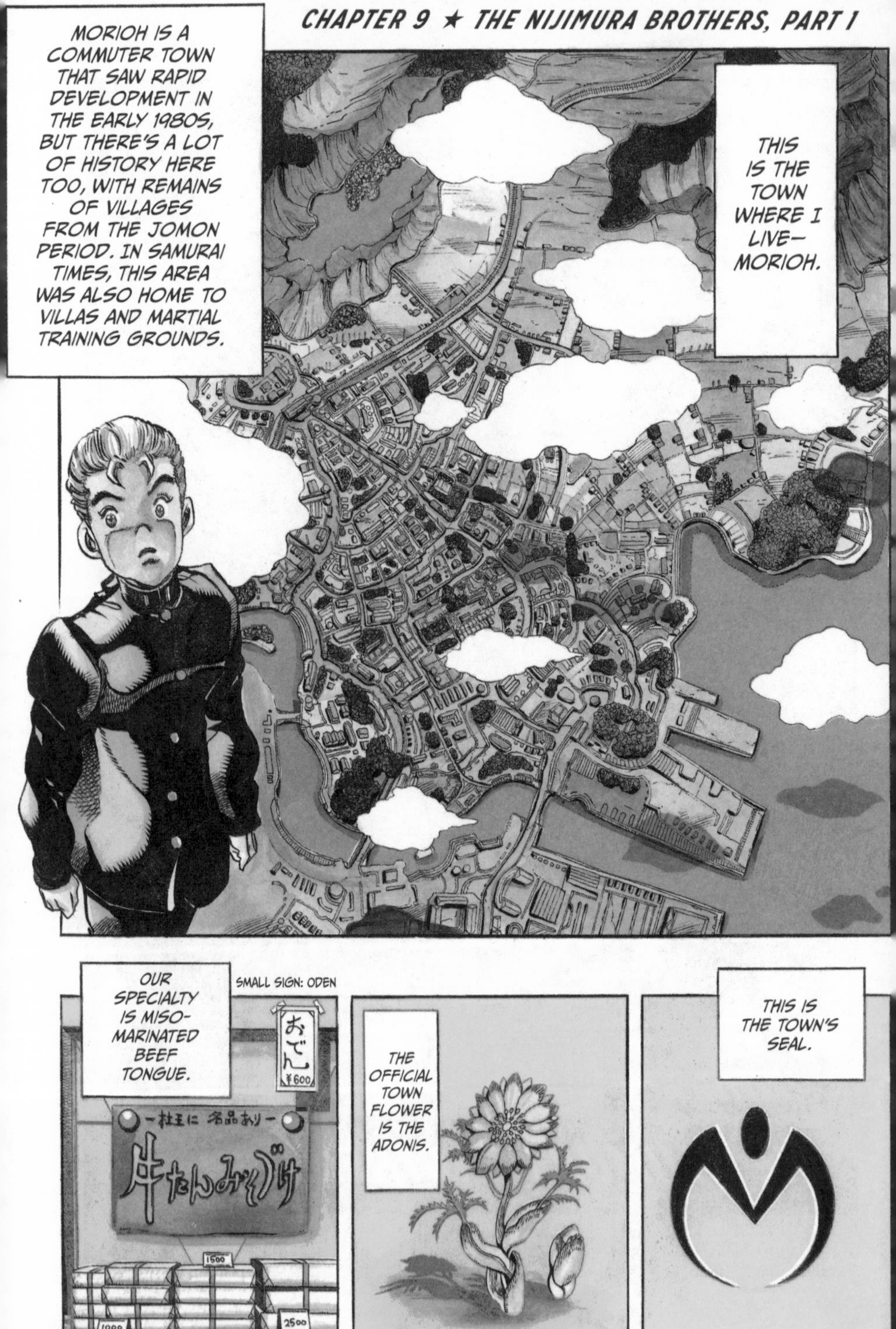
THIS IS THE TOWN WHERE I LIVE—MORIOH.
MORIOH IS A COMMUTER TOWN THAT SAW RAPID DEVELOPMENT IN THE EARLY 1980S, BUT THERE'S A LOT OF HISTORY HERE TOO, WITH REMAINS OF VILLAGES FROM THE JOMON PERIOD. IN SAMURAI TIMES, THIS AREA WAS ALSO HOME TO VILLAS AND MARTIAL TRAINING GROUNDS.
THIS IS THE TOWN'S SEAL.
THE OFFICIAL TOWN FLOWER IS THE ADONIS.
OUR SPECIALTY IS MISO-MARINATED BEEF TONGUE.
SMALL SIGN: ODEN
おでん
¥600
一杜王に 名品あり一
牛たんみそづけ
1500
1000
2500
LARGE SIGN: MORIOH'S FAMOUS MISO-MARINATED BEEF TONGUE

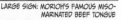

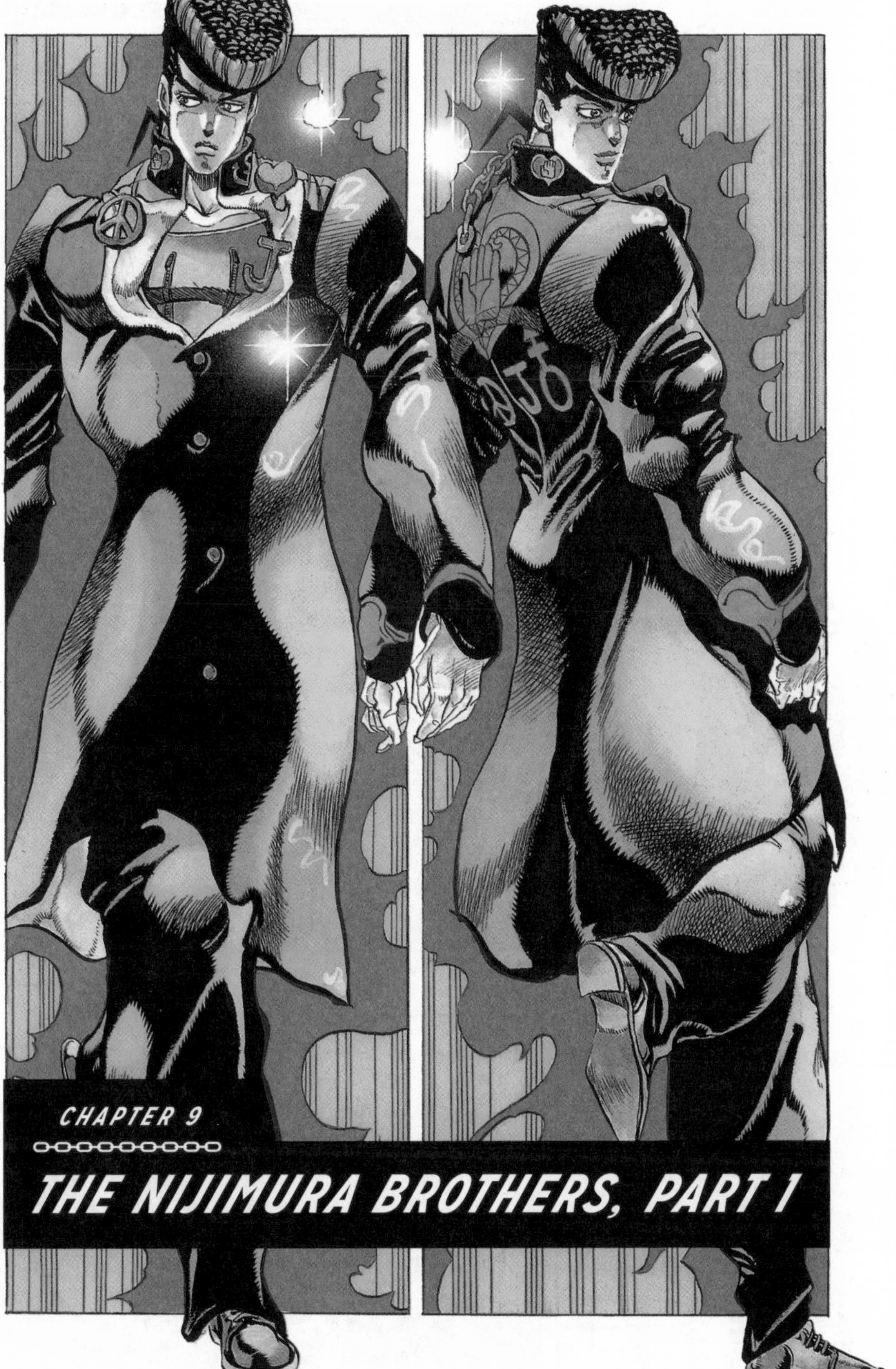

CHAPTER 9

THE NIJIMURA BROTHERS, PART 1

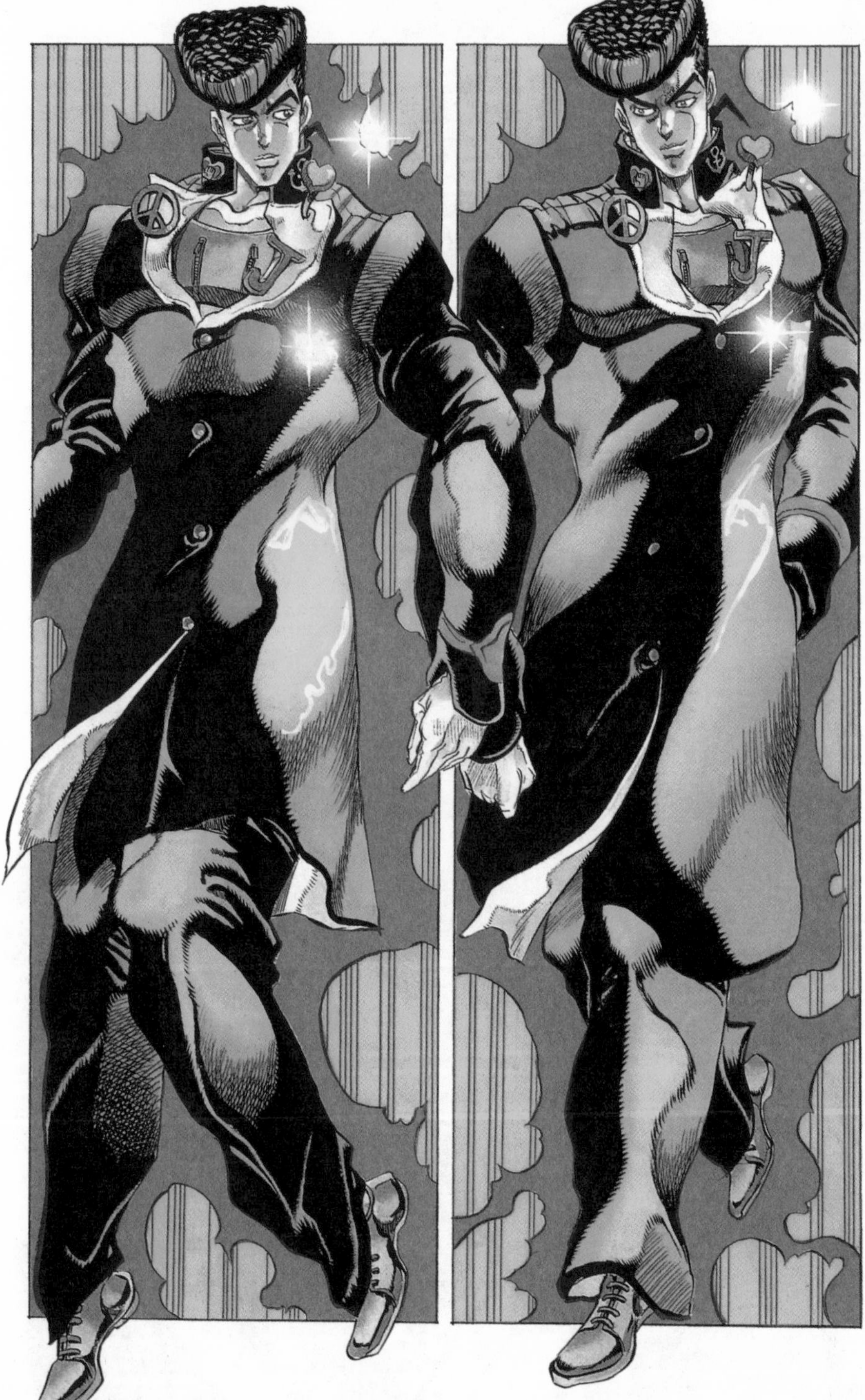

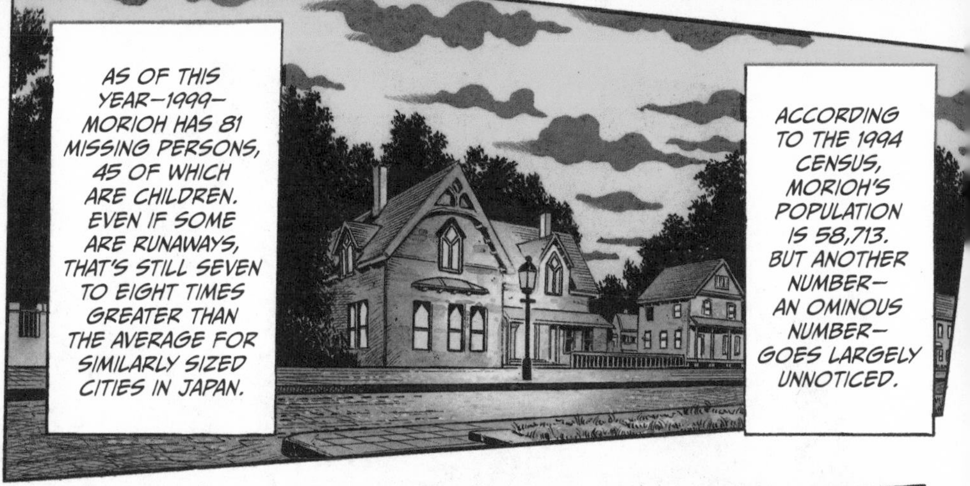
ACCORDING TO THE 1994 CENSUS, MORIOH'S POPULATION IS 58,713. BUT ANOTHER NUMBER— AN OMINOUS NUMBER— GOES LARGELY UNNOTICED.
AS OF THIS YEAR—1999— MORIOH HAS 81 MISSING PERSONS, 45 OF WHICH ARE CHILDREN. EVEN IF SOME ARE RUNAWAYS, THAT'S STILL SEVEN TO EIGHT TIMES GREATER THAN THE AVERAGE FOR SIMILARLY SIZED CITIES IN JAPAN.
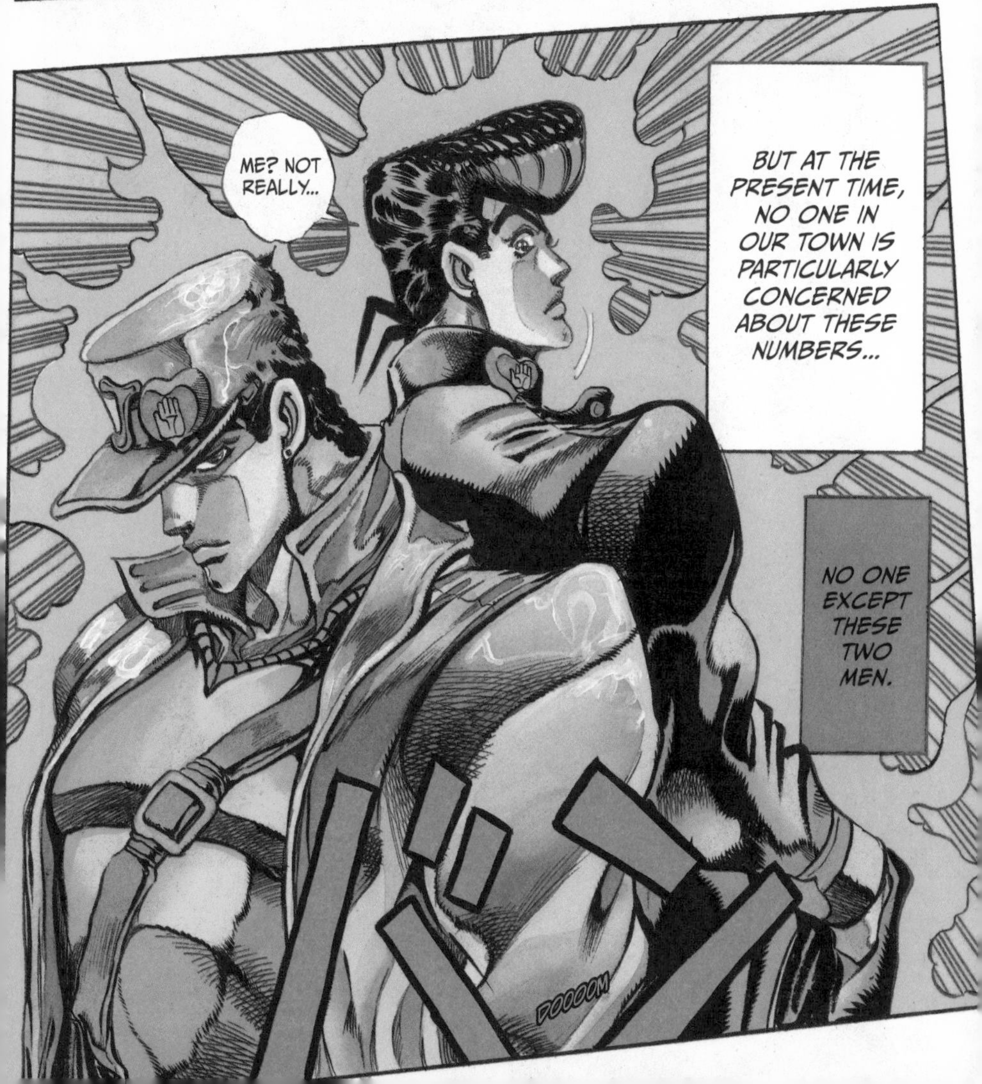
BUT AT THE PRESENT TIME, NO ONE IN OUR TOWN IS PARTICULARLY CONCERNED ABOUT THESE NUMBERS...
ME? NOT REALLY...
NO ONE EXCEPT THESE TWO MEN.
DOOOOM

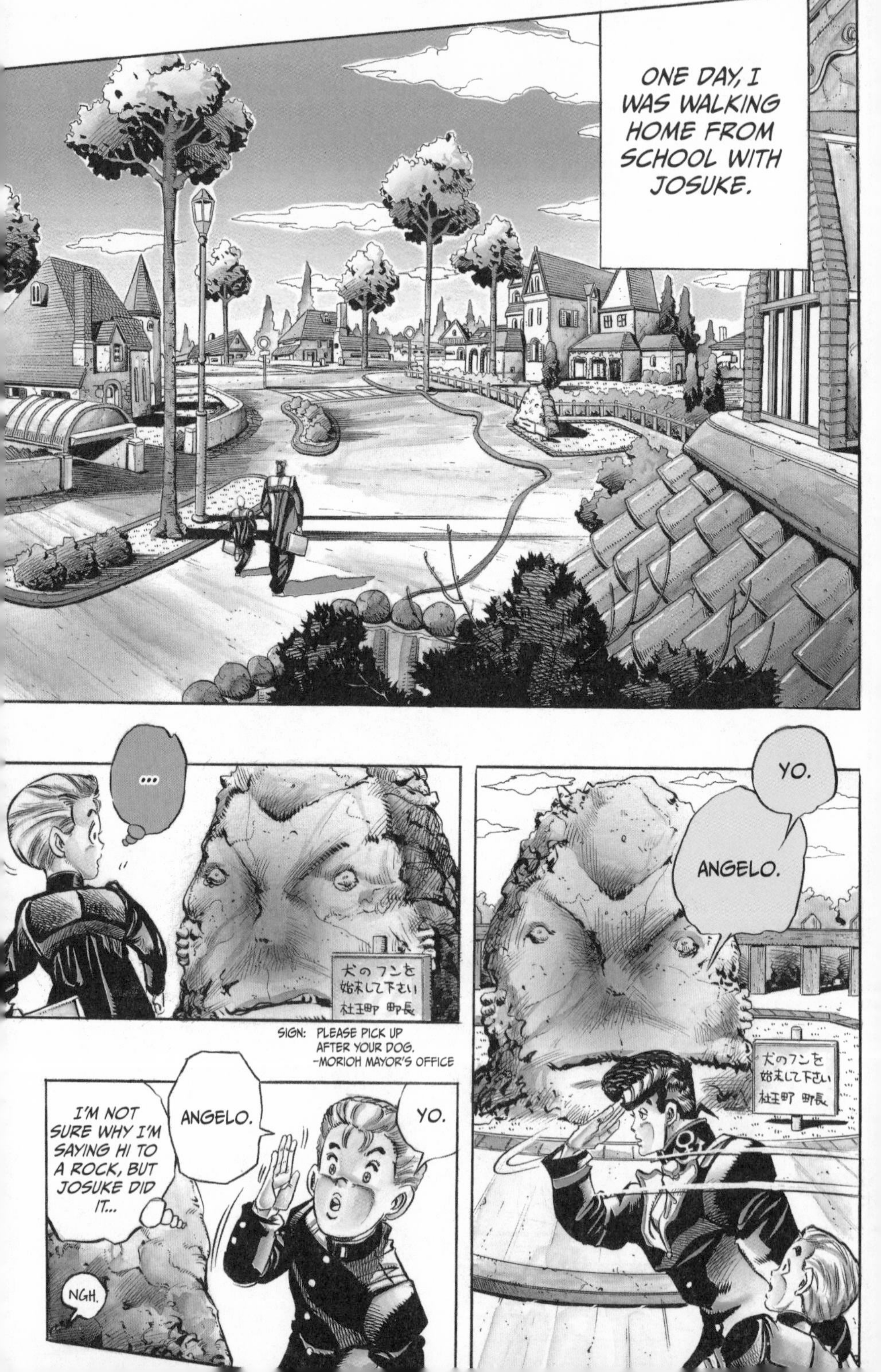
ONE DAY, I WAS WALKING HOME FROM SCHOOL WITH JOSUKE.
YO.
ANGELO.
犬のフンを始末して下さい 杜王町 町長
...
犬のフンを始末して下さい 杜王町 町長
SIGN: PLEASE PICK UP AFTER YOUR DOG. -MORIOH MAYOR'S OFFICE
YO.
ANGELO.
I'M NOT SURE WHY I'M SAYING HI TO A ROCK, BUT JOSUKE DID IT...
NGH.

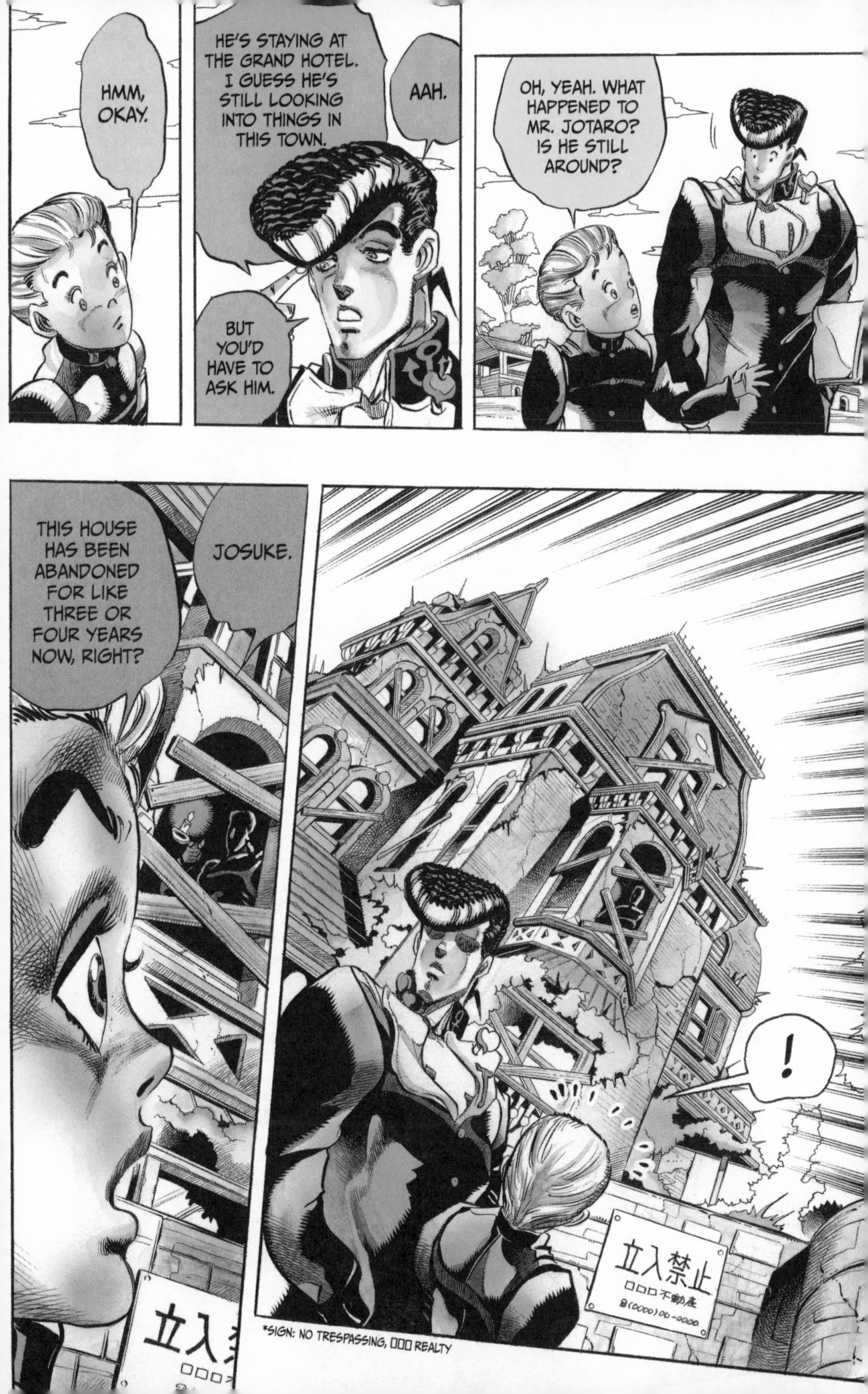
OH, YEAH. WHAT HAPPENED TO MR. JOTARO? IS HE STILL AROUND?
AAH.
HE'S STAYING AT THE GRAND HOTEL. I GUESS HE'S STILL LOOKING INTO THINGS IN THIS TOWN.
BUT YOU'D HAVE TO ASK HIM.
HMM, OKAY.
!
立入禁止
□□□不動産
JOSUKE.
THIS HOUSE HAS BEEN ABANDONED FOR LIKE THREE OR FOUR YEARS NOW, RIGHT?
立入
□□□
*SIGN: NO TRESPASSING, □□□ REALTY

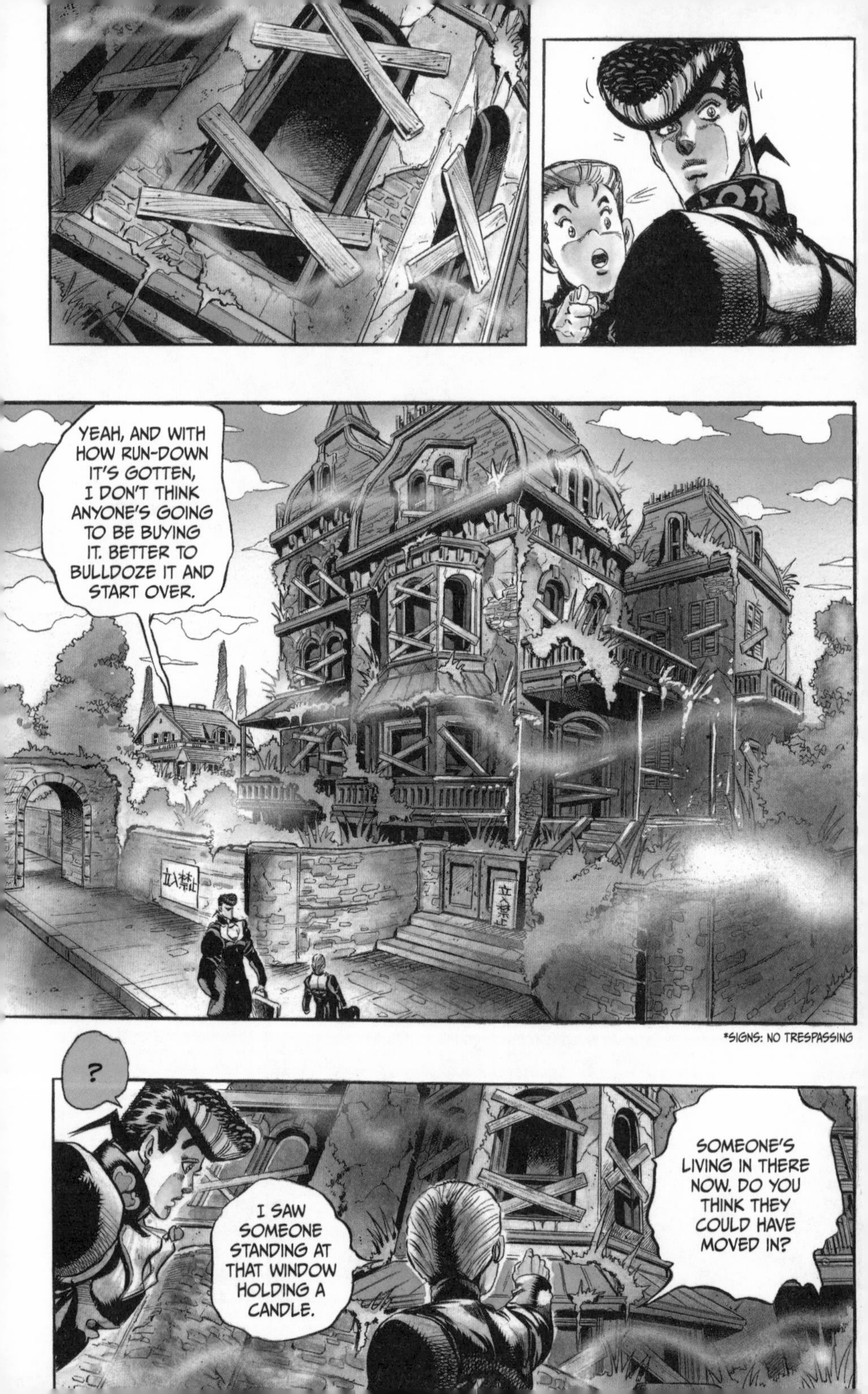
YEAH, AND WITH HOW RUN-DOWN IT'S GOTTEN, I DON'T THINK ANYONE'S GOING TO BE BUYING IT. BETTER TO BULLDOZE IT AND START OVER.
立入禁止
立入禁止
?
I SAW SOMEONE STANDING AT THAT WINDOW HOLDING A CANDLE.
SOMEONE'S LIVING IN THERE NOW. DO YOU THINK THEY COULD HAVE MOVED IN?
*SIGNS: NO TRESPASSING

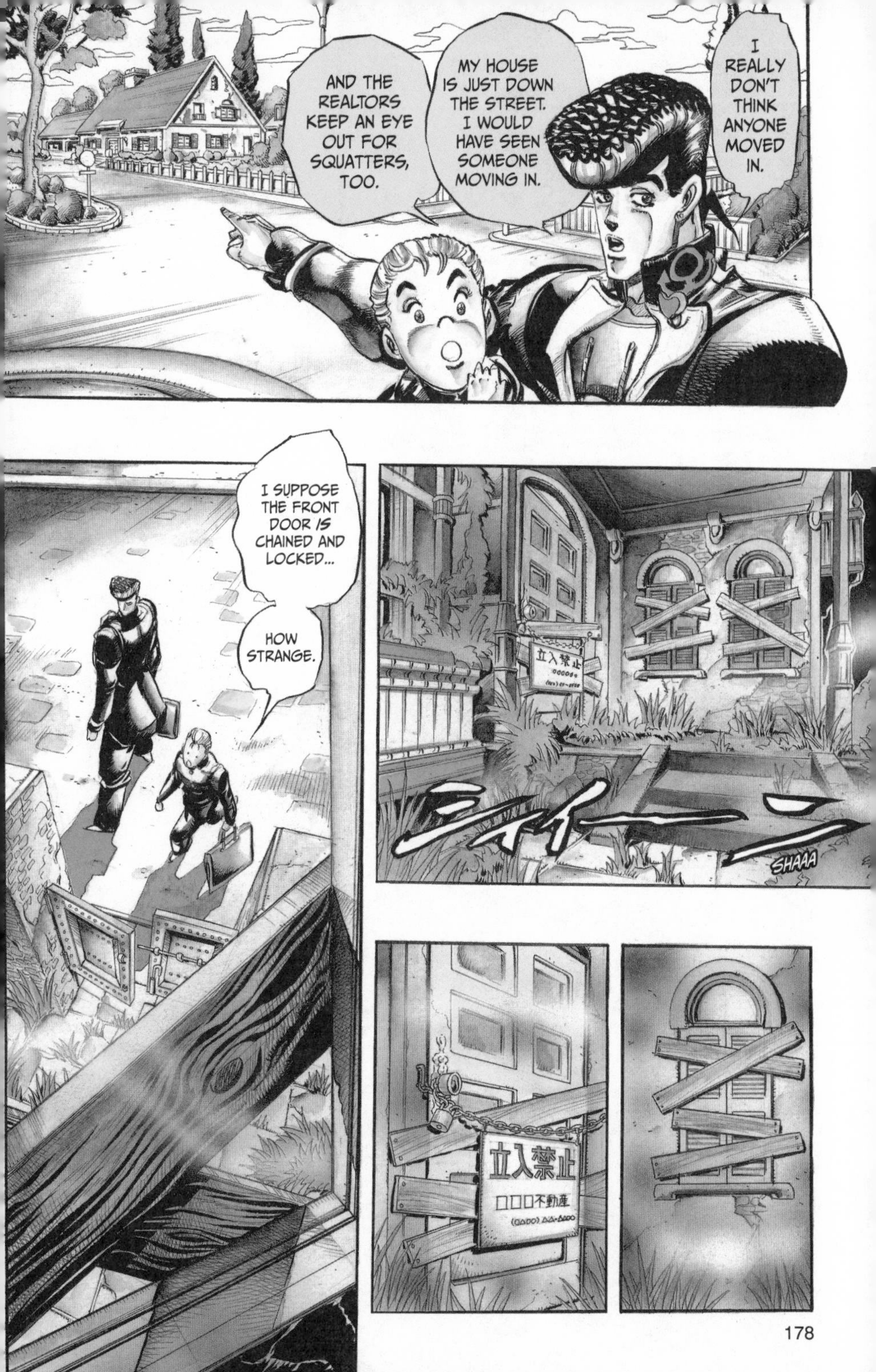
I REALLY DON'T THINK ANYONE MOVED IN.
MY HOUSE IS JUST DOWN THE STREET. I WOULD HAVE SEEN SOMEONE MOVING IN.
AND THE REALTORS KEEP AN EYE OUT FOR SQUATTERS, TOO.
立入禁止
SHAAA
立入禁止
□□□不動産
I SUPPOSE THE FRONT DOOR *IS* CHAINED AND LOCKED...
HOW STRANGE.

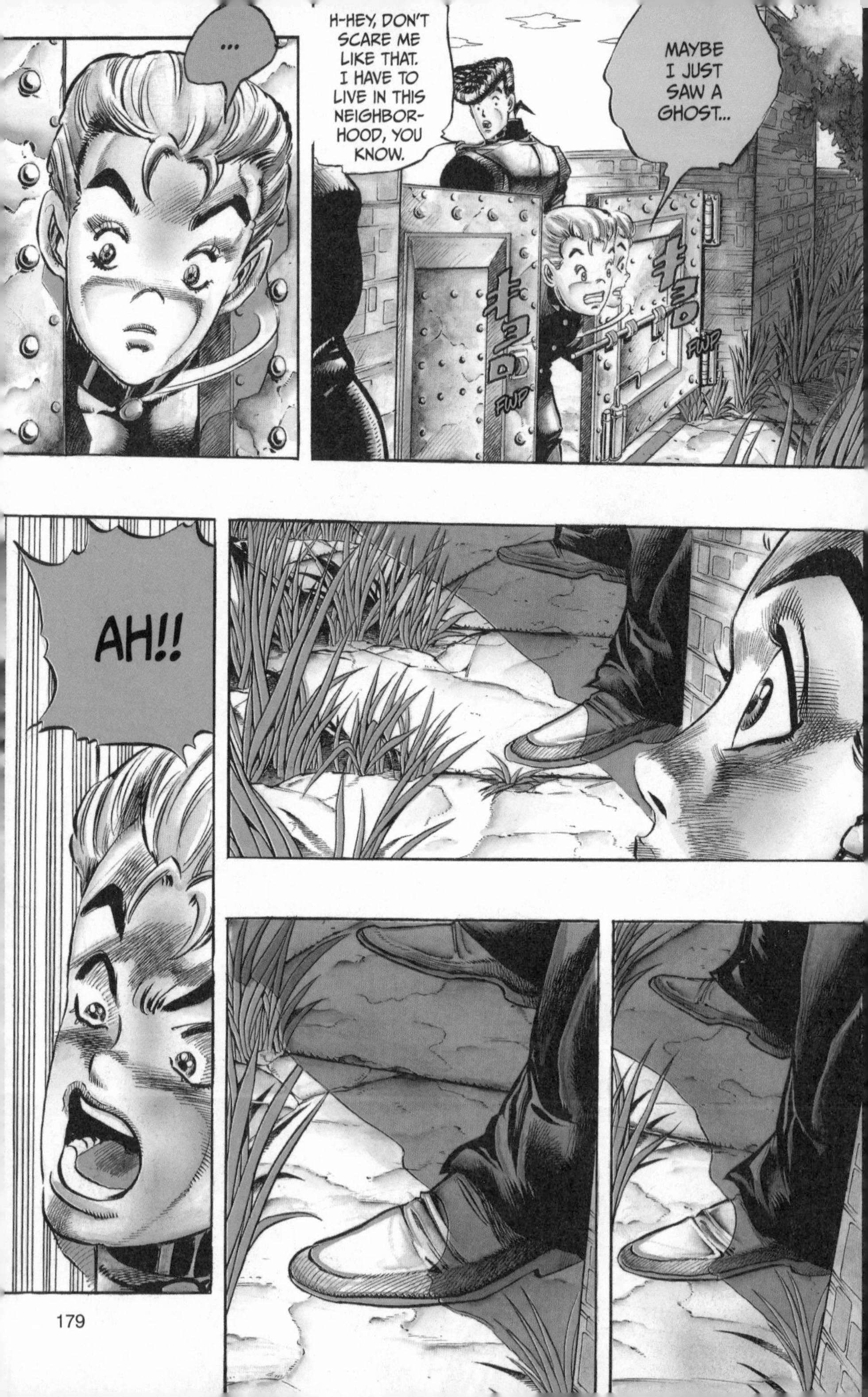
MAYBE I JUST SAW A GHOST...
H-HEY, DON'T SCARE ME LIKE THAT. I HAVE TO LIVE IN THIS NEIGHBOR-HOOD, YOU KNOW.
FWP
FWP
...
AH!!

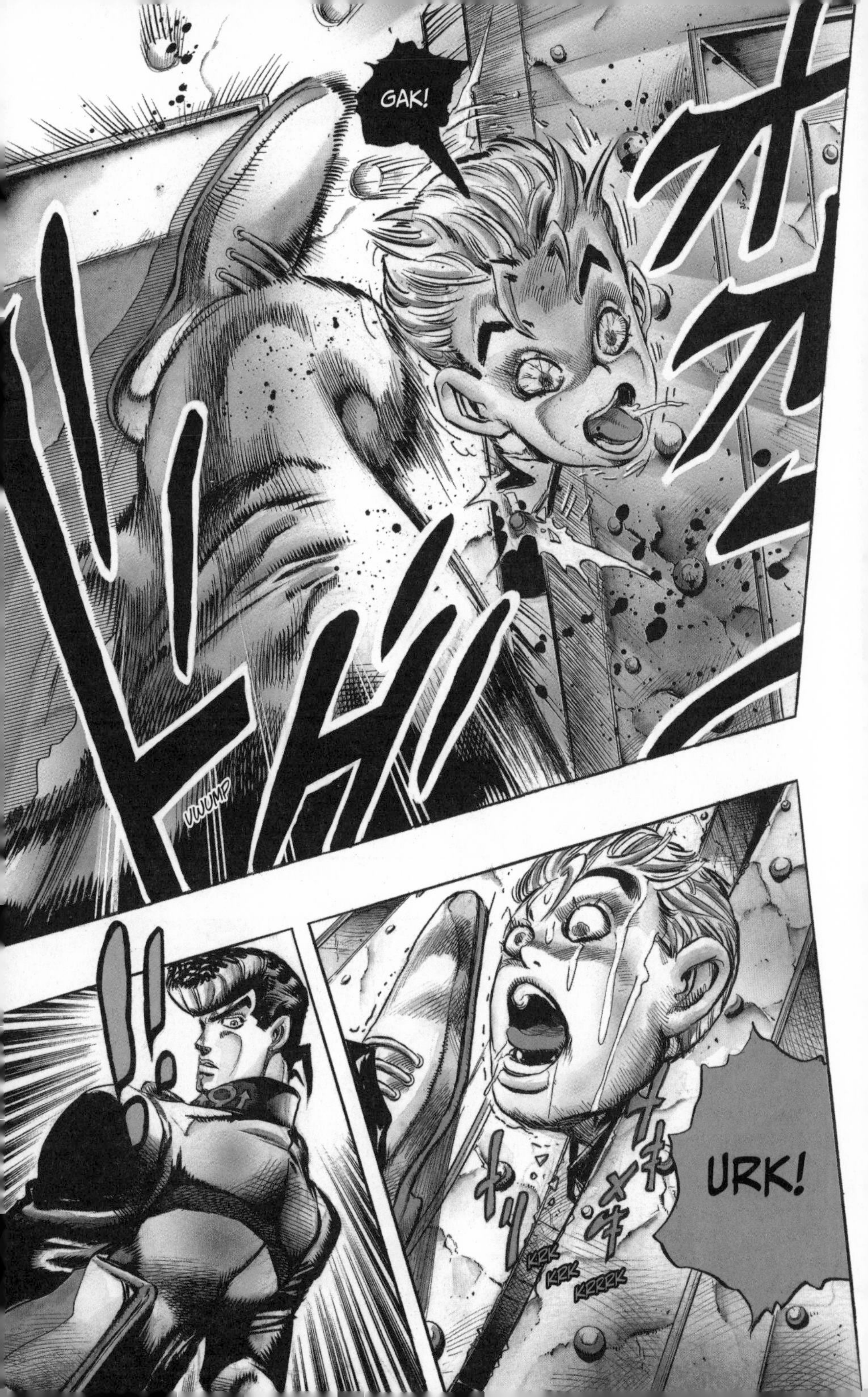
GAK!
VWUMP
URK!
KRK
KRK
KRRRK

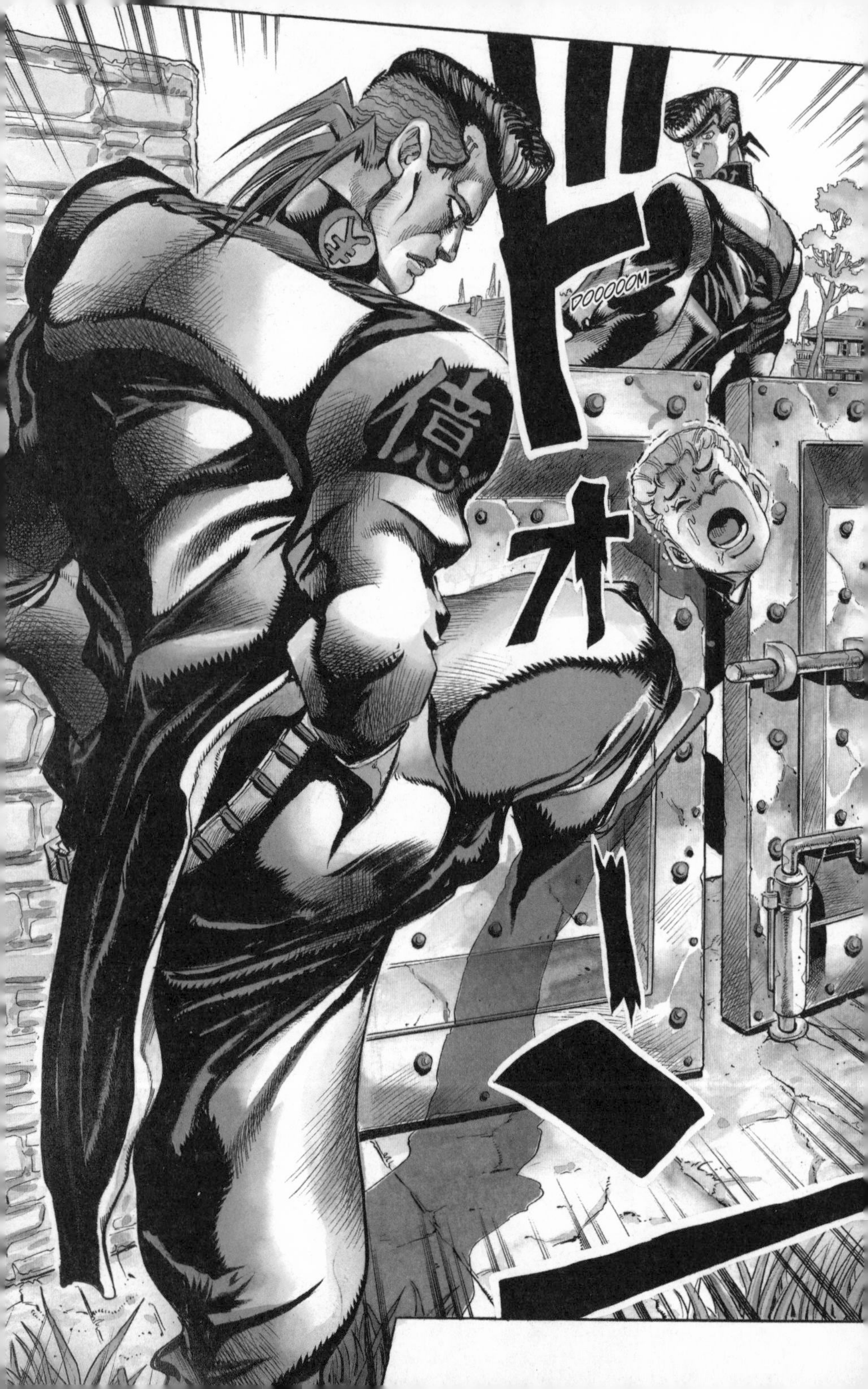
ドオオーン
DOOOOOM

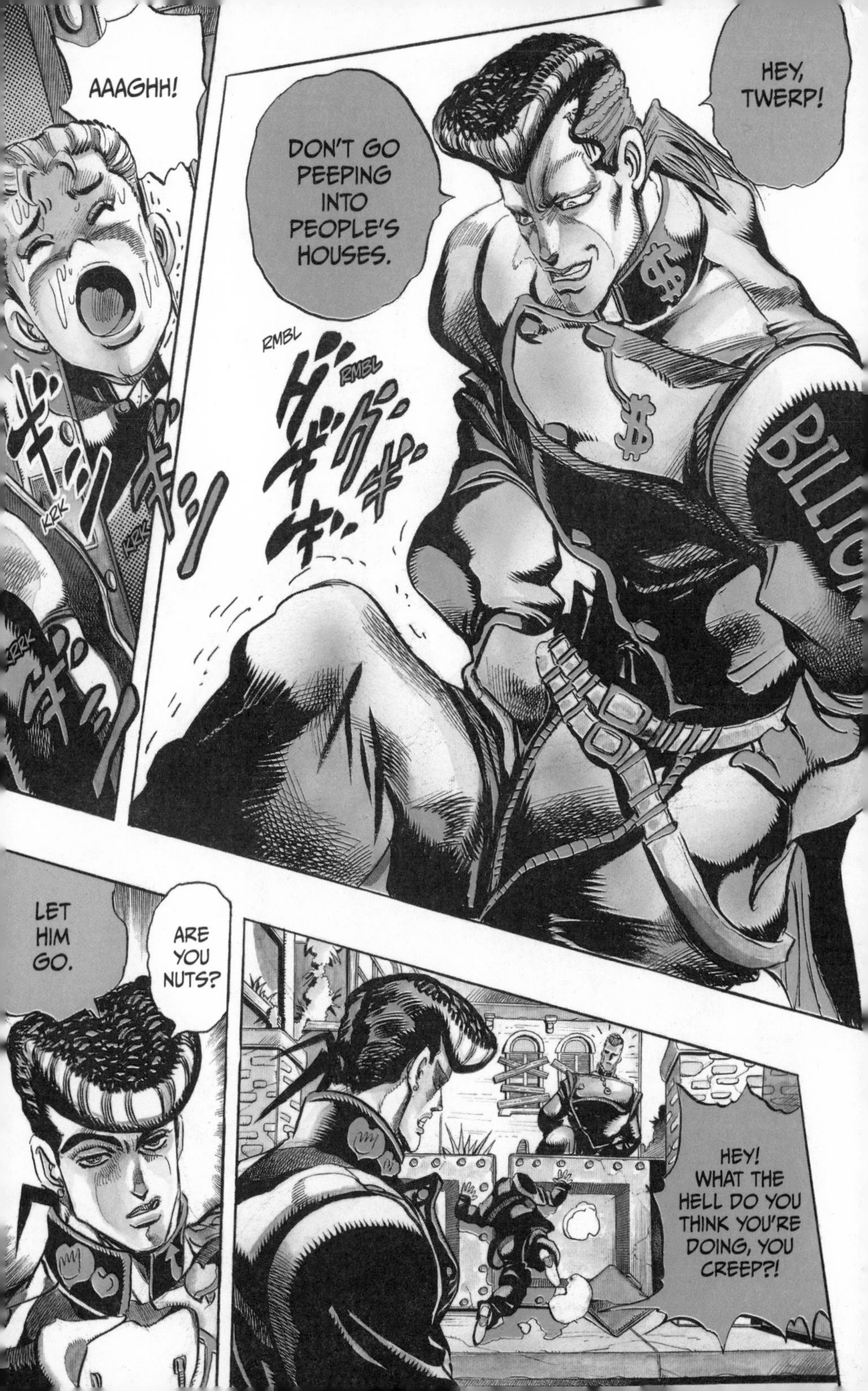
HEY, TWERP!
DON'T GO PEEPING INTO PEOPLE'S HOUSES.
RMBL
RMBL
AAAGHH!
KRK
KRK
KRRK
HEY! WHAT THE HELL DO YOU THINK YOU'RE DOING, YOU CREEP?!
ARE YOU NUTS?
LET HIM GO.

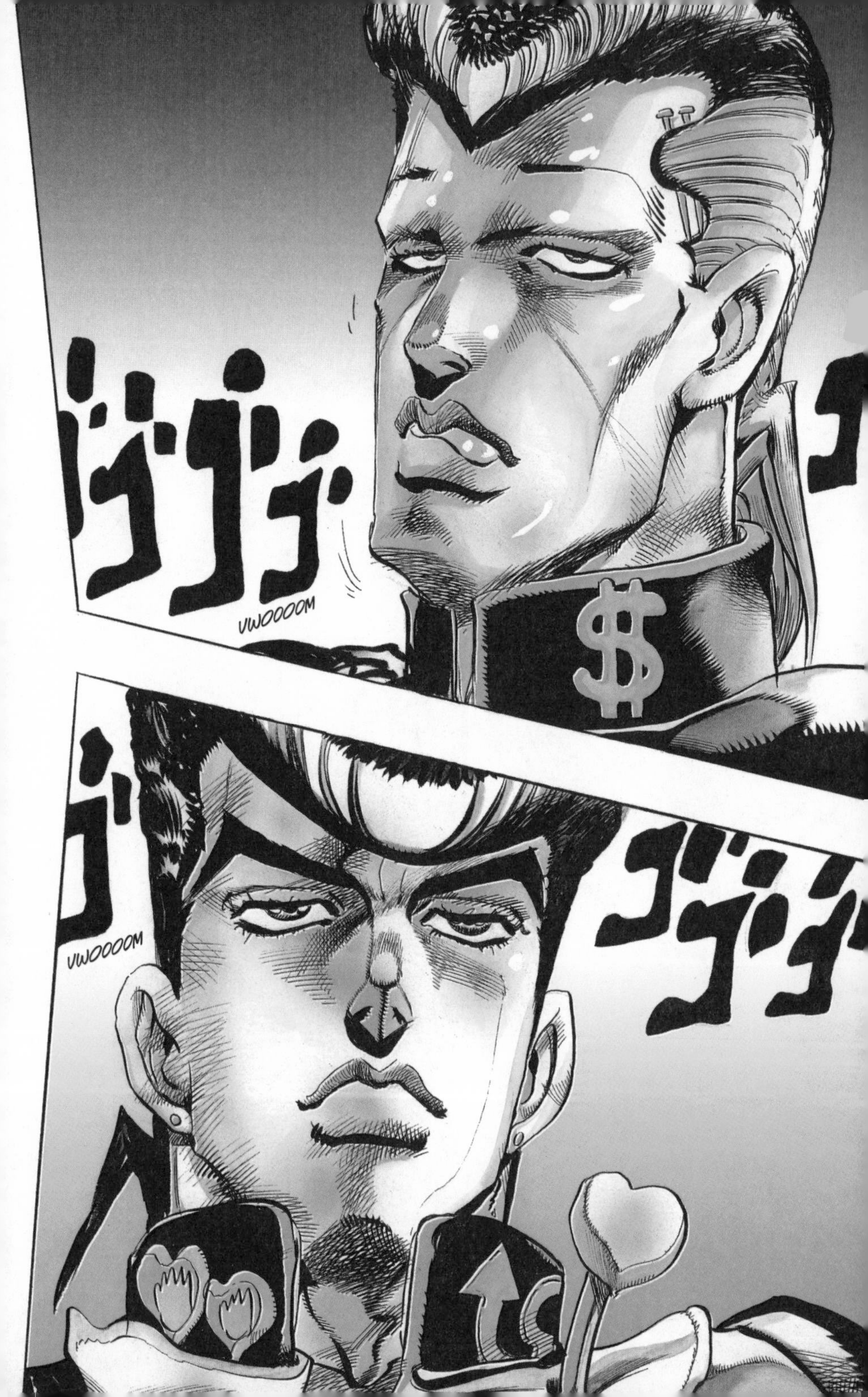
ゴゴゴ
VWOOOOM
ゴゴゴ
VWOOOOM

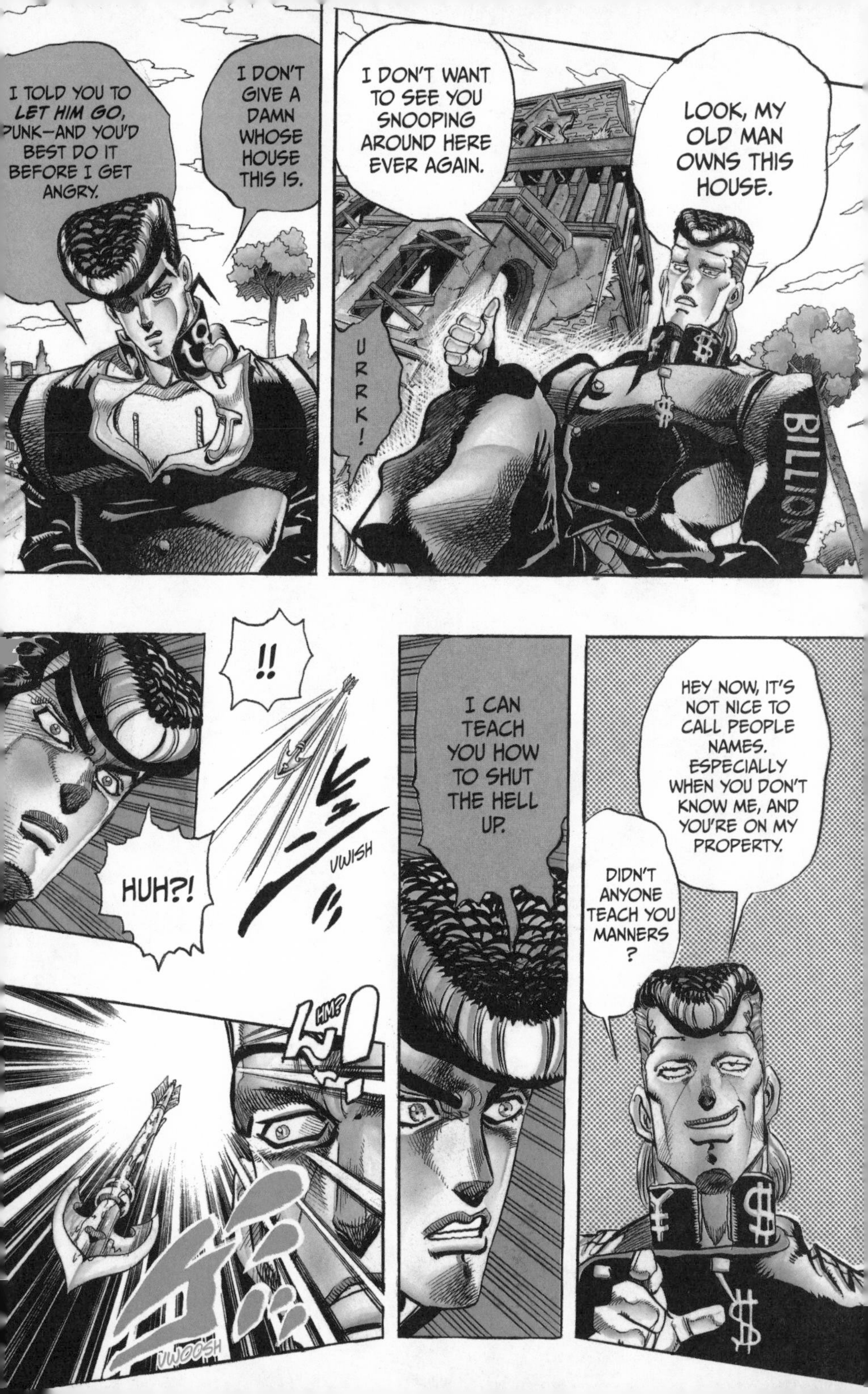
LOOK, MY OLD MAN OWNS THIS HOUSE.
I DON'T WANT TO SEE YOU SNOOPING AROUND HERE EVER AGAIN.
URRK!
I DON'T GIVE A DAMN WHOSE HOUSE THIS IS.
I TOLD YOU TO *LET HIM GO*, PUNK—AND YOU'D BEST DO IT BEFORE I GET ANGRY.
HEY NOW, IT'S NOT NICE TO CALL PEOPLE NAMES. ESPECIALLY WHEN YOU DON'T KNOW ME, AND YOU'RE ON MY PROPERTY.
DIDN'T ANYONE TEACH YOU MANNERS?
I CAN TEACH YOU HOW TO SHUT THE HELL UP.
!!
HUH?!
VWISH
HM?
VWOOSH

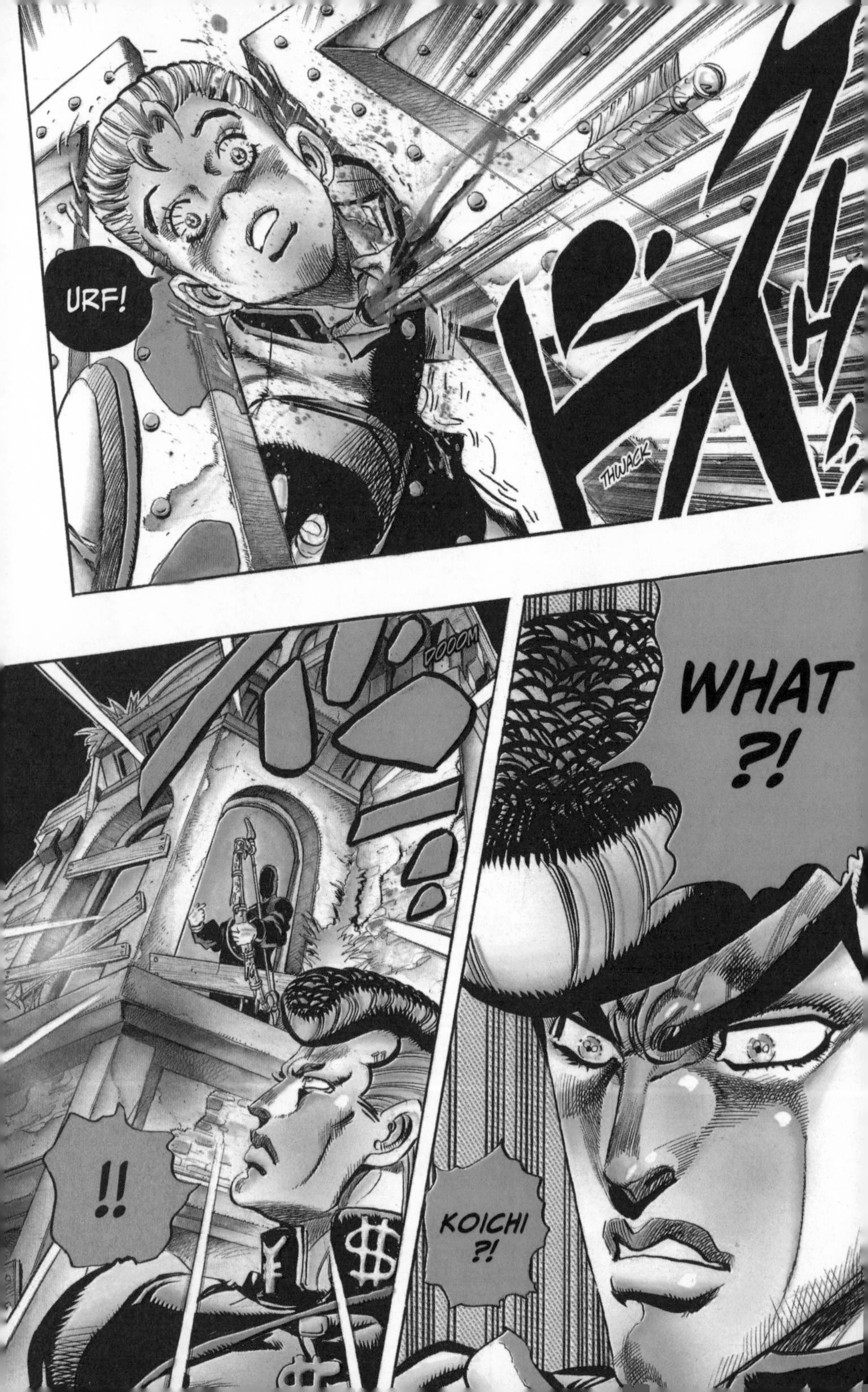
URF!
THWACK
WHAT ?!
KOICHI ?!
DOOOM
!!

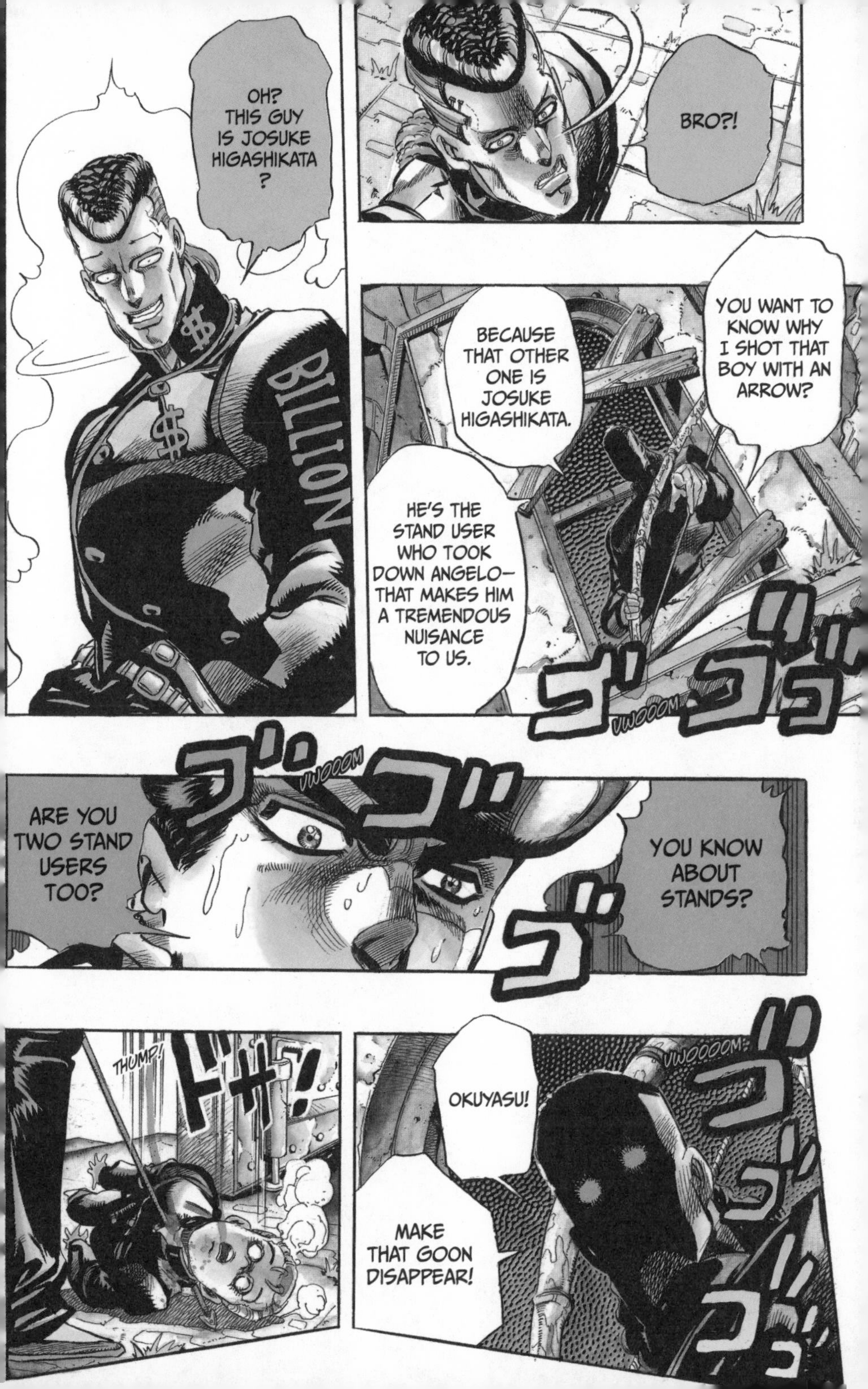
BRO?!
YOU WANT TO KNOW WHY I SHOT THAT BOY WITH AN ARROW?
BECAUSE THAT OTHER ONE IS JOSUKE HIGASHIKATA.
HE'S THE STAND USER WHO TOOK DOWN ANGELO—THAT MAKES HIM A TREMENDOUS NUISANCE TO US.
ゴゴゴ
UWOOOM
OH? THIS GUY IS JOSUKE HIGASHIKATA?
ゴゴゴ
UWOOOM
YOU KNOW ABOUT STANDS?
ARE YOU TWO STAND USERS TOO?
OKUYASU!
MAKE THAT GOON DISAPPEAR!
UWOOOOM
THUMP!

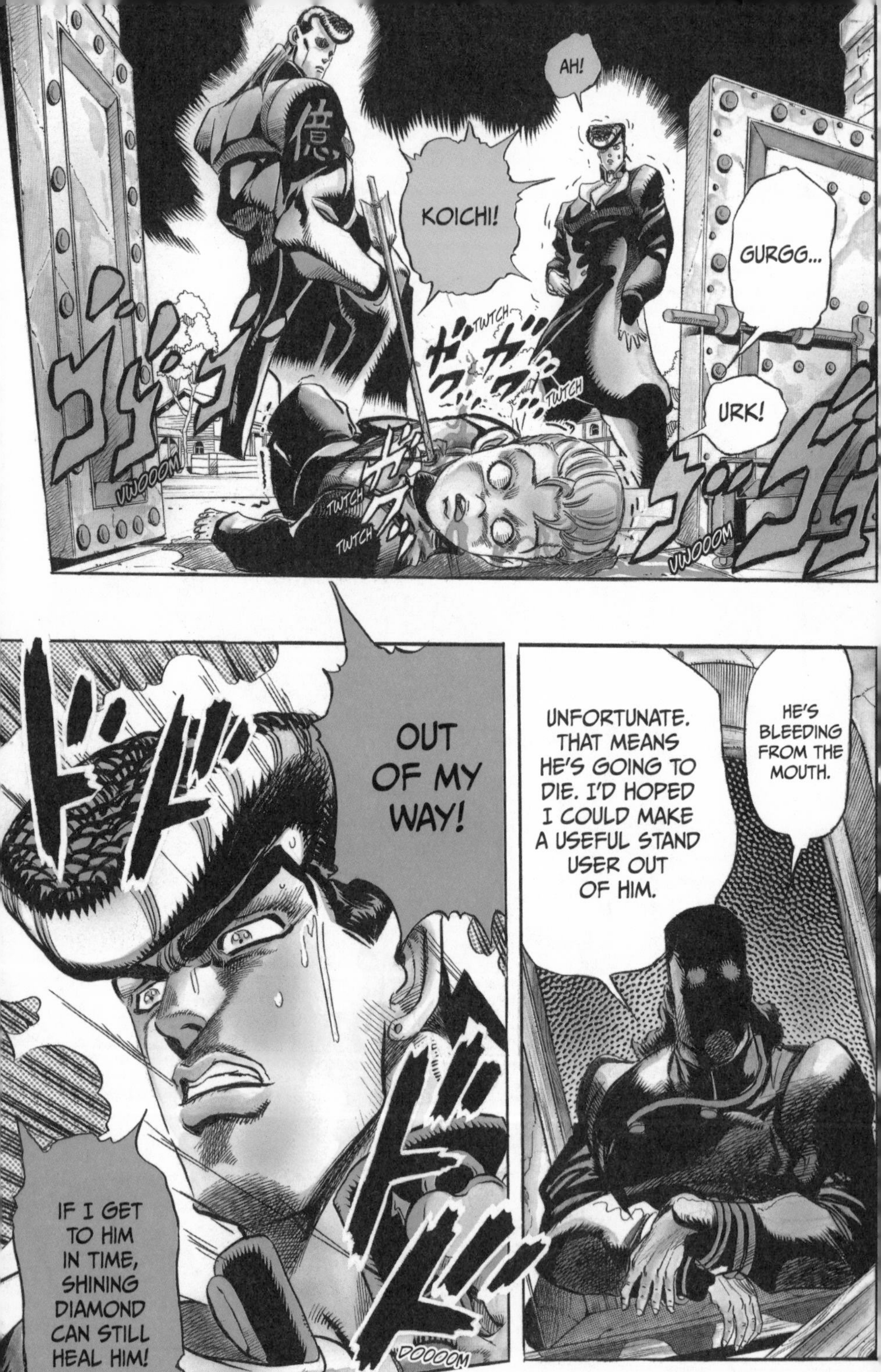
AH!
GURGG...
KOICHI!
URK!
TWTCH
TWTCH
TWTCH
TWTCH
VWOOOM
VWOOOM
HE'S BLEEDING FROM THE MOUTH.
UNFORTUNATE. THAT MEANS HE'S GOING TO DIE. I'D HOPED I COULD MAKE A USEFUL STAND USER OUT OF HIM.
OUT OF MY WAY!
IF I GET TO HIM IN TIME, SHINING DIAMOND CAN STILL HEAL HIM!
DOOOOM

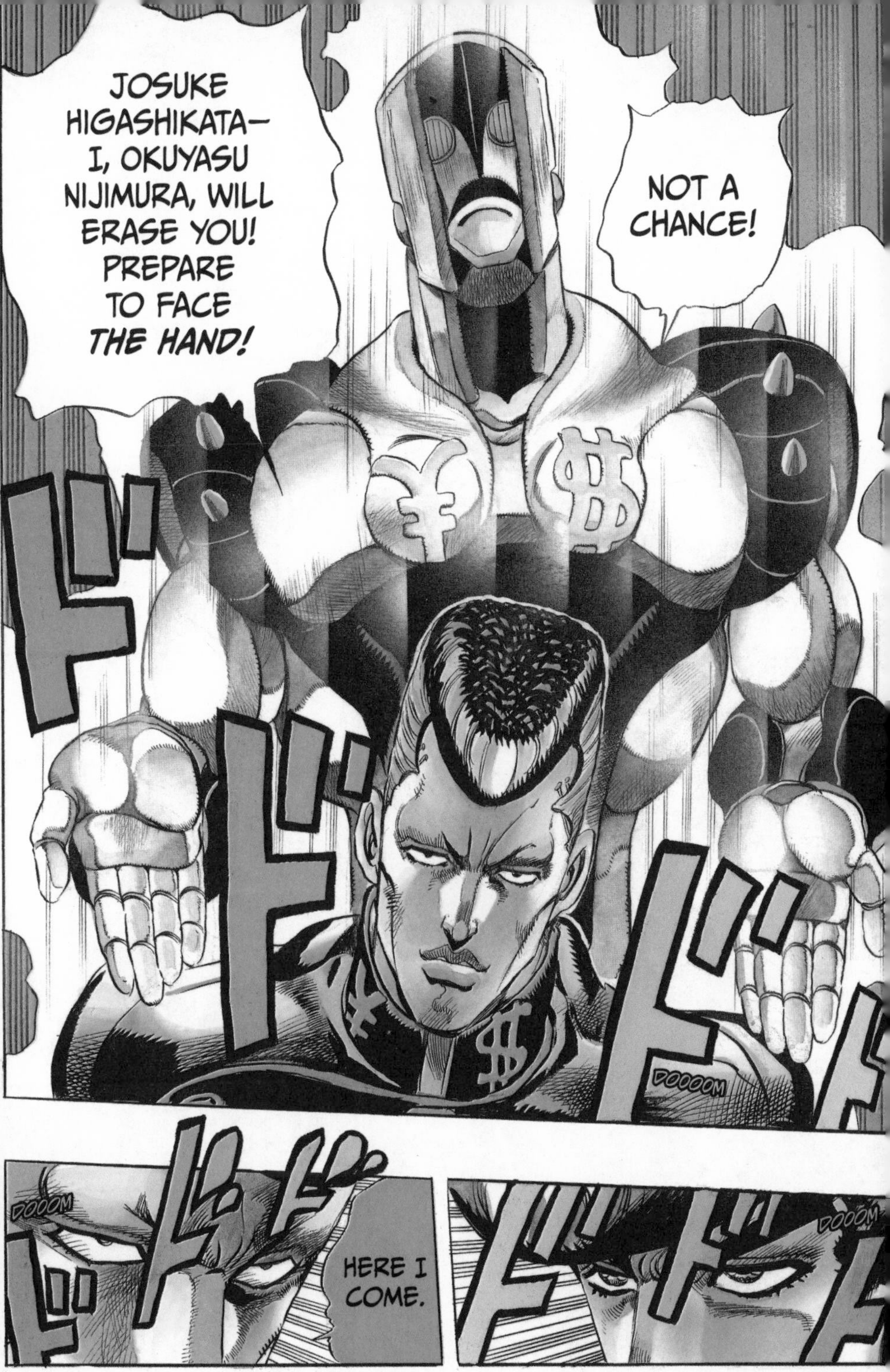
NOT A CHANCE!
JOSUKE HIGASHIKATA— I, OKUYASU NIJIMURA, WILL ERASE YOU! PREPARE TO FACE *THE HAND!*
DOOOOM
DOOOM
DOOOM
HERE I COME.

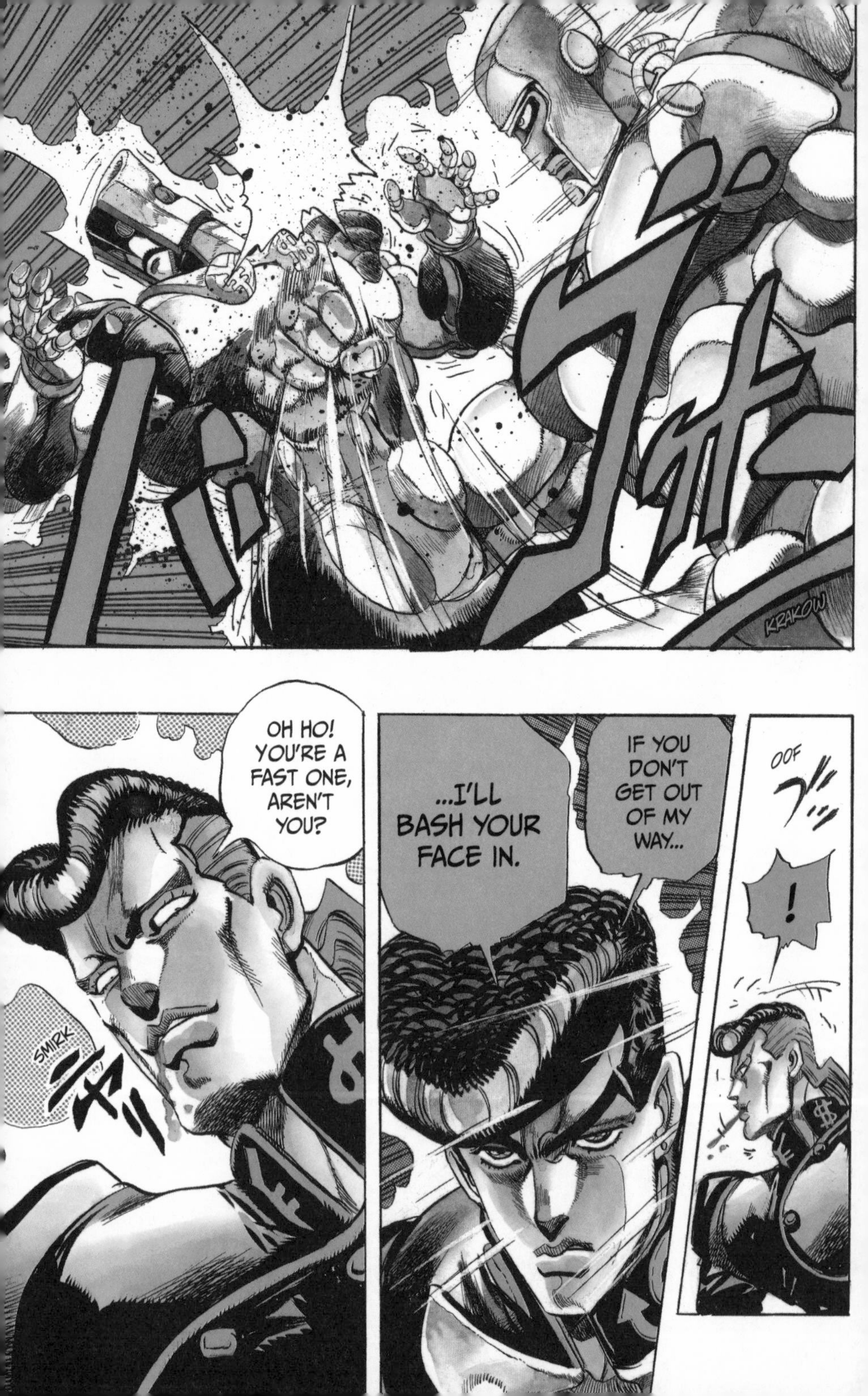
KRAKOW
OOF
!
IF YOU DON'T GET OUT OF MY WAY...
...I'LL BASH YOUR FACE IN.
OH HO! YOU'RE A FAST ONE, AREN'T YOU?
SMIRK

CHAPTER 10

THE NIJIMURA BROTHERS, PART 2

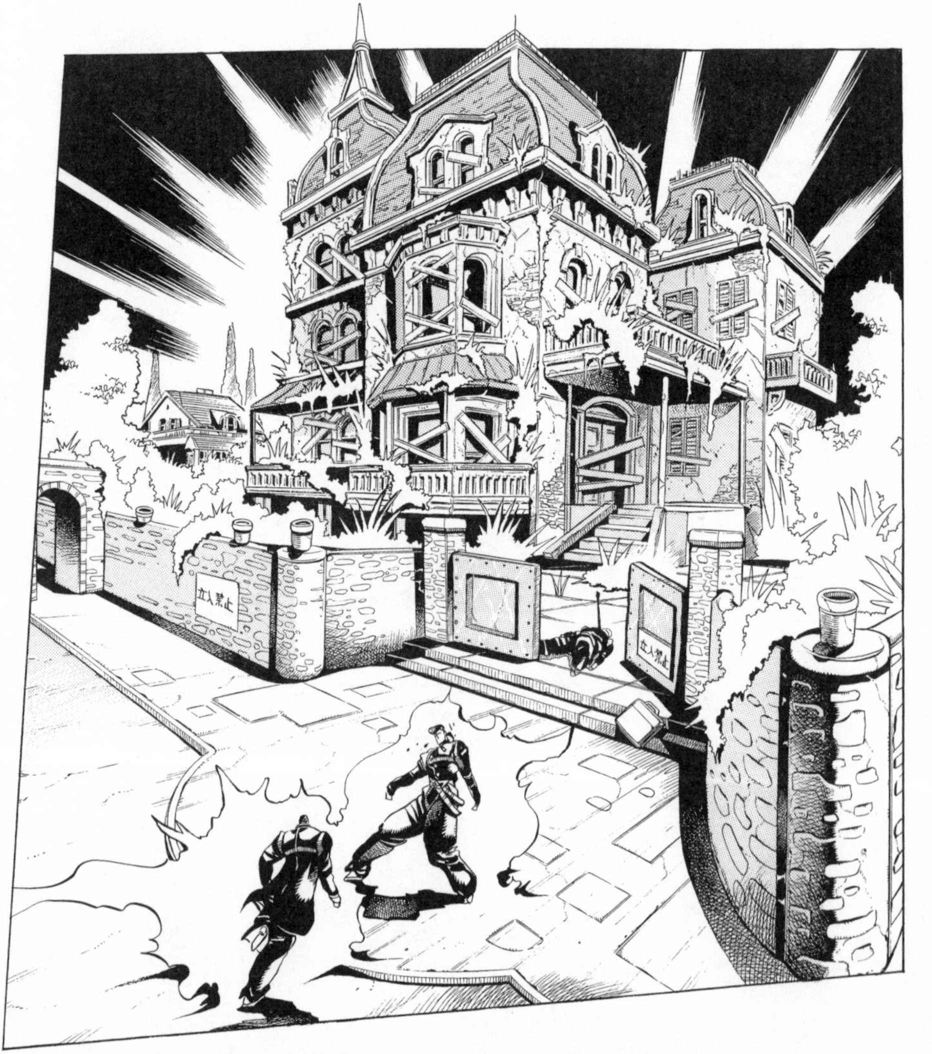
立入禁止
立入禁止

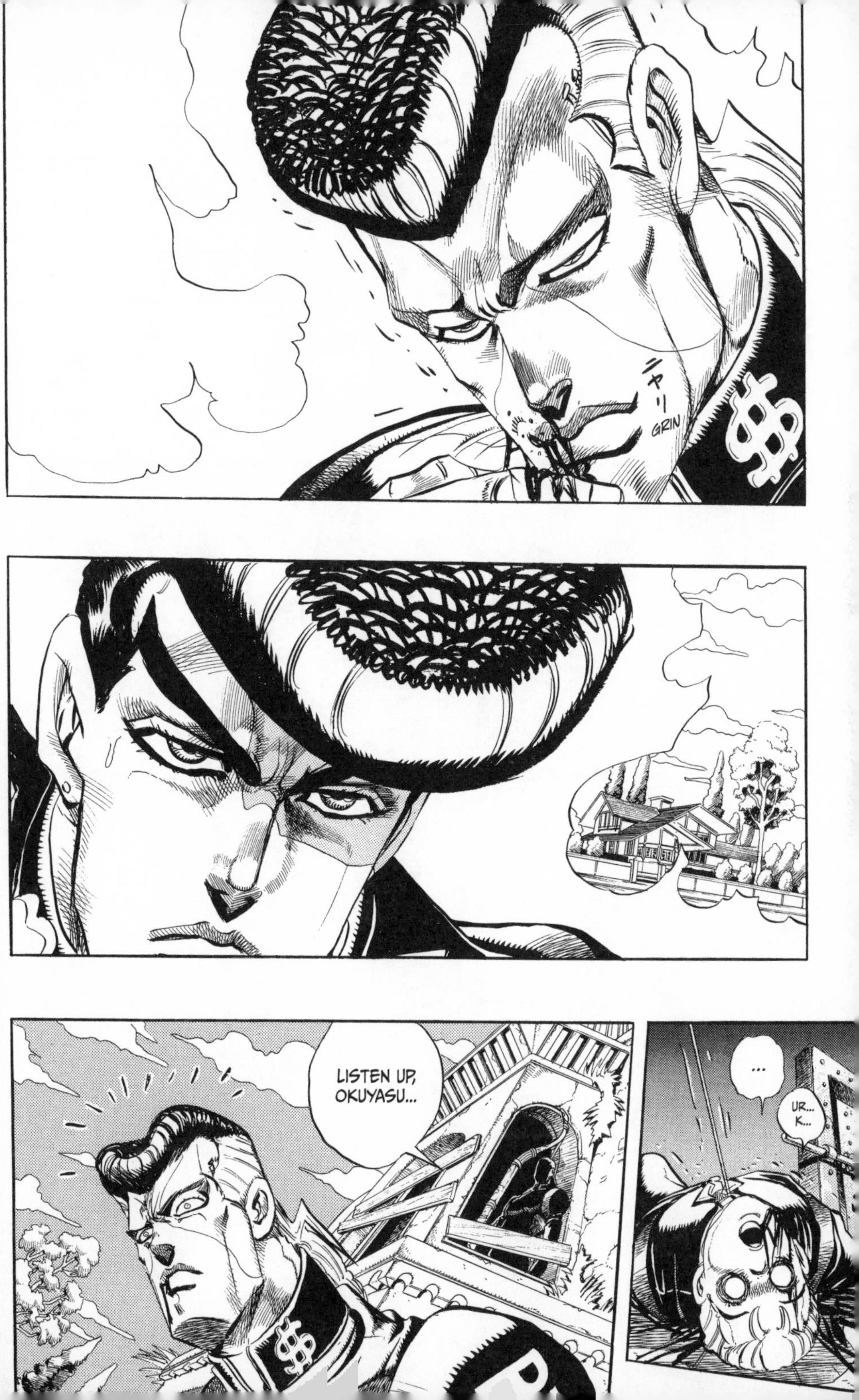
ニヤリ
GRIN
...
UR... K...
LISTEN UP, OKUYASU...

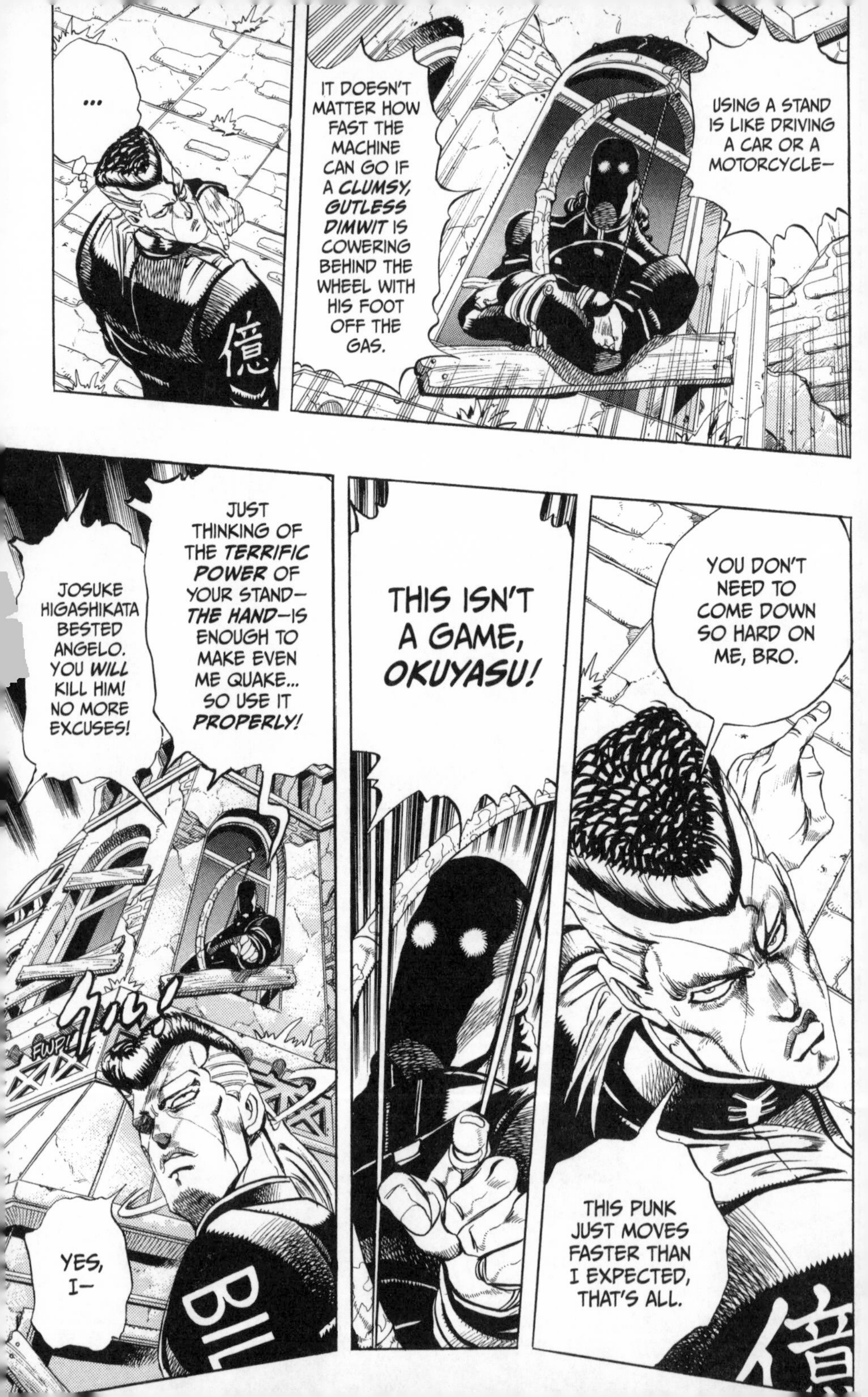
USING A STAND IS LIKE DRIVING A CAR OR A MOTORCYCLE–
IT DOESN'T MATTER HOW FAST THE MACHINE CAN GO IF A *CLUMSY, GUTLESS DIMWIT* IS COWERING BEHIND THE WHEEL WITH HIS FOOT OFF THE GAS.
...
YOU DON'T NEED TO COME DOWN SO HARD ON ME, BRO.
THIS PUNK JUST MOVES FASTER THAN I EXPECTED, THAT'S ALL.
THIS ISN'T A GAME, *OKUYASU!*
JUST THINKING OF THE *TERRIFIC POWER* OF YOUR STAND–*THE HAND*–IS ENOUGH TO MAKE EVEN ME QUAKE... SO USE IT *PROPERLY!*
JOSUKE HIGASHIKATA BESTED ANGELO. YOU *WILL* KILL HIM! NO MORE EXCUSES!
YES, I–

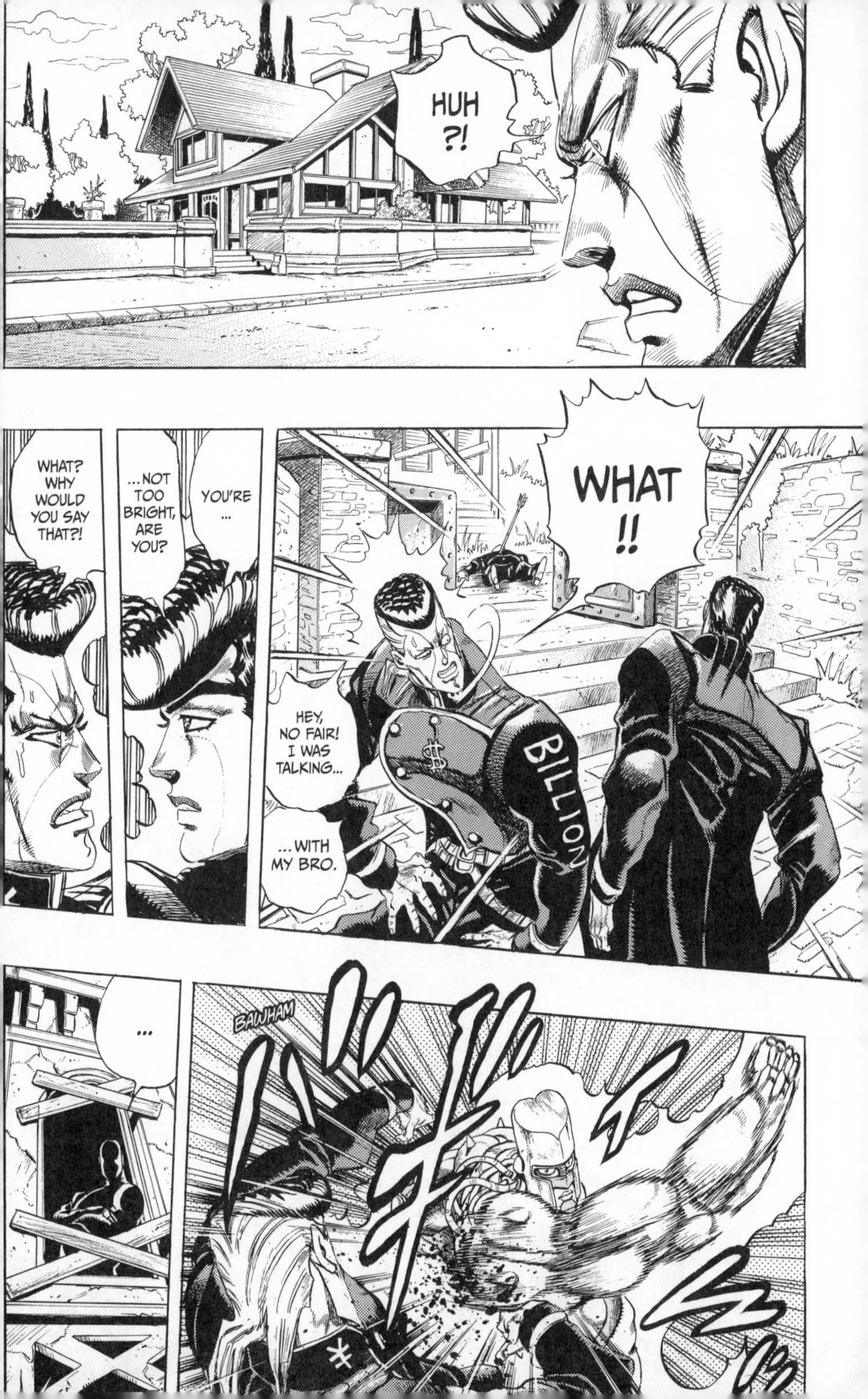
HUH ?!
WHAT !!
BILLION
HEY, NO FAIR! I WAS TALKING...
...WITH MY BRO.
YOU'RE ...
...NOT TOO BRIGHT, ARE YOU?
WHAT? WHY WOULD YOU SAY THAT?!
BAWHAM
...

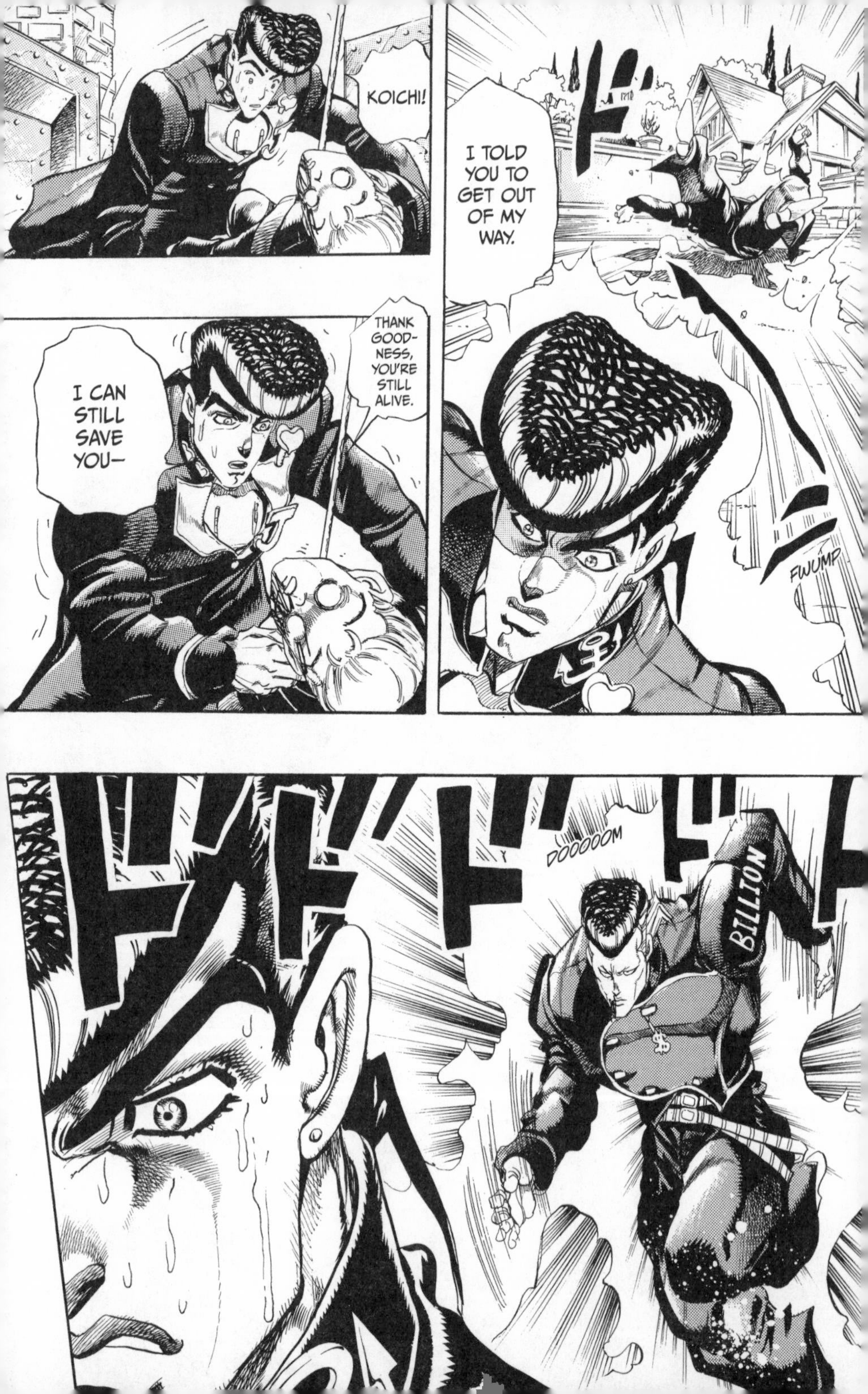
I TOLD YOU TO GET OUT OF MY WAY.
KOICHI!
FWUMP
THANK GOODNESS, YOU'RE STILL ALIVE.
I CAN STILL SAVE YOU—
DOOOOOM
BILLION

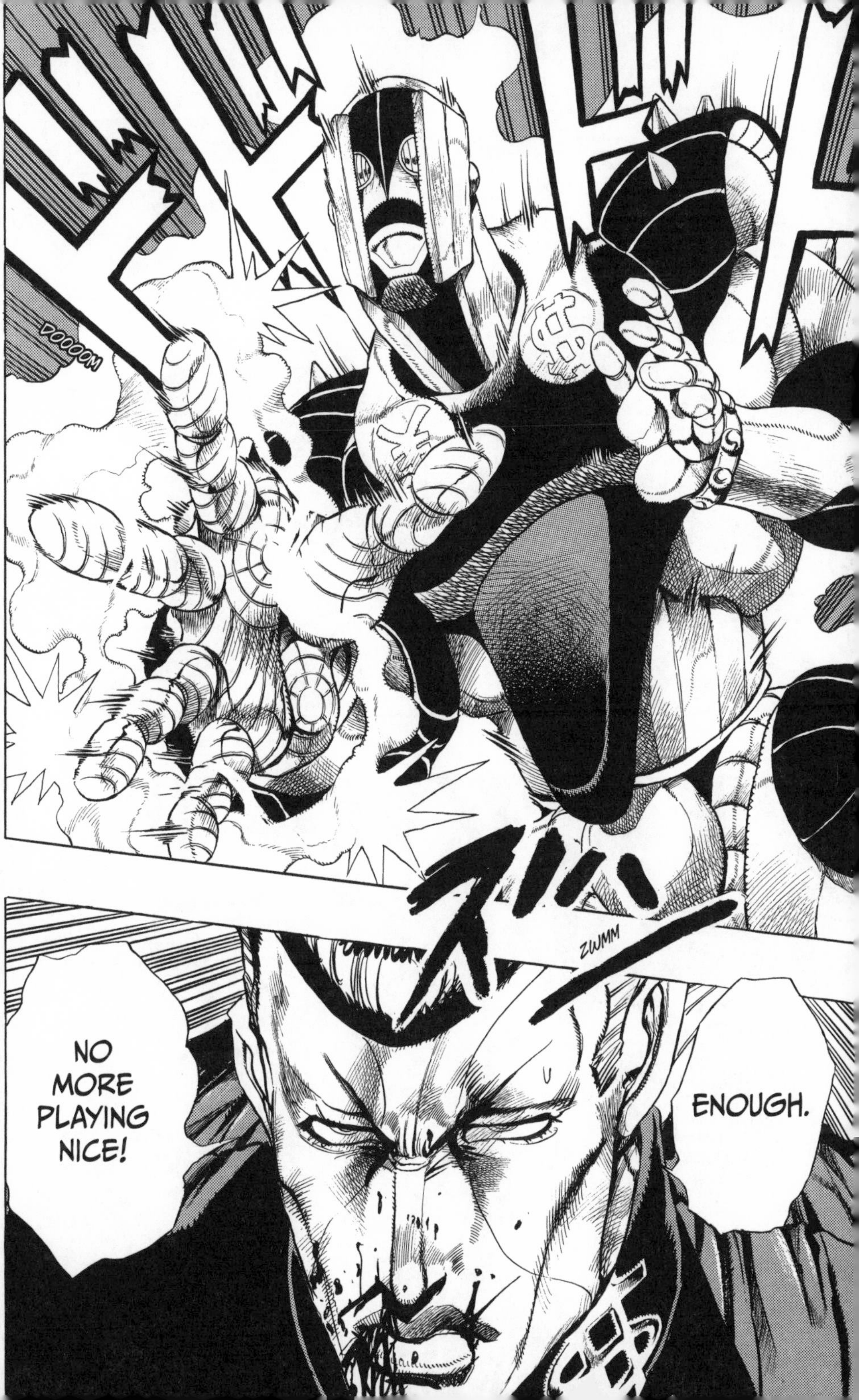
DOOOOM
ZWMM
ENOUGH.
NO MORE PLAYING NICE!

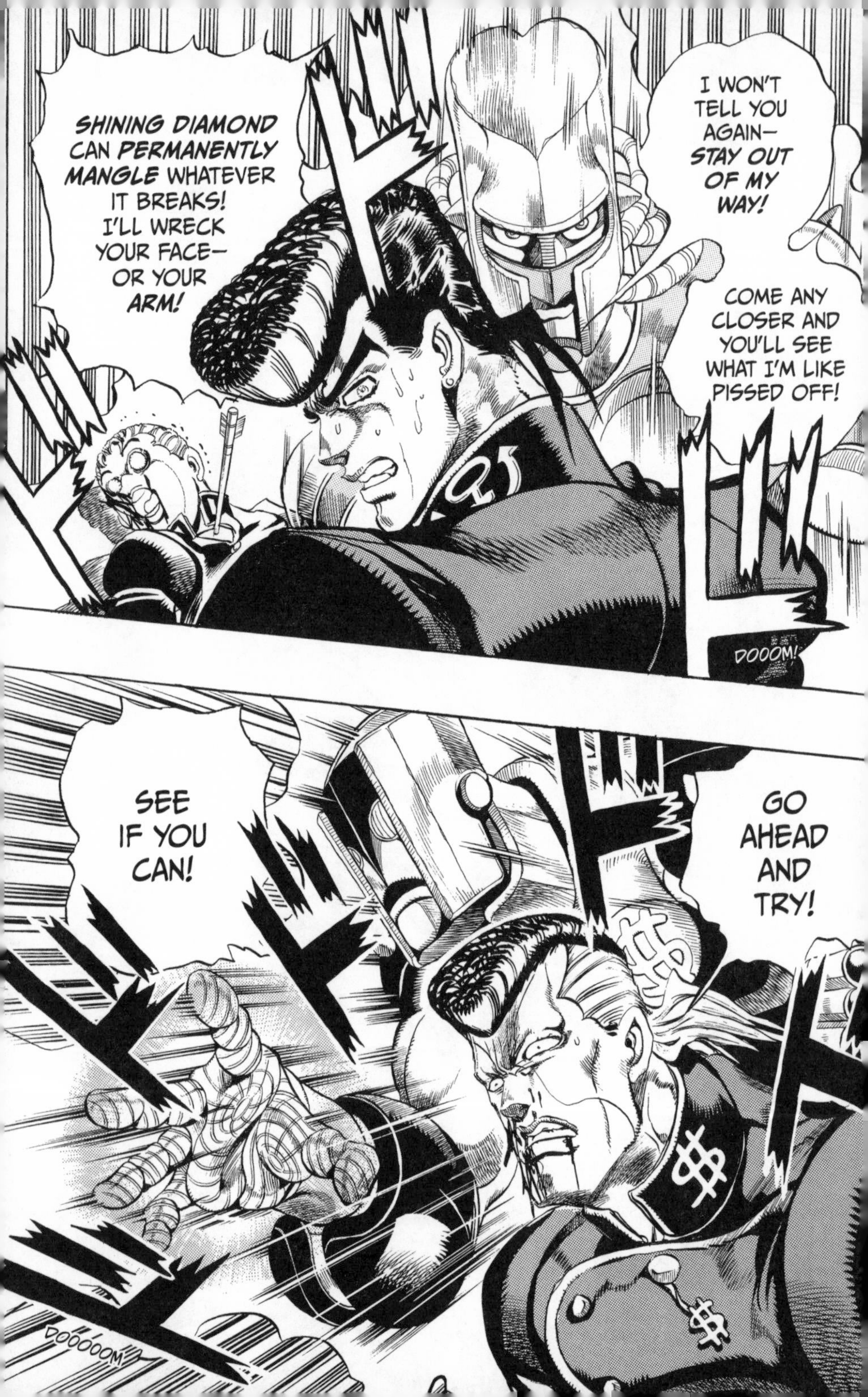
I WON'T TELL YOU AGAIN— STAY OUT OF MY WAY!
COME ANY CLOSER AND YOU'LL SEE WHAT I'M LIKE PISSED OFF!
SHINING DIAMOND CAN PERMANENTLY MANGLE WHATEVER IT BREAKS! I'LL WRECK YOUR FACE— OR YOUR ARM!
DOOOM!
GO AHEAD AND TRY!
SEE IF YOU CAN!
DOOOOOM

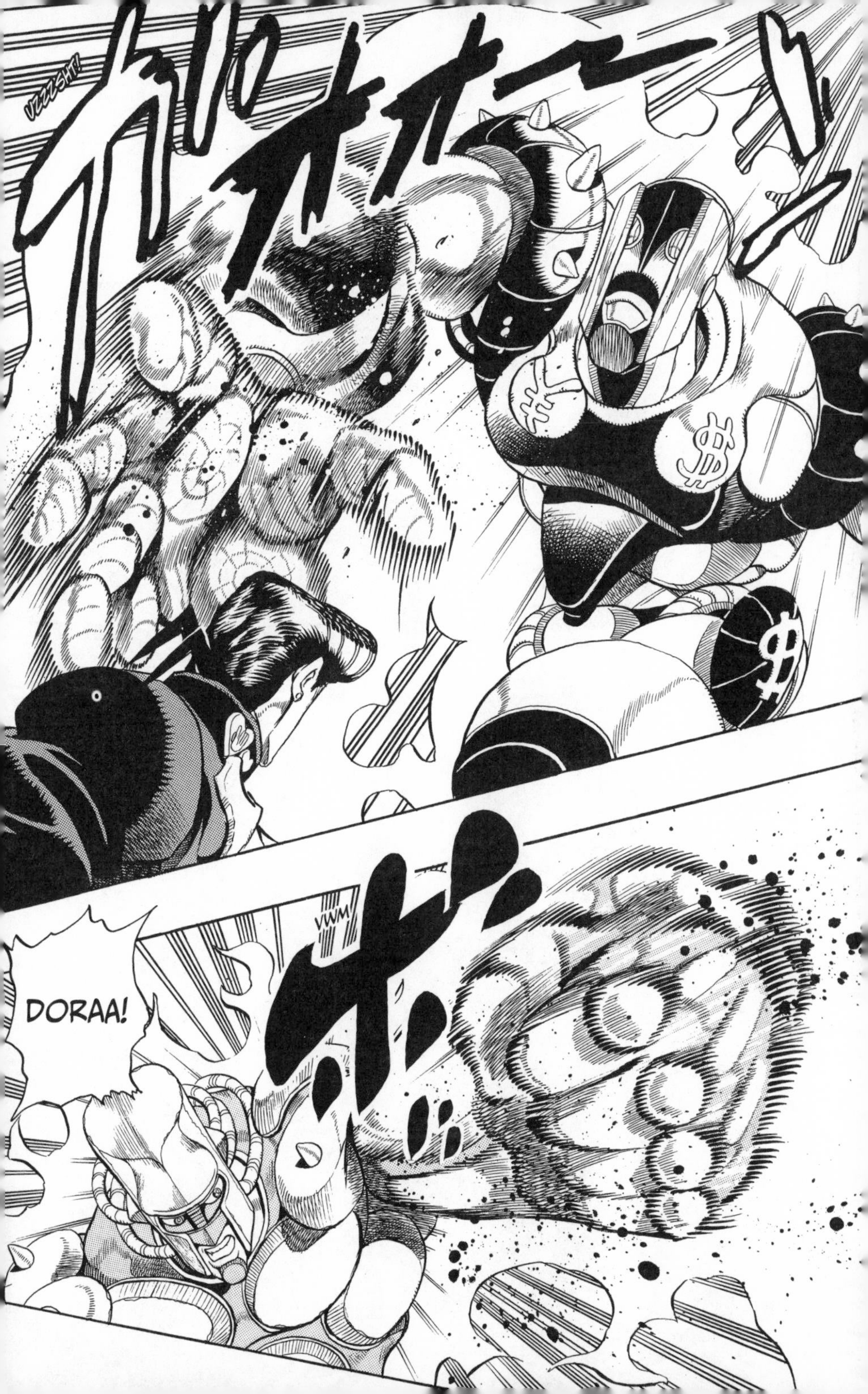
VZZZSHT!
VWM!
DORAA!

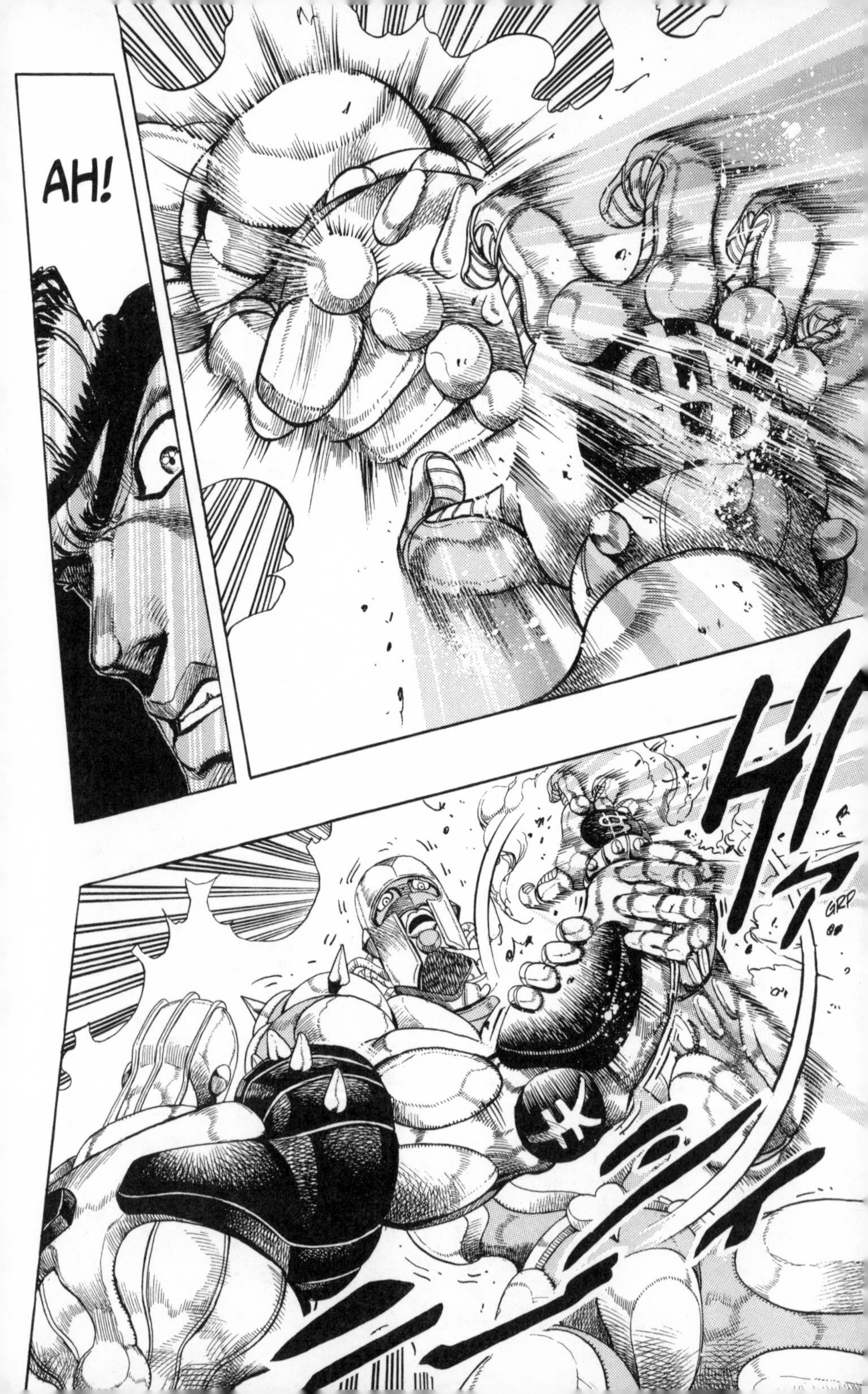
AH!
GRP

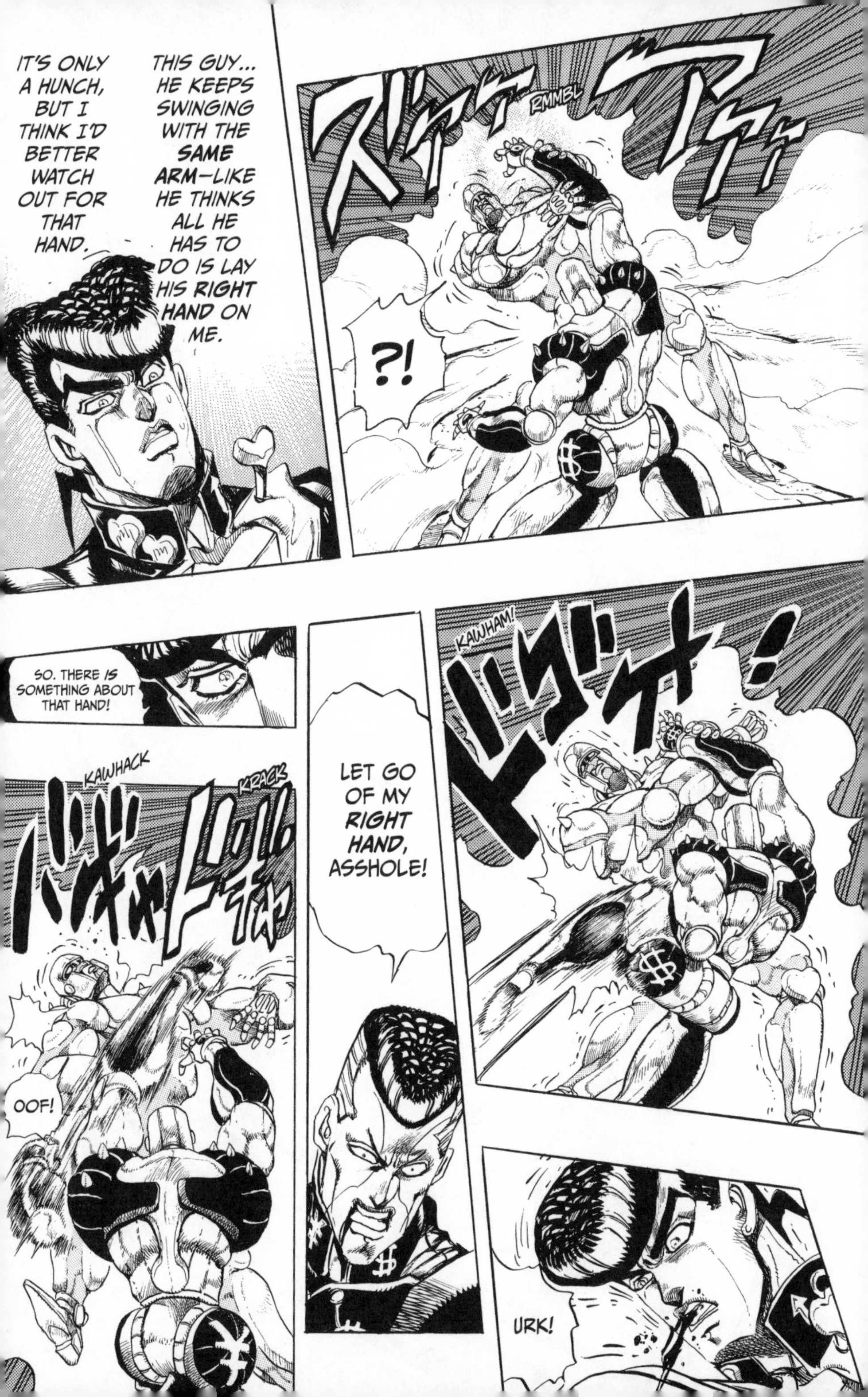
RMMBL
?!
THIS GUY... HE KEEPS SWINGING WITH THE SAME ARM—LIKE HE THINKS ALL HE HAS TO DO IS LAY HIS RIGHT HAND ON ME.
IT'S ONLY A HUNCH, BUT I THINK I'D BETTER WATCH OUT FOR THAT HAND.
KAWHAM!
URK!
LET GO OF MY RIGHT HAND, ASSHOLE!
SO. THERE IS SOMETHING ABOUT THAT HAND!
KAWHACK
KRACK
OOF!

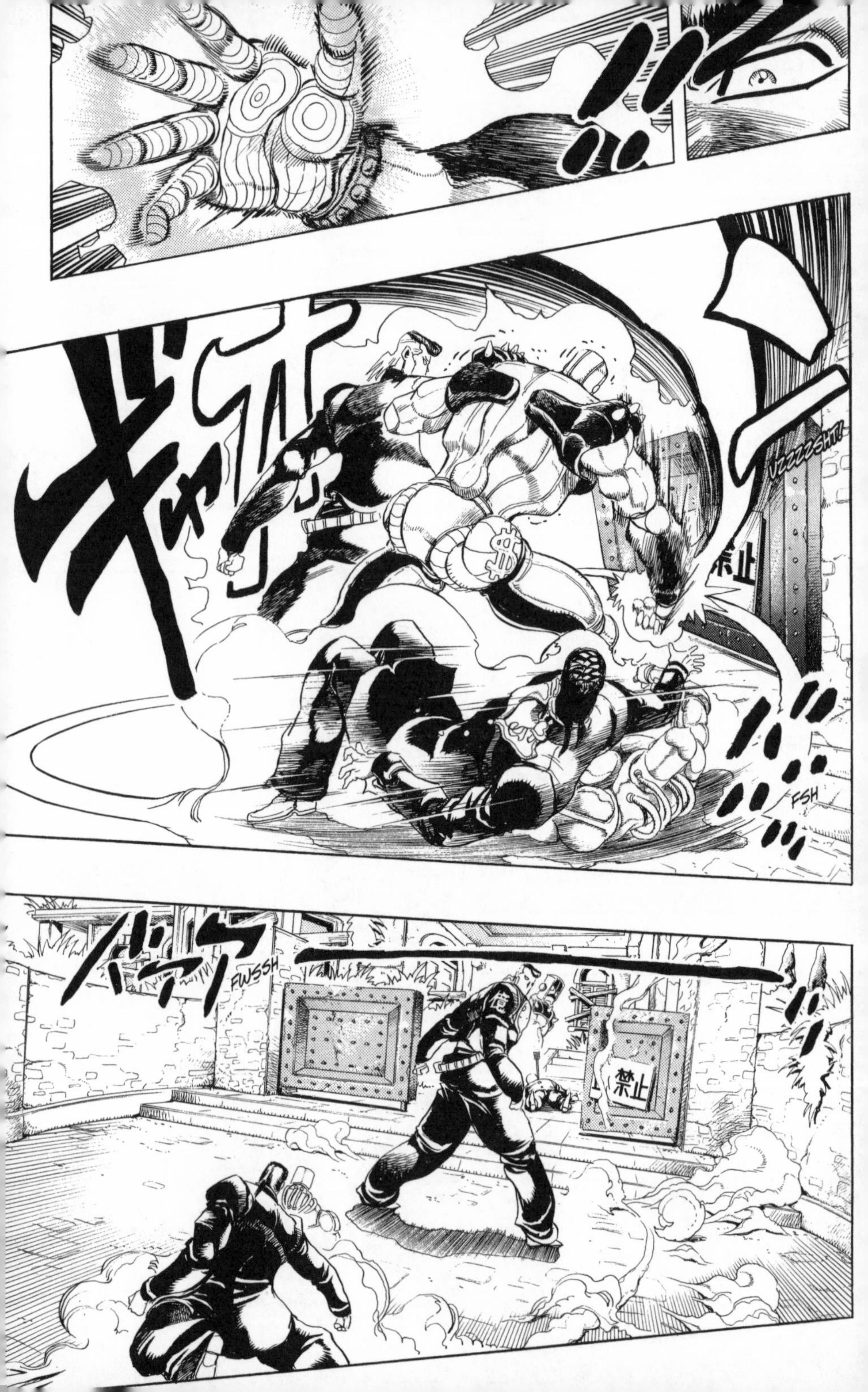
VZZZZZSHT!
禁止
FSH
FWSSH
禁止

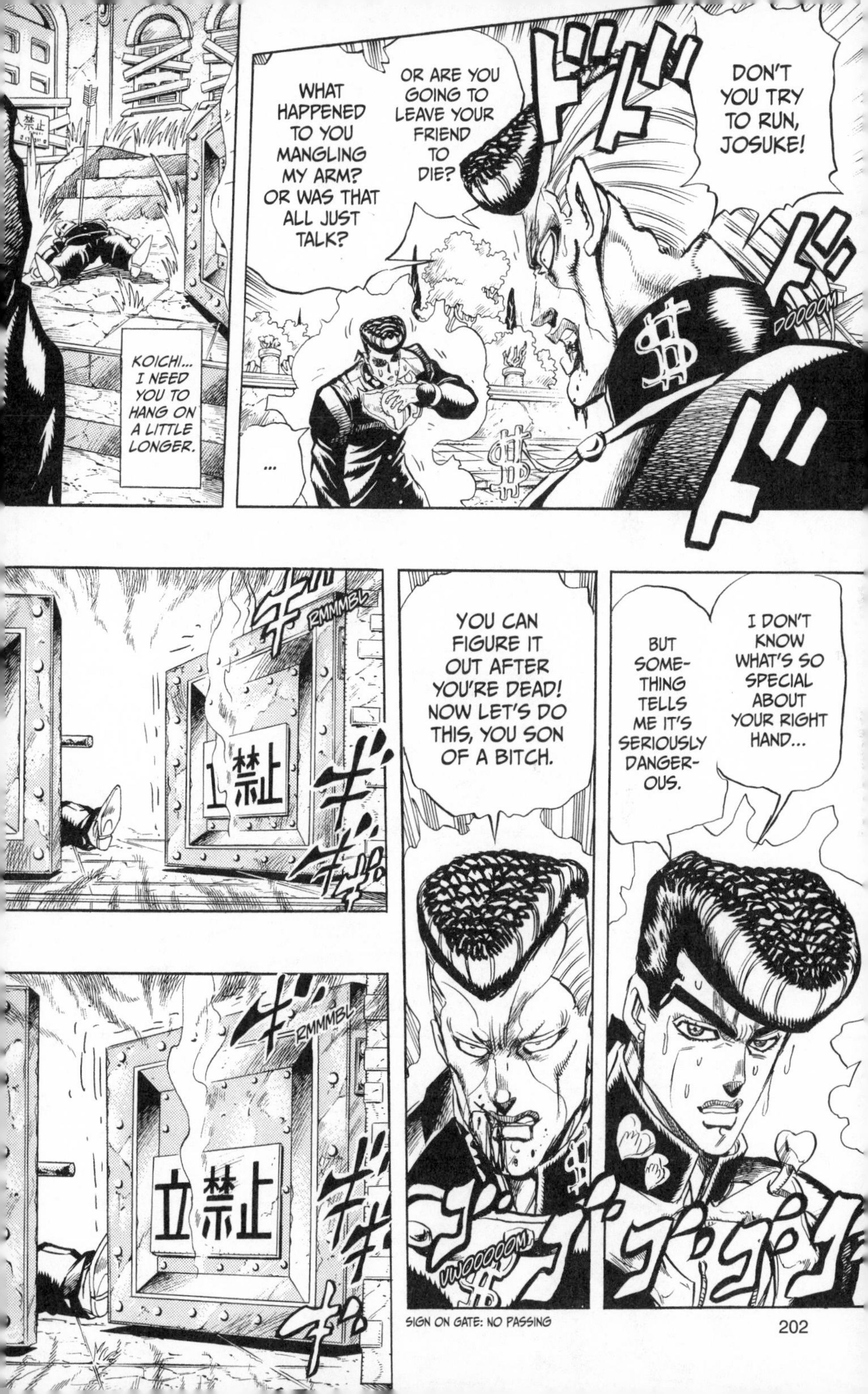
DON'T YOU TRY TO RUN, JOSUKE!
OR ARE YOU GOING TO LEAVE YOUR FRIEND TO DIE?
WHAT HAPPENED TO YOU MANGLING MY ARM? OR WAS THAT ALL JUST TALK?
DOOOOM
...
KOICHI... I NEED YOU TO HANG ON A LITTLE LONGER.
I DON'T KNOW WHAT'S SO SPECIAL ABOUT YOUR RIGHT HAND...
BUT SOME-THING TELLS ME IT'S SERIOUSLY DANGER-OUS.
YOU CAN FIGURE IT OUT AFTER YOU'RE DEAD! NOW LET'S DO THIS, YOU SON OF A BITCH.
UWOOOOOM
RMMMBL
RMMMBL

SIGN ON GATE: NO PASSING

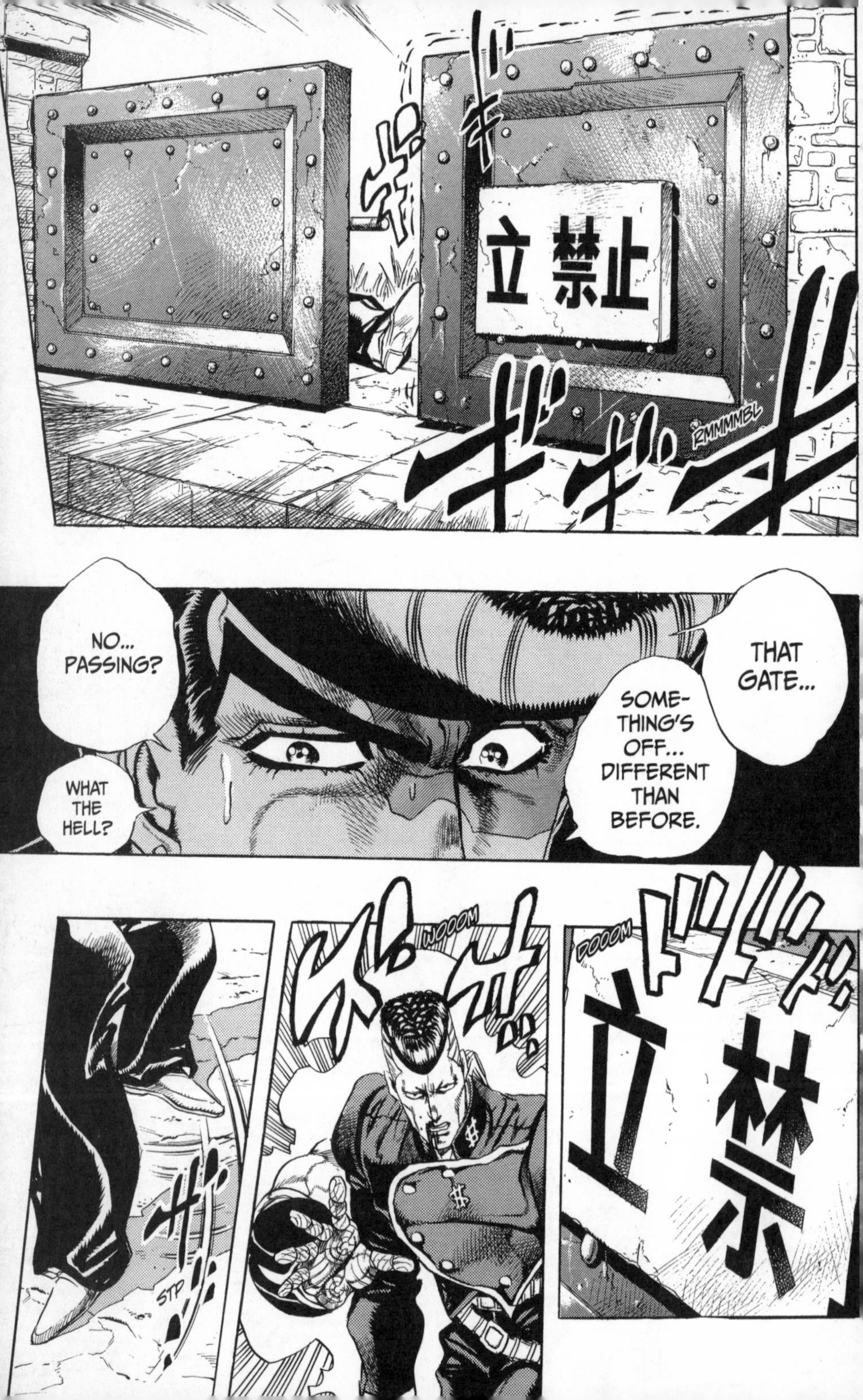
立禁止
RMMMMBL
THAT GATE...
SOME-THING'S OFF... DIFFERENT THAN BEFORE.
NO... PASSING?
WHAT THE HELL?
DOOOM
立禁
WOOOM
STP

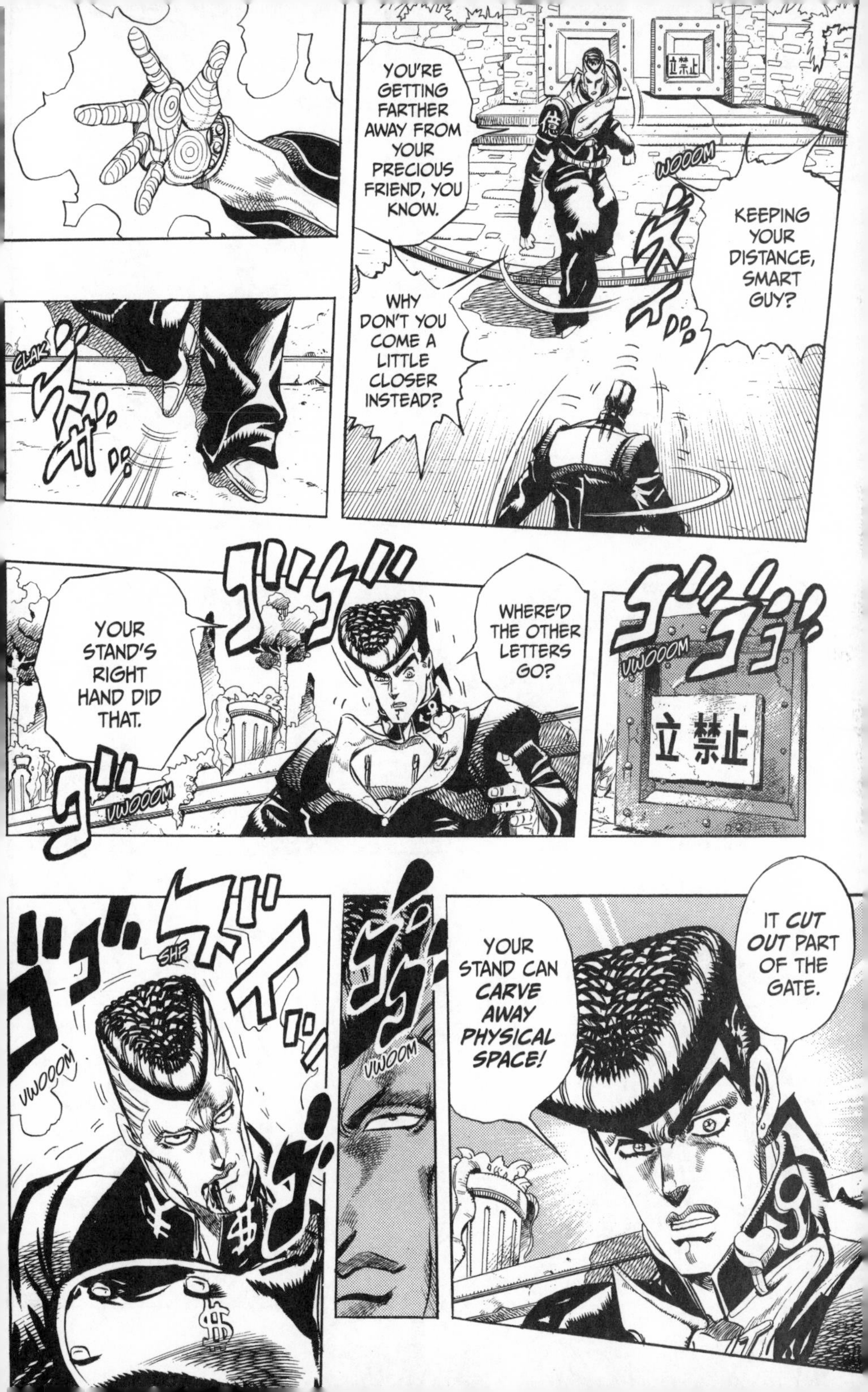

YOU'RE GETTING FARTHER AWAY FROM YOUR PRECIOUS FRIEND, YOU KNOW.
WOOOM
KEEPING YOUR DISTANCE, SMART GUY?
WHY DON'T YOU COME A LITTLE CLOSER INSTEAD?
CLAK
VWOOOM
立禁止
WHERE'D THE OTHER LETTERS GO?
YOUR STAND'S RIGHT HAND DID THAT.
VWOOOM
IT *CUT OUT* PART OF THE GATE.
YOUR STAND CAN *CARVE AWAY PHYSICAL SPACE!*
VWOOM
SHP
VWOOOM

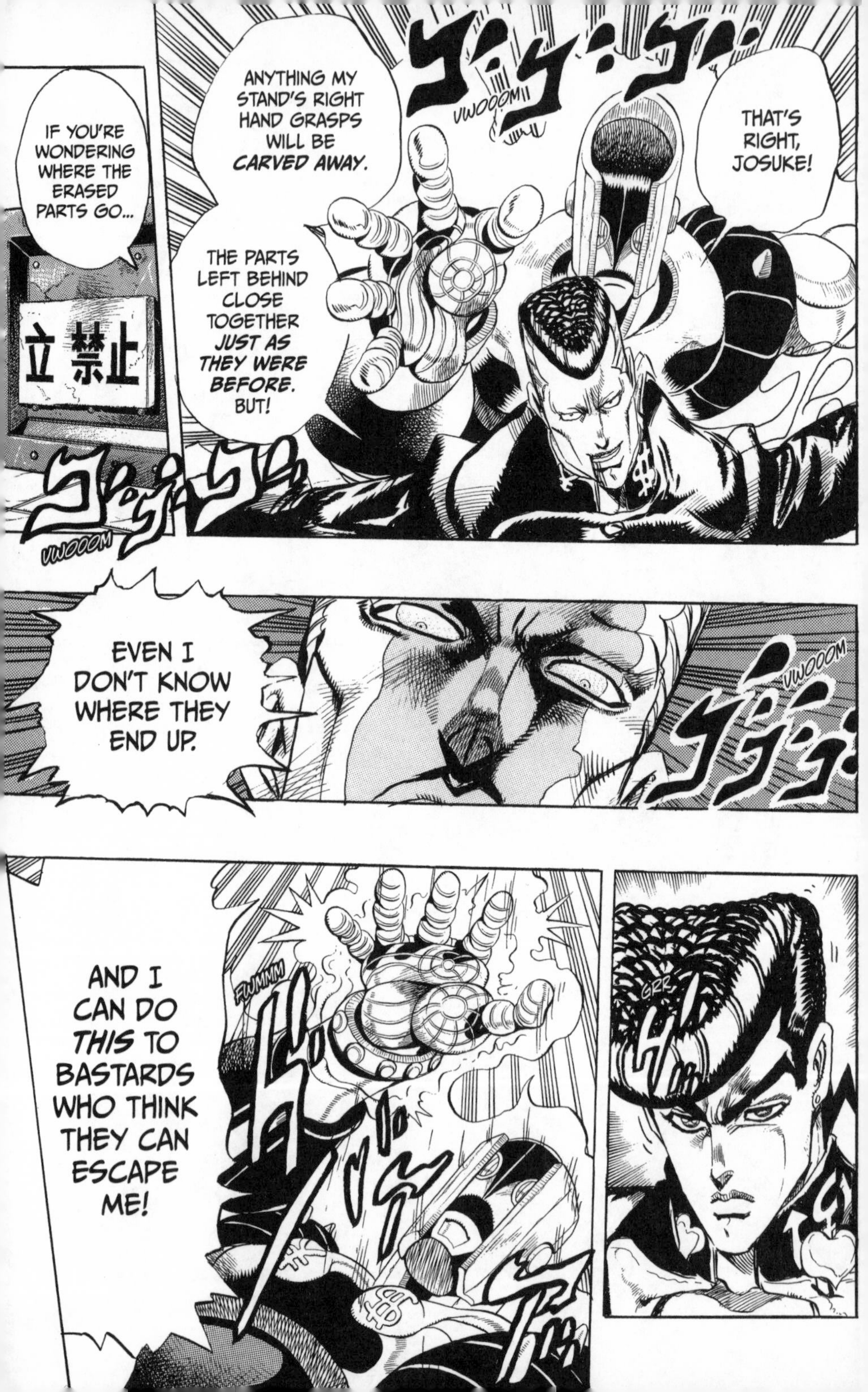
VWOOOM
THAT'S RIGHT, JOSUKE!
ANYTHING MY STAND'S RIGHT HAND GRASPS WILL BE CARVED AWAY.
THE PARTS LEFT BEHIND CLOSE TOGETHER JUST AS THEY WERE BEFORE. BUT!
IF YOU'RE WONDERING WHERE THE ERASED PARTS GO...
立禁止
VWOOOM
VWOOOM
EVEN I DON'T KNOW WHERE THEY END UP.
GRR
FWUMMM
AND I CAN DO THIS TO BASTARDS WHO THINK THEY CAN ESCAPE ME!

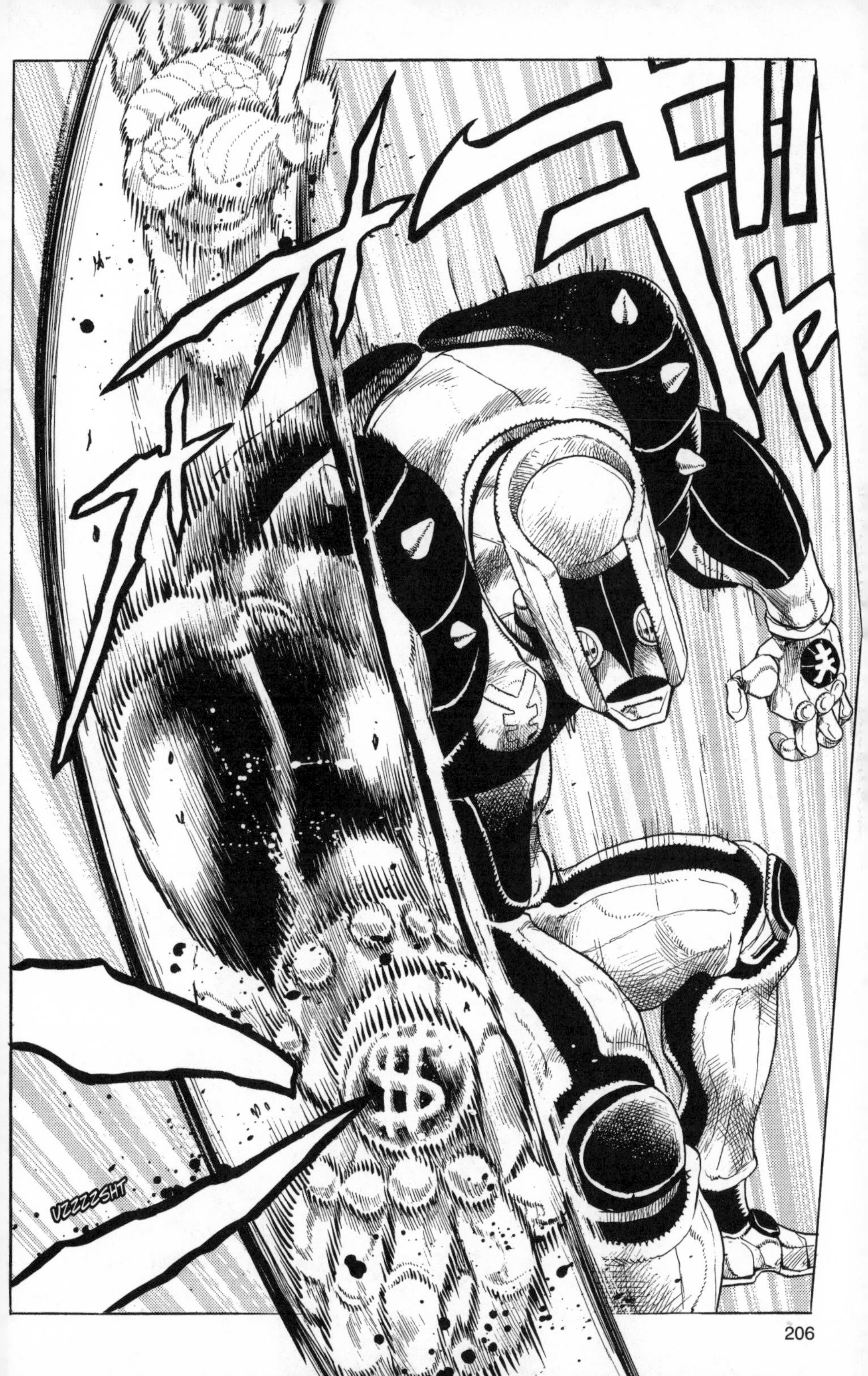
VZZZZSHT

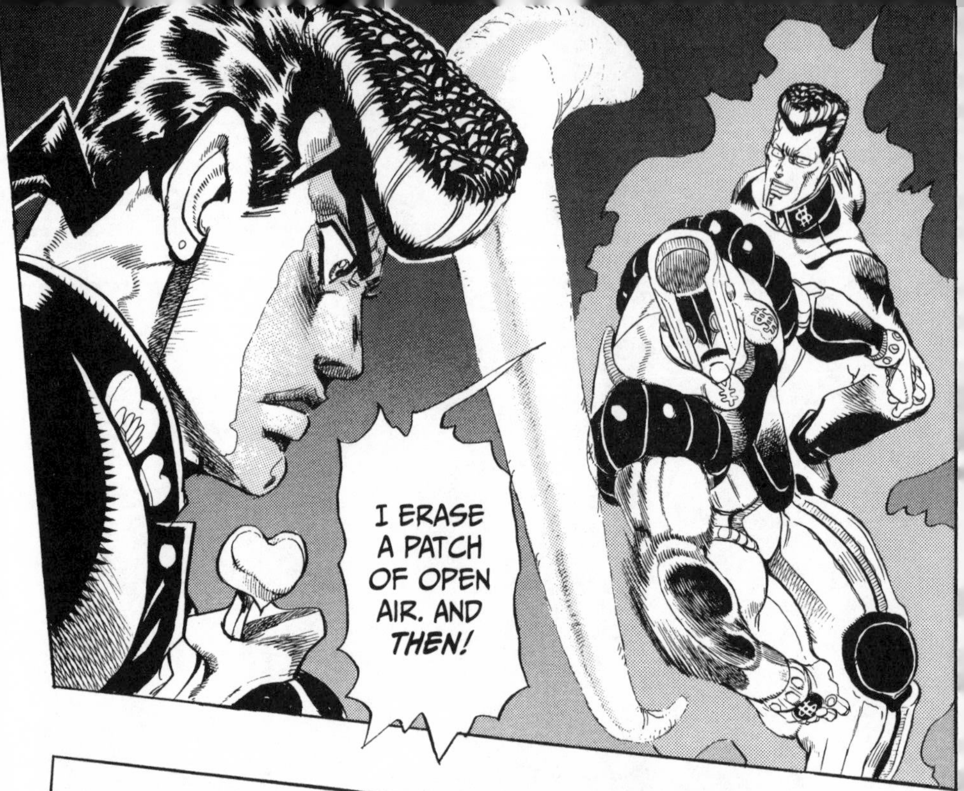
I ERASE A PATCH OF OPEN AIR. AND *THEN!*
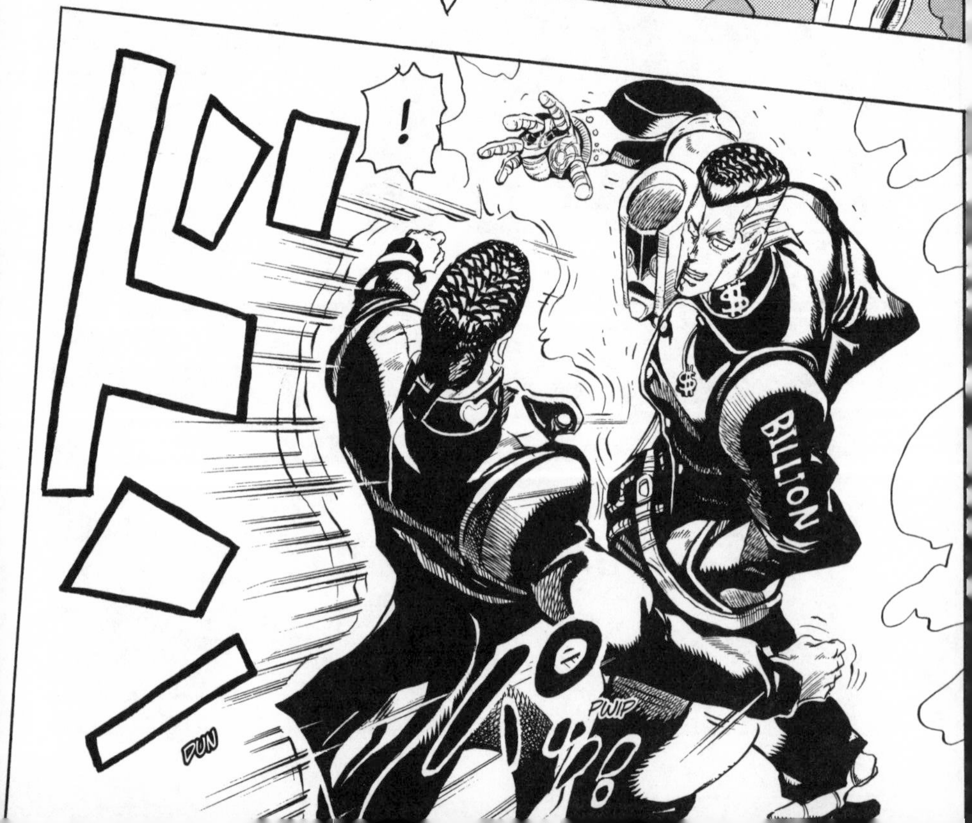
!
BILLION
PWIP
DUN

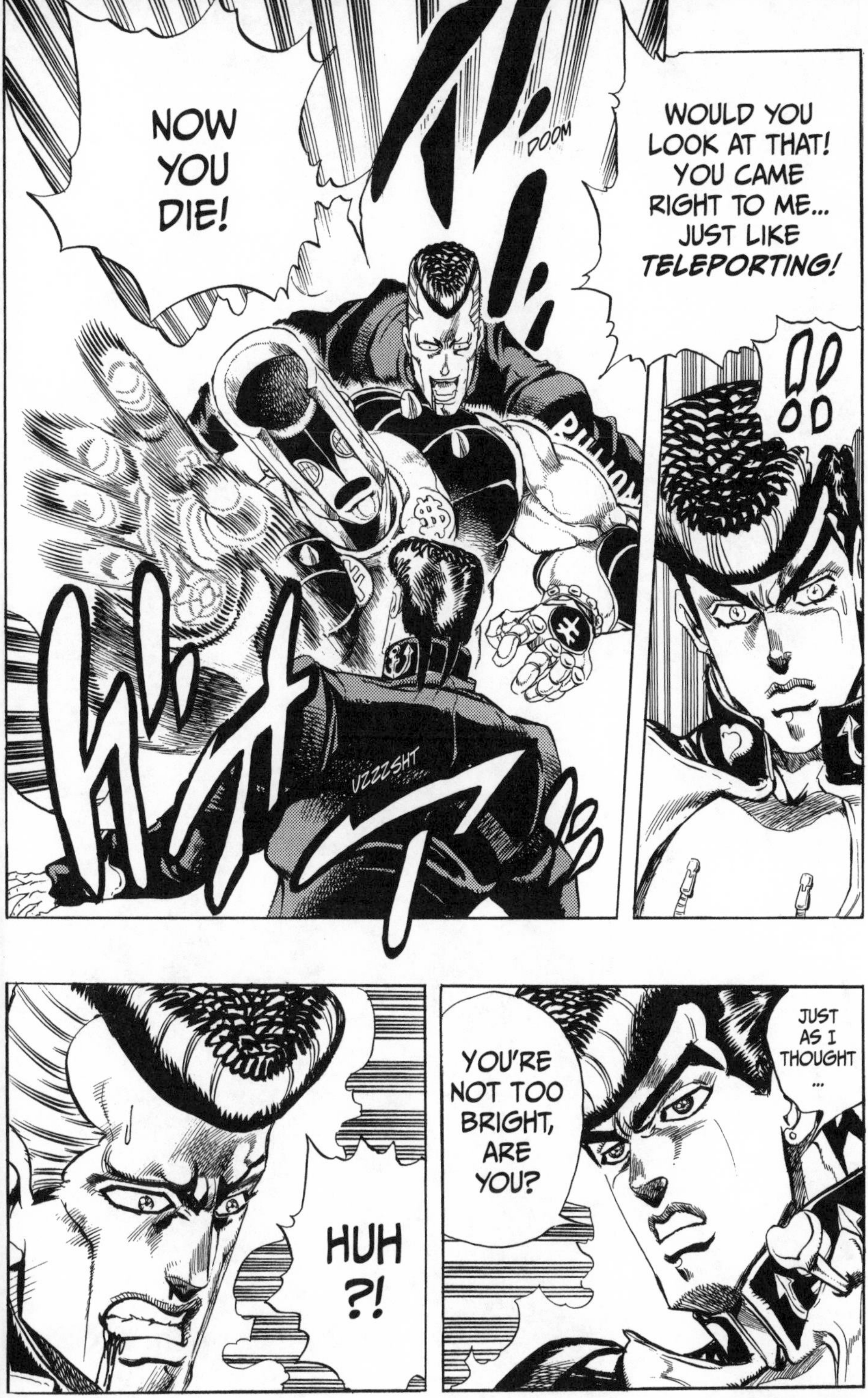
WOULD YOU LOOK AT THAT! YOU CAME RIGHT TO ME... JUST LIKE TELEPORTING!
DOOM
NOW YOU DIE!
UZZZSHT
!!
JUST AS I THOUGHT ...
YOU'RE NOT TOO BRIGHT, ARE YOU?
HUH ?!

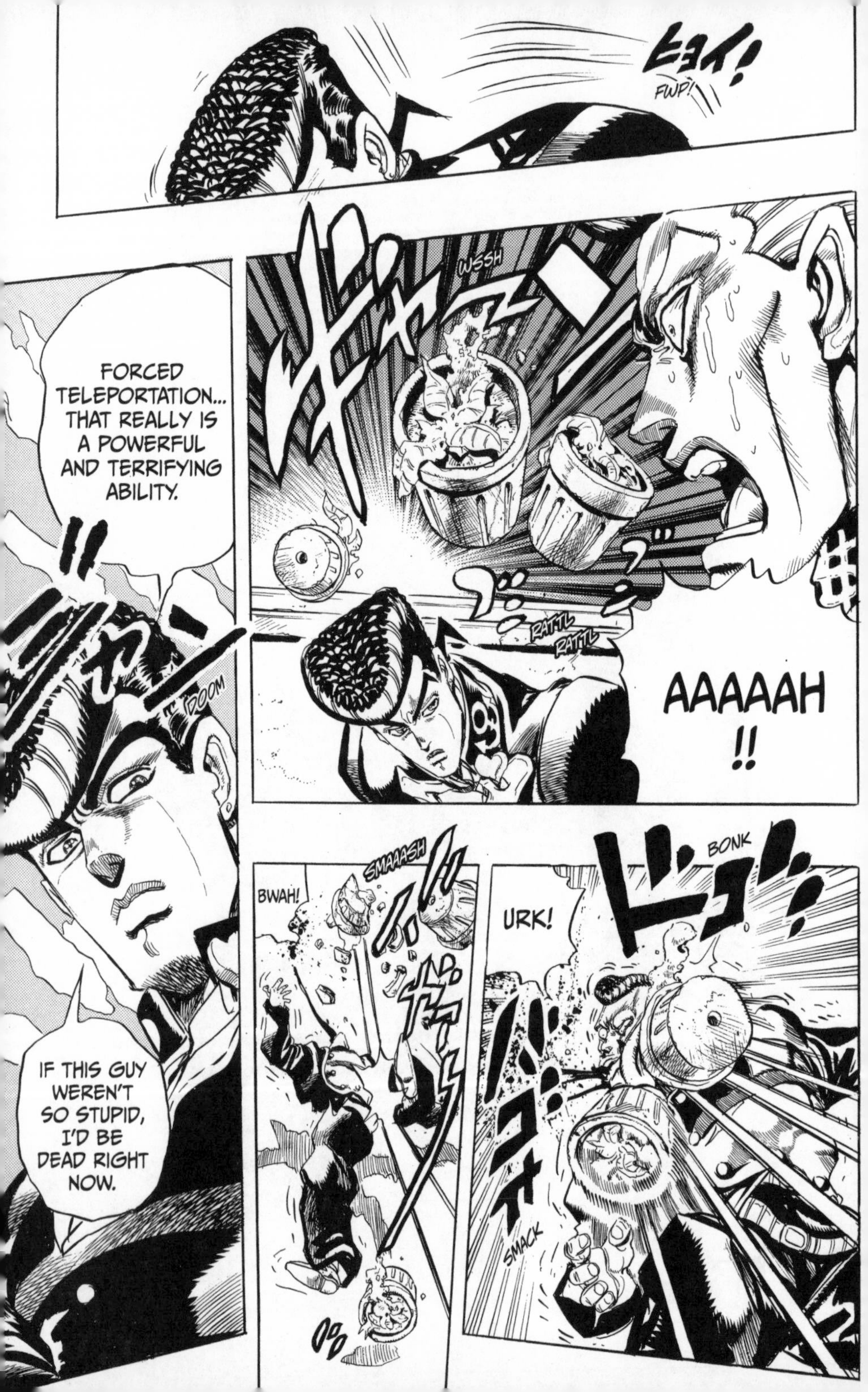

ヒョイ!
FWP!
WSSH
RATTL
RATTL
AAAAAH!!
BONK
URK!
SMACK
SMAAASH
BWAH!
FORCED TELEPORTATION... THAT REALLY IS A POWERFUL AND TERRIFYING ABILITY.
DOOM
IF THIS GUY WEREN'T SO STUPID, I'D BE DEAD RIGHT NOW.

CHAPTER 11

THE NIJIMURA BROTHERS, PART 3

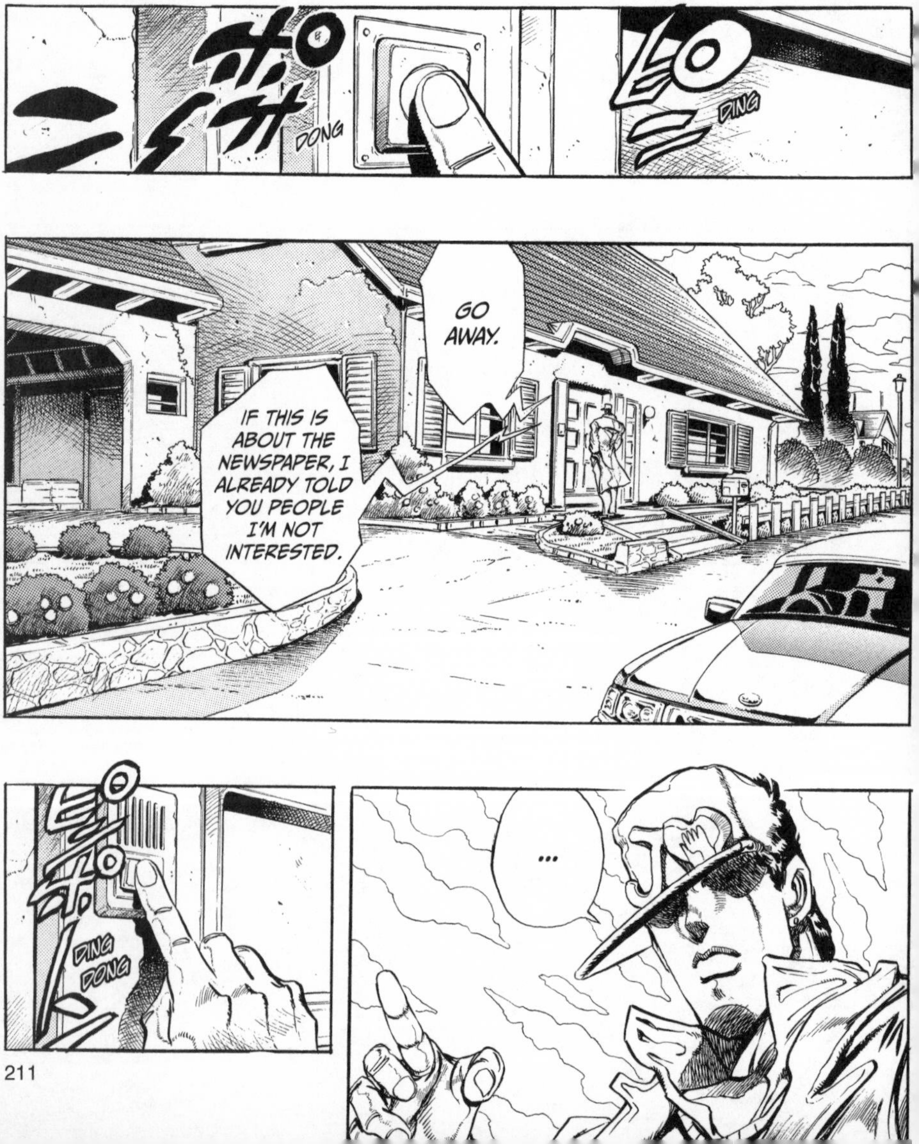
DING
DONG
GO AWAY.
IF THIS IS ABOUT THE NEWSPAPER, I ALREADY TOLD YOU PEOPLE I'M NOT INTERESTED.
...
DING DONG

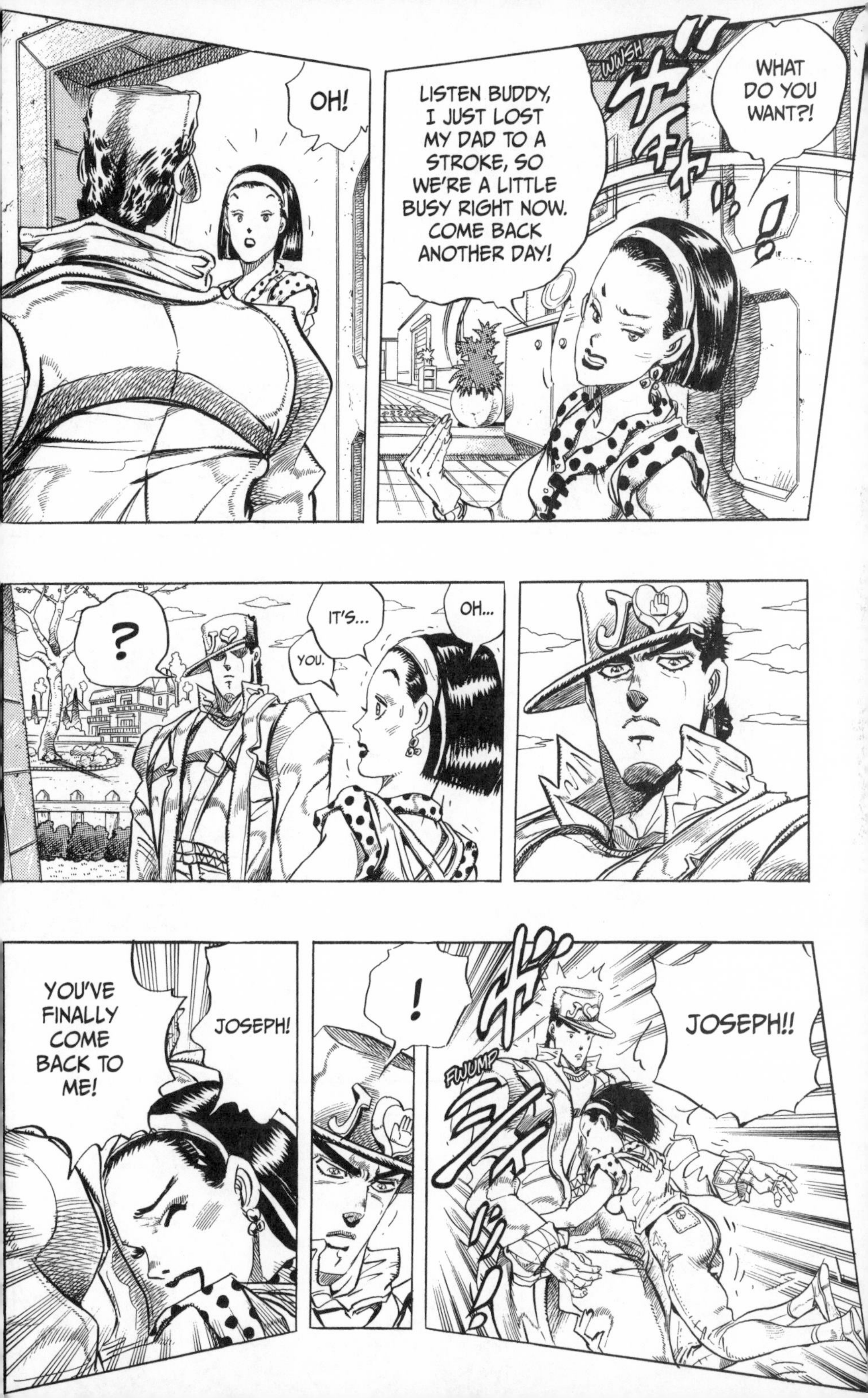
WWSH
WHAT DO YOU WANT?!
LISTEN BUDDY, I JUST LOST MY DAD TO A STROKE, SO WE'RE A LITTLE BUSY RIGHT NOW. COME BACK ANOTHER DAY!
OH!
OH...
IT'S...
YOU.
?
JOSEPH!!
FWUMP
!
JOSEPH!
YOU'VE FINALLY COME BACK TO ME!

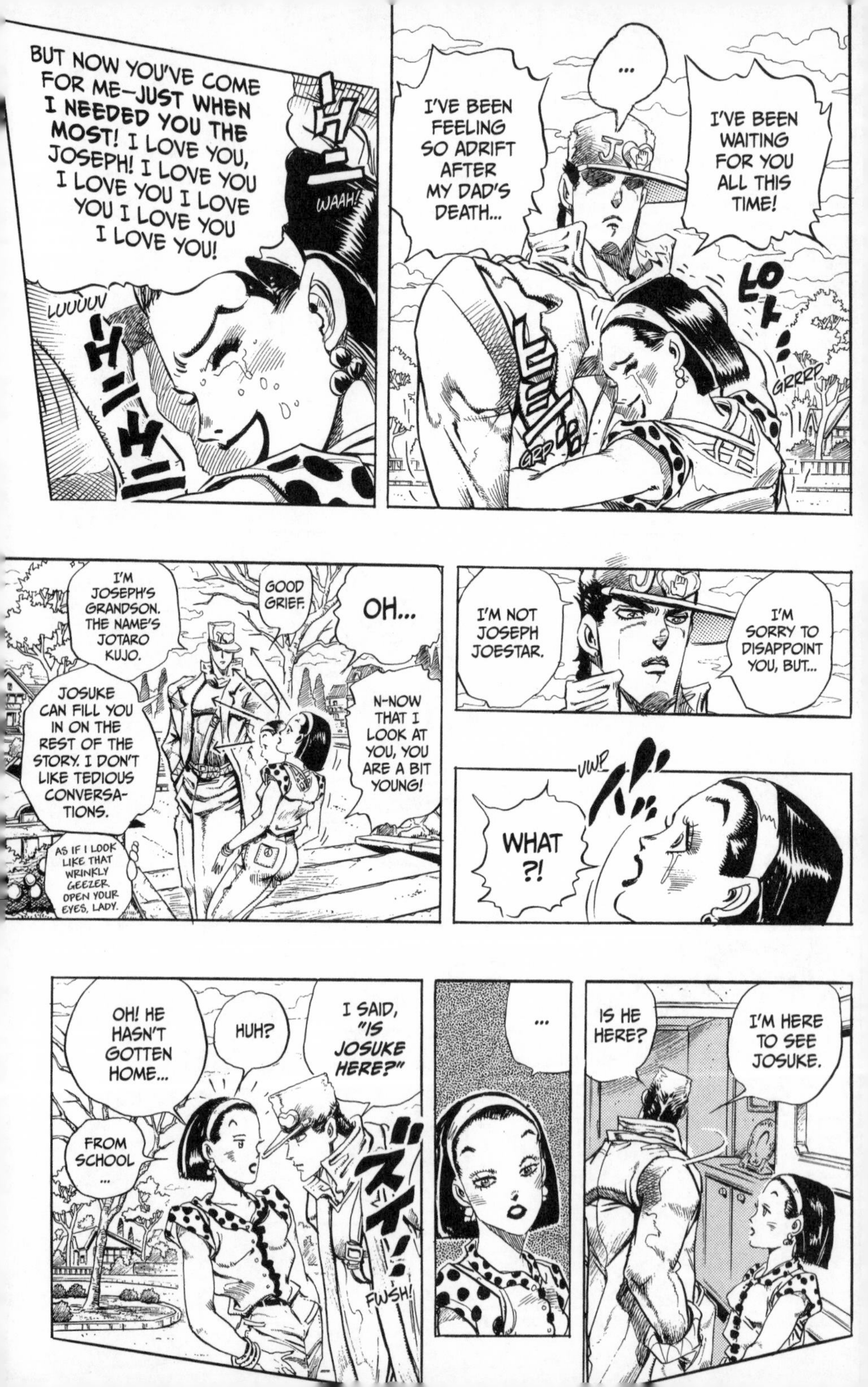
...
I'VE BEEN WAITING FOR YOU ALL THIS TIME!
I'VE BEEN FEELING SO ADRIFT AFTER MY DAD'S DEATH...
GRRRP
GRRP
BUT NOW YOU'VE COME FOR ME—JUST WHEN I NEEDED YOU THE MOST! I LOVE YOU THE JOSEPH! I LOVE YOU, I LOVE YOU I LOVE YOU I LOVE YOU I LOVE YOU I LOVE YOU!
WAAH!
LUUUUV
I'M SORRY TO DISAPPOINT YOU, BUT...
I'M NOT JOSEPH JOESTAR.
VWP
WHAT?!
OH...
GOOD GRIEF.
I'M JOSEPH'S GRANDSON. THE NAME'S JOTARO KUJO.
N-NOW THAT I LOOK AT YOU, YOU ARE A BIT YOUNG!
JOSUKE CAN FILL YOU IN ON THE REST OF THE STORY. I DON'T LIKE TEDIOUS CONVERSA-TIONS.
AS IF I LOOK LIKE THAT WRINKLY GEEZER. OPEN YOUR EYES, LADY.
I'M HERE TO SEE JOSUKE.
IS HE HERE?
...
I SAID, "IS JOSUKE HERE?"
FWSH!
HUH?
OH! HE HASN'T GOTTEN HOME...
FROM SCHOOL ...

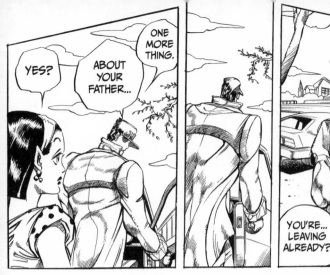

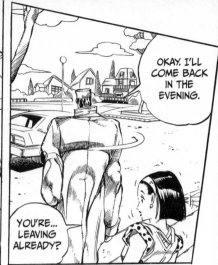

OKAY. I'LL COME BACK IN THE EVENING.
YOU'RE... LEAVING ALREADY?
ONE MORE THING.
ABOUT YOUR FATHER...
YES?
I'M SORRY ABOUT WHAT HAPPENED.
IF JOSEPH WERE AROUND, I KNOW HE'D DO WHATEVER HE COULD TO PROTECT YOU FROM THE COMING DANGER.
BUT HE'S AN OLD MAN NOW. IT WOULD HAVE BEEN IRRESPONSIBLE OF ME TO LET HIM COME.
I'M HERE IN HIS STEAD.
?
VROOOM
...

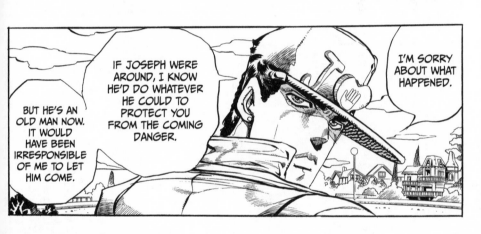

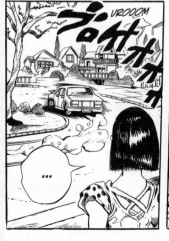

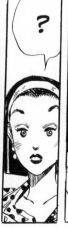

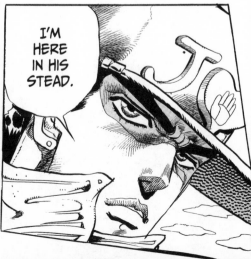

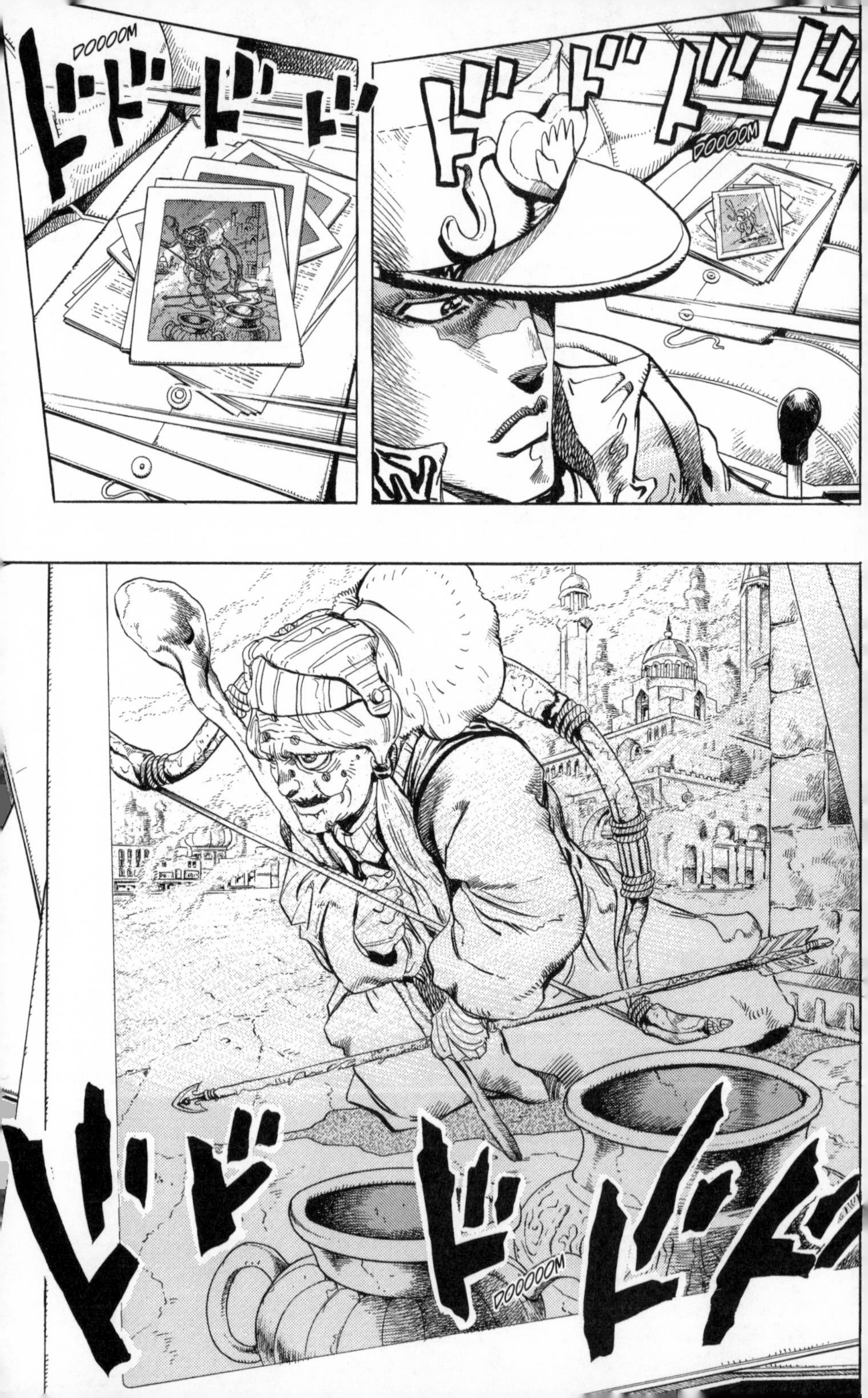

ドドドド
DOOOOM
ドドドドド
DOOOOM
ドドドドド
DOOOOOM

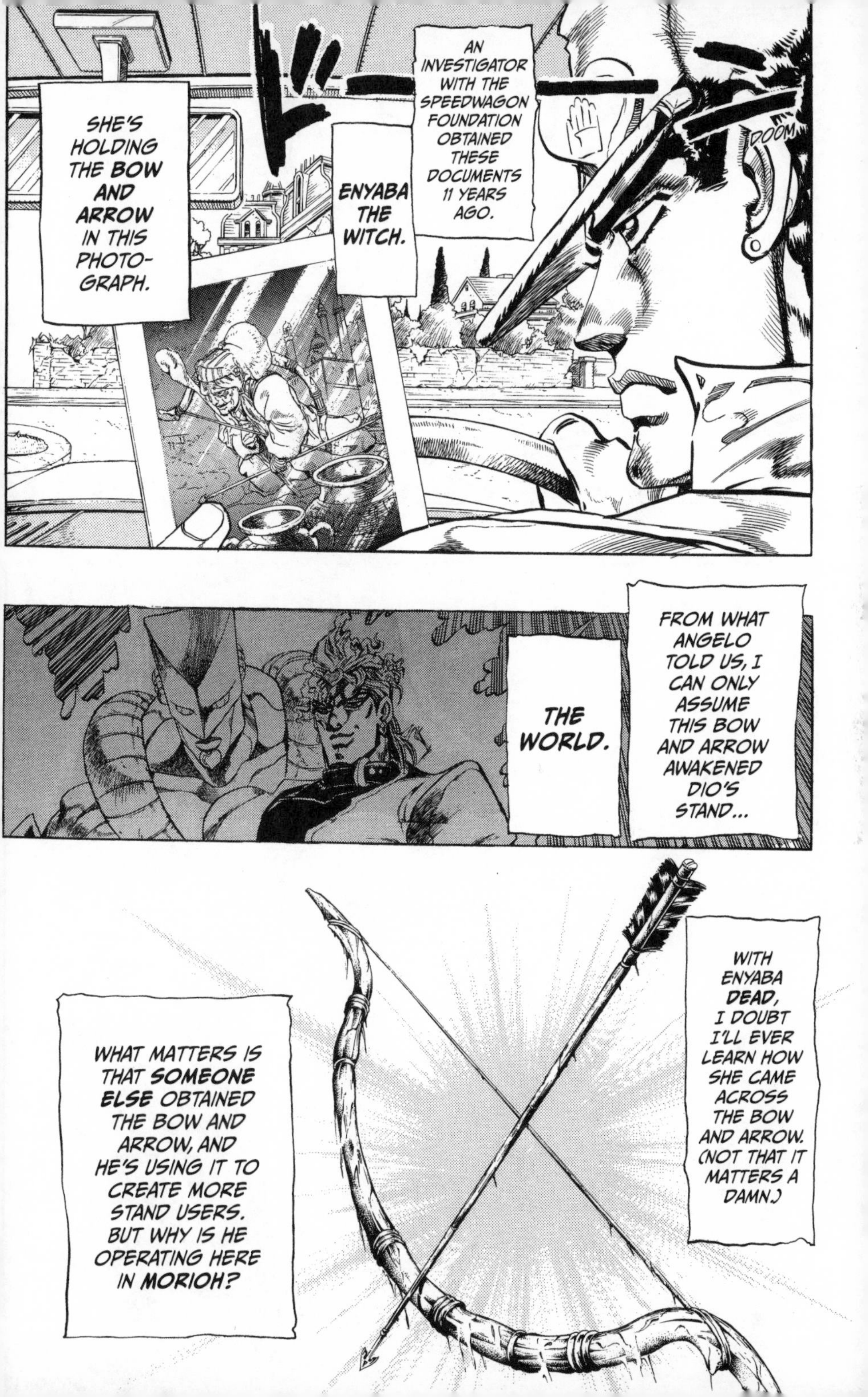
AN INVESTIGATOR WITH THE SPEEDWAGON FOUNDATION OBTAINED THESE DOCUMENTS 11 YEARS AGO.
DOOM
ENYABA THE WITCH.
SHE'S HOLDING THE BOW AND ARROW IN THIS PHOTO-GRAPH.
FROM WHAT ANGELO TOLD US, I CAN ONLY ASSUME THIS BOW AND ARROW AWAKENED DIO'S STAND...
THE WORLD.
WITH ENYABA DEAD, I DOUBT I'LL EVER LEARN HOW SHE CAME ACROSS THE BOW AND ARROW. (NOT THAT IT MATTERS A DAMN.)
WHAT MATTERS IS THAT SOMEONE ELSE OBTAINED THE BOW AND ARROW, AND HE'S USING IT TO CREATE MORE STAND USERS. BUT WHY IS HE OPERATING HERE IN MORIOH?

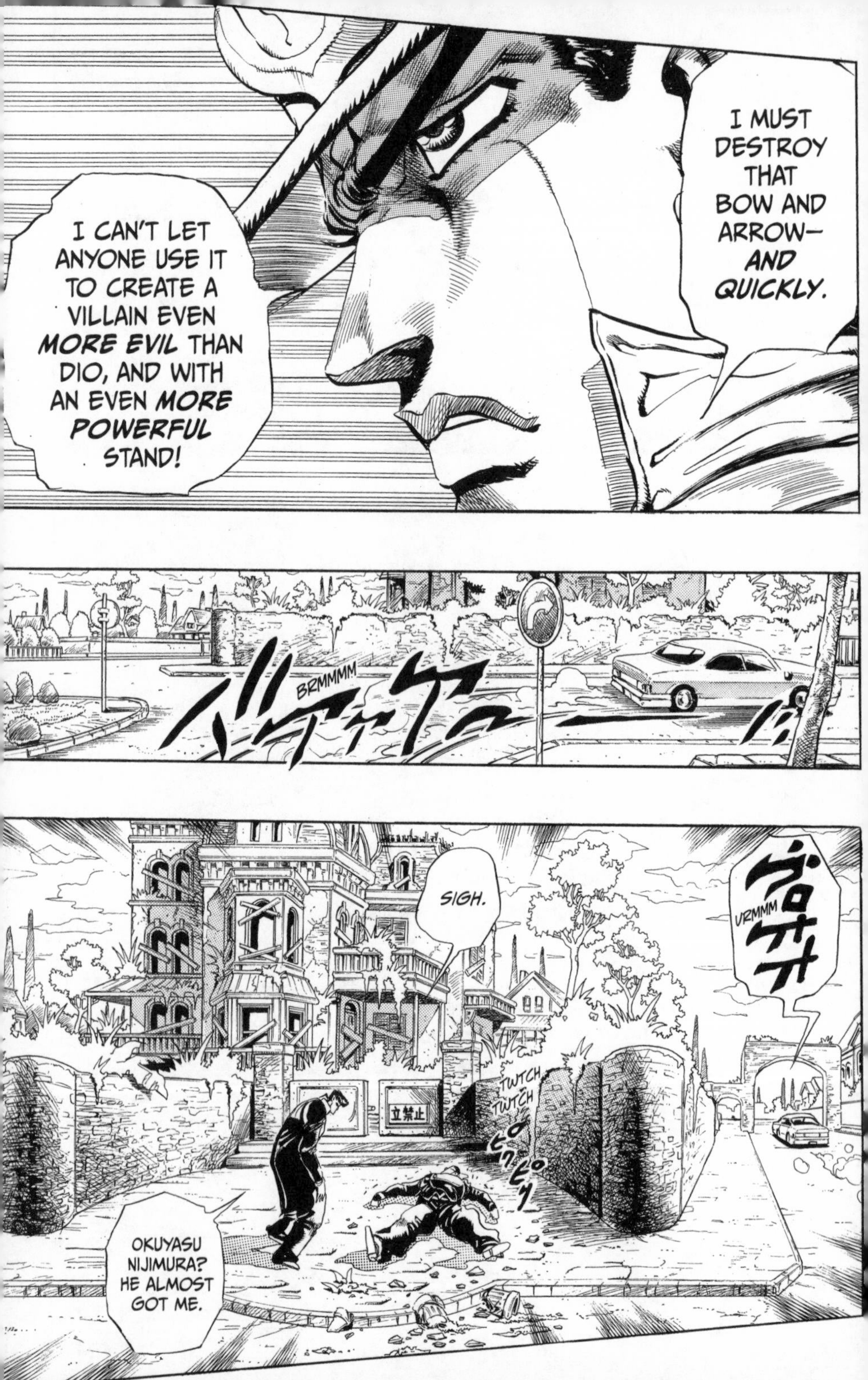
I MUST DESTROY THAT BOW AND ARROW— AND QUICKLY.
I CAN'T LET ANYONE USE IT TO CREATE A VILLAIN EVEN MORE EVIL THAN DIO, AND WITH AN EVEN MORE POWERFUL STAND!
BRMMMM
URMMM
SIGH.
TWTCH TWTCH
OKUYASU NIJIMURA? HE ALMOST GOT ME.

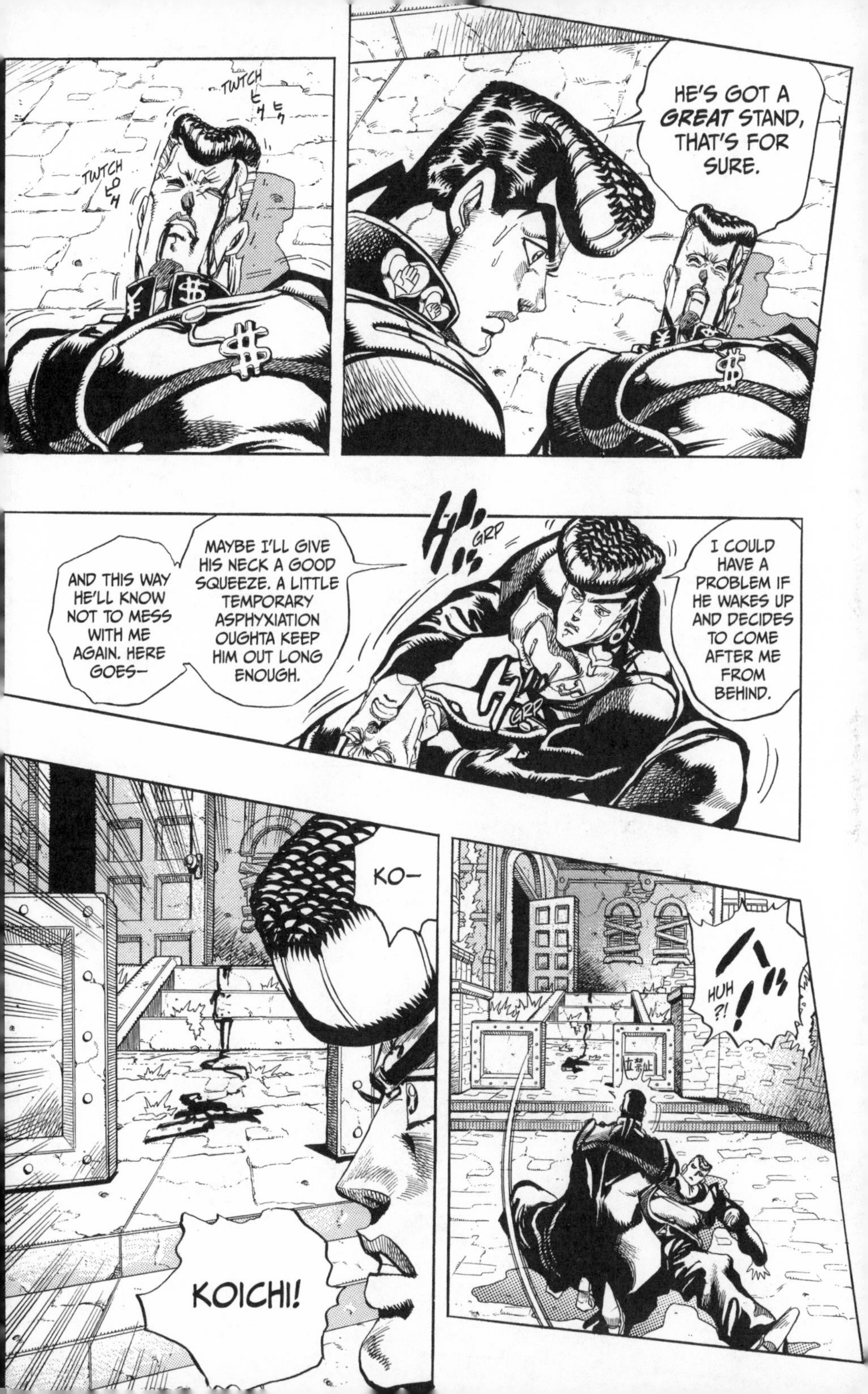
HE'S GOT A GREAT STAND, THAT'S FOR SURE.
TWTCH
TWTCH
I COULD HAVE A PROBLEM IF HE WAKES UP AND DECIDES TO COME AFTER ME FROM BEHIND.
GRP
GRP
MAYBE I'LL GIVE HIS NECK A GOOD SQUEEZE. A LITTLE TEMPORARY ASPHYXIATION OUGHTA KEEP HIM OUT LONG ENOUGH.
AND THIS WAY HE'LL KNOW NOT TO MESS WITH ME AGAIN. HERE GOES—
HUH ?!
KO—
KOICHI!

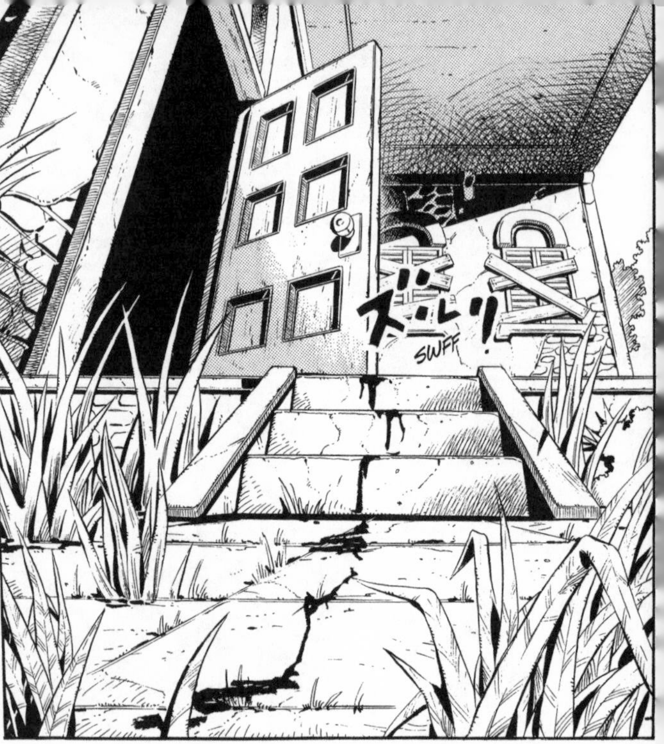
ズルリ
SWFF
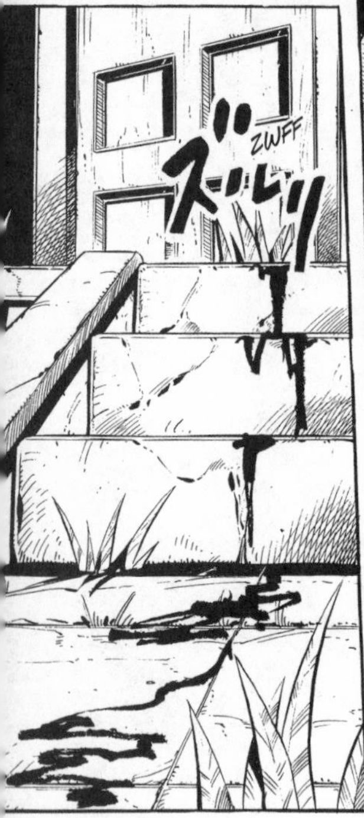
ズルリ
ZWFF
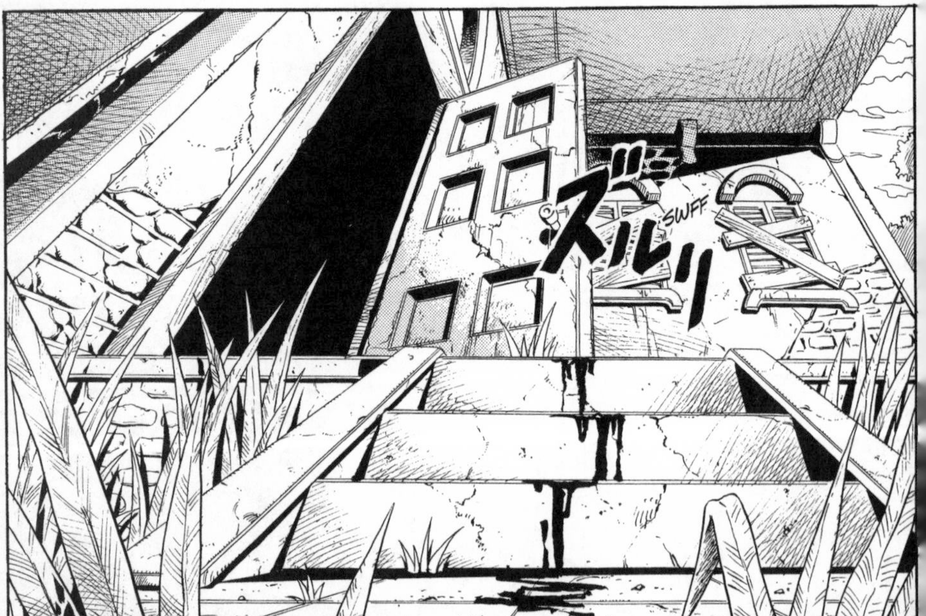
ズルリ
SWFF

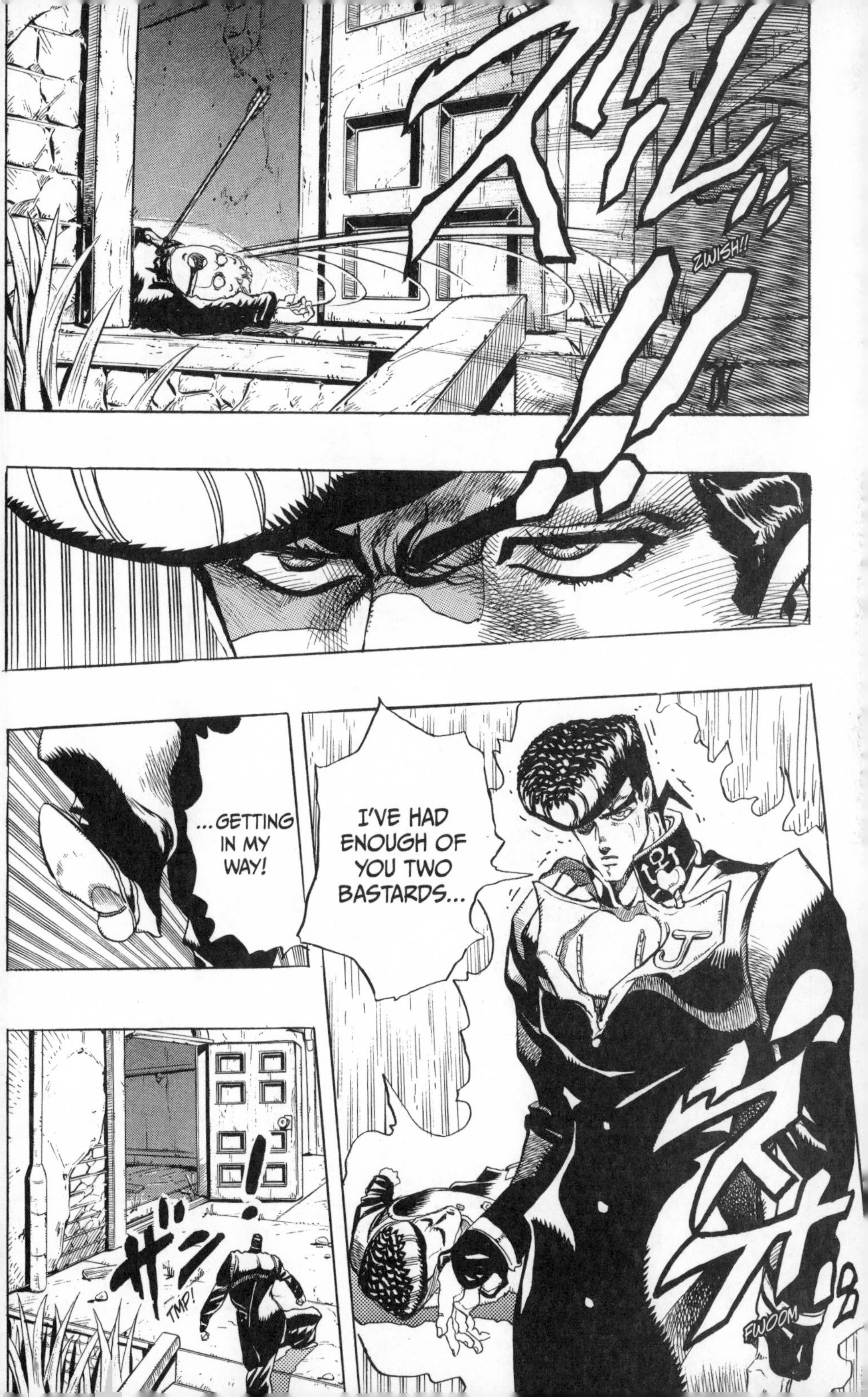
ZWISH!!
I'VE HAD ENOUGH OF YOU TWO BASTARDS...
FWOOM
...GETTING IN MY WAY!
TMP!

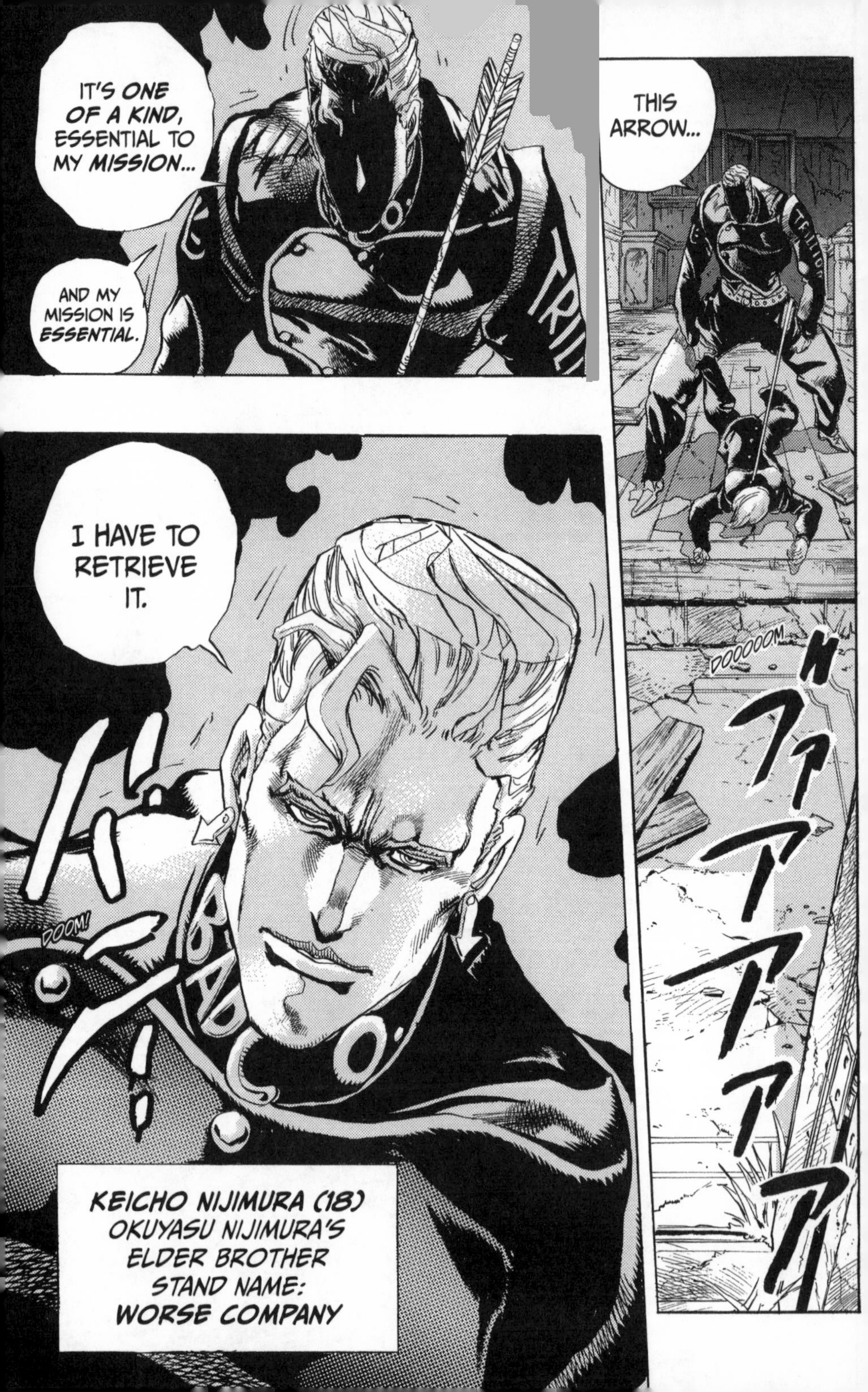
THIS ARROW...
IT'S ONE OF A KIND, ESSENTIAL TO MY MISSION...
AND MY MISSION IS ESSENTIAL.
I HAVE TO RETRIEVE IT.
DOOM!
KEICHO NIJIMURA (18) OKUYASU NIJIMURA'S ELDER BROTHER STAND NAME: WORSE COMPANY
DOOOOOM

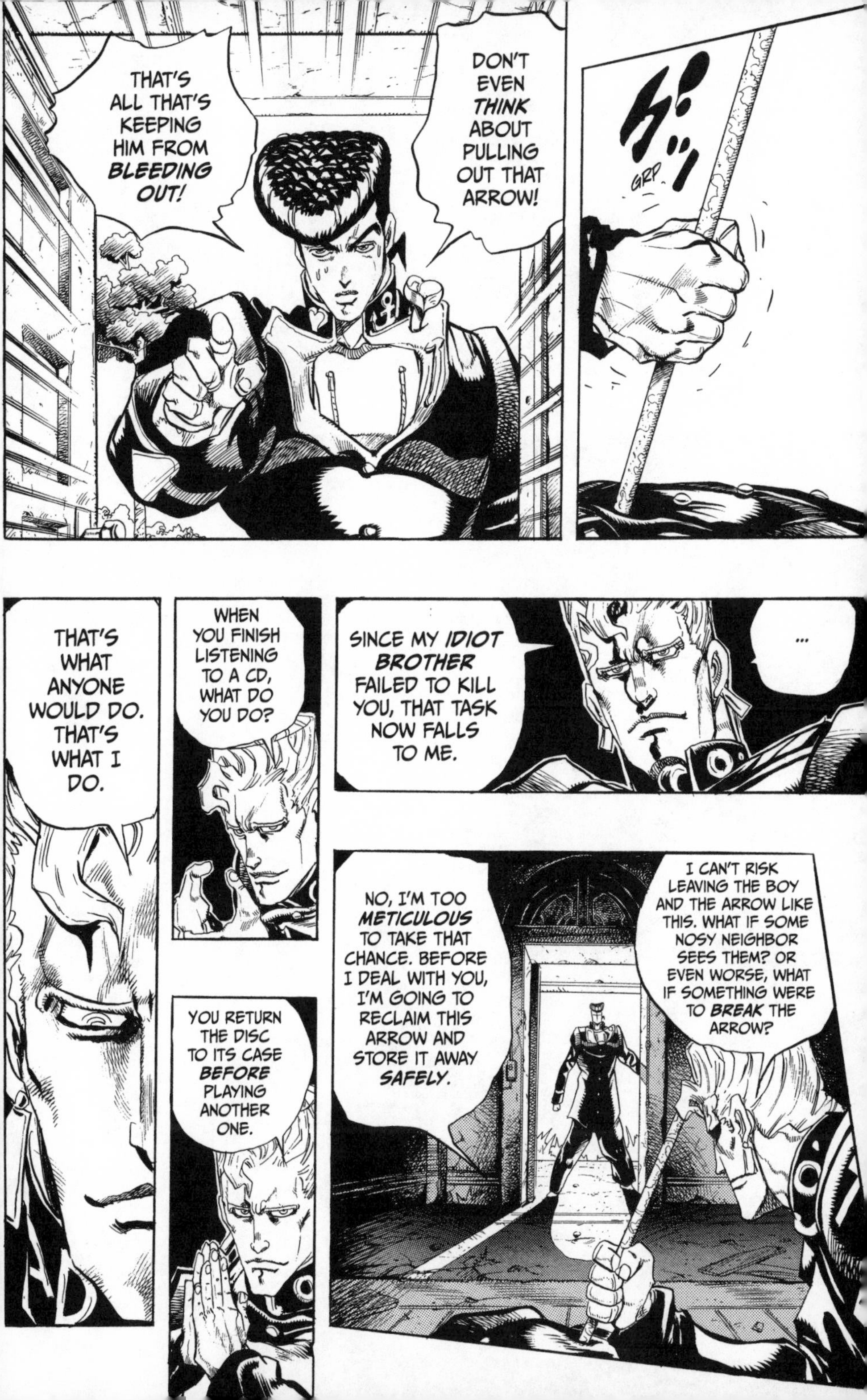

GRP
DON'T EVEN *THINK* ABOUT PULLING OUT THAT ARROW!
THAT'S ALL THAT'S KEEPING HIM FROM *BLEEDING OUT!*
...
SINCE MY *IDIOT BROTHER* FAILED TO KILL YOU, THAT TASK NOW FALLS TO ME.
I CAN'T RISK LEAVING THE BOY AND THE ARROW LIKE THIS. WHAT IF SOME NOSY NEIGHBOR SEES THEM? OR EVEN WORSE, WHAT IF SOMETHING WERE TO *BREAK* THE ARROW?
NO, I'M TOO *METICULOUS* TO TAKE THAT CHANCE. BEFORE I DEAL WITH YOU, I'M GOING TO RECLAIM THIS ARROW AND STORE IT AWAY *SAFELY.*
WHEN YOU FINISH LISTENING TO A CD, WHAT DO YOU DO?
YOU RETURN THE DISC TO ITS CASE *BEFORE* PLAYING ANOTHER ONE.
THAT'S WHAT ANYONE WOULD DO. THAT'S WHAT I DO.

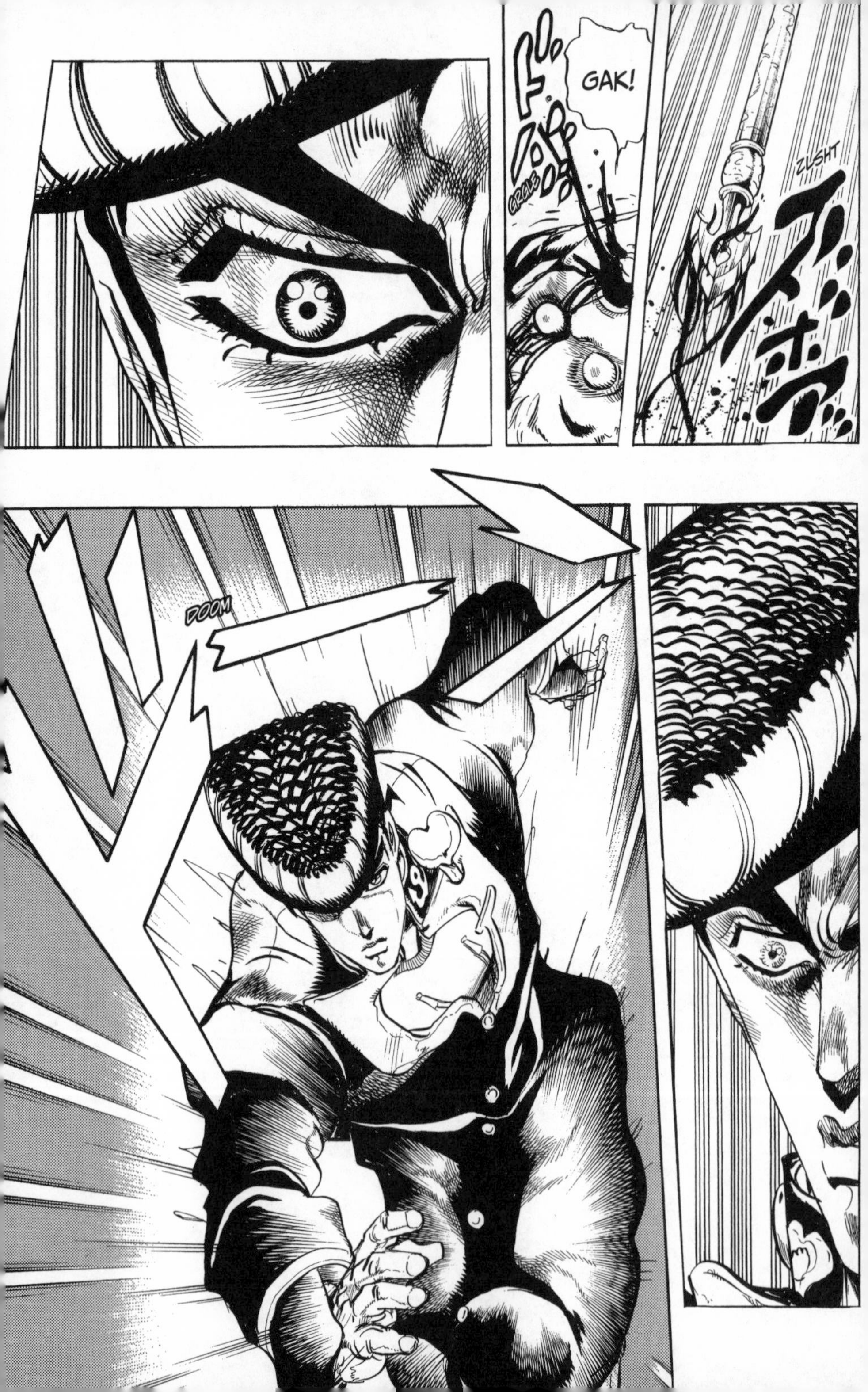
ZUSHT
GAK!
CRACK
DOOM

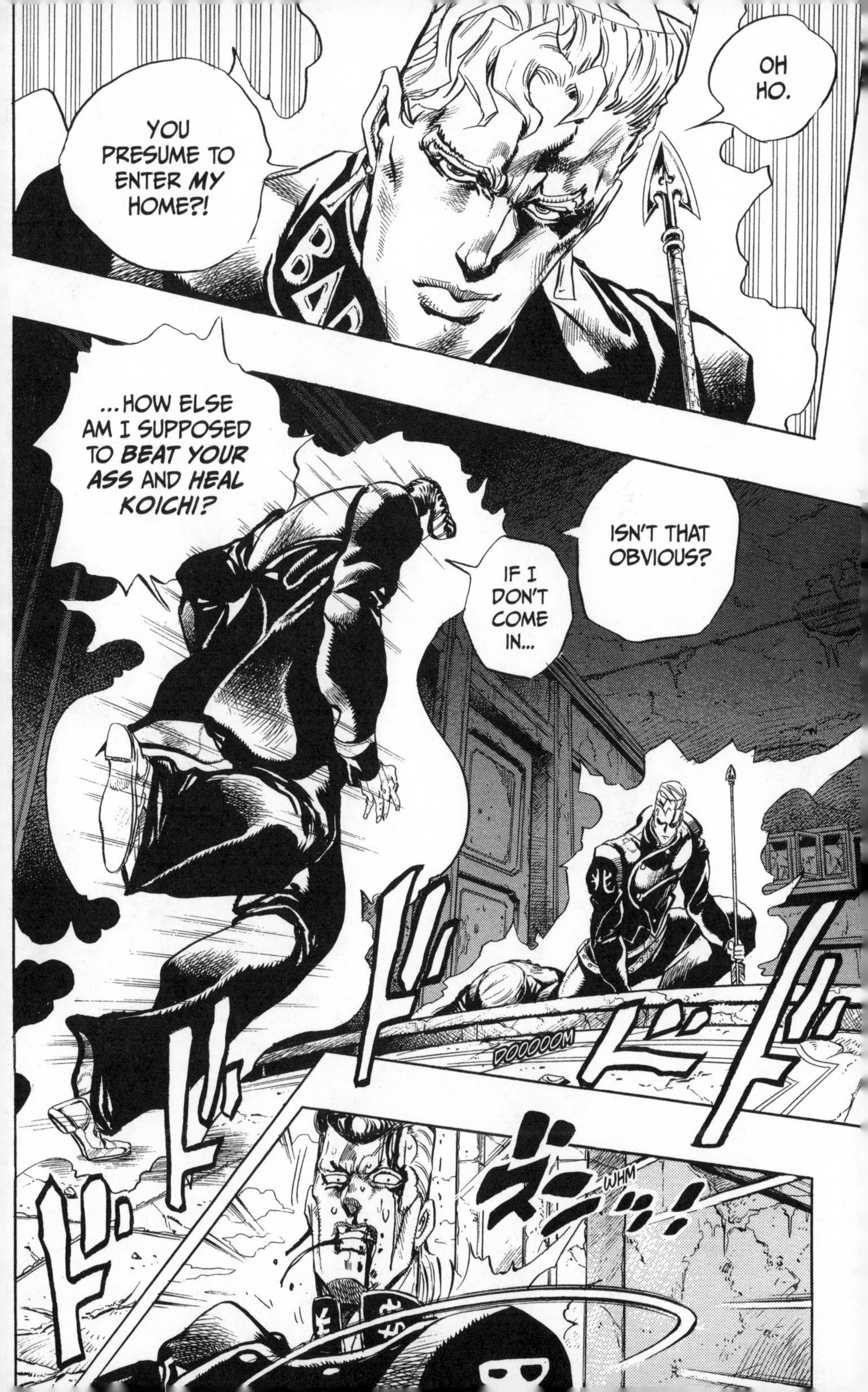

OH HO.
YOU PRESUME TO ENTER *MY* HOME?!
ISN'T THAT OBVIOUS?
IF I DON'T COME IN...
...HOW ELSE AM I SUPPOSED TO *BEAT YOUR ASS* AND *HEAL KOICHI*?
DOOOOOM
WHM

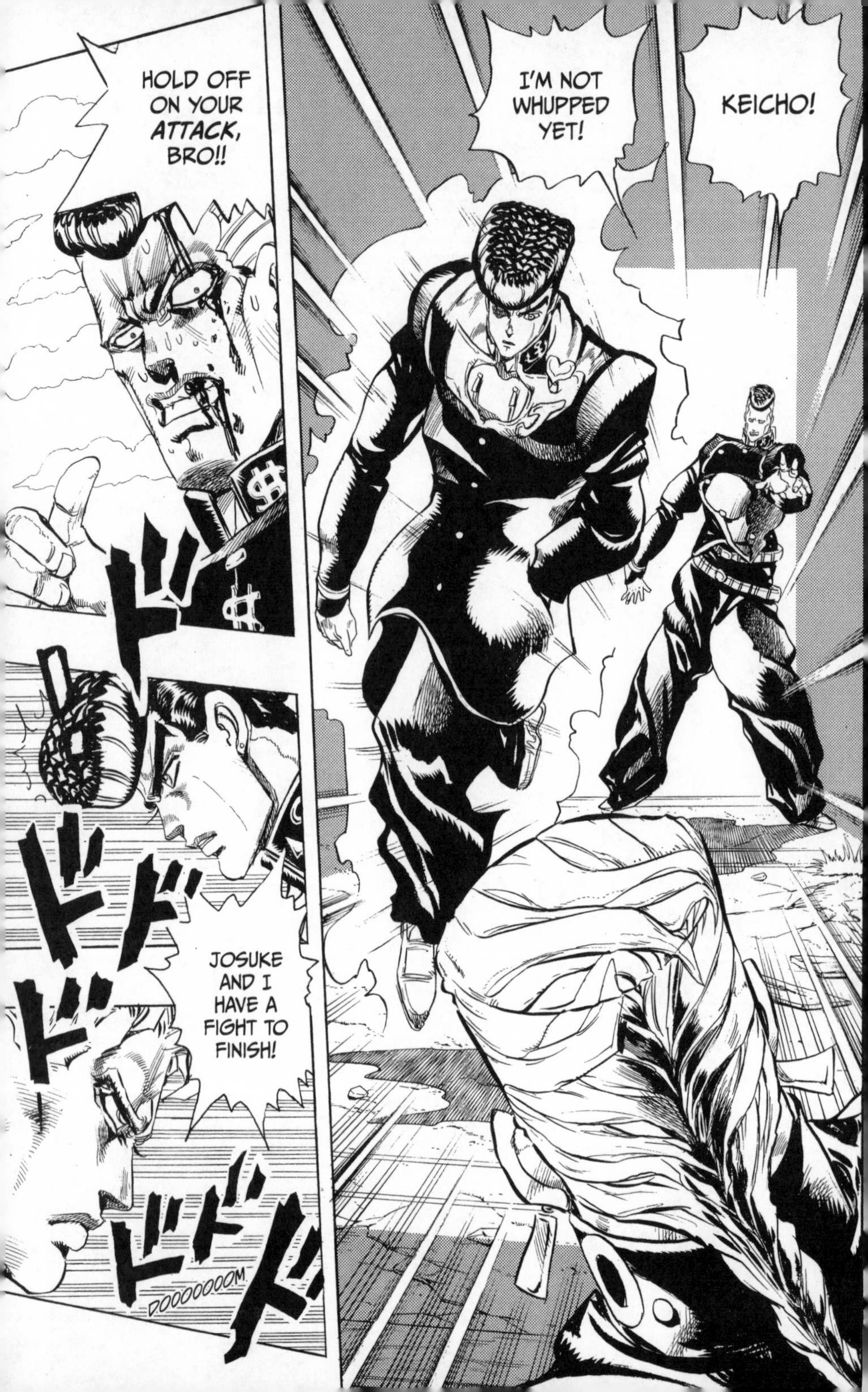
KEICHO!
I'M NOT WHUPPED YET!
HOLD OFF ON YOUR ATTACK, BRO!!
JOSUKE AND I HAVE A FIGHT TO FINISH!
DOOOOOOOM

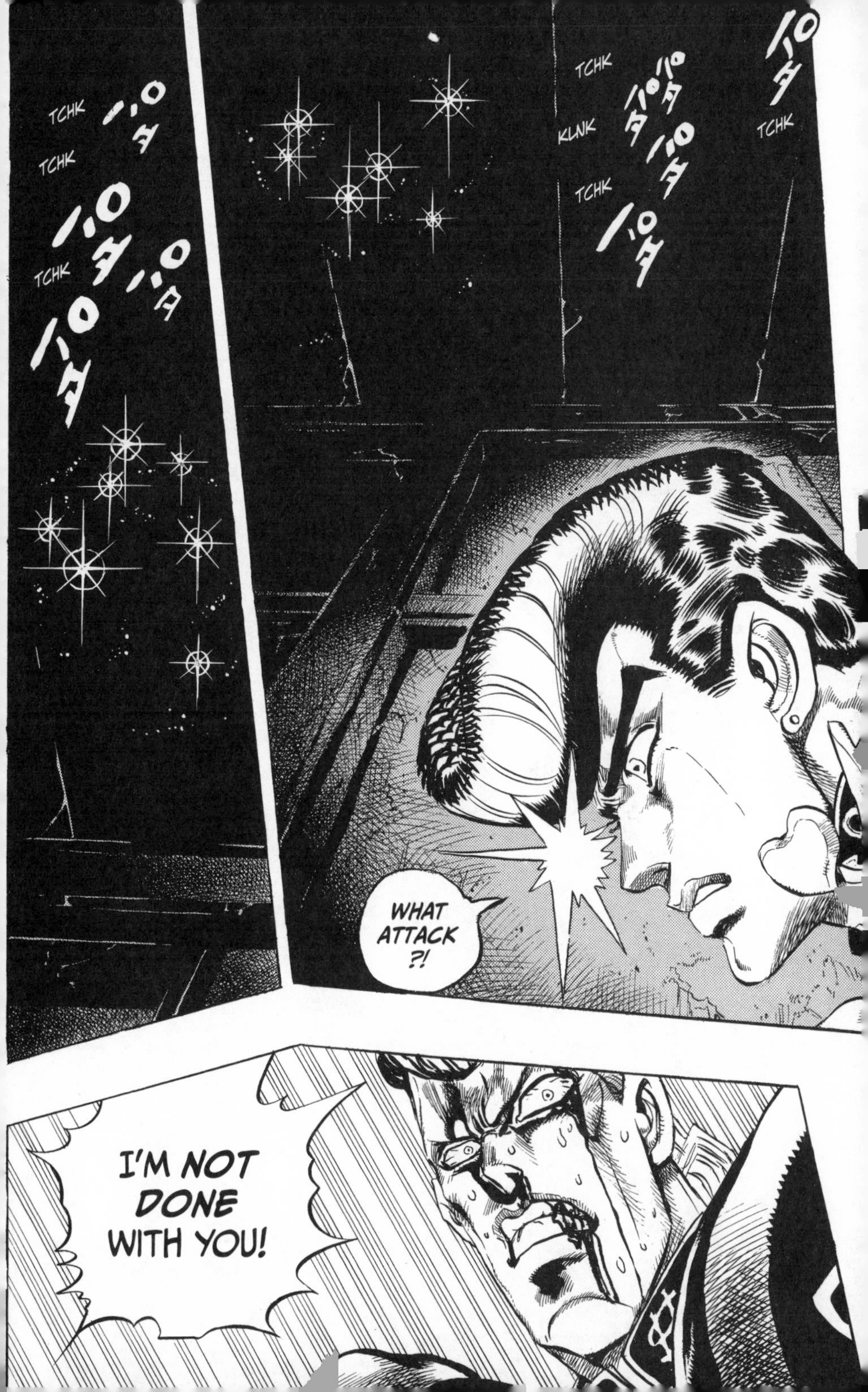
TCHK
TCHK
KLNK
TCHK
WHAT ATTACK ?!
TCHK
TCHK
TCHK
I'M NOT DONE WITH YOU!

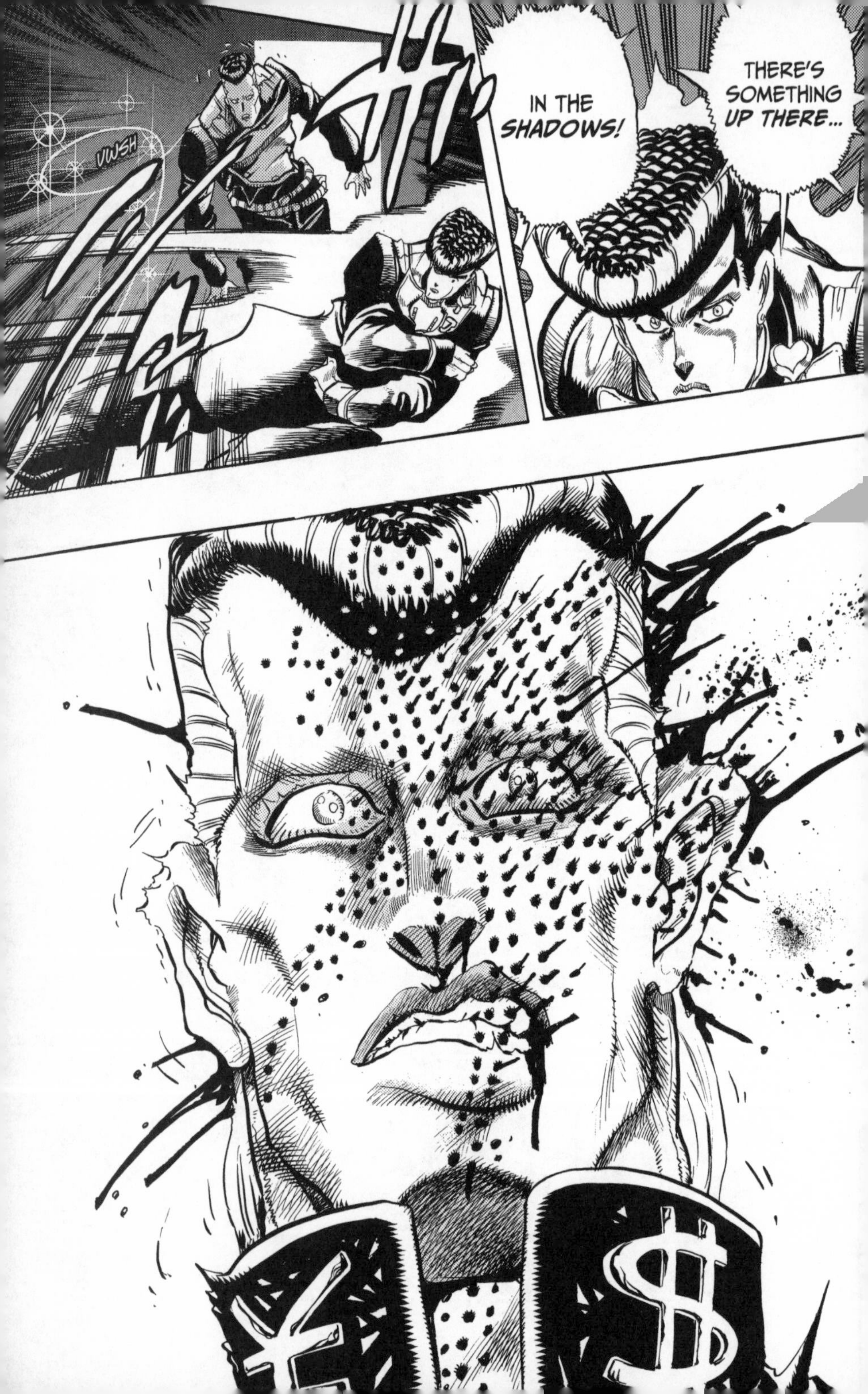
THERE'S SOMETHING UP THERE...
IN THE SHADOWS!
VWSH

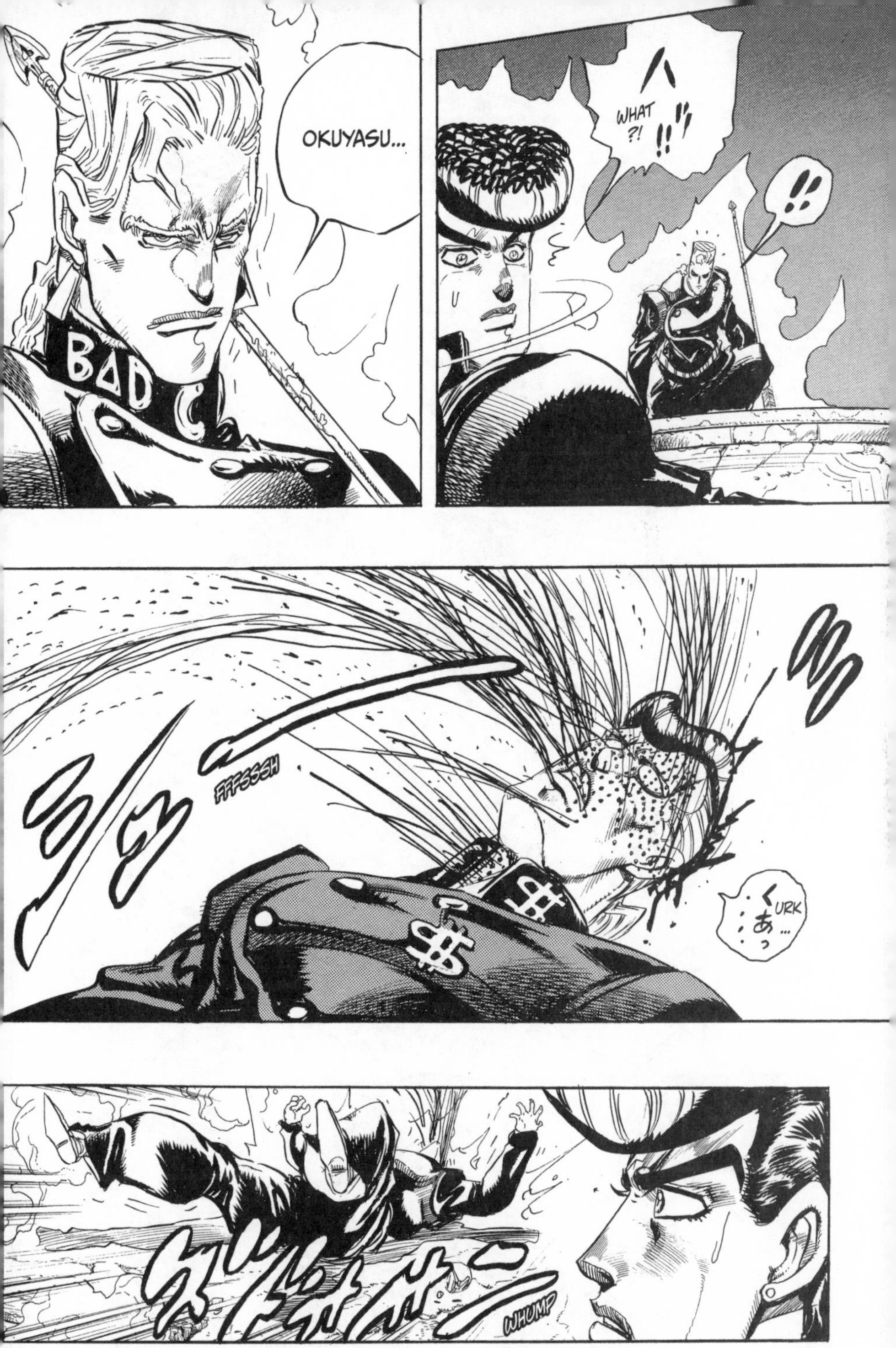
ハ WHAT ?! !!
!!
OKUYASU...
FFFSSSH
くあっ URK...
WHUMP

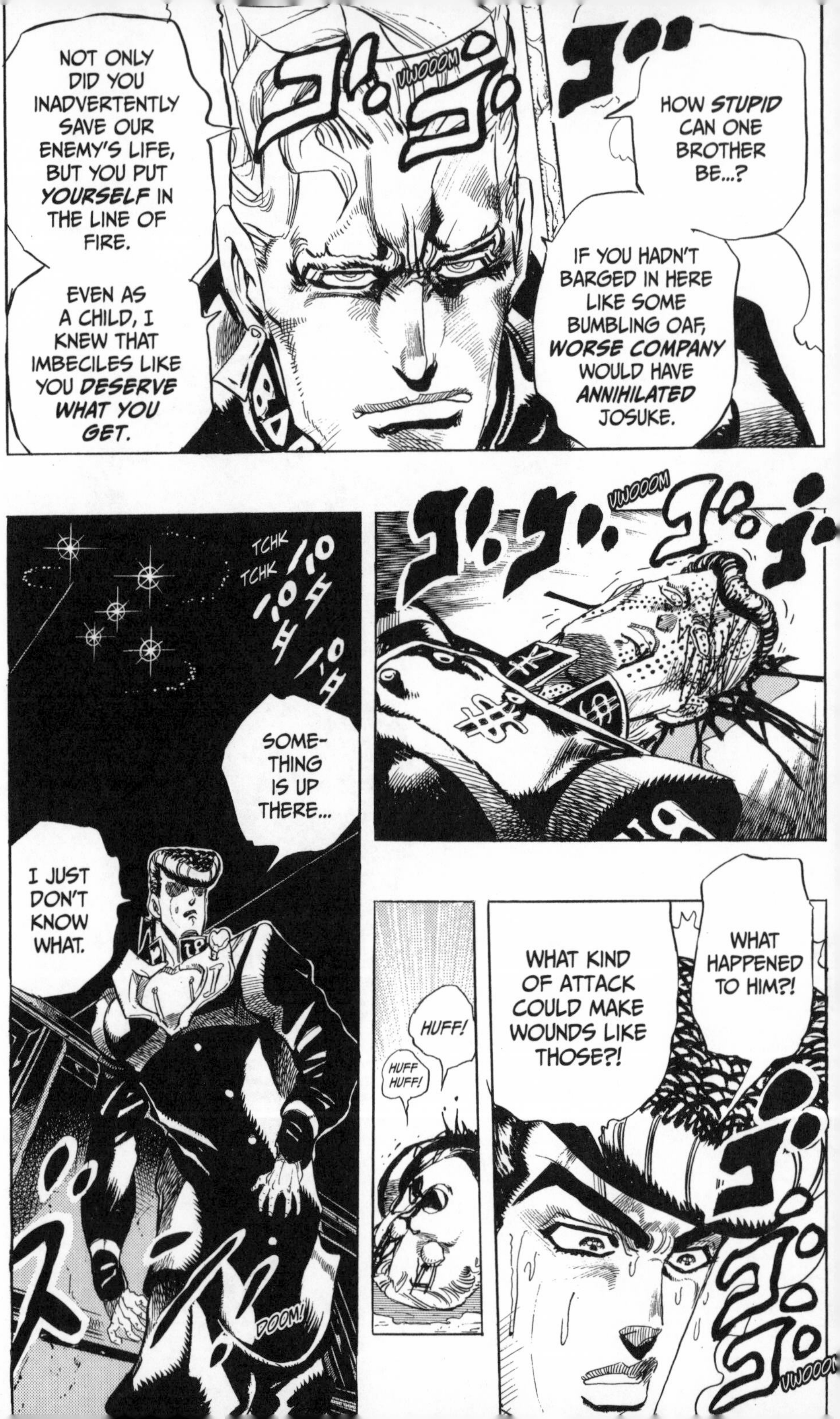
HOW STUPID CAN ONE BROTHER BE...?
VWOOOM
IF YOU HADN'T BARGED IN HERE LIKE SOME BUMBLING OAF, WORSE COMPANY WOULD HAVE ANNIHILATED JOSUKE.
NOT ONLY DID YOU INADVERTENTLY SAVE OUR ENEMY'S LIFE, BUT YOU PUT YOURSELF IN THE LINE OF FIRE.
EVEN AS A CHILD, I KNEW THAT IMBECILES LIKE YOU DESERVE WHAT YOU GET.
VWOOOM
WHAT HAPPENED TO HIM?!
WHAT KIND OF ATTACK COULD MAKE WOUNDS LIKE THOSE?!
HUFF!
HUFF HUFF!
TCHK TCHK
SOME-THING IS UP THERE...
I JUST DON'T KNOW WHAT.
DOOM!

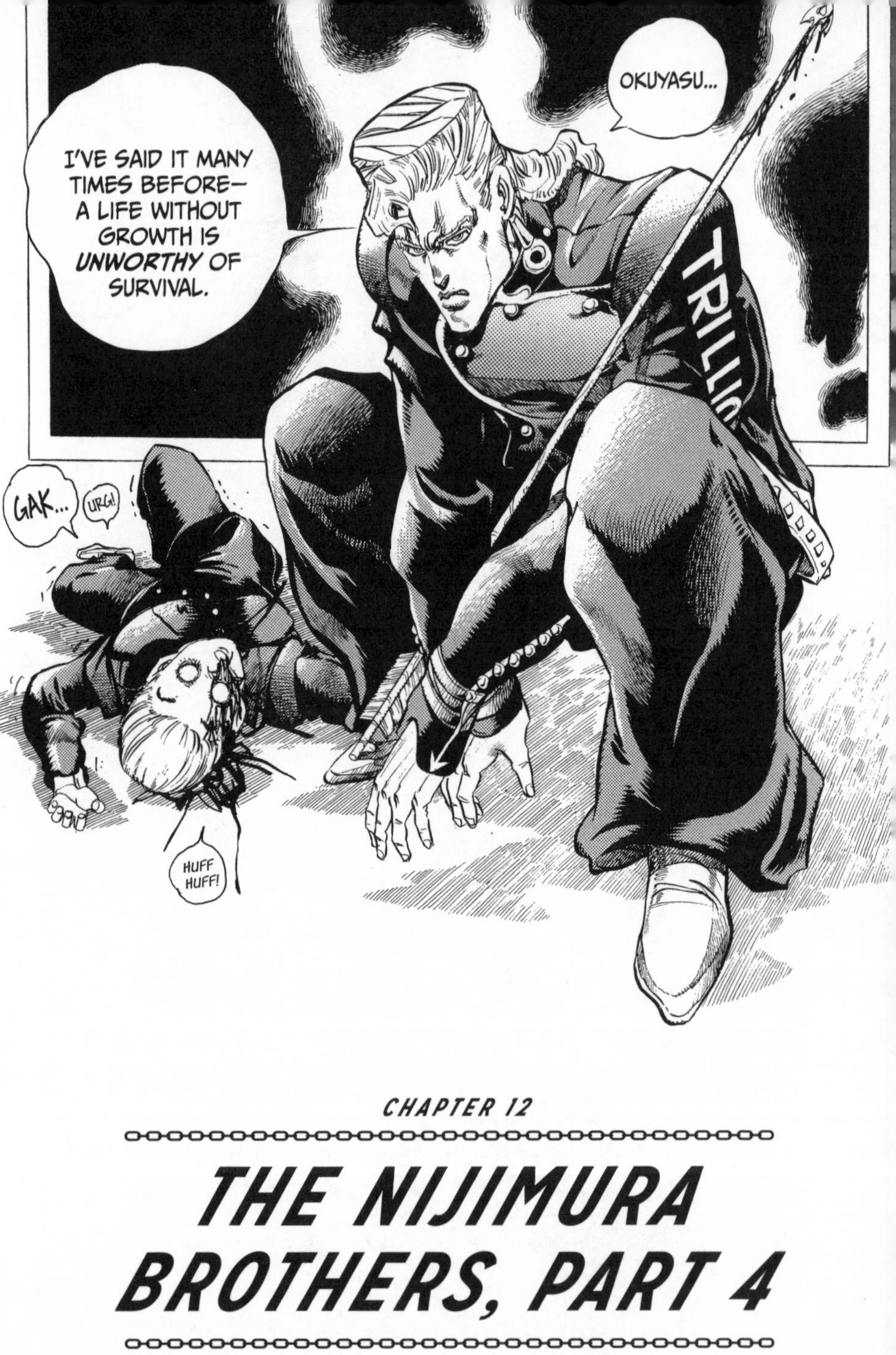
OKUYASU...
I'VE SAID IT MANY TIMES BEFORE—A LIFE WITHOUT GROWTH IS *UNWORTHY* OF SURVIVAL.
URG!
GAK...
HUFF HUFF!

CHAPTER 12

THE NIJIMURA BROTHERS, PART 4

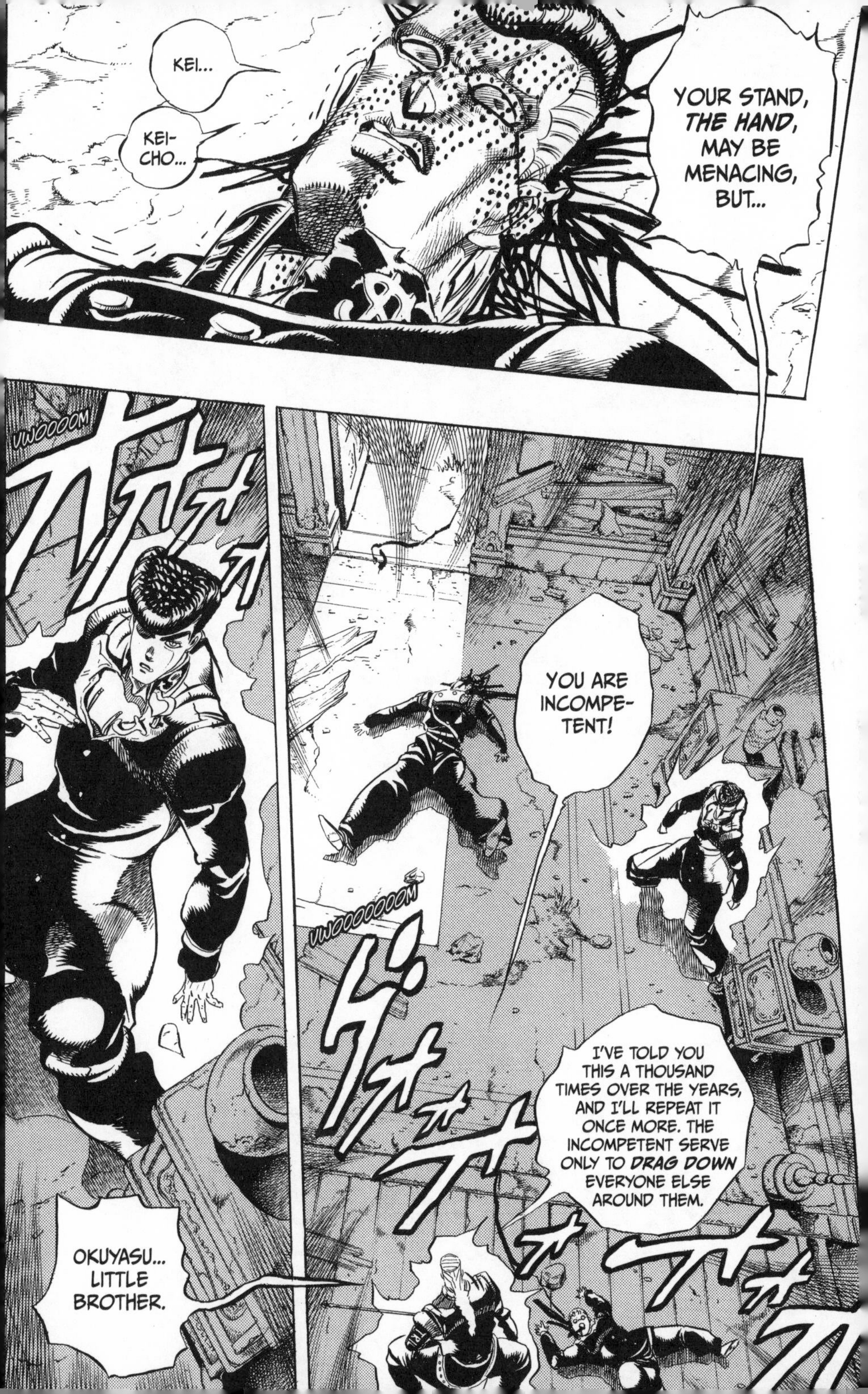
YOUR STAND, *THE HAND,* MAY BE MENACING, BUT...
KEI...
KEI-CHO...
YOU ARE INCOMPETENT!
UWOOOOOOOOM
I'VE TOLD YOU THIS A THOUSAND TIMES OVER THE YEARS, AND I'LL REPEAT IT ONCE MORE. THE INCOMPETENT SERVE ONLY TO ***DRAG DOWN*** EVERYONE ELSE AROUND THEM.
UWOOOOOM
OKUYASU... LITTLE BROTHER.

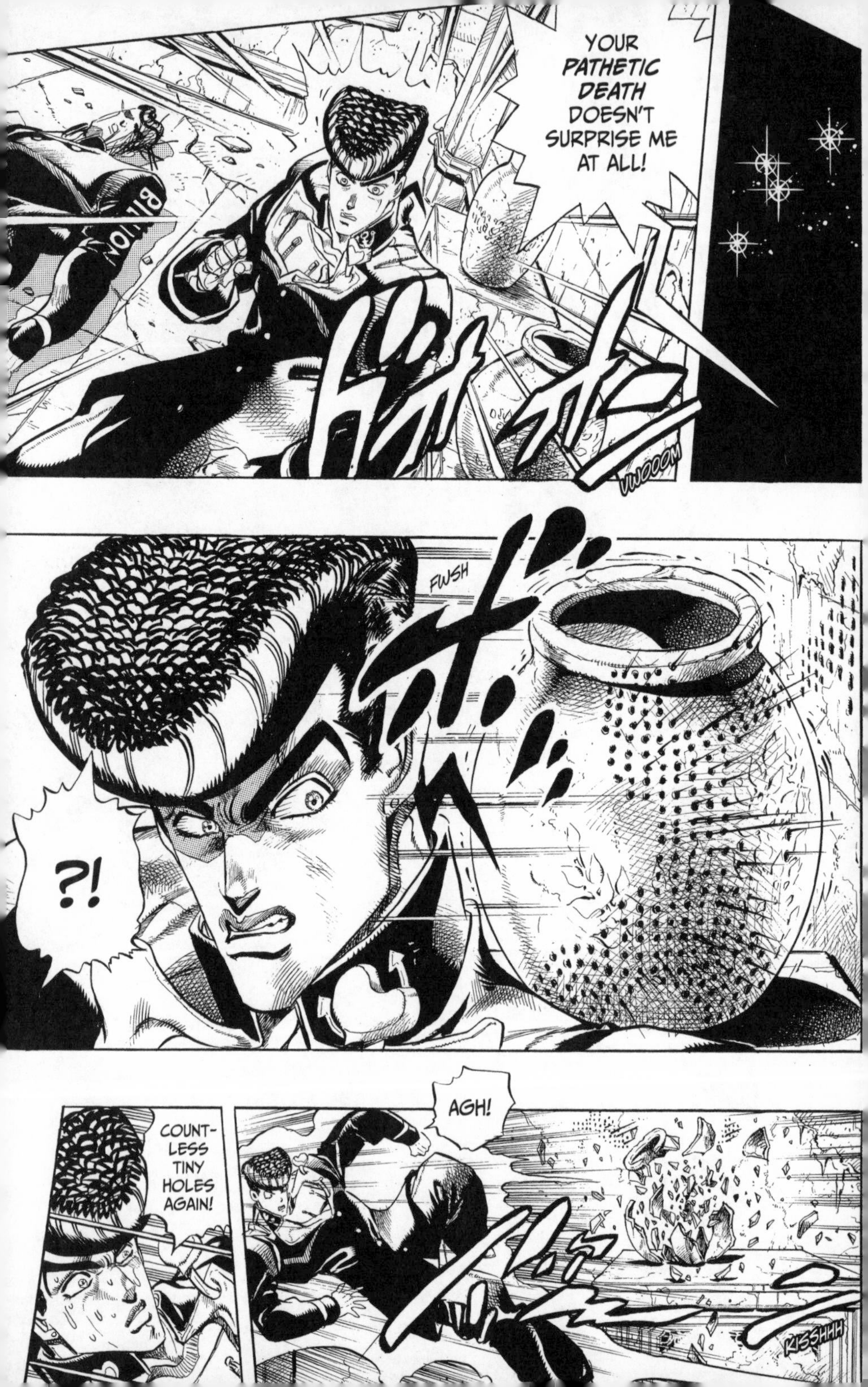
YOUR PATHETIC DEATH DOESN'T SURPRISE ME AT ALL!
VWOOOM
FWSH
?!
AGH!
KISSHHH
COUNT-LESS TINY HOLES AGAIN!

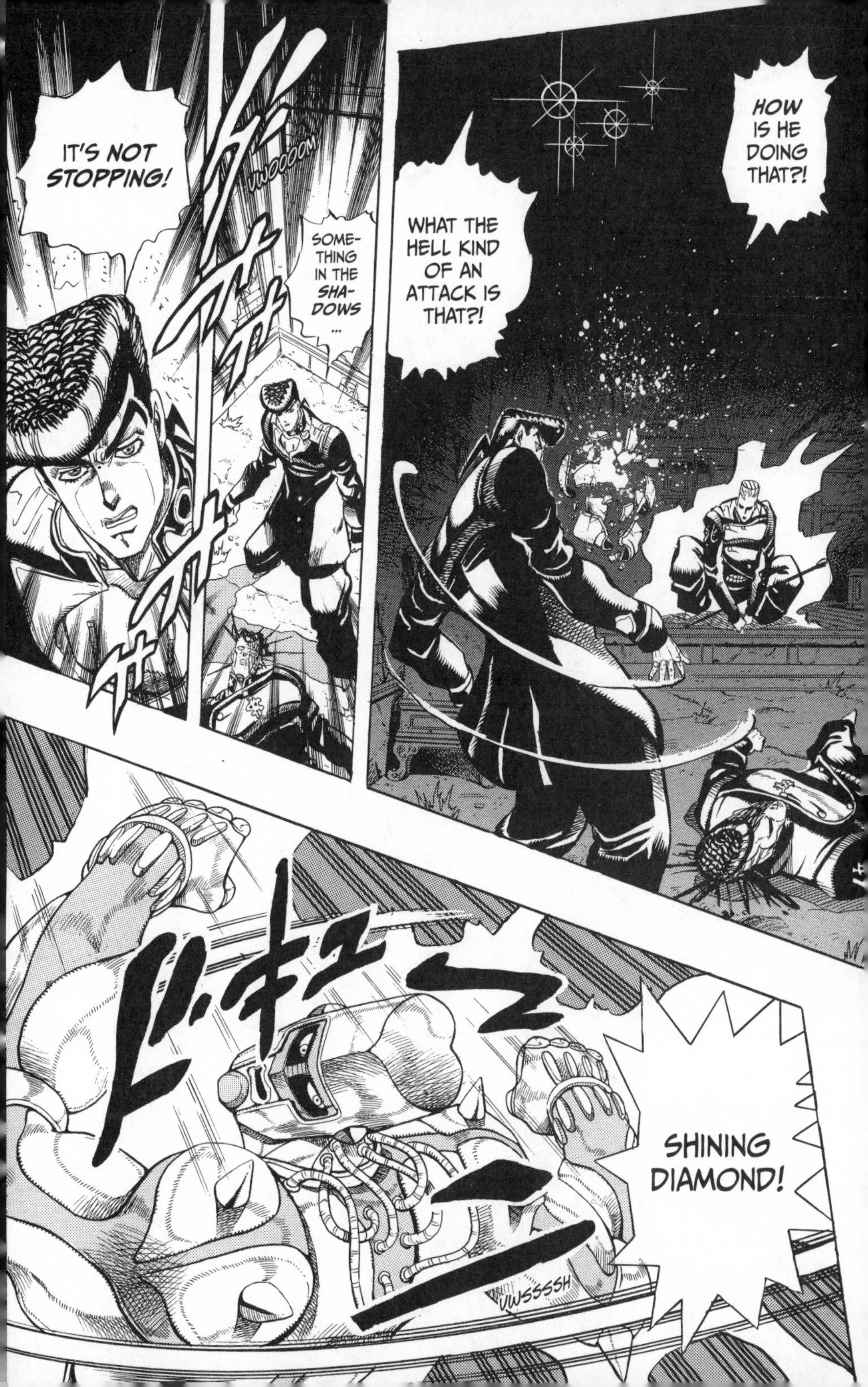
HOW IS HE DOING THAT?!
WHAT THE HELL KIND OF AN ATTACK IS THAT?!
UWOOOOM
SOME-THING IN THE SHA-DOWS...
IT'S NOT STOPPING!
SHINING DIAMOND!
VWSSSSH

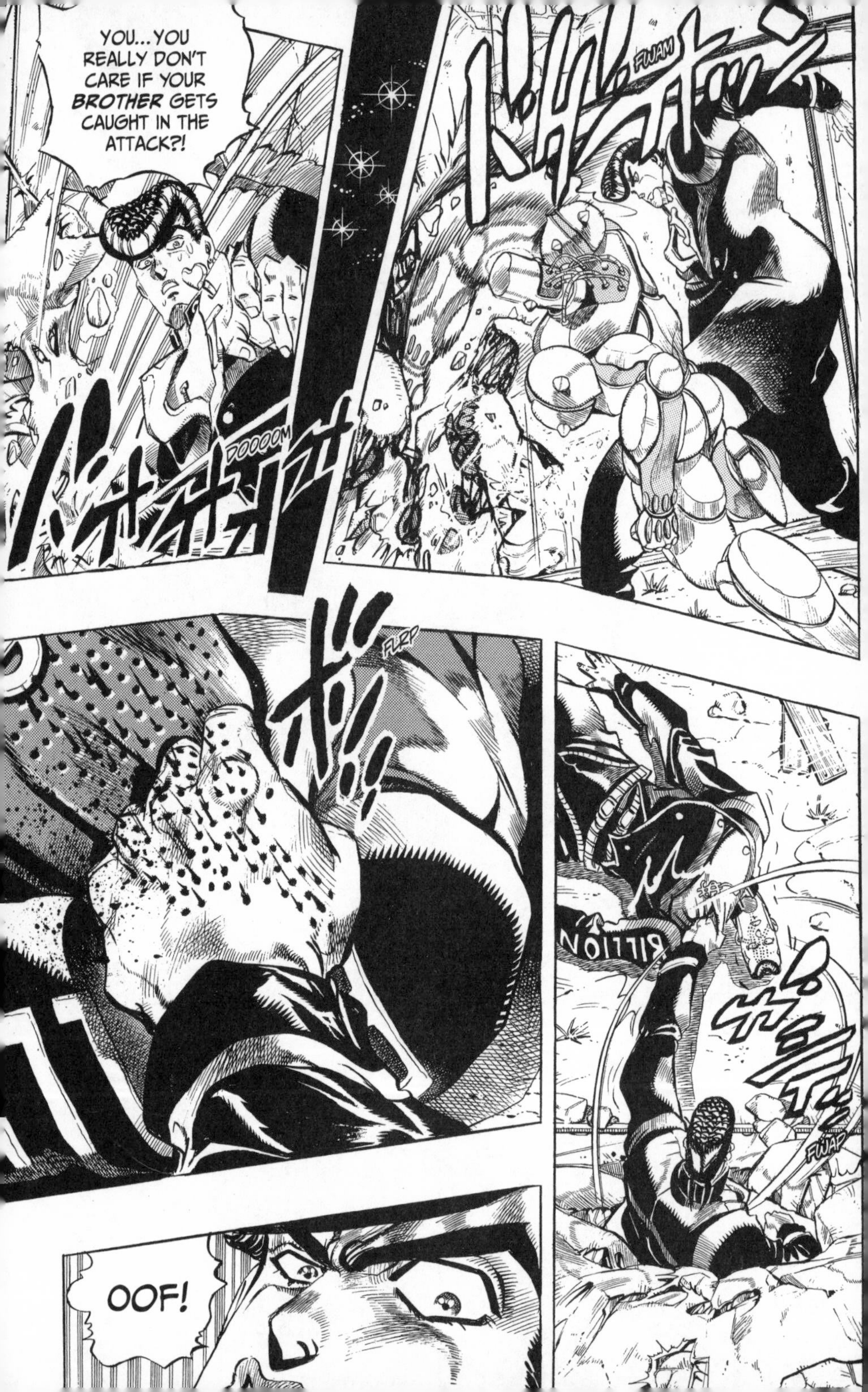
FWAM
YOU...YOU REALLY DON'T CARE IF YOUR BROTHER GETS CAUGHT IN THE ATTACK?!
DOOOOM
FWAP
FLRP
OOF!

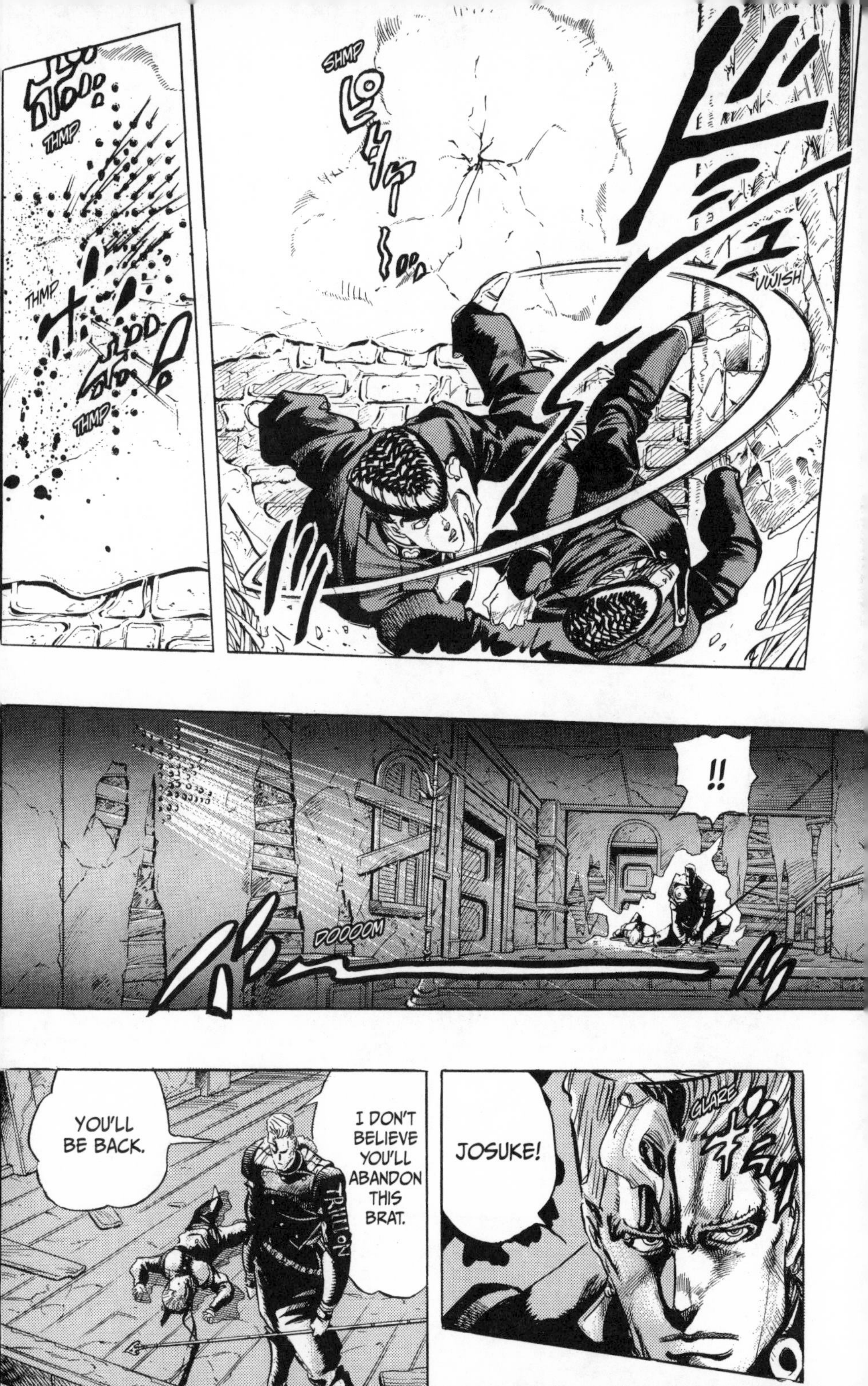
SHMP
VWISH
THMP
THMP
THMP
!!
DOOOOM
JOSUKE!
GLARE
I DON'T BELIEVE YOU'LL ABANDON THIS BRAT.
YOU'LL BE BACK.
TRILLION

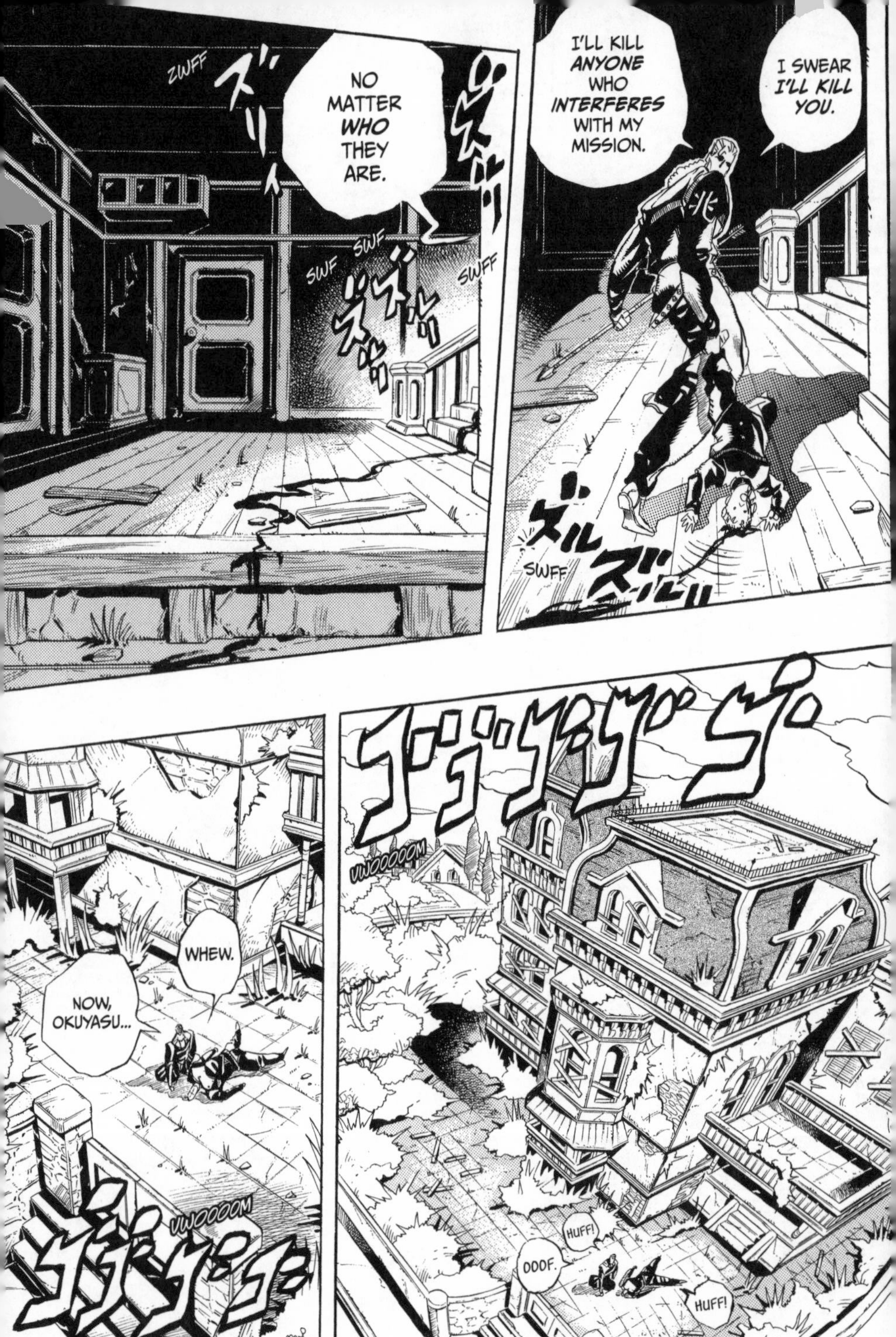
I SWEAR I'LL KILL YOU.
I'LL KILL ANYONE WHO INTERFERES WITH MY MISSION.
SWFF
NO MATTER WHO THEY ARE.
ZWFF
SWF SWF
SWFF
UWOOOOOM
HUFF!
OOOF.
HUFF!
WHEW.
NOW, OKUYASU...
UWOOOOM

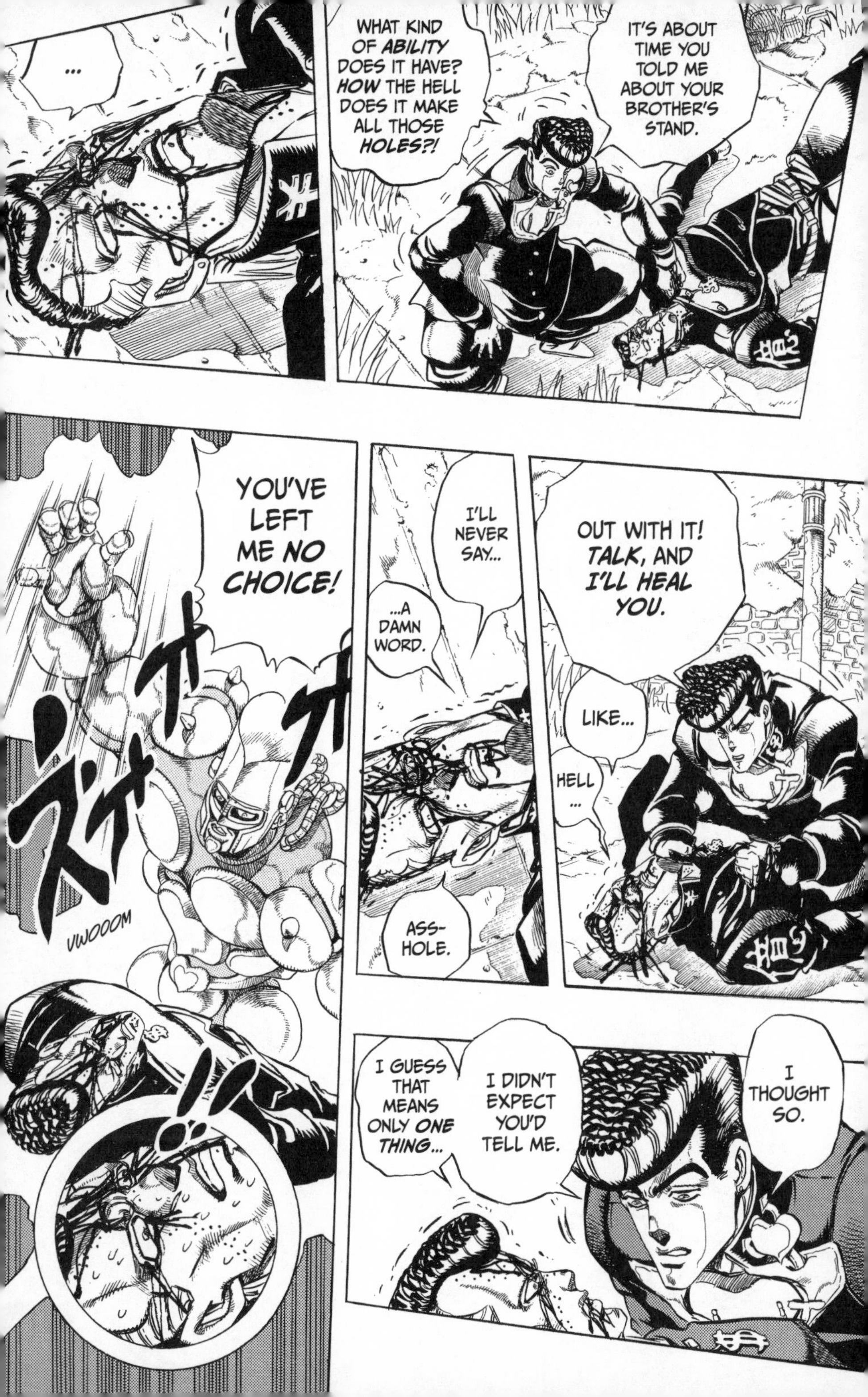
IT'S ABOUT TIME YOU TOLD ME ABOUT YOUR BROTHER'S STAND.
WHAT KIND OF *ABILITY* DOES IT HAVE? *HOW* THE HELL DOES IT MAKE ALL THOSE *HOLES?!*
...
OUT WITH IT! *TALK*, AND *I'LL HEAL YOU.*
LIKE...
HELL...
I'LL NEVER SAY...
...A DAMN WORD.
ASS-HOLE.
I THOUGHT SO.
I DIDN'T EXPECT YOU'D TELL ME.
I GUESS THAT MEANS ONLY *ONE THING...*
YOU'VE LEFT ME *NO CHOICE!*
ズオオ
VWOOOM
!!

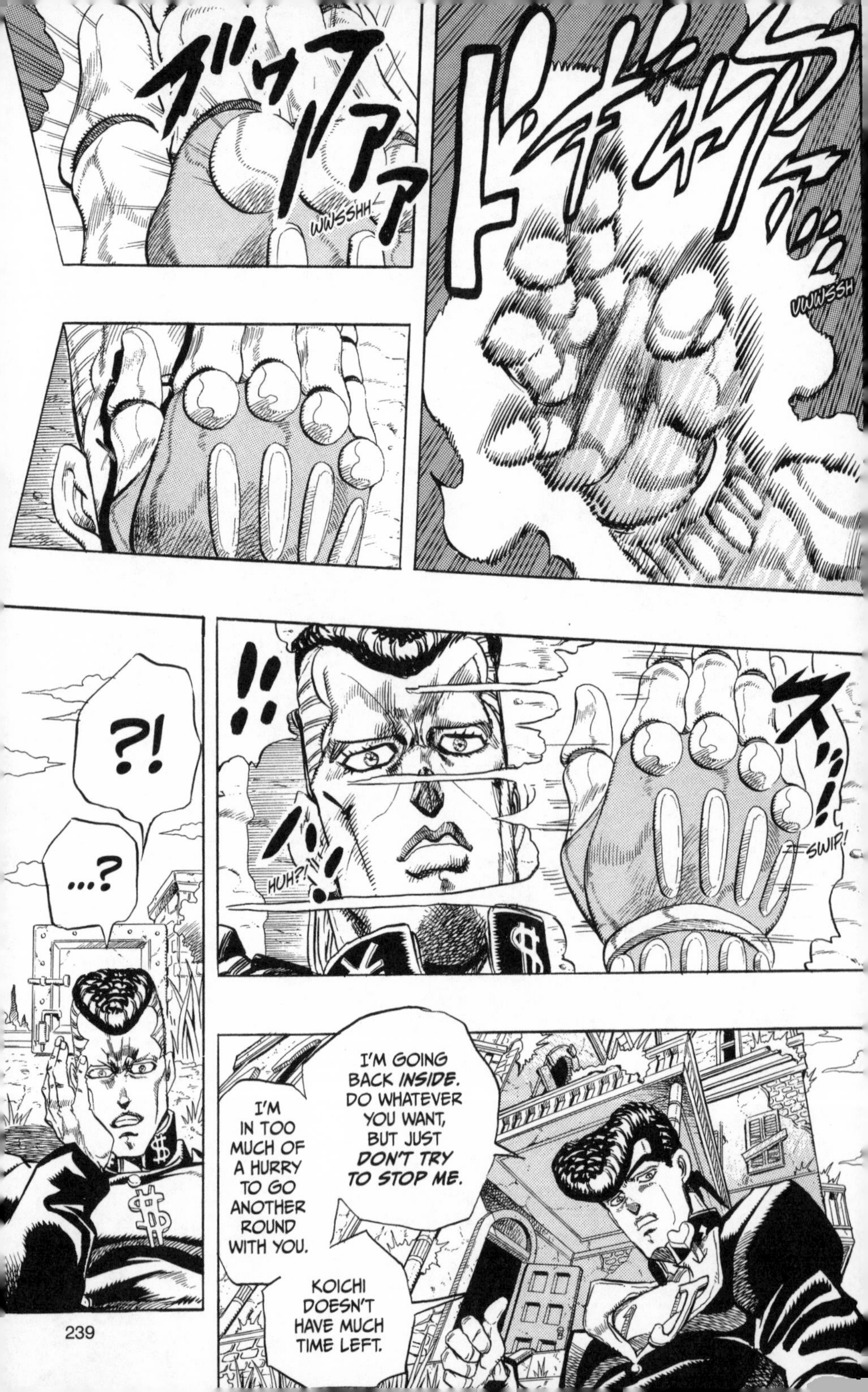
VWWSSH
WWSSHH
!!
HUH?!
SWIP!
I'M GOING BACK *INSIDE*. DO WHATEVER YOU WANT, BUT JUST ***DON'T TRY TO STOP ME***.
I'M IN TOO MUCH OF A HURRY TO GO ANOTHER ROUND WITH YOU.
KOICHI DOESN'T HAVE MUCH TIME LEFT.
?!
...?

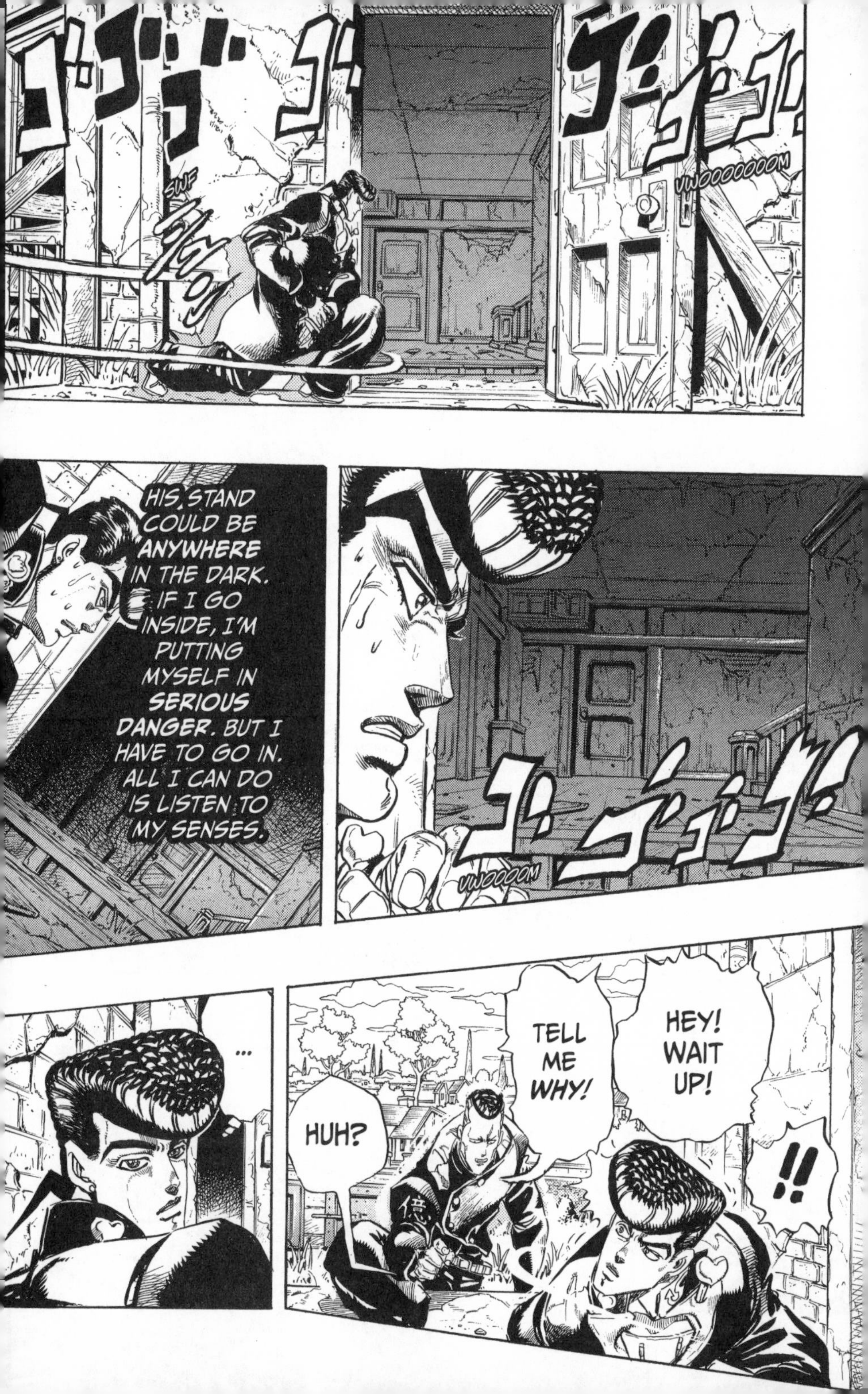
SWF
VWOOOOOOOOM
VWOOOOM
HIS STAND COULD BE ANYWHERE IN THE DARK. IF I GO INSIDE, I'M PUTTING MYSELF IN SERIOUS DANGER. BUT I HAVE TO GO IN. ALL I CAN DO IS LISTEN TO MY SENSES.
HEY! WAIT UP!
TELL ME WHY!
HUH?
!!
...

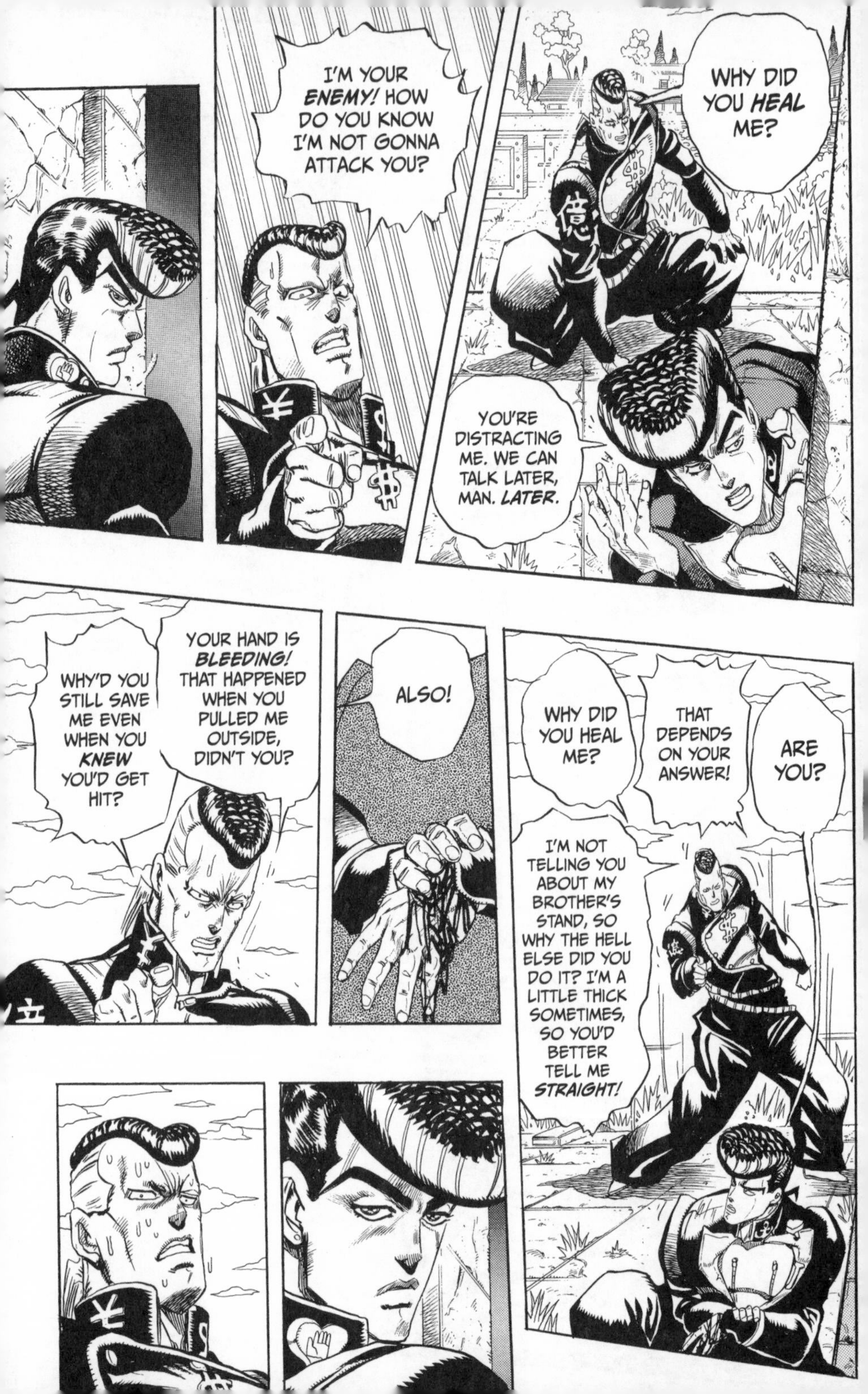
WHY DID YOU *HEAL* ME?
YOU'RE DISTRACTING ME. WE CAN TALK LATER, MAN. *LATER.*
I'M YOUR *ENEMY!* HOW DO YOU KNOW I'M NOT GONNA ATTACK YOU?
ARE YOU?
THAT DEPENDS ON YOUR ANSWER!
WHY DID YOU HEAL ME?
I'M NOT TELLING YOU ABOUT MY BROTHER'S STAND, SO WHY THE HELL ELSE DID YOU DO IT? I'M A LITTLE THICK SOMETIMES, SO YOU'D BETTER TELL ME *STRAIGHT!*
ALSO!
YOUR HAND IS *BLEEDING!* THAT HAPPENED WHEN YOU PULLED ME OUTSIDE, DIDN'T YOU?
WHY'D YOU STILL SAVE ME EVEN WHEN YOU *KNEW* YOU'D GET HIT?

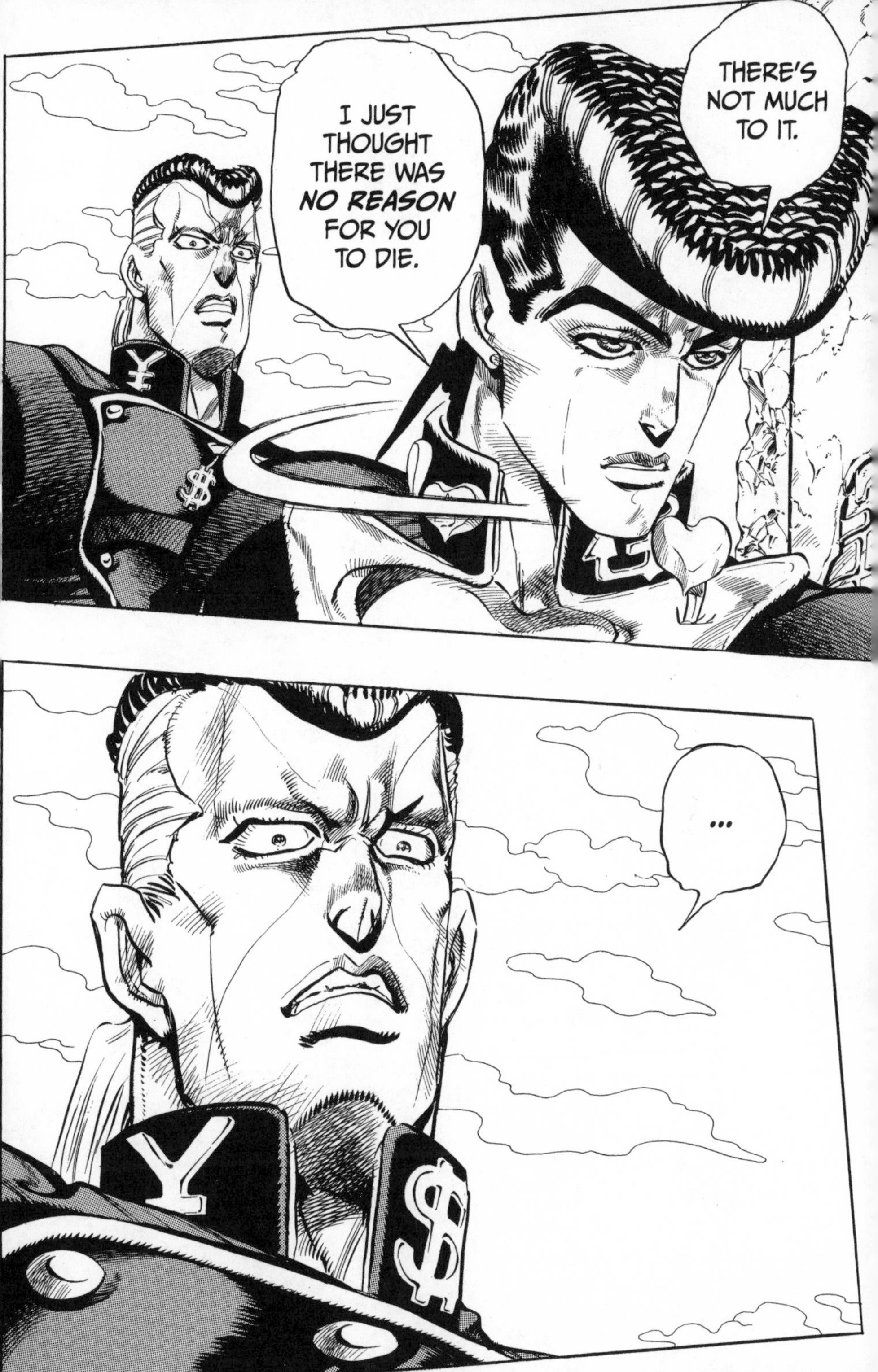
THERE'S NOT MUCH TO IT.
I JUST THOUGHT THERE WAS *NO REASON* FOR YOU TO DIE.
...

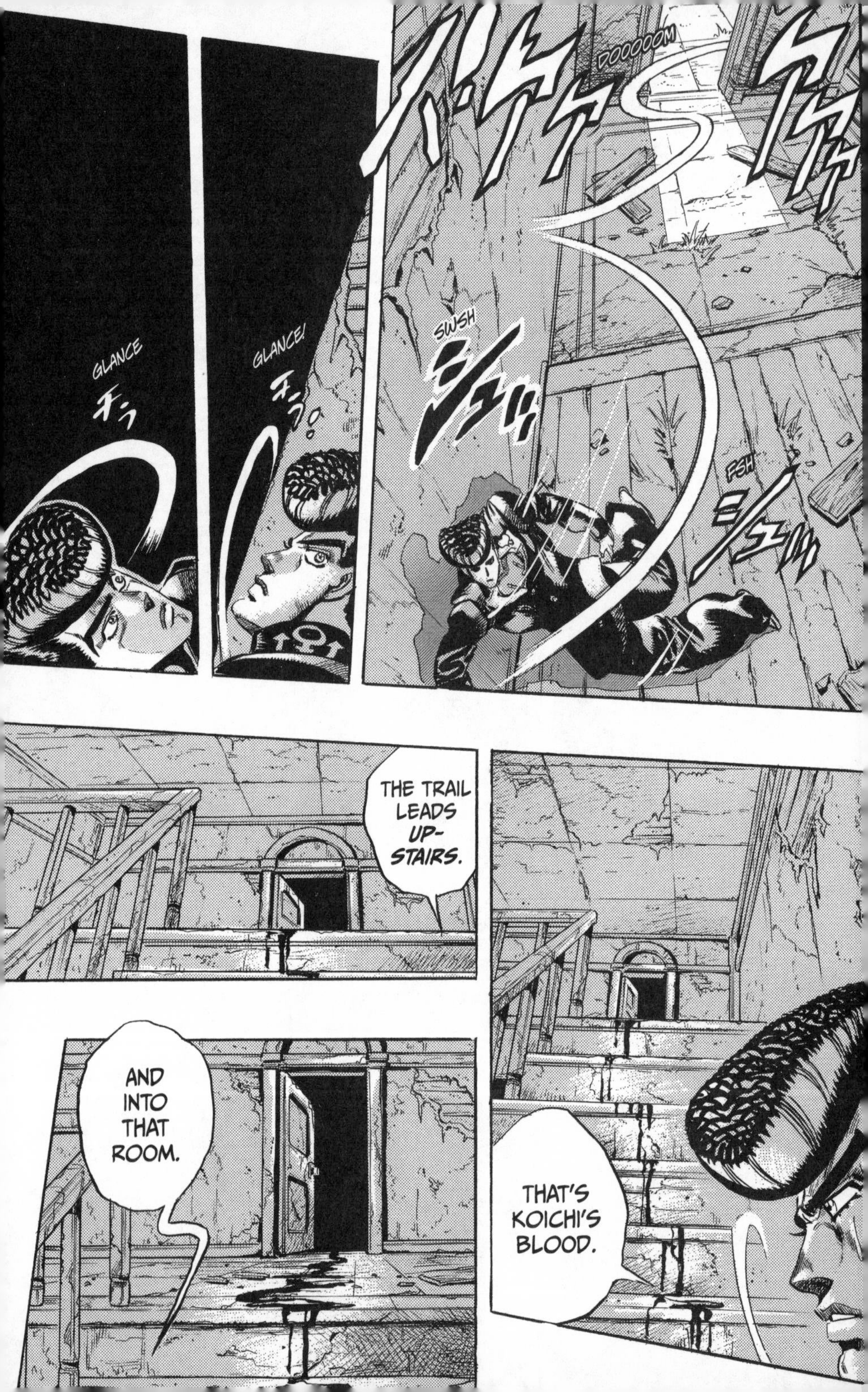
DOOOOOM
SWSH
FSH
GLANCE!
GLANCE
THAT'S KOICHI'S BLOOD.
THE TRAIL LEADS UP-STAIRS.
AND INTO THAT ROOM.

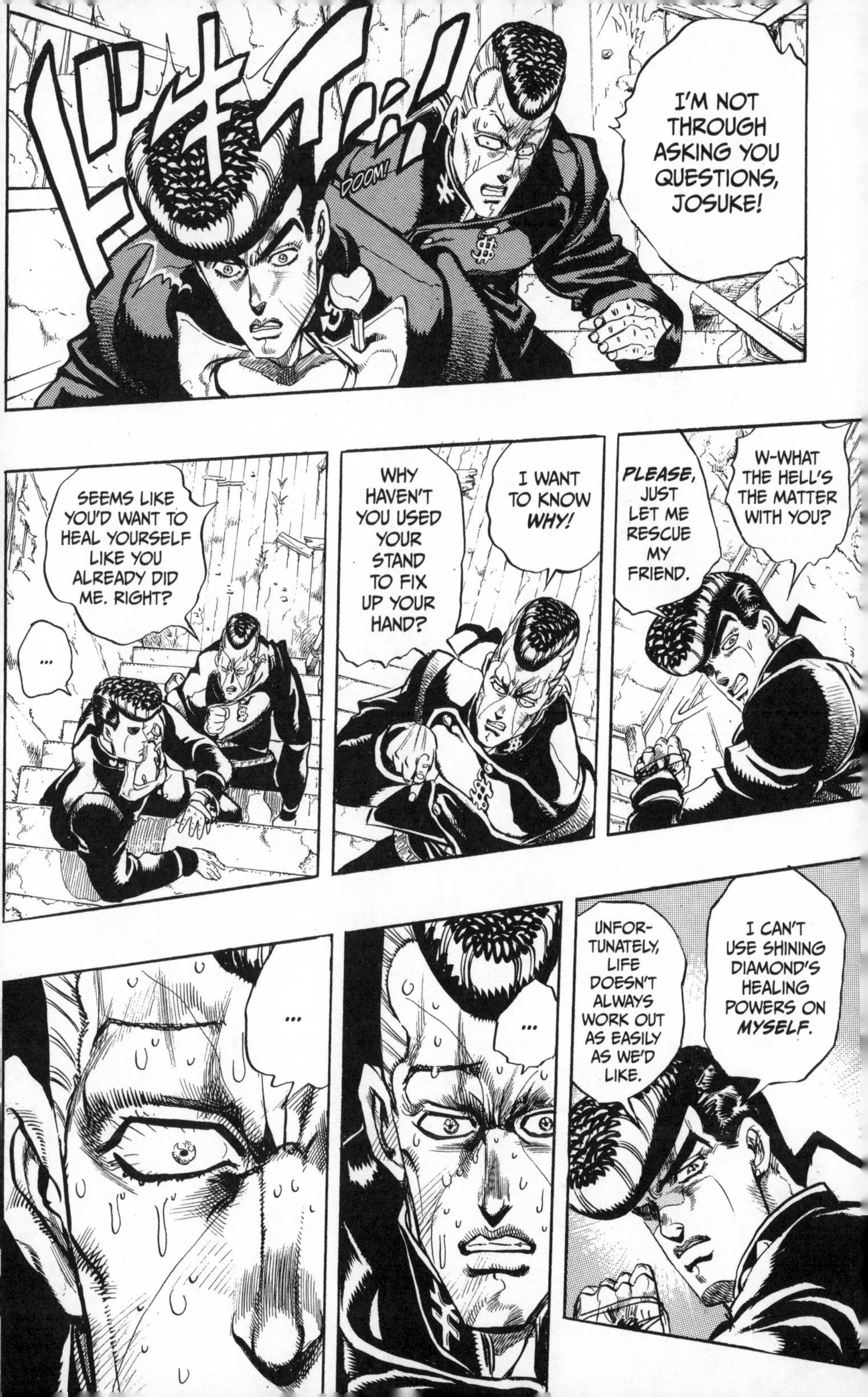
DOOM!
I'M NOT THROUGH ASKING YOU QUESTIONS, JOSUKE!
W-WHAT THE HELL'S THE MATTER WITH YOU?
PLEASE, JUST LET ME RESCUE MY FRIEND.
I WANT TO KNOW *WHY!*
WHY HAVEN'T YOU USED YOUR STAND TO FIX UP YOUR HAND?
SEEMS LIKE YOU'D WANT TO HEAL YOURSELF LIKE YOU ALREADY DID ME. RIGHT?
...
I CAN'T USE SHINING DIAMOND'S HEALING POWERS ON *MYSELF*.
UNFOR-TUNATELY, LIFE DOESN'T ALWAYS WORK OUT AS EASILY AS WE'D LIKE.
...
...

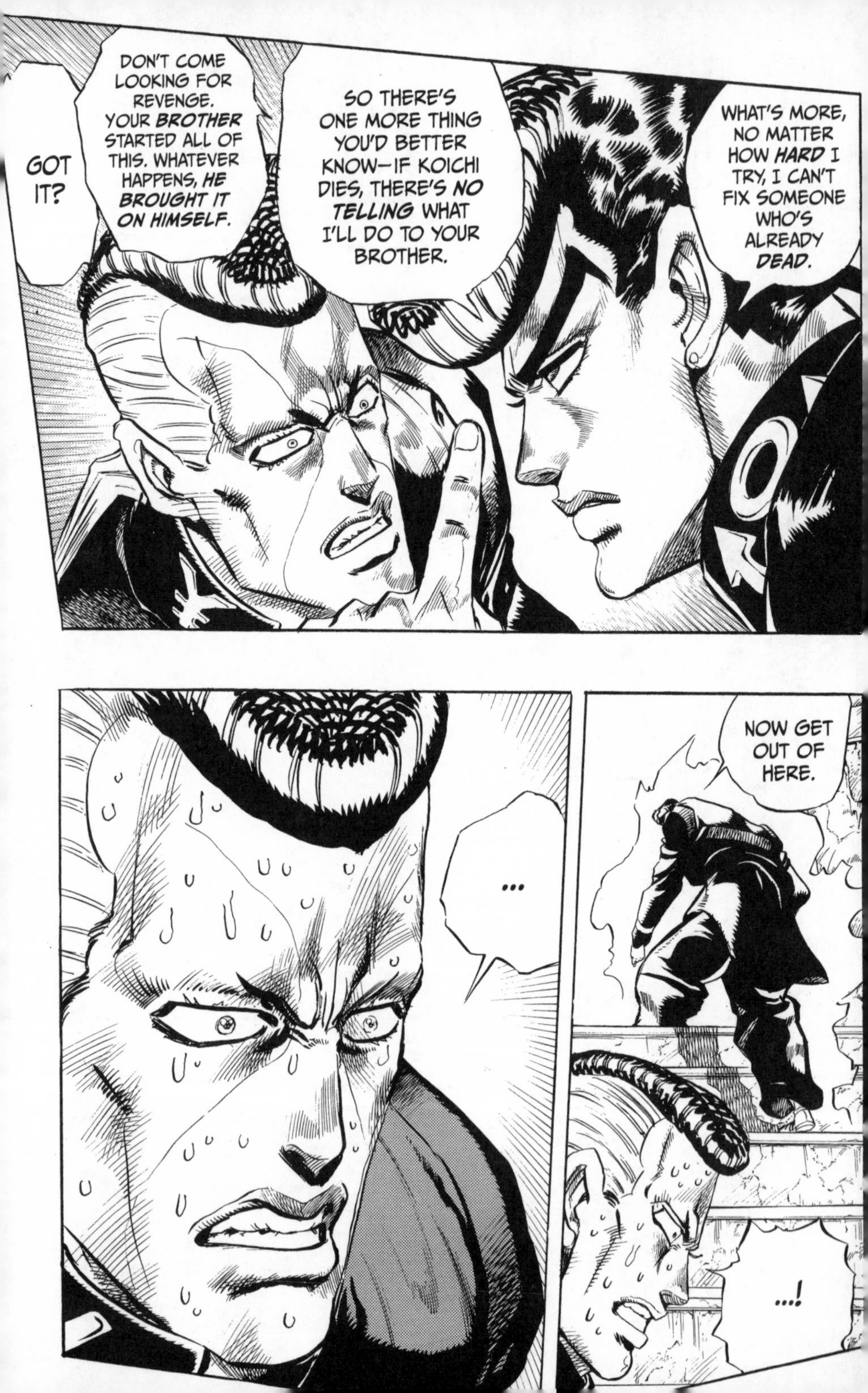
WHAT'S MORE, NO MATTER HOW HARD I TRY, I CAN'T FIX SOMEONE WHO'S ALREADY DEAD.
SO THERE'S ONE MORE THING YOU'D BETTER KNOW—IF KOICHI DIES, THERE'S NO TELLING WHAT I'LL DO TO YOUR BROTHER.
DON'T COME LOOKING FOR REVENGE. YOUR BROTHER STARTED ALL OF THIS. WHATEVER HAPPENS, HE BROUGHT IT ON HIMSELF.
GOT IT?
NOW GET OUT OF HERE.
...!
...

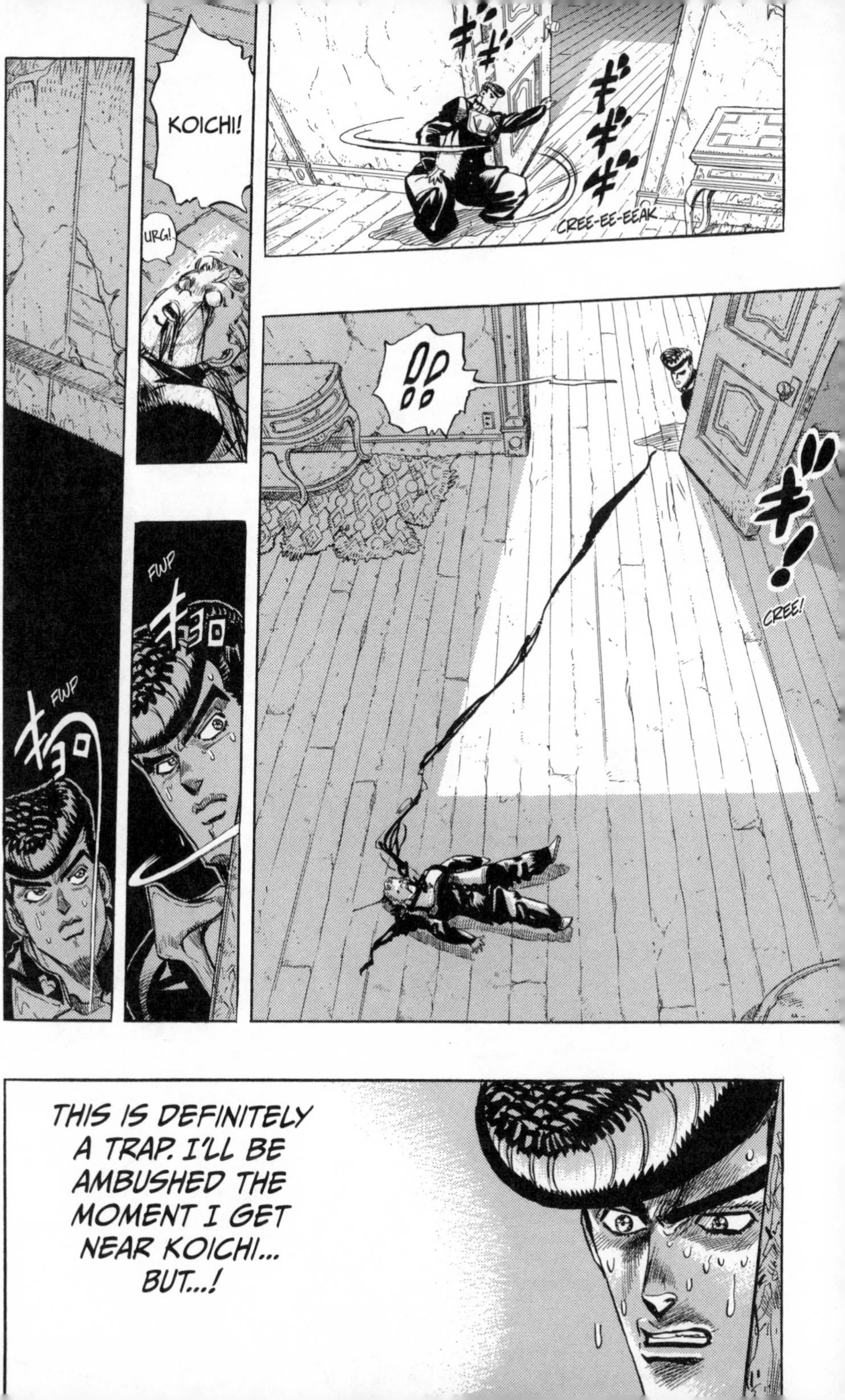
CREE-EE-EEAK
KOICHI!
URG!
!!
CREE!
FWP
FWP
THIS IS DEFINITELY A TRAP. I'LL BE AMBUSHED THE MOMENT I GET NEAR KOICHI... BUT...!

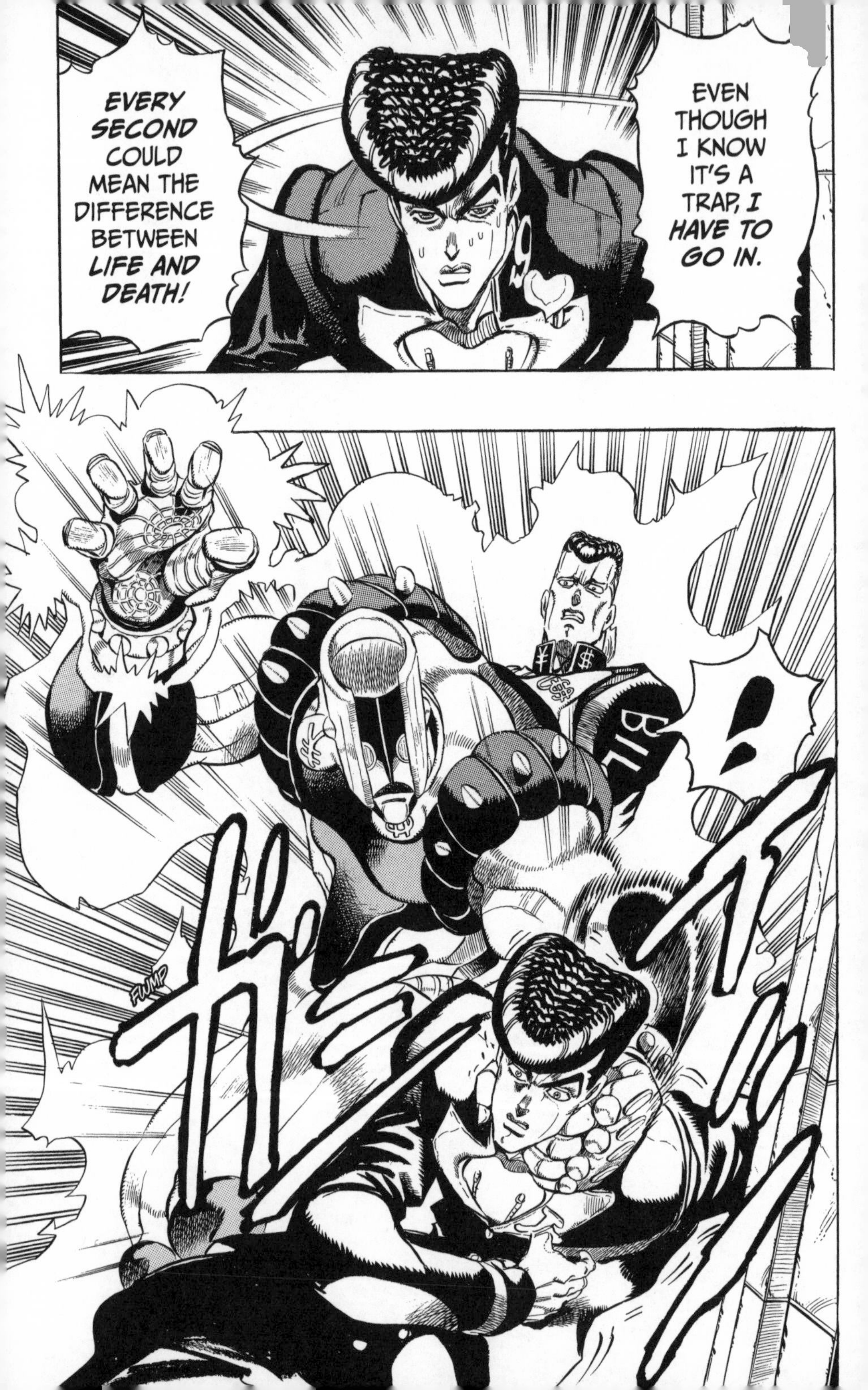
EVEN THOUGH I KNOW IT'S A TRAP, I HAVE TO GO IN.
EVERY SECOND COULD MEAN THE DIFFERENCE BETWEEN LIFE AND DEATH!
!
FWUMP

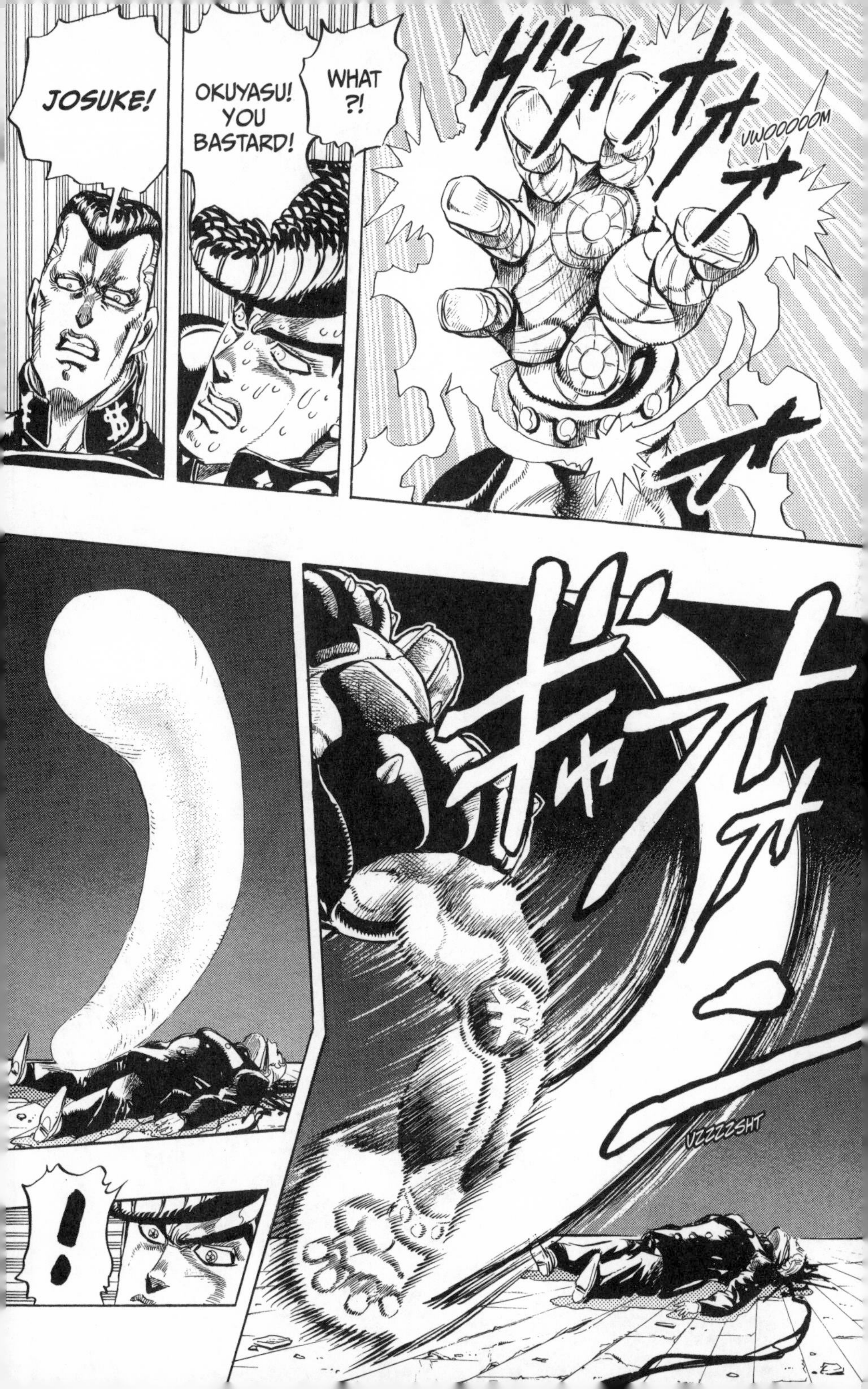
VWOOOOOM
WHAT ?!
OKUYASU! YOU BASTARD!
JOSUKE!
VZZZZSHT
!

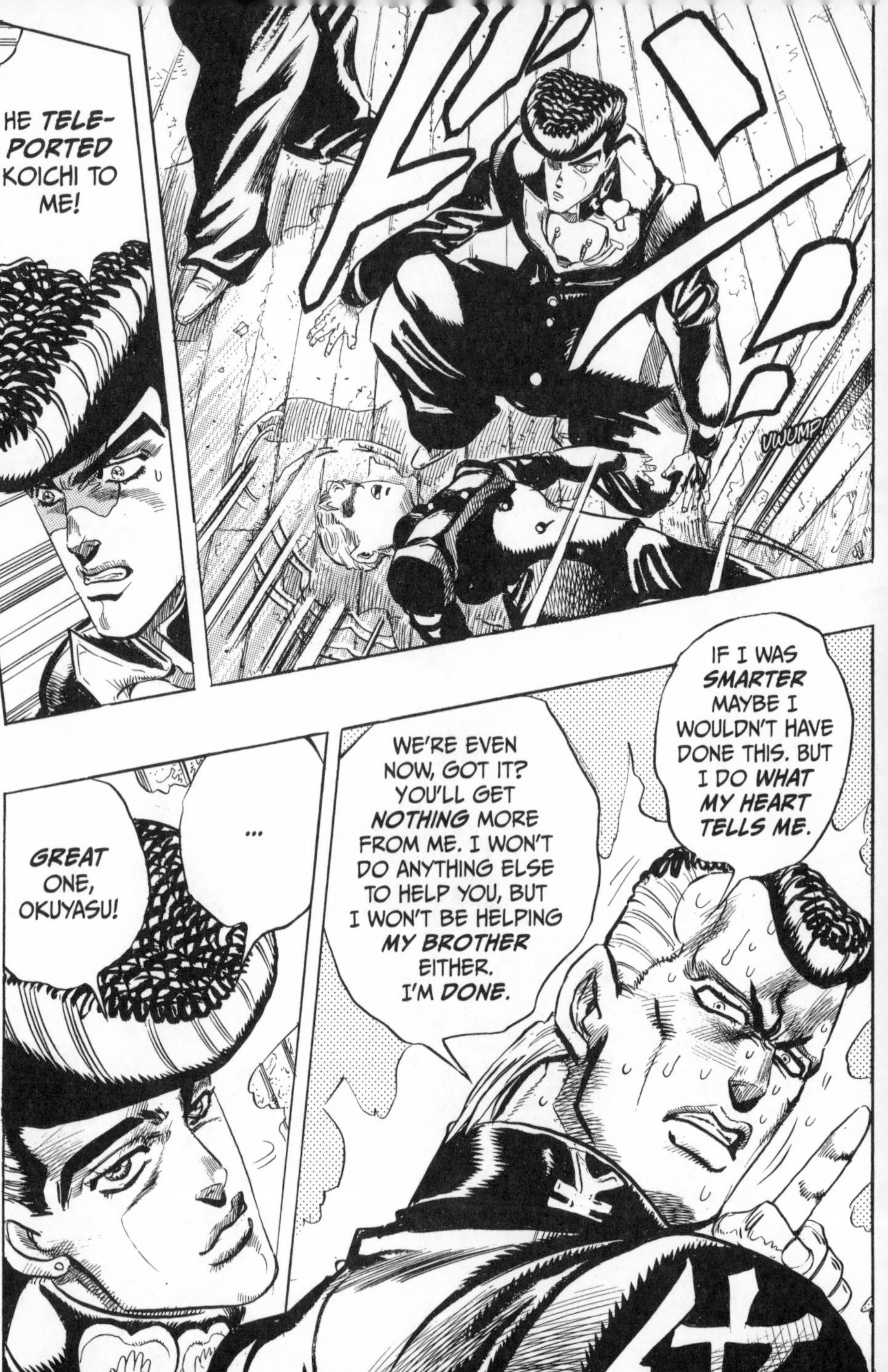
UWUMP!
HE *TELE-PORTED* KOICHI TO ME!
IF I WAS *SMARTER* MAYBE I WOULDN'T HAVE DONE THIS. BUT I DO *WHAT MY HEART TELLS ME*.
WE'RE EVEN NOW, GOT IT? YOU'LL GET *NOTHING* MORE FROM ME. I WON'T DO ANYTHING ELSE TO HELP YOU, BUT I WON'T BE HELPING *MY BROTHER* EITHER. I'M *DONE*.
...
GREAT ONE, OKUYASU!

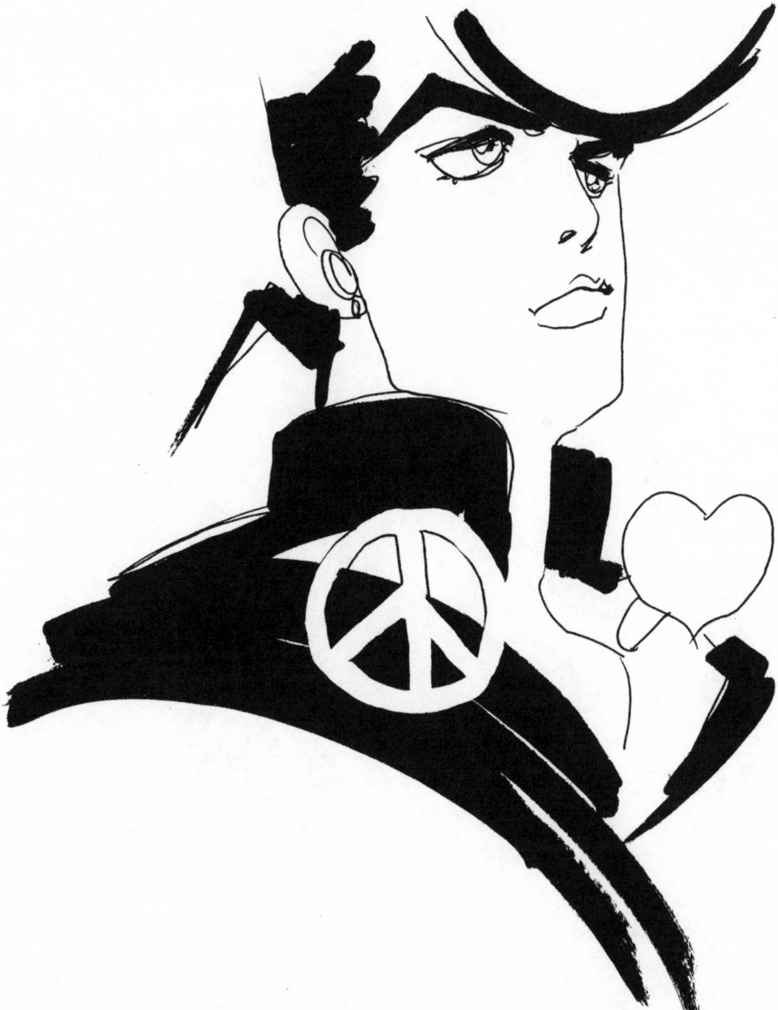

CHAPTER 13

THE NIJIMURA BROTHERS, PART 5

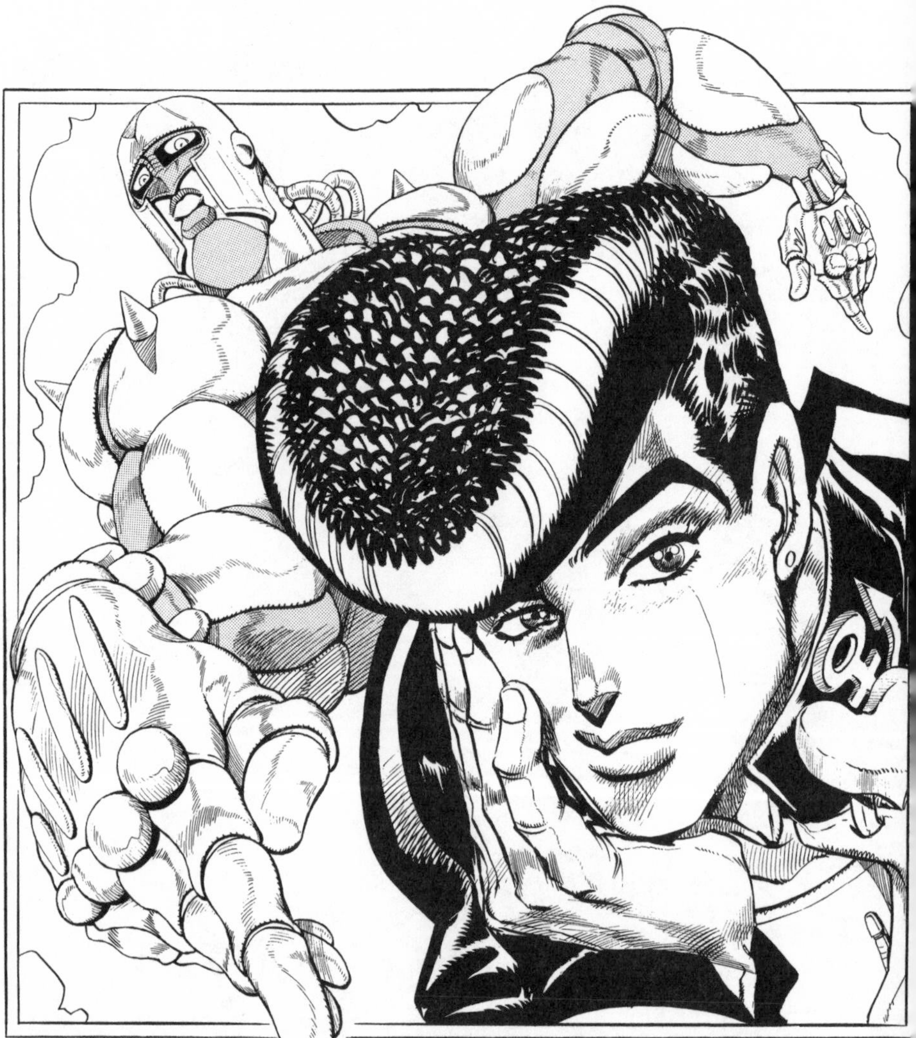

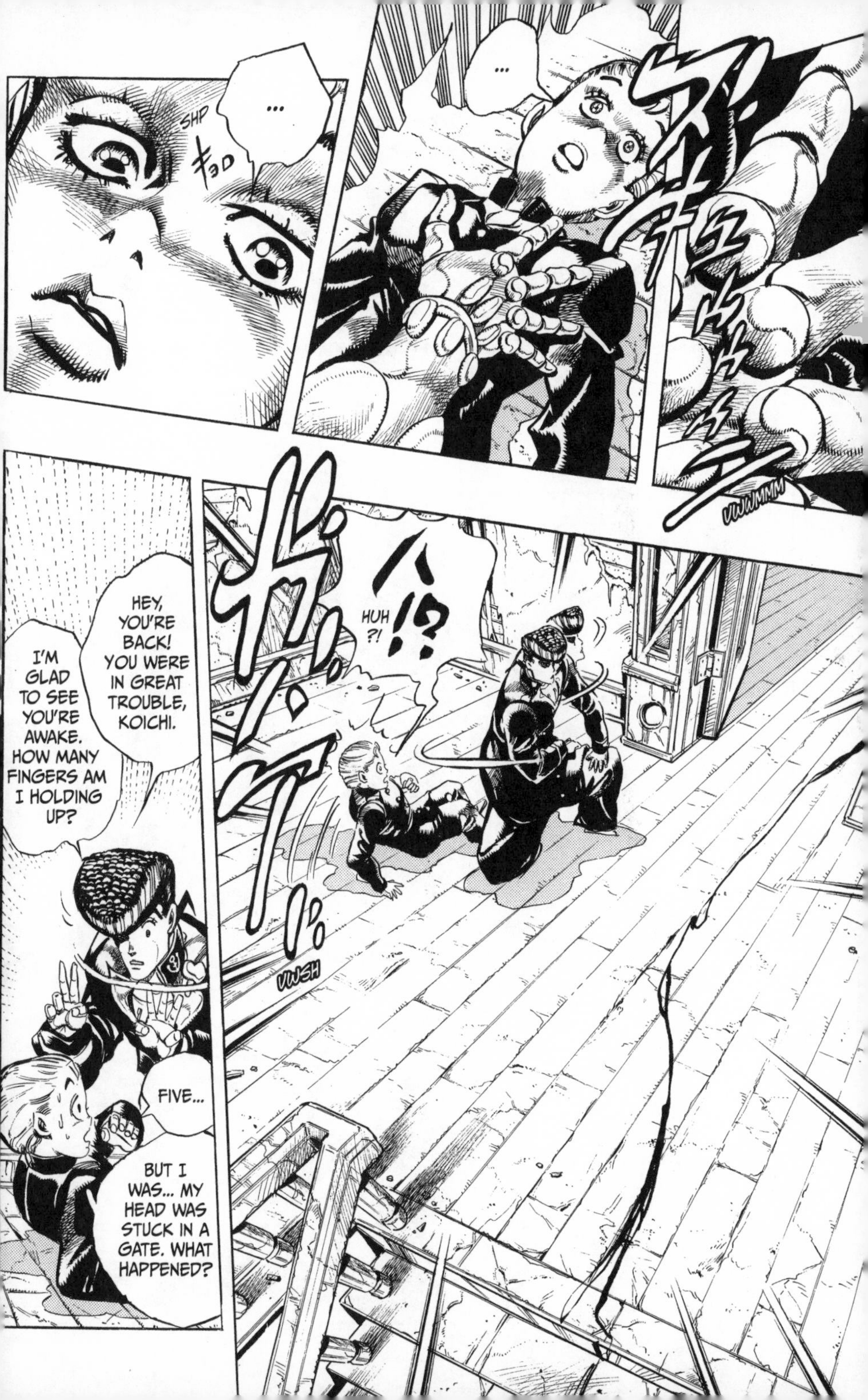

UWWMMM
...
...
SHP
HUH ?!
UWSH
HEY, YOU'RE BACK! YOU WERE IN GREAT TROUBLE, KOICHI.
I'M GLAD TO SEE YOU'RE AWAKE. HOW MANY FINGERS AM I HOLDING UP?
FIVE...
BUT I WAS... MY HEAD WAS STUCK IN A GATE. WHAT HAPPENED?

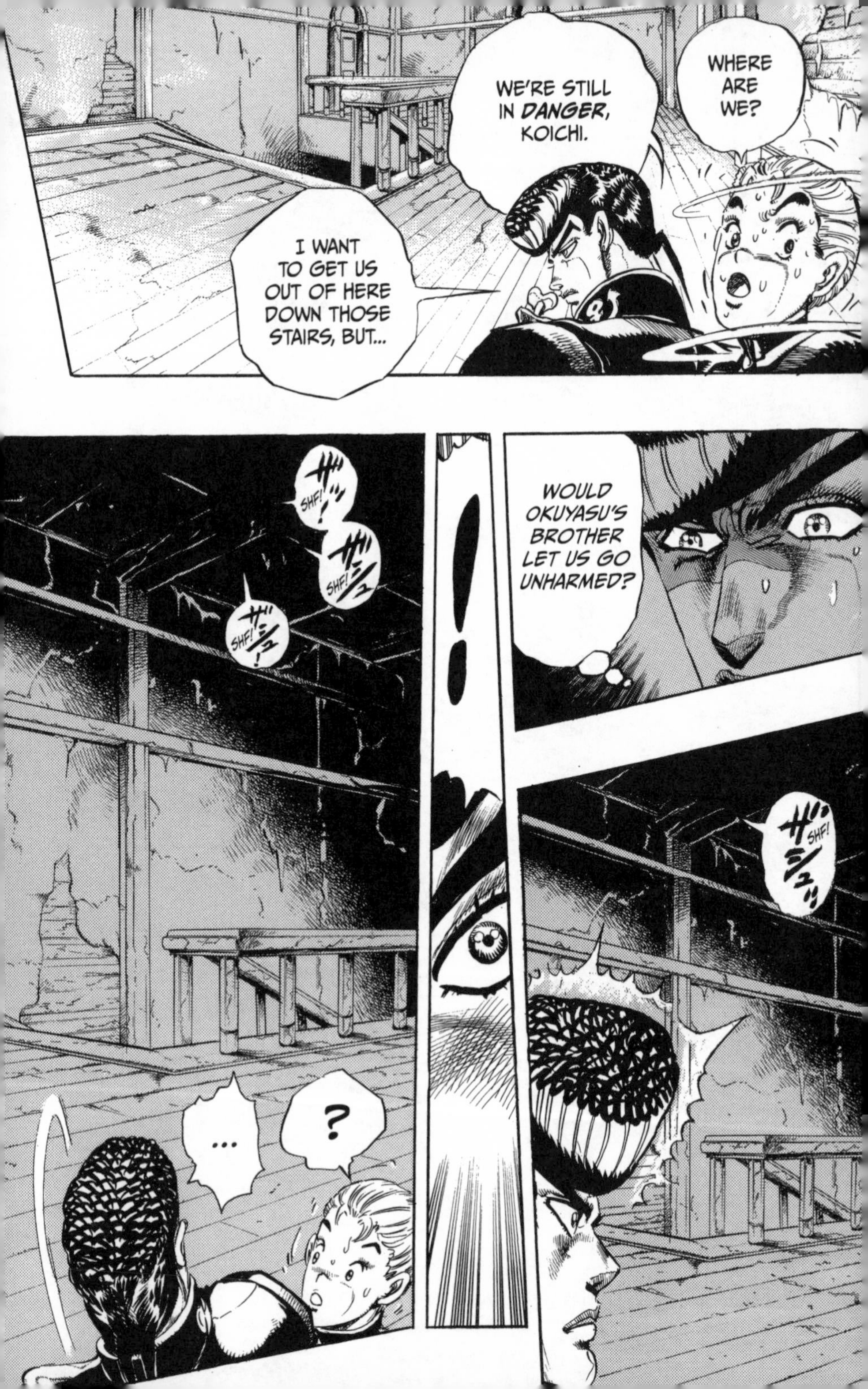

WHERE ARE WE?
WE'RE STILL IN *DANGER*, KOICHI.
I WANT TO GET US OUT OF HERE DOWN THOSE STAIRS, BUT...
WOULD OKUYASU'S BROTHER LET US GO UNHARMED?
SHF!
!
SHF!
SHF!
SHF!
?
...

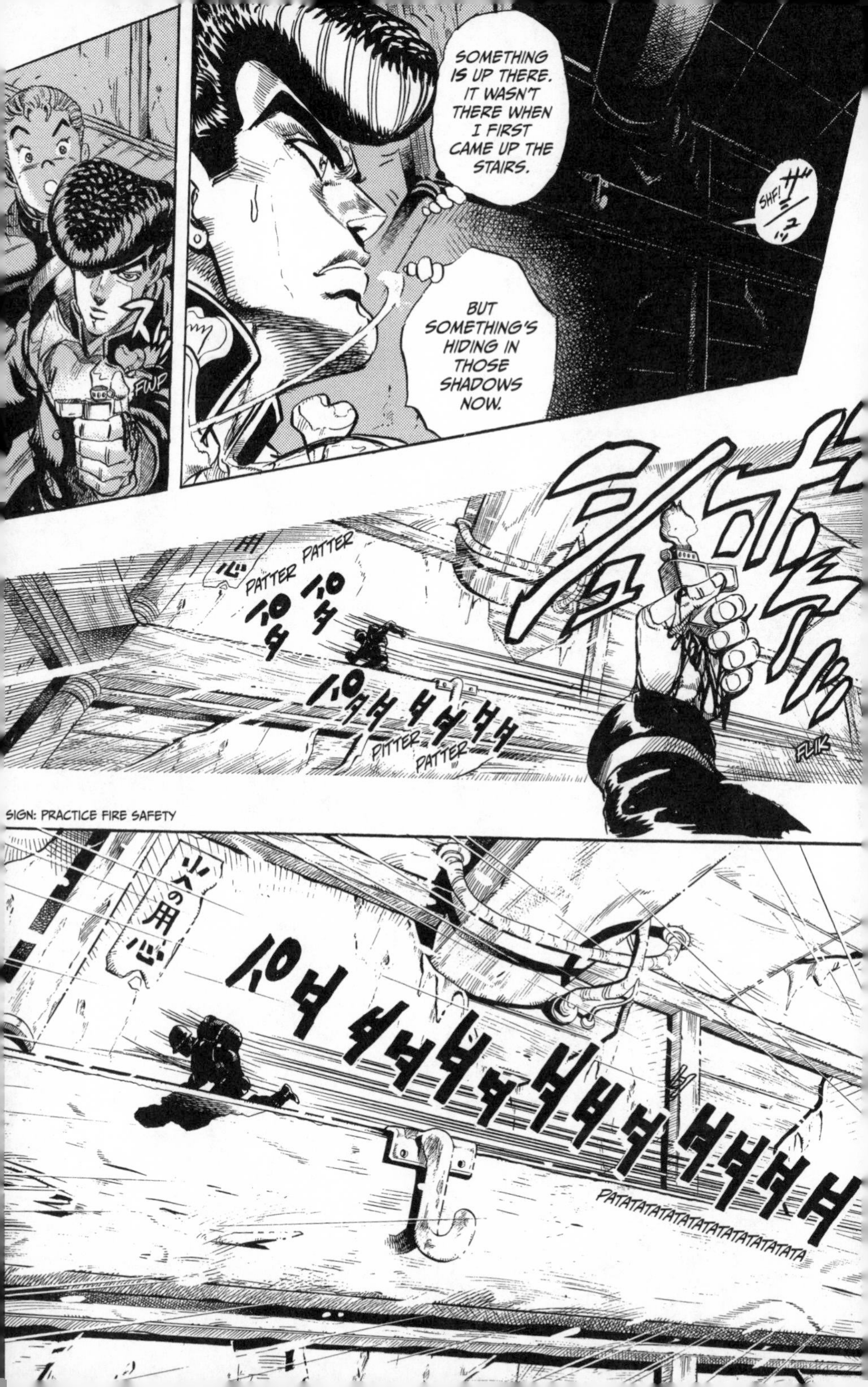
SHF!
SOMETHING IS UP THERE. IT WASN'T THERE WHEN I FIRST CAME UP THE STAIRS.
BUT SOMETHING'S HIDING IN THOSE SHADOWS NOW.
FWP
FLIK
PATTER PATTER
PITTER PATTER
SIGN: PRACTICE FIRE SAFETY
火の用心
PATATATATATATATATATATATATA

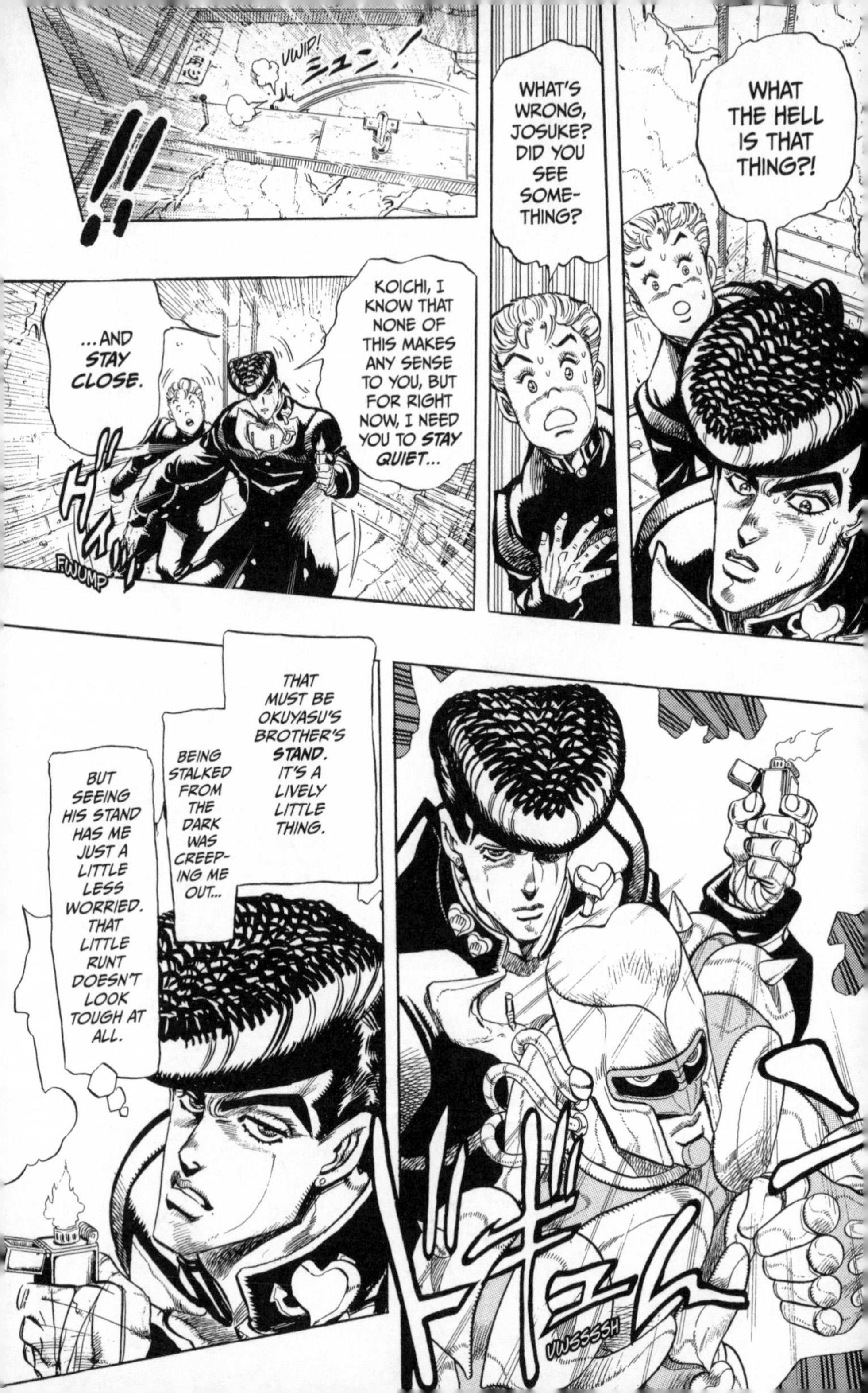
WHAT THE HELL IS THAT THING?!
WHAT'S WRONG, JOSUKE? DID YOU SEE SOME-THING?
VWIP!
シュン!
!!
KOICHI, I KNOW THAT NONE OF THIS MAKES ANY SENSE TO YOU, BUT FOR RIGHT NOW, I NEED YOU TO STAY QUIET...
...AND STAY CLOSE.
FWUMP
UWSSSSH
THAT MUST BE OKUYASU'S BROTHER'S STAND. IT'S A LIVELY LITTLE THING.
BEING STALKED FROM THE DARK WAS CREEP-ING ME OUT...
BUT SEEING HIS STAND HAS ME JUST A LITTLE LESS WORRIED. THAT LITTLE RUNT DOESN'T LOOK TOUGH AT ALL.

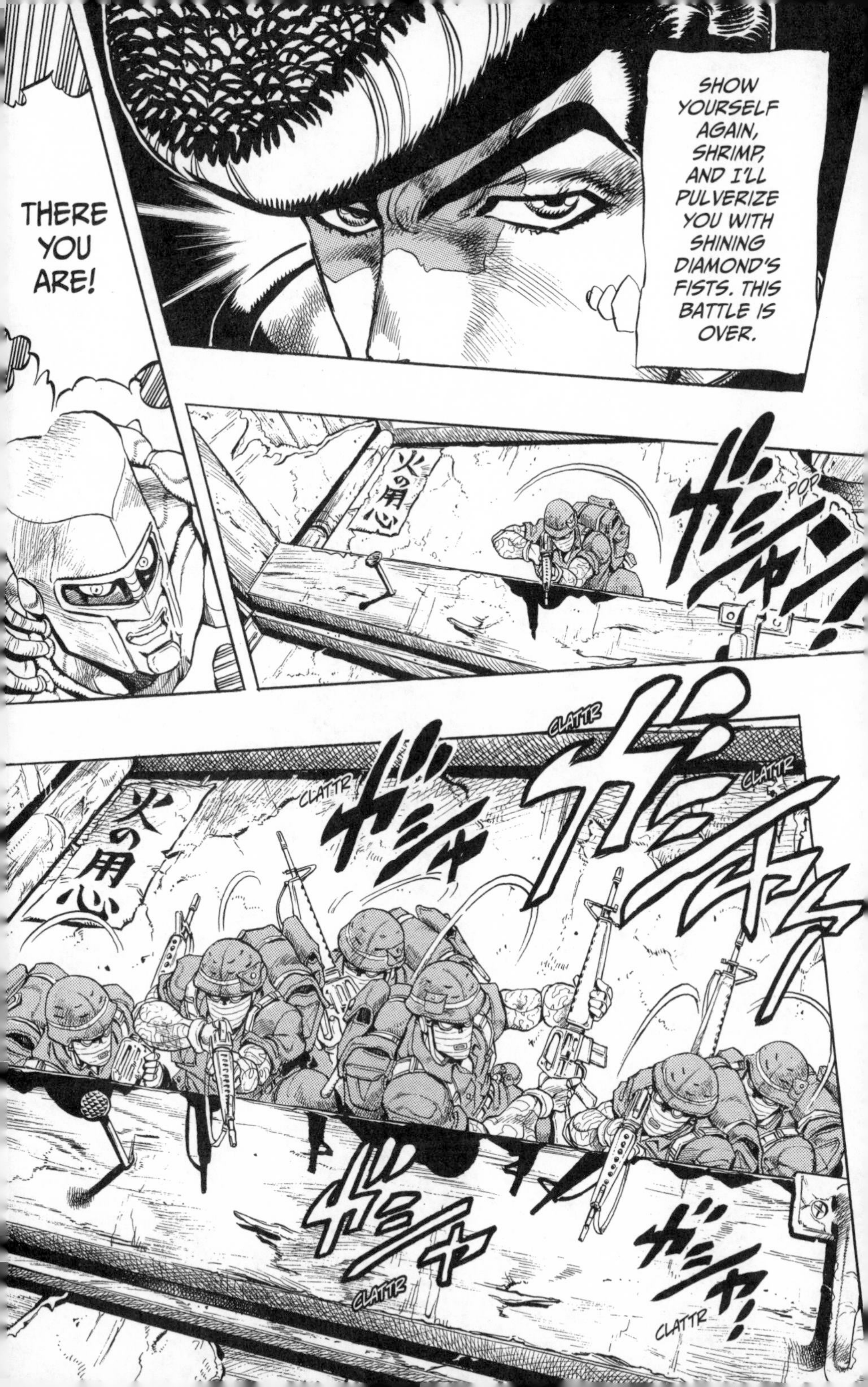
SHOW YOURSELF AGAIN, SHRIMP, AND I'LL PULVERIZE YOU WITH SHINING DIAMOND'S FISTS. THIS BATTLE IS OVER.
THERE YOU ARE!
POP
ガシャン!!
火の用心
CLATTR
CLATTR
CLATTR
火の用心
CLATTR
CLATTR

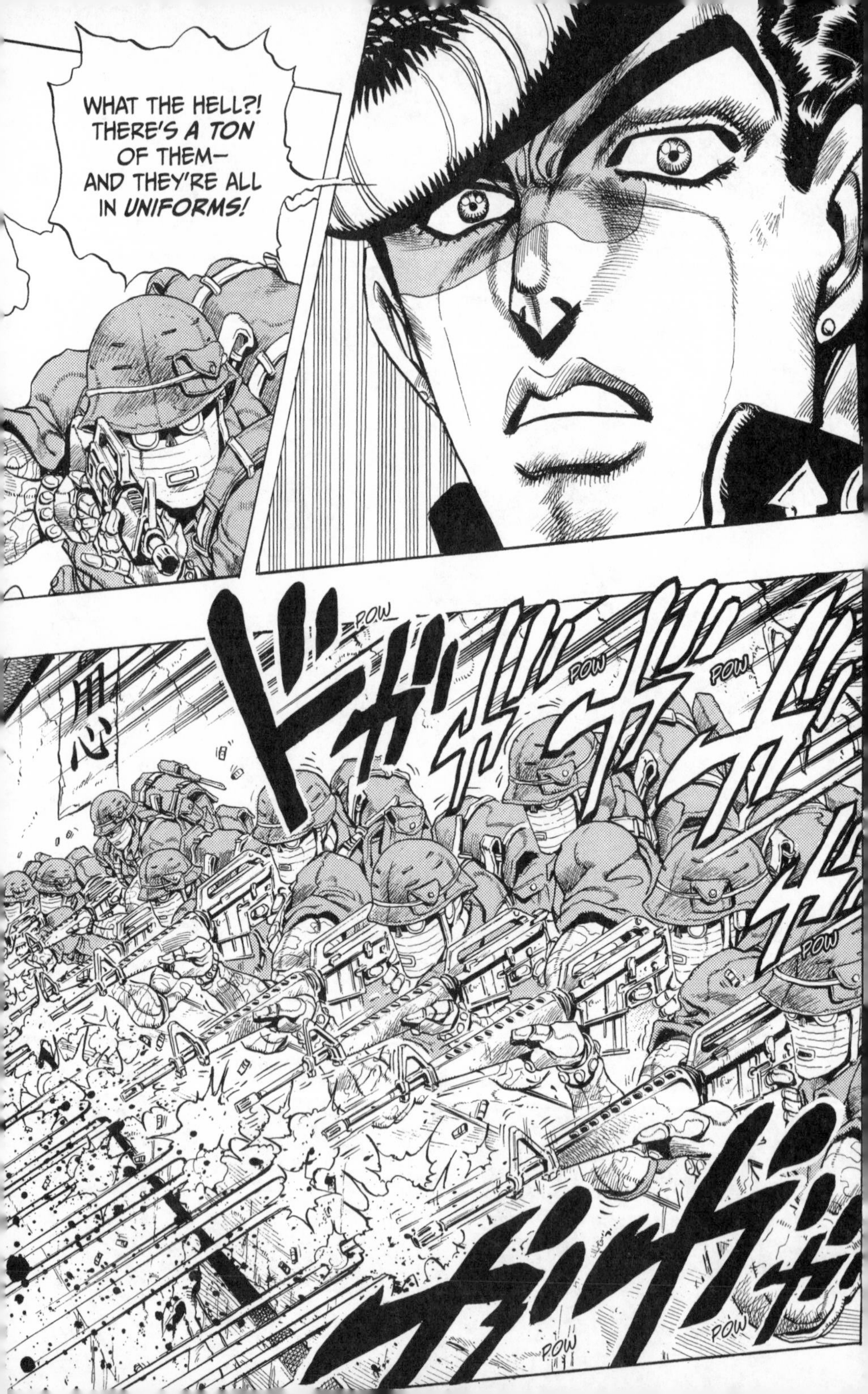
WHAT THE HELL?! THERE'S *A TON* OF THEM— AND THEY'RE ALL IN *UNIFORMS!*
POW
POW
POW
POW
用心
POW
POW

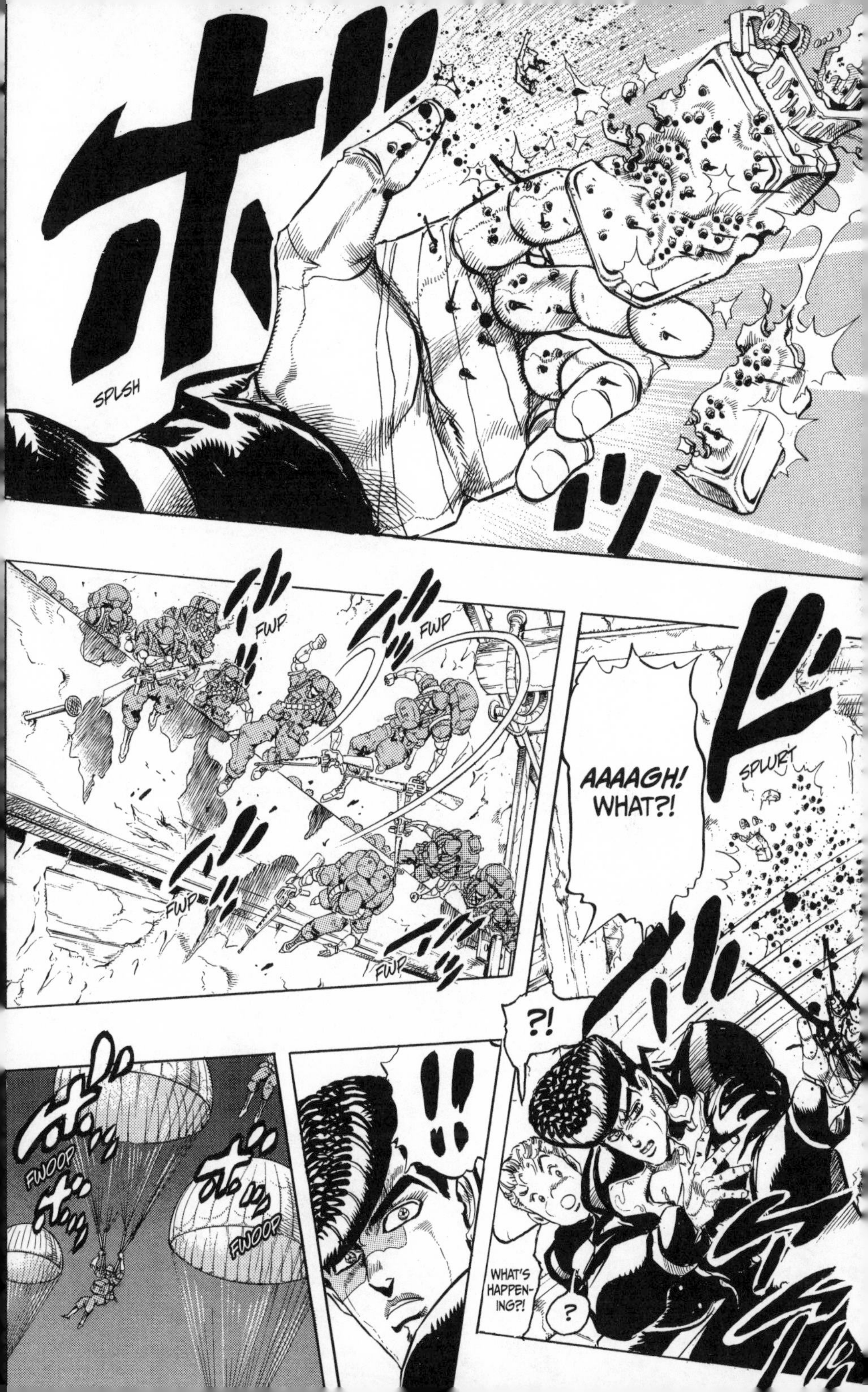
SPLSH
SPLURT
AAAAGH! WHAT?!
FWP
FWP
FWP
FWP
?!
WHAT'S HAPPEN-ING?!
?
!!
FWOOP
FWOOP

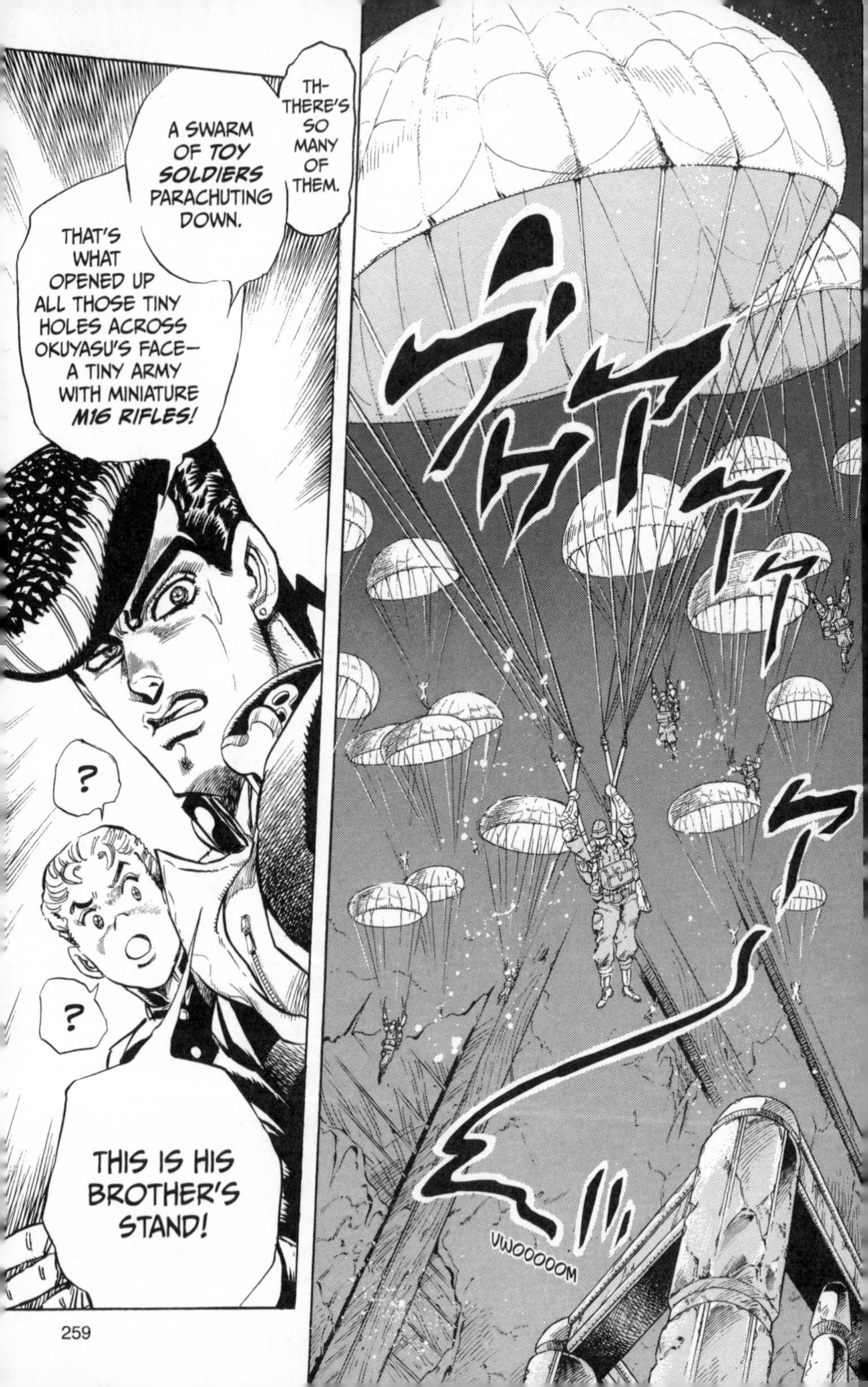
VWOOOOOM
TH- THERE'S SO MANY OF THEM.
A SWARM OF *TOY SOLDIERS* PARACHUTING DOWN.
THAT'S WHAT OPENED UP ALL THOSE TINY HOLES ACROSS OKUYASU'S FACE— A TINY ARMY WITH MINIATURE *M16 RIFLES!*
?
?
THIS IS HIS BROTHER'S STAND!

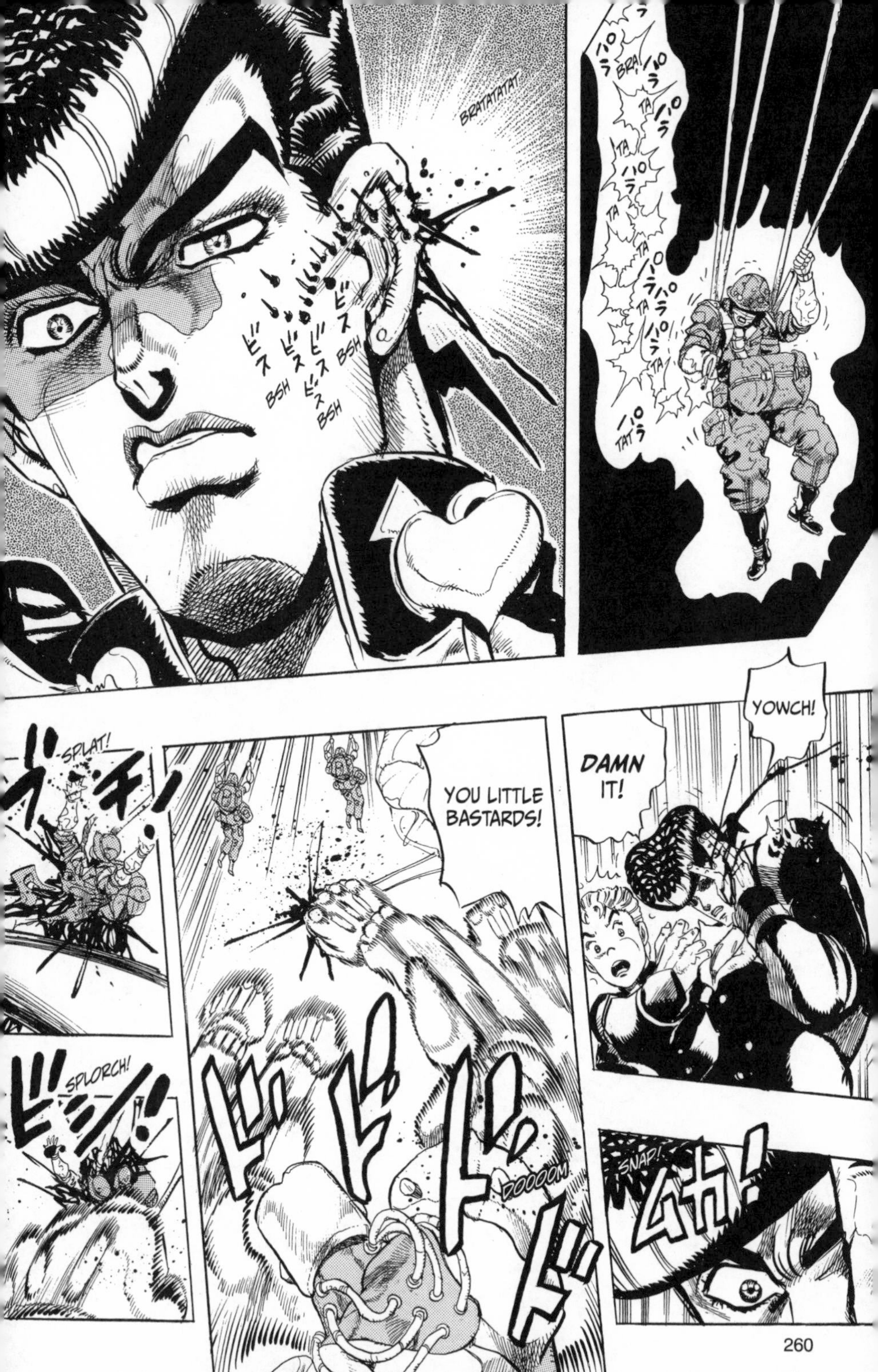

BRA!
TA
TA
TA
TA
TA
TATAT
BRATATATAT
BSH
BSH
BSH
YOWCH!
DAMN IT!
SNAP!
YOU LITTLE BASTARDS!
DOOOOM
SPLAT!
SPLORCH!

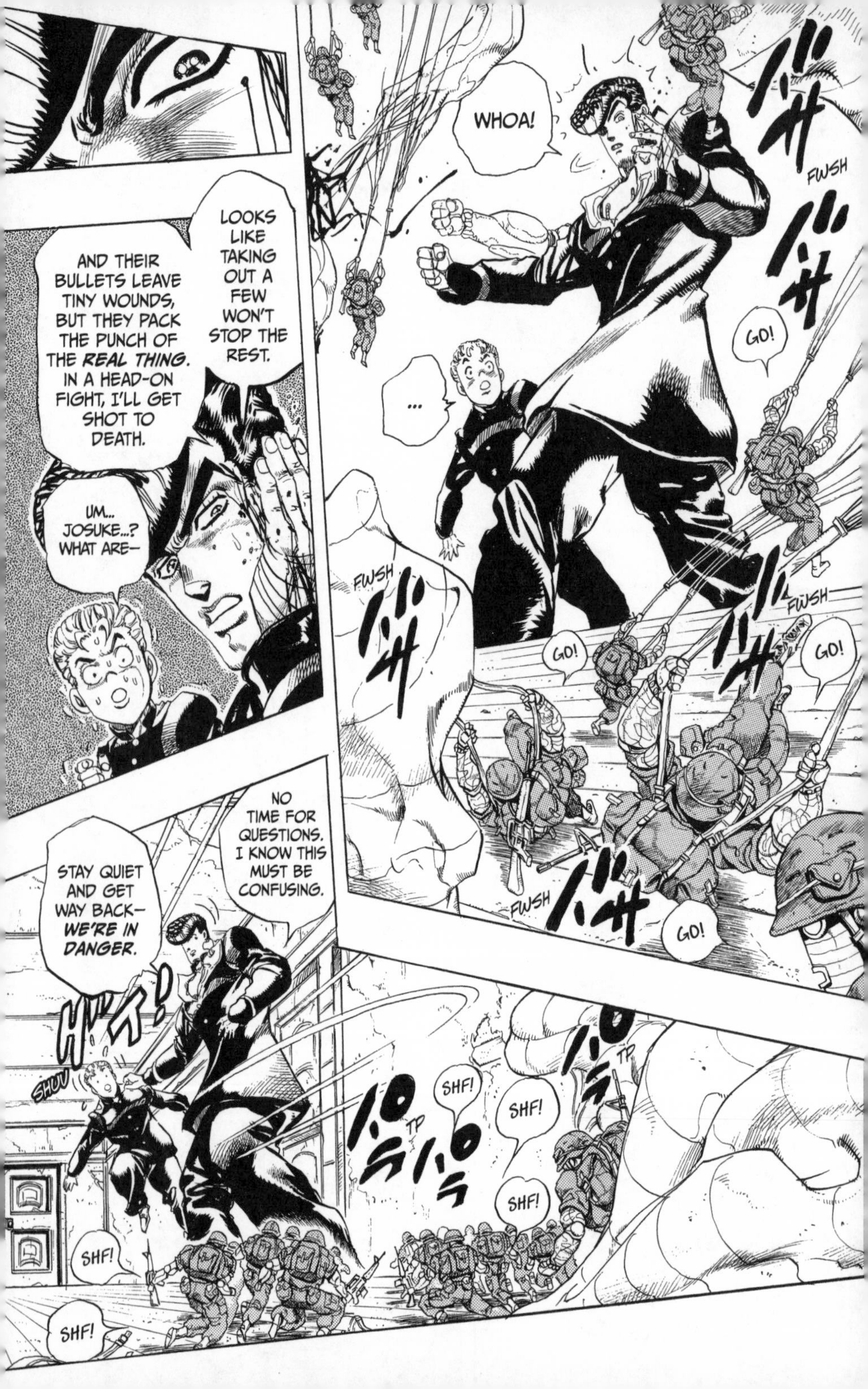
FWSH
WHOA!
GO!
...
FWSH
FWSH
GO!
GO!
FWSH
GO!
LOOKS LIKE TAKING OUT A FEW WON'T STOP THE REST.
AND THEIR BULLETS LEAVE TINY WOUNDS, BUT THEY PACK THE PUNCH OF THE ***REAL THING***. IN A HEAD-ON FIGHT, I'LL GET SHOT TO DEATH.
UM... JOSUKE...? WHAT ARE–
NO TIME FOR QUESTIONS. I KNOW THIS MUST BE CONFUSING.
STAY QUIET AND GET WAY BACK– ***WE'RE IN DANGER.***
TP
SHF!
SHF!
TP
SHF!
SHUU
SHF!
SHF!

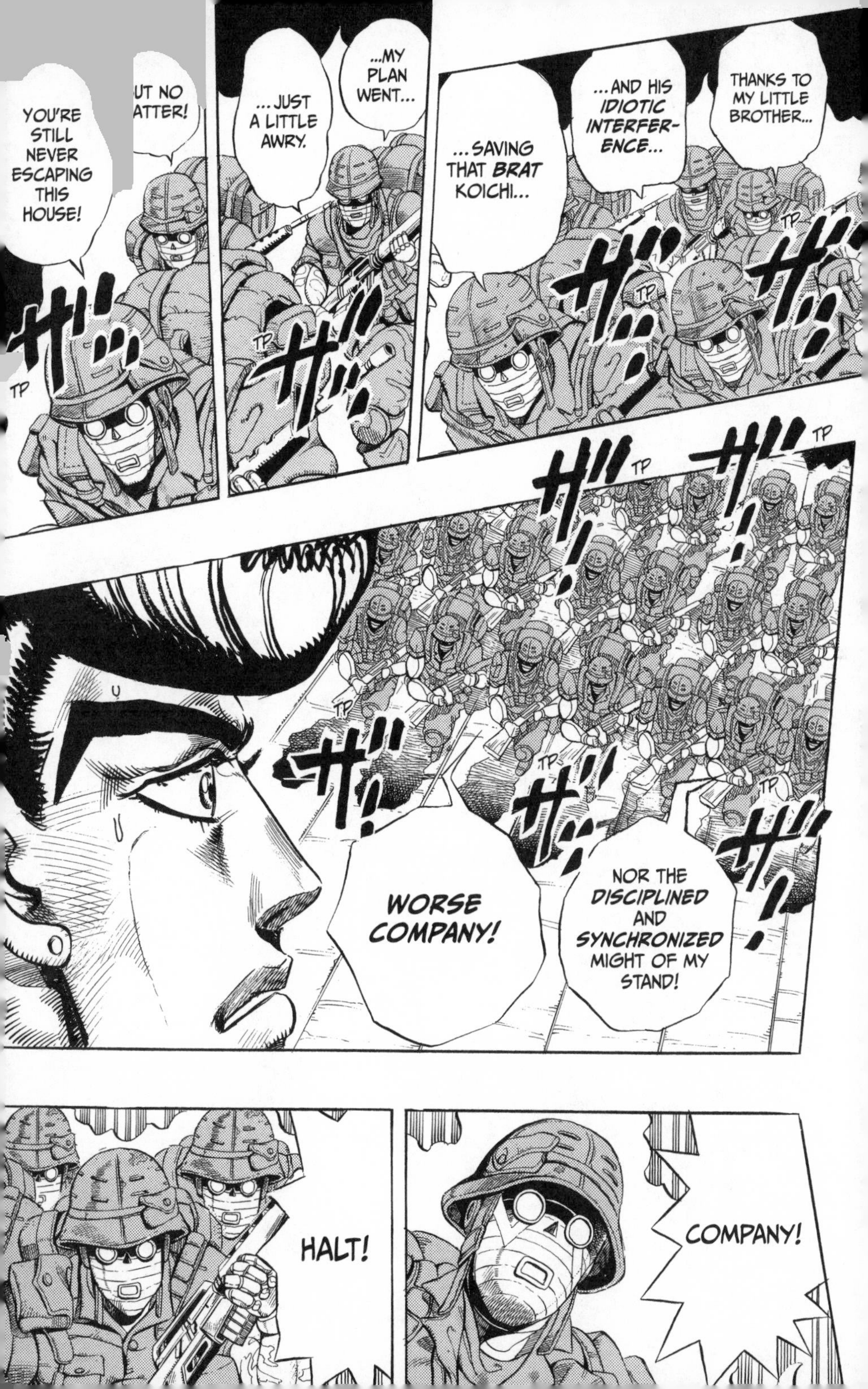

THANKS TO MY LITTLE BROTHER...
...AND HIS IDIOTIC INTERFERENCE...
...SAVING THAT BRAT KOICHI...
TP
TP
...MY PLAN WENT...
...JUST A LITTLE AWRY.
TP
UT NO ATTER!
YOU'RE STILL NEVER ESCAPING THIS HOUSE!
TP
TP
TP
TP
TP
NOR THE DISCIPLINED AND SYNCHRONIZED MIGHT OF MY STAND!
WORSE COMPANY!
COMPANY!
HALT!

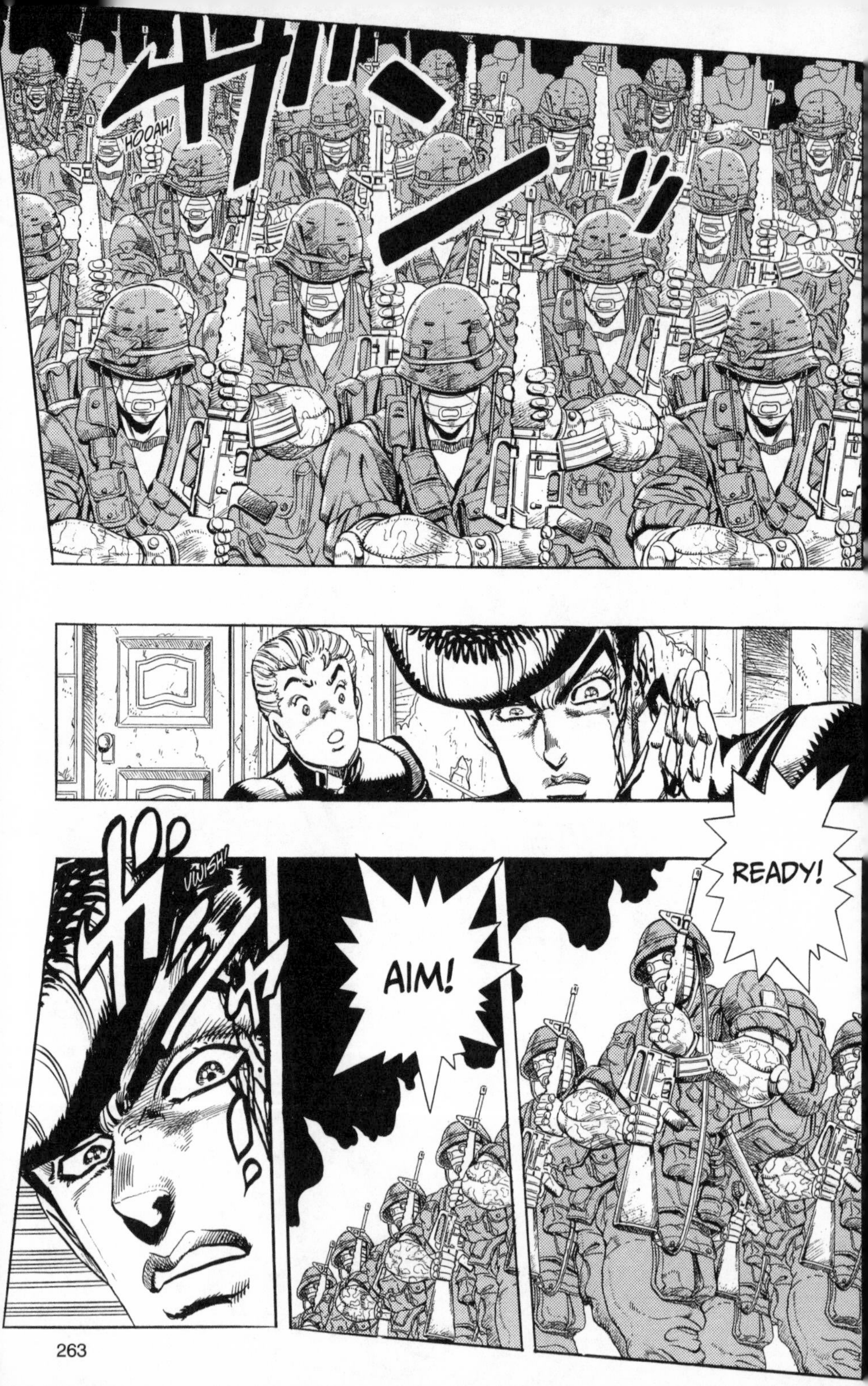
HOOAH!
READY!
AIM!
VWISH!

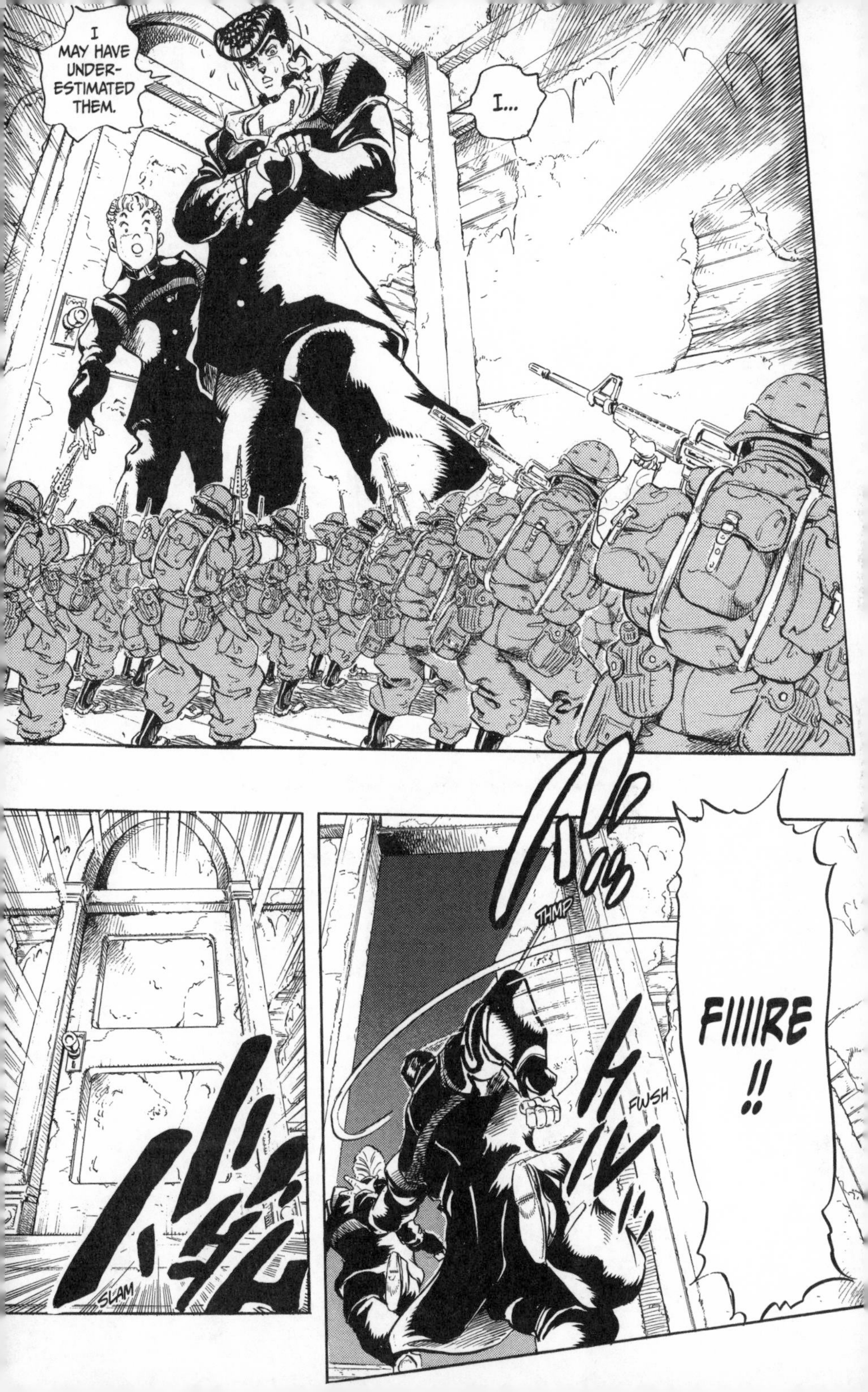
I...
I MAY HAVE UNDER-ESTIMATED THEM.
FIIIRE !!
THMP
FWSH
SLAM

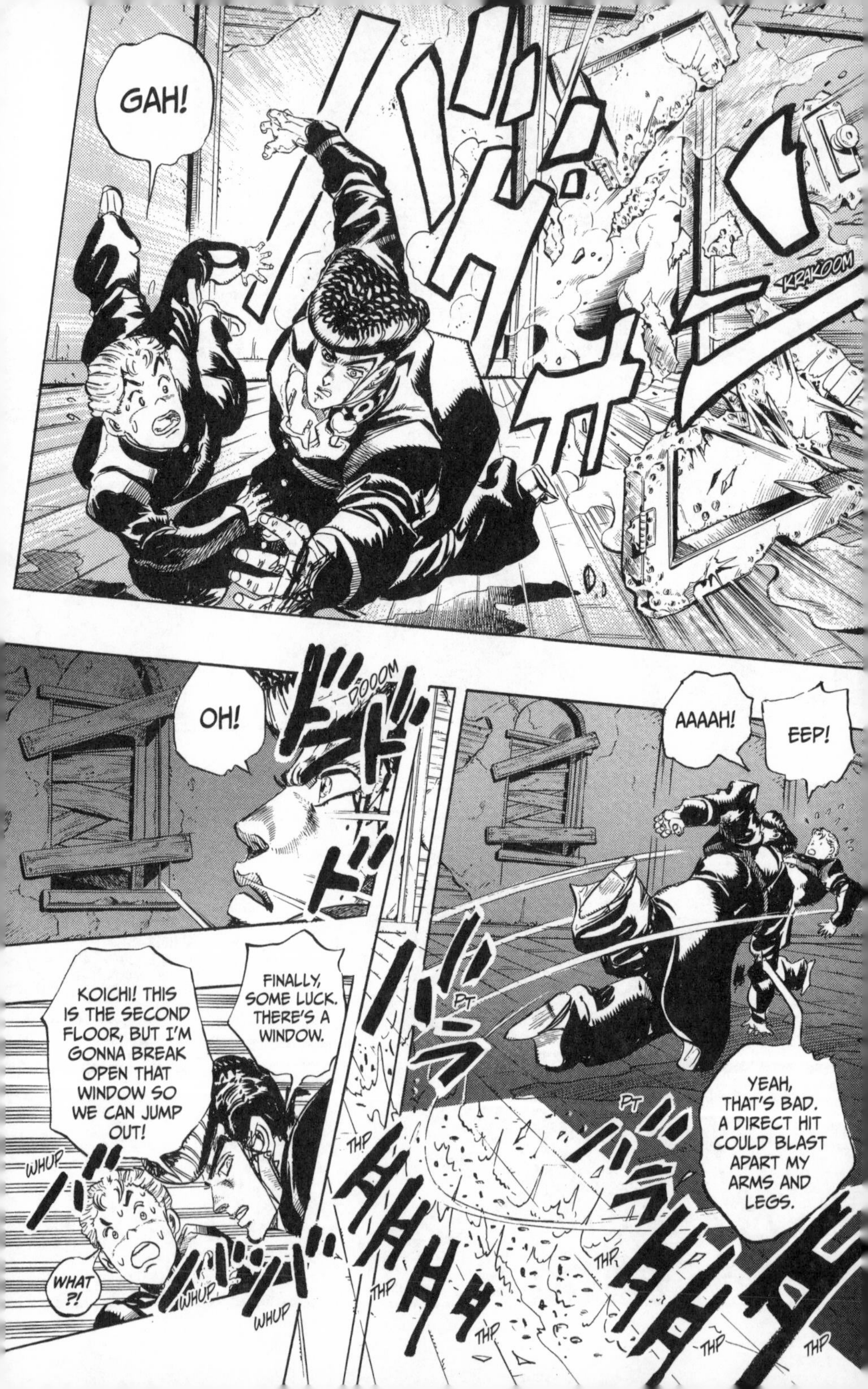
GAH!
KRAKOOM
EEP!
AAAAH!
PT
PT
YEAH, THAT'S BAD. A DIRECT HIT COULD BLAST APART MY ARMS AND LEGS.
THP
THP
THP
THP
THP
THP
DOOOM
OH!
FINALLY, SOME LUCK. THERE'S A WINDOW.
KOICHI! THIS IS THE SECOND FLOOR, BUT I'M GONNA BREAK OPEN THAT WINDOW SO WE CAN JUMP OUT!
WHUP
WHUP
WHUP
WHAT ?!

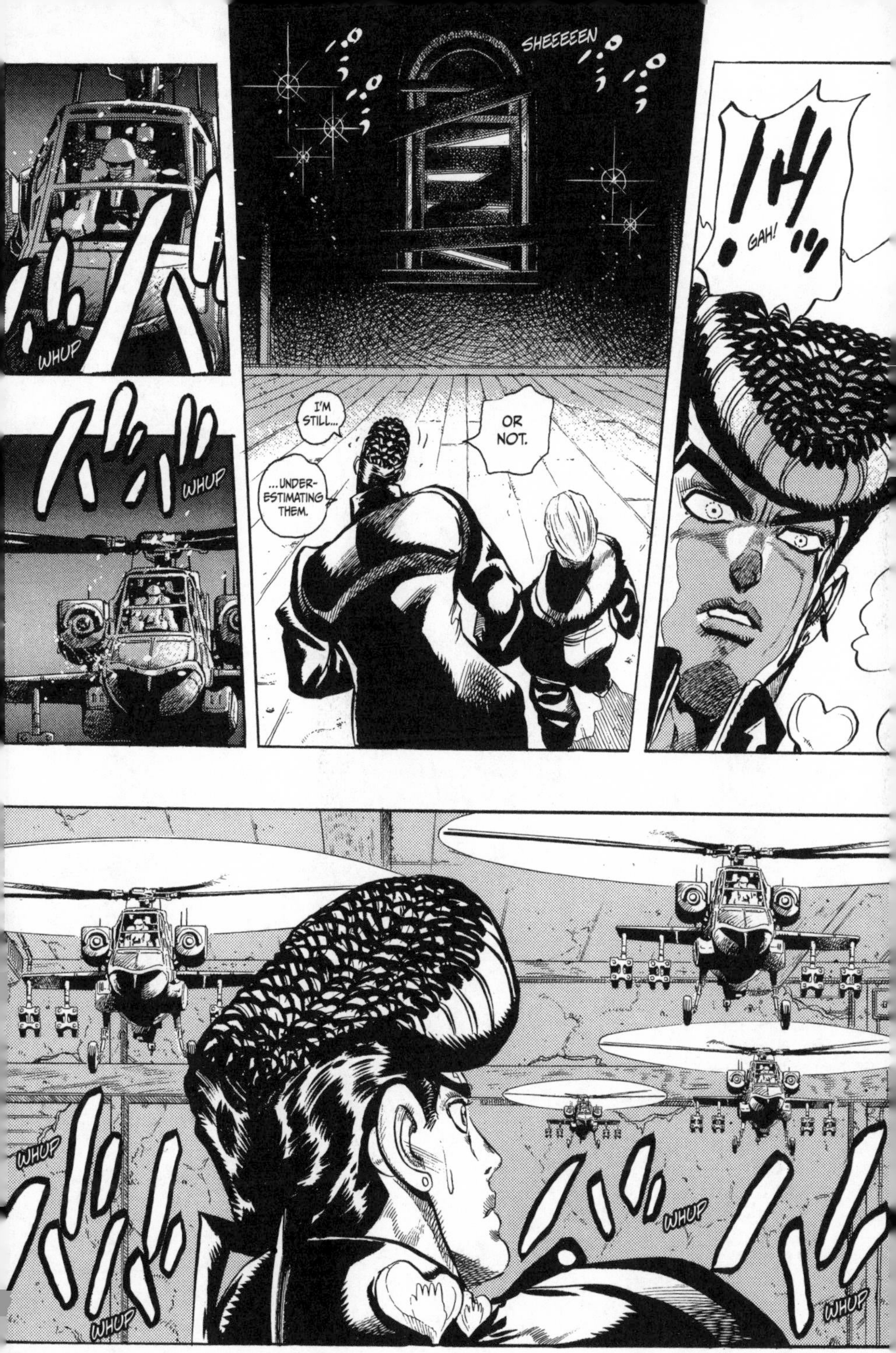

!!
GAH!
SHEEEEEN
I'M STILL...
...UNDER-ESTIMATING THEM.
OR NOT.
WHUP
WHUP
WHUP
WHUP
WHUP
WHUP

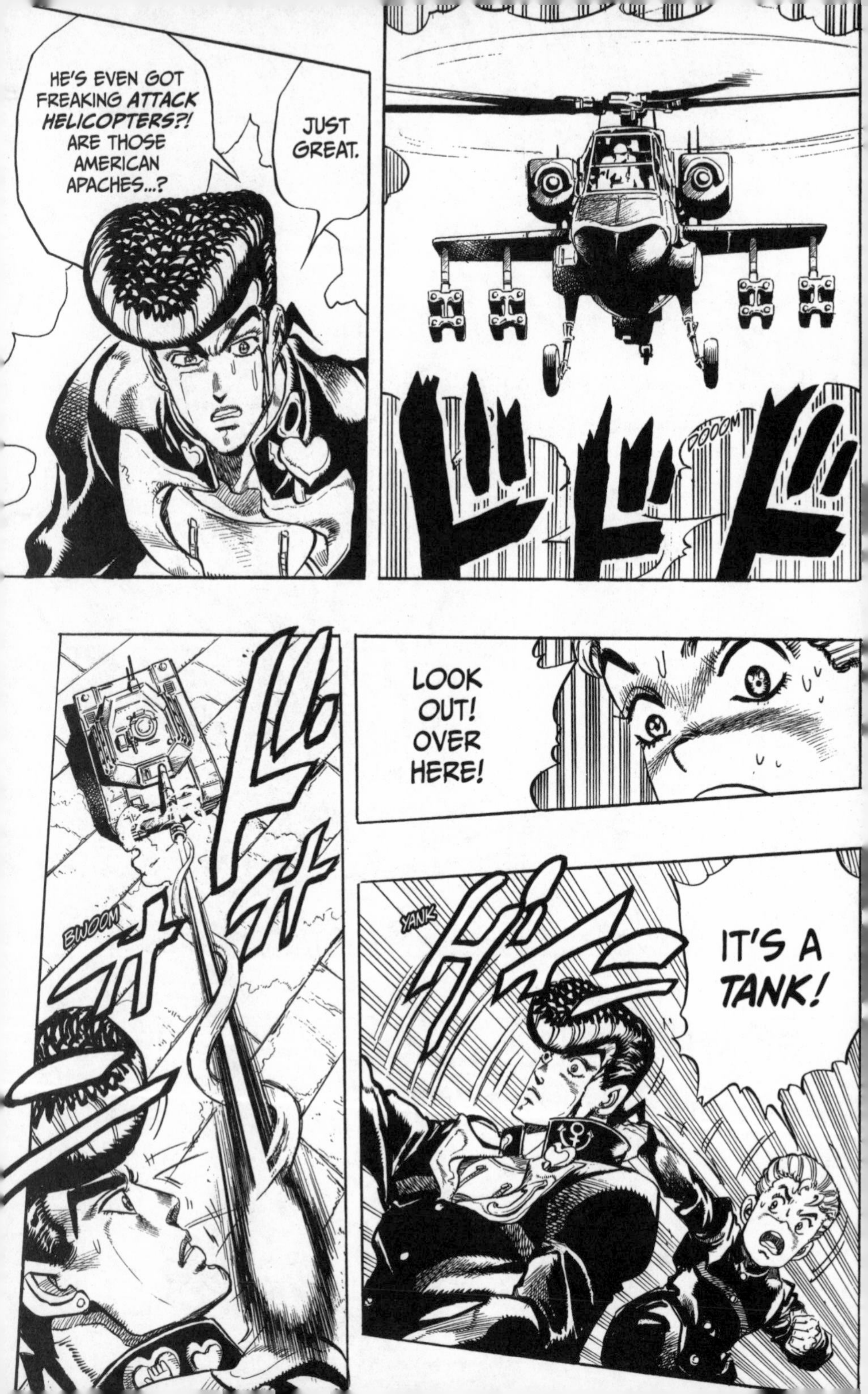
DOOOM
JUST GREAT.
HE'S EVEN GOT FREAKING *ATTACK HELICOPTERS?!* ARE THOSE AMERICAN APACHES...?
LOOK OUT! OVER HERE!
IT'S A *TANK!*
YANK
BWOOM

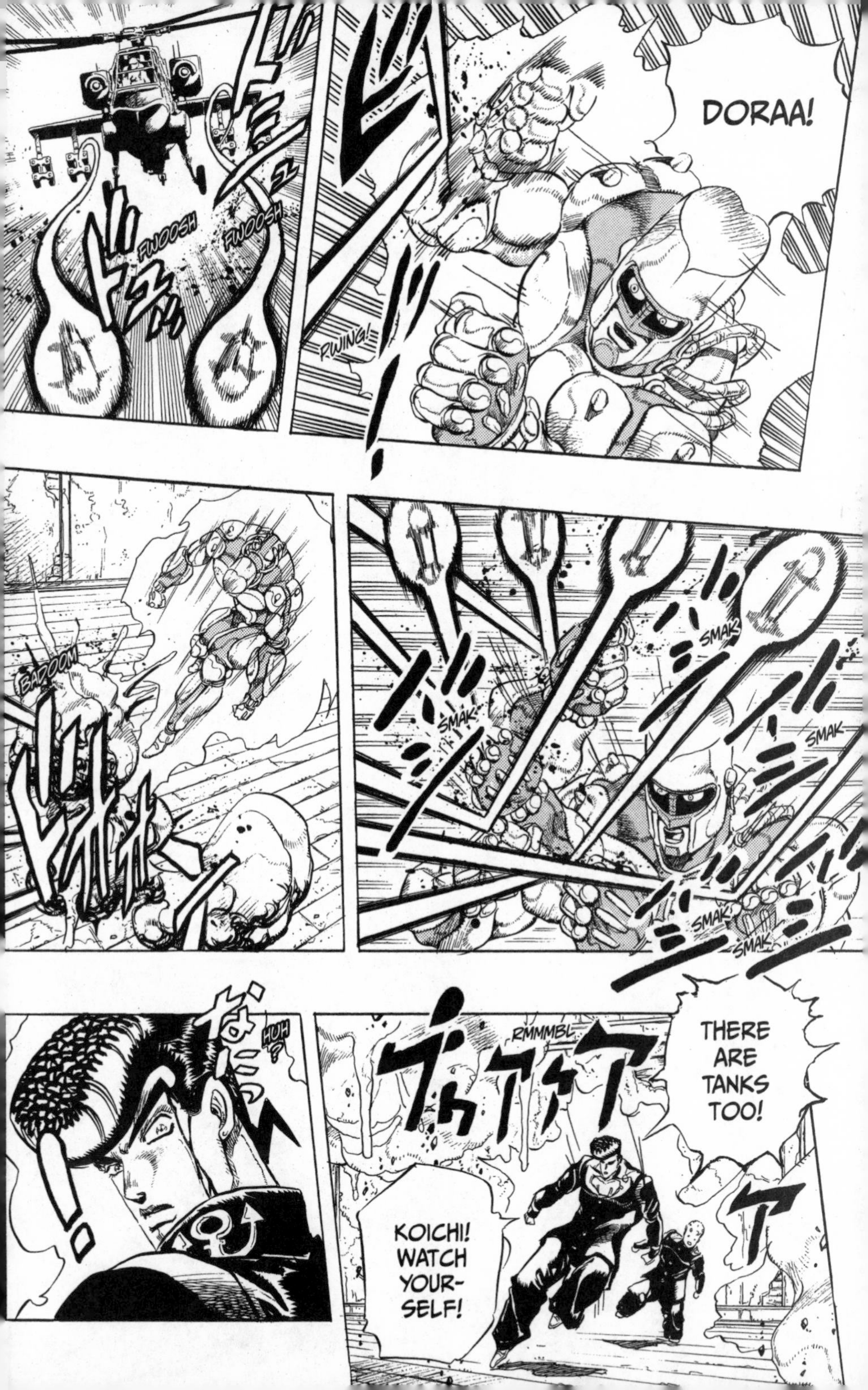
DORAA!
RWING!
FWOOSH
FWOOSH
SMAK
SMAK
SMAK
SMAK
SMAK
BADOOM
RMMMBL
THERE ARE TANKS TOO!
KOICHI! WATCH YOUR-SELF!
HUH?

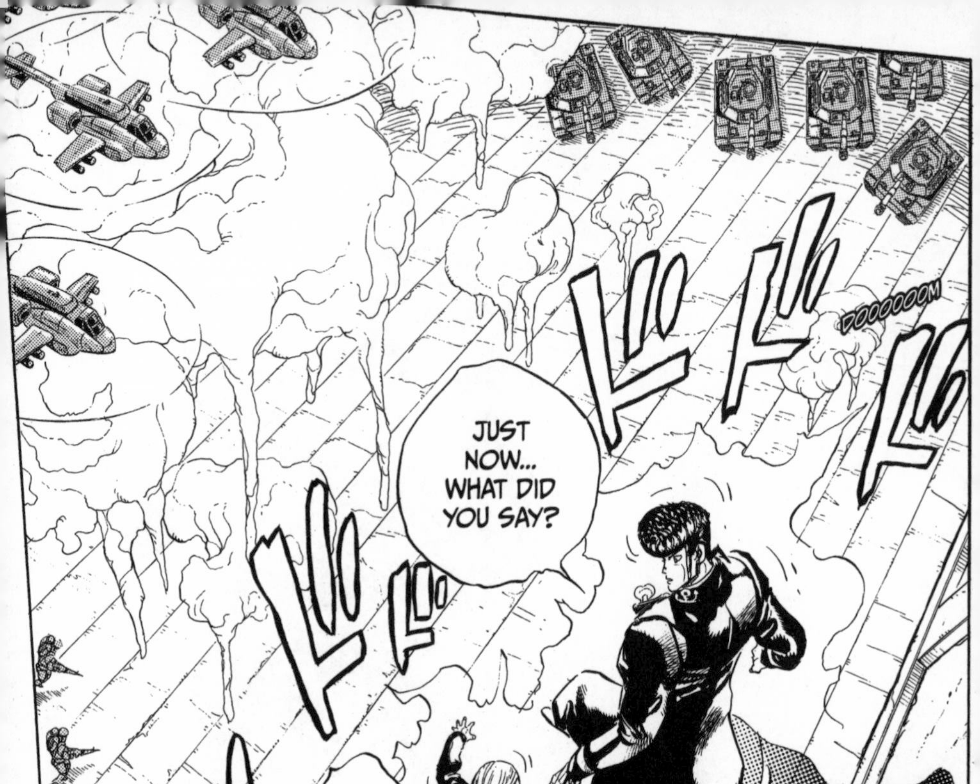
DOOOOOOM
JUST NOW... WHAT DID YOU SAY?
!!

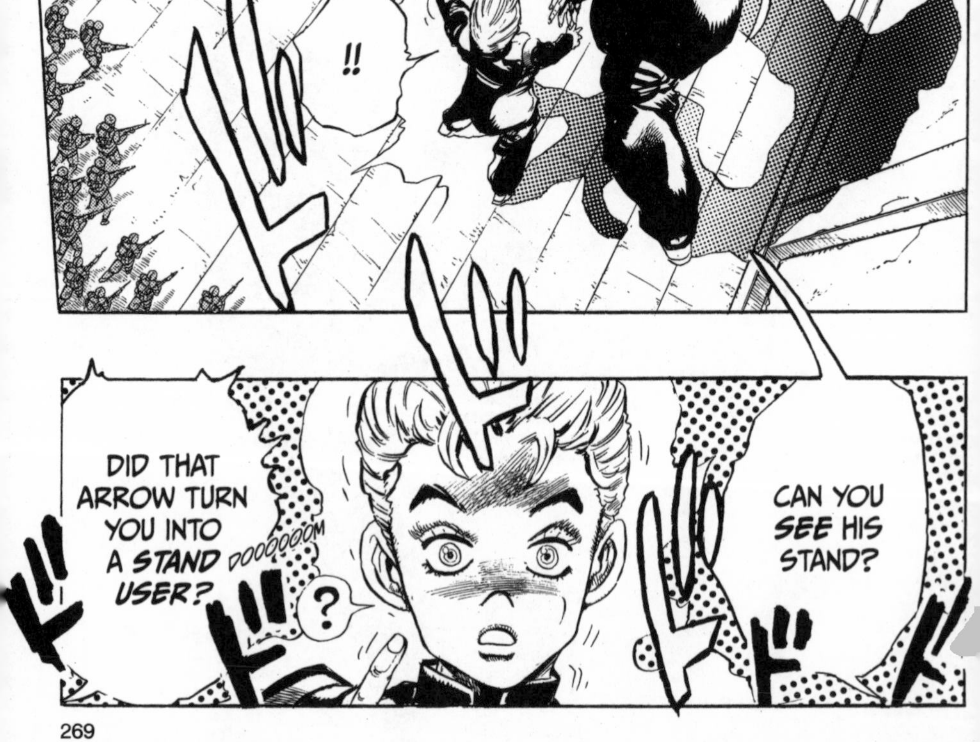
CAN YOU **SEE** HIS STAND?
DID THAT ARROW TURN YOU INTO A **STAND USER?**
DOOOOOOM
?

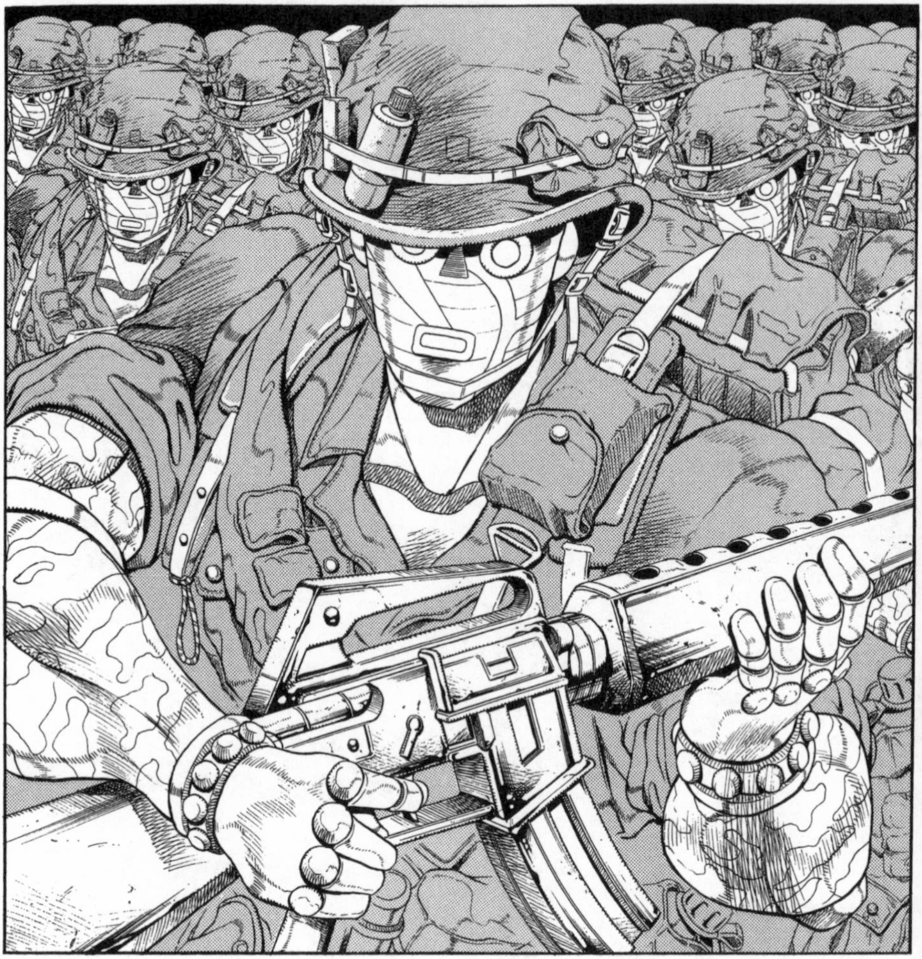

CHAPTER 14

THE NIJIMURA BROTHERS, PART 6

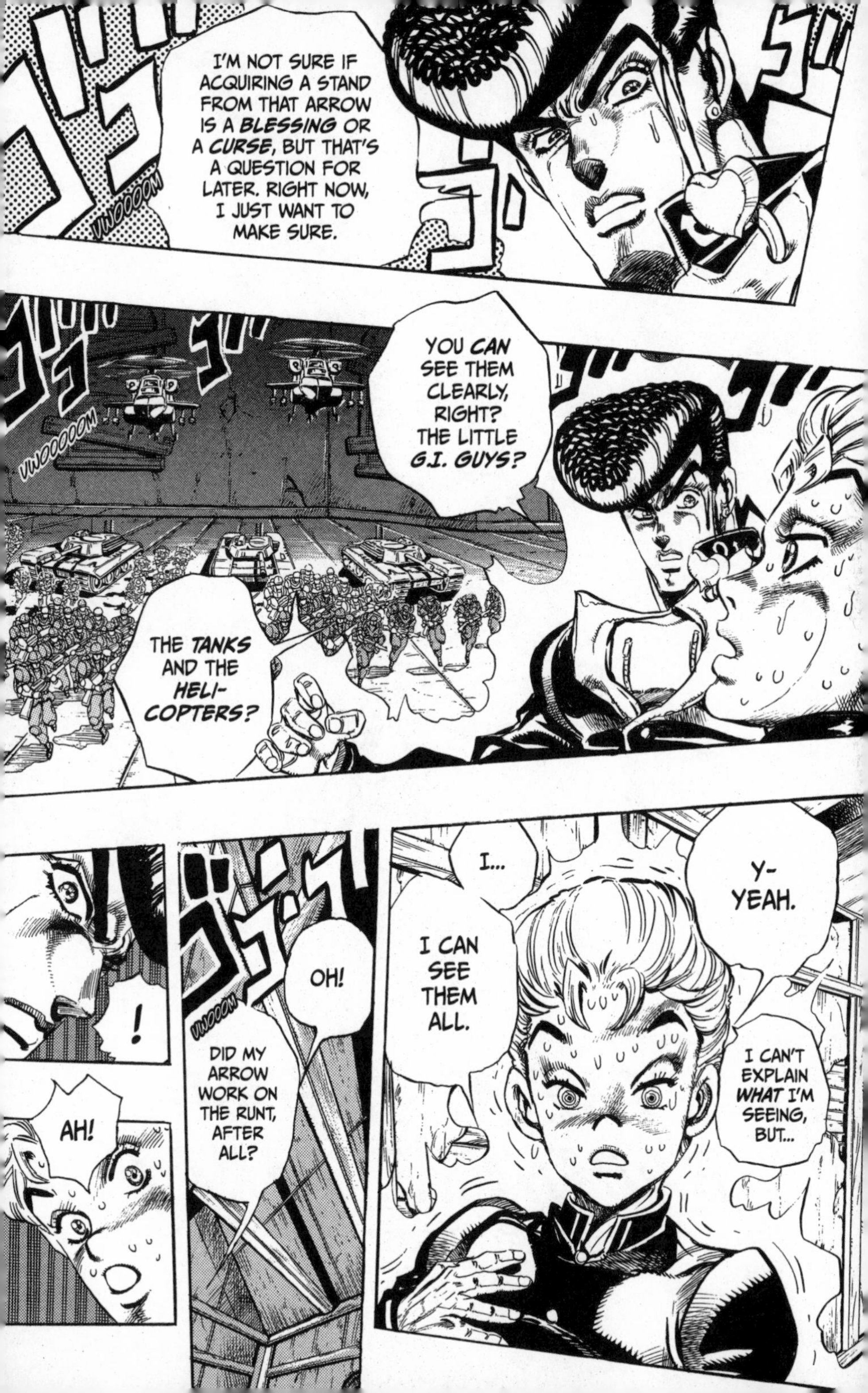
I'M NOT SURE IF ACQUIRING A STAND FROM THAT ARROW IS A ***BLESSING*** OR A ***CURSE***, BUT THAT'S A QUESTION FOR LATER. RIGHT NOW, I JUST WANT TO MAKE SURE.
VWOOOOOM
YOU ***CAN*** SEE THEM CLEARLY, RIGHT? THE LITTLE ***G.I. GUYS?***
THE ***TANKS*** AND THE ***HELI-COPTERS?***
VWOOOOOM
Y- YEAH.
I...
I CAN SEE THEM ALL.
I CAN'T EXPLAIN ***WHAT*** I'M SEEING, BUT...
OH!
DID MY ARROW WORK ON THE RUNT, AFTER ALL?
VWOOOM
!
AH!

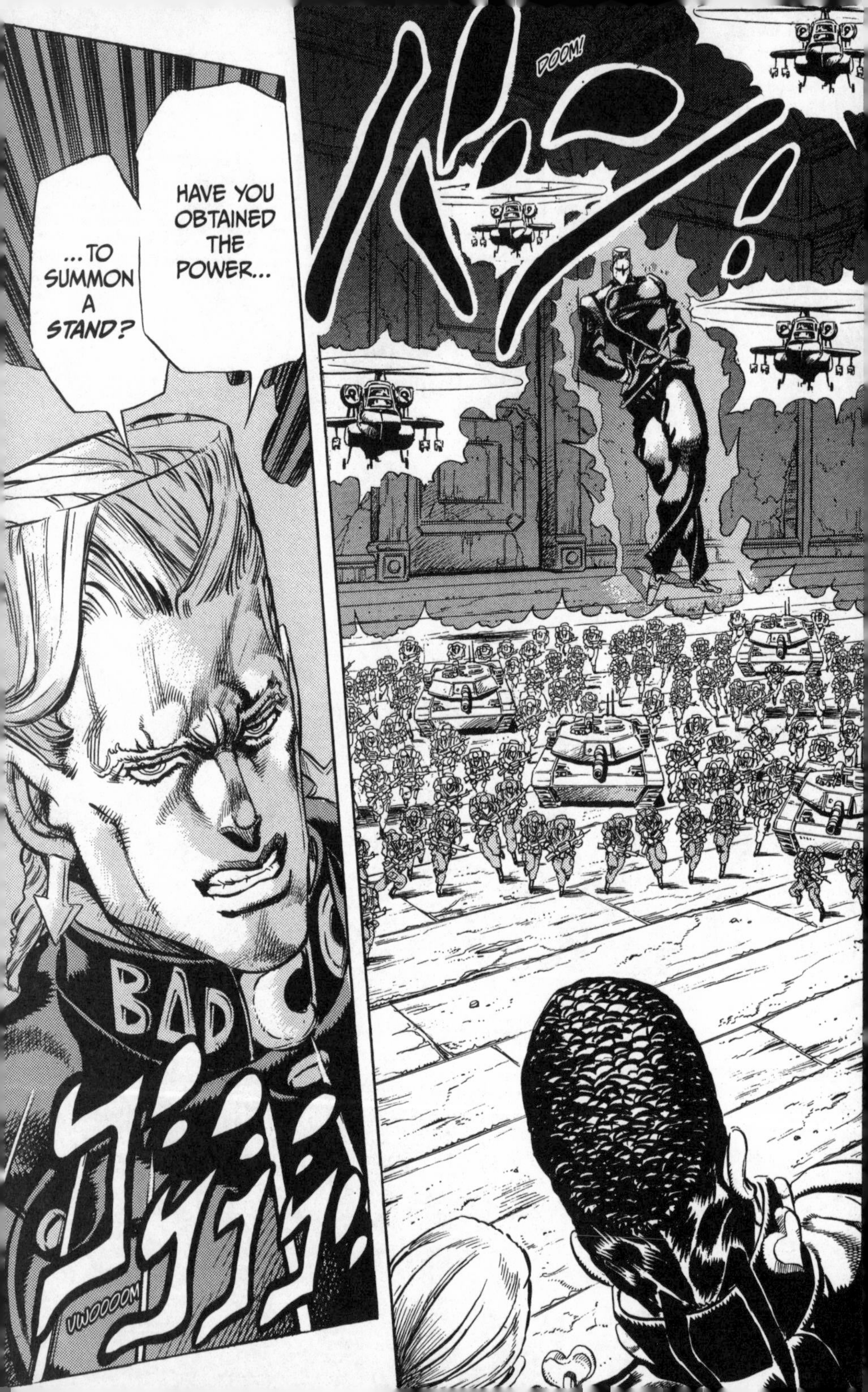
DOOM!
HAVE YOU OBTAINED THE POWER...
...TO SUMMON A STAND?
BAD
UWOOOOM

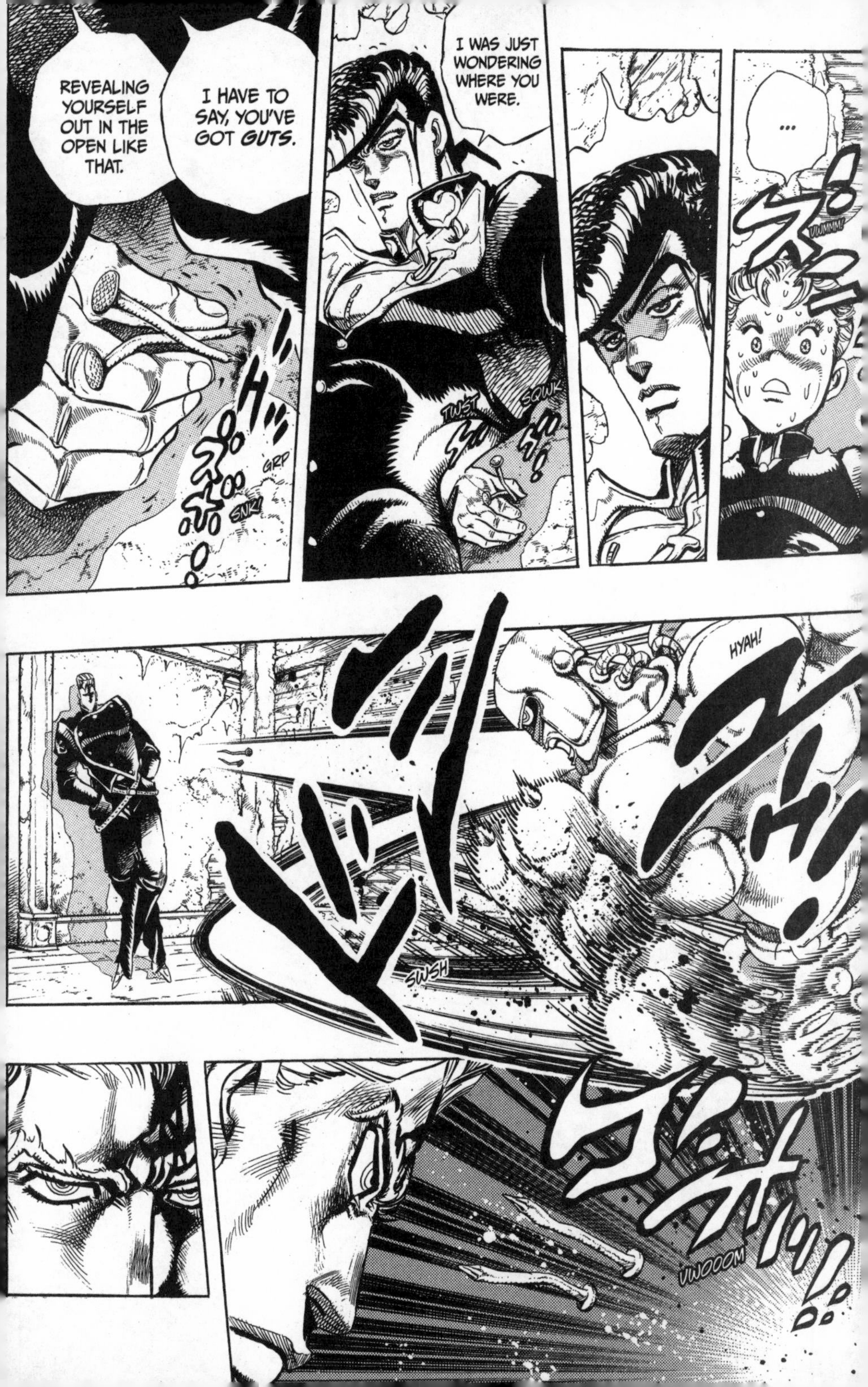
...
VWMMM
I WAS JUST WONDERING WHERE YOU WERE.
SQWK
TWIST
I HAVE TO SAY, YOU'VE GOT GUTS.
REVEALING YOURSELF OUT IN THE OPEN LIKE THAT.
GRP
SNK
HYAH!
SWSH
VWOOOM

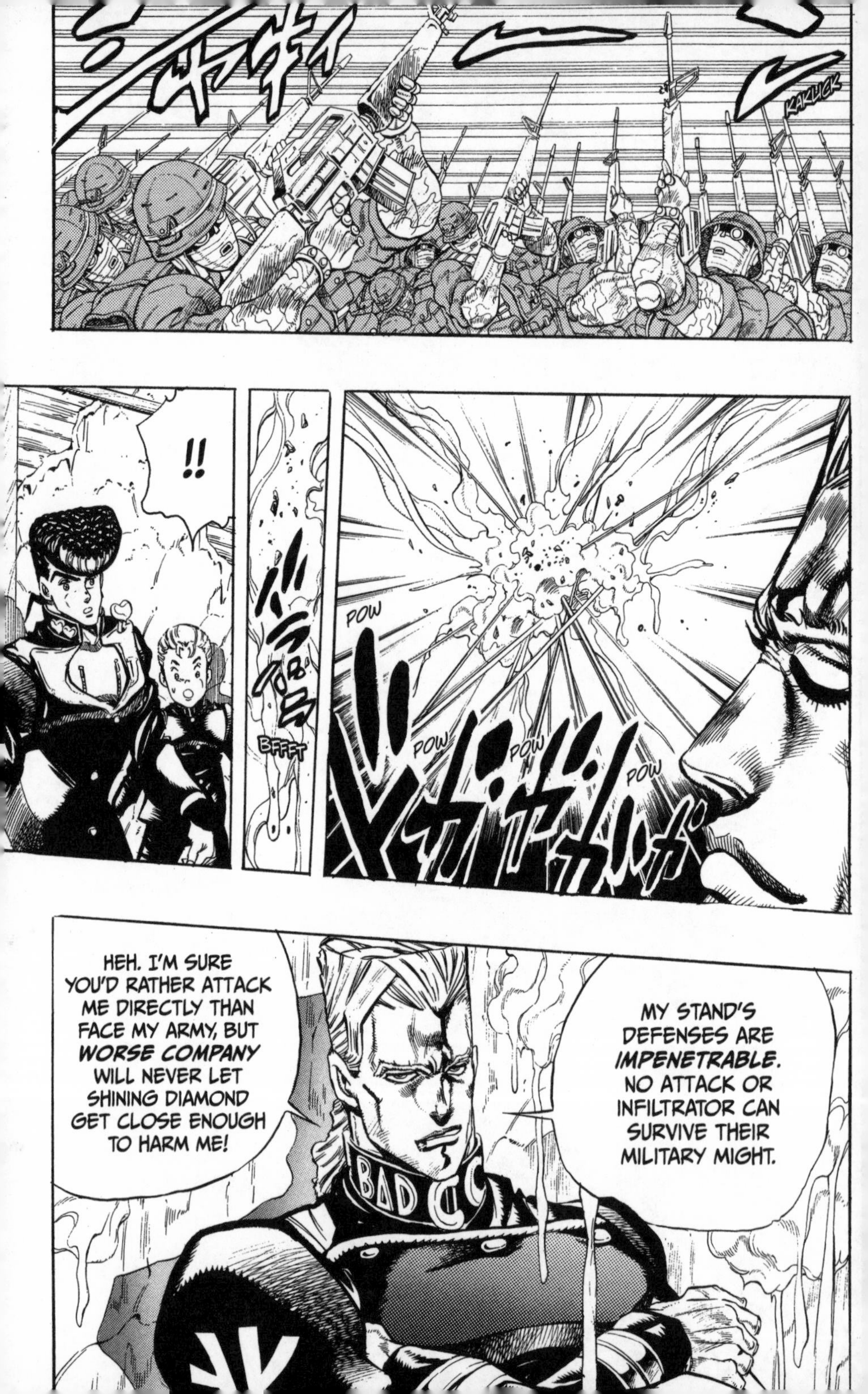
KAKLICK
POW
POW
POW
POW
BFFFT
!!
HEH. I'M SURE YOU'D RATHER ATTACK ME DIRECTLY THAN FACE MY ARMY, BUT ***WORSE COMPANY*** WILL NEVER LET SHINING DIAMOND GET CLOSE ENOUGH TO HARM ME!
MY STAND'S DEFENSES ARE ***IMPENETRABLE.*** NO ATTACK OR INFILTRATOR CAN SURVIVE THEIR MILITARY MIGHT.

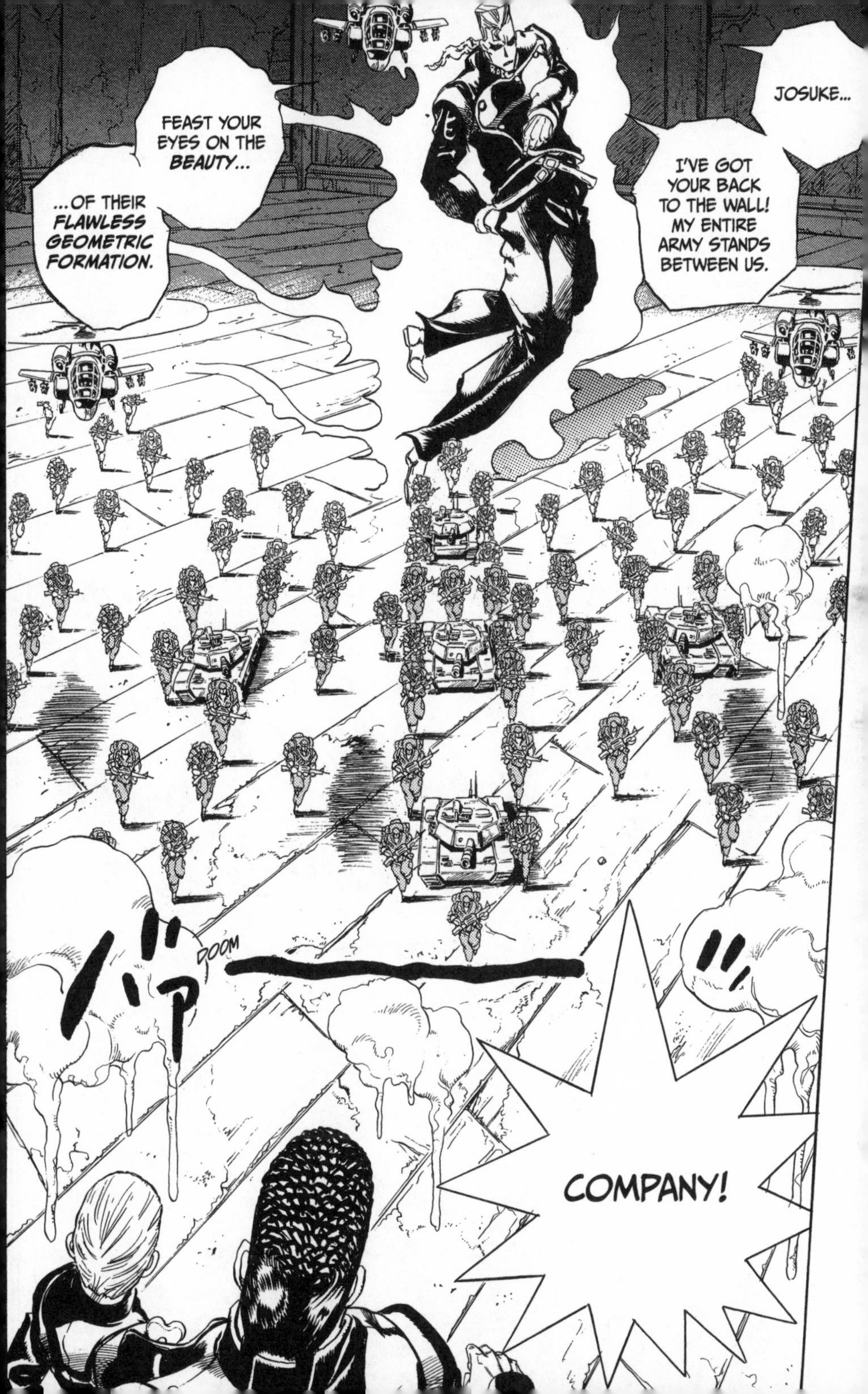
JOSUKE...
I'VE GOT YOUR BACK TO THE WALL! MY ENTIRE ARMY STANDS BETWEEN US.
FEAST YOUR EYES ON THE *BEAUTY*...
...OF THEIR *FLAWLESS GEOMETRIC FORMATION.*
DOOM
COMPANY!

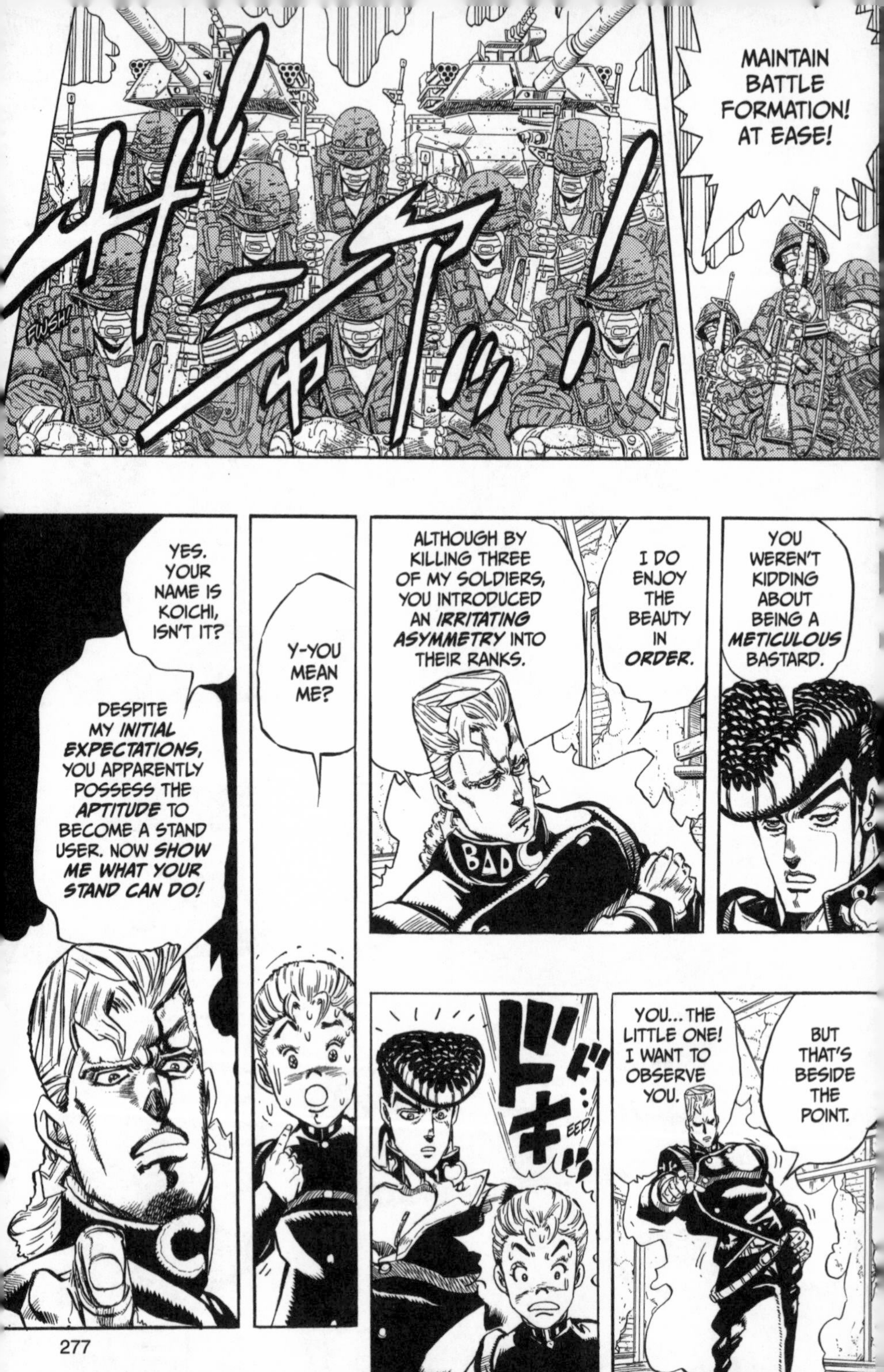

MAINTAIN BATTLE FORMATION! AT EASE!
FWISH!
YOU WEREN'T KIDDING ABOUT BEING A *METICULOUS* BASTARD.
I DO ENJOY THE BEAUTY IN *ORDER.*
ALTHOUGH BY KILLING THREE OF MY SOLDIERS, YOU INTRODUCED AN *IRRITATING ASYMMETRY* INTO THEIR RANKS.
BUT THAT'S BESIDE THE POINT.
YOU... THE LITTLE ONE! I WANT TO OBSERVE YOU.
EEP!
Y-YOU MEAN ME?
YES. YOUR NAME IS KOICHI, ISN'T IT?
DESPITE MY *INITIAL EXPECTATIONS,* YOU APPARENTLY POSSESS THE *APTITUDE* TO BECOME A STAND USER. NOW *SHOW ME WHAT YOUR STAND CAN DO!*

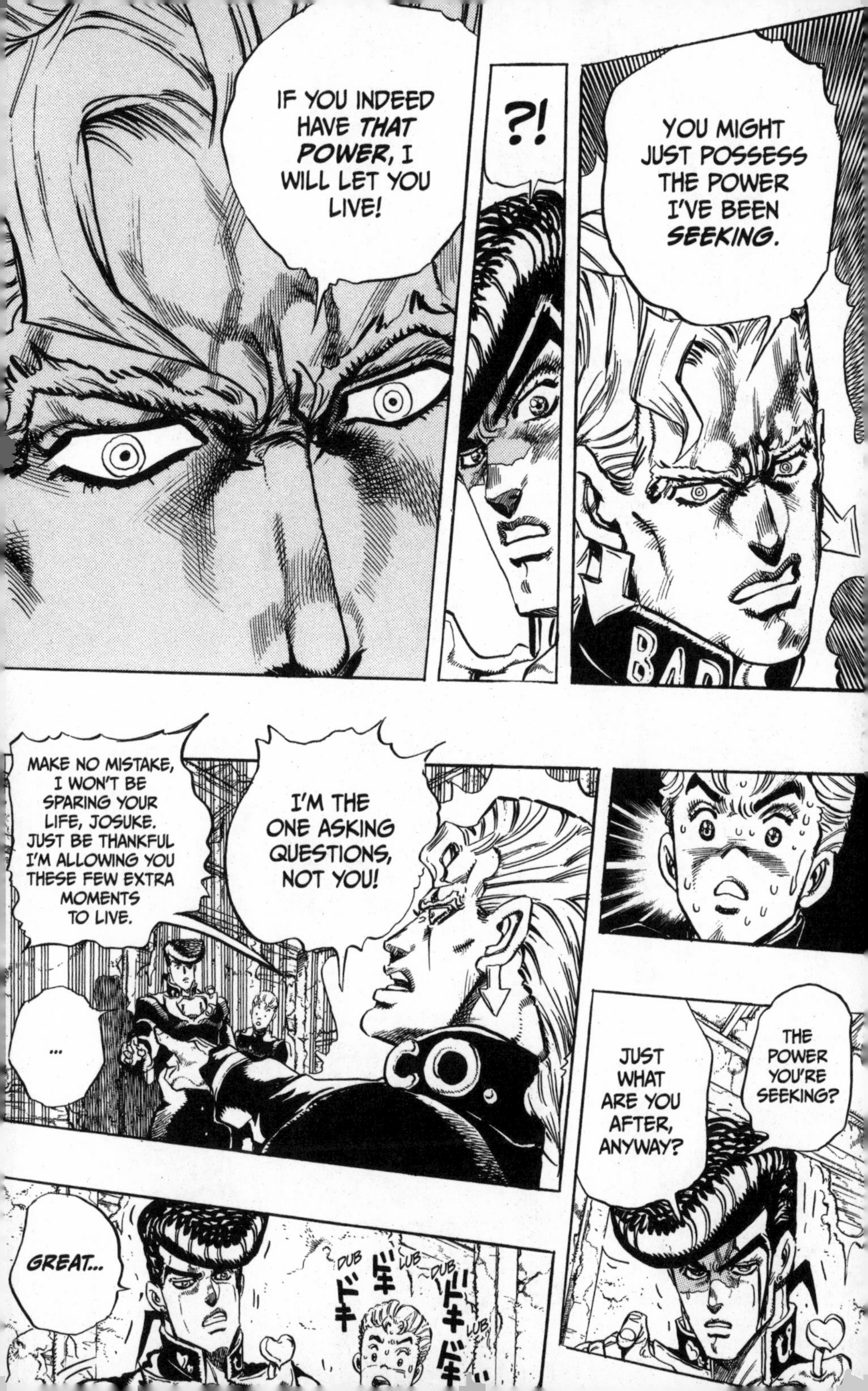
YOU MIGHT JUST POSSESS THE POWER I'VE BEEN *SEEKING.*
?!
IF YOU INDEED HAVE *THAT POWER*, I WILL LET YOU LIVE!
THE POWER YOU'RE SEEKING?
JUST WHAT ARE YOU AFTER, ANYWAY?
I'M THE ONE ASKING QUESTIONS, NOT YOU!
MAKE NO MISTAKE, I WON'T BE SPARING YOUR LIFE, JOSUKE. JUST BE THANKFUL I'M ALLOWING YOU THESE FEW EXTRA MOMENTS TO LIVE.
...
GREAT...
ドキ DUB LUB
ドキ DUB LUB

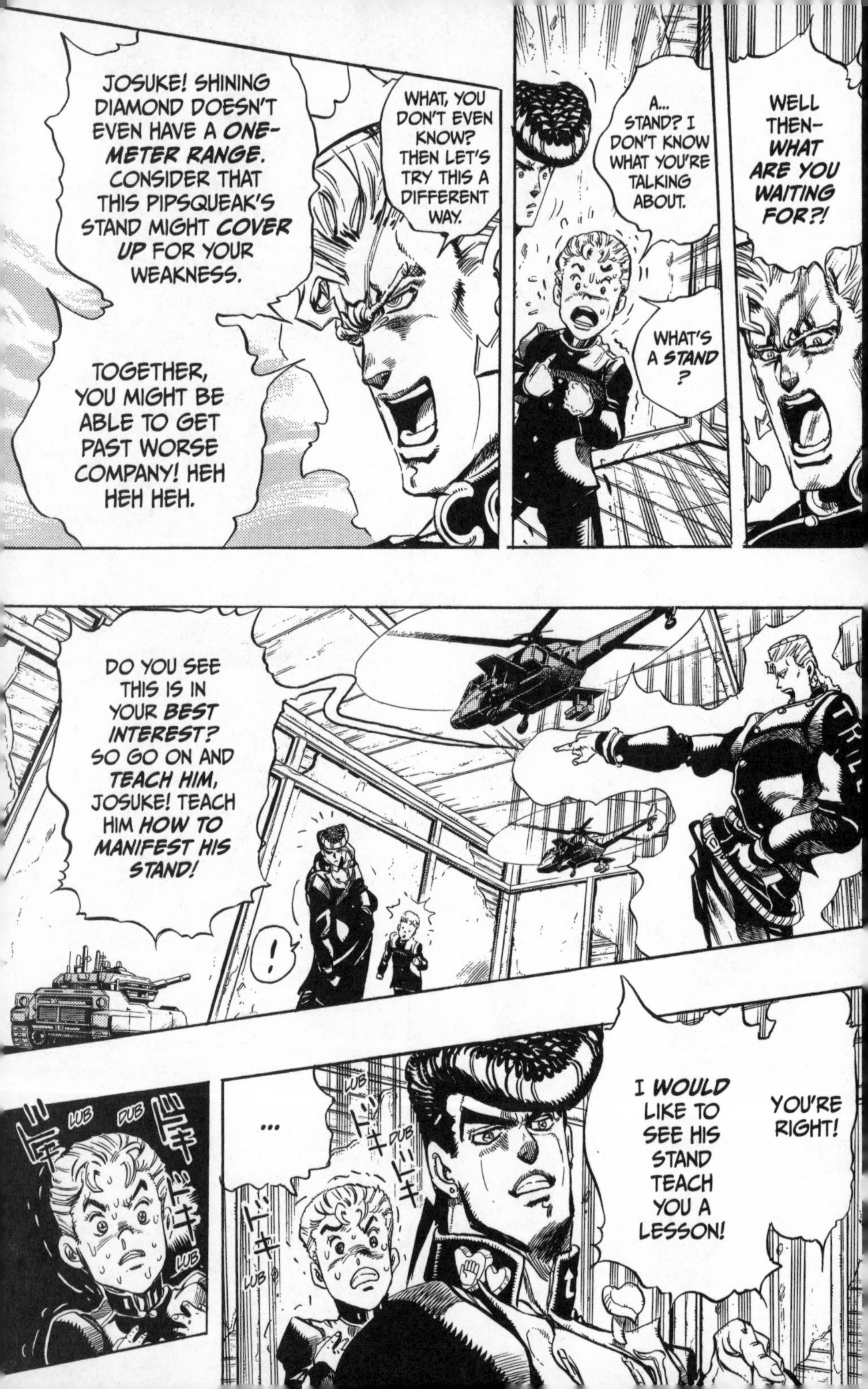
WELL THEN– WHAT ARE YOU WAITING FOR?!
A... STAND? I DON'T KNOW WHAT YOU'RE TALKING ABOUT.
WHAT'S A STAND?
WHAT, YOU DON'T EVEN KNOW? THEN LET'S TRY THIS A DIFFERENT WAY.
JOSUKE! SHINING DIAMOND DOESN'T EVEN HAVE A ONE-METER RANGE. CONSIDER THAT THIS PIPSQUEAK'S STAND MIGHT COVER UP FOR YOUR WEAKNESS.
TOGETHER, YOU MIGHT BE ABLE TO GET PAST WORSE COMPANY! HEH HEH HEH.
DO YOU SEE THIS IS IN YOUR BEST INTEREST? SO GO ON AND TEACH HIM, JOSUKE! TEACH HIM HOW TO MANIFEST HIS STAND!
!
YOU'RE RIGHT!
I WOULD LIKE TO SEE HIS STAND TEACH YOU A LESSON!
...
LUB
DUB
LUB
LUB
DUB
LUB

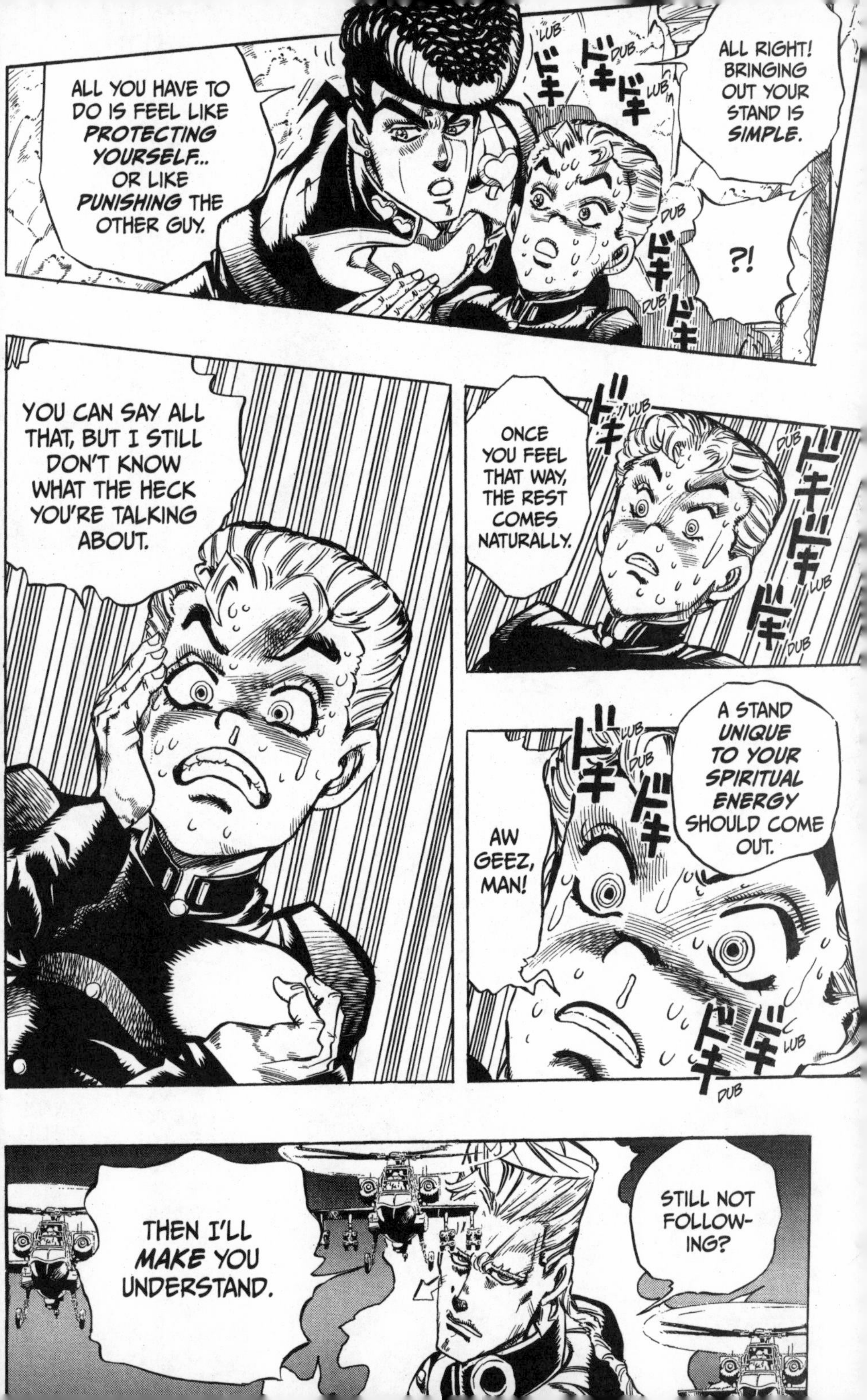
ALL RIGHT! BRINGING OUT YOUR STAND IS *SIMPLE.*
LUB DUB LUB
DUB DUB
?!
ALL YOU HAVE TO DO IS FEEL LIKE *PROTECTING YOURSELF...* OR LIKE *PUNISHING* THE OTHER GUY.
LUB DUB LUB DUB
ONCE YOU FEEL THAT WAY, THE REST COMES NATURALLY.
LUB DUB LUB
DUB
A STAND *UNIQUE TO YOUR SPIRITUAL ENERGY* SHOULD COME OUT.
LUB DUB
AW GEEZ, MAN!
YOU CAN SAY ALL THAT, BUT I STILL DON'T KNOW WHAT THE HECK YOU'RE TALKING ABOUT.
STILL NOT FOLLOW-ING?
THEN I'LL *MAKE* YOU UNDERSTAND.

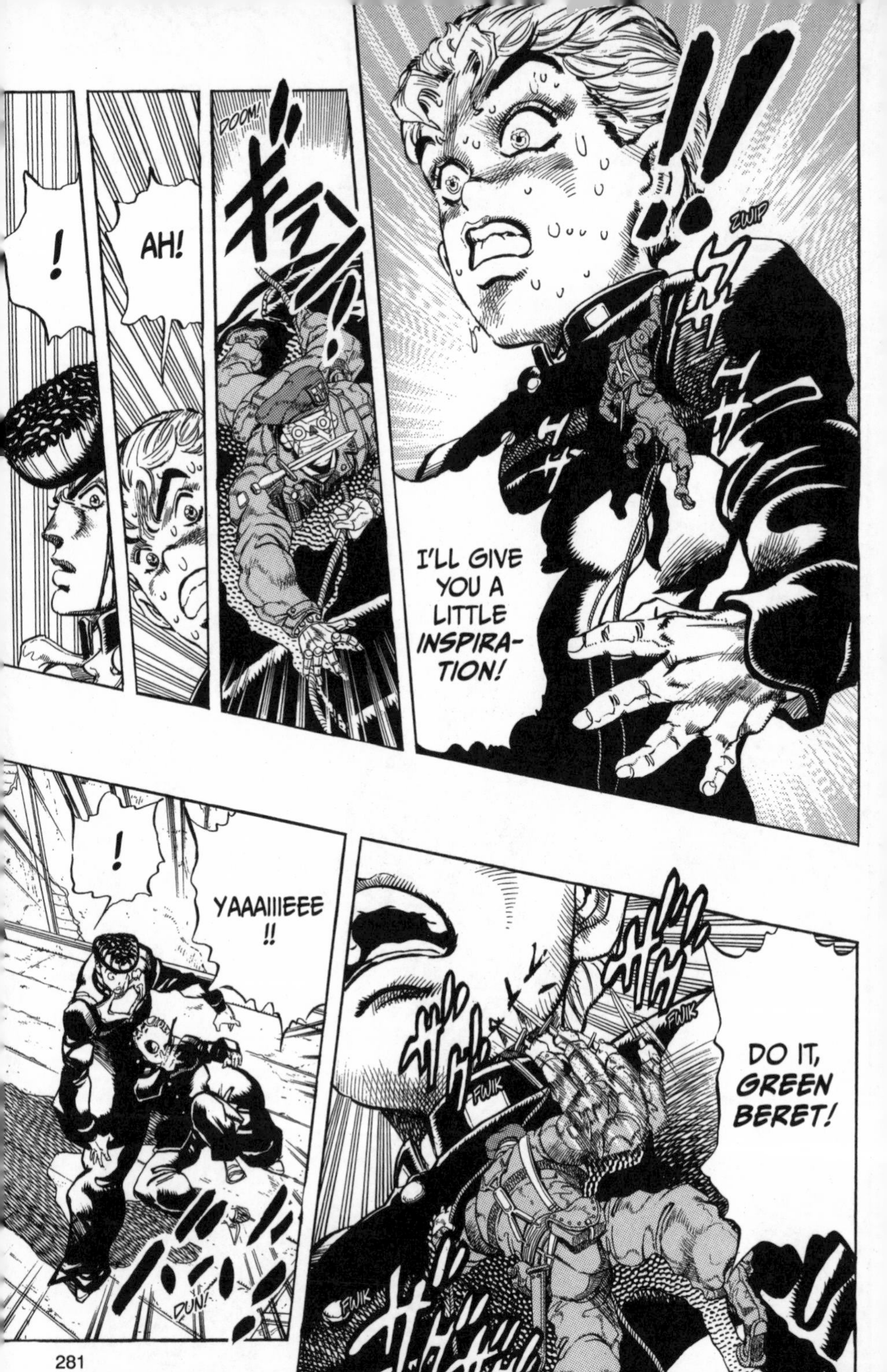
ZWIP
I'LL GIVE YOU A LITTLE INSPIRATION!
DOOM!
AH!
!
DO IT, GREEN BERET!
FWIK
FWIK
FWIK
!
YAAAIIIEEE !!
DUN!

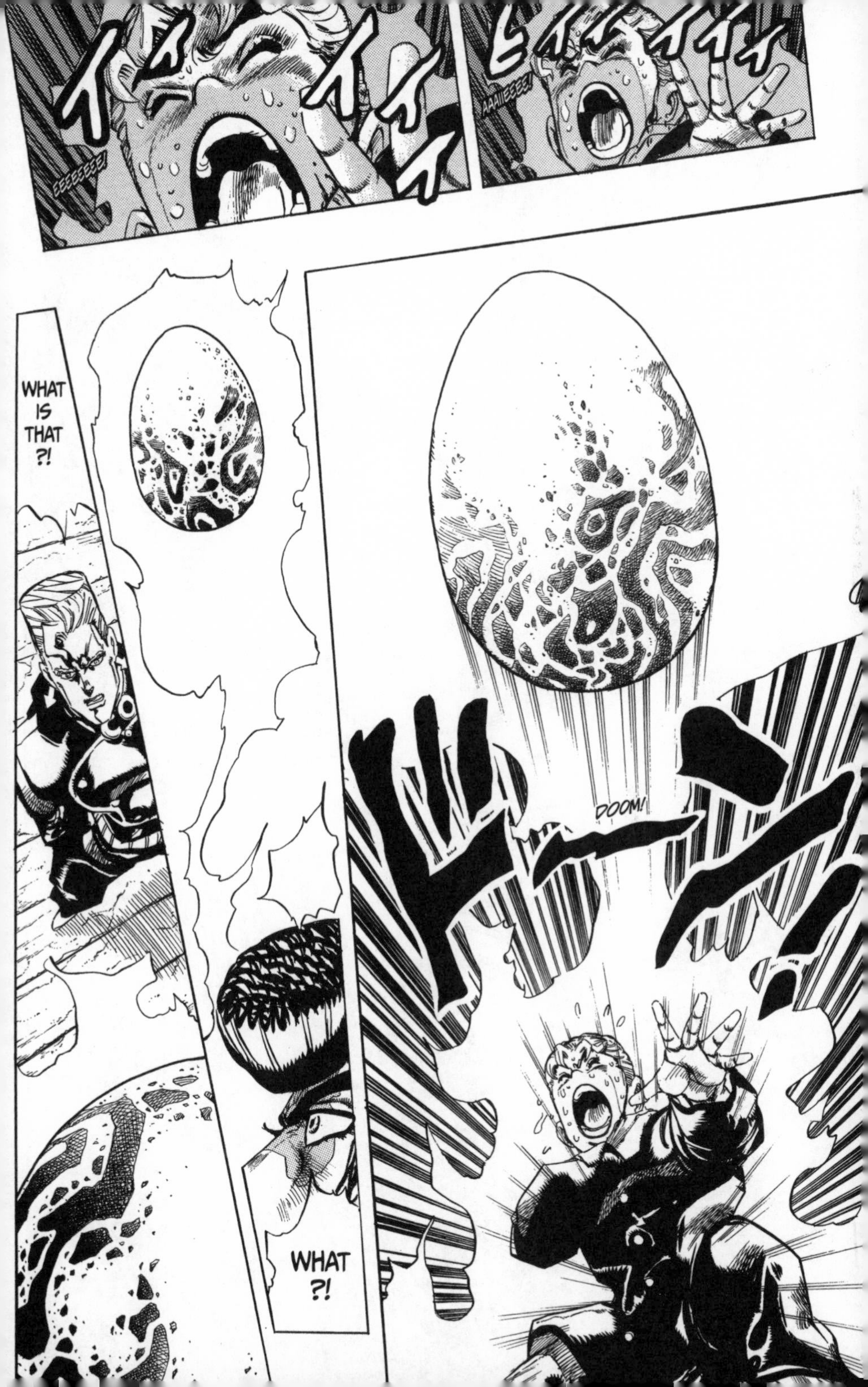
AAAIIEEEE!
EEEEEEEE!
DOOM!
WHAT ?!
WHAT IS THAT ?!

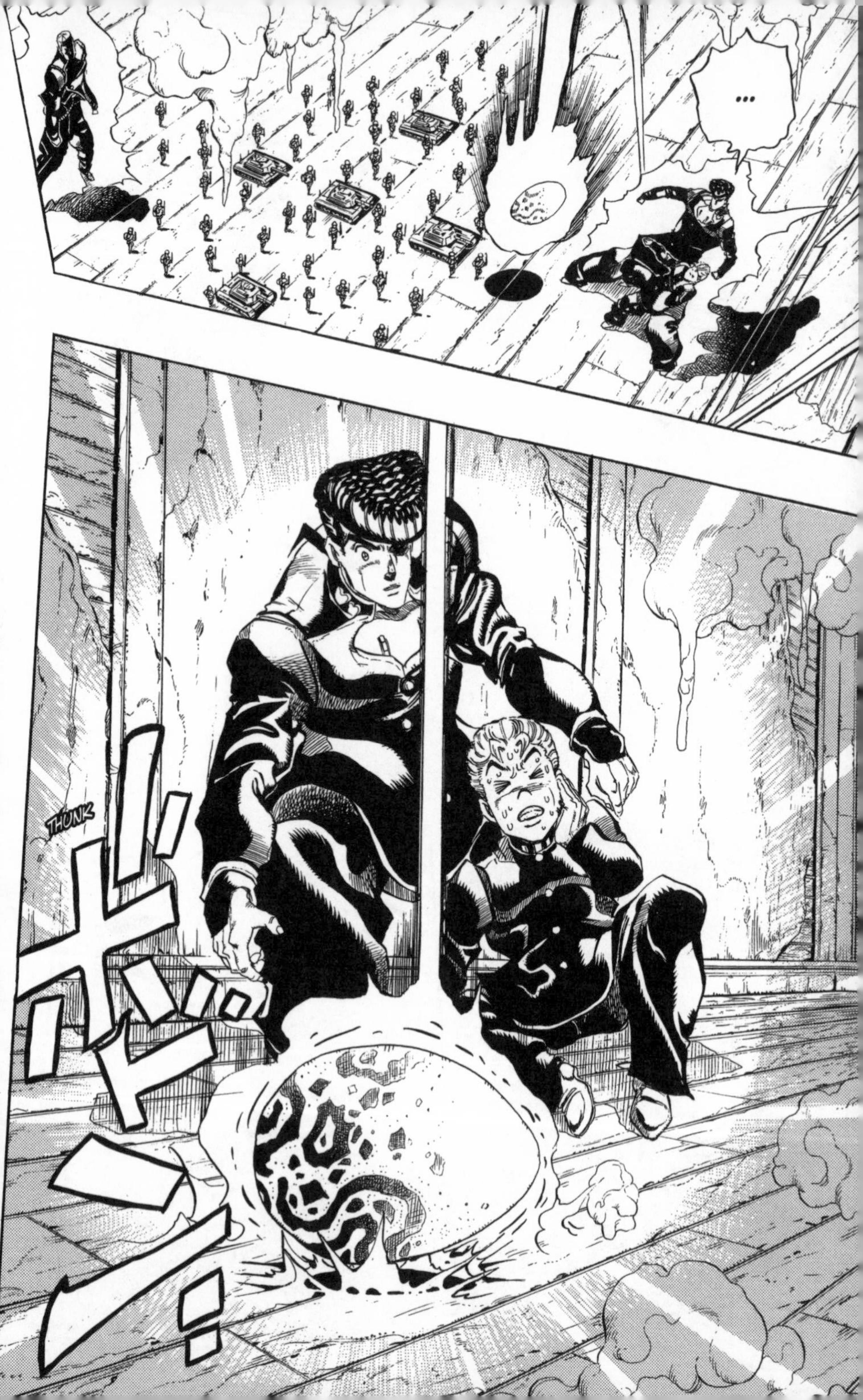
...
THUNK

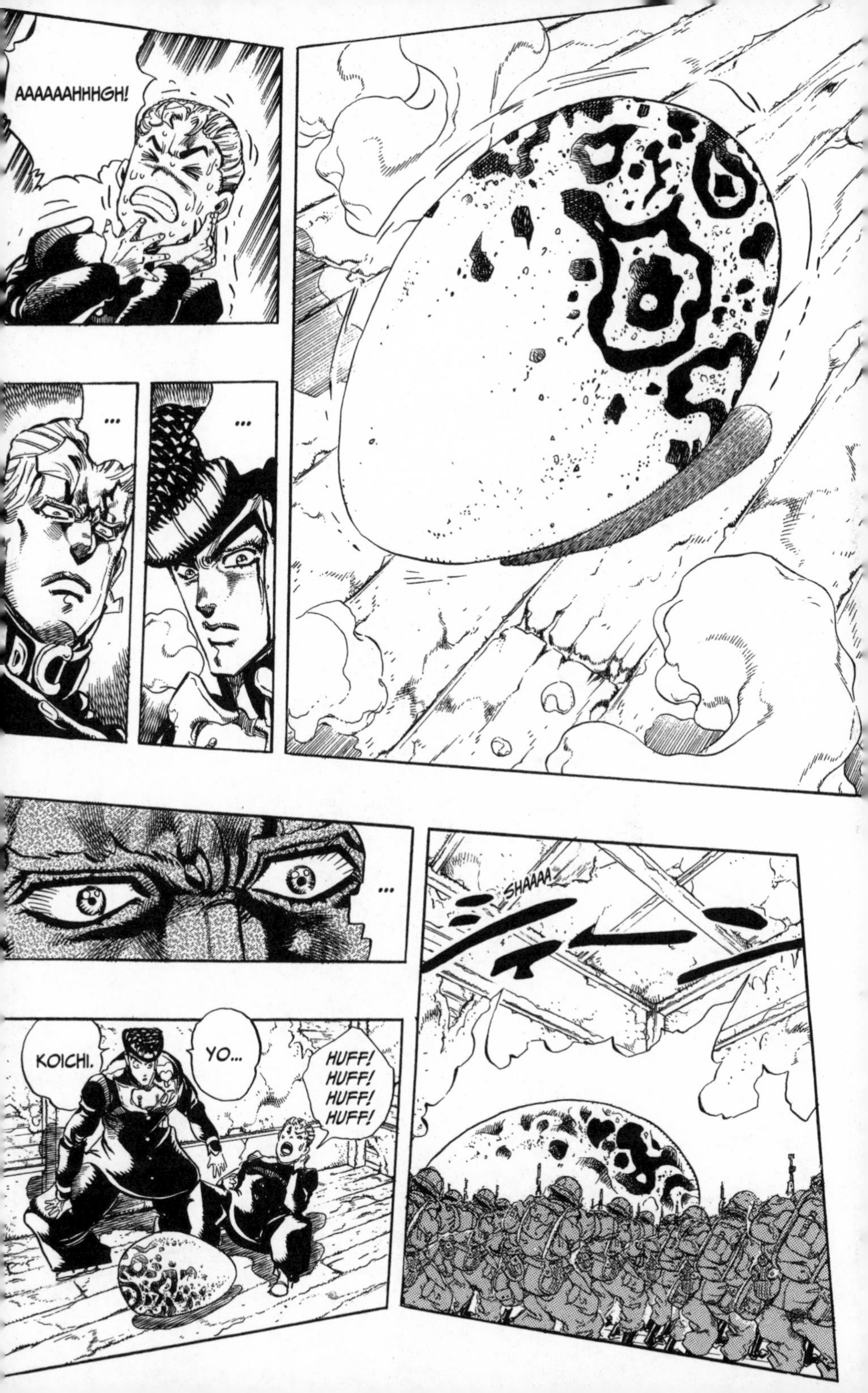
AAAAAAHHHGH!
...
...
SHAAAA
...
HUFF! HUFF! HUFF! HUFF!
YO...
KOICHI.

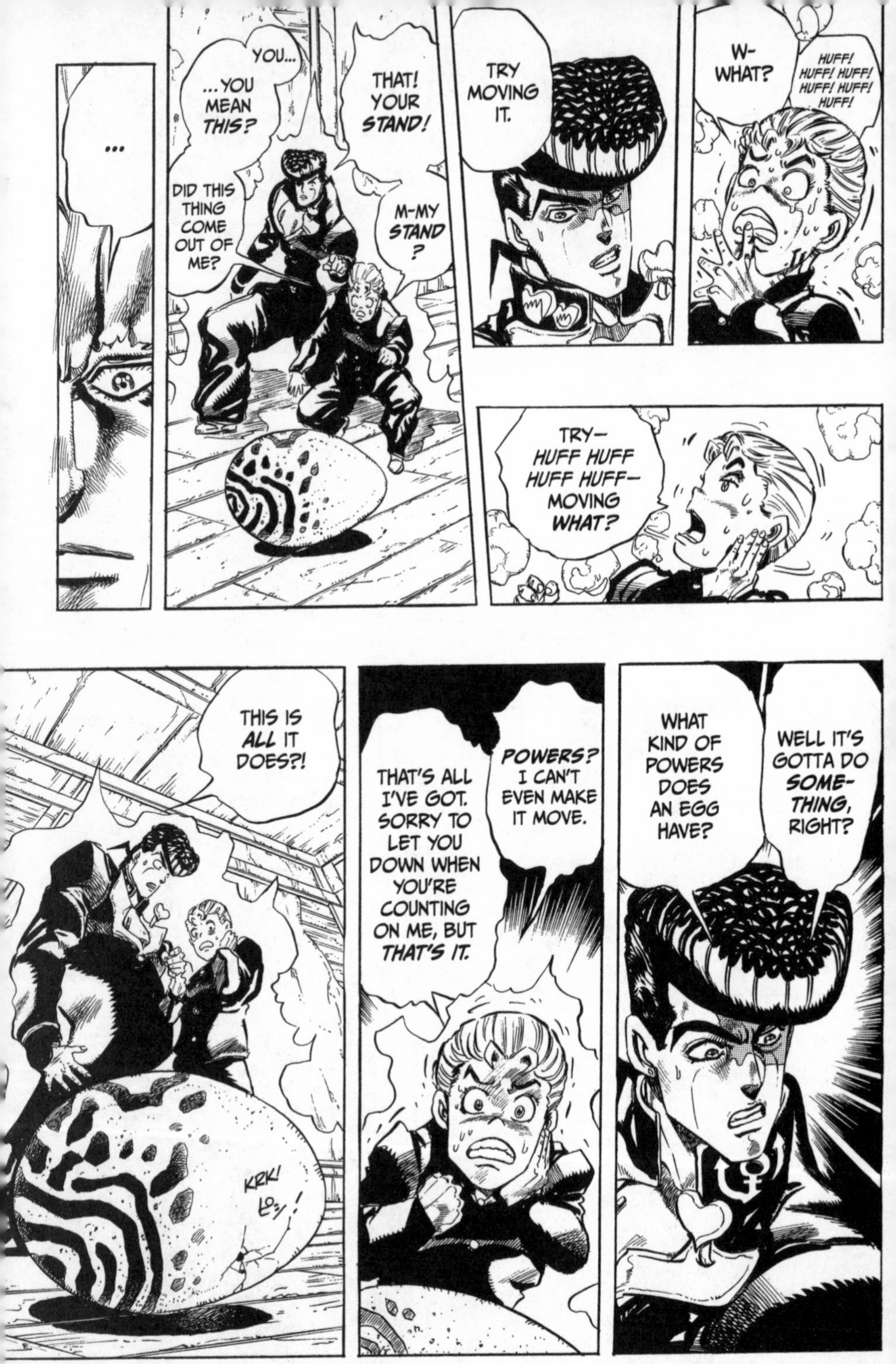
W-WHAT?
HUFF! HUFF! HUFF! HUFF! HUFF! HUFF!
TRY MOVING IT.
TRY— HUFF HUFF HUFF HUFF— MOVING WHAT?
YOU... ...YOU MEAN THIS?
THAT! YOUR STAND!
M-MY STAND?
DID THIS THING COME OUT OF ME?
...
WELL IT'S GOTTA DO SOME- THING, RIGHT?
WHAT KIND OF POWERS DOES AN EGG HAVE?
POWERS? I CAN'T EVEN MAKE IT MOVE.
THAT'S ALL I'VE GOT. SORRY TO LET YOU DOWN WHEN YOU'RE COUNTING ON ME, BUT THAT'S IT.
THIS IS ALL IT DOES?!
KRK!

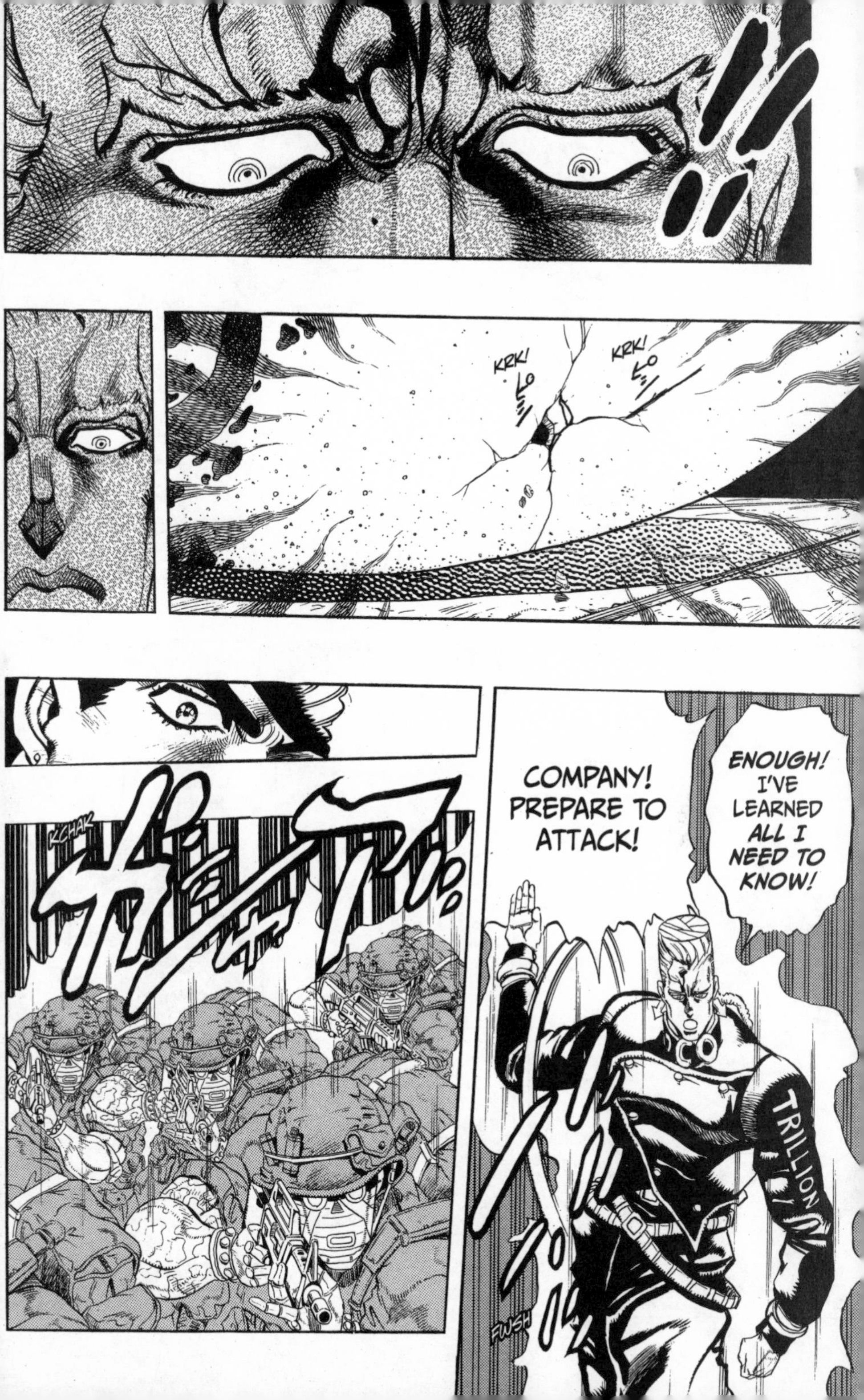
KRK!
KRK!
ENOUGH! I'VE LEARNED ALL I NEED TO KNOW!
COMPANY! PREPARE TO ATTACK!
TRILLION
FWSH
KCHAK

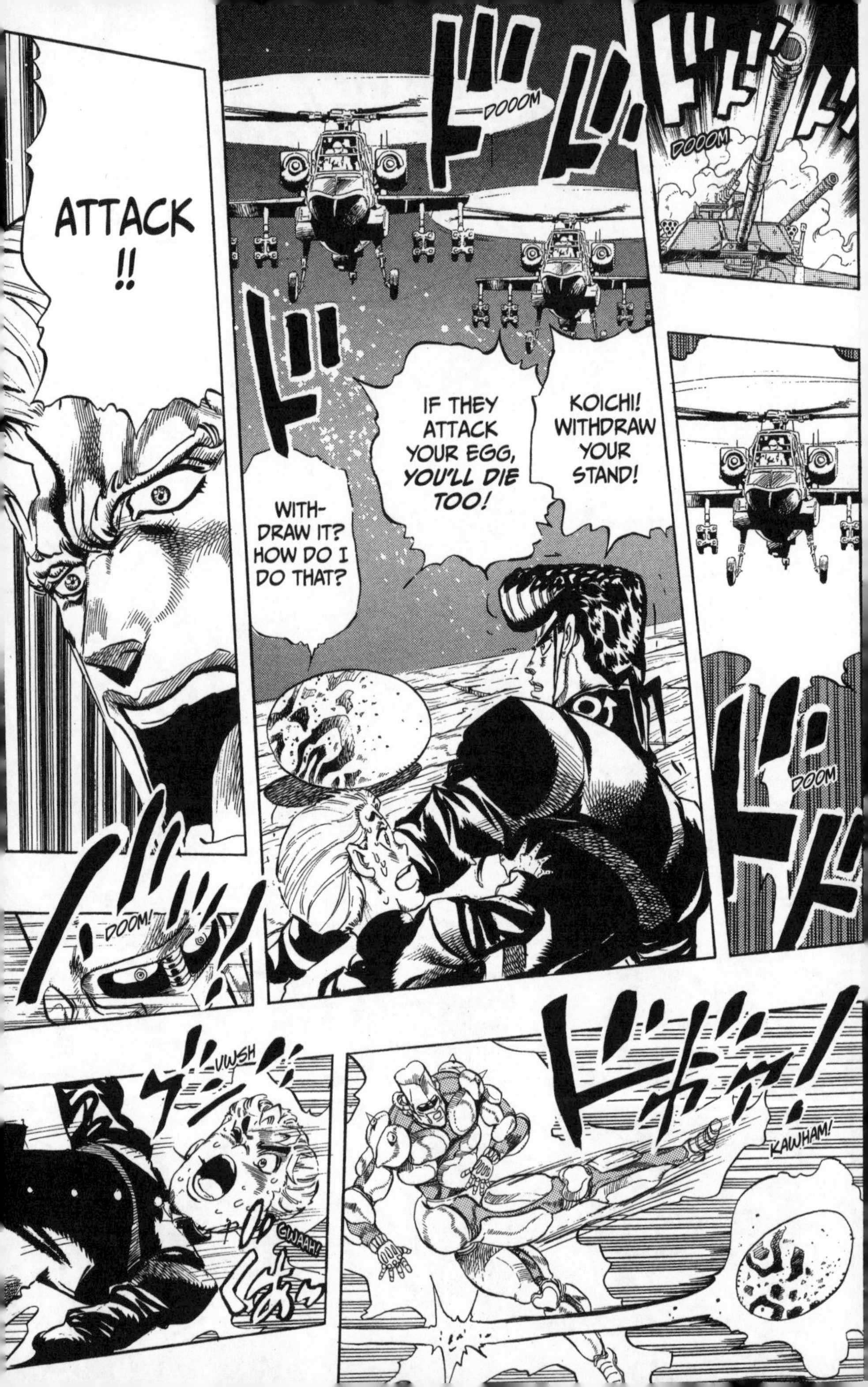
DOOOM
DOOM
DOOOM
KOICHI! WITHDRAW YOUR STAND!
IF THEY ATTACK YOUR EGG, YOU'LL DIE TOO!
WITH-DRAW IT? HOW DO I DO THAT?
ATTACK !!
DOOM!
KAWHAM!
VWSH
GWAAH!

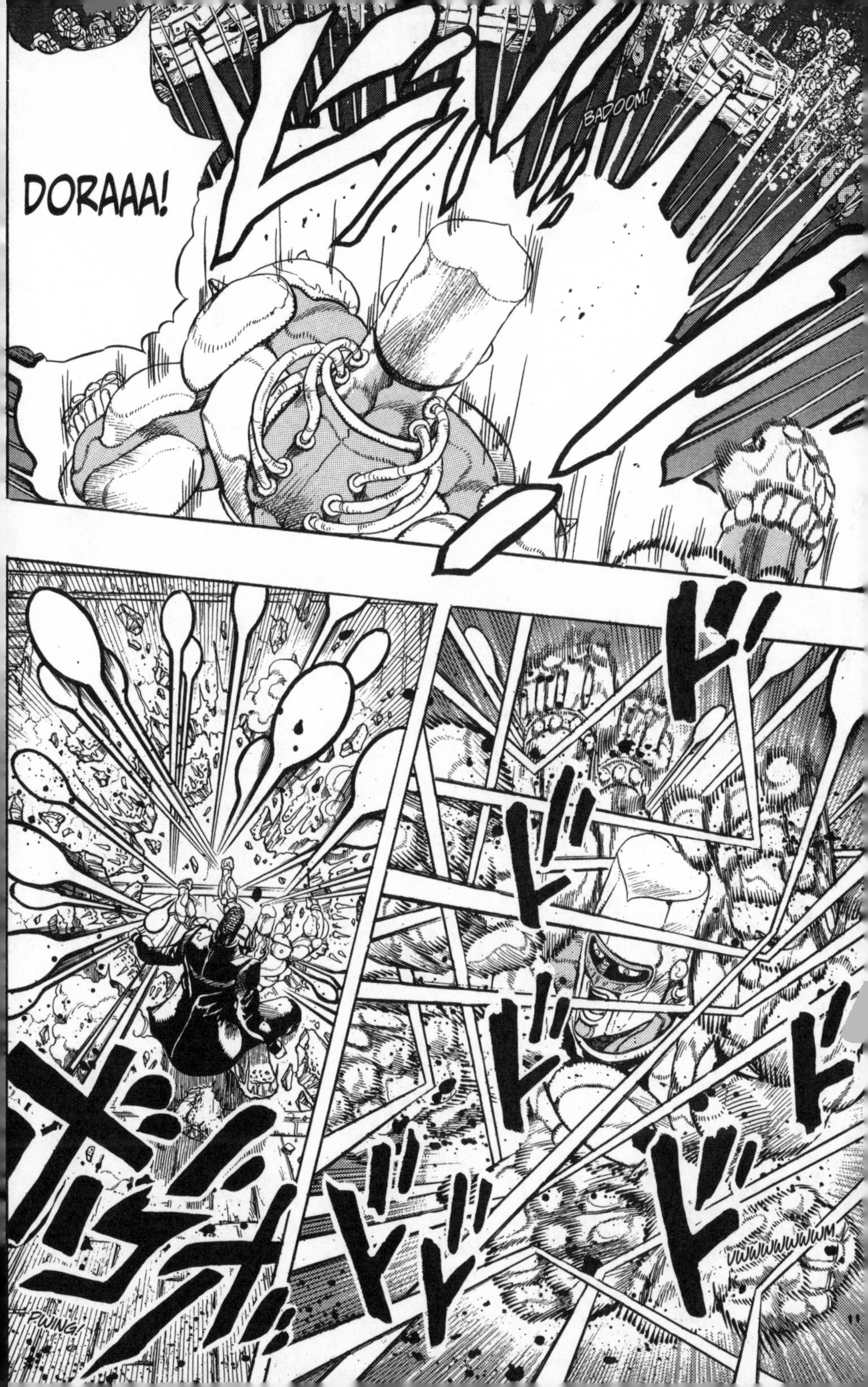
BADOOM!
DORAAA!
VWWWWWWWUM
P-WING!

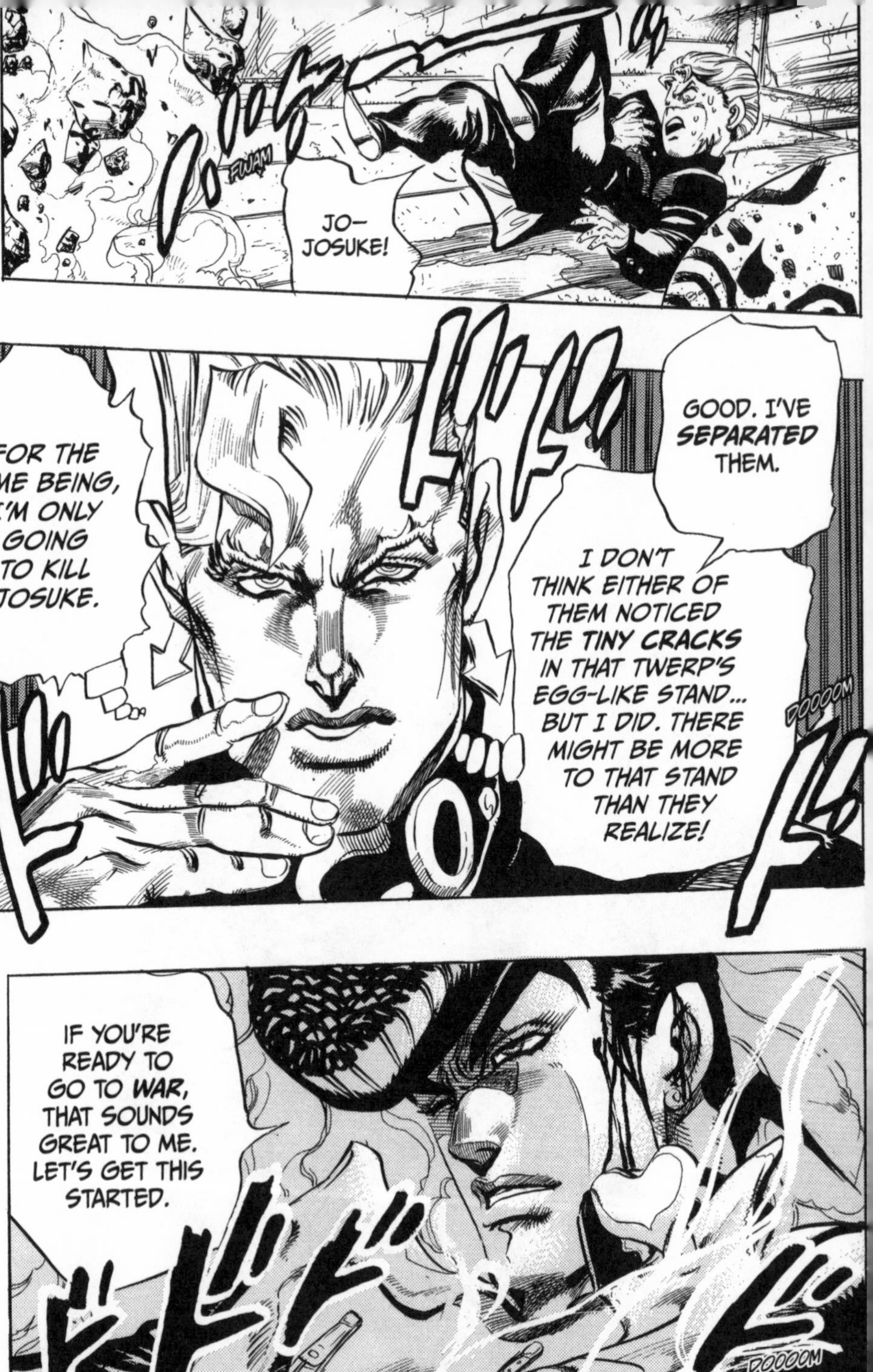
FWAM
JO—JOSUKE!
GOOD. I'VE **SEPARATED** THEM.
I DON'T THINK EITHER OF THEM NOTICED THE **TINY CRACKS** IN THAT TWERP'S EGG-LIKE STAND... BUT I DID. THERE MIGHT BE MORE TO THAT STAND THAN THEY REALIZE!
DOOOOM
FOR THE TIME BEING, I'M ONLY GOING TO KILL JOSUKE.
IF YOU'RE READY TO GO TO **WAR**, THAT SOUNDS GREAT TO ME. LET'S GET THIS STARTED.
DOOOOM

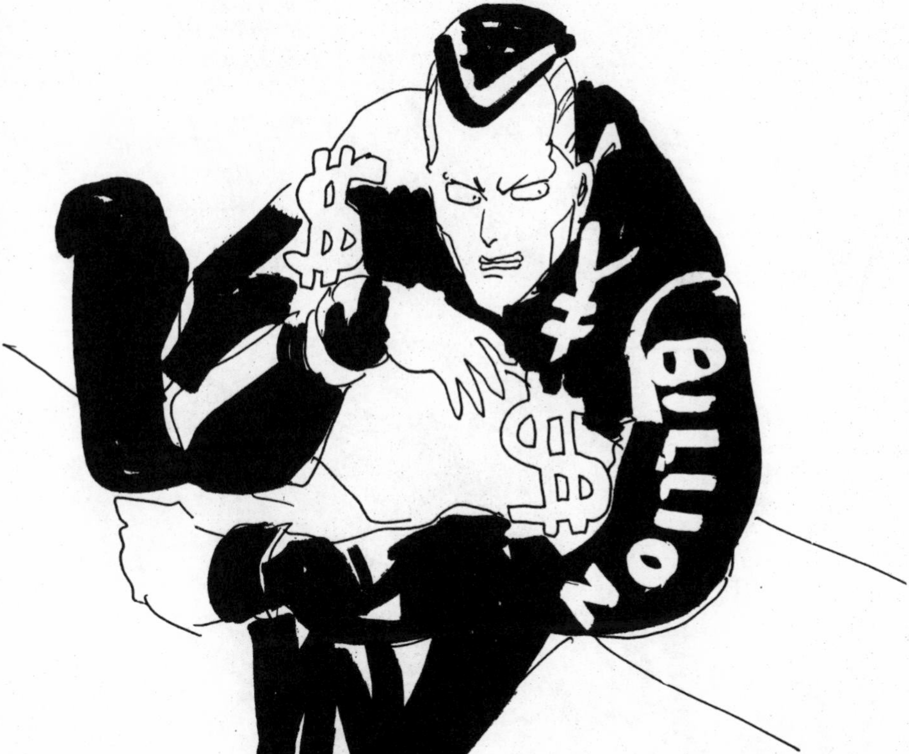
BILLION

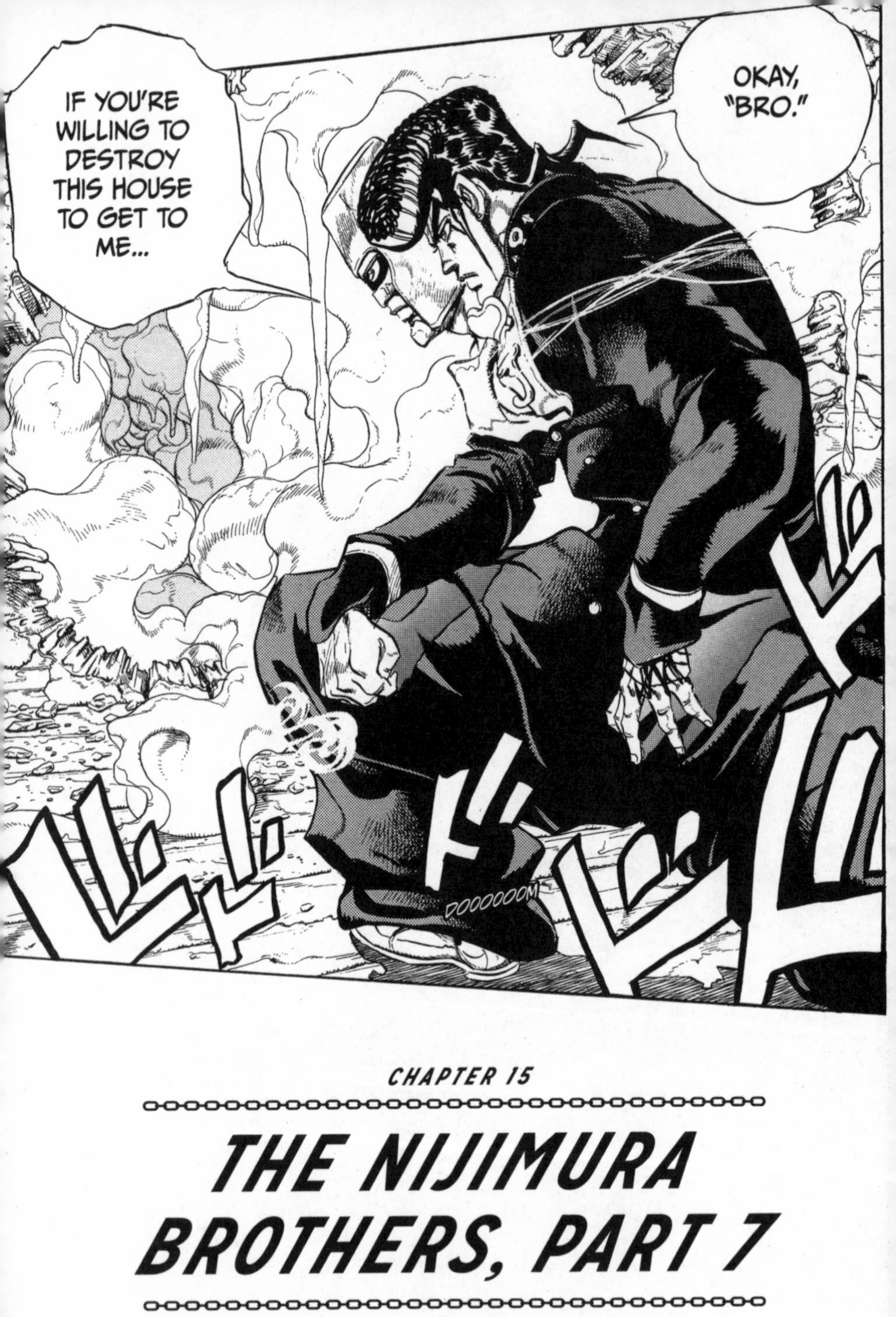
OKAY, "BRO."
IF YOU'RE WILLING TO DESTROY THIS HOUSE TO GET TO ME...
DOOOOOOM

CHAPTER 15

THE NIJIMURA BROTHERS, PART 7

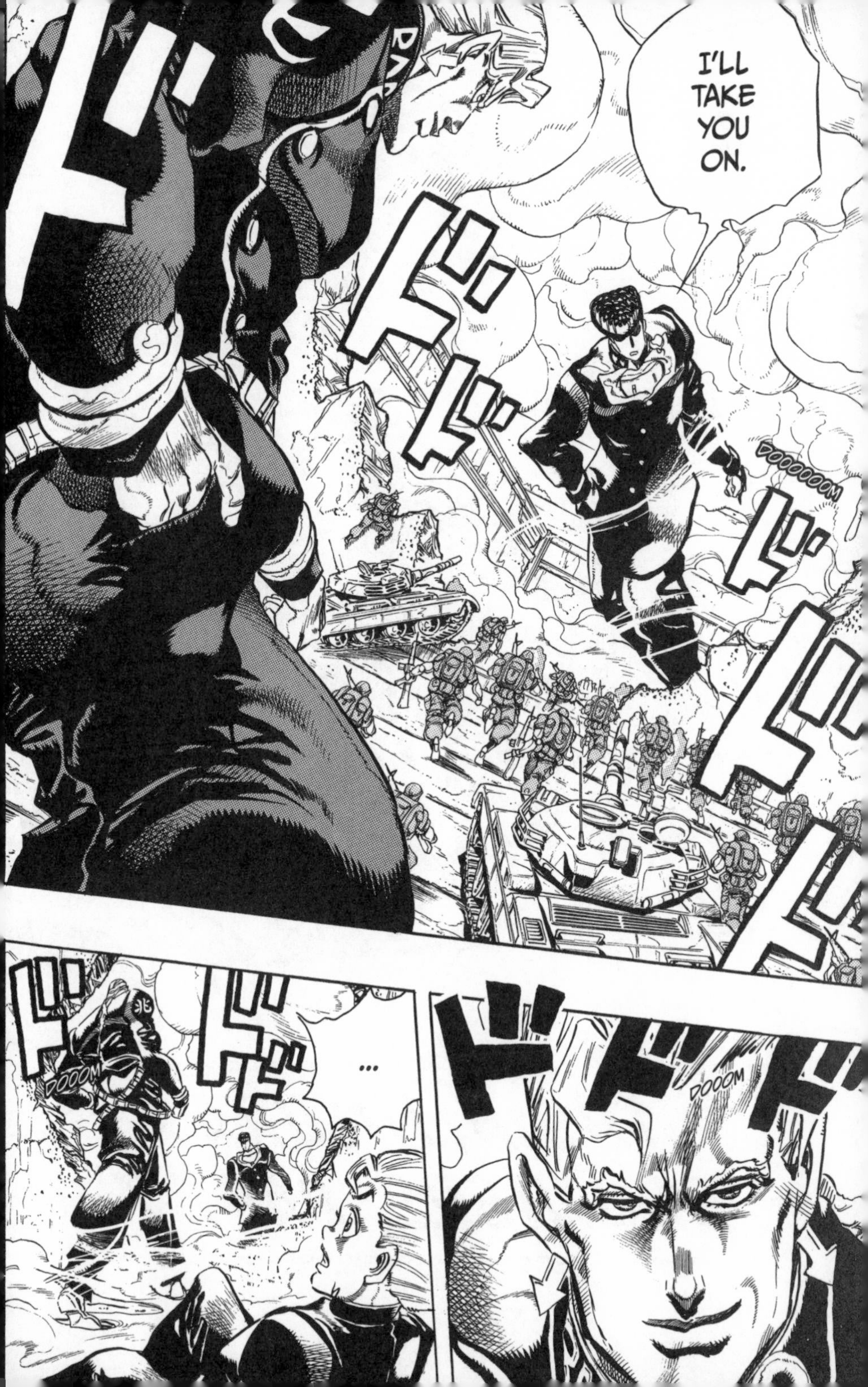
I'LL TAKE YOU ON.
DOOOOOOM
DOOOM
...
DOOOM

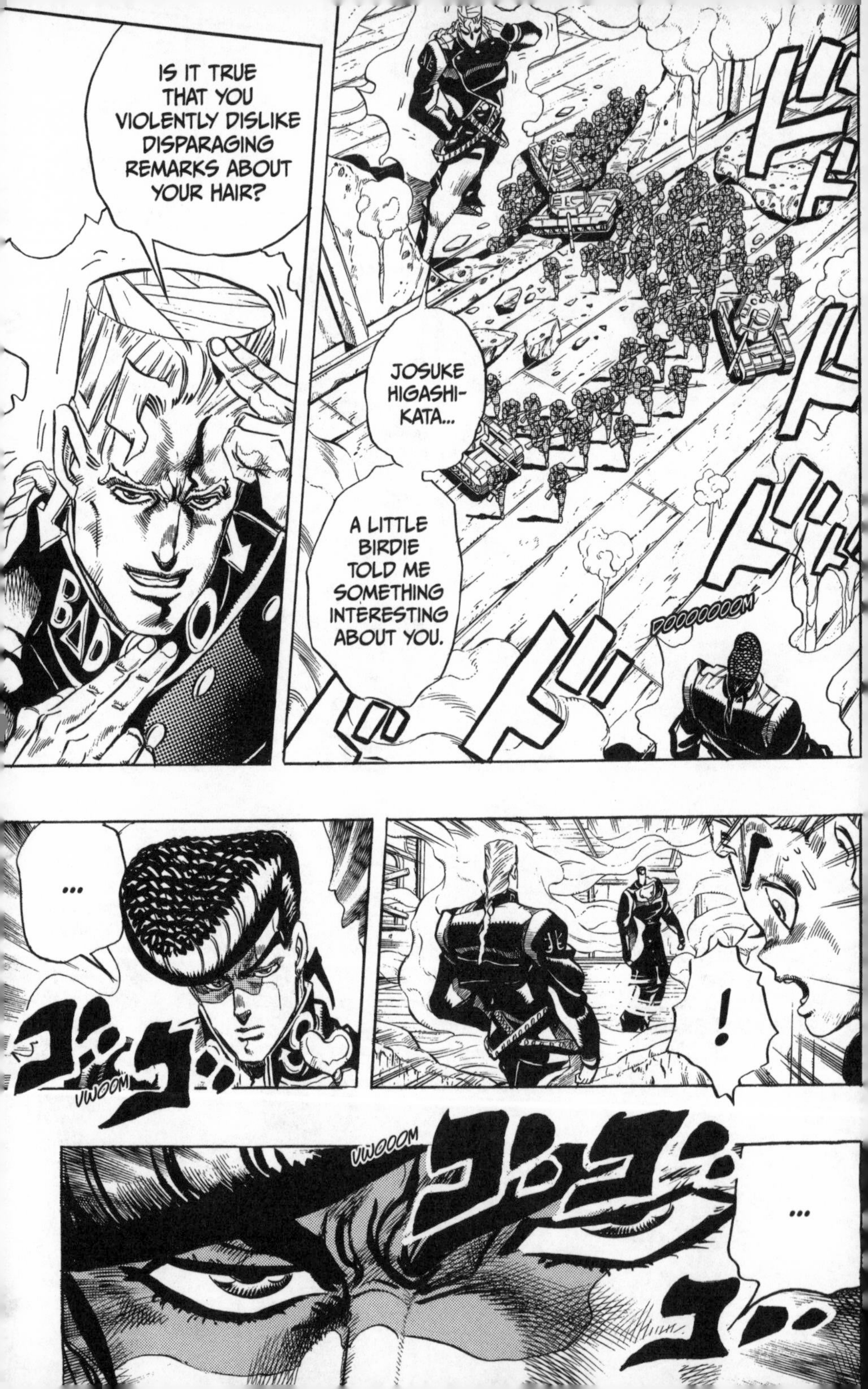
JOSUKE HIGASHI-KATA...
A LITTLE BIRDIE TOLD ME SOMETHING INTERESTING ABOUT YOU.
DOOOOOOOOM
IS IT TRUE THAT YOU VIOLENTLY DISLIKE DISPARAGING REMARKS ABOUT YOUR HAIR?
!
...
VWOOM
VWOOOM
...

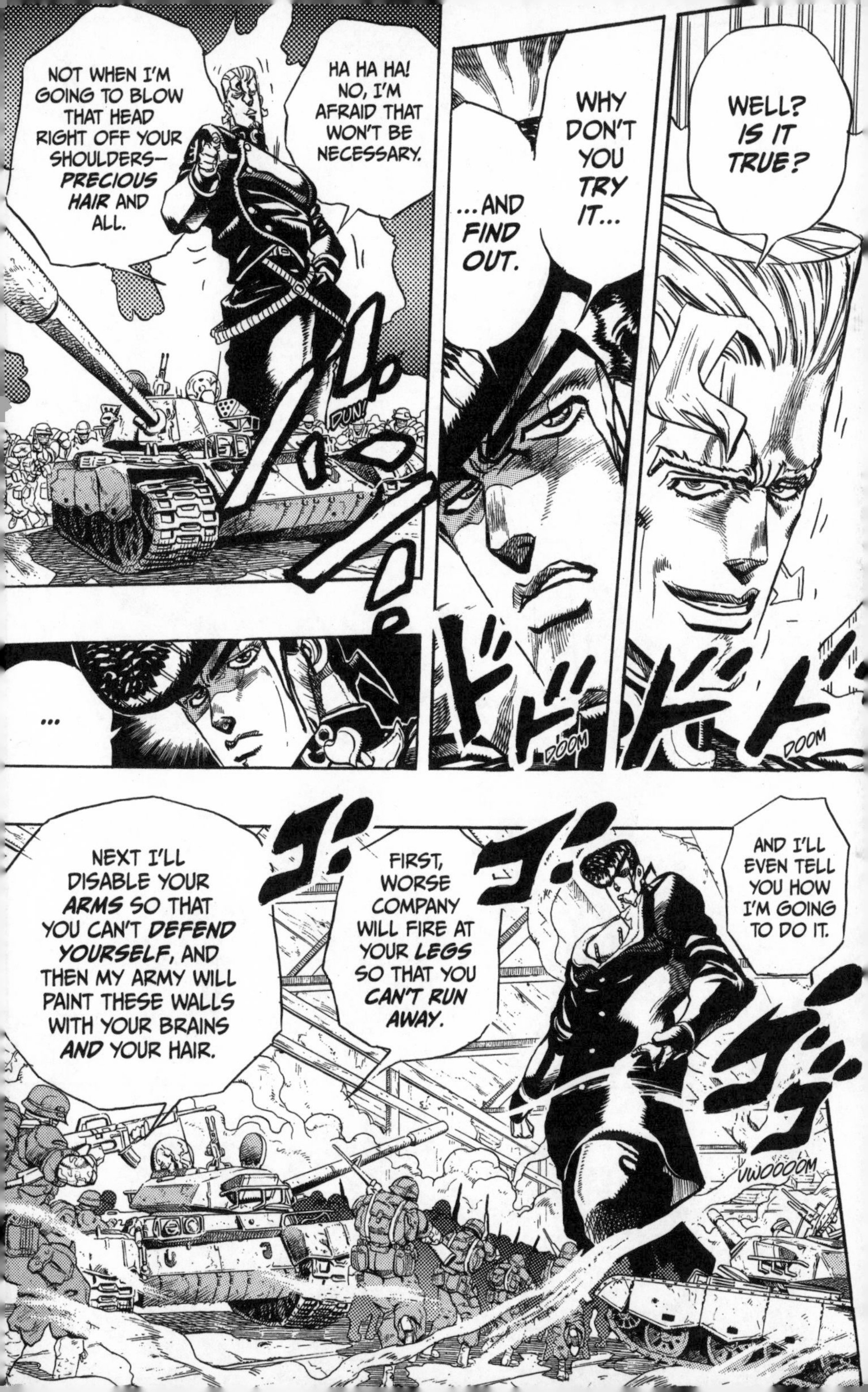

WELL? IS IT TRUE?
WHY DON'T YOU TRY IT...
...AND FIND OUT.
HA HA HA! NO, I'M AFRAID THAT WON'T BE NECESSARY.
NOT WHEN I'M GOING TO BLOW THAT HEAD RIGHT OFF YOUR SHOULDERS—PRECIOUS HAIR AND ALL.
DUN!
DOOM
DOOM
...
AND I'LL EVEN TELL YOU HOW I'M GOING TO DO IT.
FIRST, WORSE COMPANY WILL FIRE AT YOUR LEGS SO THAT YOU CAN'T RUN AWAY.
NEXT I'LL DISABLE YOUR ARMS SO THAT YOU CAN'T DEFEND YOURSELF, AND THEN MY ARMY WILL PAINT THESE WALLS WITH YOUR BRAINS AND YOUR HAIR.
VWOOOOOM

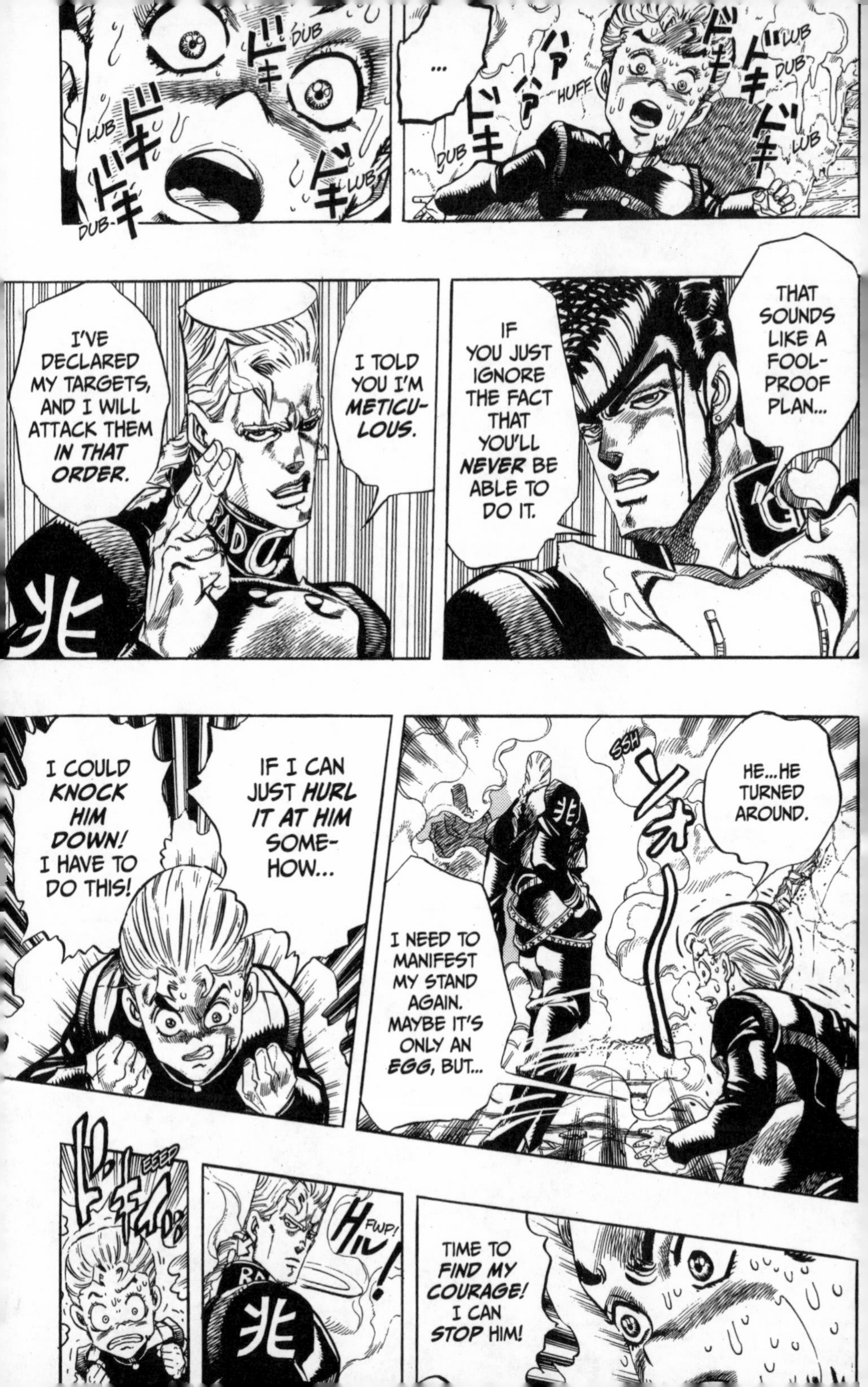
...
HUFF
LUB
DUB
LUB
DUB
LUB
DUB
LUB
DUB
THAT SOUNDS LIKE A FOOL-PROOF PLAN...
IF YOU JUST IGNORE THE FACT THAT YOU'LL NEVER BE ABLE TO DO IT.
I TOLD YOU I'M METICULOUS.
I'VE DECLARED MY TARGETS, AND I WILL ATTACK THEM IN THAT ORDER.
SSH
HE...HE TURNED AROUND.
I NEED TO MANIFEST MY STAND AGAIN. MAYBE IT'S ONLY AN EGG, BUT...
IF I CAN JUST HURL IT AT HIM SOMEHOW...
I COULD KNOCK HIM DOWN! I HAVE TO DO THIS!
TIME TO FIND MY COURAGE! I CAN STOP HIM!
FWIP!
EEEP

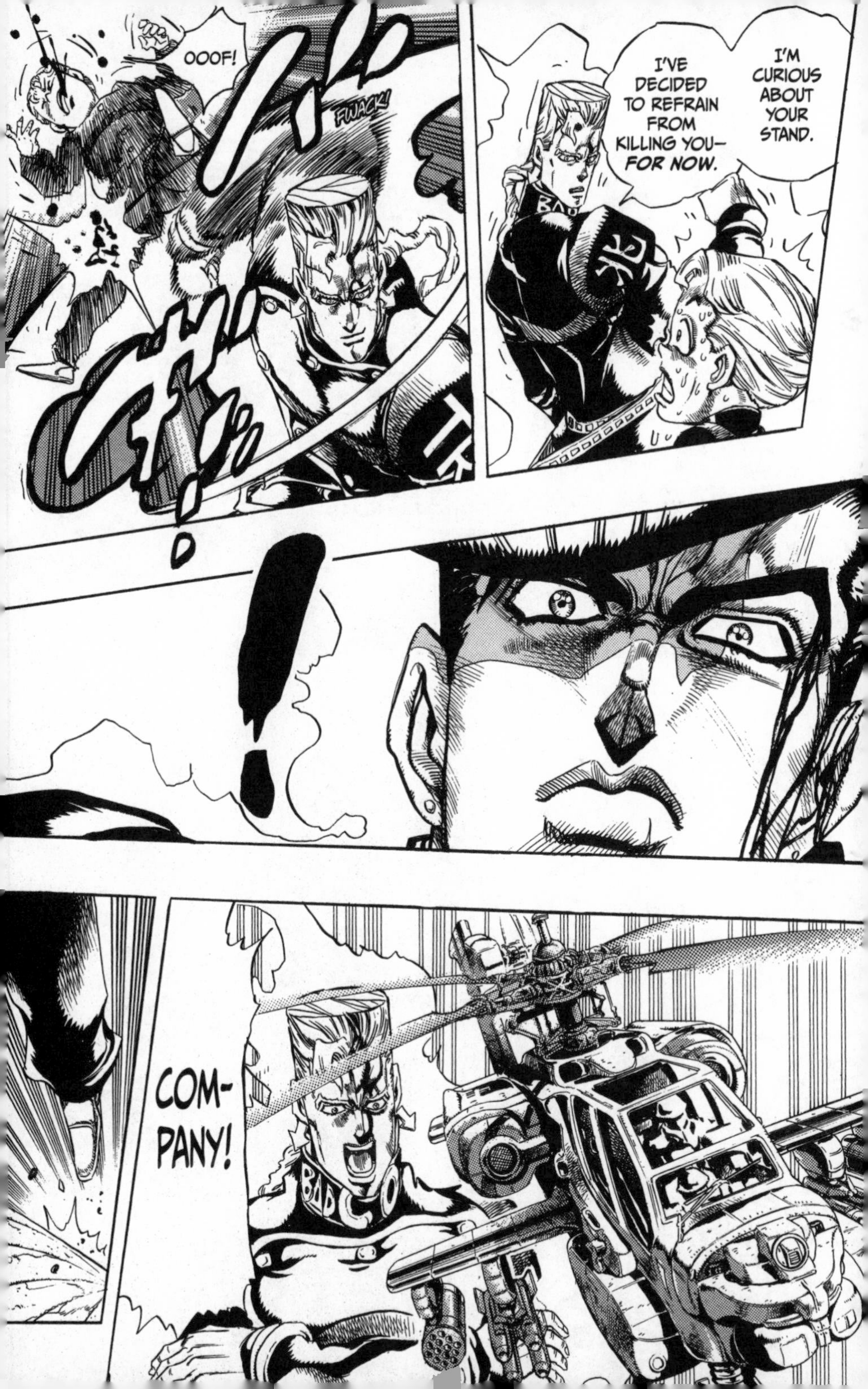
I'VE DECIDED TO REFRAIN FROM KILLING YOU—FOR NOW. I'M CURIOUS ABOUT YOUR STAND.
FWACK!
OOOF!
!
COM-PANY!

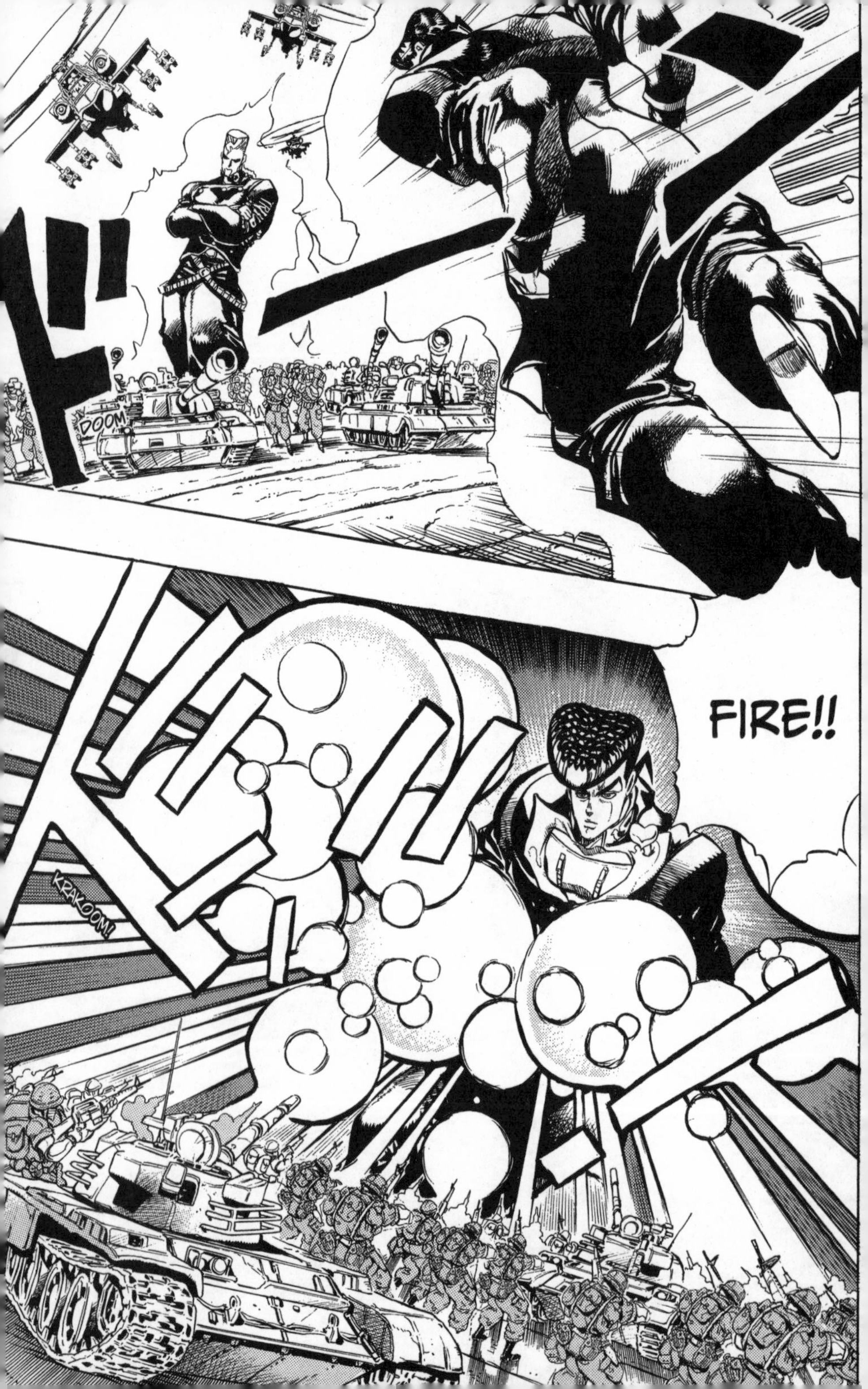
DOOM
FIRE!!
KRAKOOM!

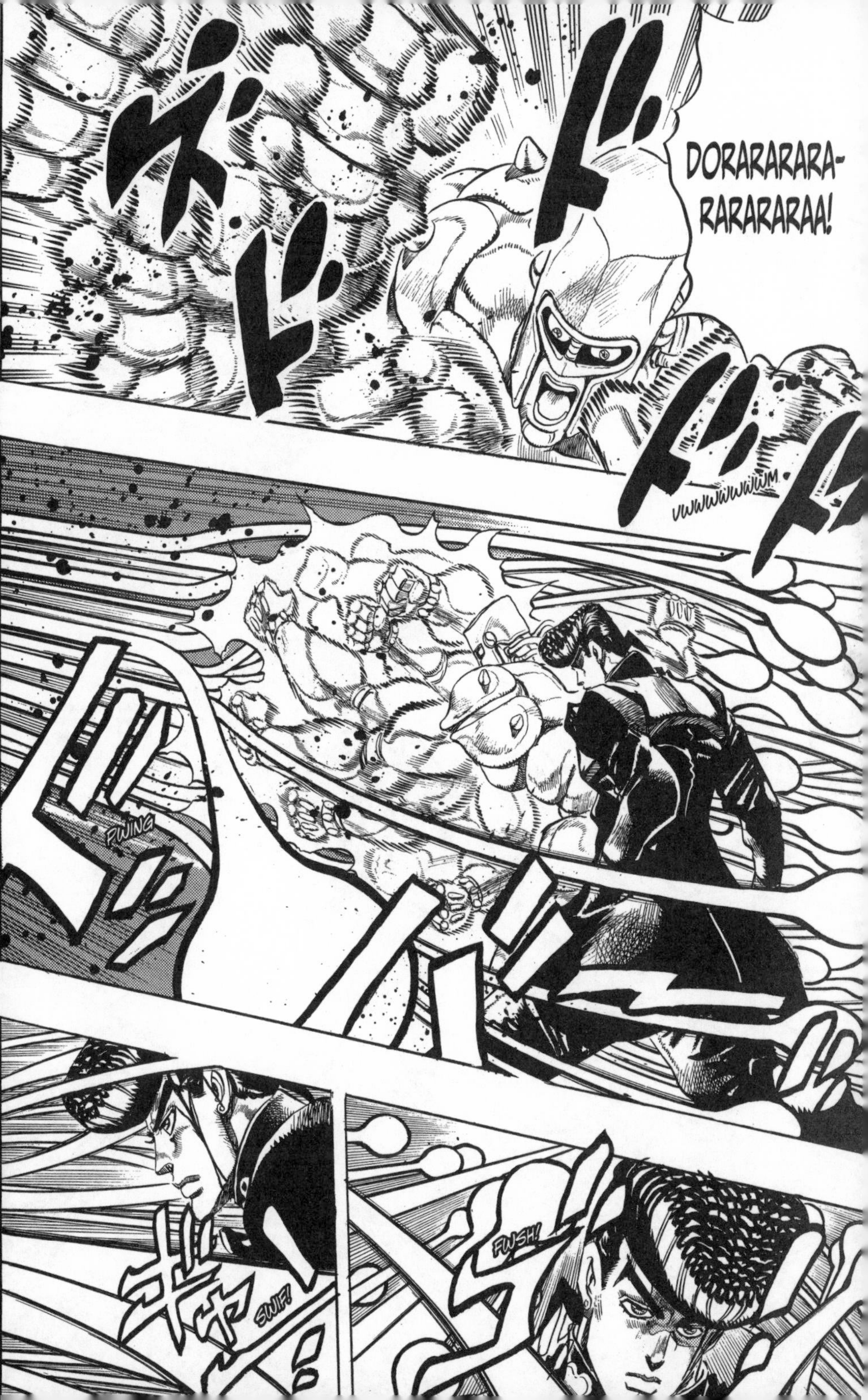
DORARARARA-
RARARARAA!
VWWWWWWWM
PWING
FWSH!
SWIF!

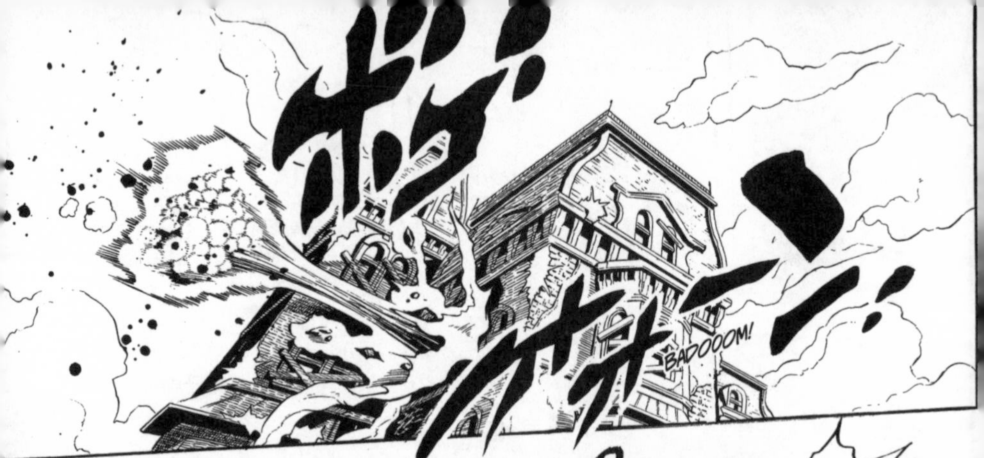
BADOOOM!
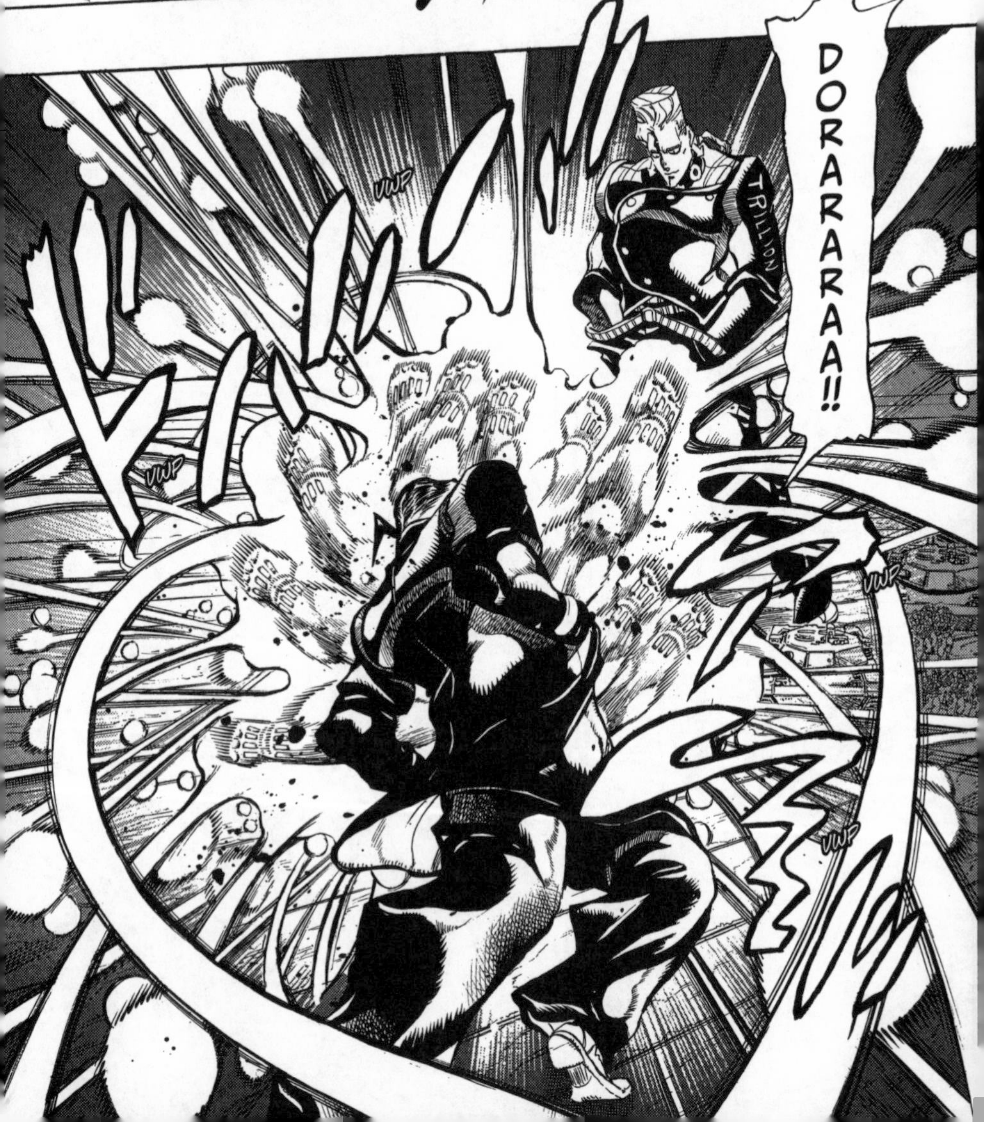
DORARARAA!!
VWP
VWP
VWP
VWP

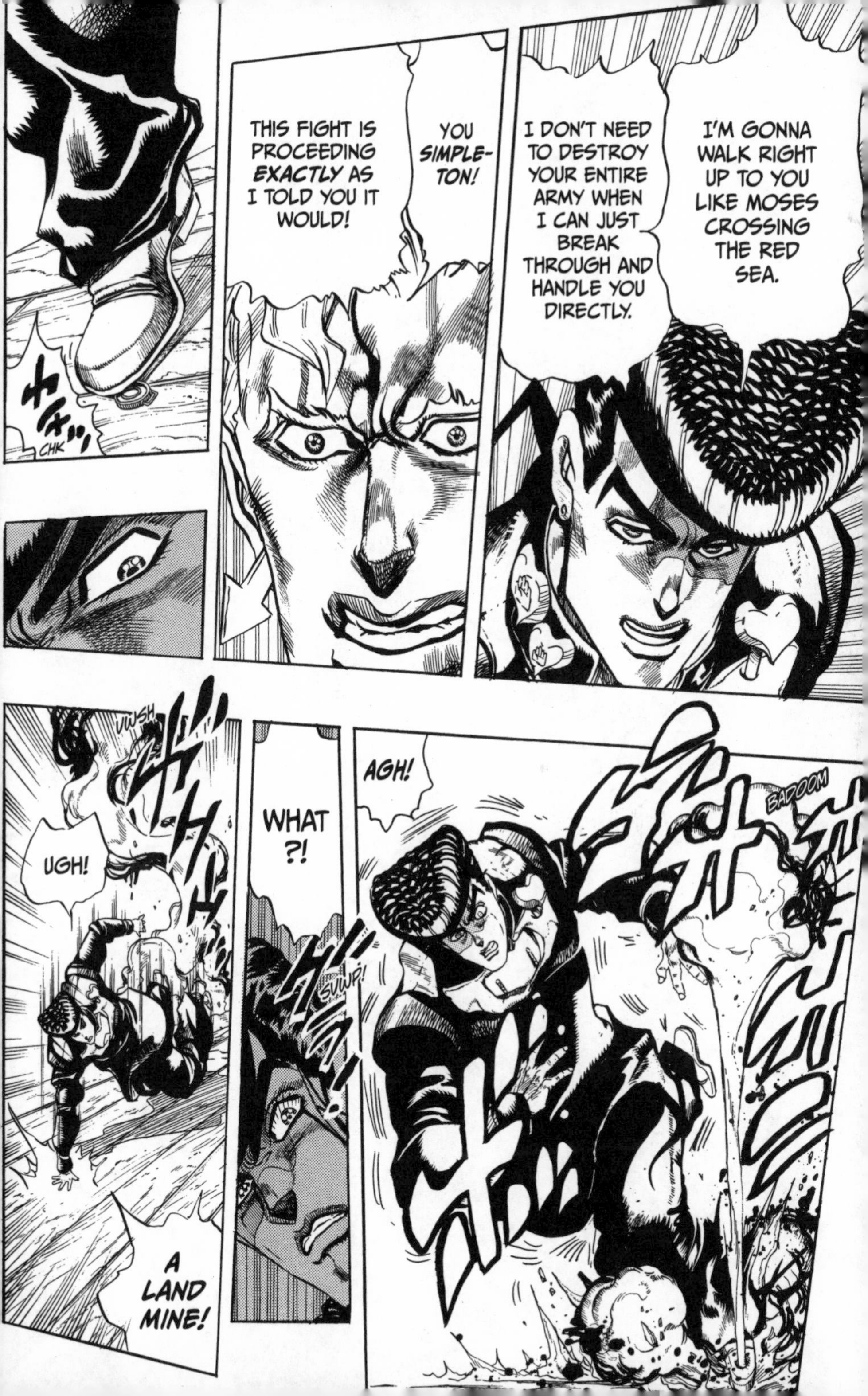

I'M GONNA WALK RIGHT UP TO YOU LIKE MOSES CROSSING THE RED SEA.
I DON'T NEED TO DESTROY YOUR ENTIRE ARMY WHEN I CAN JUST BREAK THROUGH AND HANDLE YOU DIRECTLY.
YOU SIMPLETON!
THIS FIGHT IS PROCEEDING EXACTLY AS I TOLD YOU IT WOULD!
CHK
BADOOM
AGH!
WHAT?!
SWUP!
VWSH
UGH!
A LAND MINE!

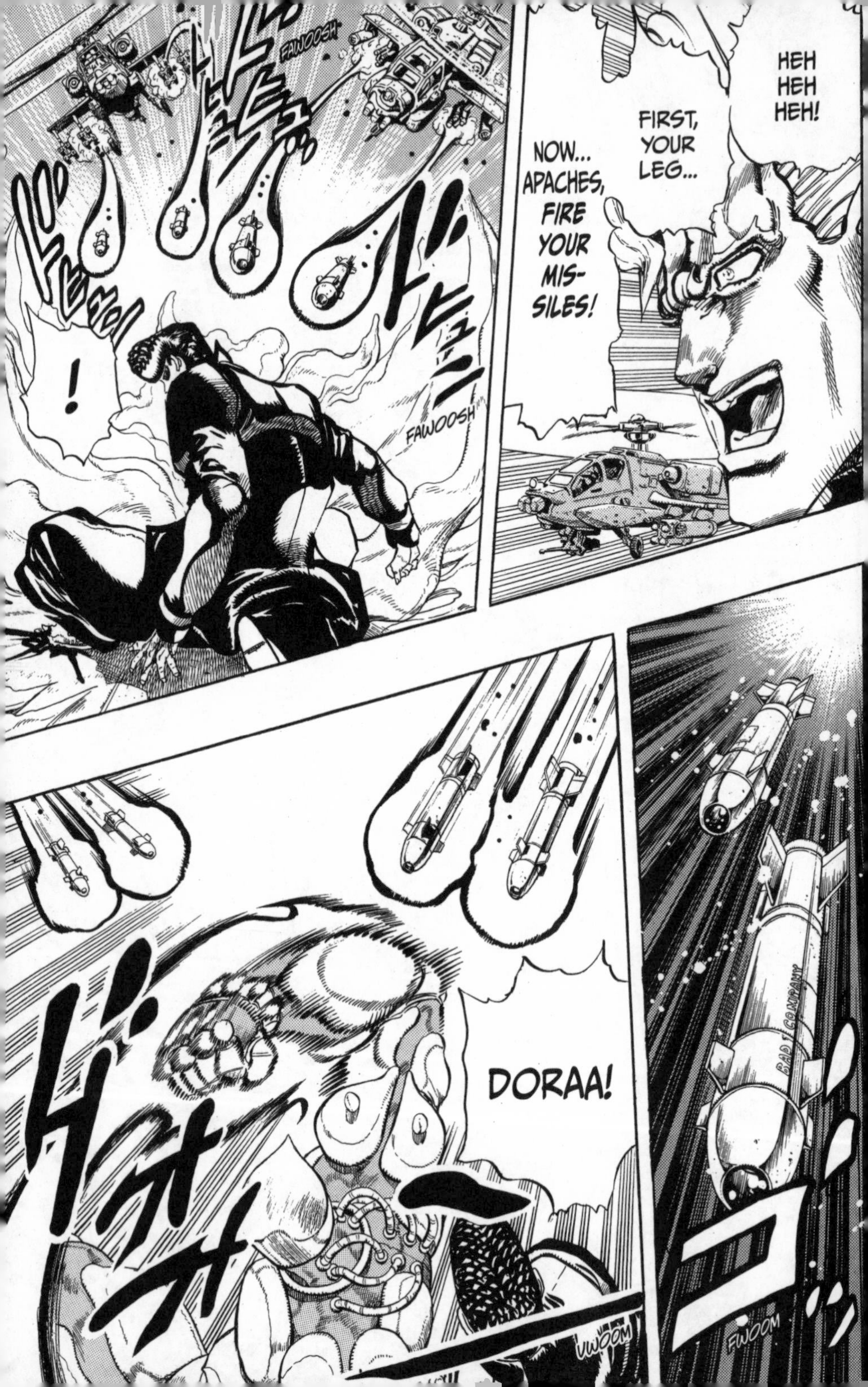
HEH HEH HEH!
FIRST, YOUR LEG...
NOW... APACHES, FIRE YOUR MISSILES!
FAWOOSH
FAWOOSH
!
BAD COMPANY
FWOOM
DORAA!
VWOOM

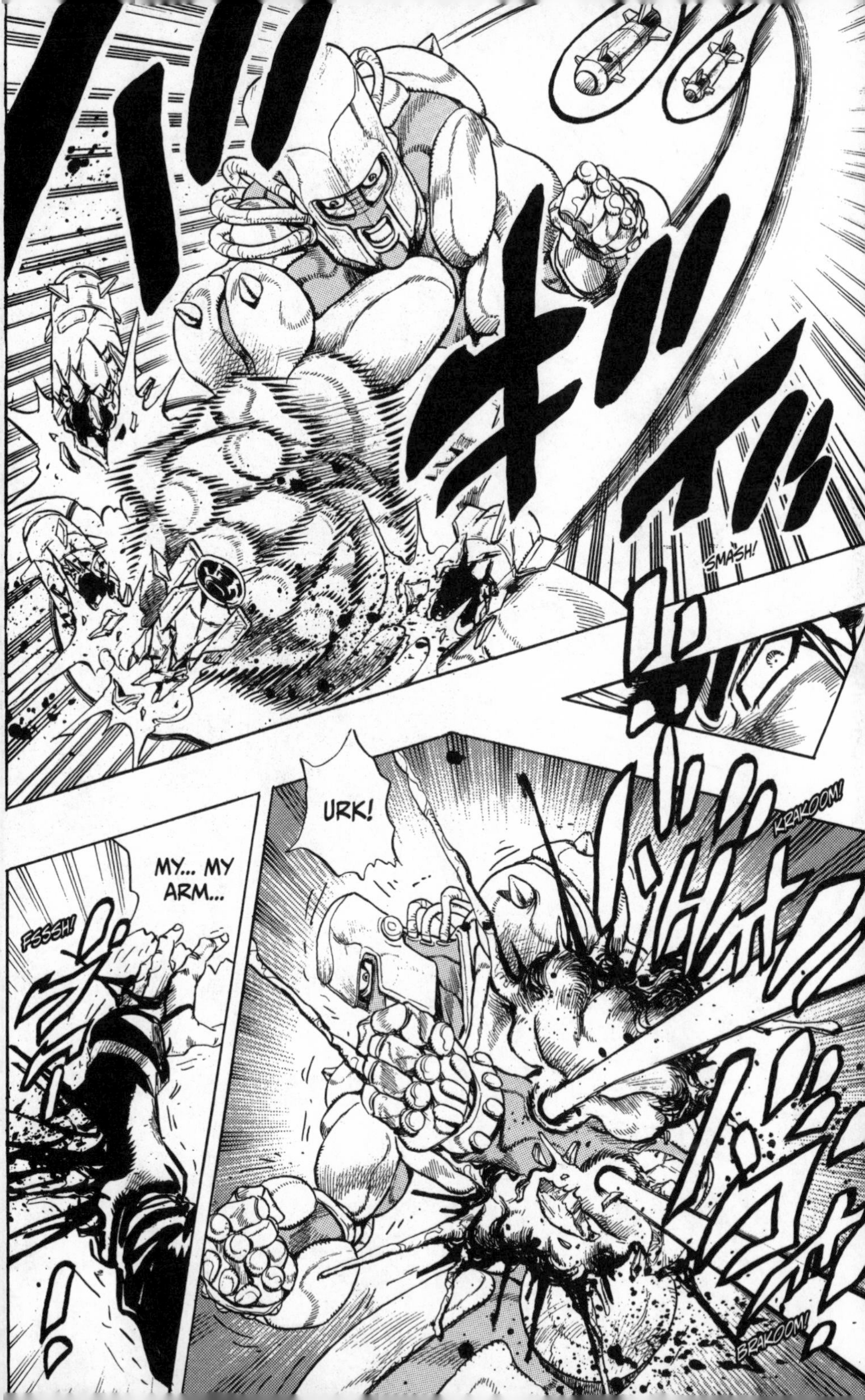
SMASH!
KRAKOOM!
URK!
BRAKOOM!
MY... MY ARM...
FSSSH!

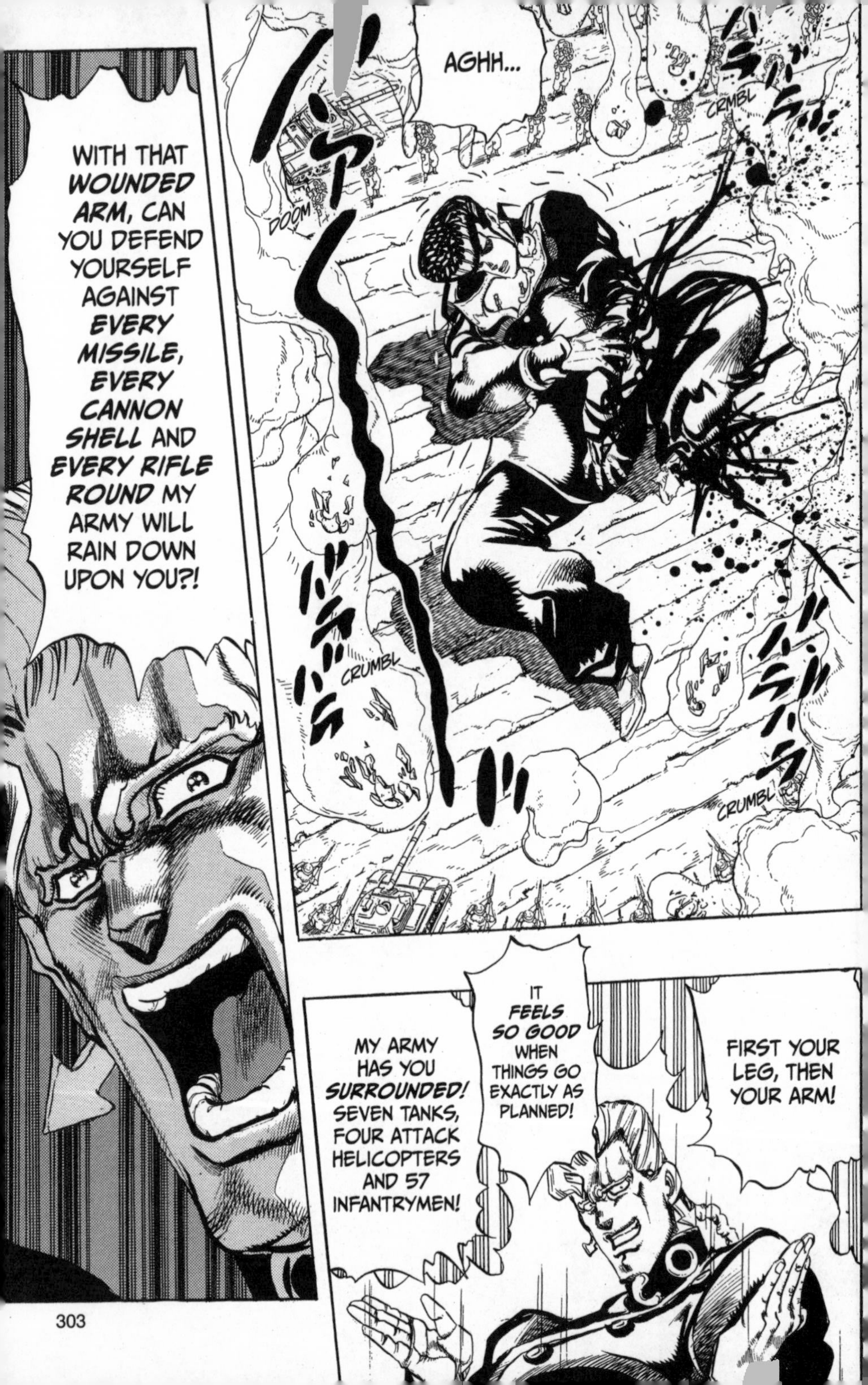
AGHH...
CRUMBL
DOOM
CRUMBL
CRUMBL
FIRST YOUR LEG, THEN YOUR ARM!
IT FEELS SO GOOD WHEN THINGS GO EXACTLY AS PLANNED!
MY ARMY HAS YOU SURROUNDED! SEVEN TANKS, FOUR ATTACK HELICOPTERS AND 57 INFANTRYMEN!
WITH THAT WOUNDED ARM, CAN YOU DEFEND YOURSELF AGAINST EVERY MISSILE, EVERY CANNON SHELL AND EVERY RIFLE ROUND MY ARMY WILL RAIN DOWN UPON YOU?!

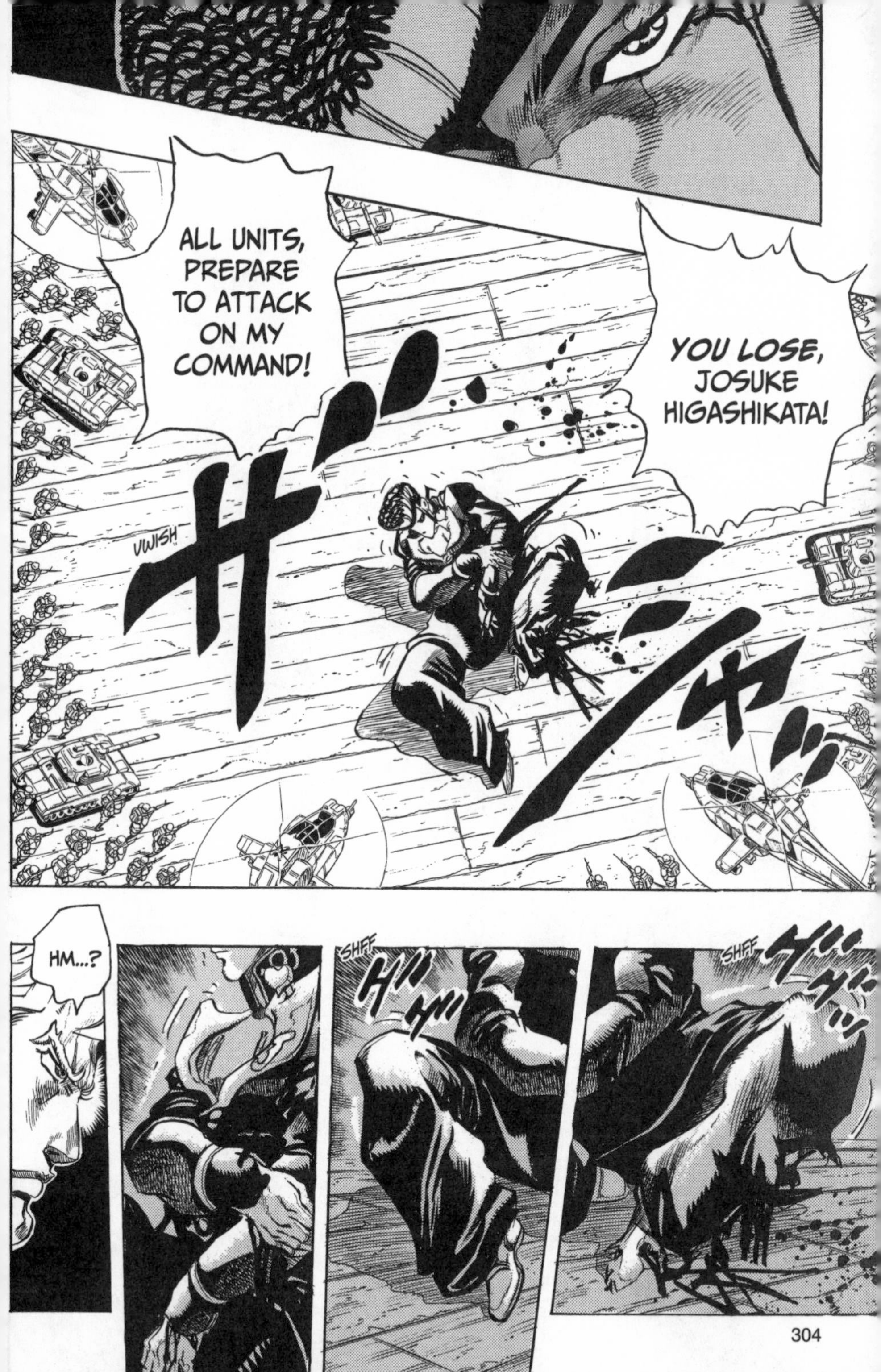
YOU LOSE, JOSUKE HIGASHIKATA!
ALL UNITS, PREPARE TO ATTACK ON MY COMMAND!
VWISH
SHFF
SHFF
HM...?

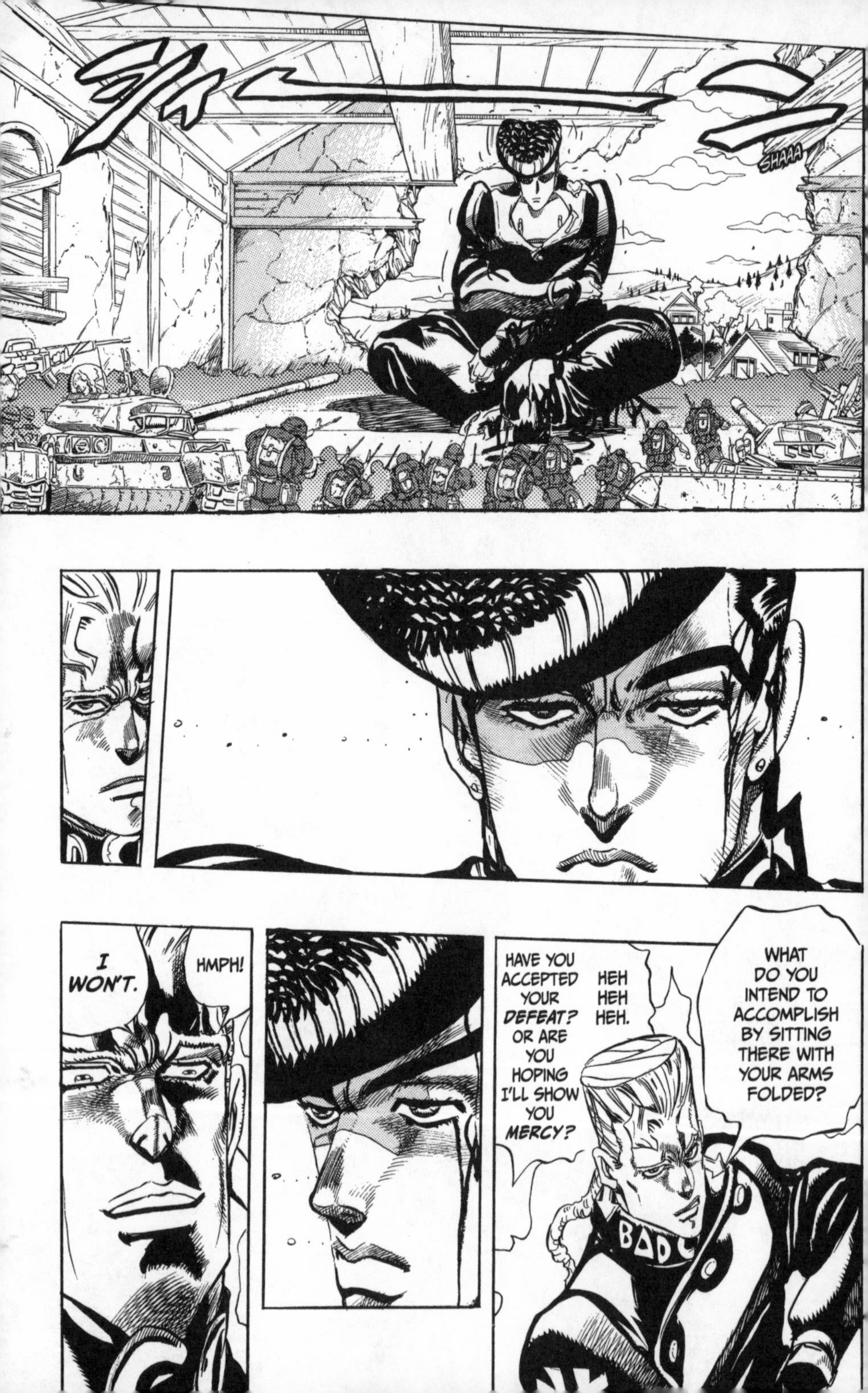
SHAAA
WHAT DO YOU INTEND TO ACCOMPLISH BY SITTING THERE WITH YOUR ARMS FOLDED?
HEH HEH HEH.
HAVE YOU ACCEPTED YOUR *DEFEAT?* OR ARE YOU HOPING I'LL SHOW YOU *MERCY?*
HMPH!
I WON'T.

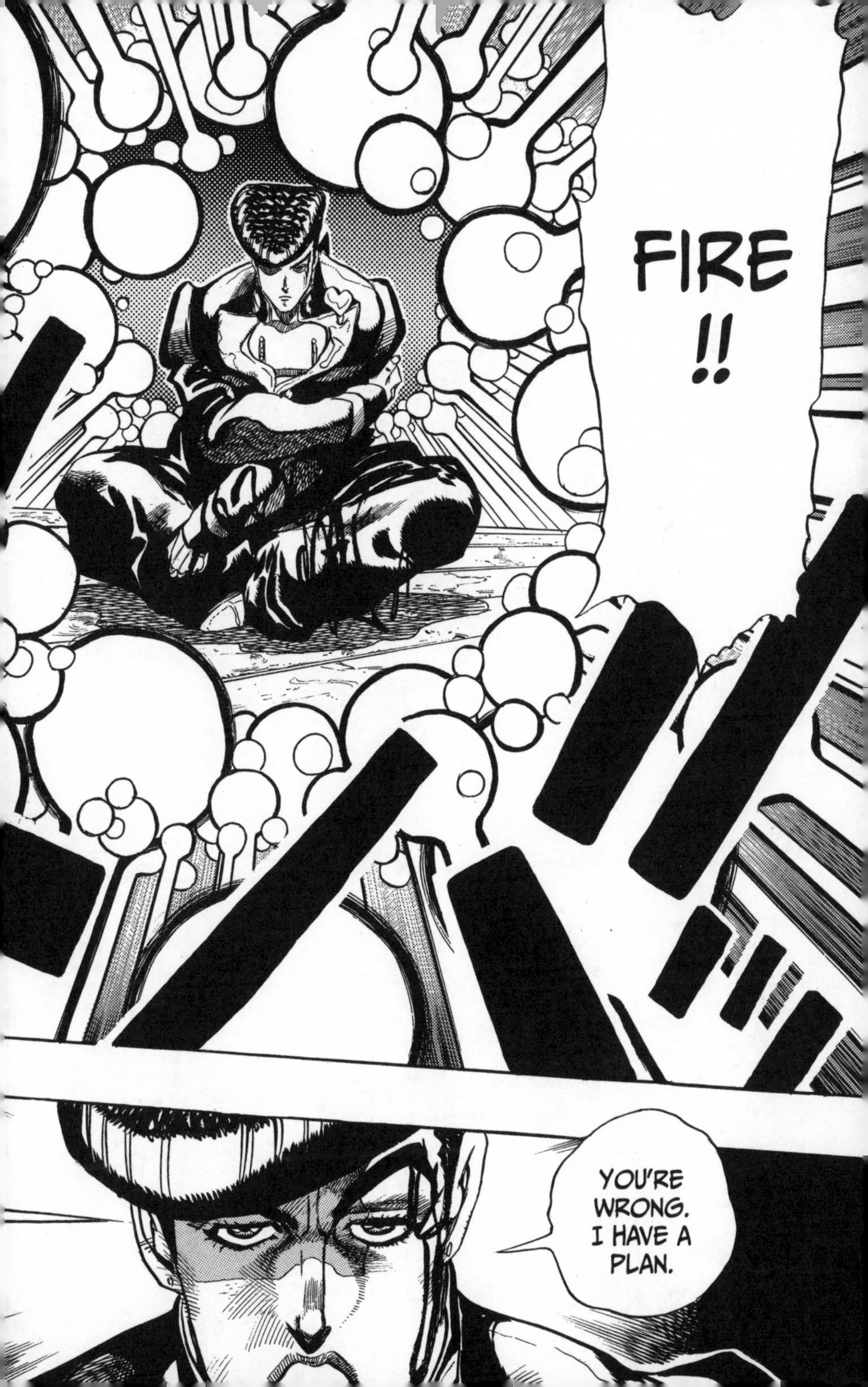
FIRE !!
YOU'RE WRONG. I HAVE A PLAN.

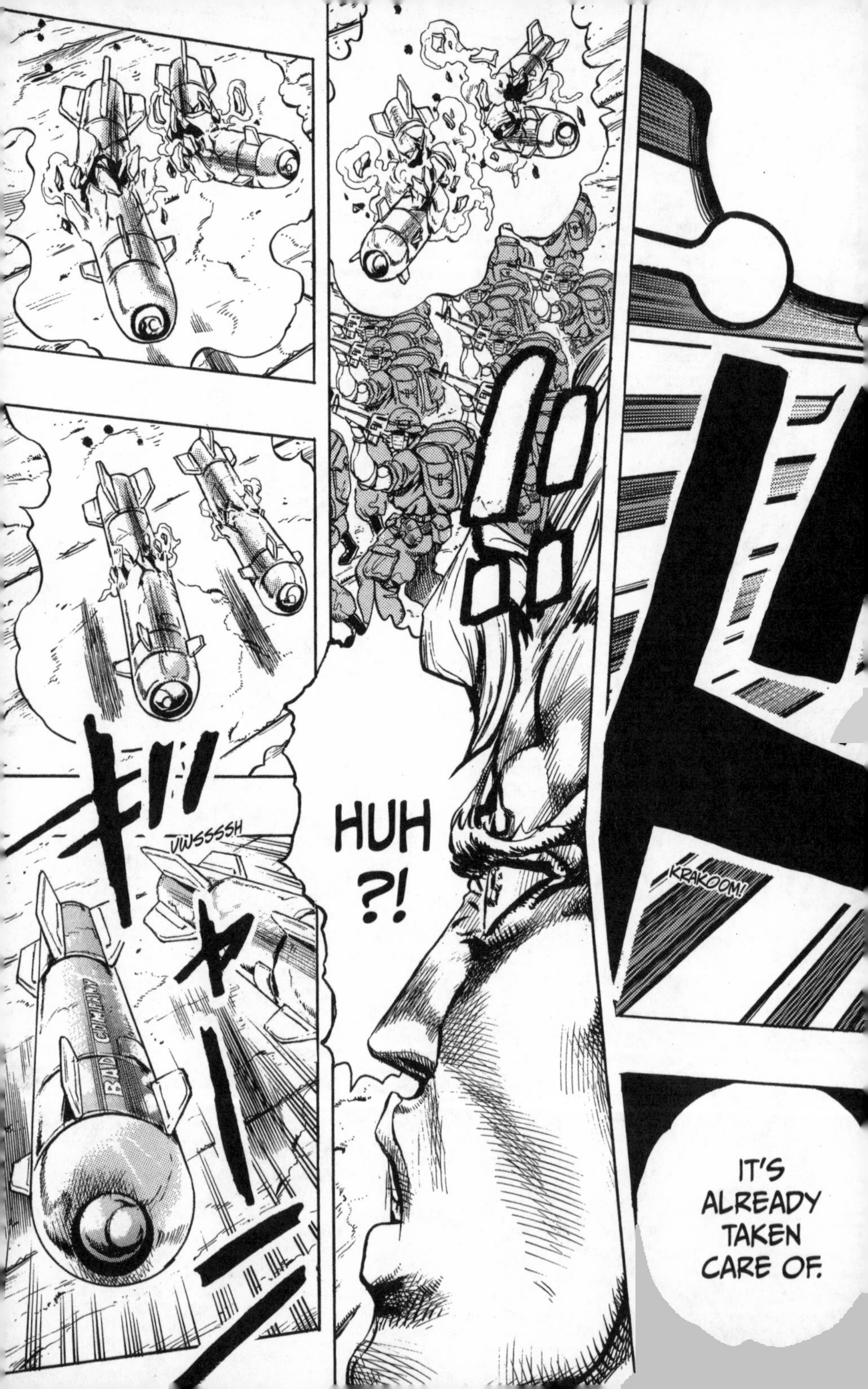
KRAKOOM!
IT'S ALREADY TAKEN CARE OF.
HUH ?!
VWSSSSH
BAD COMPANY

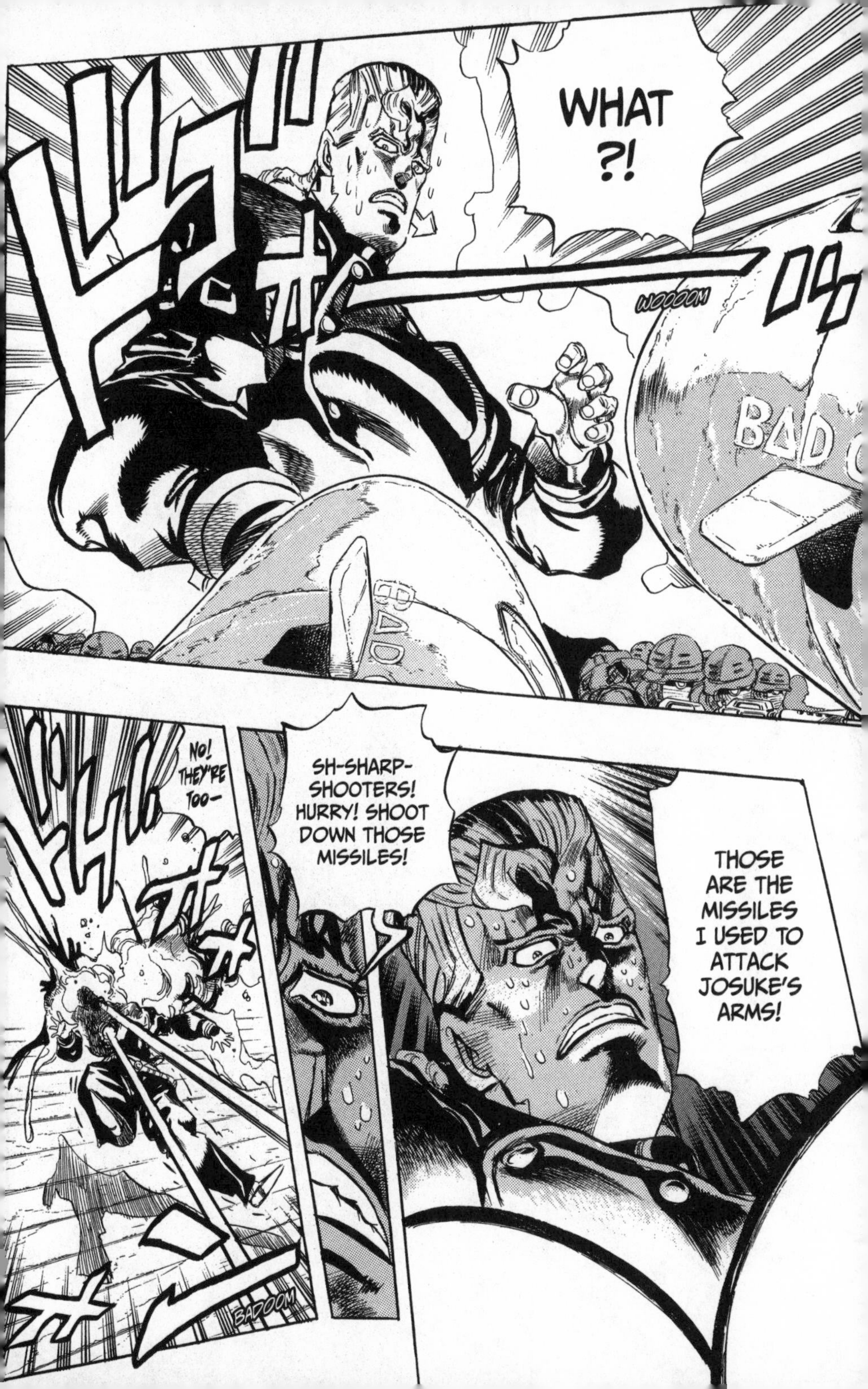
WHAT ?!
WOOOOM
THOSE ARE THE MISSILES I USED TO ATTACK JOSUKE'S ARMS!
SH-SHARP-SHOOTERS! HURRY! SHOOT DOWN THOSE MISSILES!
NO! THEY'RE TOO-
BADOOM

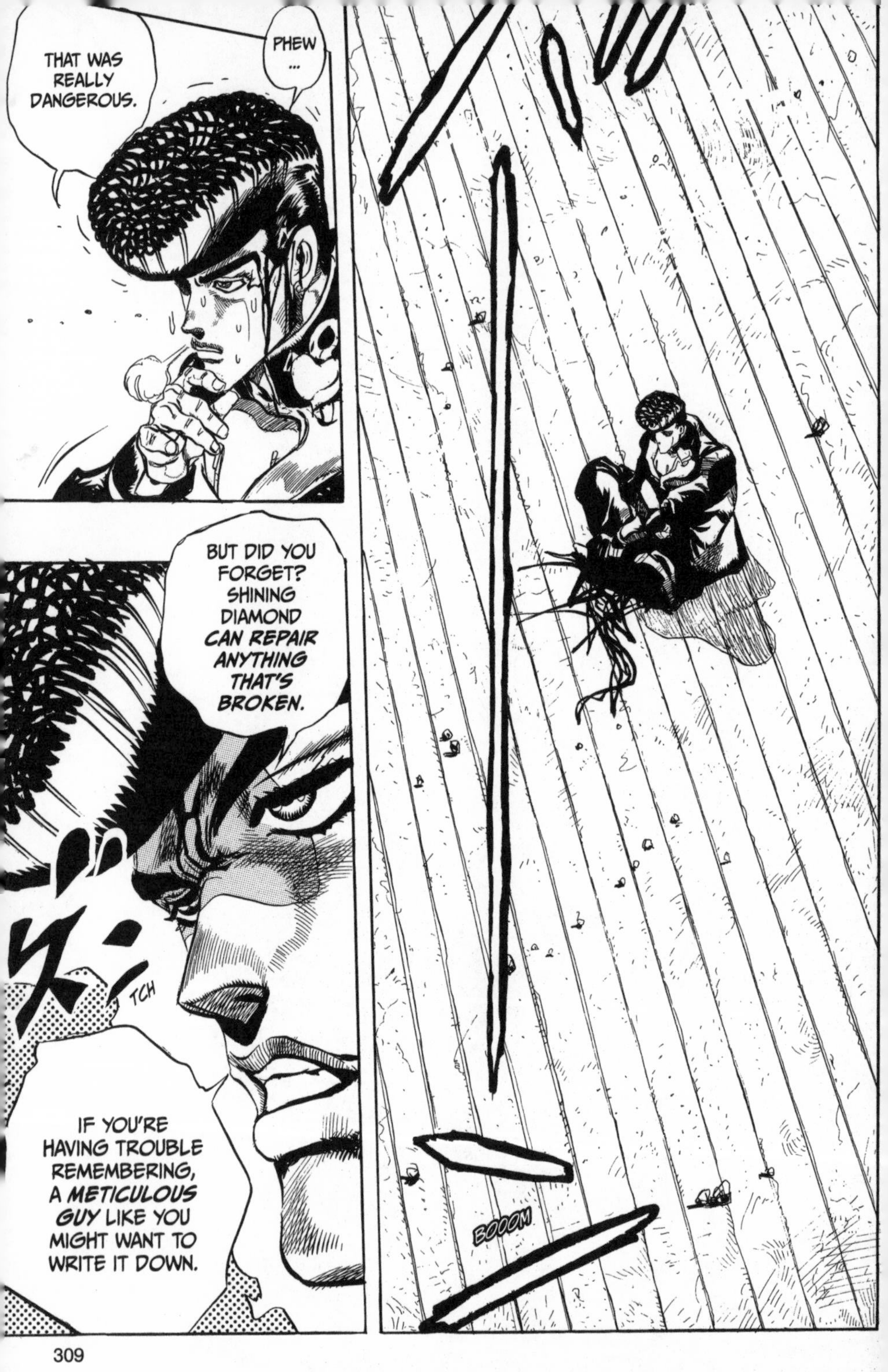
BOOOM
PHEW ...
THAT WAS REALLY DANGEROUS.
BUT DID YOU FORGET? SHINING DIAMOND CAN REPAIR ANYTHING THAT'S BROKEN.
TCH
IF YOU'RE HAVING TROUBLE REMEMBERING, A METICULOUS GUY LIKE YOU MIGHT WANT TO WRITE IT DOWN.

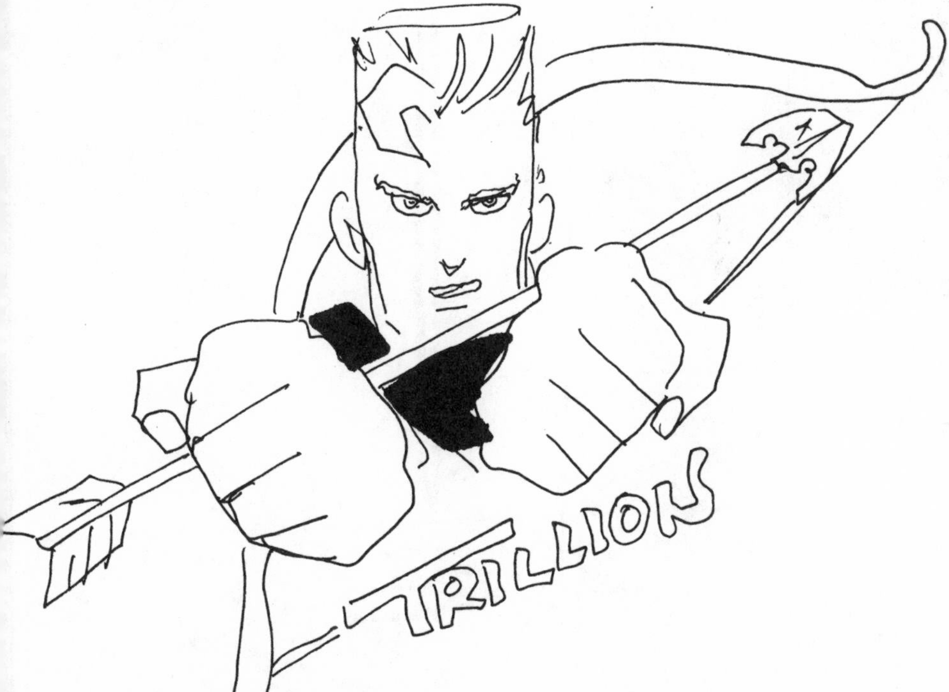
TRILLION

CHAPTER 16

THE NIJIMURA BROTHERS, PART 8

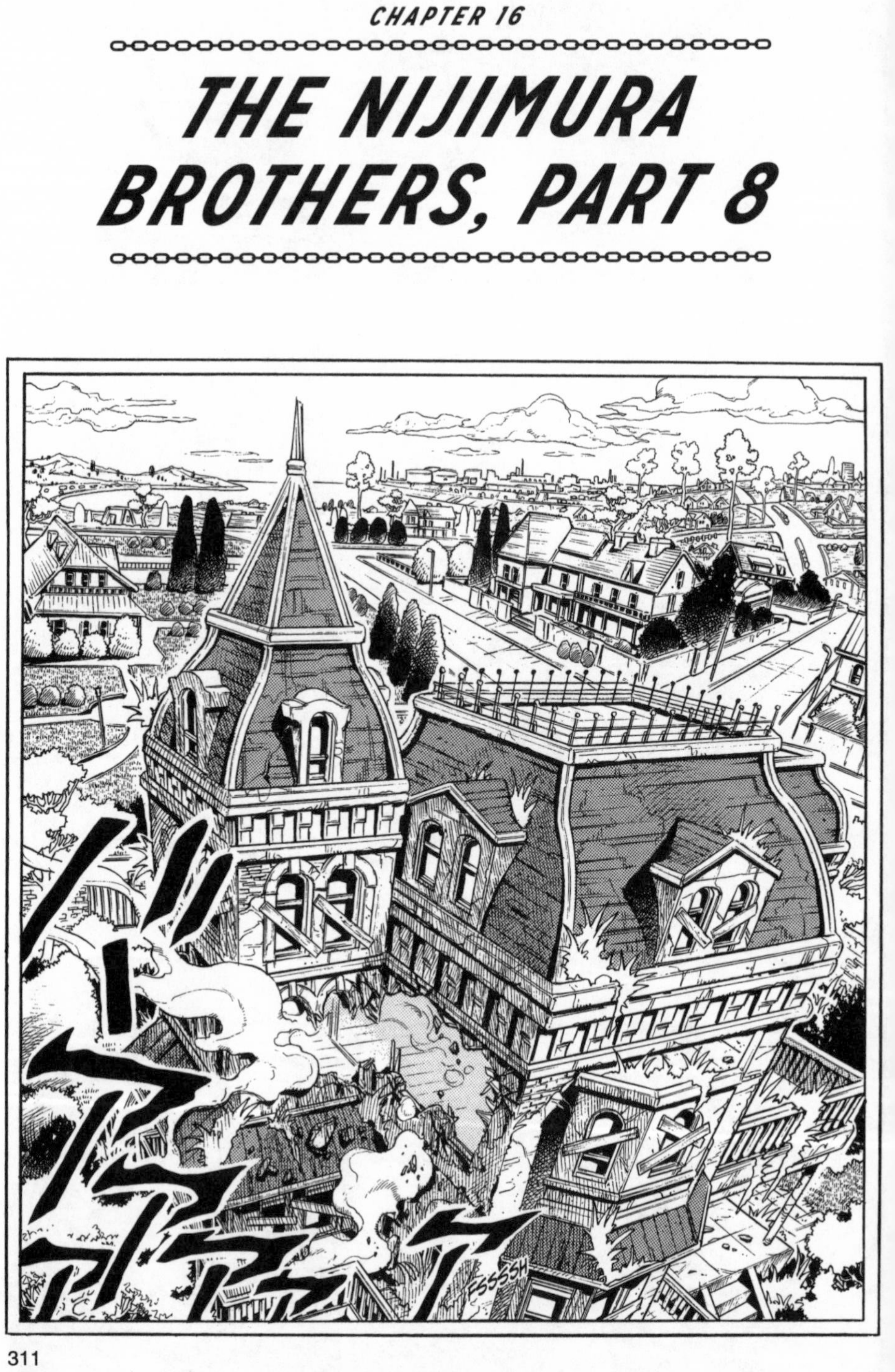
FSSSSH

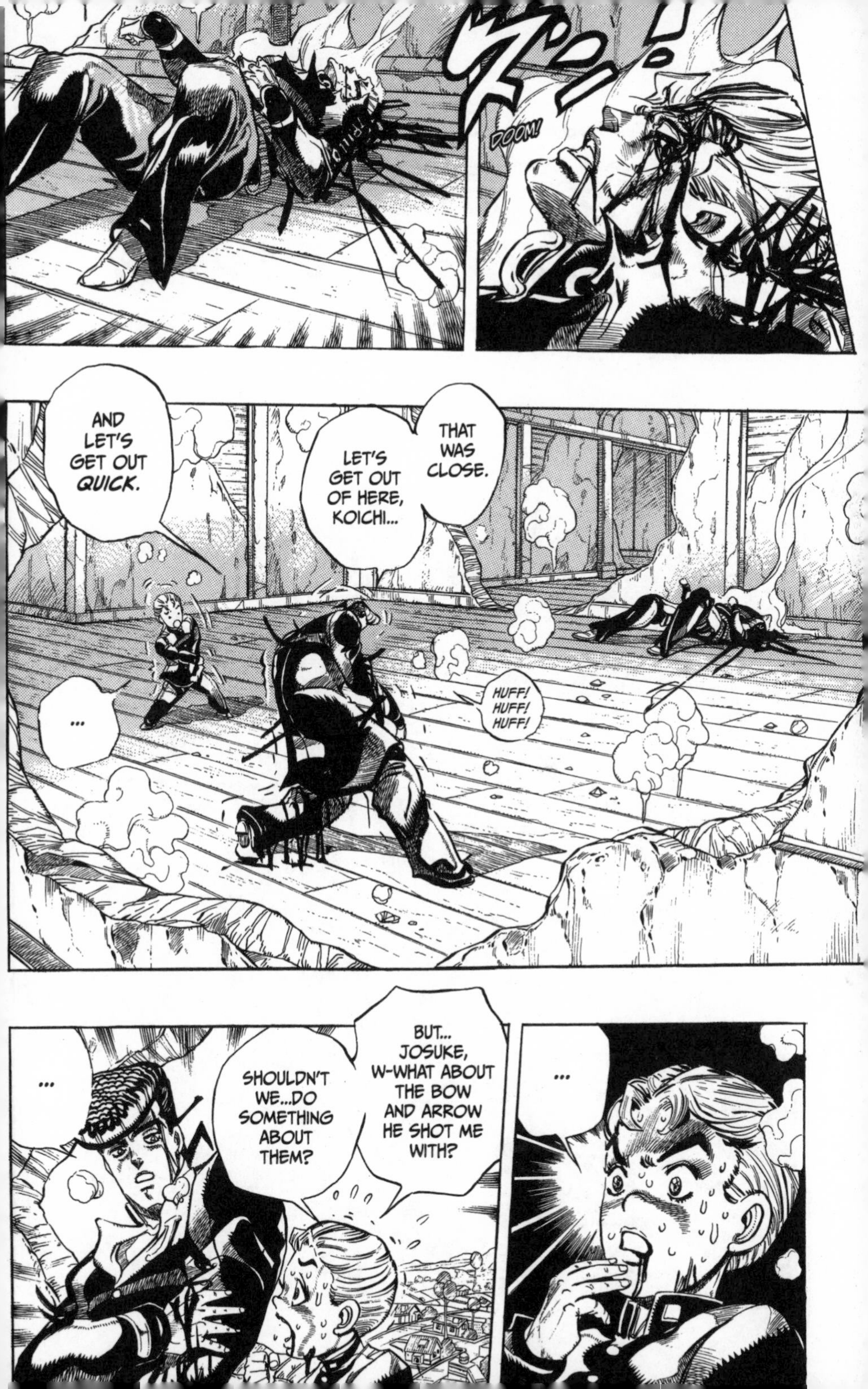
DOOM!
THAT WAS CLOSE.
LET'S GET OUT OF HERE, KOICHI...
AND LET'S GET OUT QUICK.
HUFF! HUFF! HUFF!
...
...
BUT... JOSUKE, W-WHAT ABOUT THE BOW AND ARROW HE SHOT ME WITH?
SHOULDN'T WE...DO SOMETHING ABOUT THEM?
...

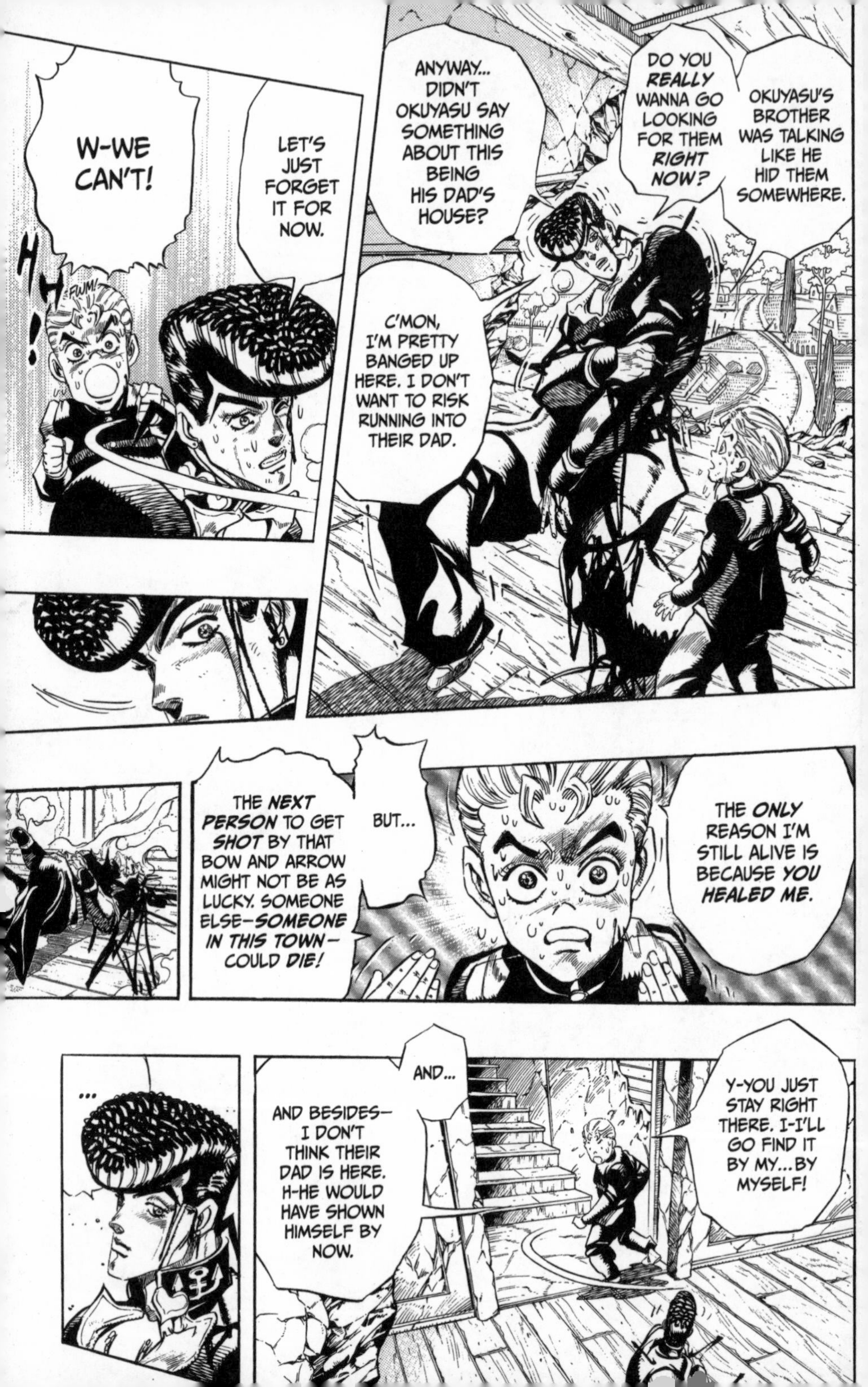

OKUYASU'S BROTHER WAS TALKING LIKE HE HID THEM SOMEWHERE.
DO YOU REALLY WANNA GO LOOKING FOR THEM RIGHT NOW?
ANYWAY... DIDN'T OKUYASU SAY SOMETHING ABOUT THIS BEING HIS DAD'S HOUSE?
C'MON, I'M PRETTY BANGED UP HERE. I DON'T WANT TO RISK RUNNING INTO THEIR DAD.
LET'S JUST FORGET IT FOR NOW.
W-WE CAN'T!
HH!
FWM!
THE ONLY REASON I'M STILL ALIVE IS BECAUSE YOU HEALED ME.
BUT...
THE NEXT PERSON TO GET SHOT BY THAT BOW AND ARROW MIGHT NOT BE AS LUCKY. SOMEONE ELSE—SOMEONE IN THIS TOWN—COULD DIE!
Y-YOU JUST STAY RIGHT THERE. I-I'LL GO FIND IT BY MY...BY MYSELF!
AND...
AND BESIDES— I DON'T THINK THEIR DAD IS HERE. H-HE WOULD HAVE SHOWN HIMSELF BY NOW.
...

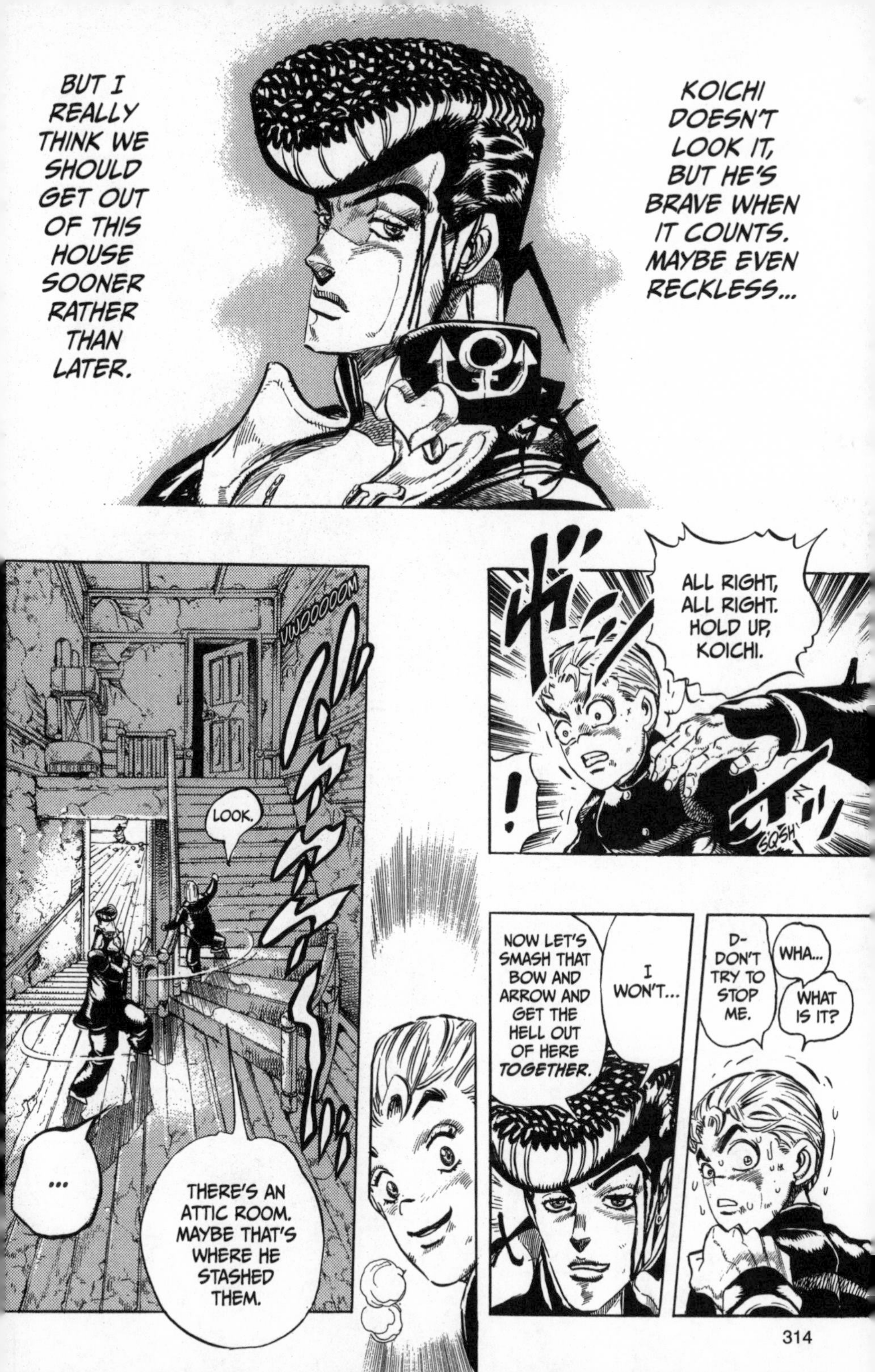
KOICHI DOESN'T LOOK IT, BUT HE'S BRAVE WHEN IT COUNTS. MAYBE EVEN RECKLESS...
BUT I REALLY THINK WE SHOULD GET OUT OF THIS HOUSE SOONER RATHER THAN LATER.
ALL RIGHT, ALL RIGHT. HOLD UP, KOICHI.
!
SQSH
WHA... WHAT IS IT?
D-DON'T TRY TO STOP ME.
I WON'T...
NOW LET'S SMASH THAT BOW AND ARROW AND GET THE HELL OUT OF HERE *TOGETHER*.
UWOOOOOM
LOOK.
...
THERE'S AN ATTIC ROOM. MAYBE THAT'S WHERE HE STASHED THEM.

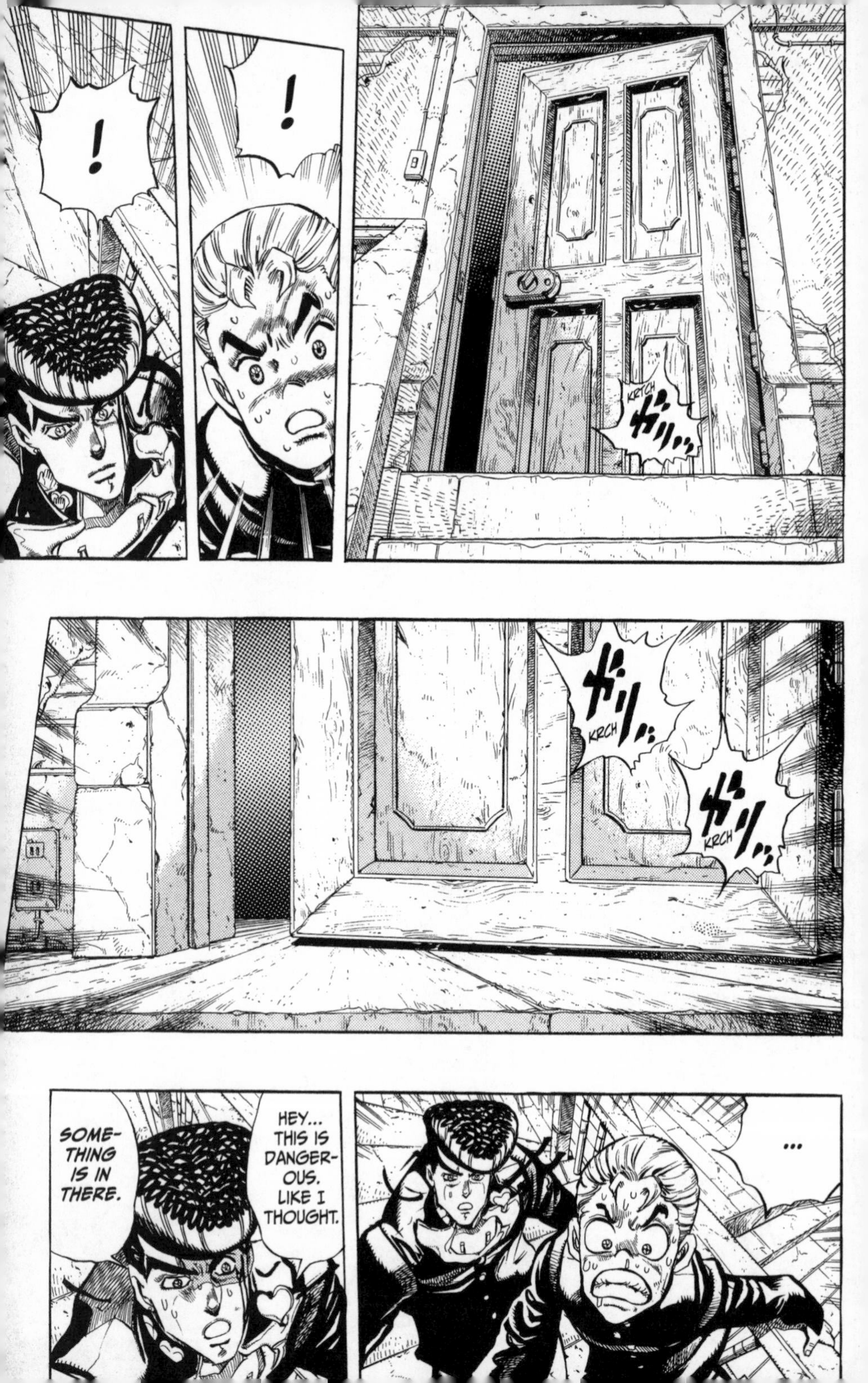

KRTCH
ガリッ
!
!
ガリッ
KRCH
ガリッ
KRCH
...
HEY... THIS IS DANGER-OUS. LIKE I THOUGHT.
SOME-THING IS IN THERE.

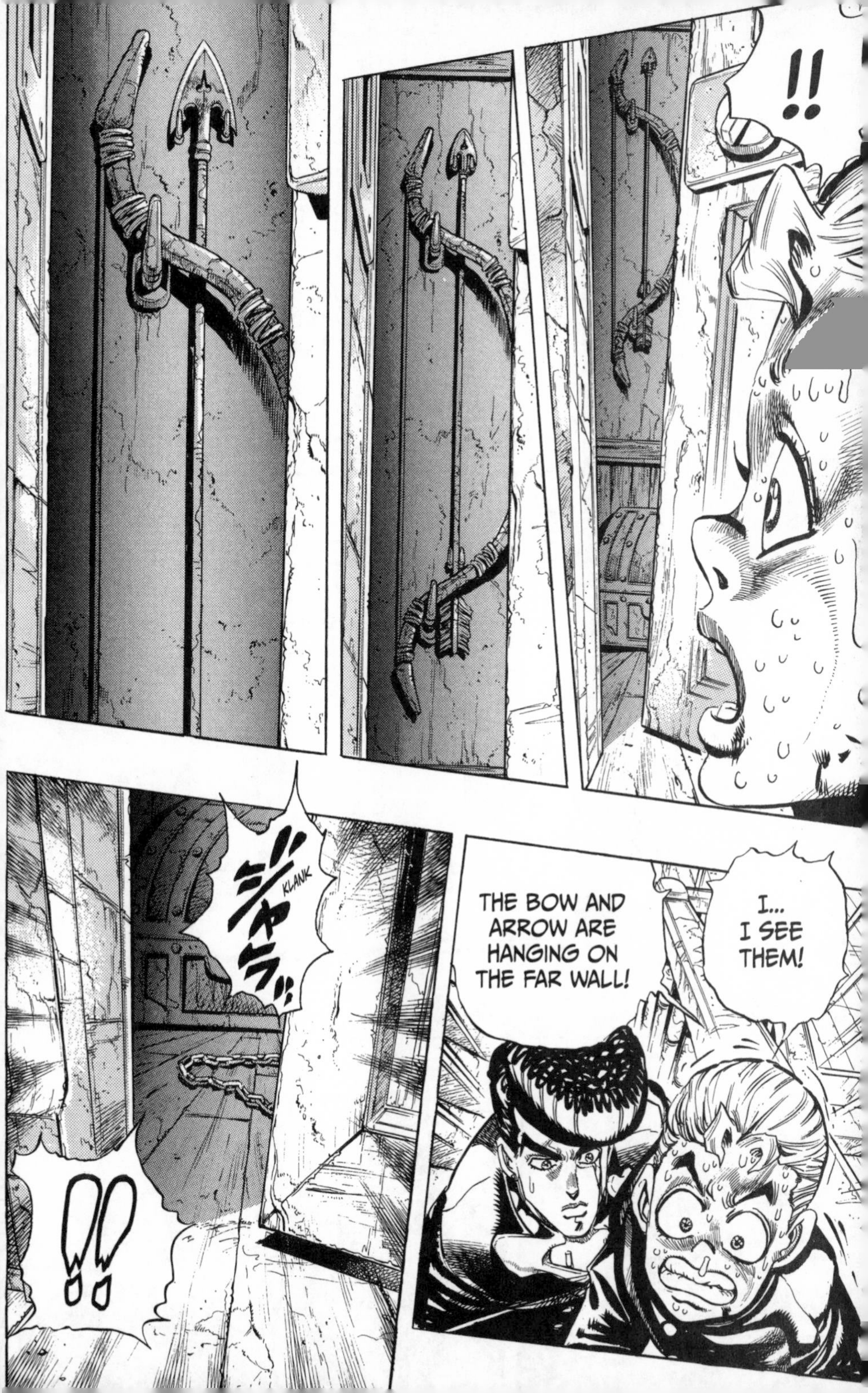
!!
I...
I SEE
THEM!
THE BOW AND
ARROW ARE
HANGING ON
THE FAR WALL!
ジャラ‼
KLANK
!!

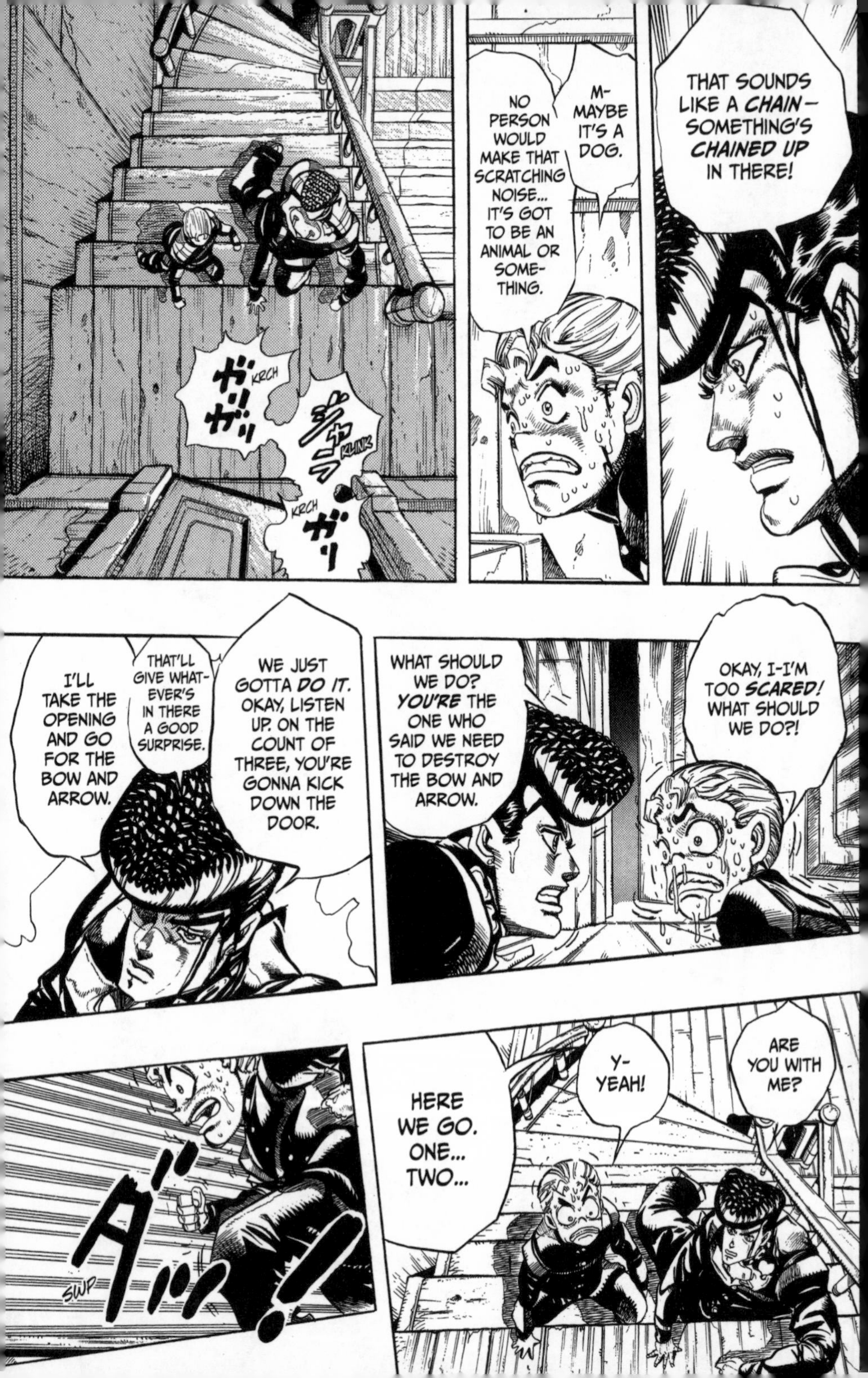
THAT SOUNDS LIKE A *CHAIN*—SOMETHING'S *CHAINED UP* IN THERE!
M-MAYBE IT'S A DOG.
NO PERSON WOULD MAKE THAT SCRATCHING NOISE... IT'S GOT TO BE AN ANIMAL OR SOMETHING.
ガリガリ KRCH
ジャラ KLINK
ガリ KRCH
OKAY, I-I'M TOO *SCARED!* WHAT SHOULD WE DO?!
WHAT SHOULD WE DO? *YOU'RE* THE ONE WHO SAID WE NEED TO DESTROY THE BOW AND ARROW.
WE JUST GOTTA *DO IT.* OKAY, LISTEN UP. ON THE COUNT OF THREE, YOU'RE GONNA KICK DOWN THE DOOR.
THAT'LL GIVE WHATEVER'S IN THERE A GOOD SURPRISE.
I'LL TAKE THE OPENING AND GO FOR THE BOW AND ARROW.
ARE YOU WITH ME?
Y-YEAH!
HERE WE GO. ONE... TWO...
ダッ!! SWP

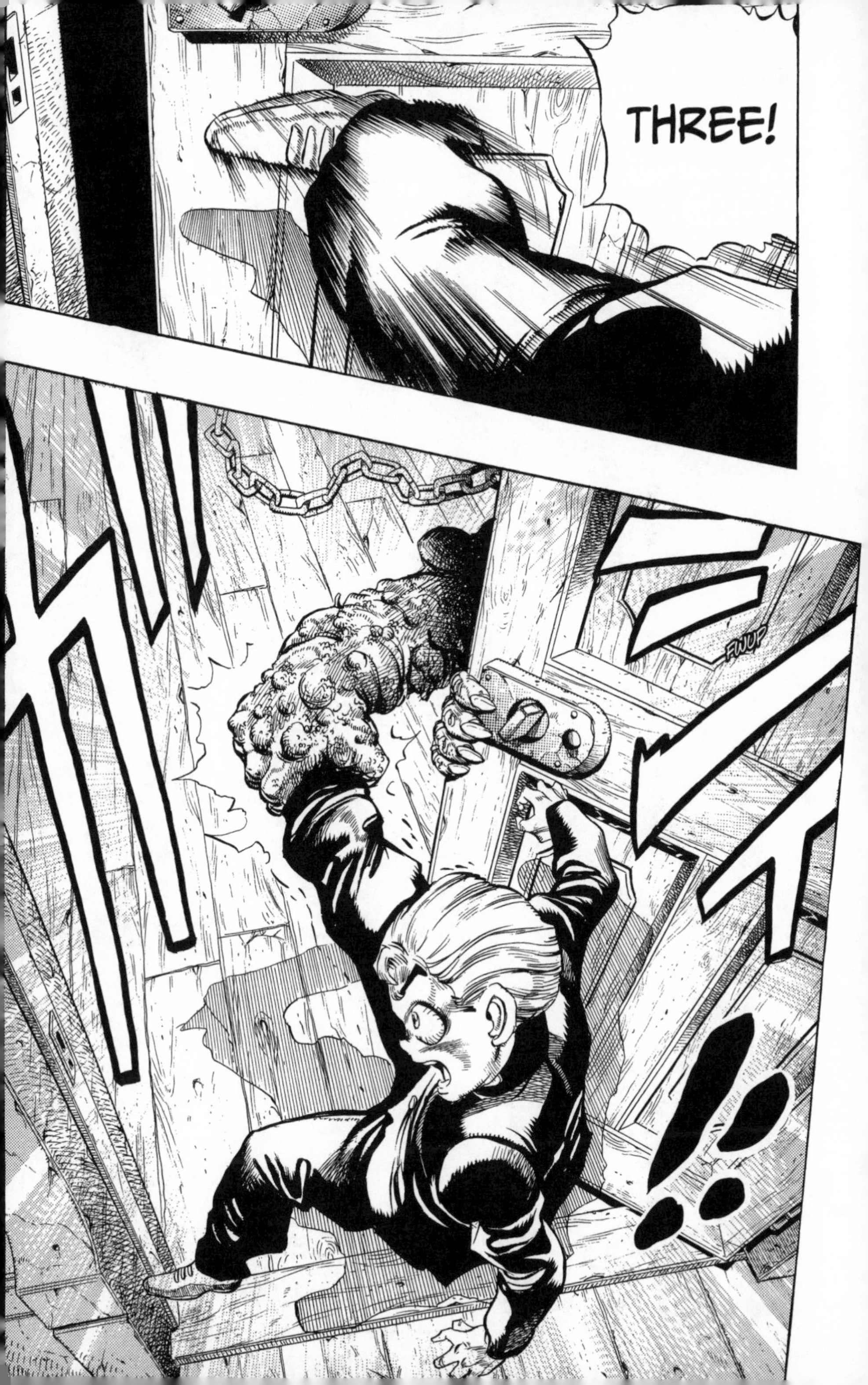
THREE!
FWUP
!!

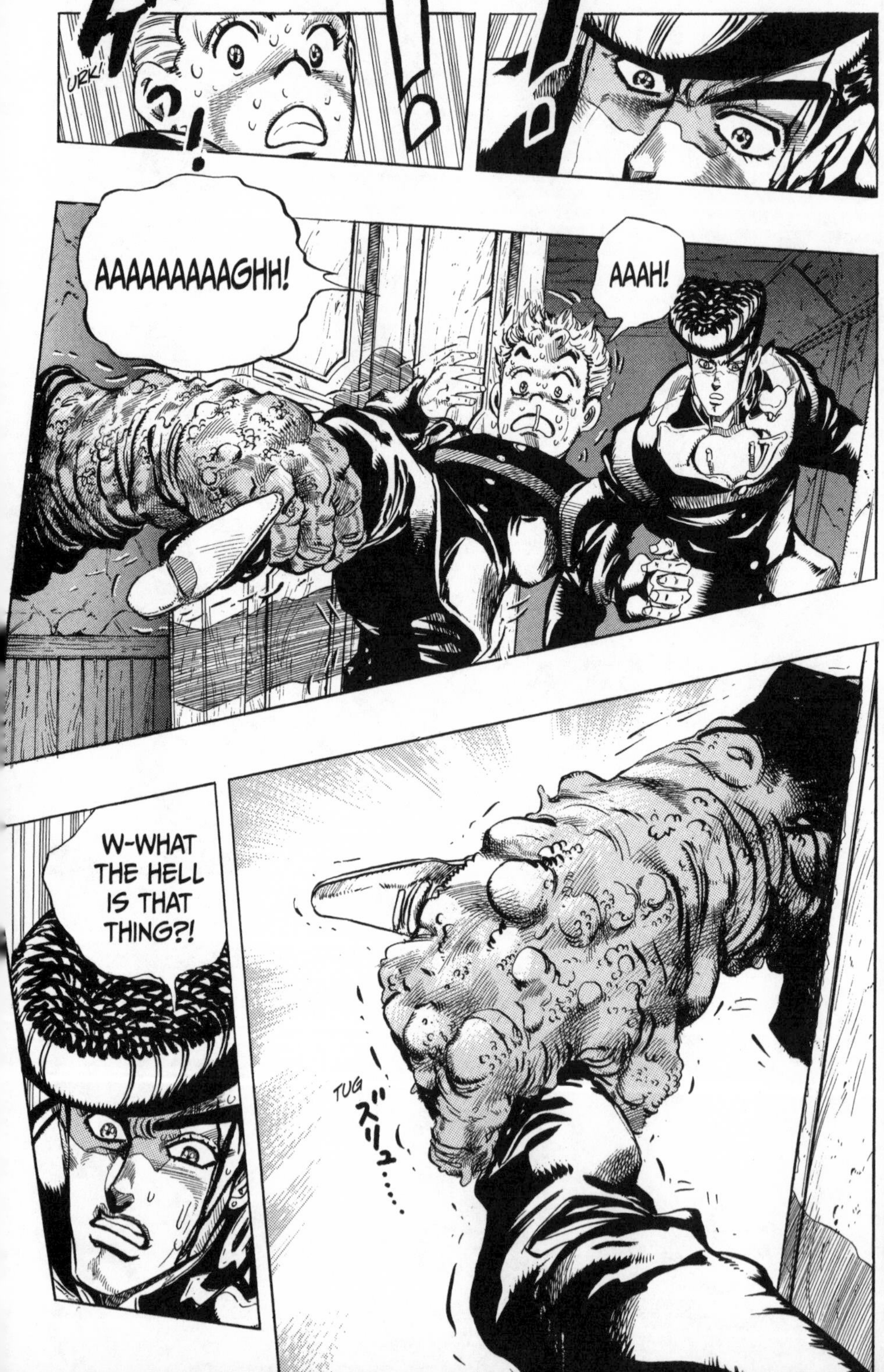
!
ゲ
URK!
!
AAAH!
AAAAAAAAAGHH!
TUG
ズリュ……
W-WHAT THE HELL IS THAT THING?!

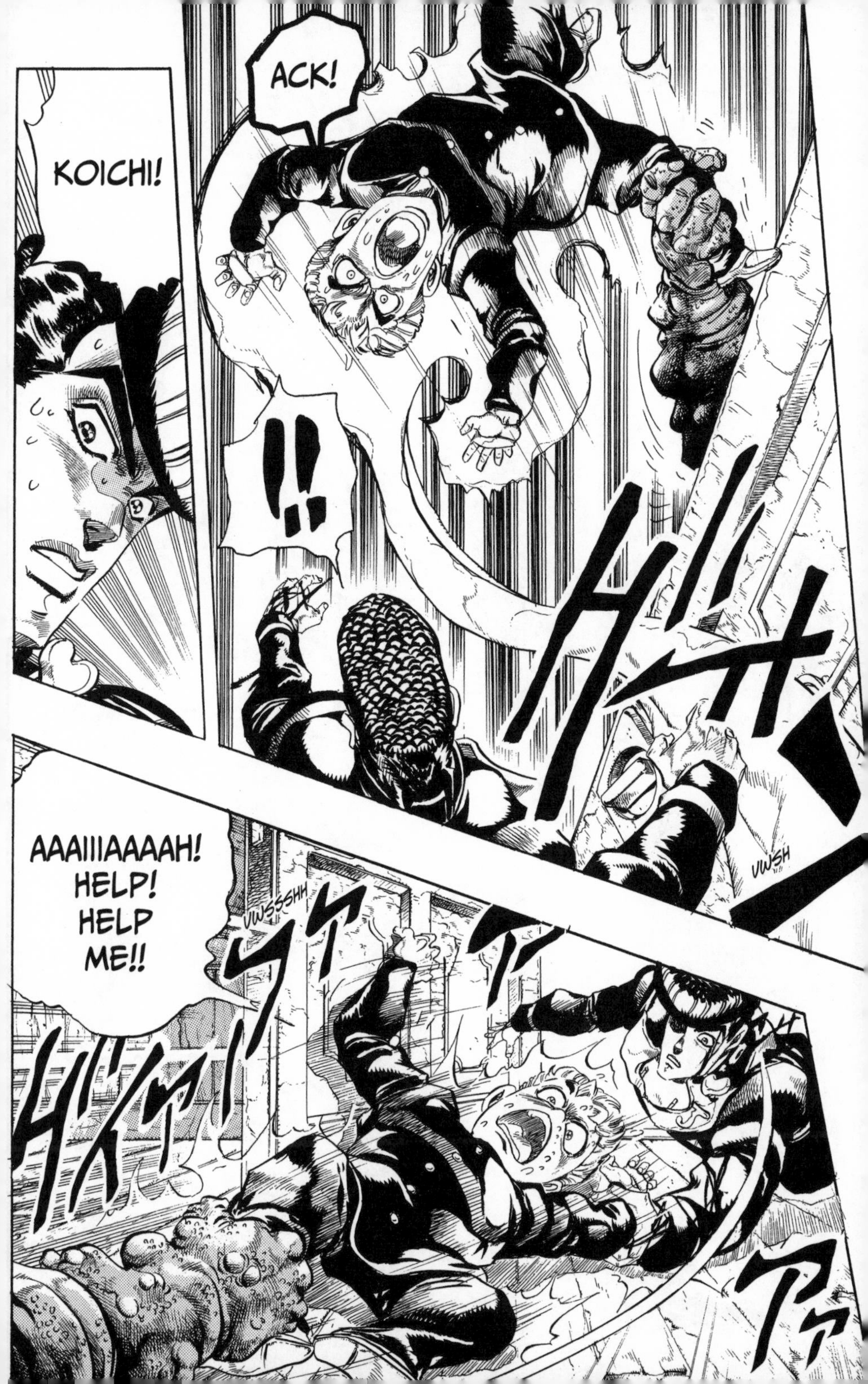
ACK!
!!
KOICHI!
VWSH
VWSSSHH
AAAIIIAAAAH! HELP! HELP ME!!

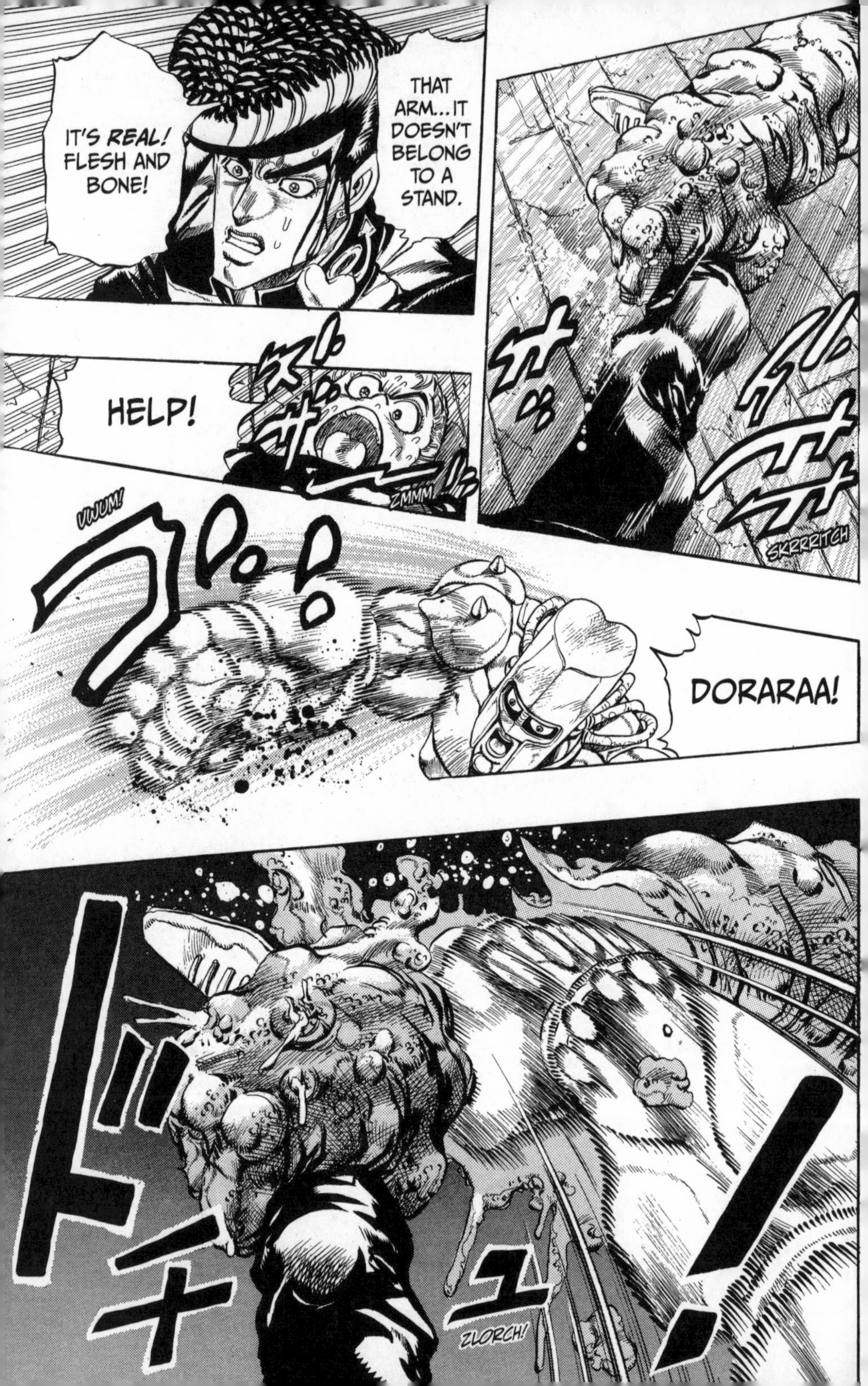
SKRRRITCH
THAT ARM... IT DOESN'T BELONG TO A STAND.
IT'S REAL! FLESH AND BONE!
ZMMM
HELP!
DORARAA!
VWUM!
ZLORCH!

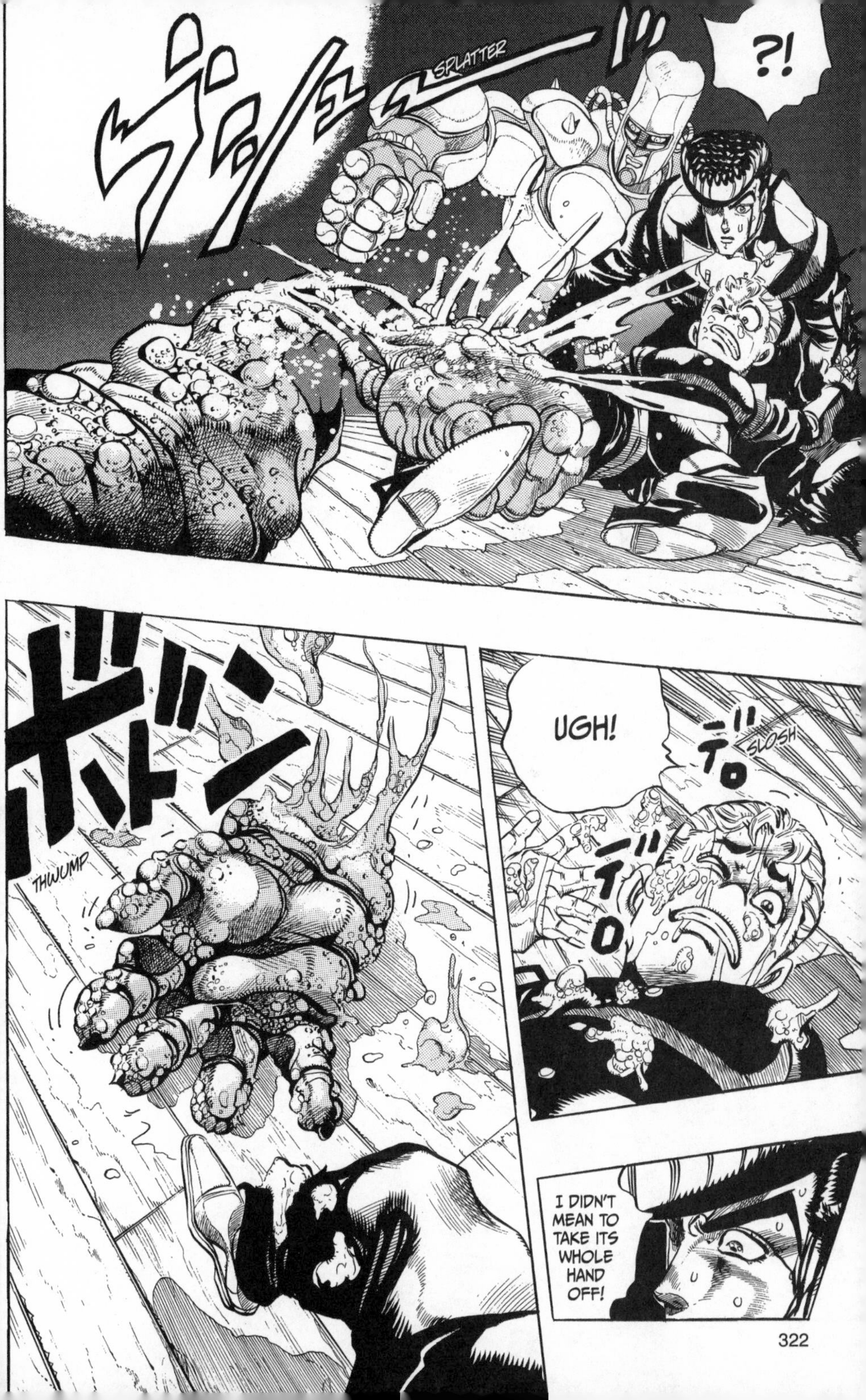
SPLATTER
?!
UGH!
SLOSH
I DIDN'T MEAN TO TAKE ITS WHOLE HAND OFF!
THWUMP

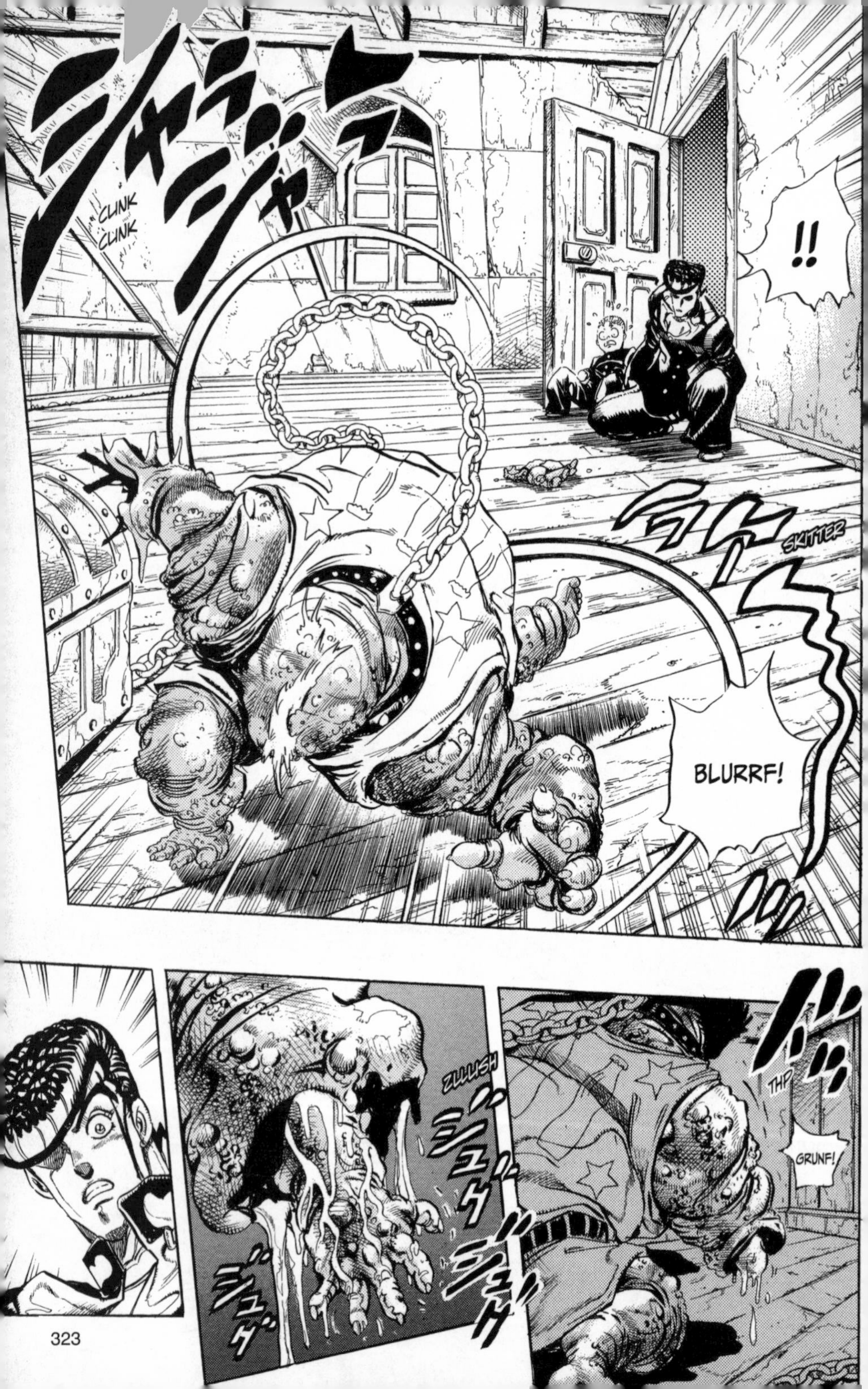
!!
SKITTER
BLURRF!
CLUNK CLUNK
THP
GRUNF!
ZLLUSH

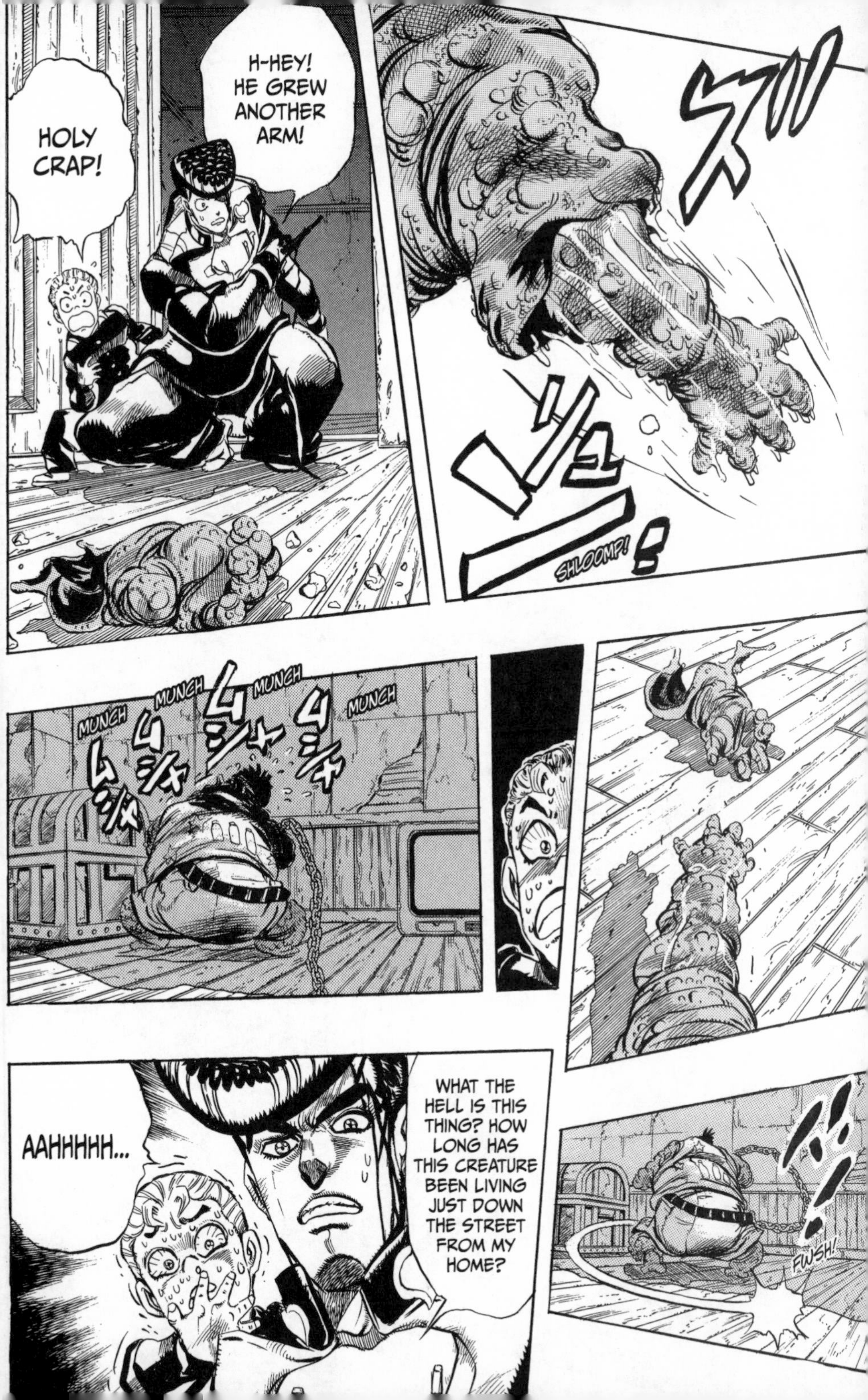
SHLOOMP!
H-HEY! HE GREW ANOTHER ARM!
HOLY CRAP!
MUNCH
MUNCH
MUNCH
MUNCH
FWUSH!
WHAT THE HELL IS THIS THING? HOW LONG HAS THIS CREATURE BEEN LIVING JUST DOWN THE STREET FROM MY HOME?
AAHHHHH...

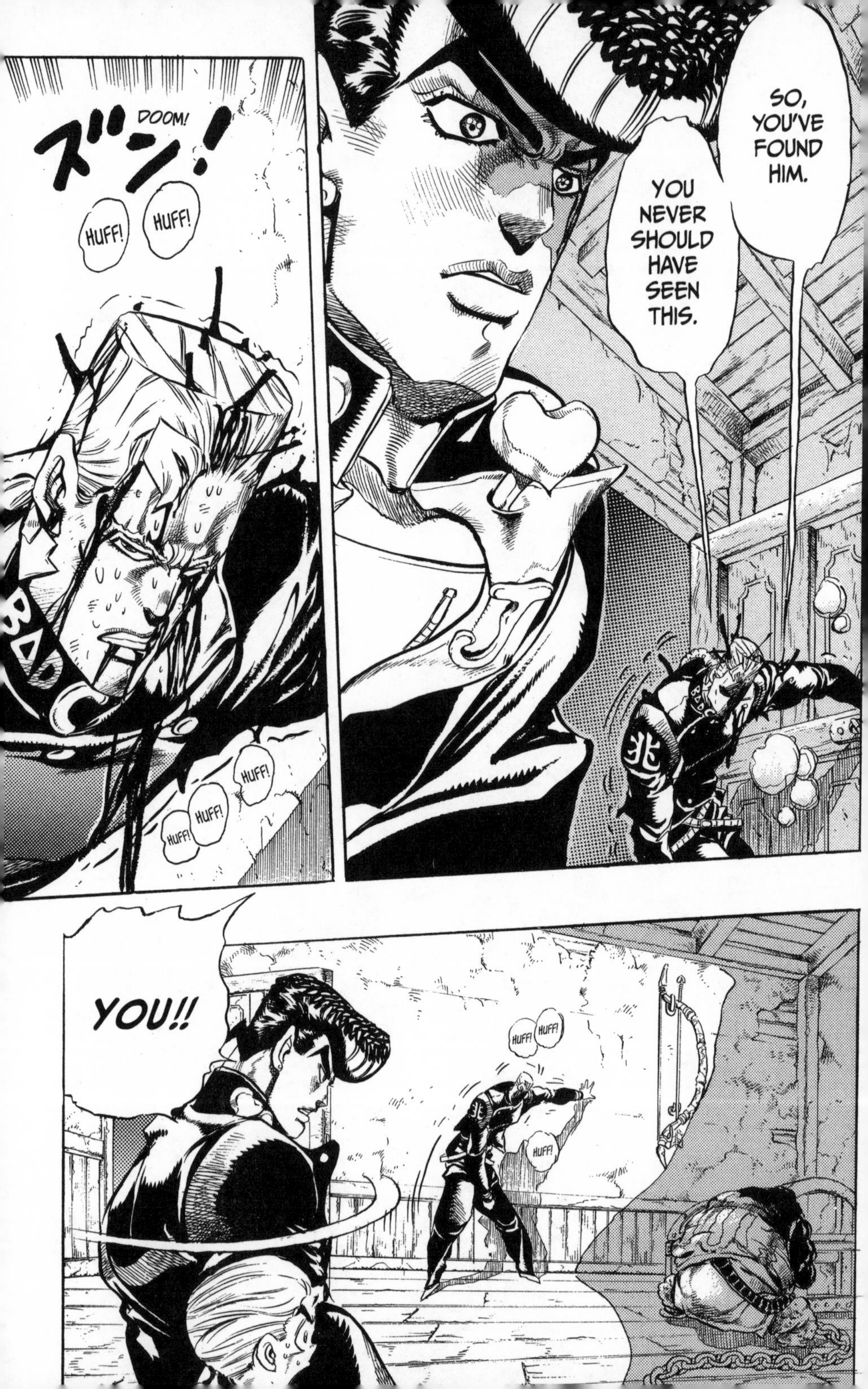
SO, YOU'VE FOUND HIM.
YOU NEVER SHOULD HAVE SEEN THIS.
ズーン!
DOOM!
HUFF!
HUFF!
HUFF!
HUFF!
HUFF!
YOU!!
HUFF!
HUFF!
HUFF!

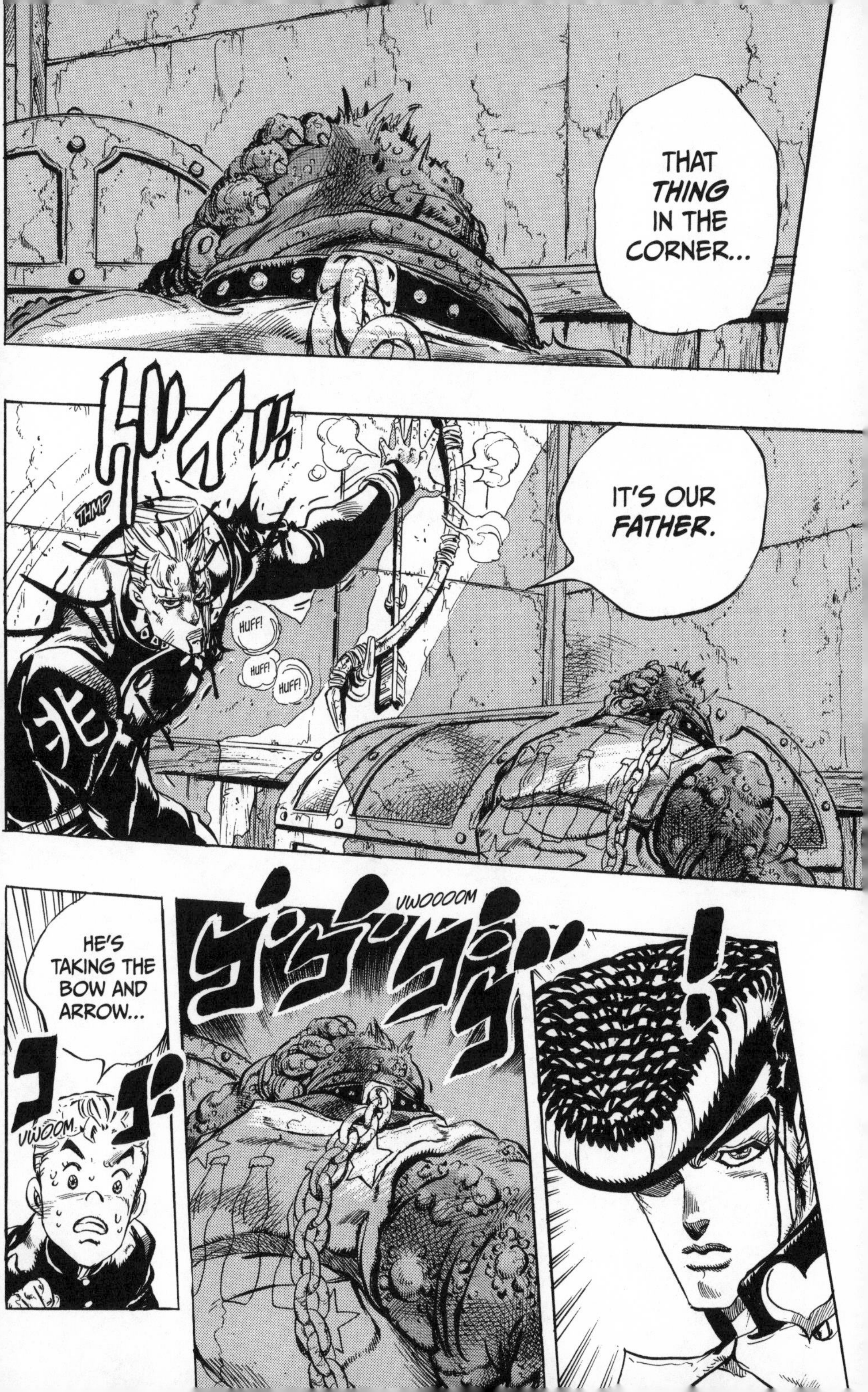
THAT THING IN THE CORNER...
IT'S OUR FATHER.
THMP
HUFF!
HUFF!
HUFF!
VWOOOOM
HE'S TAKING THE BOW AND ARROW...
VWOOM

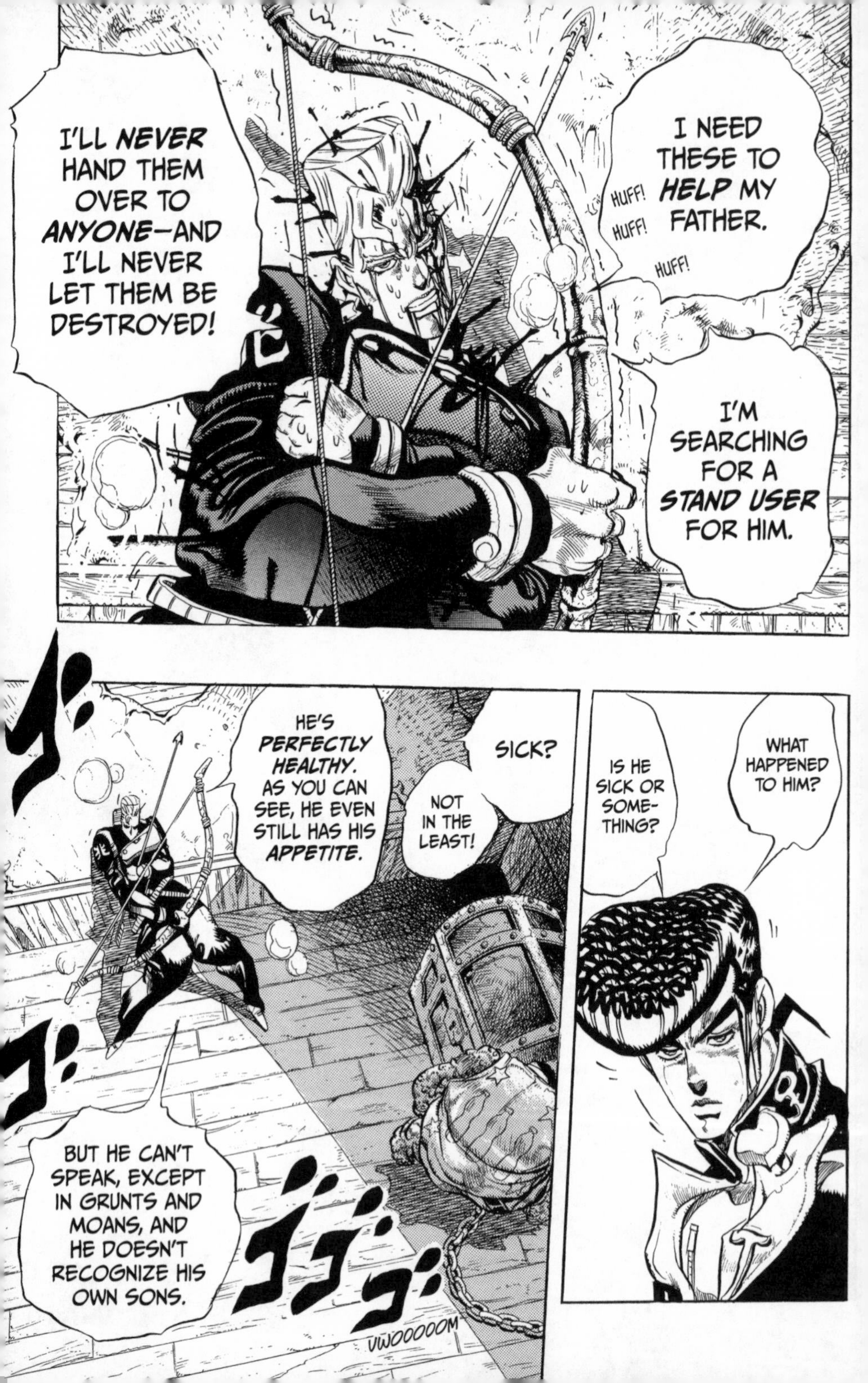
I NEED THESE TO HELP MY FATHER.
HUFF!
HUFF!
HUFF!
I'M SEARCHING FOR A STAND USER FOR HIM.
I'LL NEVER HAND THEM OVER TO ANYONE—AND I'LL NEVER LET THEM BE DESTROYED!
WHAT HAPPENED TO HIM?
IS HE SICK OR SOME-THING?
SICK?
NOT IN THE LEAST!
HE'S PERFECTLY HEALTHY. AS YOU CAN SEE, HE EVEN STILL HAS HIS APPETITE.
BUT HE CAN'T SPEAK, EXCEPT IN GRUNTS AND MOANS, AND HE DOESN'T RECOGNIZE HIS OWN SONS.
VWOOOOOM

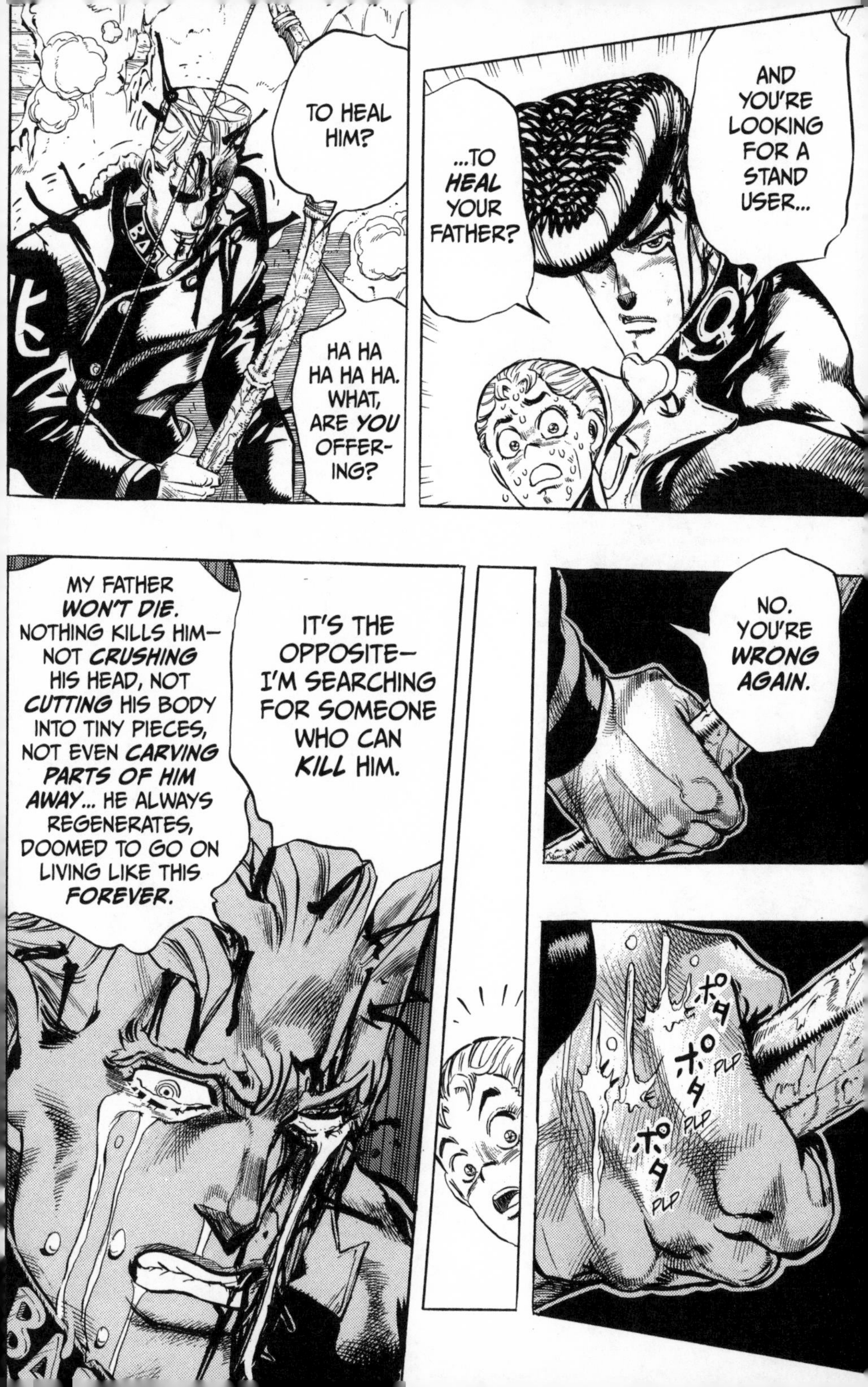
AND YOU'RE LOOKING FOR A STAND USER...
...TO HEAL YOUR FATHER?
TO HEAL HIM?
HA HA HA HA HA. WHAT, ARE YOU OFFERING?
NO. YOU'RE WRONG AGAIN.
ポタ PLP
ポタ PLP
ポタ PLP
IT'S THE OPPOSITE— I'M SEARCHING FOR SOMEONE WHO CAN KILL HIM.
MY FATHER WON'T DIE. NOTHING KILLS HIM— NOT CRUSHING HIS HEAD, NOT CUTTING HIS BODY INTO TINY PIECES, NOT EVEN CARVING PARTS OF HIM AWAY... HE ALWAYS REGENERATES, DOOMED TO GO ON LIVING LIKE THIS FOREVER.

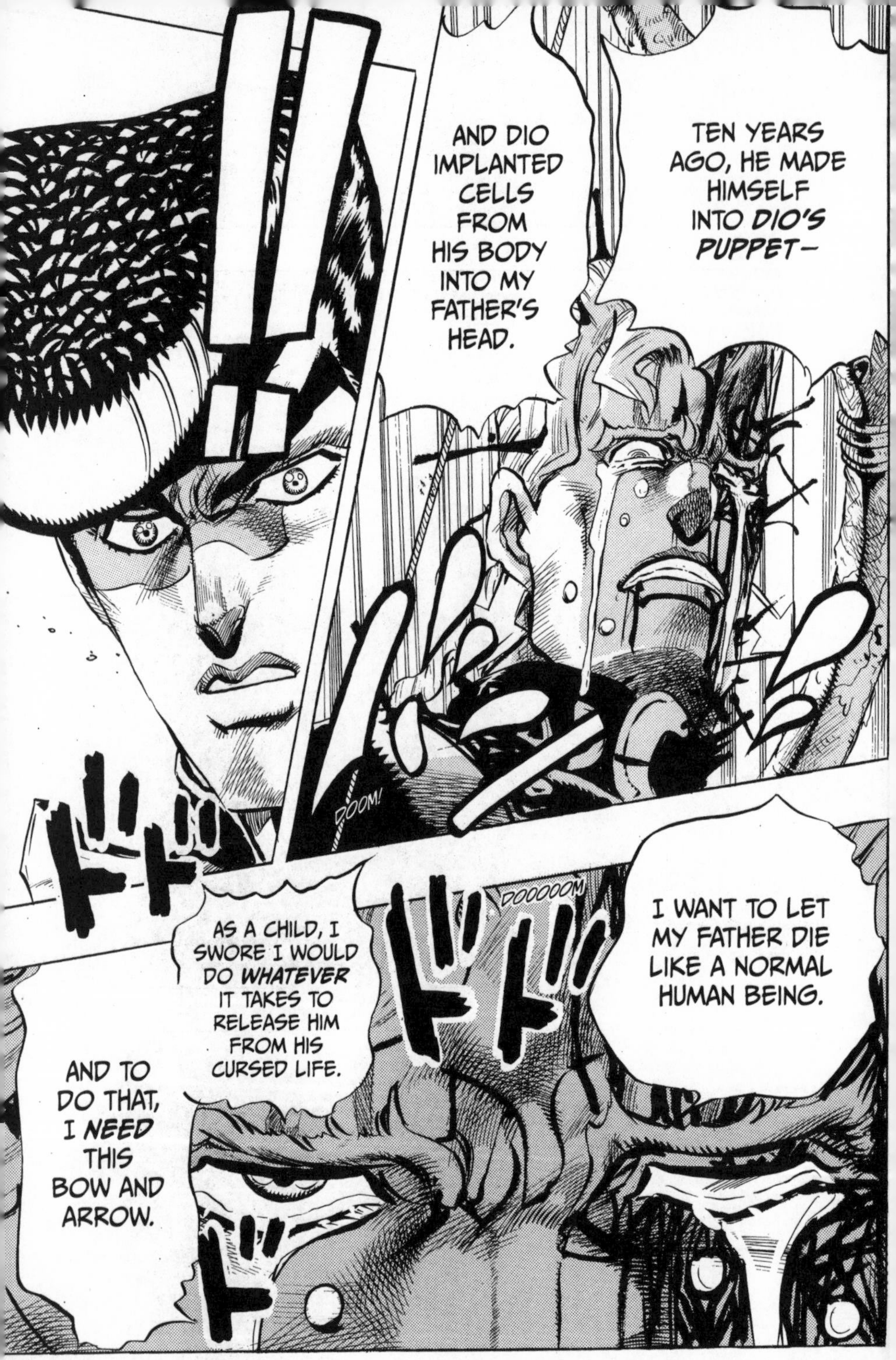
TEN YEARS AGO, HE MADE HIMSELF INTO *DIO'S PUPPET*—
AND DIO IMPLANTED CELLS FROM HIS BODY INTO MY FATHER'S HEAD.
DOOM!
I WANT TO LET MY FATHER DIE LIKE A NORMAL HUMAN BEING.
DOOOOOM
AS A CHILD, I SWORE I WOULD DO *WHATEVER* IT TAKES TO RELEASE HIM FROM HIS CURSED LIFE.
AND TO DO THAT, I *NEED* THIS BOW AND ARROW.

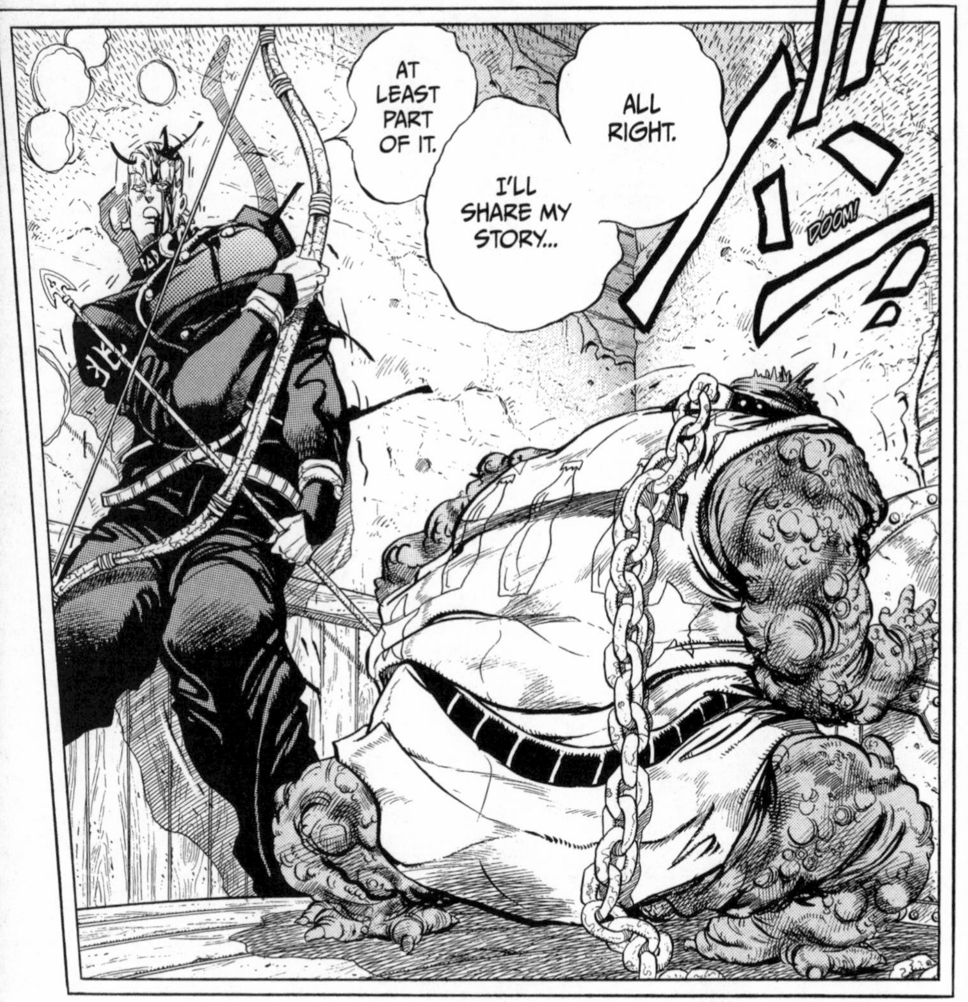
ALL RIGHT.
I'LL SHARE MY STORY...
AT LEAST PART OF IT.
DOOM!

CHAPTER 17

THE NIJIMURA BROTHERS, PART 9

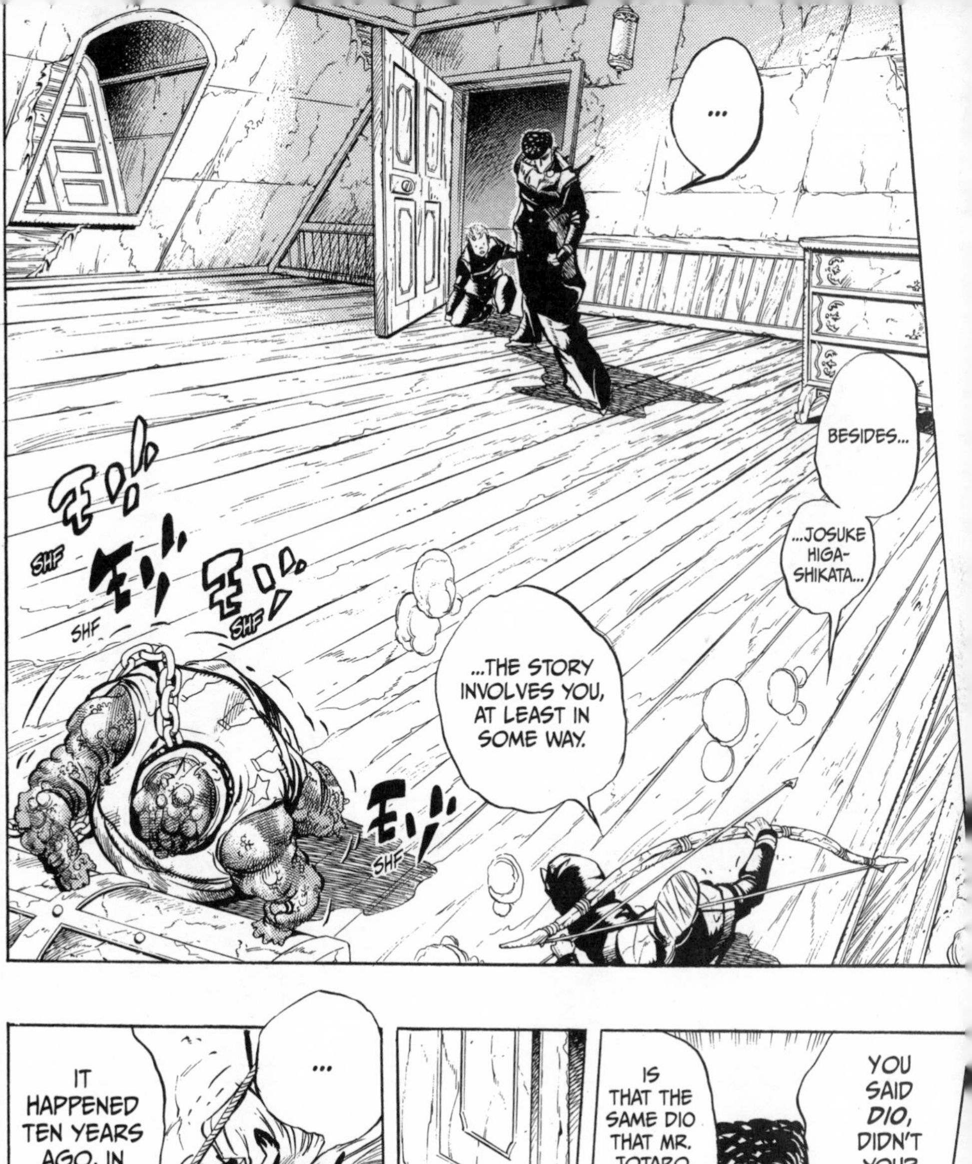
...
BESIDES...
...JOSUKE HIGASHIKATA...
...THE STORY INVOLVES YOU, AT LEAST IN SOME WAY.
SHF
SHF
SHF
SHF

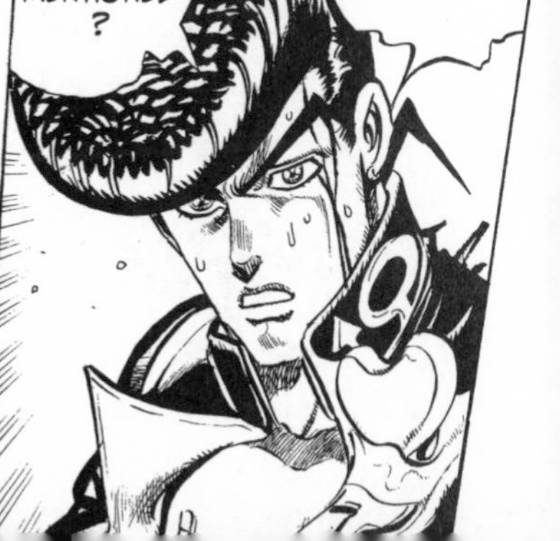
YOU SAID *DIO*, DIDN'T YOU?

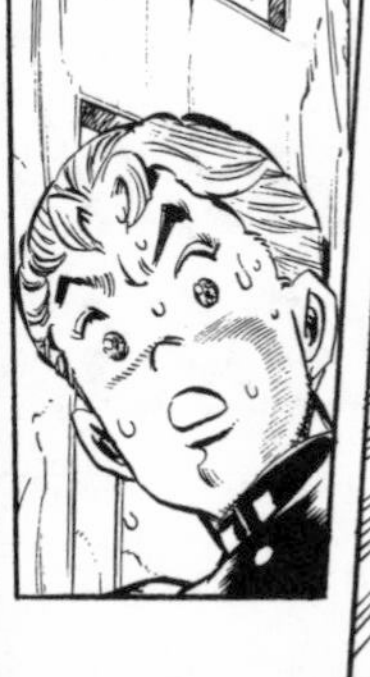
IS THAT THE SAME DIO THAT MR. JOTARO MENTIONED?

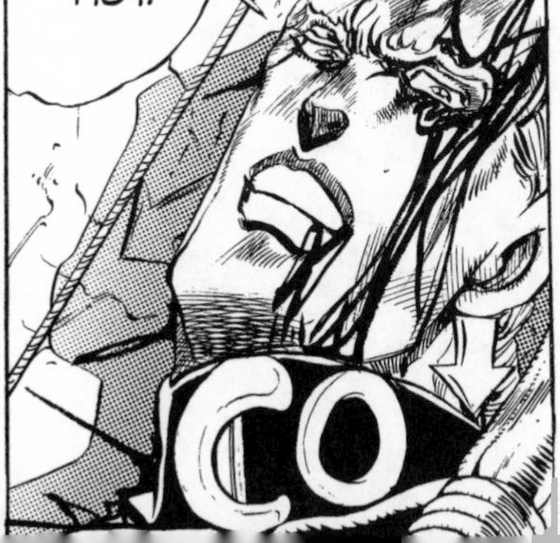
...
IT HAPPENED TEN YEARS AGO, IN 1989.

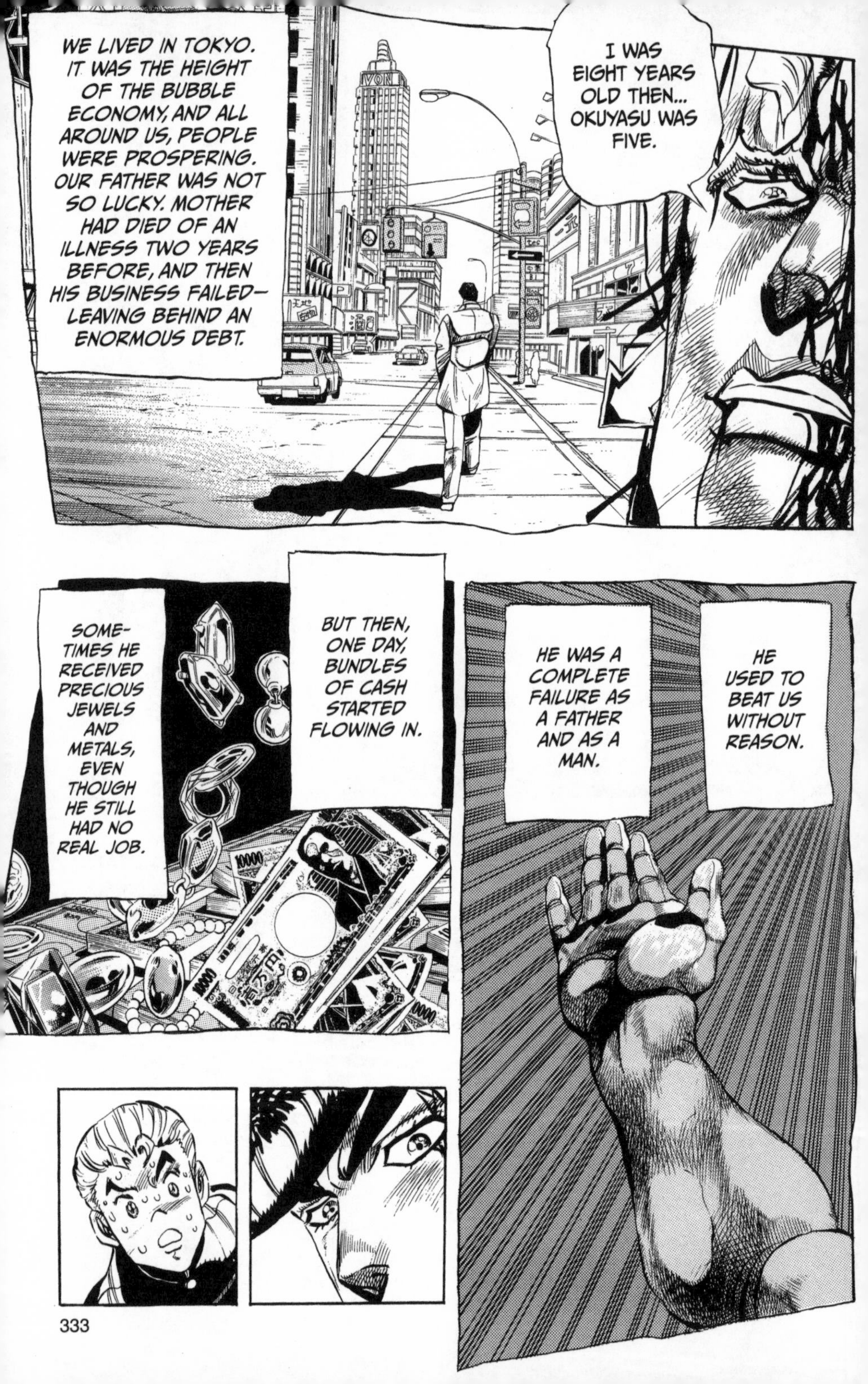
I WAS EIGHT YEARS OLD THEN... OKUYASU WAS FIVE.
WE LIVED IN TOKYO. IT WAS THE HEIGHT OF THE BUBBLE ECONOMY, AND ALL AROUND US, PEOPLE WERE PROSPERING. OUR FATHER WAS NOT SO LUCKY. MOTHER HAD DIED OF AN ILLNESS TWO YEARS BEFORE, AND THEN HIS BUSINESS FAILED—LEAVING BEHIND AN ENORMOUS DEBT.
HE USED TO BEAT US WITHOUT REASON.
HE WAS A COMPLETE FAILURE AS A FATHER AND AS A MAN.
BUT THEN, ONE DAY, BUNDLES OF CASH STARTED FLOWING IN.
SOMETIMES HE RECEIVED PRECIOUS JEWELS AND METALS, EVEN THOUGH HE STILL HAD NO REAL JOB.

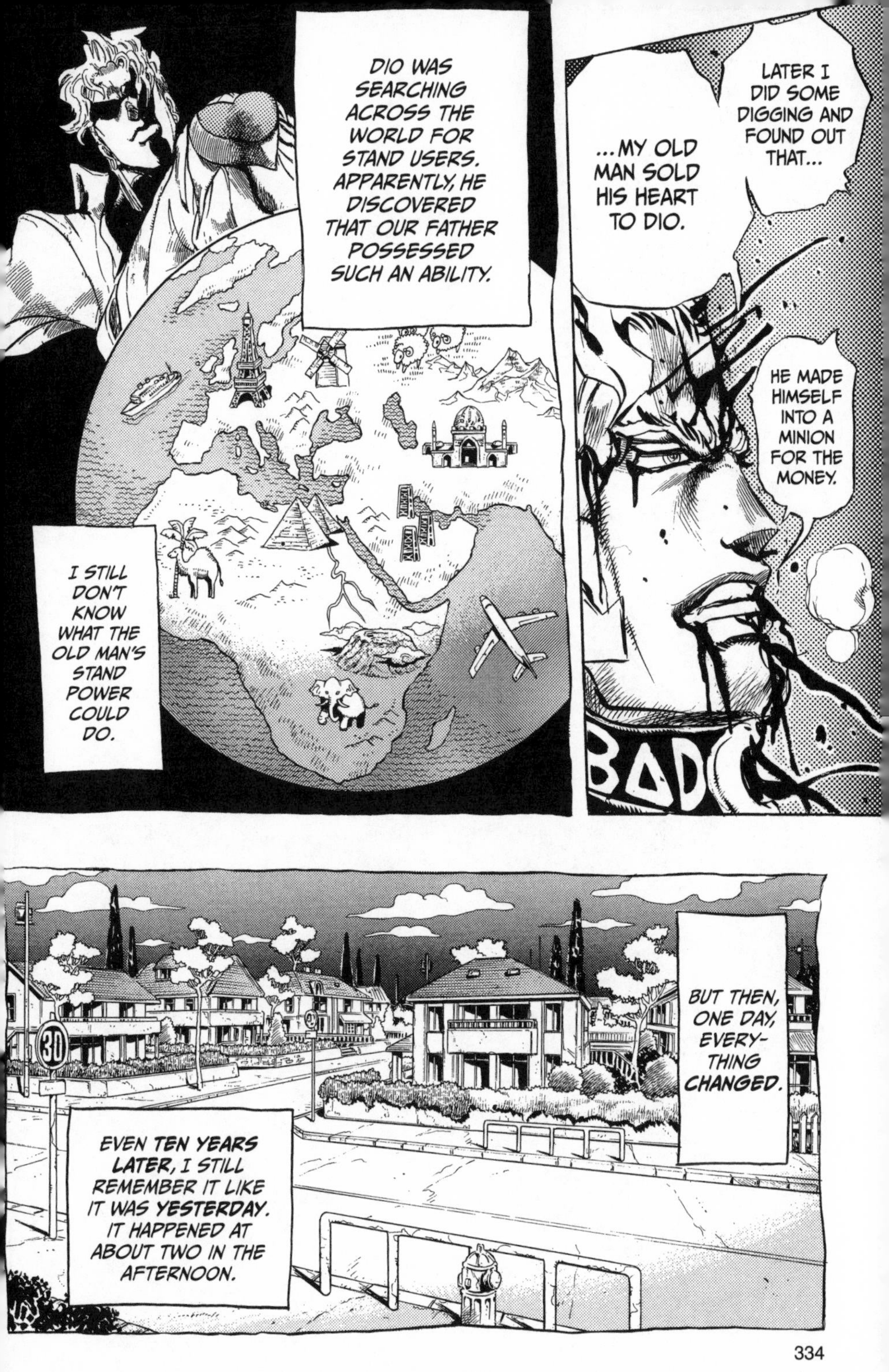
LATER I DID SOME DIGGING AND FOUND OUT THAT...
...MY OLD MAN SOLD HIS HEART TO DIO.
HE MADE HIMSELF INTO A MINION FOR THE MONEY.
BAD
DIO WAS SEARCHING ACROSS THE WORLD FOR STAND USERS. APPARENTLY, HE DISCOVERED THAT OUR FATHER POSSESSED SUCH AN ABILITY.
I STILL DON'T KNOW WHAT THE OLD MAN'S STAND POWER COULD DO.
BUT THEN, ONE DAY, EVERY-THING CHANGED.
30
EVEN TEN YEARS LATER, I STILL REMEMBER IT LIKE IT WAS YESTERDAY. IT HAPPENED AT ABOUT TWO IN THE AFTERNOON.

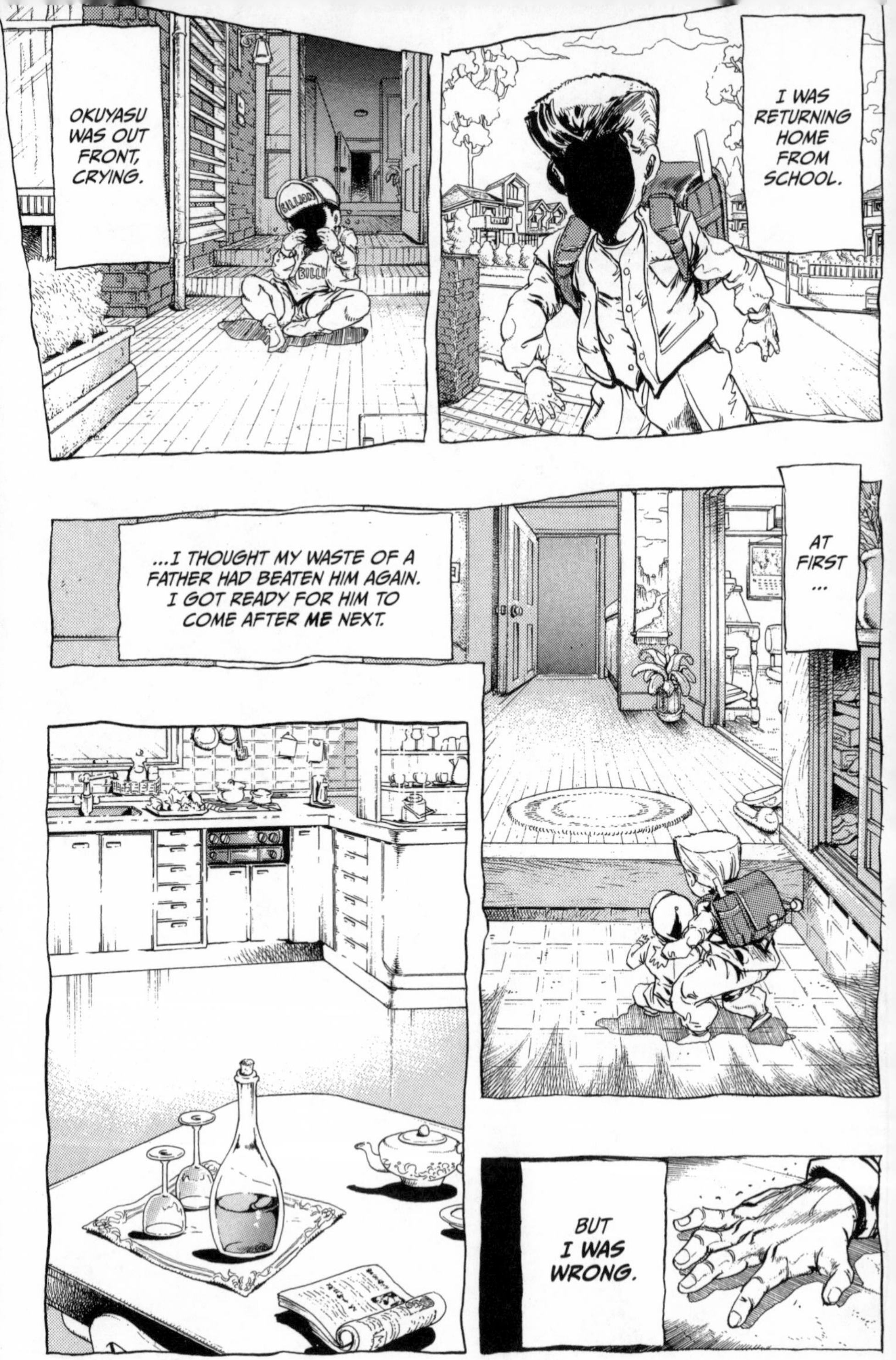
I WAS RETURNING HOME FROM SCHOOL.
OKUYASU WAS OUT FRONT, CRYING.
AT FIRST...
...I THOUGHT MY WASTE OF A FATHER HAD BEATEN HIM AGAIN. I GOT READY FOR HIM TO COME AFTER **ME** NEXT.
BUT I WAS WRONG.

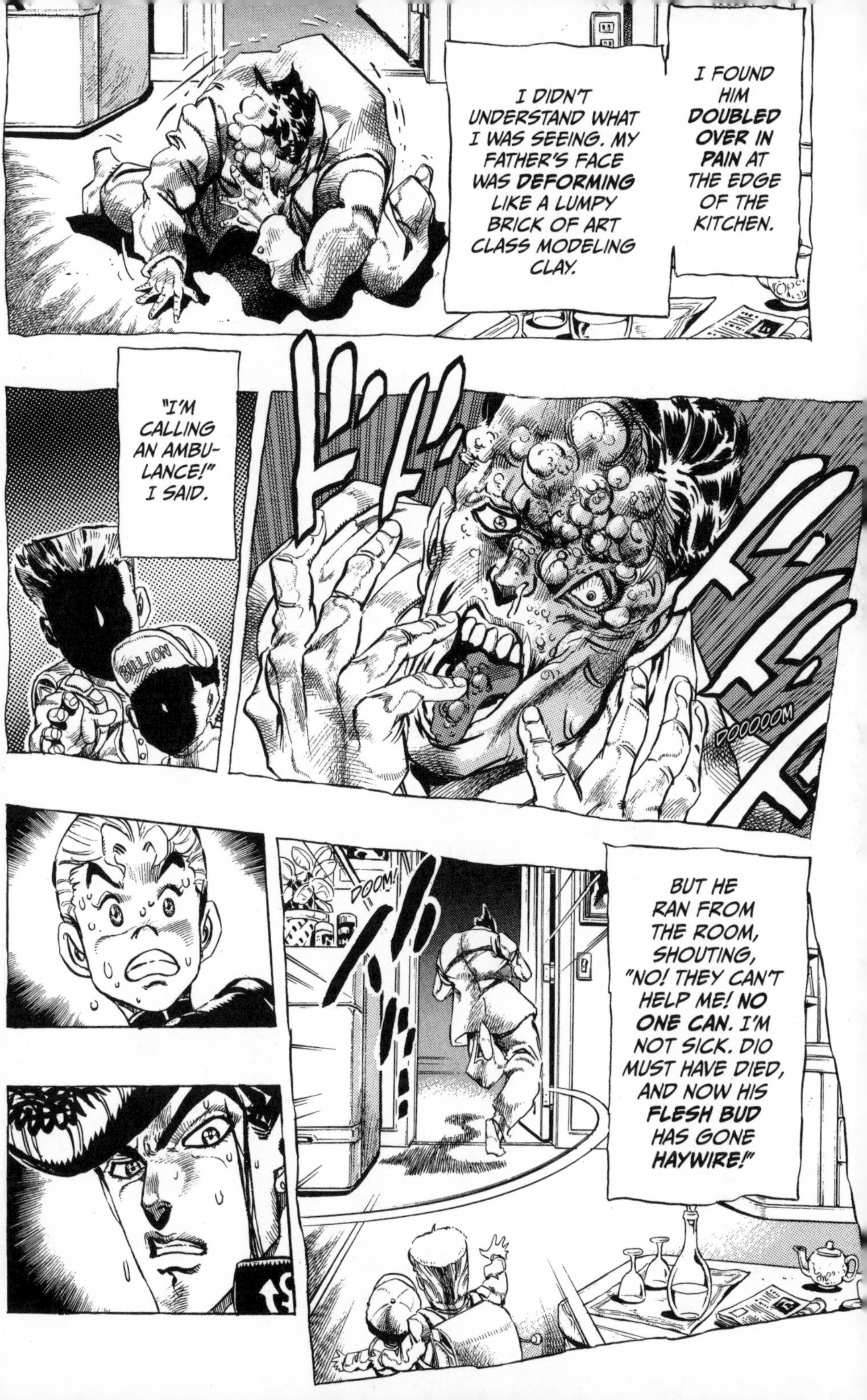

I FOUND HIM DOUBLED OVER IN PAIN AT THE EDGE OF THE KITCHEN.
I DIDN'T UNDERSTAND WHAT I WAS SEEING. MY FATHER'S FACE WAS DEFORMING LIKE A LUMPY BRICK OF ART CLASS MODELING CLAY.
DOOOOOM
"I'M CALLING AN AMBU-LANCE!" I SAID.
BILLION
BUT HE RAN FROM THE ROOM, SHOUTING, "NO! THEY CAN'T HELP ME! NO ONE CAN. I'M NOT SICK. DIO MUST HAVE DIED, AND NOW HIS FLESH BUD HAS GONE HAYWIRE!"
DOOM!

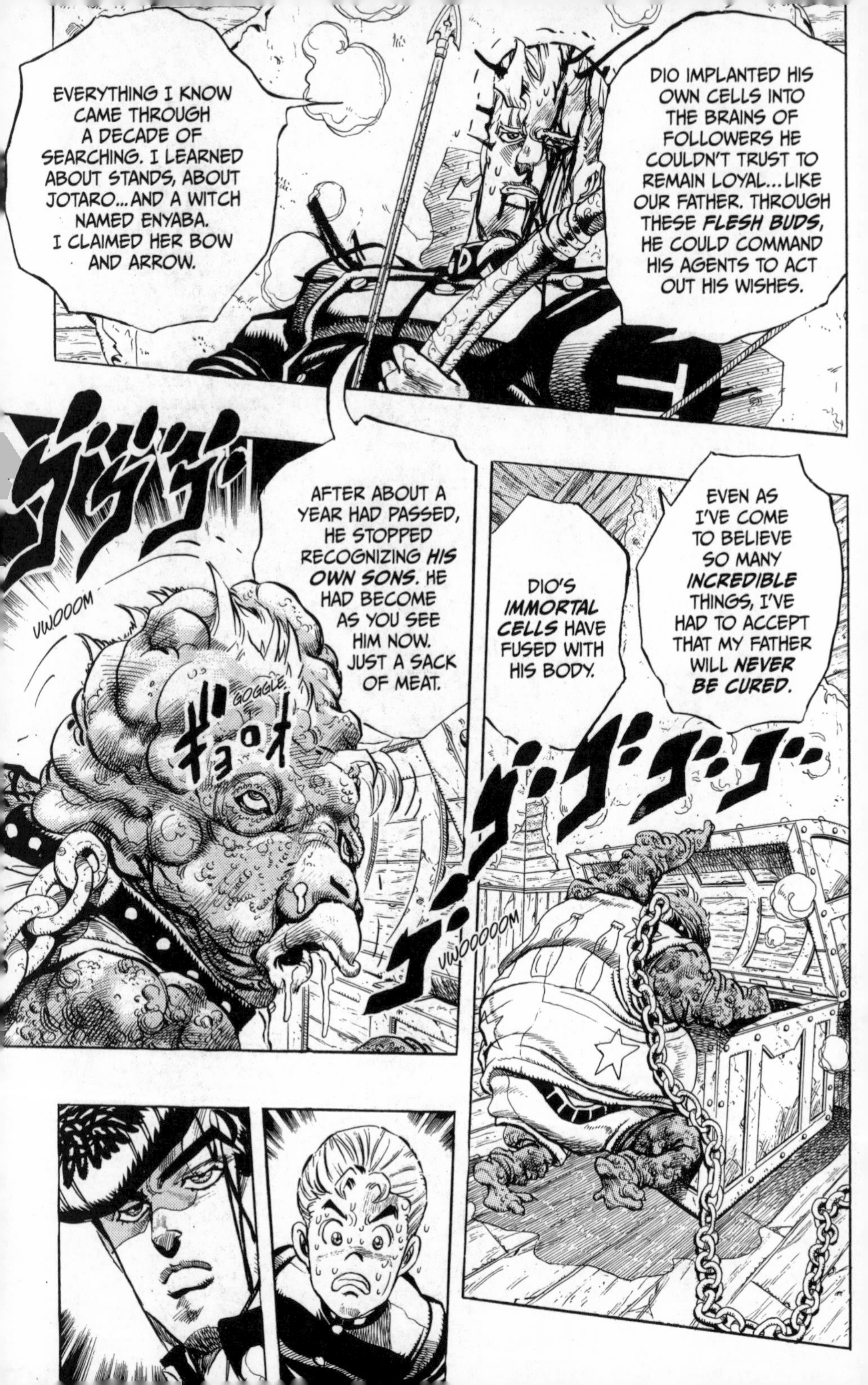
DIO IMPLANTED HIS OWN CELLS INTO THE BRAINS OF FOLLOWERS HE COULDN'T TRUST TO REMAIN LOYAL... LIKE OUR FATHER. THROUGH THESE *FLESH BUDS*, HE COULD COMMAND HIS AGENTS TO ACT OUT HIS WISHES.
EVERYTHING I KNOW CAME THROUGH A DECADE OF SEARCHING. I LEARNED ABOUT STANDS, ABOUT JOTARO... AND A WITCH NAMED ENYABA. I CLAIMED HER BOW AND ARROW.
EVEN AS I'VE COME TO BELIEVE SO MANY *INCREDIBLE* THINGS, I'VE HAD TO ACCEPT THAT MY FATHER WILL *NEVER BE CURED*.
DIO'S *IMMORTAL CELLS* HAVE FUSED WITH HIS BODY.
VWOOOOOM
AFTER ABOUT A YEAR HAD PASSED, HE STOPPED RECOGNIZING *HIS OWN SONS*. HE HAD BECOME AS YOU SEE HIM NOW. JUST A SACK OF MEAT.
VWOOOM
GOGGLE

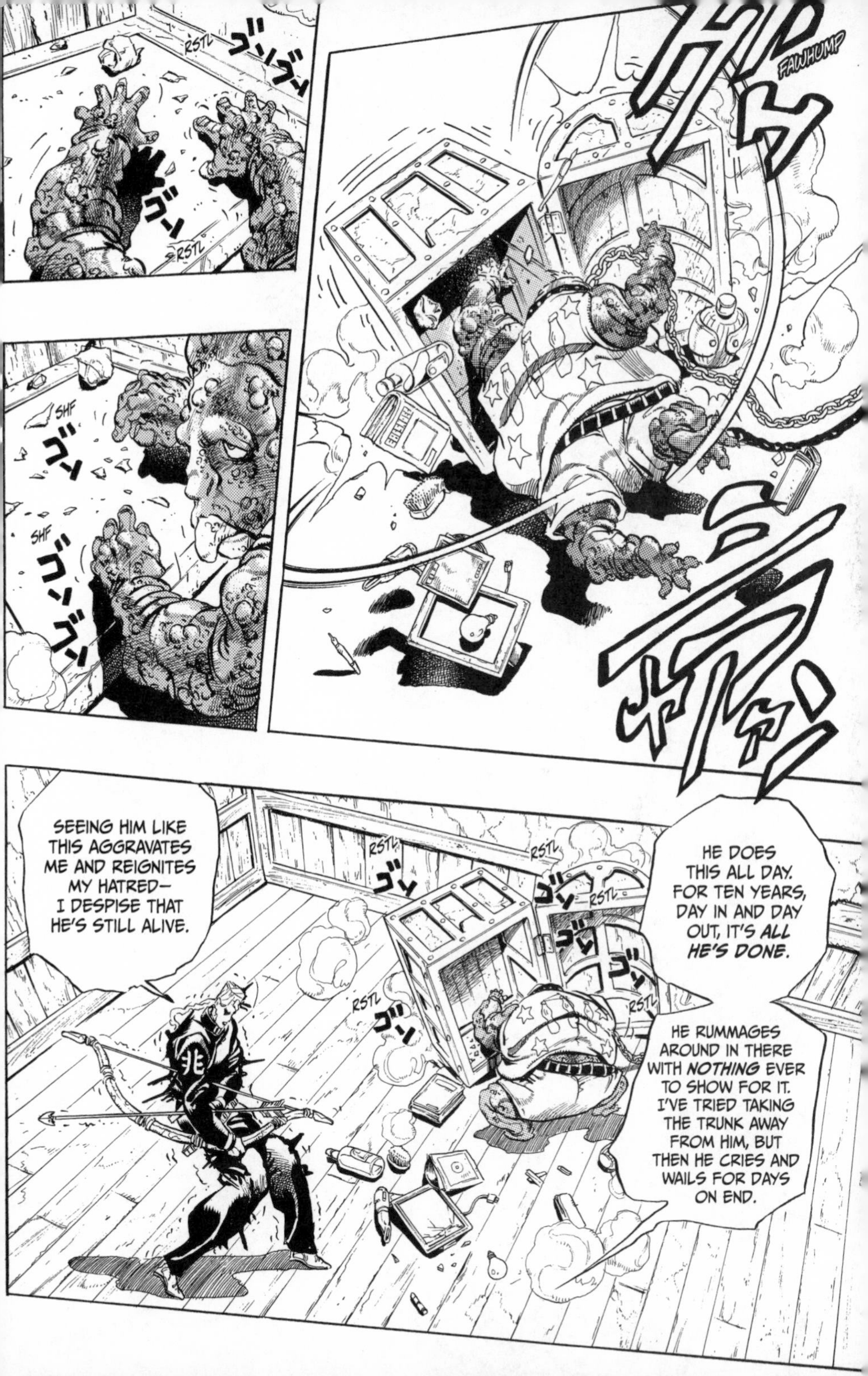
FAWHUMP
RSTL
RSTL
SHF
SHF
RSTL
RSTL
RSTL
RSTL
RSTL
HE DOES THIS ALL DAY. FOR TEN YEARS, DAY IN AND DAY OUT, IT'S *ALL HE'S DONE.*
HE RUMMAGES AROUND IN THERE WITH *NOTHING* EVER TO SHOW FOR IT. I'VE TRIED TAKING THE TRUNK AWAY FROM HIM, BUT THEN HE CRIES AND WAILS FOR DAYS ON END.
SEEING HIM LIKE THIS AGGRAVATES ME AND REIGNITES MY HATRED— I DESPISE THAT HE'S STILL ALIVE.

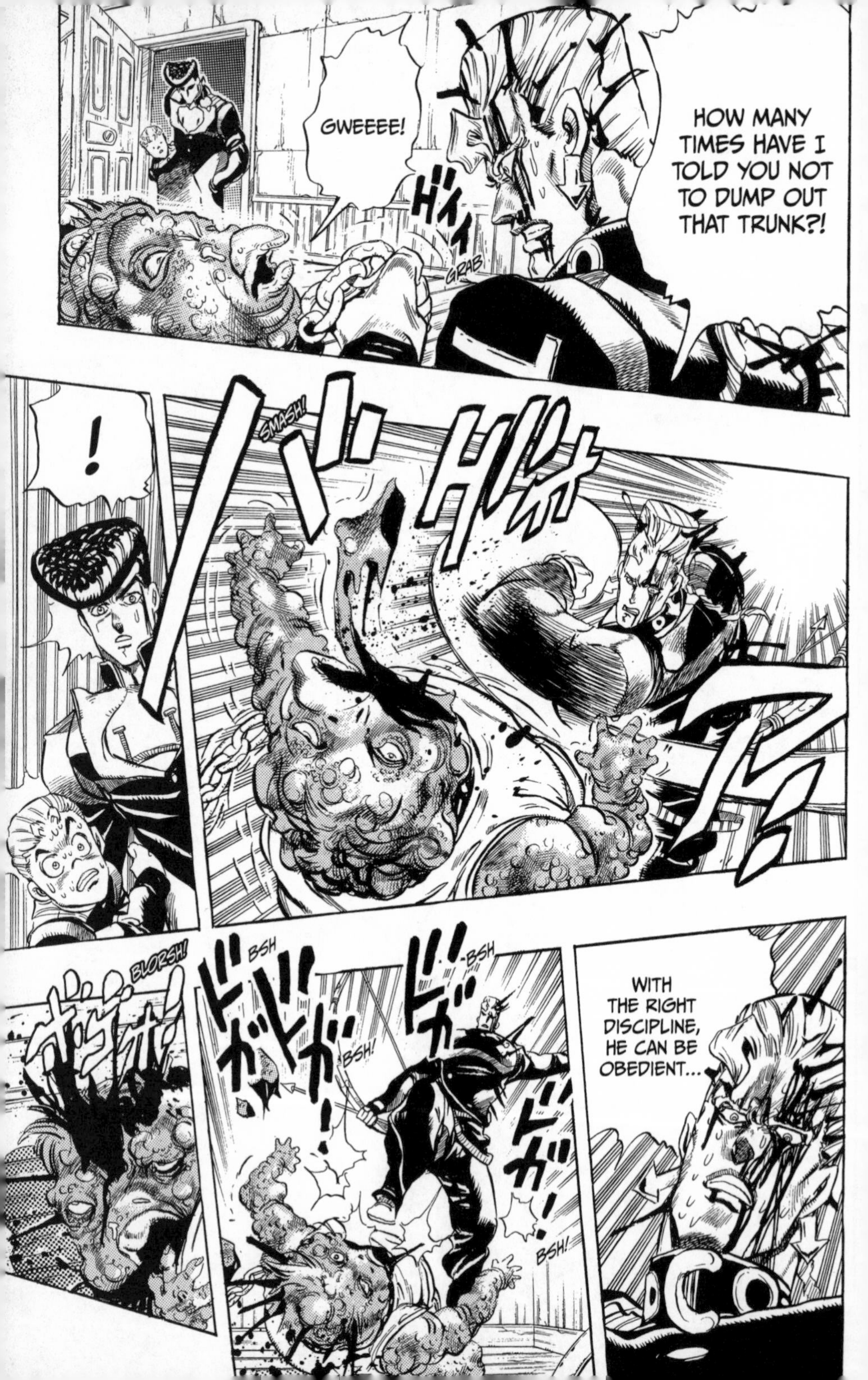
HOW MANY TIMES HAVE I TOLD YOU NOT TO DUMP OUT THAT TRUNK?!
GWEEEE!
GRAB
SMASH!
!
WITH THE RIGHT DISCIPLINE, HE CAN BE OBEDIENT...
BSH
BSH
BSH!
BSH!
BLORSH!

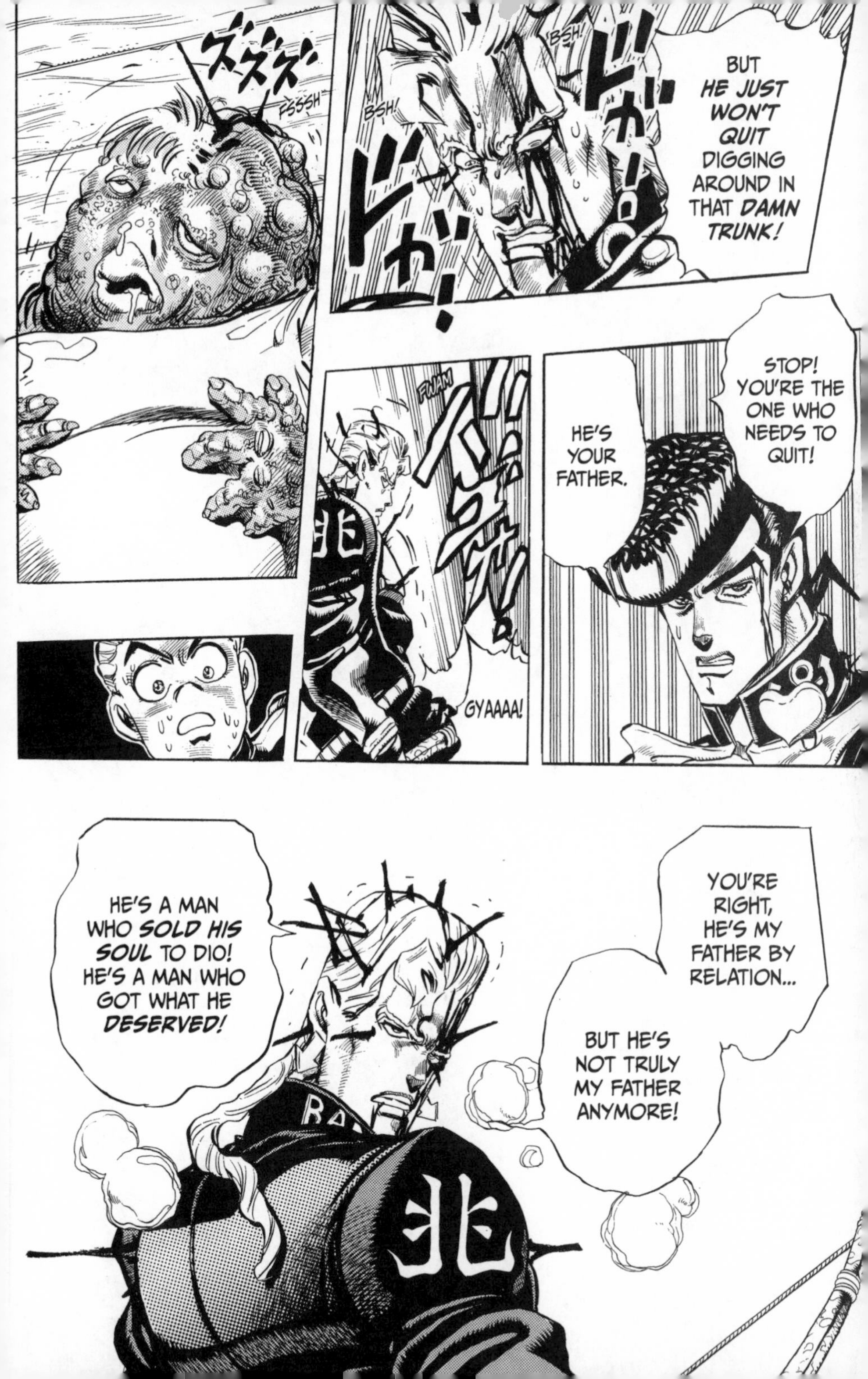
BSH!
BSH!
BUT HE JUST WON'T QUIT DIGGING AROUND IN THAT DAMN TRUNK!
FSSSH
STOP! YOU'RE THE ONE WHO NEEDS TO QUIT!
HE'S YOUR FATHER.
FWAM
GYAAAA!
YOU'RE RIGHT, HE'S MY FATHER BY RELATION...
BUT HE'S NOT TRULY MY FATHER ANYMORE!
HE'S A MAN WHO SOLD HIS SOUL TO DIO! HE'S A MAN WHO GOT WHAT HE DESERVED!

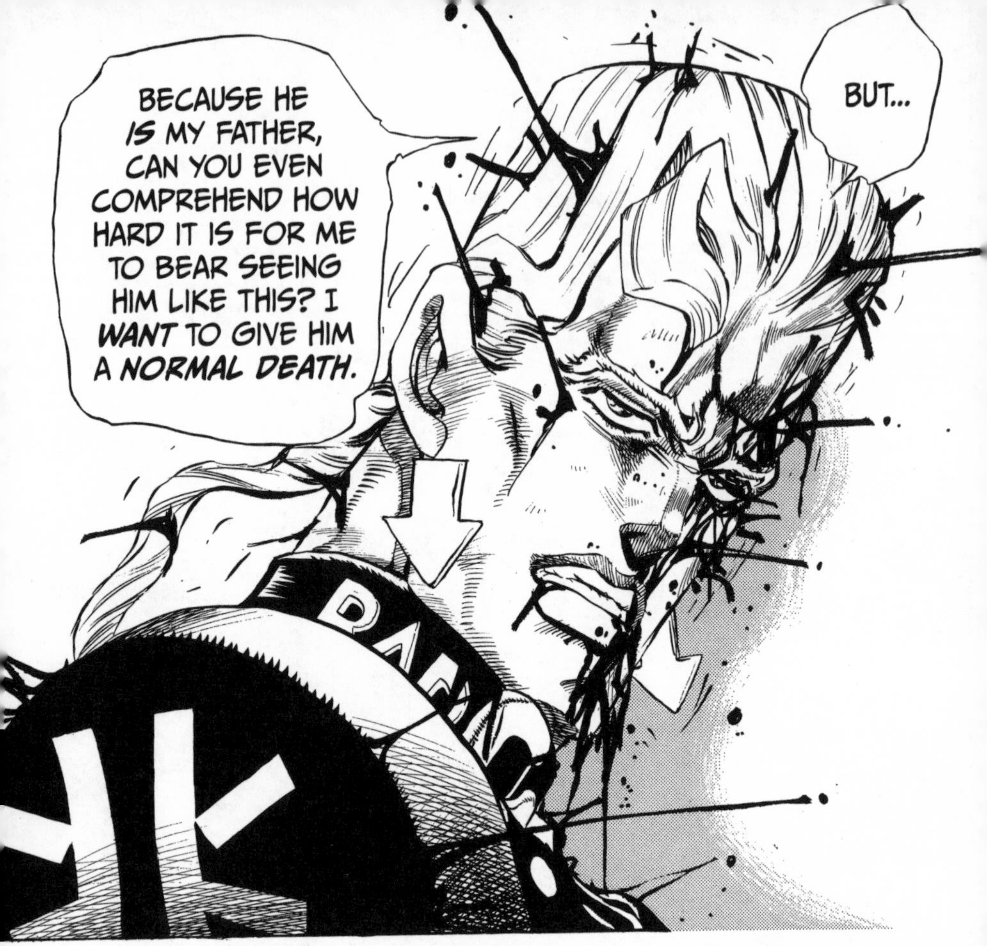
BECAUSE HE *IS* MY FATHER, CAN YOU EVEN COMPREHEND HOW HARD IT IS FOR ME TO BEAR SEEING HIM LIKE THIS? I *WANT* TO GIVE HIM A *NORMAL DEATH*.
BUT...
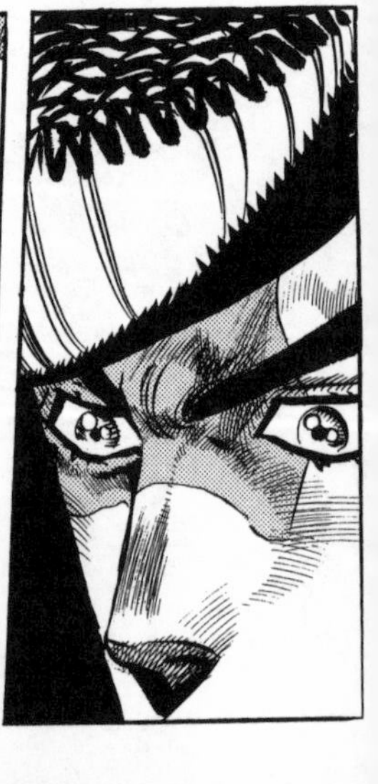
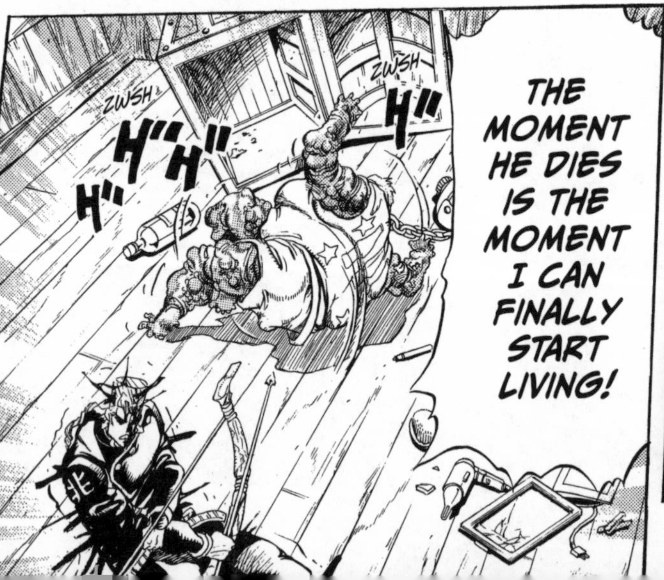
THE MOMENT HE DIES IS THE MOMENT I CAN FINALLY START LIVING!
ZWSH
H''
ZWSH
H''
H''
H''

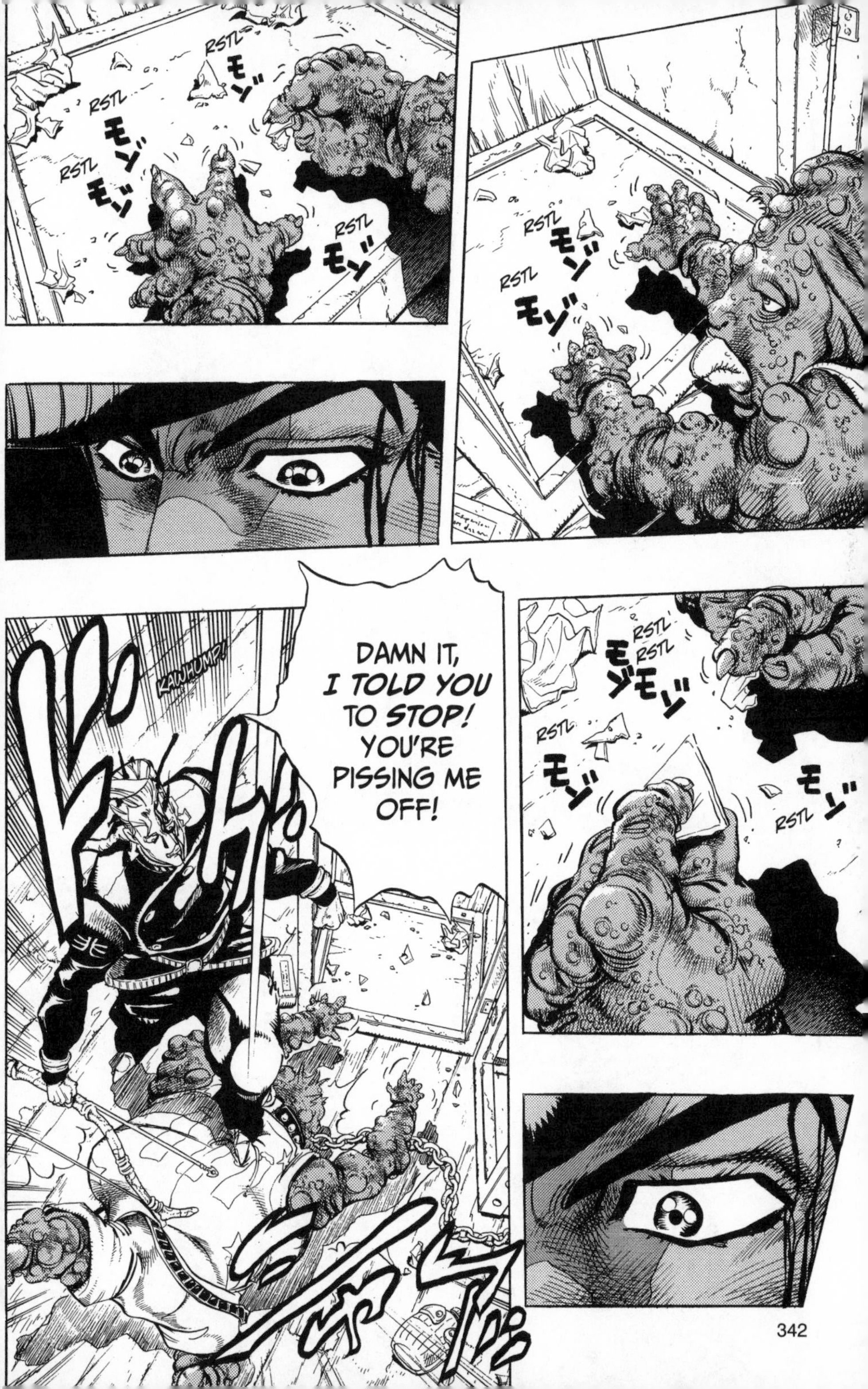
RSTL
モゾ
RSTL
モゾ
RSTL
モゾ
RSTL
モゾ
RSTL
モゾ
RSTL
モゾ
RSTL RSTL
モゾモゾ
RSTL
モゾ
モゾ
RSTL
KAWHUMP!
DAMN IT, I TOLD YOU TO STOP! YOU'RE PISSING ME OFF!

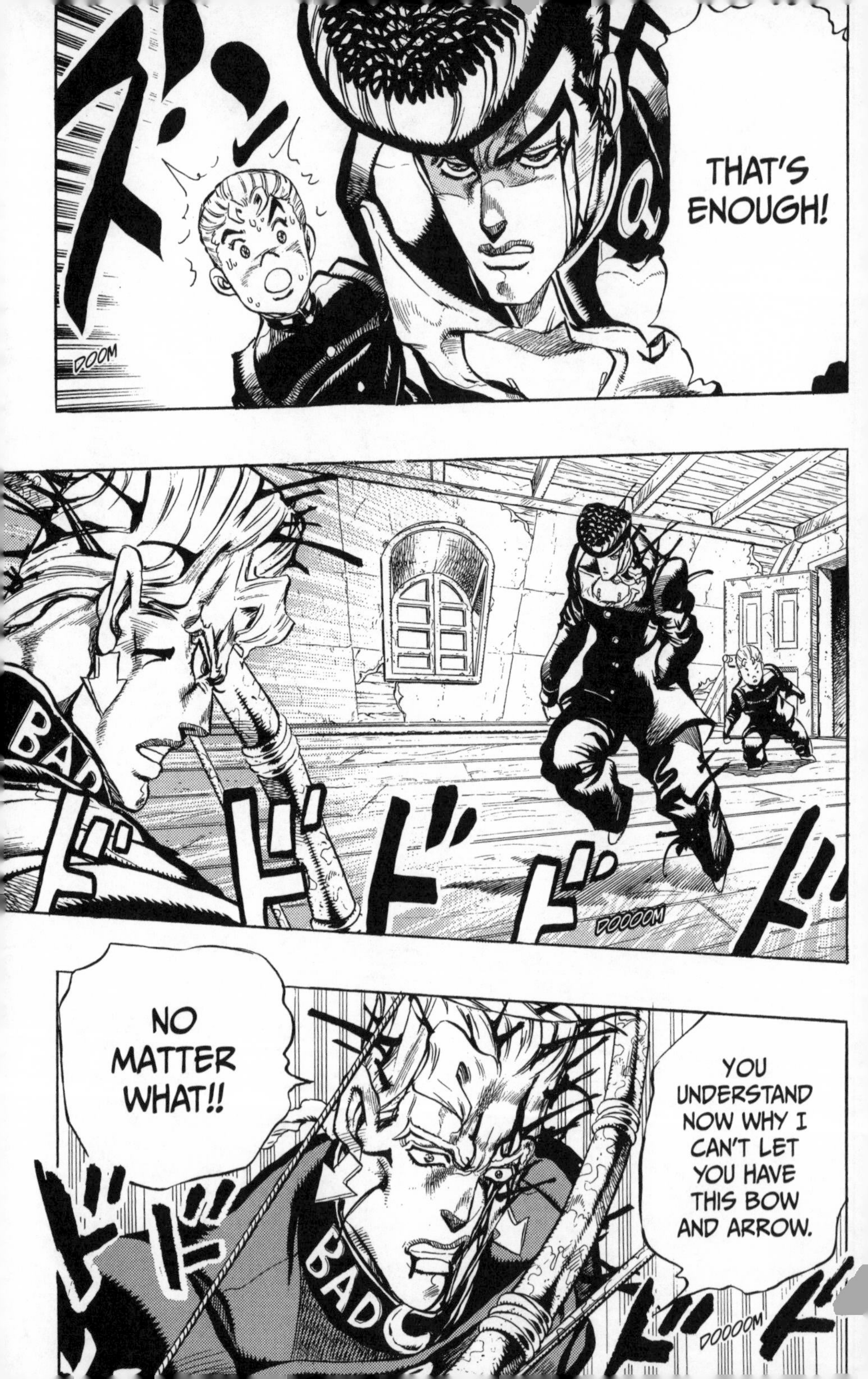
THAT'S ENOUGH!
DOOM
DOOOOM
YOU UNDERSTAND NOW WHY I CAN'T LET YOU HAVE THIS BOW AND ARROW.
NO MATTER WHAT!!
DOOOOM

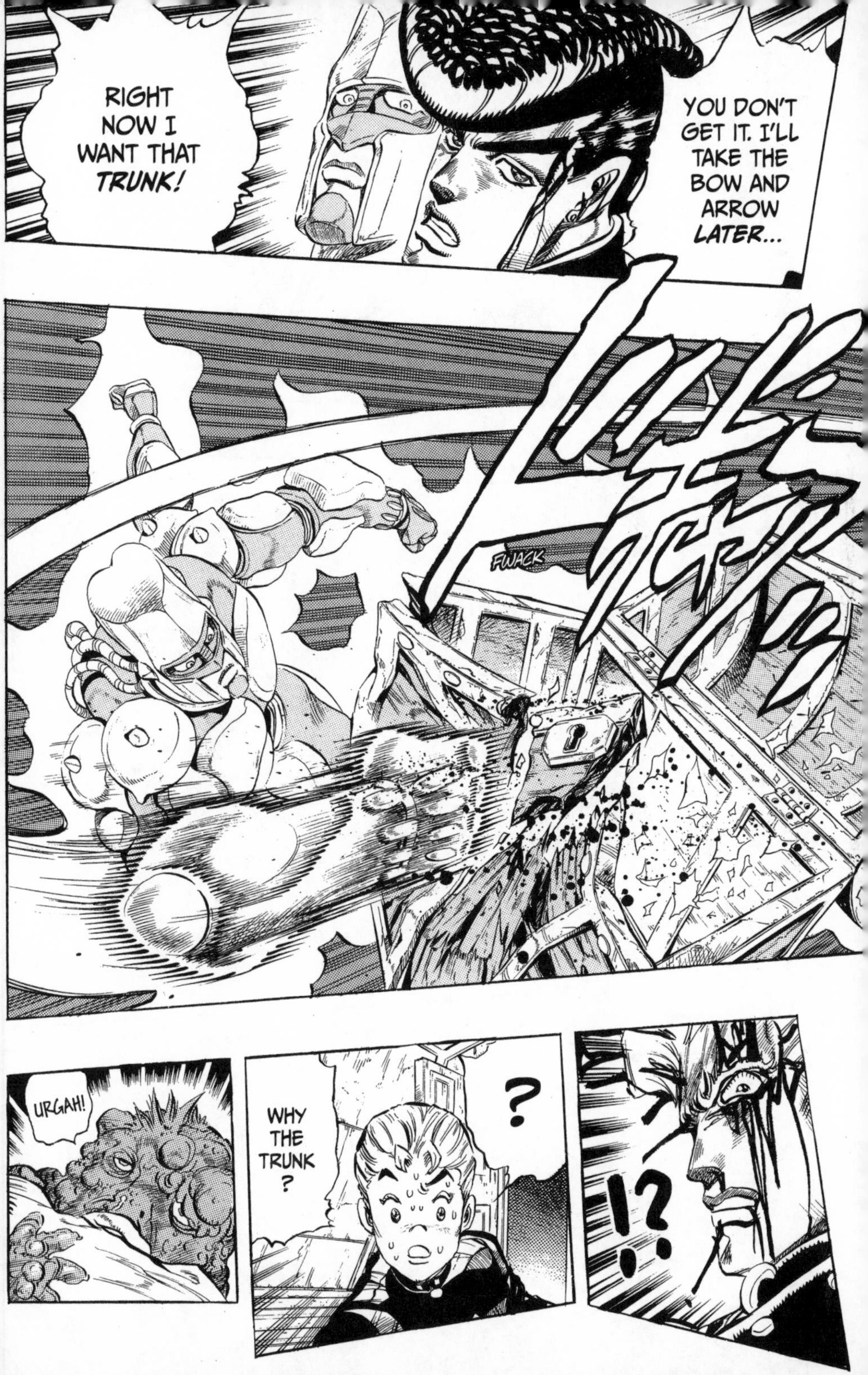
YOU DON'T GET IT. I'LL TAKE THE BOW AND ARROW LATER...
RIGHT NOW I WANT THAT TRUNK!
FWACK
!?
?
WHY THE TRUNK?
URGAH!

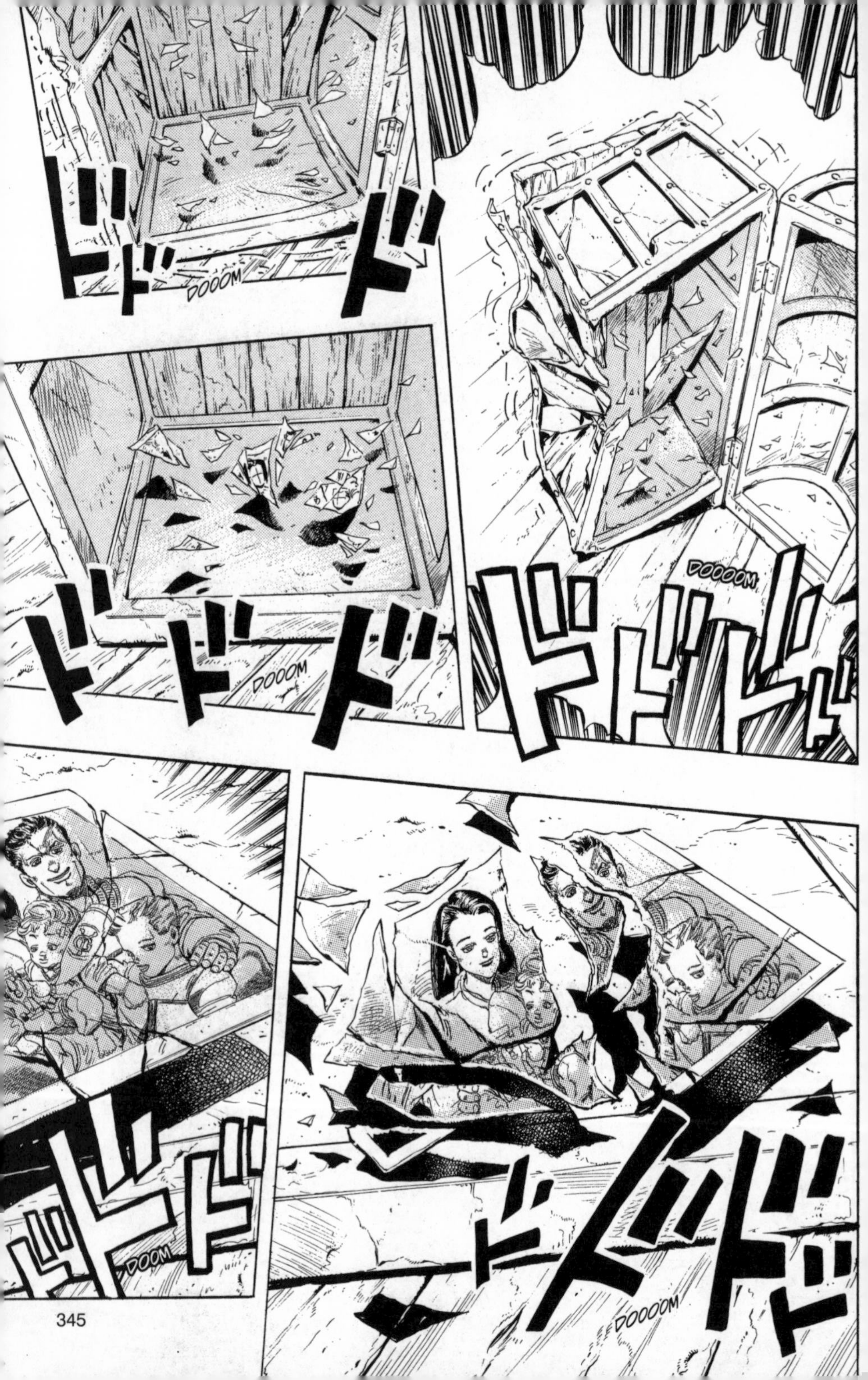
DOOOOM
DOOOM
DOOOM
DOOOOM
DOOM

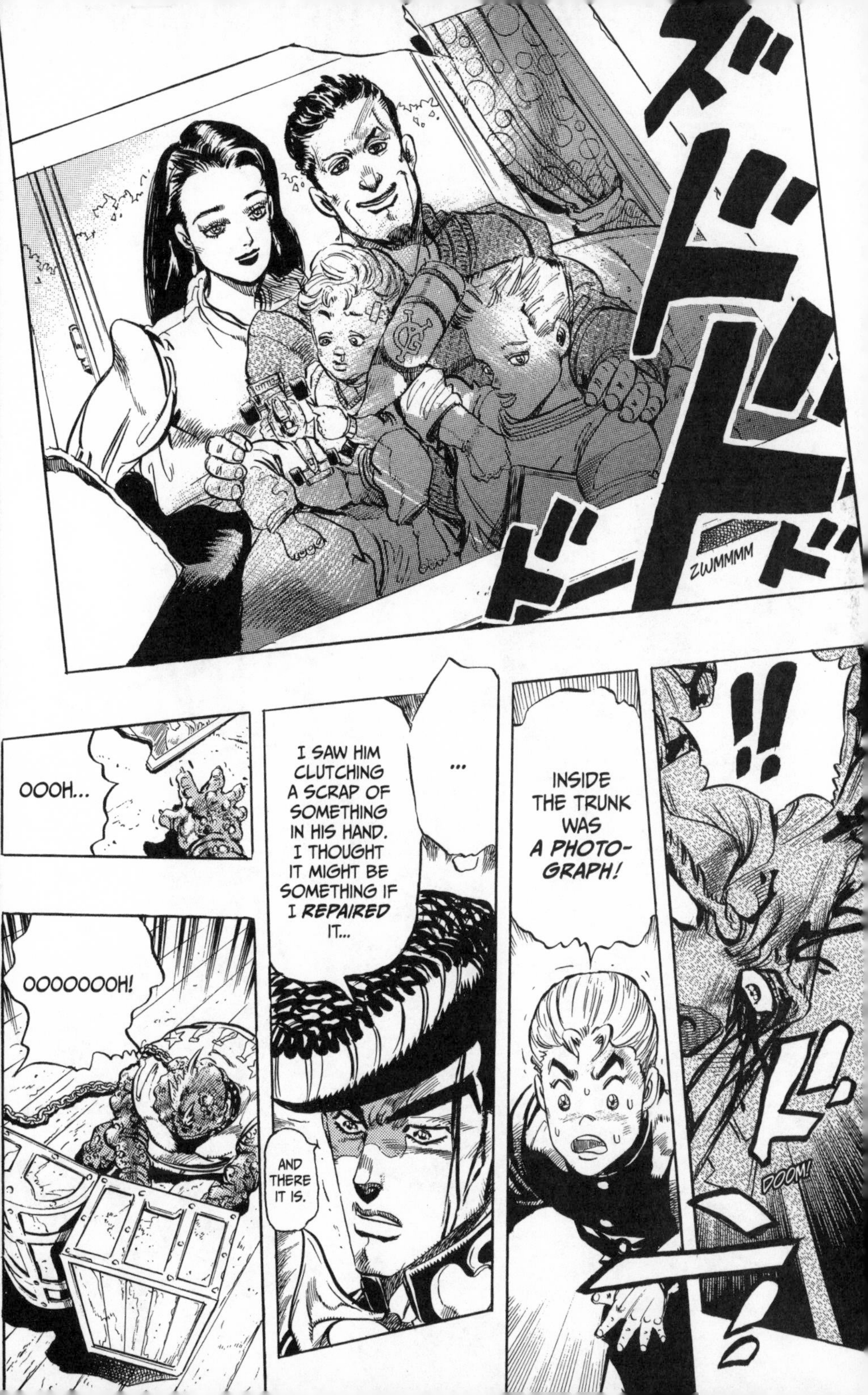
ZWMMMM
!!
DOOM!
INSIDE THE TRUNK WAS *A PHOTOGRAPH!*
...
I SAW HIM CLUTCHING A SCRAP OF SOMETHING IN HIS HAND. I THOUGHT IT MIGHT BE SOMETHING IF I *REPAIRED* IT...
AND THERE IT IS.
OOOH...
OOOOOOOH!

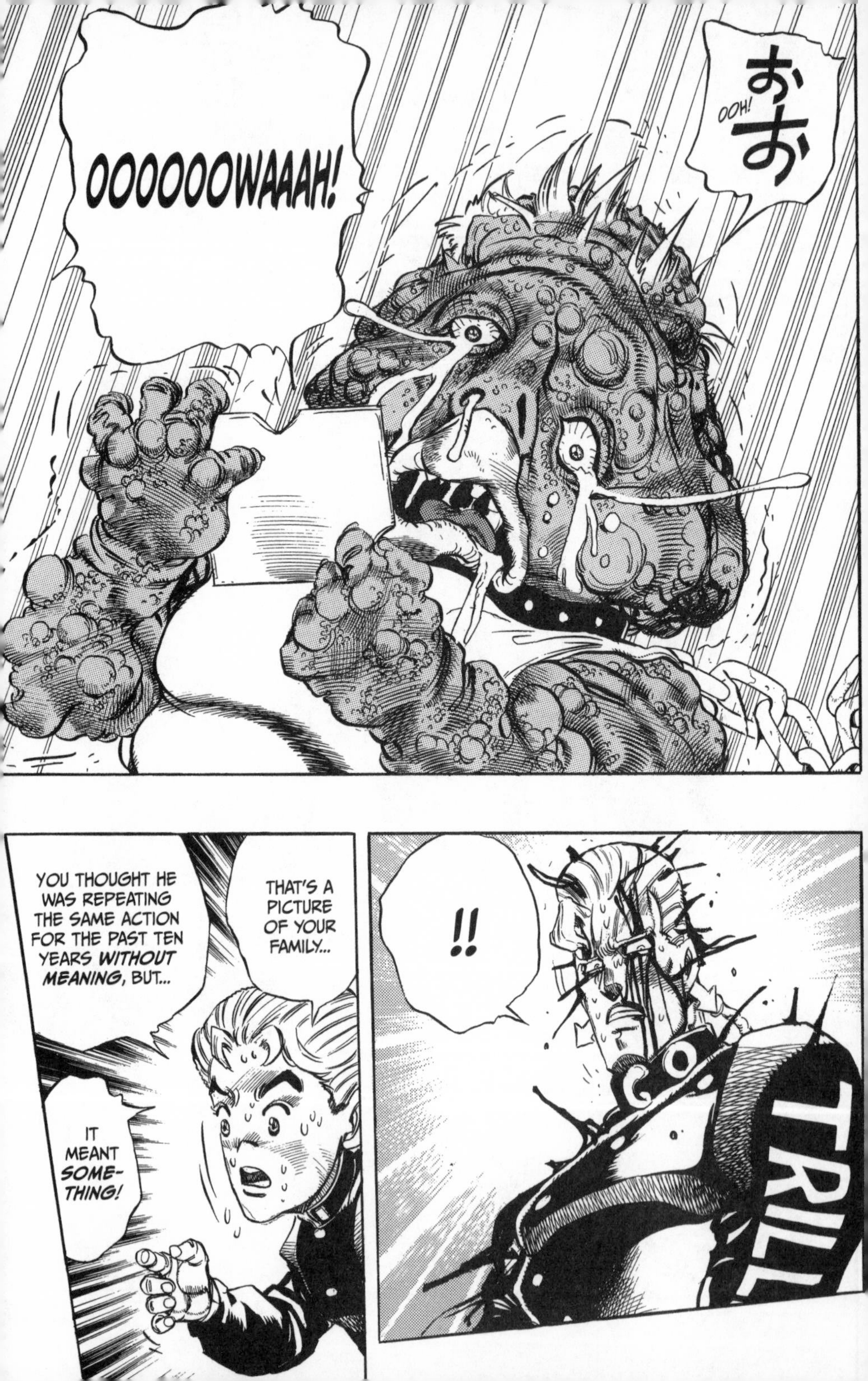
おお
OOH!
OOOOOOWAAAH!
!!
TRILL
THAT'S A PICTURE OF YOUR FAMILY...
YOU THOUGHT HE WAS REPEATING THE SAME ACTION FOR THE PAST TEN YEARS *WITHOUT MEANING*, BUT...
IT MEANT *SOME-THING!*

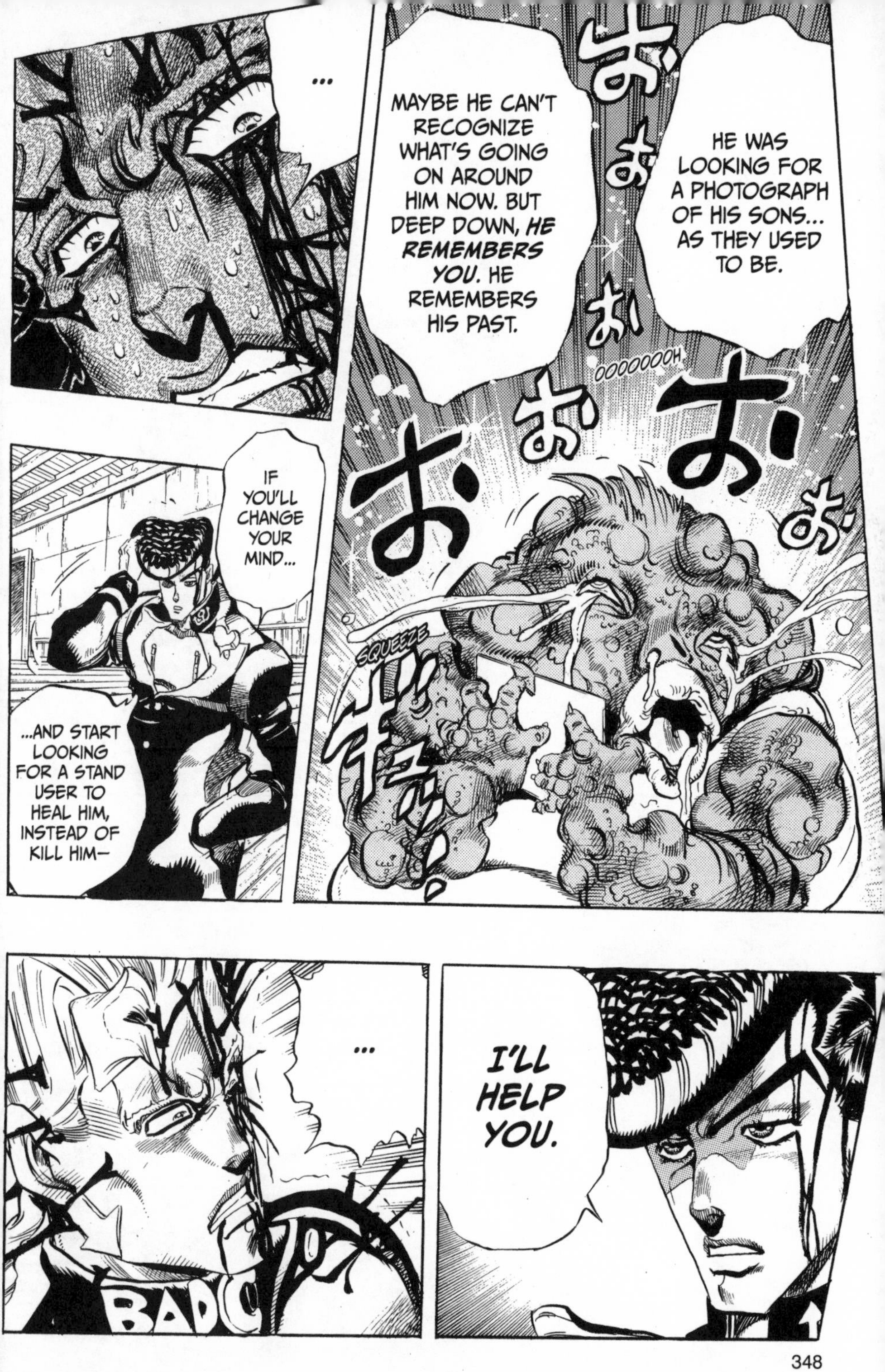
HE WAS LOOKING FOR A PHOTOGRAPH OF HIS SONS... AS THEY USED TO BE.
MAYBE HE CAN'T RECOGNIZE WHAT'S GOING ON AROUND HIM NOW. BUT DEEP DOWN, *HE REMEMBERS YOU*. HE REMEMBERS HIS PAST.
OOOOOOOOH
SQUEEZE
...
IF YOU'LL CHANGE YOUR MIND...
...AND START LOOKING FOR A STAND USER TO HEAL HIM, INSTEAD OF KILL HIM—
I'LL HELP YOU.
...
BAD

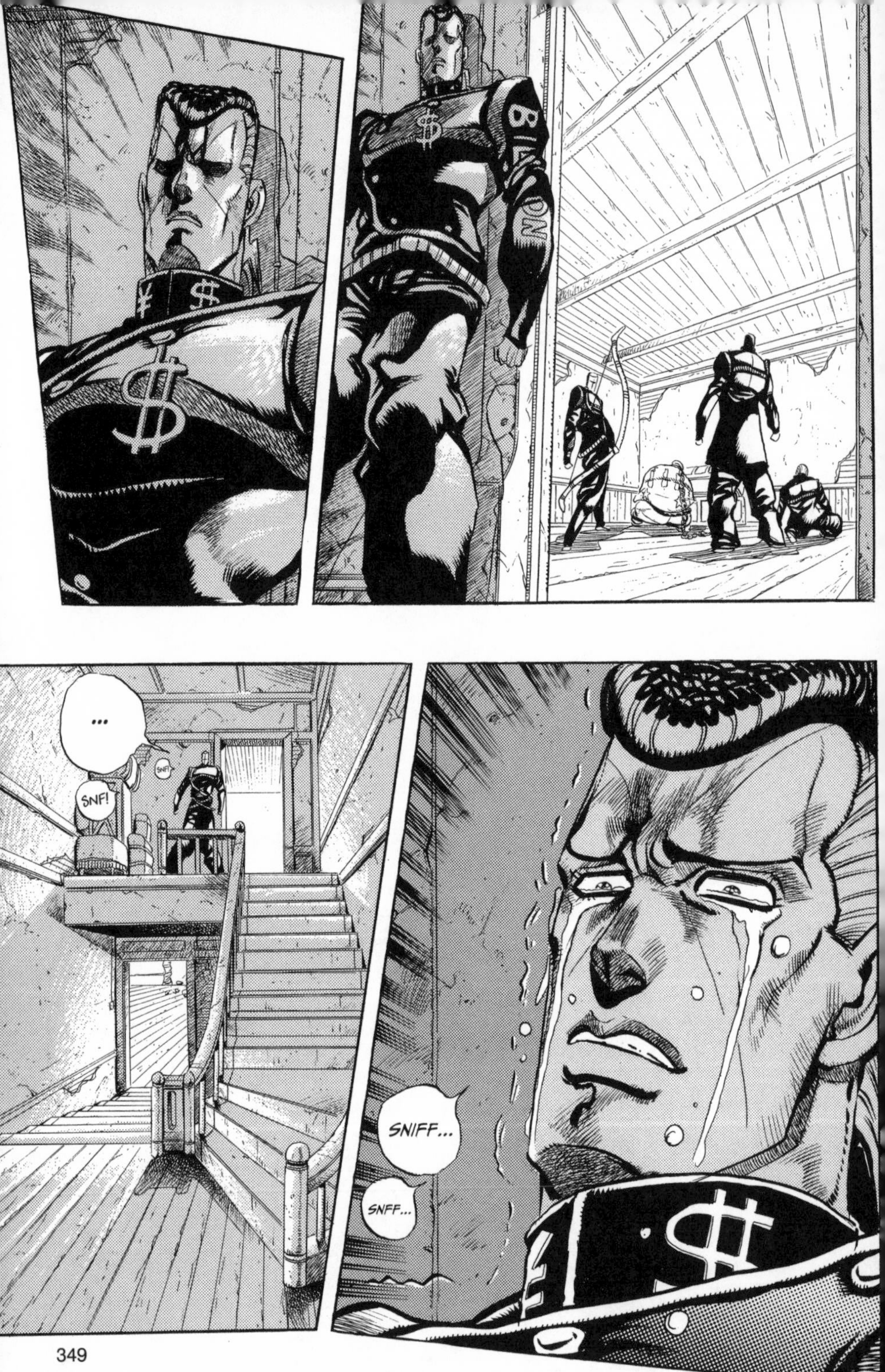
SNIFF...
SNFF...
...
SNF
SNF!

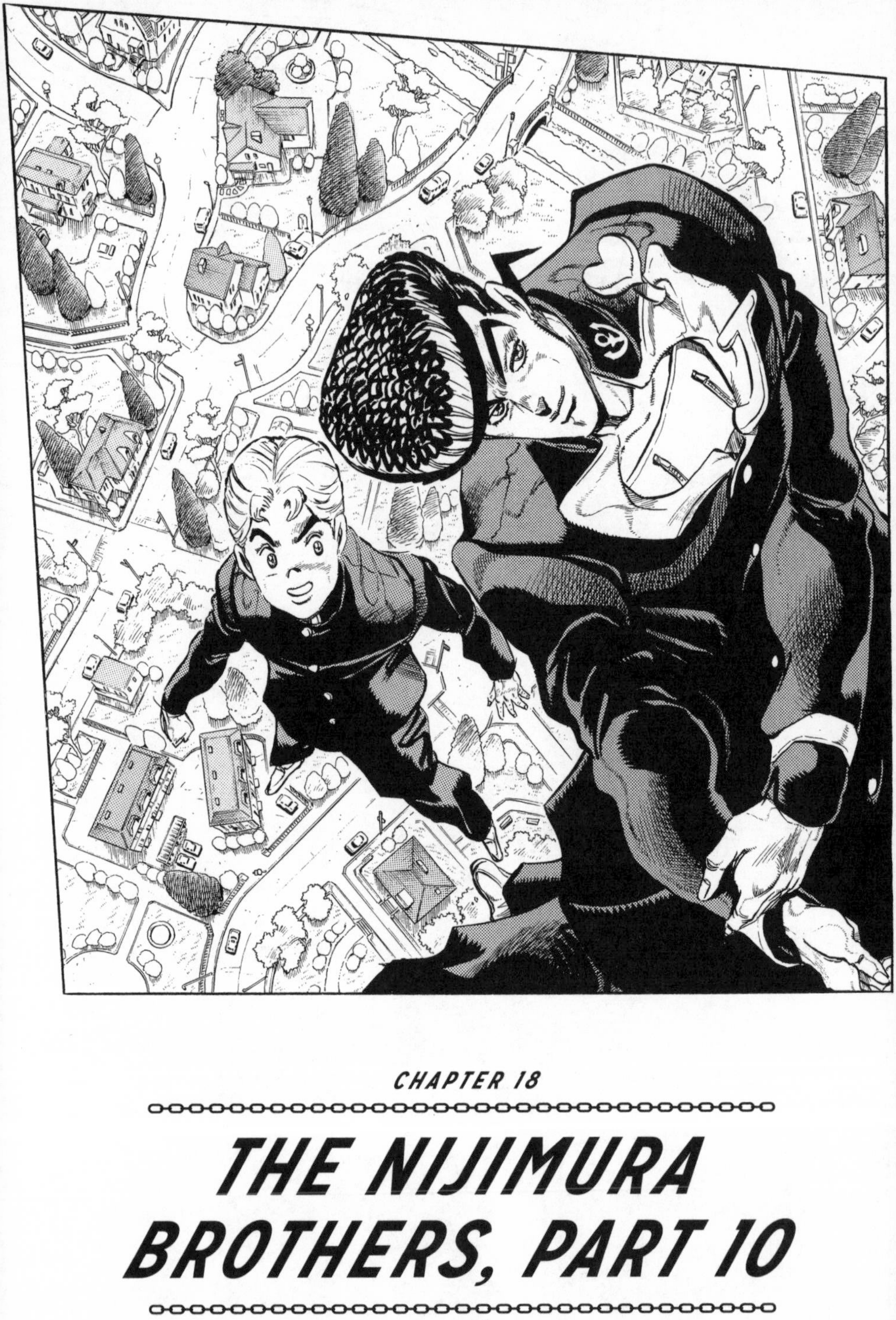

CHAPTER 18

THE NIJIMURA BROTHERS, PART 10

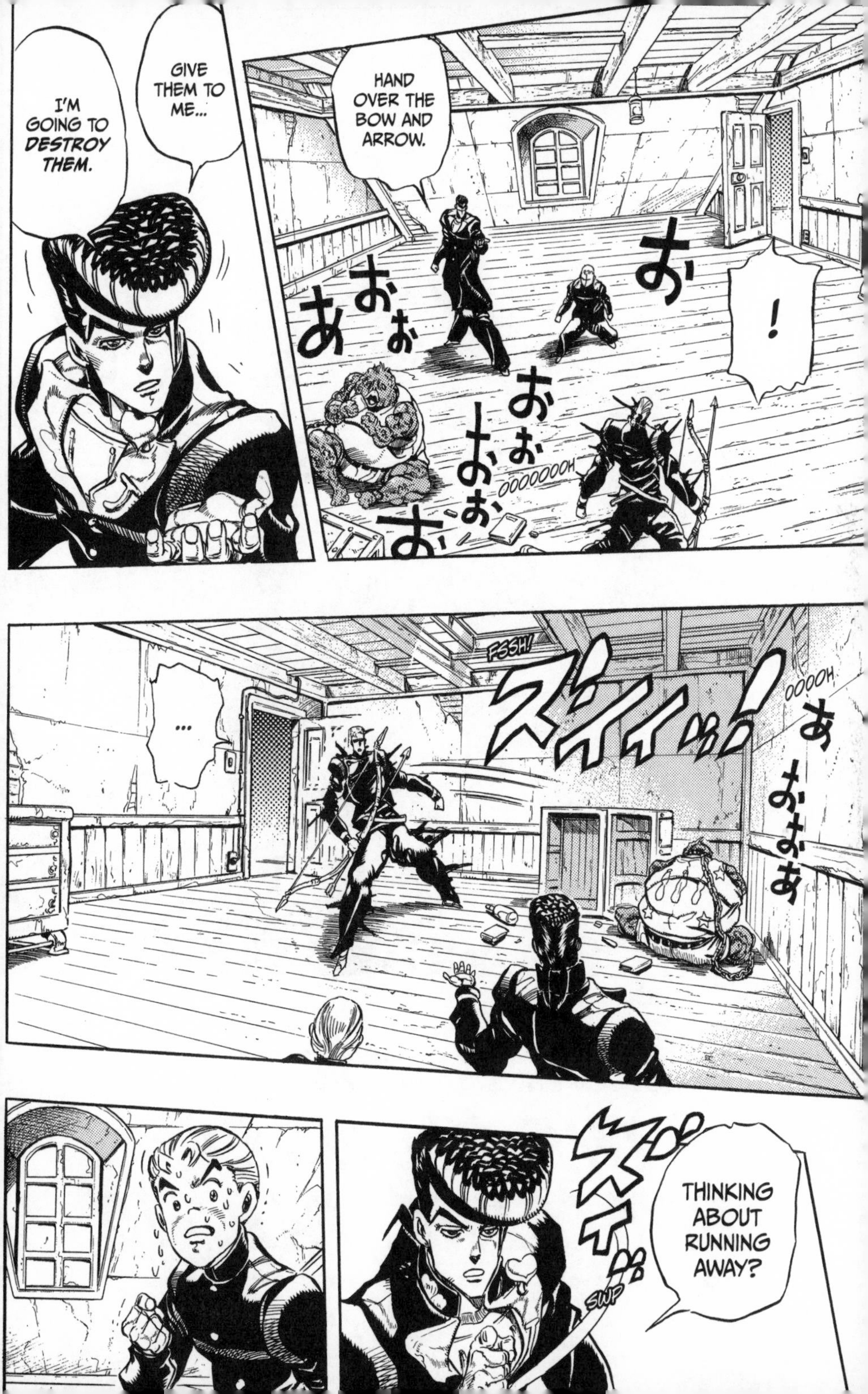
HAND OVER THE BOW AND ARROW.
!
お
あおぉ
おぉ
おぉ
お
OOOOOOOH
GIVE THEM TO ME...
I'M GOING TO DESTROY THEM.
FSSH!
スイィッ!
OOOOH
あおおあ
...
スッ
SWP
THINKING ABOUT RUNNING AWAY?

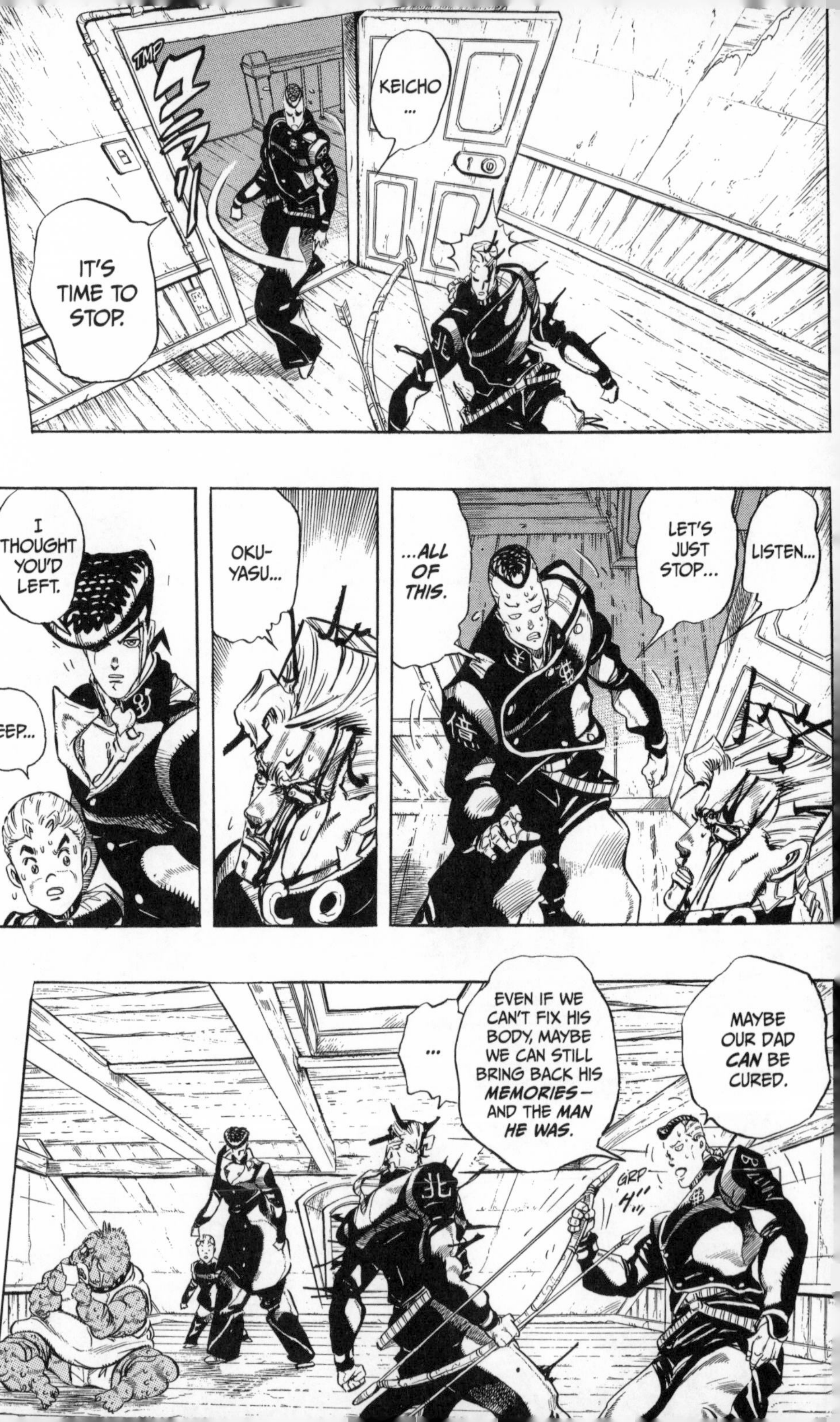
KEICHO ...
TMP
IT'S TIME TO STOP.
LISTEN...
LET'S JUST STOP...
...ALL OF THIS.
OKU-YASU...
I THOUGHT YOU'D LEFT.
EEP...
MAYBE OUR DAD CAN BE CURED.
GRP
EVEN IF WE CAN'T FIX HIS BODY, MAYBE WE CAN STILL BRING BACK HIS MEMORIES— AND THE MAN HE WAS.
...

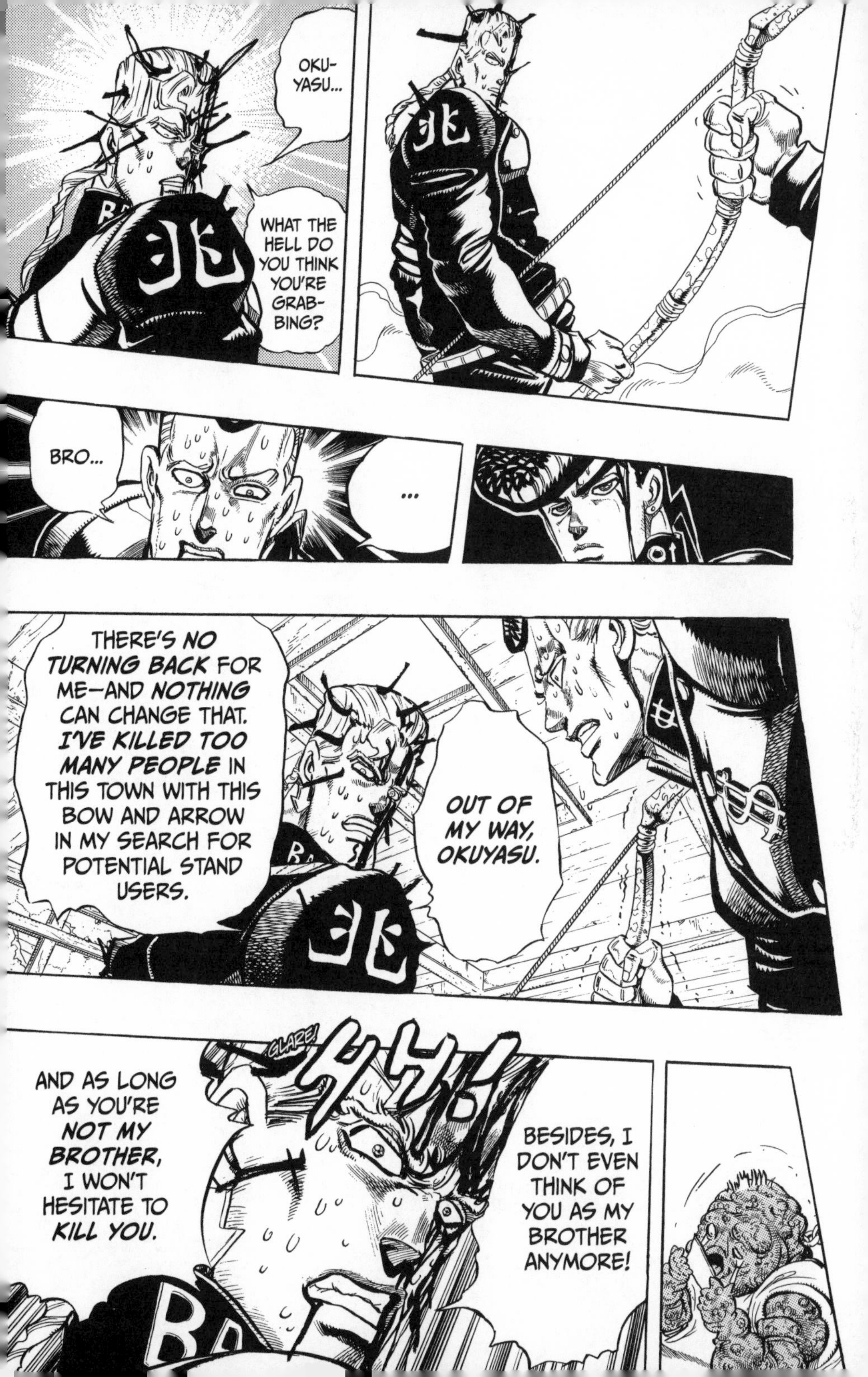
OKU-YASU...
WHAT THE HELL DO YOU THINK YOU'RE GRAB-BING?
...
BRO...
OUT OF MY WAY, OKUYASU.
THERE'S NO TURNING BACK FOR ME—AND NOTHING CAN CHANGE THAT. I'VE KILLED TOO MANY PEOPLE IN THIS TOWN WITH THIS BOW AND ARROW IN MY SEARCH FOR POTENTIAL STAND USERS.
GLARE!
AND AS LONG AS YOU'RE NOT MY BROTHER, I WON'T HESITATE TO KILL YOU.
BESIDES, I DON'T EVEN THINK OF YOU AS MY BROTHER ANYMORE!

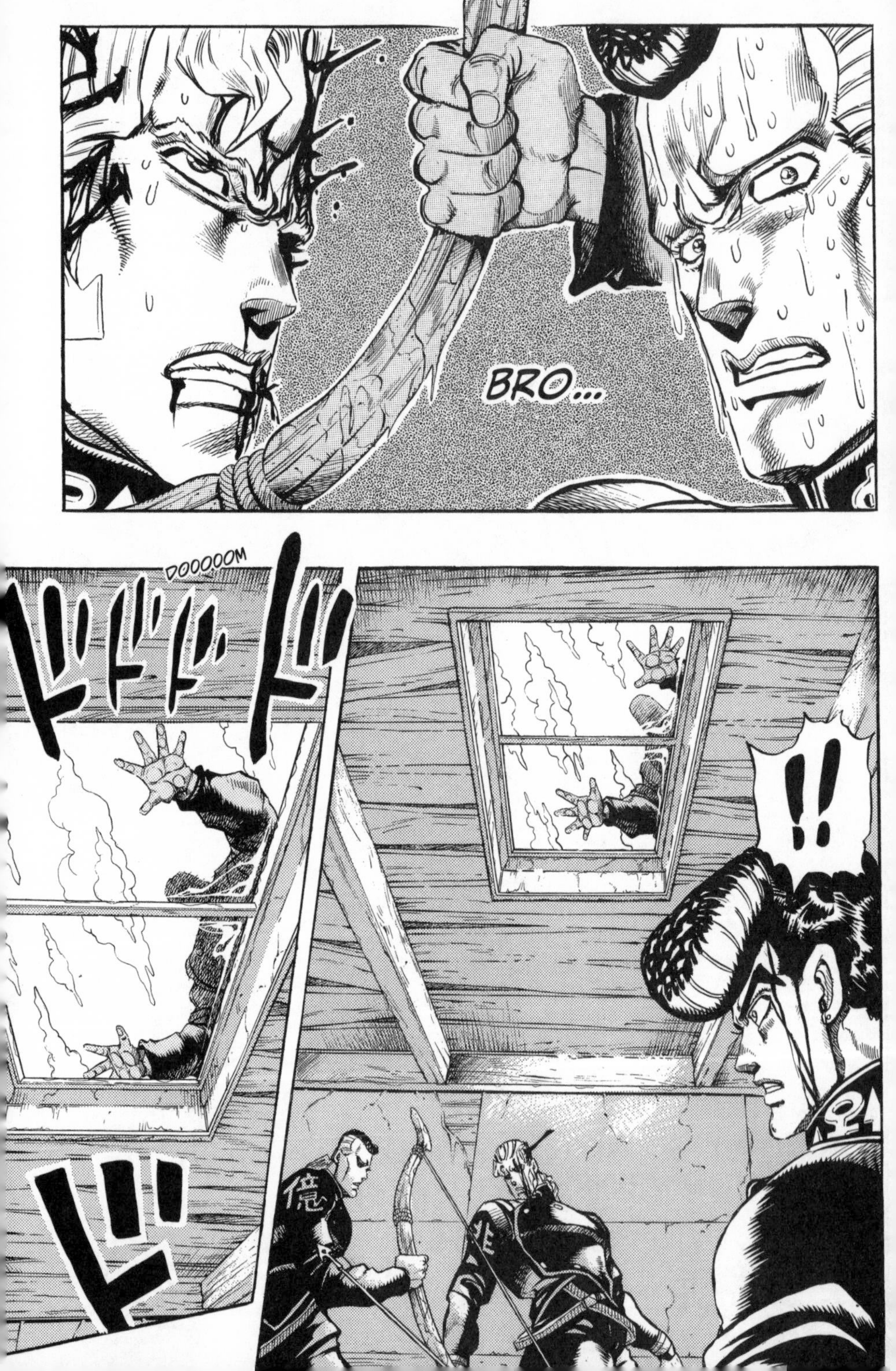
BRO...
!!
DOOOOOM
ドドドドド
ド

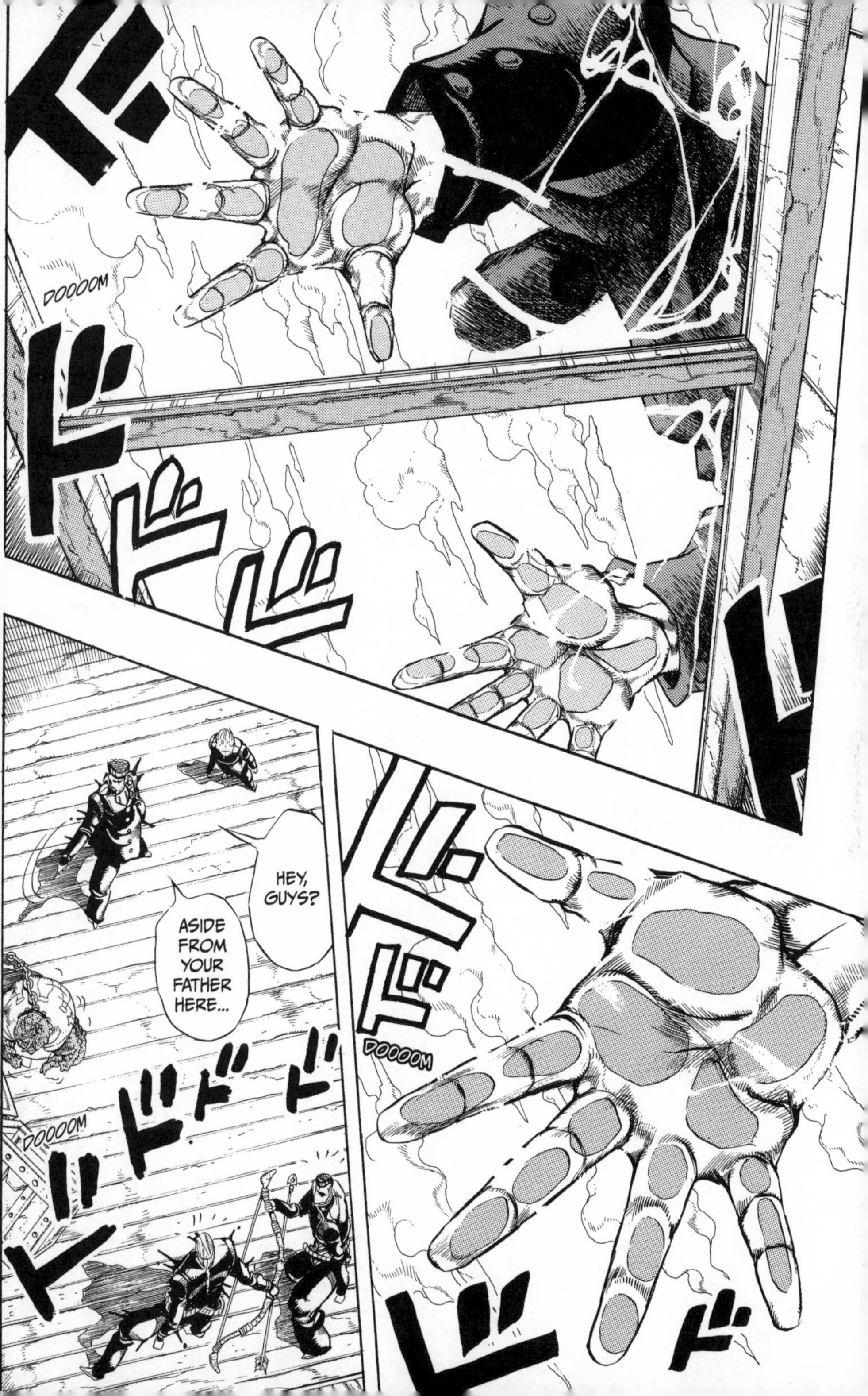
DOOOOM
DOOOOM
HEY, GUYS?
ASIDE FROM YOUR FATHER HERE...
DOOOOM

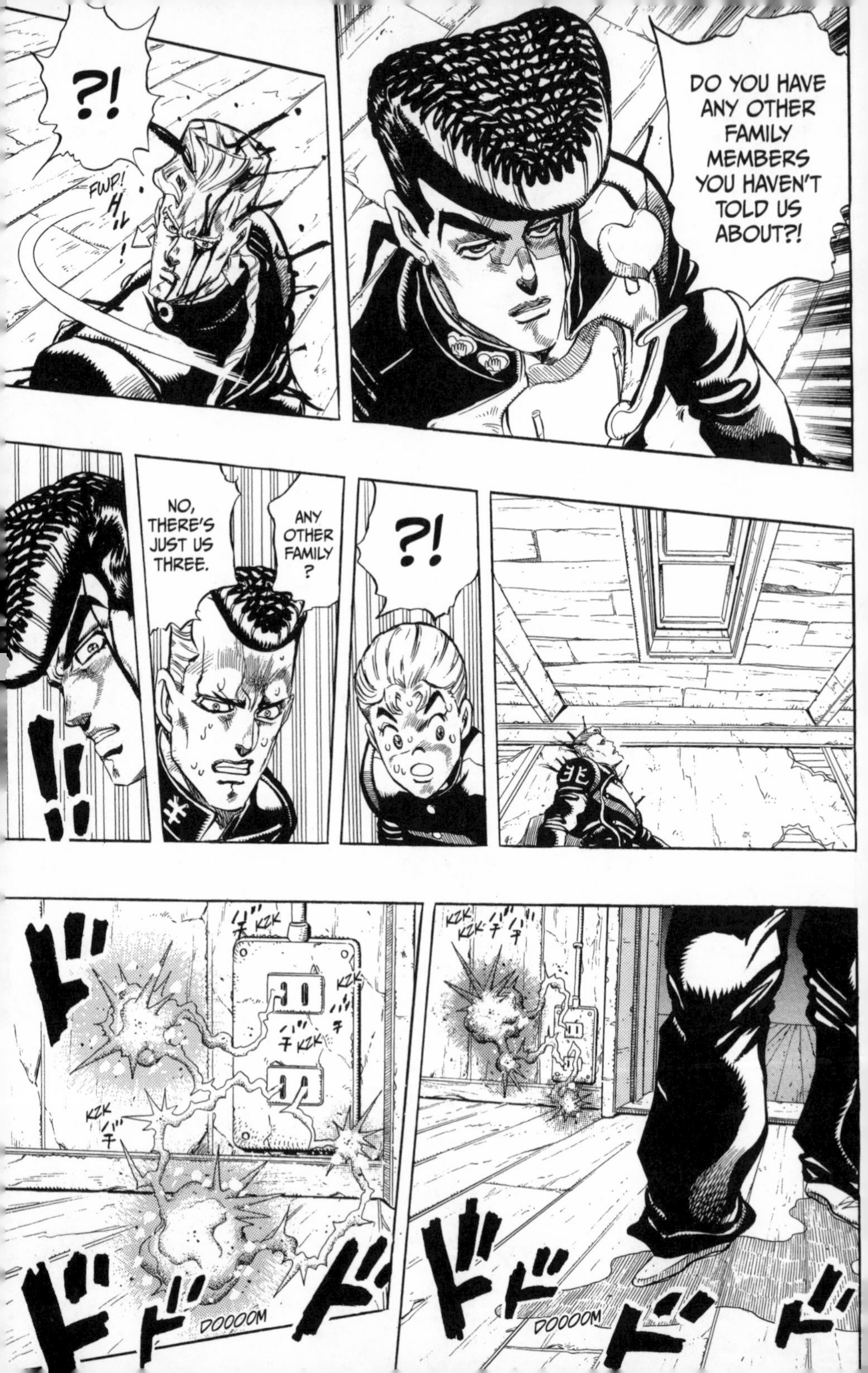
DO YOU HAVE ANY OTHER FAMILY MEMBERS YOU HAVEN'T TOLD US ABOUT?!
?!
FWP!
?!
ANY OTHER FAMILY?
NO, THERE'S JUST US THREE.
!!
KZK
KZK
DOOOOM
KZK
KZK
KZK
KZK
DOOOOM

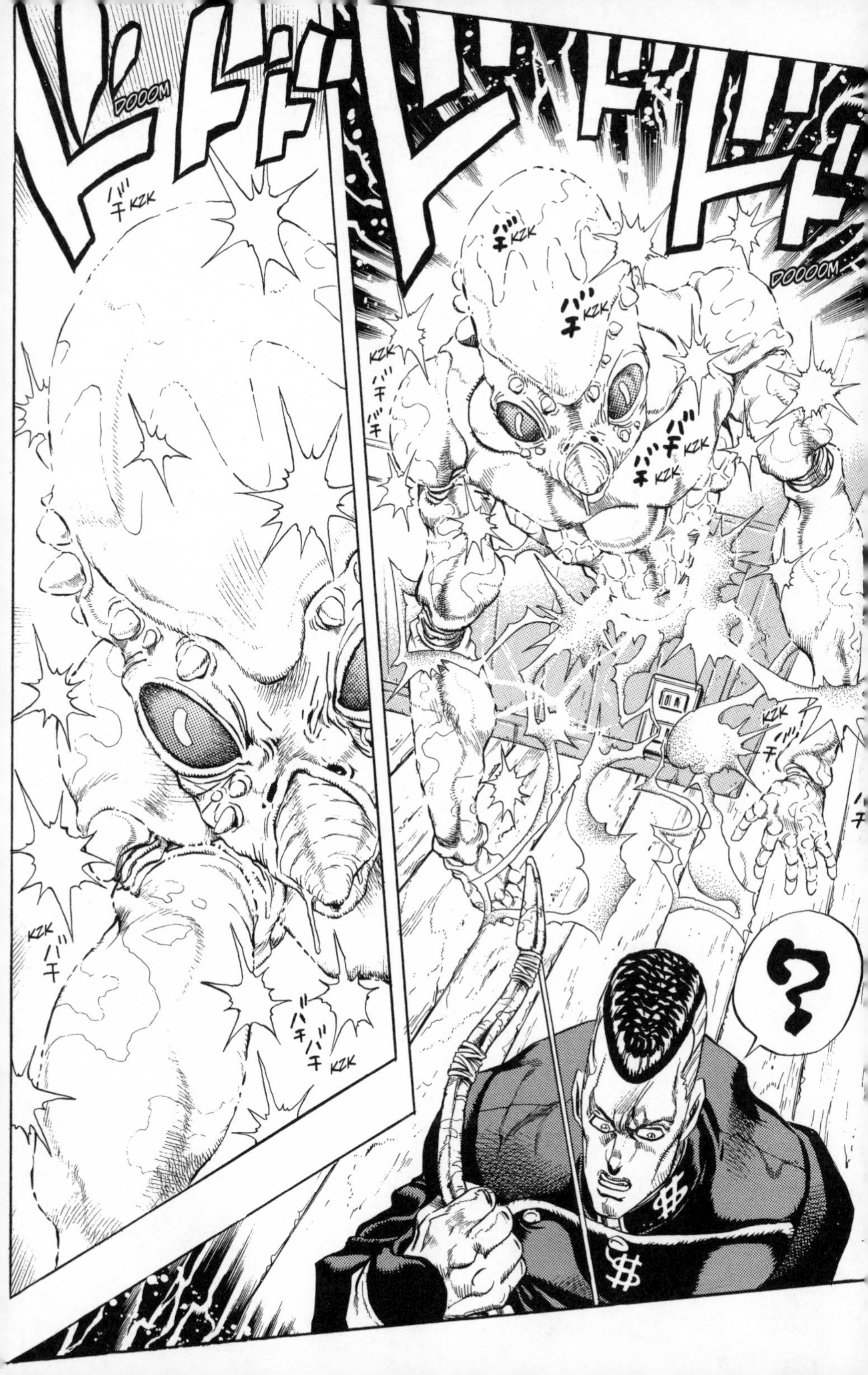
DOOOOM
バチ KZK
バチ KZK
KZK バチバチ
バチ KZK
バチ KZK
KZK バチ
?
DOOOM
バチ KZK
KZK バチ
バチバチ KZK

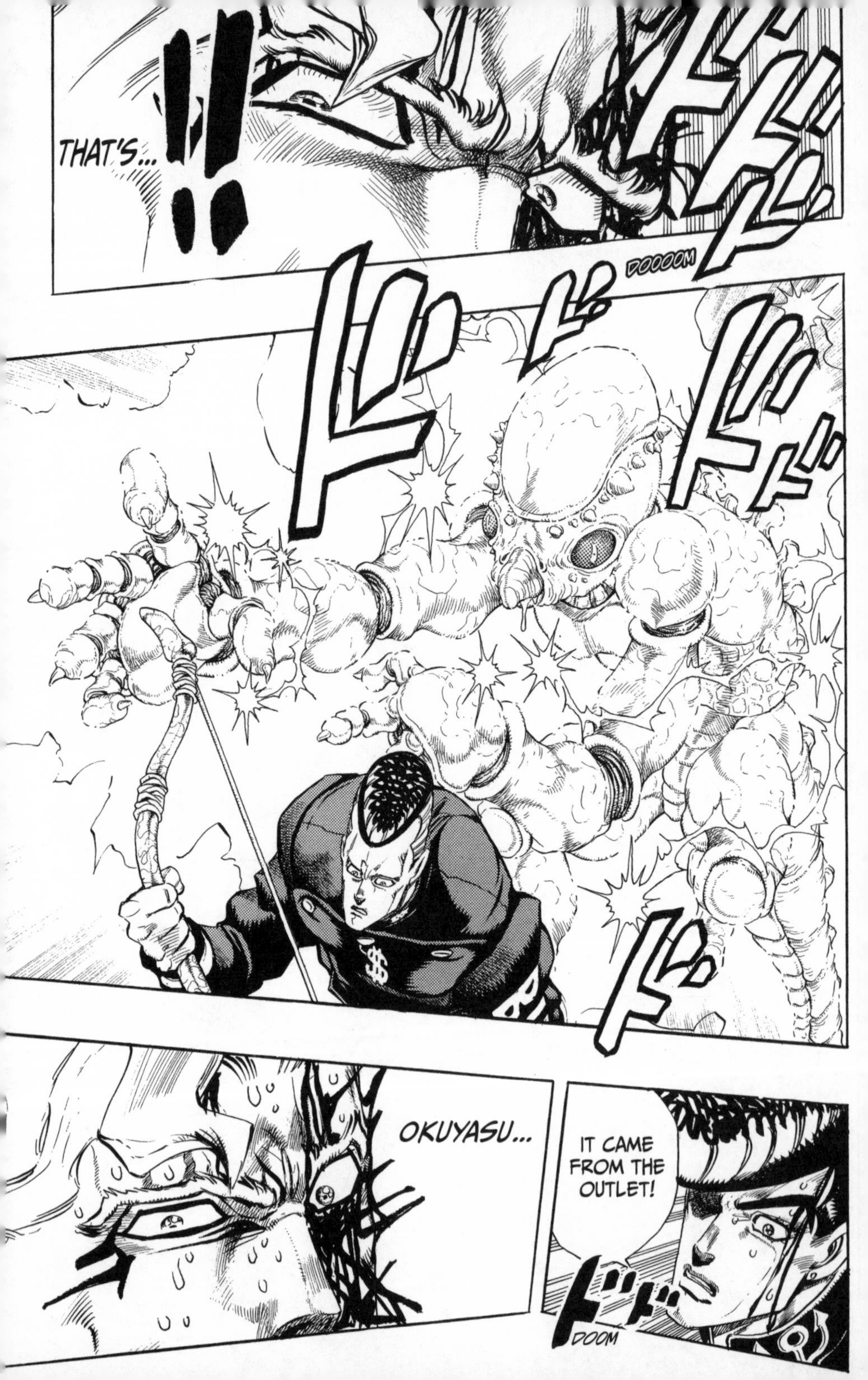
THAT'S...!!
DOOOOM
IT CAME FROM THE OUTLET!
DOOM
OKUYASU...

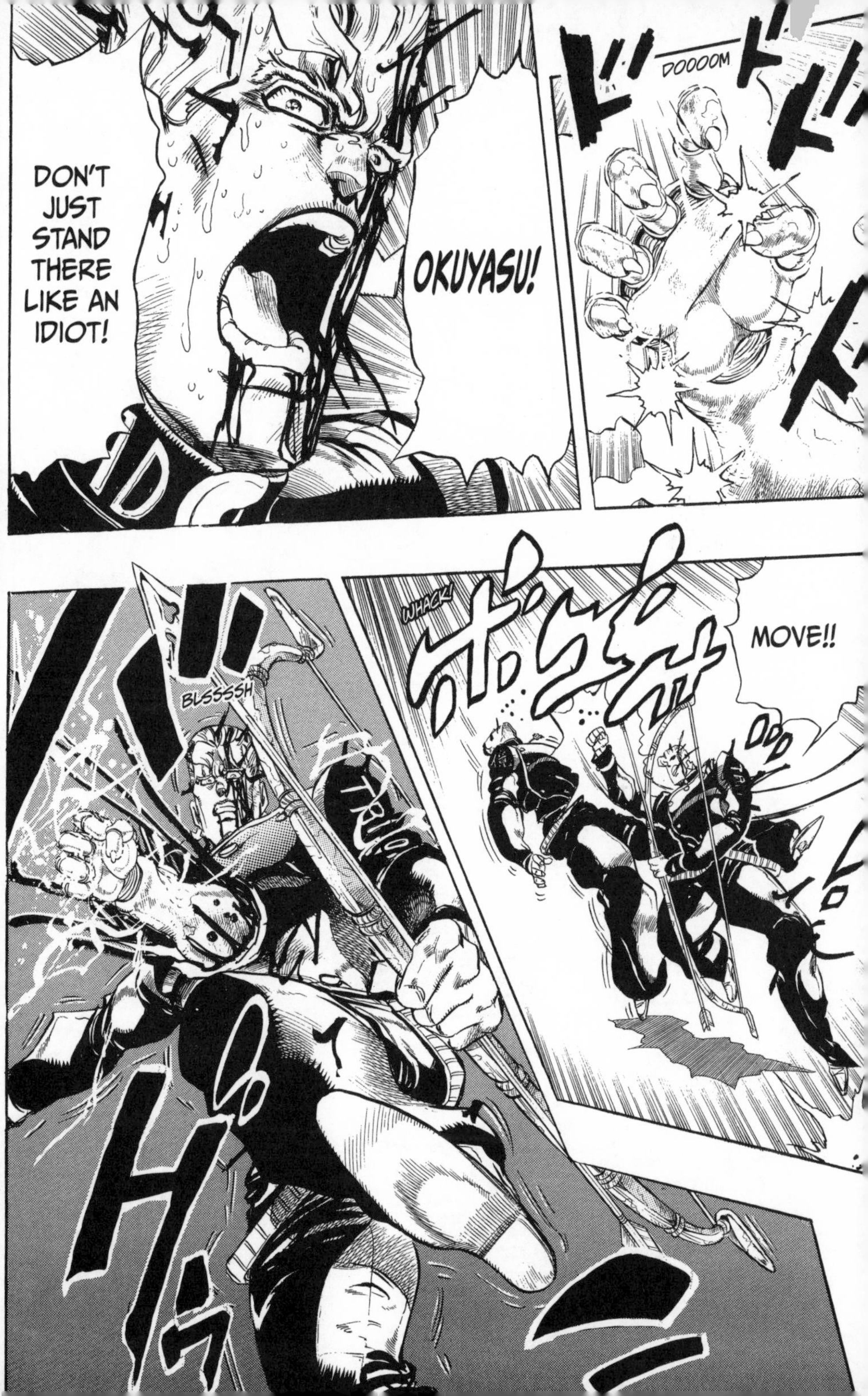
DOOOOM
OKUYASU!
DON'T JUST STAND THERE LIKE AN IDIOT!
MOVE!!
WHACK!
BLSSSSH

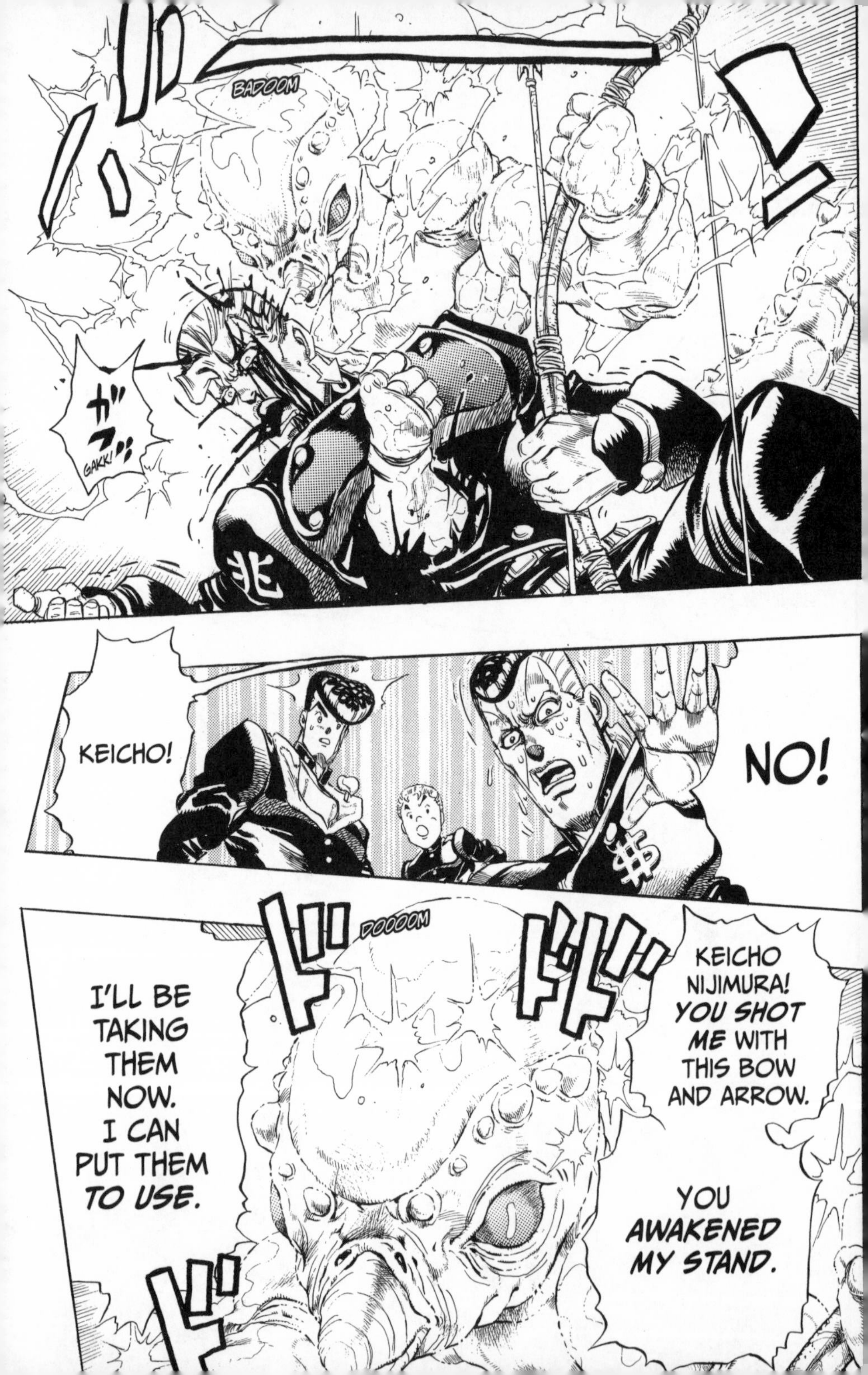
BADOOM
ガツッ
GAKK!
NO!
KEICHO!
KEICHO NIJIMURA! YOU SHOT ME WITH THIS BOW AND ARROW.
YOU AWAKENED MY STAND.
DOOOOM
I'LL BE TAKING THEM NOW. I CAN PUT THEM TO USE.

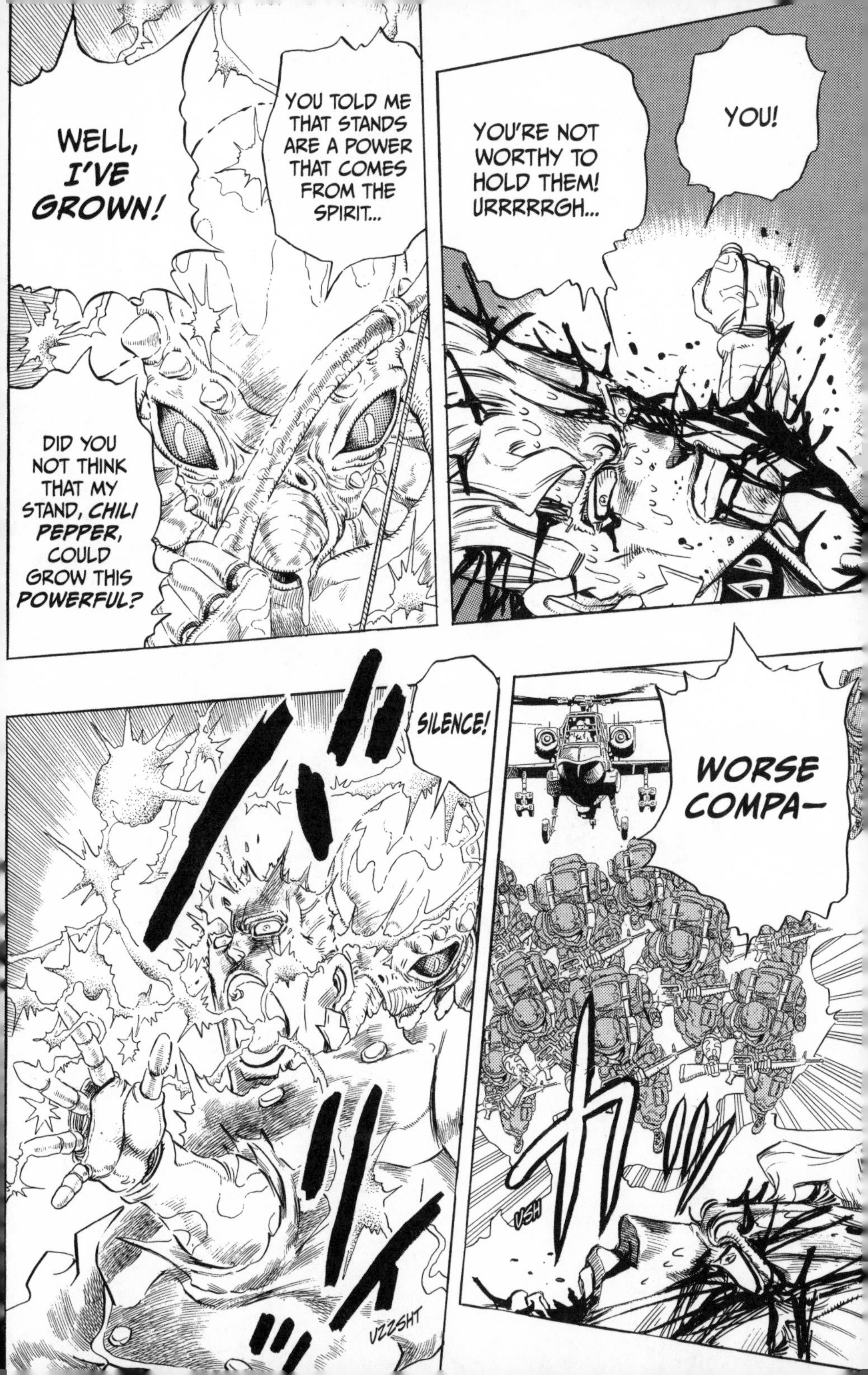
YOU!
YOU'RE NOT WORTHY TO HOLD THEM! URRRRRGH...
YOU TOLD ME THAT STANDS ARE A POWER THAT COMES FROM THE SPIRIT...
WELL, I'VE GROWN!
DID YOU NOT THINK THAT MY STAND, *CHILI PEPPER*, COULD GROW THIS *POWERFUL*?
WORSE COMPA—
VSH
SILENCE!
VZZSHT

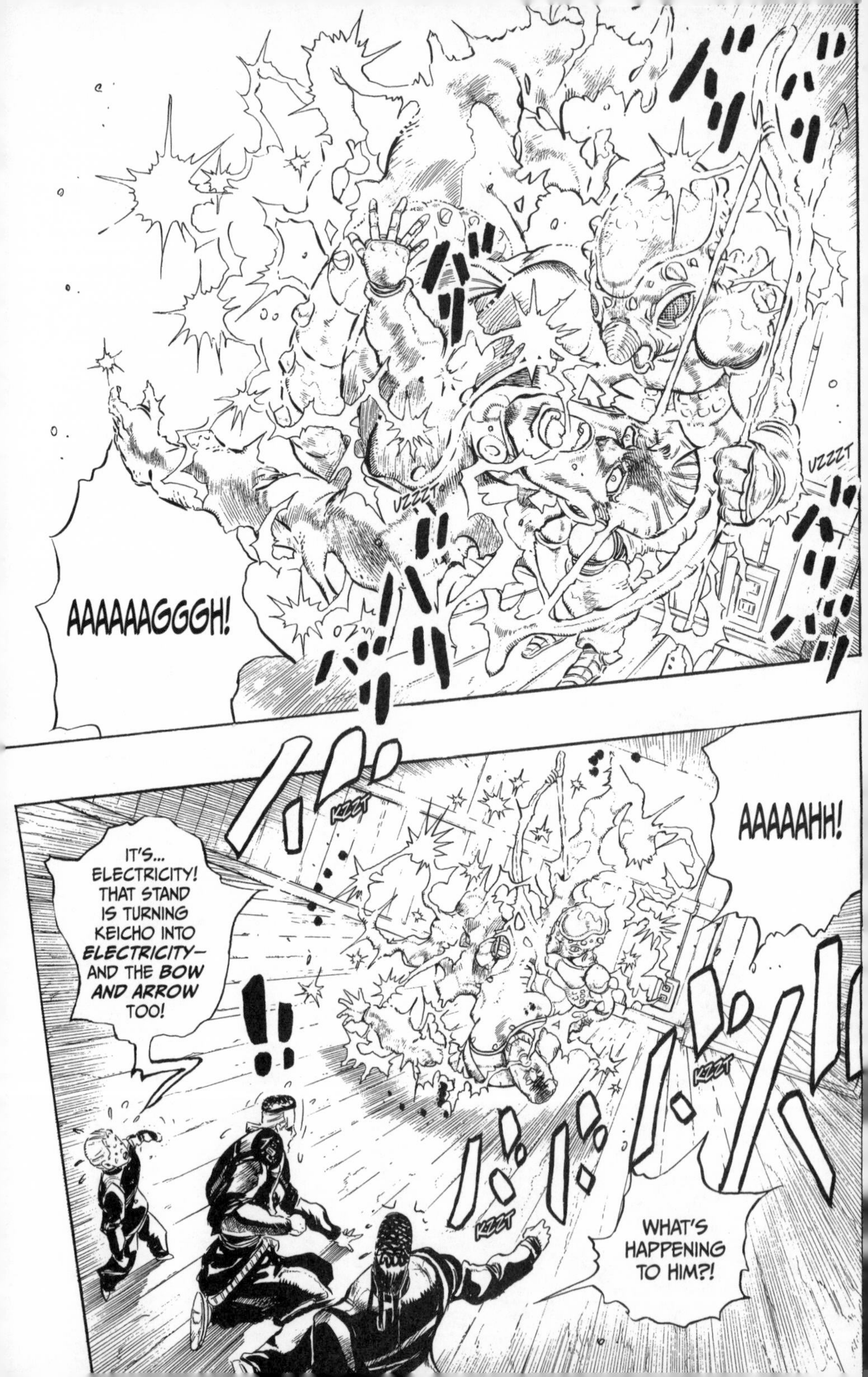
UZZZT
UZZZT
AAAAAAGGGH!
AAAAAHH!
KZZT
WHAT'S HAPPENING TO HIM?!
KZZT
KZZT
IT'S... ELECTRICITY! THAT STAND IS TURNING KEICHO INTO *ELECTRICITY*— AND THE *BOW AND ARROW* TOO!
!!

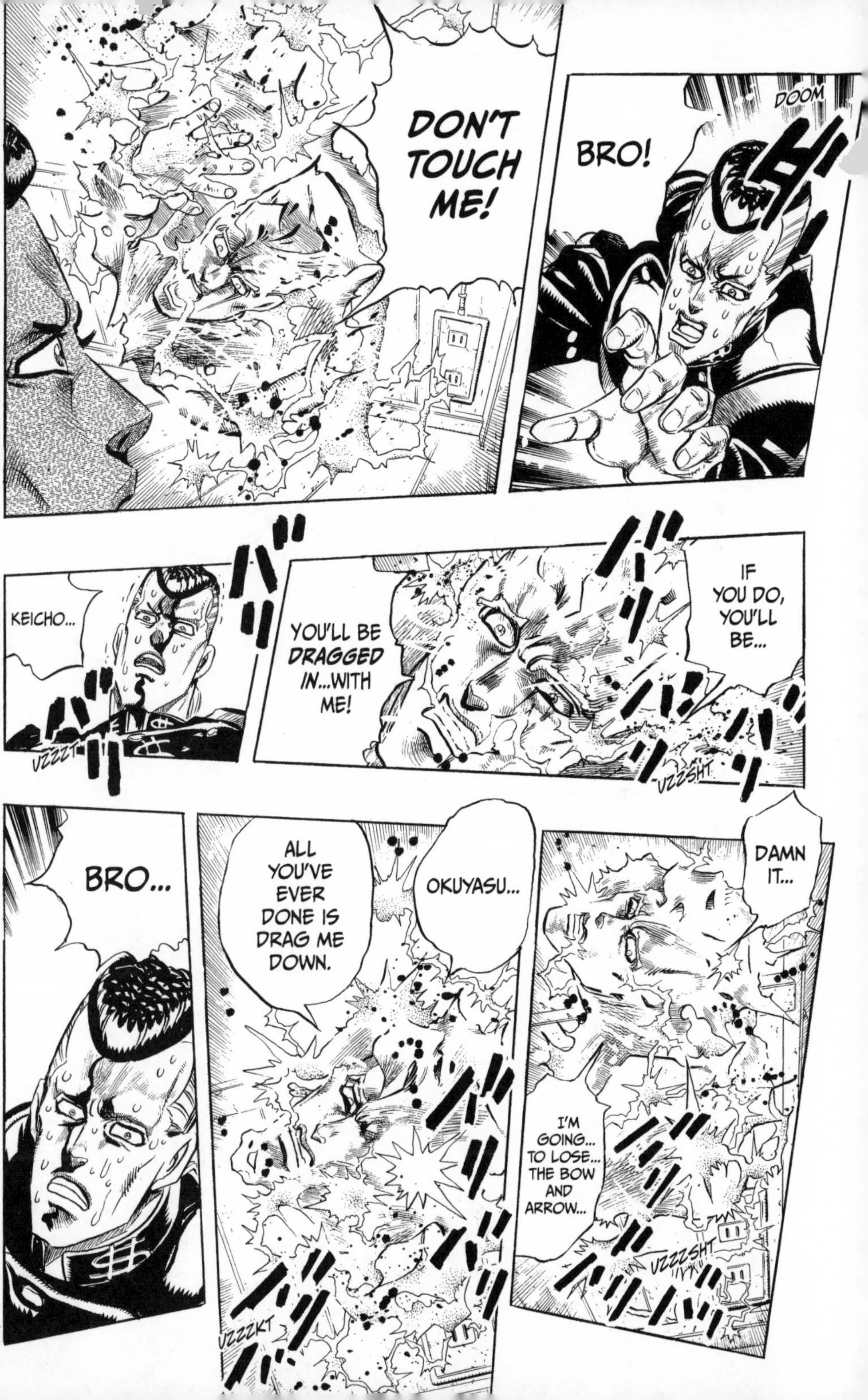
DOOM
BRO!
DON'T TOUCH ME!
IF YOU DO, YOU'LL BE...
YOU'LL BE DRAGGED IN...WITH ME!
UZZZSHT
KEICHO...
UZZZT
DAMN IT...
I'M GOING... TO LOSE... THE BOW AND ARROW...
UZZZSHT
OKUYASU...
ALL YOU'VE EVER DONE IS DRAG ME DOWN.
UZZZKT
BRO...

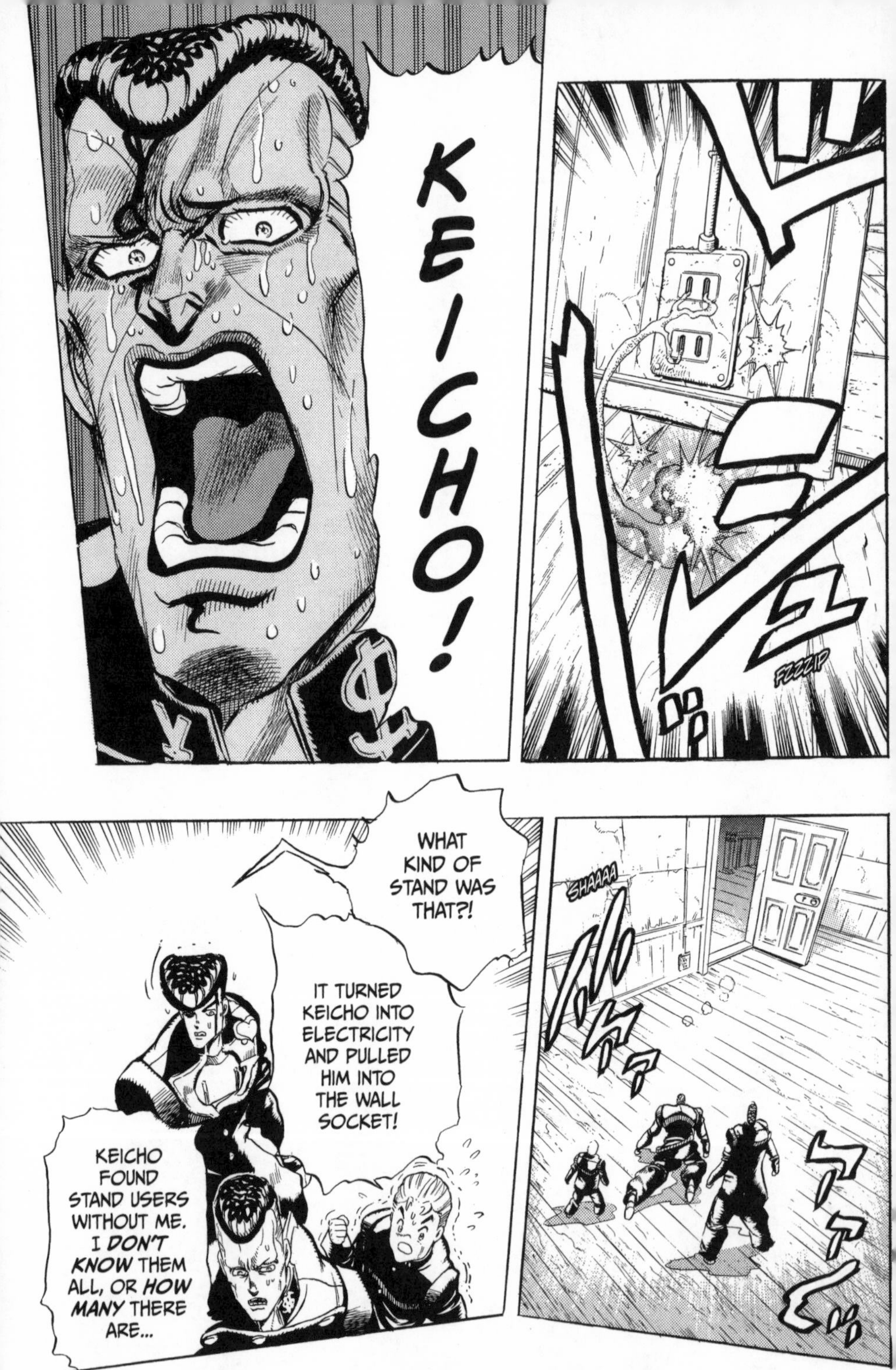
FZZZIP
KEICHO!
SHAAAA
WHAT KIND OF STAND WAS THAT?!
IT TURNED KEICHO INTO ELECTRICITY AND PULLED HIM INTO THE WALL SOCKET!
KEICHO FOUND STAND USERS WITHOUT ME. I *DON'T KNOW* THEM ALL, OR *HOW MANY* THERE ARE...

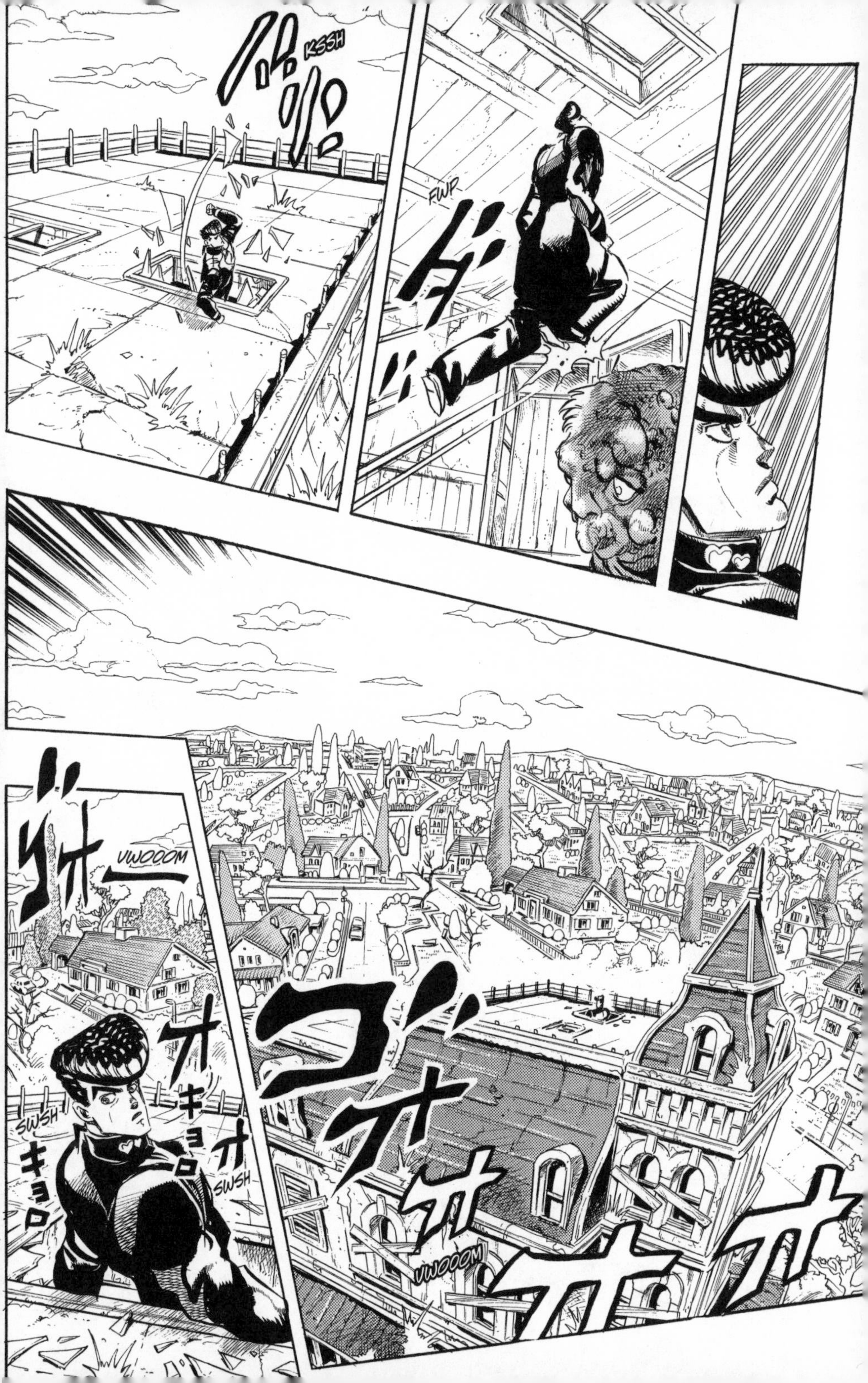
FWP
ダッ
KSSH
ゴオオオオ
VWOOOM
ゴオー
VWOOOM
キョロ
SWSH
キョロ
SWSH

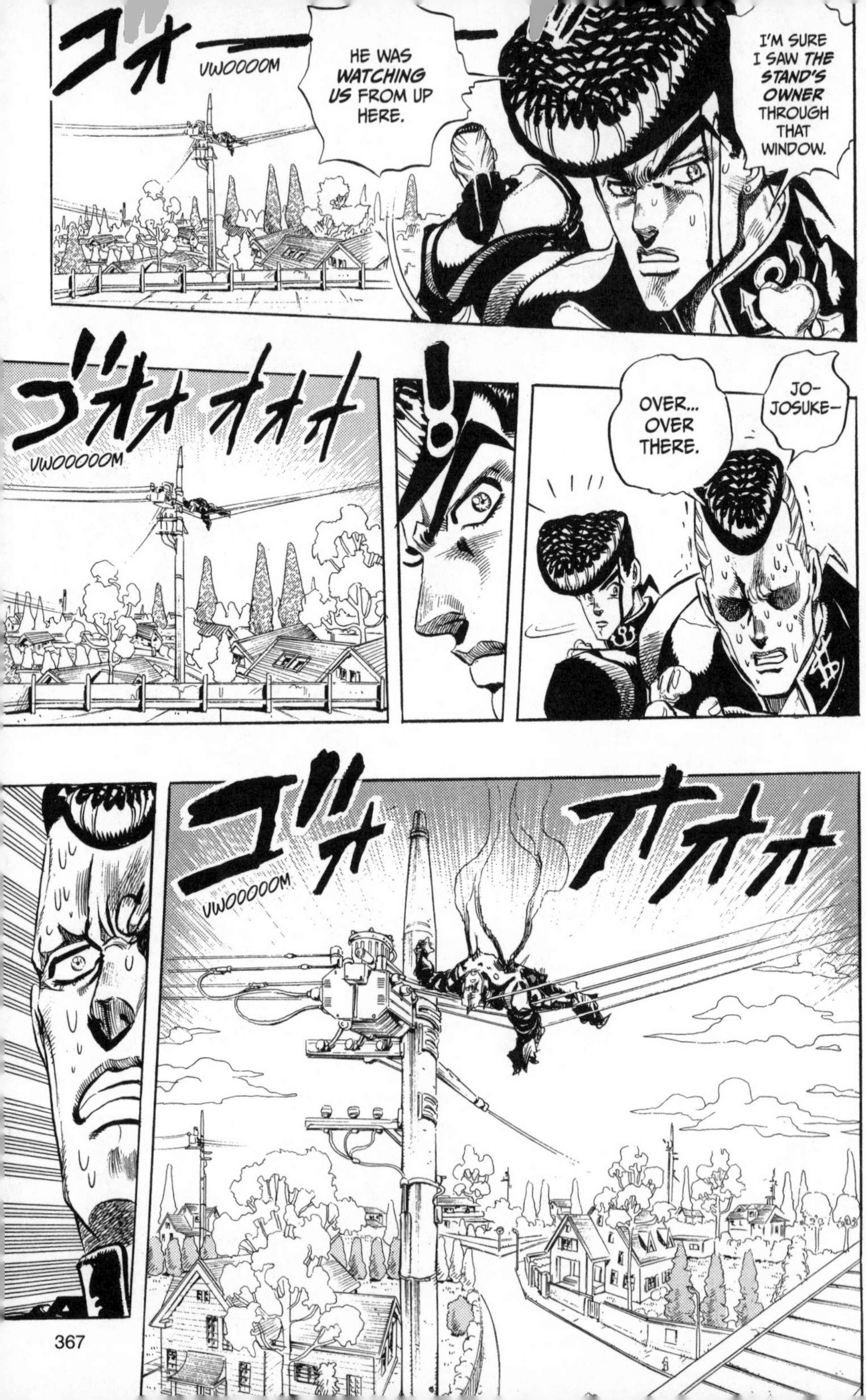
VWOOOOM
I'M SURE I SAW THE STAND'S OWNER THROUGH THAT WINDOW.
HE WAS WATCHING US FROM UP HERE.
JO-JOSUKE—
OVER... OVER THERE.
VWOOOOOM
VWOOOOOM

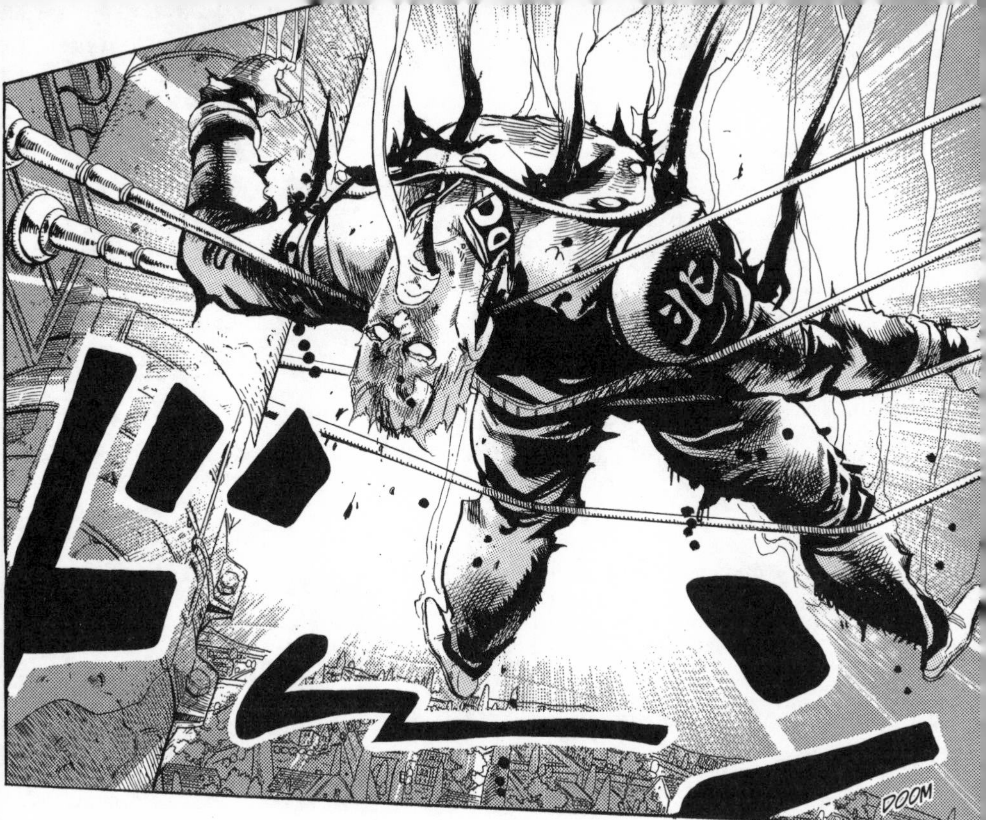
DOOM

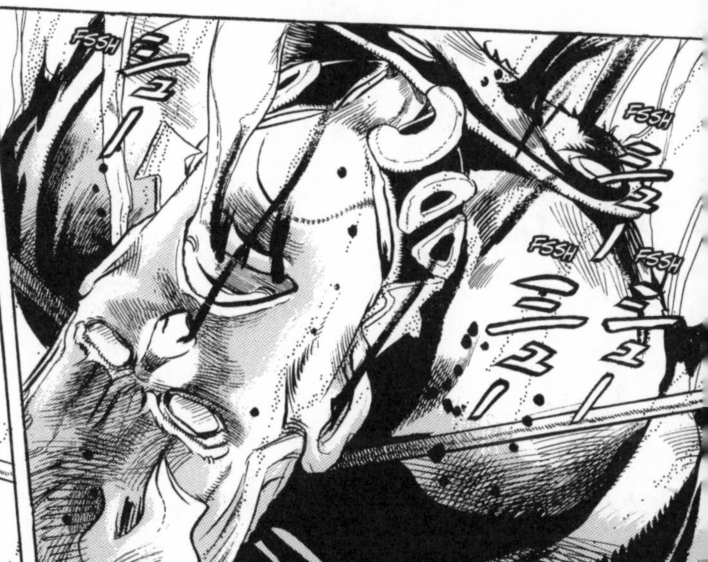
FSSH
FSSH
FSSH
FSSH

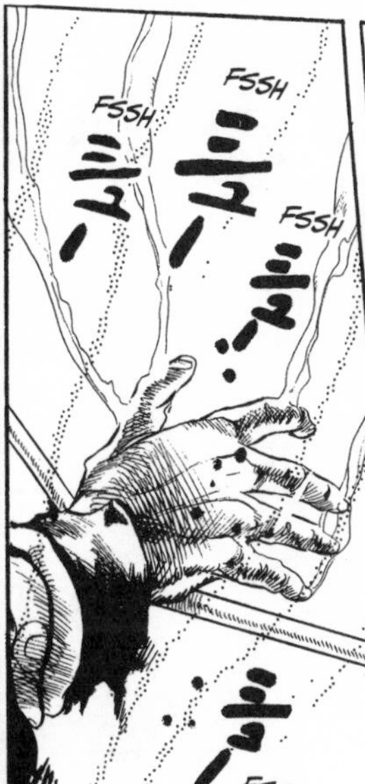
FSSH
FSSH
FSSH
FSSH

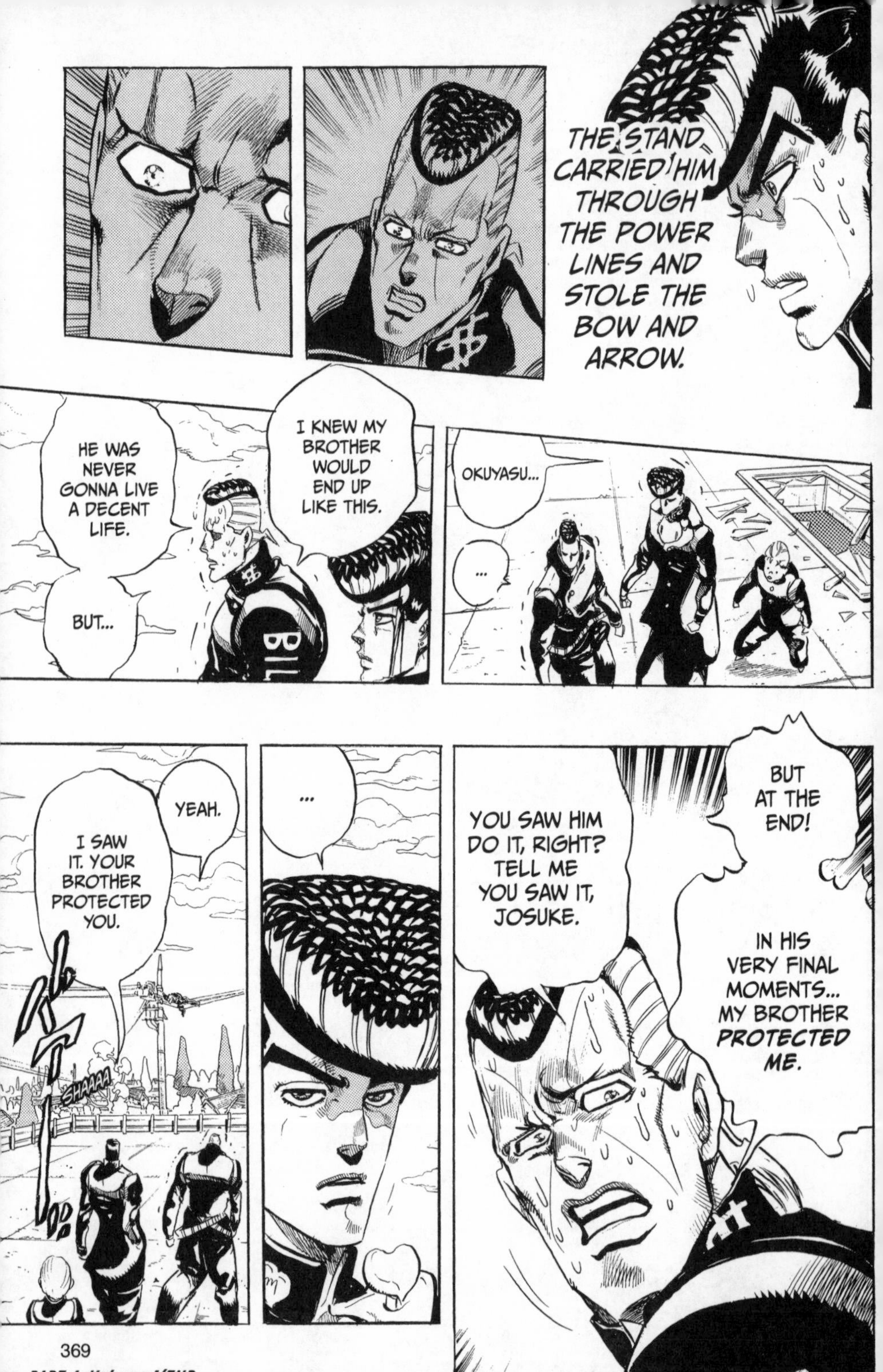
THE STAND CARRIED HIM THROUGH THE POWER LINES AND STOLE THE BOW AND ARROW.
OKUYASU...
...
I KNEW MY BROTHER WOULD END UP LIKE THIS.
HE WAS NEVER GONNA LIVE A DECENT LIFE.
BUT...
BUT AT THE END!
IN HIS VERY FINAL MOMENTS... MY BROTHER PROTECTED ME.
YOU SAW HIM DO IT, RIGHT? TELL ME YOU SAW IT, JOSUKE.
...
YEAH.
I SAW IT. YOUR BROTHER PROTECTED YOU.
SHAAAA

PART 4, Volume 1/END

AUTHOR'S
COMMENTS

There's a lot to be afraid of out there in the world—here are my top ten personal fears:

#10: Death
#9: Organisms that can cling to the ceiling (cockroaches, etc.)
#8: Delusions
#7: My acquaintances
#6: Getting an unlucky fortune
#5: Hospitals
#4: Destruction of the environment
#3: Confined spaces
#2: Strangers
And, finally, for the illustrious #1 spot: The dark

What do you think? How is my list different than yours?

When I was growing up...
  One day, my mother came down with a cold and asked me to help her.
  She said, "Would you mind going to the neighborhood doctor to get my medicine?"
  I was waiting in the reception area when the doctor came out and said, "All right, Araki-kun! Roll up your sleeve—it's time for your shot."
  "What?!" I shouted. "I'm not here for me!"
  "Just kidding," he said.
  I'd been terrified, but I also thought it was a hilarious trick. Looking back, I think that experience led me to become a manga creator.

JoJo's
BIZARRE ADVENTURE

PART 4: DIAMOND IS UNBREAKABLE
VOLUME 1
BY HIROHIKO ARAKI

DELUXE HARDCOVER EDITION
Translation: Nathan A Collins
Touch-Up Art & Lettering: Mark McMurray
Design: Adam Grano
Editor: David Brothers

Printed in the U.S.A.

Published by VIZ Media, LLC
P.O. Box 77010
San Francisco, CA 94107

10 9 8 7 6
First printing, May 2019
Sixth printing, June 2023

VIZ MEDIA   **SHONEN JUMP**

viz.com

THIS IS THE LAST PAGE

JoJo's BIZARRE ADVENTURE

has been printed in the original
Japanese format in order to preserve
the orientation of the original artwork.